CITIZENS AND

Citizens and Politics: Perspectives from Political Psychology brings together some of the current research on citizen decision making. It addresses the questions of citizen political competence from different political psychology perspectives. Some of the authors in this volume look to affect and emotions to determine how people reach political judgments, others to human cognition and reasoning. Still others focus on perceptions or basic political attitudes such as political ideology. Several demonstrate the impact of values on policy preferences. The collection features chapters from some of the most talented political scientists in the country.

James H. Kuklinski is a Professor in the Department of Political Science and the Institute of Government and Public Affairs at the University of Illinois at Urbana-Champaign.

Cambridge Studies in Political Psychology and
Public Opinion

General Editors

James H. Kuklinski
University of Illinois, Urbana-Champaign
Dennis Chong
Northwestern University

Editorial Board

Stanley Feldman, *State University of New York,
Stony Brook*
Roger D. Masters, *Dartmouth College*
William J. McGuire, *Yale University*
Norbert Schwarz, *Zentrum für Umfragen, Methoden
und Analysen (ZUMA), Mannheim, FRG*
David O. Sears, *University of California, Los Angeles*
Paul M. Sniderman, *Stanford University and Survey
Research Center, University of California, Berkeley*
James A. Stimson, *University of North Carolina*

This series has been established in recognition of the growing sophistication in
the resurgence of interest in political psychology and the study of public opinion.
Its focus will range from the kinds of mental processes that people employ when
they think about democratic processes and make political choices to the nature
and consequences of macro-level public opinion.

We expect that some of the works will draw on developments in cognitive
and social psychology and relevant areas of philosophy. Appropriate subjects
would include the use of heuristics, the roles of core values and moral principles
in political reasoning, the effects of expertise and sophistication, the roles of
affect and emotion, and the nature of cognition and information processing. The
emphasis will be on systematic and rigorous empirical analysis, and a wide
range of methodologies will be appropriate: traditional surveys, experimental
surveys, laboratory experiments, focus groups, and in-depth interviews, as well
as others. We intend that these empirically oriented studies will also consider
normative implications for democratic politics generally.

Politics, not psychology, will be the primary focus, and it is expected that most
works will deal with mass publics and democratic politics, although work on
nondemocratic publics will not be excluded. Other works will examine traditional topics in public opinion research, as well as contribute to the growing
literature on aggregate opinion and its role in democratic societies.

Series list on page following the Index

CITIZENS
AND
POLITICS

PERSPECTIVES FROM
POLITICAL PSYCHOLOGY

EDITED BY

JAMES H. KUKLINSKI

University of Illinois at
Urbana-Champaign

CAMBRIDGE
UNIVERSITY PRESS

CAMBRIDGE UNIVERSITY PRESS
Cambridge, New York, Melbourne, Madrid, Cape Town, Singapore, São Paulo, Delhi

Cambridge University Press
The Edinburgh Building, Cambridge CB2 8RU, UK

Published in the United States of America by Cambridge University Press, New York

www.cambridge.org
Information on this title: www.cambridge.org/9780521593762

First published 2001
This digitally printed version 2008

A catalogue record for this publication is available from the British Library

Library of Congress Cataloguing in Publication data

Citizens and politics: perspectives from political psychology / edited by James H. Kuklinski.
p.   cm. – (Cambridge studies in political psychology and public opinion)
ISBN 0-521-59376-X
1. Political psychology.   2. Political science – Decision making.
I. Kuklinski, James H.   II. Series.
JA74.5 .C59   2001
320´.01´9–dc21   00-059876

ISBN 978-0-521-59376-2 hardback
ISBN 978-0-521-08942-5 paperback

Contents

Contents

PART III: POLITICAL ATTITUDES AND PERCEPTIONS

PART IV: POLITICAL VALUES

Contents

List of Contributors

Gerald L. Clore, *Department of Psychology, University of Illinois, Urbana, Illinois*

Gregory Andrade Diamond, *Columbia University Law School, New York, New York*

Laura Elms, *Department of Political Science, University of California at Berkeley, Berkeley, California*

Stanley Feldman, *Department of Political Science, SUNY at Stony Brook, Stony Brook, New York*

Jill Glathar, *Department of Political Science, SUNY at Stony Brook, Stony Brook, New York*

Jennifer L. Hochschild, *Department of Politics, Princeton University, Princeton, New Jersey*

Linda M. Isbell, *Department of Psychology, University of Illinois, Urbana, Illinois*

Jennifer Jerit, *Department of Political Science, University of Illinois, Urbana, Illinois*

James H. Kuklinski, *Department of Political Science, University of Illinois, Urbana, Illinois*

Richard R. Lau, *Department of Political Science, Rutgers University, New Brunswick, New Jersey*

Milton Lodge, *Department of Political Science, SUNY at Stony Brook, Stony Brook, New York*

Michael B. MacKuen, *Department of Political Science, University of North Carolina, Chapel Hill, North Carolina*

George E. Marcus, *Department of Political Science, Williams College, Williamstown, Massachusetts*

Gregory B. Markus, *Department of Political Science, University of Michigan, Ann Arbor, Michigan*

Roger D. Masters, *Department of Government, Dartmouth College, Hanover, New Hampshire*

List of Contributors

Kathleen M. McGraw, *Department of Political Science, Ohio State University, Columbus, Ohio*

Michelle R. Nelson, *MathEngine, Inc. MathEngine, USA, Petaluma, California.*

Melissa A. Orlie, *Department of Political Science, University of Illinois, Urbana, Illinois*

Kenneth A. Rasinski, *Department of Political Science, University of Chicago, Chicago, Illinois*

David P. Redlawsk, *Department of Political Science, University of Iowa, Ames, Iowa*

David O. Sears, *Department of Political Science, UCLA, Los Angeles, California*

Sharon Shavitt, *Department of Advertising, University of Illinois, Urbana, Illinois*

Paul M. Sniderman, *Department of Political Science, Stanford University, Stanford, California*

Marco Steenbergen, *Department of Political Science, University of North Carolina, Chapel Hill, North Carolina*

Laura Stoker, *Department of Political Science, University of California at Berkeley, Berkeley, California*

Charles S. Taber, *Department of Political Science, SUNY at Stony Brook, Stony Brook, New York*

Philip E. Tetlock, *Department of Political Science, Ohio State University, Columbus, Ohio*

Prologue: Political Psychology and the Study of Citizens and Politics

JAMES H. KUKLINSKI

This volume is simultaneously a statement on the nature of mass political judgments and the capacity of a particular research perspective, political psychology, to reveal that nature. Using political psychology to explore citizen decision making is, of course, not new. Indeed, the two are so inextricably intertwined that it is difficult to imagine studying the latter without the help of the former. Even the authors of the Columbia studies of the 1940s and 1950s, who were largely sociological in orientation, used relevant psychological concepts to explain how people form political attitudes and why they vote as they do. The subsequent and continuing University of Michigan National Election Studies are deeply rooted in psychological notions such as affect, projection, and rationalization.

More recently, a group of scholars has applied (and modified) ideas and methodologies from the field of social cognition to the study of citizen political decision making. This research is new because the field of social cognition is itself quite new. One of the unifying themes of social cognition, and thus of contemporary political psychology, is information processing. People are seen not as passive receivers of environmental stimuli, but as active choosers and interpreters of them. Much of the new political psychology research examines how people reason and make inferences about politics. Other work delineates unconscious mental processes that influence the judgments people make.

Methodological approaches vary. Some scholars correlate traditional survey items, but unlike public opinion researchers more generally, they use concepts from social cognition to direct their empirical research. Others use experimental surveys, which embed experimental designs in the questionnaire items. Typically, respondents are randomly assigned to one of several versions of the same question. What varies, and the only thing that varies, is the target group. For example, some might be asked about affirmative action for blacks, others about affirmative action for women, and still others about affirmative action generally. The researcher can then compare the mean responses across the conditions to ascertain what effect, if any, reference to a particular group has. The experimental survey thus enhances the ability to make causal inferences while maintaining the ecological validity of a random sample. Finally, a few political scientists have gone into the laboratory and undertaken classical experiments. Some of this research entails measuring people's physiological responses to political stimuli.

This volume brings some of the current research on citizen decision making together. It thus affords an opportunity to answer the question "What does this endeavor called political psychology look like?" It also affords an opportunity to ascertain what contemporary political psychology, in toto, has to say about the capacity of ordinary citizens to evaluate political phenomena. These two seemingly straightforward tasks – defining the contours of political psychology and measuring citizen competence – in fact are anything but simple.

The editor originally subtitled this volume *A Political Psychology Perspective*. That the subtitle is now *Perspectives from Political Psychology* underlines a crucially important point: there is not *a* single political psychology perspective. Political psychology is far-ranging in its approaches and the topics it encompasses. In sharp contrast to rational choice, for example, political psychology does not consist of an agreed-upon set of axioms from which implications can be drawn. Some of the authors in this volume look to affect and emotions to determine how people reach political judgments, others to human cognition and reasoning. Still others focus on perceptions or basic political attitudes such as political ideology. Several demonstrate the impact of values on policy preferences.

The diversity extends even further. Those authors who investigate the impact of affect and emotions, for example, do not always adopt the same conception of identically labeled psychological phenomena. Similarly, the authors of the chapters on values vary widely in what values they choose to study. One of the chapters on political attitudes challenges the very construction of attitudes that underlies another.

Consequently, different authors use different criteria to assess citizen performance. Different criteria, in turn, imply possibly different conclusions about citizen competence. That is precisely what the reader will find. What to make of this variety of evaluations, for both the nature of citizen judgments and the utility of political psychology, is for the reader to decide. It is a decision that warrants reflection.

The book is divided into four somewhat arbitrary and not mutually exclusive parts: affect and emotions, political cognition, political attitudes and perceptions, and political values. Each part consists of an introduction, three illustrative substantive chapters, and a commentary (for reasons noted later, the political values section contains two commentaries). The commentaries summarize and integrate the three substantive chapters and offer further thoughts on the topic at hand.

Most of the chapters report ongoing research. These research programs were selected because they represent some of the best work in the field, and the goal was to bring this work together in one place and with the singular focus on citizen competence.[1] A companion volume focuses less on substantive research and more on the strengths and weaknesses of political psychology as a research enterprise. In it, scholars who practice political psychology take a hard look at the research endeavor in which they are engaged.

1 Diana Mutz and John Zaller also attended the conference. For different reasons, neither was able to contribute to this or the other volume.

Part I Affect and Emotions

Introduction

JAMES H. KUKLINSKI

Although scholars continue to distinguish affect from cognition, they recognize that the two interact in complex ways to influence political attitudes and judgments. Most of the authors in this and the following part explicitly acknowledge this reality, and some propose models that explicitly take affect and cognition as intertwined. The six chapters nonetheless fall into two groups, those that emphasize affect and emotions (Sears, Marcus and MacKuen, and Masters) and those that emphasize cognition (Lau and Redlawsk, McGraw, and Taber, Lodge, and Glathar). What ties them together is their adoption in one form or another of an information processing perspective.

CONCEPTIONS

Social psychologists distinguish affect from emotion. "Affect," according to this categorization, is a generic term encompassing not only emotions, but also mood and evaluations. "Emotions" include a whole range of specific feelings, from fear, anger, and sadness to happiness and enthusiasm. For some needs, this distinction has value. For purposes of evaluating the following chapters, the distinction is less helpful, and thus the two terms will be used interchangeably. On the other hand, affect and emotion should not be, and are not, equated with mood in the chapters that follow. Whereas emotions are caused by reactions to specific targets, moods are general feelings not directed at anyone or anything. This is not to say that mood is irrelevant to political evaluations, as Clore and Isbell note in their commentary.

The three principal chapters on emotions share three characteristics: all offer strong and very general conceptual frameworks; all hypothesize that emotions matter in politics; and all provide compelling evidence to support their hypotheses. This said, the three approaches differ in the conceptual approach they adopt and thus the kinds of questions they investigate empirically.

David Sears's chapter on affect and symbolic politics summarizes and elaborates an enduring research program that has influenced public opinion and political psychology work for years. The theory is simple and elegant. Individuals, Sears argues, learn "symbolic predispositions" early in life, and these predispositions strongly condition how people respond to political words and symbols in their current political environments. The affect in Sears's theory, in other words, has roots that go back to childhood. It shapes reactions to political words like "busing," "taxpayers," "communists," and "affirmative action" as well as to specific objects such as candidates and members of racial and ethnic groups.

The symbolic politics theory comports with all we know about the nature of ordinary citizens: they know little about politics; they profess only minimal interest in politics; they see politics as distant and complex. Symbolic reactions provide a quick and easy way for people to break through the complexity of politics and render political evaluations.

Sears extends his theory in this chapter by also demonstrating that symbolic processing, which takes the form of strong affective responses to symbols, comports with current research into how people process information from their environments. Many social psychologists and some political scientists have found that people process on-line, which means they continually update their evaluative judgments but then forget the specific information that contributed to the judgment. Like on-line processing, symbolic processing does not require storage of information in memory. Symbolic processing also comports with the universal phenomenon of automatic processing, that is, people making quick and often unconscious evaluations, and with the dominant although not totally unchallenged finding (see the chapter by Clore and Isbell) that emotions dominate cognition in everyday judgments. In a very real sense, Sears offers a compelling and an encompassing theory of politics that builds on and is compatible with what we know about psychological processes.

Marcus and MacKuen argue that to understand how citizens cope with politics, we need to understand how they learn, which in turn requires identifying the conditions under which they pay attention to politics. People will pay attention, the authors assert, when they experience heightened emotions.

But just when will this occur? The answer, Marcus and MacKuen assert, is to be found in neuroscience, specifically, in Gray's work on emotionality. Gray's conception of emotionality, which Marcus has used on several occasions, consists of three systems – fight/flight, behavioral approach, and behavioral inhibition – that collectively form the limbic system. The latter two of the three systems hold the most relevance for the study of politics. The behavioral approach system (BAS) helps us cope with the world by monitoring and assessing previously learned behaviors. When an action is deemed successful, given earlier experiences, the BAS provides immediate feedback in the form of feelings of elation, enthusiasm, and the like. Conversely, questionable behaviors lead to feelings of despair and depression. The good feelings lead us to engage the environment; the bad ones, to draw back. Thus it is the positive affect that serves as the primary diagnostic with respect to choosing a course of behavior.

Sometimes we face new and novel situations, in which case the behavioral inhibition system (BIS) system kicks in. If the incoming sensory signals meet expectations, given relevant past experiences, the BIS calms and relaxes. But, and this is especially important, when there is a mismatch between external stimuli and expectations, we feel anxious and nervous. Consequently, we attend to the new stimuli for the purpose of learning. In the case of the BIS, negative affect serves as the primary diagnostic that motivates behavior.

Together, the two systems, BAS and BIS, give us a considerable amount of valuable information. And they do so without conscious effort on our part; information processing need not mean *conscious* processing.

In their chapter, Marcus and MacKuen summarize the fruits of their research into politics that takes Gray's neurobiological perspective as its point of departure. That research takes the form of two substantively distinct programs, the first on social and political tolerance. Marcus and his Minnesota collaborators have shown, through a set of experimental surveys, that people become less tolerant of groups if the latter display threatening behavior that runs counter to normal expectations about how societal groups should and do act. On the other hand, and contrary to intuition and the authors' prediction, the likelihood of a group's gaining political power has no main or interactive effect on tolerance. People express just as much intolerance of "badly" behaving groups who have little chance to gain office or garner wide public support as of those with a good chance.

Marcus and MacKuen's studies of electoral decision making have an advantage over the tolerance research in that only the former include measures of two elements in Gray's model: anxiety and enthusiasm. The measures take the form of questions (100-point thermometers) asking respondents how anxious each of the two 1988 presidential candidates made them feel and how enthusiastic they were about them. The authors reach this conclusion: when candidates increase voters' anxiety, the latter rely more on contemporary information (their comparative enthusiasm for the two candidates) and less on standing cues such as partisanship.

In analyses not previously reported, Marcus and MacKuen demonstrate that across three presidential elections, those of 1984, 1988, and 1992, increases in voters' anxieties about the candidates strikingly increased issue voting. Less anxious voters overwhelmingly supported their parties' candidates, while more anxious voters tended to cast ballots for the candidate who was closer to their own thinking on the issues, irrespective of the candidate's party. To those who prescribe issue voting as a form of electoral accountability, Marcus and MacKuen offer a simple vehicle: heighten anxiety during the campaign.

Whereas elegant simplicity best describes Sears's theory of symbolic politics, complexity is the essence of Masters's approach. Masters takes recent findings in neuroscience, including Gray's, as his point of departure. His focus is on the structure and functioning of the brain. The structure is modular, taking the form of a series of hierarchically patterned neural pathways that are linked to the emotional centers of the brain. The process is simultaneous parallel processing, which in simple terms means that the brain at any point in time deals with an incredibly large number of environmental stimuli. But it does not just passively accept these stimuli; to the contrary, internally generated neural activity can alter them considerably.

This neuroscience-based perspective leads Masters to a highly significant conclusion: because attitudes and perceptions are emergent phenomena that arise from neural activity, it is extremely difficult to predict what these attitudes and perceptions will be. To use a term that Masters borrows from chaos and complexity theory, the dynamics will be nonlinear. This perspective comports with recent neuroscience research that views the neurons in the human brain as competing for space, with some winning out, often unpredictably, over others to form a thought.

What, then, are the implications for empirical research? One response might be despair. Social scientists can never understand the dynamics underlying perceptions and attitude formation, nor will they ever be able to predict. An alternative, which Masters adopts, is to acknowledge the complexity and then investigate as much of it as possible. This, in turn, requires very fine-tuned analysis that examines small parts of the dynamics in great detail. Like Marcus and MacKuen, Masters advocates the inclusion of interaction terms in statistical models; it is not clear, however, that statistical interactions alone can capture empirically what Masters proposes conceptually.

Masters uses his many careful studies into the effects of facial displays on emotional responses and attitude change to illustrate his points. He also sets out an almost overwhelming list of factors that can condition emotional responses to facial displays. Master has set out on a journey more demanding than most, and his decade of carefully planned and conducted studies represents an impressive first step or two.

The three chapters on emotion, when juxtaposed, raise a battery of interesting questions about the way political psychologists might proceed in the future. The most fundamental are these: (1) Should political scientists borrow more heavily from research that looks at the "hard wiring" of the brain? (2) If political psychologists indeed take this route, what will be the value added? Will we be better able to explain aspects of mass public opinion and voting behavior? (3) If Masters is correct in his assertion that the brain functions in complex and, more important, unpredictable ways, just how far can political psychologists go with this perspective? Are we traveling down a road that will lead us to intractable problems? One way in which to include more of the materialistic research would be to turn some of the neuropsychological findings into premises from which we then draw implications for politics. At the moment, however, neuropsychology is itself in search of fundamental answers. Finally, (4) can studies that begin with the functioning of the brain answer inevitable (and already existent) criticisms that political psychologists are too reductionist and thus have little to say about politics? Although Masters and Marcus and MacKuen take a big step toward countering that claim, the crucial test will entail showing how these micro level studies can speak to the nature of collective opinion, which is the level at which ordinary citizens' preferences normally enter the political process (see the chapters by Luskin, MacKuen, and Stimson in the accompanying volume).

Clore and Isbell's reaction to the three chapters both expands the discussion of emotions, generally and in political judgment, and raises additional questions. Their discussion is rooted in Clore's earlier work. Emotions provide consciously available information, Clore and Isbell state, but only following (usually) unconscious appraisals of the personal significance of situations. In other words, feelings are closely linked to beliefs and cognition. If this is true, it therefore follows that the kinds of survey measures of emotions that political psychologists often use – "has Ronald Reagan ever made you feel angry?" – can be contaminated, incorporating both emotions *and* prior relevant beliefs. Whether these measures identify truly independent effects of emotions thus remains an open question. The authors recommend the use of mood manipulations, which are independent of any beliefs about a political object, to ascertain whether affect has a direct effect.

Clore and Isbell contend that emotions and feelings do have a direct effect, which manifests itself in people asking themselves, "How do I feel about it?" But this raises a crucial concern: do people use only the target-specific feelings or do they misattribute irrelevant mood and affect as part of their reaction to the target? For example, people might draw on their emotions regarding waving flags and patriotic music to evaluate a candidate rather than on their emotion-based information about the candidate alone. The authors present laboratory evidence that such misattribution can and does happen; in many cases, however, it appears that people adjust for their own affective misattributions, that is, they recognize their response to irrelevant feelings.

Gray's theory of emotion and the "How do I feel about it?" or affect-as-information perspective represent alternative explanations of how emotions influence political judgments. In many instances, the two views offer the same predictions; in the Lakatosian spirit of competing programs and paradigms, Clore and Isbell propose conducting critical tests that might help to choose between them.

EMOTIONS AND THE QUALITY OF POLITICAL JUDGMENTS

Students of politics care about emotions primarily because they can affect the quality of political judgments and decision making. When they work at the level of unconsciousness, emotions can have an especially pernicious effect, which is the central theme in the chapters by Sears and Masters. Symbols and elite rhetoric, Sears argues, can evoke emotional responses that are deeply rooted in early socialization. Thus "welfare," with all its racial connotations, generates markedly less citizen support than "helping the poor." "Affirmative action" serves as a lightning rod for citizen wrath, even though – and especially when – people do not fully understand the program's purpose. Masters's research raises troubling questions about the ability to hold elected leaders accountable in the electronic age. Merely *seeing* a leader, he demonstrates, influences people's attitudes. Television watchers perceive a leader's facial expression, which evokes an emotion (such as anger or happiness), which in turn conditions their attitudes toward the leader. This final effect, it should be underlined, occurs independently of cognitive factors such as the evaluation of issue agreement with the leader. Masters ends on an unsettling note: "[T]he failure to revise our theoretical and practical assumptions in the face of changing scientific findings could be fatal to the very survival of constitutional government." Strong stuff, needless to say.

But so is Marcus and MacKuen's conclusion, which could not stand in stronger contrast to Masters's. Their evidence points to the positive effect that emotions can have on democratic decision making. "Absent increased anxiety and enthusiasm, political campaigns will be stagnant affairs of habit and dull regularity." That is because increased anxiety increases attention to the sources of that anxiety and thus enhances political learning. In short, Marcus and MacKuen see emotions playing not only a positive role in political choice but, in terms of accountability, an essential one. To perform adequately, democratic societies need their citizens to bring feelings and emotions to bear.

So why the strikingly different conclusions between Sears and Masters, on the one hand, and Marcus and MacKuen (and, to a great extent, Clore and Isbell), on the other? Most obviously, the authors are studying different processes and different types of affective responses. Indeed, one can easily lose sight of the fact that the authors purport to be studying the same phenomenon – emotions. This should serve as a warning that any "theory" of emotions in politics is, at best, in its infancy. We need an integration of all the perspectives included in this part, and more. "Emotions" is a catchall term that encompasses everything from anger to joy and elation. What we ultimately need to know is (1) which emotions affect which judgments, (2) when those effects occur, and (3) which form they take. Take anxiety, for example. One might hypothesize, in accord with Marcus and MacKuen, that anxiety increases issue voting and that in the absence of *any* feelings of anxiety people use a standing decision rule. But what about the situation in which anxiety seems to overwhelm everything else? Does this level of anxiety *still* enhance democratic politics? Or is there a curvilinear relationship that remains undetected? Does the same relationship obtain, say, with respect to happiness?

There might be a second reason why Marcus and MacKuen end on a more positive note than Sears and Masters. The latter began their research programs at a time when cognition ruled supreme in political psychology. Implicit in the dominance of this perspective was the assumption that thinking and reasoning – cognition – are superior to visceral reaction. Marcus and MacKuen entered the fray at the very time that social psychology itself was undergoing a metamorphosis; increasingly, psychologists searched for and began to find the positive functions of emotions in decision making. In other words, when political psychologists borrow concepts and methods from psychology, they typically buy into the implicit assumptions that accompany those concepts and methods. These assumptions, in turn, influence the conclusions that the borrowers reach.

The authors represented in part I are too sophisticated to think in dichotomous terms such as that emotions either have a positive *or* a negative effect on political judgments. That said, accepting another discipline's implicit assumptions when borrowing from it happens more often than not. Political psychologists can best attain a balanced conception of emotions and mass politics by explicating what those assumptions are.

I

The Role of Affect in Symbolic Politics

DAVID O. SEARS

Humans often are intensely emotionally involved in remote and abstract political events with only modest direct personal costs and benefits. These involvements have energized many of history's most devastating social, political, and religious conflicts. Why such intense emotions are evoked by situations with so little that is tangible and personal at stake has long been a central puzzle for social scientists. This chapter proposes one psychological approach to the problem.

Political symbols often evoke and mobilize human emotions. Virtually every American war has been fought around such rallying symbols. The Boston Tea Party symbolized the colonials' rebellion against British authority. The Confederacy's attack on Fort Sumter and "Remember the *Maine!*" were the great rallying cries for the Civil War and the Spanish-American War, respectively. The sinking of the *Lusitania* served the same purpose as America entered World War I and the "sneak attack on Pearl Harbor" for World War II. A less successful effort to create the same kind of rallying symbol was the Tonkin Bay incident in 1965, which succeeded in momentarily mobilizing support for the Vietnam War in Congress but not in the general public. Nonetheless, the Vietnam War had its share of wonderfully symbolic phrases, such as the American officer's statement that "we had to destroy it [a Vietnamese town] to save it," symbolizing for many the pointlessness of that conflict.

People can serve as powerful symbols. Jesus, hanging on the cross, is perhaps the most widely known. Revolutionary symbols are familiar to all of us: George Washington, Simon Bolivar, Garibaldi, Lenin, Castro, or Martin Luther King, Jr. People can also symbolize social evils. Marie Antoinette's supposed "let them eat cake" comment, or Nero's fiddling while Rome burned, are examples. Adolf Hitler symbolized the Nazi horror. Richard Nixon, perhaps cursed forever by the Herblock cartoon character crawling out of a sewer, symbolized deceptiveness and sleaze for many in the Watergate affair. Willie Horton, during the 1988 presidential campaign, came to symbolize a whole complex of problems in modern society: the supposed mixture of sexuality and violence in black males and the excessive permissiveness of the liberal Democratic crime policy. The supposed villainy of Saddam Hussein stimulated widespread support for a remote war with little apparent connection to American interests.

Symbols are particularly useful for distinguishing the bad guys from the good guys. There is the spendthrift Congress ("tax and spend, tax and spend"), the Communists, the Ku Klux Klan (KKK), Wall Street, drug kingpins, welfare queens, and Somalian warlords. Or we have "good Americans," "honest working-class people," "the taxpayers," "senior citizens," or even "the people." We have "flower children," "brothers" and "homeboys" in urban ghettoes, "war veterans," and "resistance fighters" (some more credible than others, perhaps, such as the distinction between France in 1943 and Nicaragua in 1983). "Woodstock" symbolized a Rousseauian ideal of peace and brotherhood.

When presented to us, these political symbols rivet our attention and evoke strong emotion. These emotions are dominated by a simple good–bad, like–dislike evaluative dimension. But beyond that, they may also take a wide variety of more specific forms. "Hatred" is not too extreme a word for the emotions behind hate-based crimes (Berk, 1989) and the more extreme forms of xenophobia, such as in the killing in Bosnia. Religious disputes in Northern Ireland, Lebanon, Kashmir, Afghanistan, and the Caucasus evoke hatreds as well. Some mixture of shame and rage may lie behind the most violent of these events (see Retzinger, 1991; Scheff, 1992). "Anger" is the more appropriate label for emotions associated with the antigovernment affect of the tax revolt in the 1970s and 1980s (as in "I'm mad as hell, and I won't take it anymore"; Jarvis, 1978; see also Sears and Citrin, 1985). The Ross Perot campaign of 1992 seems also to have exploited this strain in popular feeling (Craig, 1993), as did such earlier nativist and racist leaders as Gerald L. K. Smith, Father Gerald Coughlin, Joseph McCarthy, and George Wallace (Lipset and Raab, 1979). Fear seems to motivate repression of minorities such as blacks. Disgust has perhaps also accompanied racial prejudice in the United States and other ethnocentrisms such as European anti-Gypsy, anti-Semitic, and anti-guest-worker or anti-immigrant attitudes. The many instances of genocide increasingly recorded by social scientists are presumably founded on such emotions (see Kuper, 1981; Staub, 1989).

Our language for positive emotions in mass politics may be more impoverished, but many supporters of Franklin D. Roosevelt, or of John F. Kennedy or of Fidel Castro in the early 1960s, no less than the supporters for such charismatic leaders as Hitler or Lenin, surely experienced powerfully passionate affections. One should not fail to mention the grandiose "moments of madness" when "all seemed possible," such as in the 1848 European rebellions or the student revolts of the late 1960s or the Cultural Revolution.

This chapter offers a theory of individual psychology, described as a theory of symbolic politics, to explain these powerful mass political emotions. Usually, I will argue, these emotions center on some enduring evaluative predisposition toward relevant political symbols. To understand such emotions properly may require going well beyond such simple predispositions into the treacherous ground of more complex emotions, as these examples suggest. But I would argue that a simpler theory is an indispensable starting point and one that is sufficient for many purposes.

A PSYCHOLOGICAL THEORY OF SYMBOLIC POLITICS

Let us begin with a "simple theory of symbolic politics," as first proposed.[1] It holds that people acquire stable affective responses to particular symbols through a process of classical conditioning, most crucially relatively early in life. The term "political symbol" refers to any affectively charged element in a political attitude object; it is not intended as a singular or special class of those elements.

These learned dispositions may or may not persist throughout adult life, but the strongest, called "symbolic predispositions," do. The most important of these in American politics include party identification, political ideology, and racial prejudice. Later in life, people respond to the daily flow of political attitude objects consistently with these standing predispositions.

Any given attitude object is composed of one or more symbolic elements, and each element conveys some meaning to the individual. Whether the symbolic meaning of an object is fully apparent in its manifest content, or is dependent on some cognitive structure it elicits in the individual, is not prejudged by the use of the term "symbolic meaning"; all that is intended is that the symbol convey some meaning to the individual. Attitudes toward the object as a whole reflect some combination of the affects previously conditioned to the specific symbols included in it. For example, attitudes toward "forced busing to integrate whites and blacks" would depend on affects toward such symbols as "force," "busing," "integration," "whites," and "blacks."

---

1 The most complete earlier descriptions of the psychology of "a simple theory of symbolic politics" have appeared in Sears, Lau, Tyler, and Allen (1980), Sears (1983), and Sears, Huddy, and Schaffer (1986).

The Role of Affect in Symbolic Politics

The adult individual has numerous predispositions (that is, learned affective responses that have been conditioned to specific symbols). When these symbols become salient later on, they should evoke consistent evaluations through a process of "transfer of affect" or cognitive consistency (see Lorge and Curtiss, 1936; Osgood and Tannenbaum, 1955).[2] This assumes that people simply transfer affects from one symbol to another when they are linked to one another. As a result, the symbolic politics process is characterized by rather unthinking, reflexive, affective responses to remote attitude objects, rather than by calculations of probable costs and benefits (whether personal or not).

There are five key propositions in the theory that bear on the role of affect in symbolic politics:

1. Attitudinal predispositions that have a major impact on the adult's evaluation of political attitude objects can be identified. The strongest of these are described as "symbolic predispositions."
2. Symbolic predispositions are strong attitudes normally acquired through classical conditioning in early life (though not necessarily in the preadult years). Their strength is dependent on a variety of factors, most prominently the frequency and consistency of exposure to pairings of the political symbol with the evaluation in question.
3. These symbolic predispositions remain relatively stable throughout adult life.
4. The symbolic meaning of an attitude object evokes particular symbolic predispositions and thereby influences evaluations of it.
5. The process by which symbols evoke predispositions ("symbolic processing") is automatic and affective. Among other things, cost–benefit calculations play a relatively modest role.

Symbolic Predispositions

The core of the symbolic politics process is that standing learned predispositions are evoked by political symbols in the current informational environment. Most of the relevant research has concerned the origins, nature, and effects of these symbolic predispositions. These represent one

---

2 The "transfer of affect" theory is best described in terms of affective consistency rather than cognitive consistency, but congruity theory does not fundamentally differ from it (or indeed from the other cognitive consistency theories) in this respect; all deal primarily with reconciling inconsistent affects rather than with the cognitive processes that bind them together. For exceptions, see Abelson (1959, 1968).

David O. Sears

end of a continuum of attitudes varying in affective strength, at the other of which presumably are "nonattitudes," which are highly unstable, unrelated to other attitudes, and unlikely to influence other preferences (Converse, 1970).[3] They can be identified using three criteria: of all the individual's attitudes, they are the most stable over time (stability), yield the most consistent responses over similar attitude objects (constraint), and have the most influence on attitudes toward other objects (power; see Sears, 1969). Racial prejudice is a good example: it is quite stable over time (Converse and Markus, 1979; Sears, 1983), relatively consistent over racially relevant areas such as schools, jobs, and housing (Sears, 1988), and powerful in determining preferences toward racial policies and black candidates (Sears and Kosterman, 1991).

Much research has documented the influence of such predispositions on other political attitudes. Simple examples can be drawn from two of the most passionate and divisive political disputes in recent American history. One is the role of racial prejudices in producing antibusing (for school integration) attitudes. Their dominant role has been repeatedly documented, both in national (Sears, Hensler, and Speer, 1979) and local (McConahay, 1982; Sears and Allen, 1984) studies. Similarly, religiosity and other forms of moral conservatism are strong determinants of antiabortion attitudes (Blauwkamp, Fastnow, and Kellstedt, 1992; Luker, 1984; Sears and Huddy, 1990). In neither case do any other measured variables even approach the explanatory power of such predispositions.

This pattern holds across a wide variety of other studies on other issues. A typical study (Sears, Lau, Tyler, and Allen, 1980) used a national survey of adults, with attitudes toward major policy issues (unemployment, national health insurance, busing, and law and order) as dependent variables. The predictors were the major symbolic predispositions (party identification, ideology, and racial attitudes) and indicators of self-interest. The symbolic predispositions had strong effects, while self-interest had virtually none.

Similarly, policy and candidate preferences have often been shown to be influenced by standing party identification (e.g., Campbell, Converse, Miller, and Stokes, 1960), social values (Feldman, 1988), racial attitudes (Sears, 1988), and antagonisms toward such groups as the Communists, Nazis, and the KKK (Sullivan, Pierson, and Marcus, 1982). Whites' racial attitudes influence opposition to affirmative action and black candidates (Jessor, 1988; Kinder and Sears, 1981; Sears, Citrin, and

---

3 Fazio's recent work on the automatic activation of attitudes asserts a very similar underlying continuum in the strength of object–evaluation associations, though he refers to it as an "attitude–nonattitude continuum" (1993, p. 758).

18

Kosterman, 1987; Sears and Kosterman, 1991); political ideology, opposition to communism, and support for the military influenced support for the Vietnam War (Lau, Brown, and Sears, 1978); party identification, ideology, and racial attitudes influenced support for the California tax revolt (Sears and Citrin, 1985); and basic values activated by symbols of injustice, inequity, or immorality produced mass protests (Sears and Citrin, 1985; Sears and McConahay, 1973).

The second proposition is that such symbolic predispositions are acquired relatively early in life. Extensive research on political socialization has investigated children's and adolescents' early affective responses to such symbols as the flag, the president, stigmatized racial groups, and the political parties (e.g., Easton and Dennis, 1969; Hyman, 1959; Katz, 1976). This early learning presumably yields such predispositions as party identification, racial prejudices, ethnic identities, basic values, nationalism, and attachment to various symbols of the nation and regime.

The third proposition is that these early acquired predispositions persist through life. Early researchers on political socialization believed that childhood and early adolescent experiences were formative (Easton and Dennis, 1969; Hyman, 1959), whereas Mannheim (1952) pinpointed late adolescence as a critical period for the acquisition of lasting attitudes. "Revisionist" theorists (e.g., Franklin, 1984), in contrast, hold that short-term forces continue to influence symbolic predispositions (such as party identification) through adulthood.

Such disputes have led to the formulation of several alternative models of attitude change (and susceptibility to change) across the life span (Alwin, 1991; Sears, 1975, 1983) and to empirical tests among them. Extensive research has indicated support for both the "persistence" and the "impressionable years" viewpoints (see Sears, 1989, for a review; also see Alwin and Krosnick, 1988; Alwin, Cohen, and Newcomb, 1991; Green and Palmquist, 1990; Sears, 1983). Especially interesting recent work has been done on the conditions for long-term attitude stability (Niemi and Jennings, 1991; Sears, Zucker, and Funk, 1992), and especially on socialization experiences later in the life span (Sigel, 1989).[4]

---

4 There is an active debate between "traditional" and "revisionist" views of persistence, with the latter asserting considerably more influence during adulthood of short-term forces on long-standing predispositions than does the former. The revisionists' strongest claims center on attitude changes in young adulthood, however; the burden of evidence suggests stability rather than change in later adulthood (see Alwin, Cohen, and Newcomb, 1991; Green and Palmquist, 1990, 1992; Sears and Funk, 1990).

David O. Sears

Symbolic Meaning

Our fourth proposition suggests that symbolic meaning influences evaluations of the attitude object. And changes in symbolic meaning should do so as well. The symbols contained in the object can vary cross-sectionally among individuals at one time point or longitudinally within individuals over time. The effects of changes in symbolic meaning have been investigated in a number of contexts.

Only recently has attention begun to be be devoted to the role of the evoking political symbols. At the simplest level, naturalistic wording variations sometimes show dramatic effects on evaluations of public policy (though they do not always do so). Support for intervention in the Korean War was considerably greater when it was described as intended "to stop the Communist invasion of South Korea" than when it was simply described as "the war in Korea" (Mueller, 1973). Most people strongly oppose spending for "welfare" but support "helping the poor," "public assistance programs to the elderly and the disabled," and programs "for low-income families with dependent children," which together comprise a major portion of welfare spending (see Sears and Citrin, 1985; Smith, 1987). Whites overwhelmingly oppose "busing" but support "racial integration of the schools" (Schuman, Steeh, and Bobo, 1985; Sears, Hensler, and Speer, 1979). In each case the differences may be due to a variety of factors, but it seems likely that the presence of affectively loaded symbols such as "Communists," "welfare," or "blacks" or other minority cultures is a critical factor.

A second point concerns the level of abstraction of political symbols. The conventional wisdom in political science and social psychology has been that abstract attitude objects are processed differently than concrete ones. Converse (1964) argued that relatively few voters possess abstract ideological conceptualizations that would permit the deduction of specific policy attitudes. On the other hand, deductive hierarchical structures play a more prominent role in contemporary social psychology, as "top-down" or "theory-driven" processing helps "cognitive misers" to minimize psychologically costly information-processing efforts (Fiske and Taylor, 1991; Hurwitz and Peffley, 1987).

The simple symbolic politics view is quite different from either view of abstract attitude objects. It assumes that processing of political symbols depends on the evaluations associated with them, not on the symbols' level of abstraction. Several findings indicate that political symbols presented at different levels of abstraction but referring to the same underlying reality do draw different responses, but because of the differences in their manifest contents (and, presumably, the evaluations associated with them), not because of differences in abstraction. For example, most Americans prefer, in the abstract, "less government" to "more government." On the other hand, a large majority also consistently prefer that government services in specific areas (such as the schools, police, public health, etc.) be at least maintained at current levels, not cut. But there is no evidence that these two sets of attitude objects are processed very differently, despite the difference in levels of abstraction: in one extensive study, both were explained by the same predispositions (party identification, ideology, and racial attitudes), and both had similar effects upon support for tax cuts (Sears and Citrin, 1985). A simple symbolic politics theory would explain the less favorable evaluation of the more abstract object as principally due to the different manifest symbolic content presented at each level of abstraction (and the different conditioned associations to those different symbols), not to the difference in level of abstraction per se (also see Sears et al., 1986).

A third case in point concerns social groups as attitude objects. Much social science theory holds that they are not treated like other political symbols; rather, they have special psychological meaning. For example, the conventional wisdom in social psychology has been that one's group identity is psychologically central to the individual, with self-esteem partially dependent upon perceiving one's own group as superior to other groups (Tajfel, 1982). Similarly, a "sense of group position" is thought likely to generate racial prejudice when the dominant group feels threatened by other groups (Blumer, 1958). And groups are thought to be the most "central" of political attitude objects, so that political parties are perceived in terms of which groups they favor or oppose, with voters adopting "ideologies by proxy" from the beliefs of their own groups, providing the psychological foundation for ego-involved attitudes (Campbell et al., 1960; Converse, 1964; Sherif and Cantril, 1947). Similarly, group interest is said to be a powerful determinant of one's political preferences (Bobo, 1983; Sniderman and Tetlock, 1986).

The symbolic politics view, in contrast, is that a group represents an attitude object like any other and therefore evokes affective responses in the same manner. Groups may behave like other political symbols, mainly evoking symbolic predispositions (as in patriotism or nationalism or class solidarity), and so may be best described in terms of symbolic politics (see Conover, 1988; Jessor, 1988; Sears, 1988). For example, people's willingness to extend civil liberties to a group depends on their evaluations of the group (Stouffer, 1955; Sullivan et al., 1982).

But more than that, support for policies or candidacies associated with a particular group should be influenced quite specifically by

David O. Sears

evaluations of that group and not of other groups. So whites' attitudes toward racial policies and black candidates are influenced by their evaluations of blacks but not of whites (Sears and Kosterman, 1991), and non-Hispanics' attitudes toward bilingual education are influenced by evaluations of Hispanics (but not of other minorities or whites; Sears and Huddy, 1990). Similarly, racial equality values influence support for racial policies, and gender equality values influence support for gender policies, but neither set of values influences issues affecting the other group (Sears, Huddy, and Schaffer, 1986).

Symbolic Processing

The theory of symbolic politics also describes a distinctive mode of information processing, which might be called "symbolic processing." Most notably, it proceeds in terms of strong affective responses to political symbols. When we hear the word "democracy" we have a strong and immediate positive affect; when we hear the word "Nazi" we have a strong and immediate negative response. Affect is central to this process, then, since political symbols are assumed to evoke strong emotions in the individual.

A contemporary illustration of affectively driven symbolic processing is "hot button" political advertising. Political campaigns devote much of their attention to trying to discover what issues or symbols evoke an emotional response, that is, what hits voters' hot buttons. The assumption is, as one specialist put it, that "voting is a matter of the heart, what you *feel* about someone, rather than a matter of the mind.... [The mind] takes what the heart feels, and interprets it" (Diamond and Bates, 1984, p. 316). Certainly the hot button formula of many modern political ads, such as Lyndon Johnson's Daisy spot, George Bush's "revolving-door justice" spot, or Ronald Reagan's "morning in America" ads, aim to evoke gut-level, affective responses (Kosterman, 1991).

Two recent experiments provide examples. Perdue, Dovidio, Gurtman, and Tyler (1990) demonstrated that pairing nonsense syllables with in-group designators such as "we" or "ours" led to more favorable evaluations of the nonsense syllables than did pairing them with such out-group designators as "they" or "theirs," even when the latter were presented only briefly and subliminally prior to the nonsense syllables. In another experiment, Americans responded more negatively to foreign than to American leaders when shown television clips without audio tracks. Interestingly enough, this negative response to foreign leaders disappeared when the audio information was supplied, suggesting that the negative affect was an immediate, primary, and noncognitive response to the leaders' foreignness (see Warnecke, Masters, and Kempter, 1992).[5]

A second aspect of symbolic processing is that evaluation of the attitude object is cumulative and rapidly becomes detached from its informational origins. This is described by the notion of "on-line processing" (as opposed to "memory-based processing"; see Hastie and Park, 1986). The individual makes an evaluative judgment as relevant information is encountered and then essentially keeps only a running tally, simply retrieving and updating that summary evaluation with later information but forgetting the actual pieces of evidence that contributed to it. Indeed, there is much evidence from experimental studies of impressions and attitudes that affective change is generally only weakly correlated with memory for the information that originally induced the change (see Anderson and Hubert, 1963; Fiske and Taylor, 1991). In experiments on political information processing, similarly, Lodge and his colleagues (1993) find that candidate evaluations are responsive to campaign messages, and indeed, the cumulative evaluation continues to reflect those message effects for some time. But the contents of the specific messages are themselves quickly forgotten.

Third, symbolic processing involves a relatively swift, reflexive, automatic triggering of an appropriate predisposition by a political symbol, guided by pressures toward affective consistency (Lorge and Curtiss, 1936; Osgood and Tannenbaum, 1955). In general, these consistency pressures are assumed to operate quickly and nondeliberatively. Consistent with this view, much of our research has shown that rational calculations of self-interest are weak forces in mass politics (Sears and Funk, 1991).

Fourth, affect often dominates cognition. Which of them plays the more important role in mass politics is an old debate, originally framed by James Madison in the *Federalist Papers* as pitting passion against reason (see Marcus, Sullivan, Theiss-Morse, and Barnum, 1989). Many have attempted to contrast the empirical impact of the two, going back at least to the work of Rosenberg (1960) and Carlson (1956) in the early days of consistency theory.

In more recent work, the dominance of simple evaluative predispositions can perhaps be seen in the ineffectiveness of (content-rich)

---

5 While the difference between positive and negative affect is crucial to a symbolic politics theory, it does not concern itself with qualitatively different *kinds* of affect in each category. For example, fear is not differentiated from anger, or hope from pity, contrary to some current theories of emotion (see Marcus, 1990; Roseman, Abelson, and Ewing, 1986; Weiner, 1974). It may be that such distinctions will be valuable in the future.

short-term forces in altering (highly affective) long-term partisan commitments (Green and Palmquist, 1990, 1992). Granberg and Brown (1989) report several conceptually similar findings in a study of candidate evaluations and the vote. Candidate evaluations were more closely related to the vote than were cognitions about the candidates; the stability of evaluations of parties and candidates, and the association of evaluations with the vote, were only minimally affected by the number of relevant cognitions held by the individual; and the evaluative ambivalence of the individual's cognitions, not their number, was the critical influence on all these indicators of partisan strength. Finally, Rahn and her colleagues (1994) find that the "reasons" voters give for their votes tend to be rationalizations of their evaluative preferences rather than derivations of their votes from their "reasons." Early deciders and the highly politically involved are especially likely to muster extensive cognitive rationalization for their prior preferences.

ATTITUDE ACCESSIBILITY AND AUTOMATIC ACTIVATION

This symbolic politics theory has emerged from cross-sectional surveys of the general population. However, the phenomena it focuses on, and the underlying theory, are quite similar to those developed in contemporary laboratory social psychology.

It has long been recognized that evaluation is central to such core phenomena of social psychology as social perception, interpersonal attraction, attitudes, and prejudice. Early experiments on impression formation showed that the warm–cold dimension is an especially central dimension of person perception (Asch, 1946; Kelley, 1950). Later, Osgood, Suci, and Tannenbaum (1957) demonstrated that evaluation is the central dimension of meaning in a wide variety of areas of life; its importance is in no way limited to person perception.

More recently, Zajonc (1980, 1984) also believes that evaluation is a universal component of all perception and meaning. But he goes on to propose that affect is a separate system altogether from cognition and, in his "affective primacy" hypothesis, that affect is primary, basic, inescapable, irrevocable, difficult to verbalize, capable of being elicited with minimal stimulus input, often dependent on cognition, and quite separate from content or knowledge (see also Murphy and Zajonc, 1993). That is, affective reactions are primary; they do not depend on prior cognitive appraisals and, indeed, may become completely separated from the content on which they were originally based (though perhaps later cognitively justified). In this sense, affect does not depend upon deliberate, rational, or conscious thought and may not even depend on unconscious mental activity.[6]

The clearest applications of such affect-driven theories to experimental studies of attitudes use the concepts of "attitude accessibility" (Fazio, 1986) and "automatic attitude activation" (Bargh, Chaiken, Govender, and Pratto, 1992). Both lines of work extend basic memory models to the case of attitudes (also see the recent synthesis by Greenwald and Banaji, 1995). This approach begins with the assumption that long-term memory is an "associative network," a system of nodes connected by associational links (Anderson, 1983). For example, "the Democrats support racial quotas" is stored as two nodes (the Democrats, racial quotas) and the link associating them (supports). Recall begins at one node, and activation spreads along the links between nodes (Collins and Loftus, 1975). These links are strengthened each time they are activated.

To apply the model to attitudes requires thinking of "an attitude [as] essentially an association between a given object and a given evaluation" stored in long-term memory (Fazio, 1986, p. 214). The nodes of the network could be any kind of attitude object. When the attitude object is encountered, the attitude is activated and enters consciousness (i.e., is accessed). The process of activation is said to be an automatic, spontaneous one; it does not require reflection or attention (Fazio, Sanbanmatsu, Powell, and Kardes, 1986). The key point for the present discussion is that evaluation is central to the process.

Automatic Processing

This approach views attitudes as spontaneously and automatically activated in the presence of the attitude object. Swift evaluative responses are the hallmark of the accessing of attitudes: people quickly classify objects as either good or bad. This automatic processing can occur without conscious goals, control, attention, or awareness, and so it places minimal demands on processing capacity (Bargh, 1988, 1989). One example is the experimental evidence produced by Murphy and Zajonc (1993) that only affective primes work with extremely brief

---

6 There are objections to the Zajonc view. Lazarus (1984) has argued that prior cognitive appraisal, especially of the personal significance of the stimulus, is necessary before the affective response occurs. Similarly, Weiner (1986) contends that cognitive attributions precede emotions; for example, making an internal attribution for a positive outcome produces pride, whereas making an external, controllable attribution for a negative event produces anger.

(probably subawareness) exposure durations; only with longer exposure durations do cognitive primes influence judgment. In other words, affective responses immediately and almost reflexively influence judgment, even when there is minimal or no cognitive participation.

There are several versions of this automatic processing process, and they have a good deal in common, so they will be cited briefly here. One version distinguishes *automatic* from *controlled* processing (Shiffrin and Schneider, 1977). Automatic processing involves the spontaneous activation of a well-learned set of associations that have been developed through repeated activation in memory. An example offered by Devine (1989) is of conventional American racial stereotypes. They are learned early in life, before children develop the cognitive ability to evaluate them critically. Devine argues that they represent a frequently activated, well-learned set of associations that are automatically activated in the presence of a group member (or symbolic equivalent of the target group) for virtually all Americans. In contrast, "controlled processing" is voluntary and requires conscious effort and active control by the individual. An example is the "theory of reasoned action" (Ajzen and Fishbein, 1980), which contends that behavior follows from behavioral intentions, which in turn are derived from attitudes toward the action and normative expectations, in a quite conscious and deliberate way.

A second distinction, discussed earlier, is between *on-line* and *memory-based* processing (Hastie and Park, 1986). In on-line processing, the individual keeps a running tally of evaluation of the attitude object. Each new piece of information is simply absorbed as an incremental updating of that running tally, but the information itself is not necessarily stored. When the attitude is primed, the current stored summary evaluation is retrieved, not the raw information on which it was based. As a result, evaluation is independent of memory of the details. In contrast, in memory-based processing, attitudes are dependent on the retrieval of specific pieces of information from memory, and are predictable from the mix of pro and con information retrieved from memory (McGraw, Lodge, and Stroh, 1990). Experiments by Lodge, McGraw, and Stroh (1989) found that on-line processing dominated in "impression-driven" conditions, in which individuals were presented with various pieces of information about a political candidate and then were asked whether they liked or disliked the candidate. Memory-based processing appeared only in a "memory-driven" condition, in which they instructed the person simply to try to understand the information.

A third distinction is between *category-based* and *piecemeal* processing (Fiske and Pavelchak, 1986). In category-based processing, perceivers categorize other individuals immediately upon encountering them, rapidly and at a perceptual level rather than as a consequence of deliberate and conscious thought. The category carries an "affective tag" that transfers immediately to the evaluation of the target individual. Fiske and Neuberg (1990) argue that category-based processes typically have priority over more attribute-oriented, individuating processes, or "piecemeal processing," in which the stimulus person is processed in terms of his or her own individual attributes, with each individual piece of information being reviewed and integrated into the overall impression. A similar distinction has been developed by Brewer (1988), between "category-based" and "person-based" processing, in her "dual-process model of impression formation."

Several recently developed psychological concepts parallel what we have described as symbolic processing, then: the automatic activation of attitudes, automatic processing, on-line processing, and category-based processing. All are highly affective rather than contentful or cognitive; spontaneous rather than deliberate; cognitively effortless, making minimal demands on cognitive processes; automatic rather than intentional or voluntary; and oriented around symbolic representations.

A fourth distinction does not parallel these quite as neatly: between "peripheral" or "heuristic" processing, on the one hand, and "central" or "systematic" processing, on the other (Chaiken, 1980; Petty and Cacioppo, 1986). The former describes attitude change resulting from cues other than the merits of the arguments, such as source expertness or attractiveness. The latter emphasizes deliberate and thoughtful processing of persuasive arguments, evaluating each for its validity. Peripheral/heuristic processing does parallel a piece of the symbolic or automatic processing picture in that the individual responds without thoughtful review of the details of the arguments. But it misses an equally central element: the swift and reflexive affective response based on strong object–evaluation associations (Kosterman, 1991). Central/systematic processing would seem to correspond more closely to controlled processing in that attitude change is dependent on piecemeal review of the individual arguments.

Priming

Priming is a key concept in attitude activation: "the mere presentation of an attitude object toward which the individual possesses a strong evaluative association would automatically activate the evaluation" (Fazio, 1989, p. 157). For example, presenting positively evaluated words, even if only momentarily or subliminally, can speed the response to other positively valenced stimuli (with symmetrical effects of priming negative affects; Devine, 1989; Fazio et al., 1986; Perdue et al., 1990).

David O. Sears

Activating an accessible construct through priming should increase its impact over other attitudes, judgments, and behavior. For example, priming a particular trait construct gives it more weight in impression formation. Bargh, Lombardi, and Higgins (1988) presented subjects with a group of four words that contained the critical priming trait (e.g., "she, *outgoing*, is, was"), then an ambiguous description of a person's behavior (e.g., "he monopolized the telephone where he lived"), and then asked for one word best describing this type of person. The primed adjective was more likely to be given.

Priming political attitudes has been shown experimentally to enhance their impact on candidate evaluations. Sherman and colleagues (1990) activated the categories of either foreign affairs (by presenting words such as "diplomat") or the economy (e.g., "fiscal"). Then they described a political candidate who was experienced in one area but inexperienced in the other. Evaluations of the candidate were most influenced by his level of experience in the area that had previously been primed. Similarly, "agenda-setting effects" show that emphasizing a particular issue in television news broadcasts increases that issue's weight in viewers' evaluations of presidential performance (Iyengar and Kinder, 1987). This can be thought of as another kind of priming effect: watching network coverage of a particular issue primes the individual's attitudes toward that issue, making them more accessible and more influential.

Chronic Accessibility

Some attitudes are more accessible than others on a long-term basis: "like any construct based on associative learning, the strength of the attitude can vary . . . this associative strength may determine the accessibility of the attitude from memory" (Fazio, 1986, p. 214). Spontaneous activation, without prompting from situational cues or even extensive exposure to the attitude object itself, should by this theory occur most readily with highly accessible attitudes, that is, those with especially strong associative links between attitude object and evaluation. Even if not directly primed, they will dominate other attitudes. Less strong attitudes must be more explicitly primed to have an effect, either through exposure to the attitude object or prompting from situational cues (Higgins and King, 1981).

This dimension of chronic accessibility, reflecting the strength of object–evaluation association, is analogous to a number of other concepts that bear on underlying attitude strength, such as "ego involvement" (Sherif and Cantril, 1947), "attitude centrality" (Converse, 1964), "attitude importance" (Krosnick, 1988), "conviction" about one's attitude (Abelson, 1988), or "public commitment" to an attitude (Hovland, Campbell, and Brock, 1957). In the language of symbolic politics, sym-

28

bolic predispositions anchor one end of this dimension and nonattitudes the other (Sears, 1983).[7]

The link between accessibility and attitude strength lies in the notion that attitudes are evaluations stored (along with relevant information) in long-term memory and varying in associative strength. Accessibility in memory does provide one potential explanation for the effects of attitude strength on resistance to change or influence over other attitudes. For example, Krosnick (1989) has suggested that the effects of attitude importance are due to accessibility; more important attitudes are more accessible, and therefore more easily evoked and more likely to influence other attitudes. Similarly, Fazio and his colleagues argue that more accessible attitudes produce higher attitude–behavior consistency, such as between preelection candidate preference and actual vote (e.g., Fazio et al., 1986; Fazio and Williams, 1986).

There is some controversy about whether or not strong (more accessible) attitudes are indeed more readily activated than weak ones in laboratory studies. Fazio's (1993) view is that strong attitudes are activated much more readily than weak attitudes, while Bargh's view (see Bargh, Chaiken, Govender, and Pratto, 1992; Chaiken and Bargh, 1993) is that all attitudes are automatically activated. In this dialogue there is some consensus that strong attitudes are more readily activated but debate over whether idiosyncratic or consensual determinants of attitude strength are more important.

It should be noted, though, that laboratory studies are generally working at the tepid end of the affective continuum. For truly strong object–evaluation associations (as the Fazio theory requires), one might want to look at attitude objects with extremely long histories. "Collective memories," or "public memories" (see Brown, Shevill, and Rips, 1986; Schuman and Scott, 1989), such as those of World War II or of the assassination of President John F. Kennedy, might offer better representatives of the strong-predisposition camp. Memories of group oppression are likely to be especially significant, such as the cultural conflicts surrounding collective memories of the American West (Novotny, 1992).

---

7 Not everyone would agree that all these concepts can be reduced to a single dimension of attitude strength. Raden (1985) and Krosnick and Schuman (1988) raise such questions, and others (Johnson and Eagly, 1989) distinguish three different versions of ego involvement, of which "valuerelevant" (i.e., "position involvement") most parallels attitude strength. It should also be noted that the psychological mainsprings of these various concepts vary somewhat. Sherif and Cantril (1947) and Converse (1964) suspect that the strongest ego involvements were anchored in some sense of group identity, while Abelson (1968) describes "conviction" as deriving from emotional commitment, ego preoccupation, and cognitive elaboration.

David O. Sears

In short, the core idea of a symbolic politics theory, as it has been developed in survey research on political behavior, is that strongly held affective predispositions are triggered automatically by attitude objects with relevant symbolic meaning. Quite independently, recent experimental work on attitudes has treated them in parallel fashion, as elements in an associative network that vary in the strength of the object–evaluation association (i.e., in attitude strength). Those with the strongest associations are most accessible in memory and are evoked most automatically when primed with relevant stimuli. The notion of symbolic processing of political symbols relevant to symbolic predispositions would seem to have much in common with the notions of automatic processing of objects that activate chronically accessible attitudes, on-line processing, and category-based processing. All of them would seem to contrast with the concepts of controlled processing, memory-based processing, attribute-based processing, or central processing. But these latter literatures have been developed on the basis of experimental laboratory research.

Most social psychologists seem to feel that automatic processing dominates in ordinary life: "It appears that most daily behaviors are not sufficiently consequential to induce people to undertake a controlled analysis" (Fazio, 1986, p. 238); "category-based processes seem to be the default option . . . under ordinary conditions, people simply do not pay enough attention to individuate each other" (Fiske and Neuberg, 1990, p. 21); "person-based encoding is the exception rather than the rule in . . . complex information settings" (Brewer, 1988, p. 3); and "on-line processing is . . . psychologically realistic in placing minimal information-processing demands on voters" (Lodge et al., 1989, p. 416) and is more common than memory-based processing (also see Fiske and Taylor, 1991; Hastie and Park, 1986).

This might imply that symbolic processing would dominate mass politics as well. But this does not necessarily follow because the conditions of mass politics are special ones (like those of any specialized realm of human life). So which of these modes of processing best fits the natural conditions of mass politics? To answer this question, we need to review the conditions under which automatic as opposed to more controlled processing takes place. And then we need to ask how common they are in mass politics.

For one thing, *time pressure* and *limited attention*, and indeed limited cognitive resources in general, promote category-based processing (Fiske and Neuberg, 1990). These, of course, are perennially at the heart of the problem with public participation in politics. It is clear that ordinary people usually do not have a great deal of political information (Kinder and Sears, 1985; Sears, 1969). Nor do they pay close attention to the political media; even though television is ubiquitous in our society, it usually receives diffused and distracted attention from the public, and that is particularly true of political messages (Kinder and Sears, 1985; Sears and Kosterman, 1991). The incentives for public attentiveness are minimal, and there are many other demands on people's time, so politics is plainly one area of life in which decision-making shortcuts are likely to be found. Indeed, the cognitive miser may be just as rational as Downs's (1957) rational nonvoter. So the generally poor information and weak attention of the mass public should favor symbolic processing.

Category-based processing requires the presence of *appropriate categories*, strongly established categories, and consistency of the target with the category (Fiske and Neuberg, 1990). To be sure, nonattitudes abound in politics. But both politicians and journalists try to frame issues and candidates in terms that can be readily linked to widespread, consensually understood predispositions. That is, the information environment in mass politics is heavily biased toward widely understood and shared categories. When that process is successful, the public is likely to be very effective in making its will(s) known; if it is unsuccessful, the public will flounder and its voice is likely to be dimly heard.

Symbolic processing should be most common under conditions of *strong object–evaluation associations*. True, the mass public's attitudes toward the detailed issues of public life are frequently not very consistent or stable (Converse, 1964, 1970; Zaller and Feldman, 1992). On the other hand, they do have quite strong and stable attitudes toward the continuing political symbols of the era, and those are the attitudes that are evoked most often (Converse and Markus, 1979; Sears, 1983).

On-line processing is enhanced by an *impression set*, in which the individual's goal is to develop an impression of another person, whereas memory-based processing is enhanced by the goal of remembering the informational details (Fiske and Taylor, 1991). And in fact, an impression set is the ordinary person's orientation toward politics. The main practical decisions voters must make are choices between candidates, which require impressions of those rivals. This is the focal point of much mass political conversation as well: "what do you think of X?"

A considerable body of experimental work argues that central processing, and consequent close attention to the merits of the arguments, are stimulated by *personal involvement* in the outcomes of the issues (Johnson and Eagly, 1989; Petty and Cacioppo, 1986). In the political behavior literature this variable has been described as "self-interest" or

31

the personal impact of political issues (Sears and Funk, 1991). Similarly, outcome interdependence with another person motivates closer attention to the details of that person's nature, especially short-term, task-oriented outcome dependence on the target (Fiske and Neuberg, 1990). However, such situations are relatively rare in politics. For the most part, the political choices faced by ordinary citizens do not have a major impact on their personal lives (Green, 1988; Sears and Funk, 1991).

Moreover, there is a good deal of evidence that people do not induce political preferences from the details of their own personal experiences. Rather, people appear to be slow to draw societal-level implications from *personal*-level information and vice versa; the two seem to be cognitively compartmentalized. Extensive reviews of the literature on the political effects of self-interest have been published elsewhere and need not be reiterated here. The best evidence is that self-interest has relatively little impact on political attitudes (Sears and Funk, 1991). On the few occasions that self-interest does have large effects on public opinion, they tend to be cognitively quite narrow.

For all these reasons, then, I would argue that strongly affective symbolic processing (or, in social psychological language, automatic processing) is most likely under the conditions that hold most commonly in mass politics. Of course, there are exceptions; sometimes people do have the advantages of extended campaigns and a great deal of information, sometimes they do not have handy categories to apply, sometimes they do not need to arrive at a fast impression, and sometimes personal considerations are quite salient.

Yet it is not self-evident that even these seemingly infertile conditions foreclose symbolic processing. The California tax revolt met most of these conditions: a campaign that lasted for years, not months, with extensive media coverage, no particularly central personalized leaders, and important and well-publicized personal implications. Yet it proved to be vintage symbolic politics, mixed with some other elements, to be sure (Sears and Citrin, 1985). In my view, it is difficult for mass politics to escape the conditions that most encourage symbolic processing.

SOME IMPLICATIONS FOR DEMOCRATIC THEORY

Let me close with two observations about the implications of this work for how we think about democratic governance. As Page and Shapiro (1992) have wisely noted in their book, a variety of perspectives on the general public is possible. Theirs is one of a fairly sensible and rational public, doing as well as can be expected given the limited and biased information it is given. The image conveyed by the symbolic politics approach is rather different: emotional and reflexive responses to political symbols, relatively heedless of instrumentalities or realities. To be sure, this view is of the public in the aggregate, and it concedes that it is not a good representation of the individual.

The symbolic politics model is most obviously geared to the political conditions under which manipulation of the public is most likely to occur. By the reasoning laid out here, such efforts should be least fruitful on stimuli that have a clear, unambiguous, and consensual meaning. It has been difficult, for example, to change the meaning of busing because it is so widely viewed as a racial issue. On the other hand, manipulation should be easier on issues or candidates that lack consensual or manifest symbolism. When a new candidate, such as Michael Dukakis or Bill Clinton, comes onto the political scene, he is something of a black box, whose profile can be molded to elicit either positive or negative underlying predispositions – though presumably within some constraints based on reality.

Controlling the public agenda is required in order to control the symbolic meaning of an attitude object. Such control is politically consequential both in influencing overall public support for the object and in influencing which predisposition it evokes. By manipulating the meaning of an issue like crime, for example, as the Republican campaign did with the Willie Horton commercials in 1988, one can manipulate the role of a powerful and damaging predisposition such as racism. Similarly, regimes often manipulate national symbols to evoke loyalty and patriotism, as frequently has been done in recent times to mobilize secessionist sentiments in formerly Communist nations.[8]

The normative impact of the symbolic politics process on democratic governance depends to a great extent upon what symbols are salient in the public arena. If the symbols evoke the uglier set of our predispositions – prejudice, ethnocentrism, nationalism, hostility toward the weak and disadvantaged – that is what we are likely to get. If the symbols appeal to our better sides – to our communitarian spirit, our selflessness, our idealism – that is what we are likely to get. Political elites are to a considerable extent prisoners of their times; events dictate, to some extent, what is placed upon the public agenda. But let us not forget that no theory of good or bad times will explain variation in our own leaders' appeals to the better or to the worse sides of human nature. In our own

8 This ignores the possibility that in some natural situations the direction of causality will be reversed: the predisposition itself may influence which symbolic meaning the attitude object takes on, rather than vice versa. For example, a particular set of political protests can "mean" an ugly resurgence of nationalism or an inspiring liberation from an imperial oppressor, depending on one's predisposition. We are not here addressing this particular sequence.

country, the chaos of a new nation, civil war, or a great depression have generated some of our most uplifting presidencies. As V. O. Key pointed out years ago (1961), political elites bear a considerable responsibility for the choices they offer the general public, and therefore a considerable responsibility for the direction it then turns.

References

Abelson, R. P. (1959). Modes of resolution of belief dilemmas. *Journal of Conflict Resolution*, 3, 343–352.
(1968). Psychological implication. In R. P. Abelson, E. Aronson, W. J. McGuire, T. M. Newcomb, M. J. Rosenberg, and P. H. Tannenbaum (Eds.), *Theories of cognitive consistency: A sourcebook* (pp. 112–139). Chicago: Rand McNally.
(1988). Conviction. *American Psychologist*, 43, 267–275.
Ajzen, I., and Fishbein, M. (1980). *Understanding attitudes and predicting social behavior*. Englewood Cliffs, NJ: Prentice-Hall.
Alwin, D. F. (1991). Aging, personality and social change. In D. L. Featherman, R. M. Lerner, and M. Perlmutter (Eds.), *Life-span development and behavior* (Vol. 12). Hillsdale, NJ: Erlbaum.
Alwin, D. F., Cohen, R. L., and Newcomb, T. M. (1991). *Aging, personality and social change: Attitude persistence and change over the life-span*. Madison: University of Wisconsin Press.
Alwin, D. F., and Krosnick, J. A. (1988). Aging, cohorts, and change in political orientation: exploring the aging–attitude stability relationship. Paper presented at the annual meeting of the International Society of Political Psychology, Secaucus, NJ.
Anderson, J. R. (1983). *The architecture of cognition*. Cambridge, MA: Harvard University Press.
Anderson, N. H., and Hubert, S. (1963). Effects of concomitant verbal recall on order effects in personality impression formation. *Journal of Verbal Learning and Verbal Behavior*, 2, 379–391.
Asch, S. E. (1946). Forming impressions of personality. *Journal of Abnormal and Social Psychology*, 41, 258–290.
Bargh, J. A. (1988). Automatic information processing: Implications for communication and affect. In L. Donohew, H. E. Sypher, and E. T. Higgins (Eds.), *Communication, social cognition, and affect* (pp. 9–32). Hillsdale, NJ: Erlbaum.
(1989). Conditional automaticity: Varieties of automatic influence in social perception and cognition. In J. S. Uleman and J. A. Bargh (Eds.), *Unintended thought* (pp. 3–51). New York: Guilford Press.
Bargh, J. A., Chaiken, S., Govender, R., and Pratto, F. (1992). The generality of the automatic attitude activation effect. *Journal of Personality and Social Psychology*, 62, 893–912.
Bargh, J. A., Lombardi, W. J., and Higgins, E. T. (1988). Automaticity of chronically accessible constructs in person × situation effects on person perception: it's just a matter of time. *Journal of Personality and Social Psychology*, 55, 599–605.

Berk, R. A. (1989). Thinking about hate-motivated crimes. Unpublished manuscript, UCLA.

Blauwkamp, J. M., Fastnow, C. L., and Kellstedt, L. A. (1992). Religion and abortion attitudes: An update and extension of the Luker thesis. Presented at the annual meeting of the American Political Science Association, Chicago.

Blumer, H. (1958). Race prejudice as a sense of group position. *Pacific Sociological Review*, *1*, 3–7.

Bobo, L. (1983). Whites' opposition to busing: Symbolic racism or realistic group conflict? *Journal of Personality and Social Psychology*, *45*, 1196–1210.

Brewer, M. B. (1988). A dual process model of impression formation. In T. K. Srull and R. S. Wyer, Jr. (Eds.), *Advances in social cognition.* (Vol. 1, pp. 1–36). Hillsdale, NJ: Erlbaum.

Brown, N. R., Shevell, S. K., and Rips, L. J. (1986). Public memories and their personal context. In D. C. Rubin (Ed.), *Autobiographical memory* (pp. 137–158). Cambridge, U.K.: Cambridge University Press.

Campbell, A., Converse, P. E., Miller, W. E., and Stokes, D. E. (1960). *The American Voter*. New York: Wiley.

Carlson, E. R. (1956). Attitude change through modification of attitude structure. *Journal of Abnormal and Social Psychology*. *52*, 256–261.

Chaiken, S. (1980). Heuristic versus systematic information processing and the use of source versus message cues in persuasion. *Journal of Personality and Social Psychology*, *39*, 752–766.

Chaiken, S., and Bargh, J. A. (1993). Occurrence versus moderation of the automatic attitude activation effect: Reply to Fazio. *Journal of Personality and Social Psychology*, *64*, 759–765.

Collins, A. M., and Loftus, E. F. (1975). A spreading-activation theory of semantic processing. *Psychological Review*, *82*, 407–428.

Conover, P. J. (1988). The role of social groups in political thinking. *British Journal of Political Science*, *18*, 51–76.

Converse, P. E. (1964). The nature of belief systems in mass publics. In D. E. Apter (Ed.), *Ideology and discontent* (pp. 206–261). New York: Free Press of Glencoe.

(1970). Attitudes and non-attitudes: Continuation of a dialogue. In E. R. Tufte (Ed.), *The quantitative analysis of social problems* (pp. 168–189). Reading, MA: Addison-Wesley.

Converse, P. E., and Markus, G. B. (1979), Plus Ça change . . . : The new CPS election study panel. *American Political Science Review*, *73*, 32–49.

Craig, S. C. (1993). The angry voter? Politics and popular discontent in the 1990's. Paper presented at the 1993 annual meeting of the Midwest Political Science Association, Chicago.

Devine, P. G. (1989). Stereotypes and prejudice: Their automatic and controlled components. *Journal of Personality and Social Psychology*, *56*, 5–18.

Diamond, E., and Bates, S. (1984). *The spot: The rise of political advertising on television*. Cambridge, MA: MIT Press.

Downs, A. (1957). *An economic theory of democracy*. New York: Harper-Row.

Easton, D., and Dennis, J. (1969). *Children in the political system: Origins of political legitimacy*. New York: McGraw-Hill.

Fazio, R. H. (1986). How do attitudes guide behavior? In R. M. Sorrentino and E. T. Higgins (Eds.), *Handbook of motivation and cognition: Foundations of social behavior* (pp. 204–243). New York: Guilford Press.

(1989). On the power and functionality of attitudes: The role of attitude accessibility. In A. R. Pratkanis, S. J. Breckler, and A. G. Greenwald (Eds.), *Attitude structure and function* (pp. 153–179). Hillsdale, NJ: Erlbaum.

(1993) Variability in the likelihood of automatic attitude activation: Data reanalysis and commentary on Bargh, Chaiken, Govender, and Pratto (1992). *Journal of Personality and Social Psychology*, 64, 753–758.

Fazio, R. H., Jackson, J. R., Dunton, B. C., and Williams, C. J. (1995). Variability in automatic activation as an unobtrusive measure of racial attitudes: A bona fide pipeline? *Journal of Personality and Social Psychology*, 69, 1013–1027.

Fazio, R. H., Sanbanmatsu, D. M., Powell, M. C., and Kardes, F. R. (1986). On the automatic activation of attitudes. *Journal of Personality and Social Psychology*, 50, 229–238.

Fazio, R. H., and Williams, C. J. (1986). Attitude accessibility as a moderator of the attitude–perception and attitude–behavior relations: An investigation of the 1984 presidential election. *Journal of Personality and Social Psychology*, 51, 505–514.

Feldman, S. (1988). Structure and consistency in public opinion: the role of core beliefs and values. *American Journal of Political Science*, 32, 416–440.

Fiske, S. T., and Neuberg, S. L. (1990). A continuum of impression formation, from category-based to individuating processes: Influences of information and motivation on attention and interpretation. *Advances in Experimental Social Psychology*, 23, 1–74.

Fiske, S. T., and Pavelchak, M. A. (1986). Category-based versus piecemeal-based affective responses: Developments in schema triggered affect. In R. M. Sorrentino and E. T. Higgins (Eds.), *The Handbook of Motivation and Cognition: Foundations of Social Behavior* (pp. 167–203). New York: Guilford Press.

Fiske, S. T., and Taylor, S. E. (1991). *Social cognition* (2nd ed.). New York: McGraw-Hill.

Franklin, C. H. (1984). Issue preferences, socialization, and the evolution of party identification. *American Journal of Political Science*, 28, 459–478.

Granberg, D., and Brown, T. A. (1989). On affect and cognition in politics. *Social Psychology Quarterly*, 52, 171–182.

Green, D. P. (1988). Self-interest, public opinion, and mass political behavior. Unpublished doctoral dissertation, University of California, Berkeley.

Green, D. P., and Palmquist, B. (1990). Of artifacts and partisan instability. *American Journal of Political Science*, 34, 872–902.

(1992). How stable is party identification? Paper presented at the annual meeting of the American Political Science Association, Chicago.

Greenwald, A. G., and Banaji, M. R. (1995). Implicit social cognition: Attitudes, Self-esteem, and Stereotypes. *Psychological Review*, 102, 4–27.

Hastie, R., and Park, B. (1986). The relationship between memory and judgment depends on whether the judgment task is memory-based or on-line. *Psychological Review*, 93, 258–268.

Higgins, E. T., and King, G. (1981). Accessibility of social constructs: information processing consequences of individual and contextual variability. In N. Cantor and J. R. Kihlstrom (Eds.), *Personality, cognition, and social interaction* (pp. 69–122). Hillsdale, NJ: Erlbaum.

Hovland, C. I., Campbell, E., and Brock, T. C. (1957). The effects of "commitment" on opinion change following communication. In C. I. Hovland, *Order of presentation in persuasion.* New Haven: Yale University Press.

Hurwitz, J., and Peffley, M. (1987). How are foreign policy attitudes structured? A hierarchical model. *American Political Science Review, 81,* 1099–1120.

Hyman, J. (1959). *Political socialization.* Glencoe, IL: Free Press.

Iyengar, S., and Kinder, D. R. (1987). *News that matters: Television and American opinion.* Chicago: University of Chicago Press.

Jarvis, H. (with Pack, R.). (1979). *I'm mad as hell.* New York: Berkley Books.

Jessor, T. (1988). Personal interest, group conflict, and symbolic group affect: Explanations for whites' opposition to racial equality. Unpublished doctoral dissertation, Department of Psychology, University of California, Los Angeles.

Johnson, B. T., and Eagly, A. H. (1989). Effects of involvement on persuasion: A meta-analysis. *Psychological Bulletin, 106,* 290–314.

Katz, P. A. (1976). The acquisition of racial attitudes in children. In P. A. Katz (Ed.), *Towards the elimination of racism* (pp. 125–156). Elmsford, NY: Pergamon Press.

Kelley, H. H. (1950). The warm–cold variable in first impressions of persons. *Journal of Personality, 18,* 431–439.

Key, V. O., Jr. (1961). *Public Opinion and American Democracy.* New York: Knopf.

Kinder, D. R., and Sears, D. O. (1981). Prejudice and politics: Symbolic racism versus racial threats to the good life. *Journal of Personality and Social Psychology, 40,* 414–431.

(1985). Public opinion and political action. In G. Lindzey and E. Aronson (Eds.), *Handbook of social psychology* (Vol. 2, 3rd ed., pp. 659–741). New York: Random House.

Kosterman, R. J. (1991). Political spot advertising and routes to persuasion: The role of symbolic content. Unpublished doctoral dissertation, University of California, Los Angeles.

Krosnick, J. A. (1988). The role of attitude importance in social evaluation: A study of policy preferences, presidential candidate evaluation, and voting behavior. *Journal of personality and social psychology, 55,* 196–210.

(1989). Attitude importance and attitude accessibility. *Personality and Social Psychology Bulletin, 15,* 297–308.

Krosnick, J. A., and Schuman, H. (1988). Attitude intensity, importance, and certainty and susceptibility to response effects. *Journal of Personality and Social Psychology, 54,* 940–952.

Kuper, L. (1981). *Genocide: Its political uses in the 20th century.* New Haven, CT: Yale University Press.

Lau, R. R., Brown, T. A., and Sears, D. O. (1978). Self-interest and civilians' attitudes toward the Vietnam war. *Public Opinion Quarterly, 42,* 464–483.

Lazarus, R. S. (1984). On the primacy of cognition. *American Psychologist, 39,* 124–129.

Lipset, S. M., and Raab, E. (1978). *The politics of unreason* (2nd ed.). Chicago: University of Chicago Press.

Lodge, M., McGraw, K. M., and Stroh, P. (1989). An impression-driven model of candidate evaluation. *American Political Science Review, 83,* 399–419.

Lodge, M., Steenbergen, M., and Brau, S. (1993). The non-persistence of memory: learning and forgetting in the process of candidate evaluation.

Paper presented at the annual meeting of the Midwest Political Science Association, Chicago.

Lorge, I., and Curtiss, C. C. (1936). Prestige, suggestion, and attitudes. *Journal of Social Psychology*, 7, 386–402.

Luker, K. (1984). *Abortion and the politics of motherhood*. Berkeley: University of California Press.

Mannheim, K. (1952). The problem of generations. In P. Kecskemeti (Ed.), *Essays on the sociology of knowledge* (pp. 276–320). London: Routledge & Keagan Paul.

Marcus, G. E. (1990). Emotions and politics: Hot cognitions and the rediscovery of passion. Paper presented at the annual meeting of the International Society of Political Psychology, Washington, DC.

Marcus, G. E., Sullivan, J. L., Theiss-Morse, E., and Barnum, D. (1989). Reason and passion in political life. Paper presented at the Symposium on Democratic Theory, Williams College.

McConahay, J. B. (1982). Self-interest versus racial attitudes as correlates of anti-busing attitudes in Louisville: Is it the buses or the blacks? *Journal of Politics*, 44, 692–720.

McGraw, K. M., Lodge, M., and Stroh, P. (1990). On-line processing in candidate evaluation: The effects of issue order, issue importance, and sophistication. *Political Behavior*, 12, 41–58.

Mueller, J. E. (1973). *War, presidents, and public opinion*. New York: Wiley.

Murphy, S. T., and Zajonc, R. B. (1993) Affect, cognition, and awareness: Affective priming with optimal and suboptimal stimulus exposures. *Journal of Personality and Social Psychology*, 64, 723–739.

Niemi, R. G., and Jennings, M. K. (1991). Issues and inheritance in the formation of party identification. *American Journal of Political Science*, 35, 970–988.

Novotny, P. (1992). "Where never is heard a discouraging word." Collective memory and historical forgetting in "The West as America: Reinterpreting images of the frontier, 1820–1920." Paper presented at the annual meeting of the American Political Science Association, Chicago.

Nunn, C. Z., Crockett, J. H., Jr., and Williams, J. A., Jr. (1978). *Tolerance for nonconformity: A national survey of Americans' changing commitment to civil liberties*. San Francisco: Jossey-Bass.

Osgood, C. E., Suci , G. J., and Tannenbaum, P. H. (1957). *The measurement of meaning*. Urbana: University of Illinois Press.

Osgood, C. E., and Tannenbaum, P. (1955). The principle of congruity and the prediction of attitude change. *Psychological Review*, 62, 42–55.

Page, B. I., and Shapiro, R. Y. (1992). *The rational public: Fifty years of trends in Americans' policy preferences*. Chicago: University of Chicago Press.

Perdue, C. W., Dovidio, J. F., Gurtman, M. B., and Tyler, R. B. (1990). Us and them: Social categorization and the process of intergroup bias. *Journal of Personality and Social Psychology*, 59, 475–486.

Petty, R. E., and Cacioppo, J. T. (1986). *Communication and persuasion: Central and peripheral routes to attitude change*. New York: Springer-Verlag.

Raden, D. (1985). Strength-related attitude dimensions. *Social Psychology Quarterly*, 48, 312–330.

Rahn, W. M., Krosnick, J. A., and Breuning, M. (1994). Rationalization and derivation processes in survey studies of political candidate evaluation. *American Journal of Political Science*, 38, 582–600.

Retzinger, S. M. (1991). *Violent emotions: Shame and rage in marital quarrels.* Newbury Park, CA: Sage.

Roseman, I., Abelson, R. P., and Ewing, M. F. (1986). Emotion and political cognition: Emotional appeals in political communication. In R. R. Lau and D. O. Sears (Eds.), *Political cognition: The 19th annual carnegie symposium on cognition* (pp. 279–294). Hillsdale, NJ: Erlbaum.

Rosenberg, M. J. (1960), Cognitive reorganization in response to the hypnotic reversal of attitudinal effect. *Journal of Personality, 28,* 39–63.

Scheff, T. J. (1992). Emotion and illness: Anger, bypassed shame and heart disease. *Perspectives on Social Problems, 3,* 17–134.

Schuman, H., and Scott, J. (1989). Generations and collective memories. *American Sociological Review, 54,* 359–381.

Schuman, H., Steeh, C., and Bobo, L. (1985). *Racial trends in America: Trends and interpretations.* Cambridge, MA: Harvard University Press.

Sears, D. O. (1969). Political behavior. In G. Lindzey and E. Aronson (Eds.), *Handbook of social psychology* (Vol. 5, rev. ed., pp. 315–458). Reading: MA: Addison-Wesley.

(1975). Political socialization. In F. I. Greenstein and N. W. Polsby (Eds.), *Handbook of political science* (Vol. 2, pp. 93–153). Reading, MA: Addison-Wesley.

(1983). The persistence of early political predispositions: The roles of attitude object and life stage. In L. Wheeler and P. Shaver (Eds.), *Review of Personality and Social Psychology* (Vol. 4, pp. 79–116). Beverly Hills, CA: Sage.

(1988). Symbolic racism. In P. A. Katz and D. A. Taylor (Eds.), *Eliminating racism: Profiles in controversy* (pp. 53–84). New York: Plenum Press.

(1989). Whither political socialization research? The question of persistence. In Ichilov (Ed.), *Political socialization, citizenship education, and democracy* (pp. 69–97). New York: Teachers College Press.

Sears, D. O., and Allen, H. M., Jr. (1984). The trajectory of local desegregation controversies and whites' opposition to busing. In N. Miller and M. B. Brewer (Eds.), *Groups in contact: The psychology of desegregation* (pp. 123–151). New York: Academic Press.

Sears, D. O., and Citrin, J. (1985). *Tax revolt: Something for nothing in California* (enlarged ed.). Cambridge, MA: Harvard University Press.

Sears, D. O., Citrin, J., and Kosterman, R. (1987). Jesse Jackson and the Southern White Electorate in 1984. In L. W. Moreland, R. P. Steed, and T. A. Baker (Eds.), *Blacks in Southern politics* (pp. 209–225). New York: Praeger.

Sears, D. O., and Funk, C. L. (1990). The persistence and crystallization of political attitudes over the life-span: The Terman Gifted Children Panel. Paper presented at the Annual Meeting of the American Sociological Association, Washington, DC.

(1991). The role of self-interest in social and political attitudes. In M. Zanna (Ed.), *Advances in Experimental Social Psychology* (Vol. 24, pp. 1–91). Orlando, FL: Academic Press.

Sears, D. O., Hensler, C. P., and Speer, L. K. (1979). Whites' opposition to "busing": Self-interest or symbolic politics? *American Political Science Review, 73,* 369–384.

Sears, D. O., Huddy, L., and Schaffer, L. (1986). A schematic variant of symbolic politics theory, as applied to racial and gender equality. In R. R. Lau and D. O. Sears (Eds.), *Political cognition: The 19th annual Carnegie symposium on cognition* (pp. 159–202). Hillsdale, NJ: Erlbaum.

Sears, D. O., and Huddy, L. (1990). On the origins of political disunity among women. In L. A. Tilly and P. Gurin (Eds.), *Women, politics, and change* (pp. 249–277). New York: Russell Sage.

Sears, D. O., and Kosterman, R. (1991). Is it really racism? The origins and dynamics of symbolic racism. Paper presented at the annual meeting of the Midwestern Political Science Association, Chicago.

Sears, D. O., Lau, R. R., Tyler, T. R., and Allen, H. M., Jr. (1980). Self-interest vs. symbolic politics in policy attitudes and presidential voting. *American Political Science Review, 74,* 670–684.

Sears, D. O., and McConahay, J. B. (1973). *The politics of violence: The new urban blacks and the Watts riot.* Boston: Houghton-Mifflin. Reprinted by University Press of America, 1981.

Sears, D. O., Zucker, G., and Funk, C. (1992). Gender and ideological change in the 1960s and 1970s: A longitudinal study. Paper presented at the annual meeting of the American Political Science Review, Chicago.

Sherif, M., and Cantril, H. (1947). *The psychology of ego-involvements.* New York: Wiley.

Sherman, S. J., Mackie, D. M., and Driscoll, D. M. (1990). Priming and the differential use of dimensions in evaluation. *Personality and Social Psychology Bulletin, 16,* 405–418.

Shiffrin, R. M., and Schneider, W. (1977). Controlled and automatic human information processing: II. Perceptual learning, automatic attending, and a general theory. *Psychological Review, 84,* 127–190.

Sigel, R. S. (Ed.). (1989). *Political learning in adulthood.* Chicago: University of Chicago Press.

Smith, T. W. (1987). That which we call welfare by any other name would smell sweeter: An analysis of the impact of question wording on response patterns. *Public Opinion Quarterly, 51,* 75–83.

Sniderman, P. M., and Tetlock, P. E. (1986). Reflections on American racism. *Journal of Social Issues, 42,* 173–187.

Staub, E. (1989). *The roots of evil: The origins of genocide and other group violence.* New York: Cambridge University Press.

Stouffer, S. A. (1955). *Communism, conformity, and civil liberties.* New York: Doubleday.

Sullivan, J. L., Piereson, J., and Marcus, G. E. (1982). *Political tolerance and American democracy.* Chicago: University of Chicago Press.

Tajfel, H. (Ed.) (1982). *Social identity and intergroup relations.* Cambridge, MA: Cambridge University Press.

Warnecke, A. M., Masters, R. D., and Kempter, G. (1992). The roots of nationalism: Nonverbal behavior and xenophobia. *Ethology and Sociobiology, 13,* 267–282.

Weiner, B. (1974). *Achievement motivation and attribution theory.* Morristown, NJ: General Learning Press.
  (1986). *An attributional theory of motivation and emotion.* New York: Springer-Verlag.

Zajonc, R. B. (1980). Feeling and thinking: Preferences, need no inferences. *American Psychologist, 35,* 151–175.
  (1984). On the Primacy of affect. *American Psychologist, 39,* 117–123.

Zaller, J., and Feldman, S. (1992). A simple theory of the survey response: Answering questions vs. revealing preferences. *American Journal of Political Science, 36*(3), 579–616.

2

Emotions and Politics: The Dynamic Functions of Emotionality

GEORGE E. MARCUS
MICHAEL B. MacKUEN

> It is usually more difficult to discover the right question than it is to find
> the answer. It is precisely at this point that the unexamined and unstated
> assumptions we make are most likely to defeat us, for the questions we
> ask grow out of the assumptions we make. . . . The assumptions we make
> tend to determine what we investigate, what kinds of techniques we use,
> and how we evaluate the evidence.
>
> (Schattschneider, 1948, p. 21)

Centuries ago, Western culture joined together two normative commitments, reason and democracy. While not everyone has shared those
commitments, few would disagree with the claim that democracy's
prospects are dependent on our capacity for reason, for leaders and
followers alike. Together with those commitments, which we endorse, is
a further presumption that passions undermine and degrade our reasoning capacity.

That presumption, that reason enables and passion disables, is largely
to blame for the generally one-sided attention to the study of how
humans reason. The dominant tradition in Western culture holds that it
is through greater and better reliance on reason that humanity will
progress to a better world. Through reason, humanity can remake itself
and the world. Alas, if only humans were reasonable creatures!

Western culture, long ago, made a normative commitment to reason
and held prospects for democracy to be dependent on fuller reliance on
reason. Thus, reason and progress came to be joined in opposition to
passion. We propose another solution. This chapter argues that affective
intelligence augments and works cooperatively with reason. Rather than
working antagonistically, and with detrimental consequences, our theory
of affective intelligence argues that emotionality sustains our capacity to
use reason in precisely those circumstances when the benefits of reason
are most required and most warranted. If we can find some measure of

George E. Marcus and Michael B. MacKuen

support to sustain this approach, then it may be that democracies' prospects do depend jointly on reason and passion.

THEORIZING ABOUT DEMOCRATIC POLITICS

There is no escape from the problem of ignorance, because nobody knows enough to run the government.

(Schattschneider, 1960, p. 137)

We will concern ourselves with how citizens confront situations that require judgment because that is traditionally a capacity held to be pre-eminently within the domain of reason and because the ability to make an informed judgment is a capability that is almost universally held to be central to democratic politics. Of course, not all situations do require judgment – that is, decisions arrived at by reflective and formal reconsideration. Most of the decisions we make during a normal day are executed swiftly and rather automatically. Still, it remains the very stuff of politics for activists and leaders, both established and new, to try to excite people about the importance of their issue or program and to try to generate a willingness to reflect on and consider the issue from their perspective. People have means of responding to such initiatives. They can respond to the claims and counterclaims of activists, special interests, and politicians as they generally have in the past, by reliance on their habitual dispositions, such as partisanship, or they can set aside their prejudices and dispositions and respond with an open mind.

People have the capacity to rely on their habits, a conclusion that focuses on the historical continuity of decisions people make, reflecting the controlling force of dispositions. But we argue that people also have the capacity to set aside their dispositions and make a judgment, a decision that reflects their best contemporary thinking. We can be more precise about the crucial questions that arise when we shift from a "trait," or dispositional view of citizens, to a "state," or dynamic and interactive view of citizens. Put another way, people have the capacity to rely on what they have previously learned (the dispositions rule), *and* they have the capacity to set aside their repertoire of previously learning and engage in new learning. These questions are:

- When do people rely on previously learned dispositions, habits, and behavioral routines?
- When does new learning take place?
- More specifically, when do people pay attention and to what?
- How does learning occur?
- More specifically, who learns and who does not?

42

What is most needed, then, is a theory of political learning. To provide such a theory will require us to expand our view beyond the cognitive focus of much of political psychology.

WHAT PSYCHOLOGICAL LITERATURE SHOULD WE DRAW ON TO UNDERSTAND EMOTIONS?

The choices are three: the psychodynamic literature, academic social psychology, and neuroscience. We have elected to rely on the last because it has the most detailed theoretical formulations of the three, along with the most robust and varied methodological approaches (including drug, neurological, neurochemical, animal, twin studies, and other approaches).[1] And, within neuroscience, we have used with some success, Jeffrey Gray's theory of emotionality and personality (Gray, 1981, 1985a, 1985b, 1987a, 1987b, 1990).

Gray's model of emotionality describes three systems that collectively form the limbic system. The three systems are (1) the Fight/Flight system; (2) the Behavioral Approach System, and (3) the Behavioral Inhibition System. Importantly, the limbic system processes and manages reinforcers. In psychology, the term "reinforcer" is used to describe the effect of reward, on the one hand, and that of nonreward and punishment, on the other. Reinforcers strengthen or weaken linkages between actions undertaken and reactions to that experience. Put more simply, positive reinforcers are good things (e.g., food) or signs related to good things (e.g., a bell that regularly accompanies the arrival of food). Negative reinforcers are those that disappoint (e.g., something good that was anticipated to arrive but did not) or that punish. Positive reinforcers strengthen existing linkages between actions undertaken and reactions to that experience. They also are essential to learning new behavioral routines. Negative reinforcers weaken existing relationships and interrupt normal ongoing actions. By assigning emotional significance to sensory information, identifying some stimuli as positive and others as negative

---

1 It is only lately that social psychology, the usual feeding ground of those who study American public opinion and political psychology, has begun to reexamine its usual methods of treating affect. For much of the past few decades, social psychology has justified the exclusion of affect by concluding, erroneously, that affect is merely derivative of cognition. One study looms large in this context (Schachter & Singer, 1962). The proclaimed subordination of affect presumes that cognition is the driving force in human affairs and that affective responses are little more than twitches resulting from cognitive operations (Fiske & Pavelchak, 1985). It is not surprising, then, that the claim that affective processes are parallel and independent, in part, of cognition (Zajonc, 1980, 1982; Zajonc & Markus, 1984) generated some initial heat (Lazarus, 1982, 1984).

reinforcers, the limbic system plays an essential interpretive function. Thus, the limbic system is fully involved with learning and memory. As we shall see, the limbic system divides the management of reinforcers among three distinct systems, each with a distinct strategic focus. As we shall also see, these systems involve considerable cognitive but not conscious processing. The term "cognition," among political scientists, has generally become confused with "consciousness." They are not the same thing, as cognition can and does occur without awareness (Lewicki, 1986).

Thus, feelings and their changing states play an informing role. Information processing is not a singular activity. It has multiple modalities; some are based in cognition and some are based in affect. A fuller information processing paradigm must account for how feeling states, as well as thoughts, react to sensory stimulations of various kinds. This will require that affective processes be theoretically described and, further, that the various interrelationships of affective and cognitive processes be detailed. Gray's theory provides such an account, and we provide a brief explication.

The first system, the Fight/Flight system, differs from the other two systems in that it deals with controlling innate responses to unconditioned punishment and nonreward. It does not deal with mediated, conditioned, or secondary stimuli. We shall here ignore this system because it has limited application to politics. However, when it is engaged, its role is quite powerful.

The two remaining systems, the Behavioral Approach System and the Behavioral Inhibition System, deal primarily with conditioned and/or secondary reinforcers – that is, stimuli that are not in themselves informative, but that the subject has learned to associate with either good or bad consequences. The most important point to make about these two systems is that they are fully engaged in learning. They are information-processing systems that yield mood changes as the product of their evaluations.

According to Gray's theory and research, emotions provide ongoing assessments, much as the change in readings provided by a thermometer tells us the temperature or the movement of numbers on a digital clock tells us the time. And changes in our feelings constitute changes in these assessments. The two dimensions, positive affect and negative affect, provide us with strategic diagnoses of two crucial aspects of our experience. Further, each system of emotional response has specific motivational implications (Mayer and Gaschke, 1988; Mayer, Salovey, Gomberg-Kaufman, and Blainey, 1991), each is intimately involved in personality (Mayer, Mamberg, and Volanth, 1988; Watson and Clark, 1991), and each is central to social communication and cooperation (Chance, 1976).

Emotions and Politics

The Behavioral Approach System

The first system, the Behavioral Information System, controls the expression of emotions that fall into the group most commonly called "positive affect." When our feelings are focused on ourselves, changes in our mood, from gloomy to enthusiastic, tell us that we are bursting with confidence, energy, and eagerness. Alternatively, when our mood changes in the direction of depression, we conclude that we are exhausted and beaten. When our feelings are focused on those we depend on or are identified with – family, friends, or political leaders, for example – our moods reflect what we have recently experienced or anticipate experiencing. Our trust has been confirmed or we have been disappointed and let down. When focused on ourselves, these feelings gauge self-mastery; when attendant on those we rely upon, these feelings gauge our confidence and trust in others.

According to Gray, the moods of depression-enthusiasm provide crucial ongoing information on how well we are conducting ourselves and how well our previously learned behaviors are enacted. Thus, when a president's approval rating goes up, we can be sure that the public's confidence in the president's leadership has been strengthened. Recent studies that examine the influence of each dimension of emotional response show that it is this dimension, measuring the moods of trust and mastery, that is powerfully related to voting (Abelson, Kinder, Peters, and Fiske, 1982; Marcus, 1988). Gray calls this dimension of emotional assessment the "Behavioral Approach System," suggesting that we will engage those actions that we feel enthusiastic about and draw back from those that cause us despair.

Learning is a central feature of this system. It is concerned with motivated, not reflexive, behavior. This distinguishes the behavioral approach and inhibition systems from the fight/flight systems. These two systems deal with mediated stimuli or secondary reinforcers, and, as a result, they are more relevant to politics and to everyday experience. Secondary reinforcers are those stimuli that have acquired the status of reinforcers by their association with the experience of reward, nonreward, and punishment. Most of our experience relies on such associations rather than with direct response to unmediated experiences of reward and punishment.

The Behavioral Approach System modulates enthusiasm, elation, hope, and relief, as well as the affects that mark depression. It is also an incentive system providing emotional cues to the execution of strategic actions. Strategic progress is signaled by generating moods of growing confidence, and failure is signaled by generating a mood of depression. The Behavioral Approach System gauges the success or failure of recalled

45

actions, contemporary experience, and anticipated activities that fall within the category of previously learned behaviors.

The ability to undertake strategic actions, that is, actions designed to achieve a purpose, requires swift feedback on the intermediate success of each action in the sequence of actions. The emotions of the Behavioral Approach System provide precisely this information. When this feedback is not present, there is *no* ability to comprehend the success or failure of any subject initiated action. So, it is not surprising that variations in this dimension are powerful predictors of the willingness to engage in previously learned actions (Sacks and Bugental, 1987; Seligman, 1975). Positive moods have been found to predict helping behavior (Carlson, Charlin, and Miller, 1988), and they are the best single predictor of which candidate a citizen will support (Rahn, Aldrich, Borgida, and Sullivan, 1990).

Those who have been engaged in the information-processing paradigm frequently offer the observation that gathering information is costly (a convenient explanation for why people are not as fully informed as to satisfy the expectations of some expert). A more useful insight to offer is that all physical effort is costly and leads to exhaustion. The willingness to undertake a course of action must be based on the continual gauging of the prospects of success, the anticipated effort, and the current stock of physical and psychic resources.[2] It is the Behavioral Approach System that provides this assessment by the specific shifts of mood that define the positive affect dimension. Shifts in the direction of increased elation strengthen the motivation to expend effort and strengthen confidence in a successful outcome. Shifts in the direction of increased depression weaken the motivation to expend effort and undermine confidence that the outcome will prove successful.

The Behavioral Inhibition System

Psychologists have long known that it is important to differentiate between responses associated with threat and anxiety, on the one hand, and responses associated with inner collapse and failure of will, on the other hand (Ax, 1953; Batson, Fultz, and Schoenrade, 1987; Beck, Brown, Steer, Eidelson, and Riskind, 1987). Gray's identification of two

2 While the purpose of this exposition does not include clinical applications, it would not be inappropriate to point out the intimate relationship between the mood of depression (inability to experience even successful actions as positive) and passivity. Thus, the inability of this part of the limbic system to affix the mood of enthusiasm properly prevents individuals from gaining the essential feedback that enables ongoing action to be undertaken even under optimal circumstances.

systems of learning, one dedicated to monitoring and assessing previously learned behaviors and one dedicated to recognition of novelty and threat, underscores the importance of treating emotional responses as compounds of these two ongoing processes (Marcus, 1988; Marcus and MacKuen, 1993).

Life is full of surprises, and two kinds of surprises are crucial.[3] As we confront our world, we often come across new and unpredictable people and circumstances. And, at various times, there are people and circumstances that we find threatening. Recall that the behavioral approach system provides people with an understanding, an emotional report card, on actions that are already in one's repertoire of habits and learned behaviors. The second system, the Behavioral Inhibition System, scans the environment for novelty and intrusion of threat. This system generates moods of calmness and relaxation when the match of incoming sensory signals against anticipated normal execution of plans indicates nothing of concern. It generates moods of increasing nervousness and anxiety when the comparison of environmental information and what would be expected from normal execution of plans indicates a mismatch. This system serves to warn us that we confront a circumstance we may be ill equipped to handle and to warn us that some situations and some people are dangerous. And, because it is a warning, the shift in mood to increased anxiety is not by itself sufficient. This system also inhibits ongoing action – hence its name – and redirects attention away from the matters at hand and toward the novel or threatening stimuli.

Gray's theory suggests that while people rely on their feelings to assess how well they and those they rely upon are doing, they also rely on their feelings – a different group of feelings – to scan their experience for signs of threat and uncertainty. What is interesting about this second dimension of emotion is that Gray's theory suggests that the onset of increased anxiety stops ongoing activity and orients attention to the threatening appearance so that learning can take place. This aspect of the theory is important; we will return to it later when we discuss the political ramifications and applications of Gray's theory.

The Behavioral Inhibition System is also a learning system. It produces behavioral and affective responses, not conscious thoughts. As this system is linked to higher conscious systems, it will provoke thinking in specified circumstances. This system cycles continually. It compares sensory information about the world with expectations obtained from the Behavioral Approach System. So long as the comparison shows no

---

3 To a psychologist, the first surprise defines settings of uncertainty (circumstances in which the unfolding events cannot be anticipated); the second surprise defines settings that are anticipated to be punishing or unrewarding.

discrepancy between expectation and reality, the system generates a sense of calm and the Behavioral Inhibition System remains unobtrusive. However, when the system detects unexpected and/or threatening stimuli, it generates a mood of increasing anxiety. It interrupts on-going activity and shifts attention away from the previous focus and toward the intrusive stimuli (MacLeod and Mathews, 1988; Pratto and John, 1991).

The Behavioral Inhibition System has a particular role relevant to politics. One consequence of the activation of this system is learning. When moods are calm and ongoing actions are tranquilly performed, there is little incentive to learn. When anxiety increases, habituated and previously learned behavior is interrupted. Anxiety signals that our focus of concern needs to be shifted and that we must be ready and capable of applying new approaches to the unexpected appearance of novelty or threat. In other words, an increase in the level of anxiety, but not terror, is a motivation for learning.

The Mood Systems and Political Opinion and Political Behavior

Just as the experience of color is generated by different specific types of cells in the eye, the limbic region of the brain interprets sensory data with at least three different systems to produce mood. Just as we cannot experience a pure color generated by only one type of cell, we cannot experience a single mood generated by only one of these three systems. Our emotional experience is a composite generated by these dynamic systems. The description of the two mediated mood systems, each supporting learning, suggests that the modulations of each system influence political behavior in important but distinctive ways (Derryberry, 1991).

Finally, we wish to emphasize that what is crucial to the strategic function of the mood systems is the distinction between what we already know how to do and the wary scanning of the immediate environment. In the familiar environment, we can safely practice already learned behaviors; in the unfamiliar world, we are much more hesitant to act. The mood system, in the Behavioral Inhibition System, includes a dedicated threat recognition system. The primary purpose of this system is to enable us to recognize quickly the appearance of the novel, the un-familiar, and the threatening. The identification of "we" and "they" is a central part of our feelings about the world.

In the most fundamental way, we are born to understand and experience the world, and the social interactions we engage in, with a partisan perspective. Our emotional responses to events, groups, proposals, and individuals depend primarily upon whether they fall within our familiar circle or represent the strange, the unfamiliar, or the threatening. While reliance on reason may encourage us to endorse universal norms and principles, our feelings will continue to be influenced by whether actions or people appear to us as familiar or strange (Lanzetta and Englis, 1989).

The Gray model, and the conception of emotionality as a form of intelligence, are not the only theoretical formulations that suggest that humans make good use of emotional reactions to guide their thoughts and actions. Clore and Salovey have each suggested that moods may be important sources of information that people use to gauge their circumstances effectively (Mayer, DiPaolo, and Salovey, 1990; Salovey, 1992; Salovey and Mayer, 1990; Schwarz and Clore, 1983). Two principal advantages are offered by Gray's account. First, it is based on studies that explore how the brain (both of human and of other species) works rather than surmises based on perceptions of how humans make judgments. Second, Gray's account offers a far more precise statement of how affective information is gathered and the impact of affective intelligence on other cognitive functions and behavior. Thus, though Gray's account is unlikely to be the final word, it does offer greater theoretical specificity and a neurological foundation that other approaches lack.

EMPIRICAL SUPPORT

Gray's work on emotions suggests that we can offer a good deal more than just a new set of variables to be added to the multivariate mix. What we gain is a quite specific (perhaps fully specified) model that incorporates feeling, thinking, and acting. Most fundamental is the placement of emotional reactions at the core of the model. Emotional reactions shape when we think, what we ponder, when we shift attention, and when and to whom we bond as well as shun. Emotional reactions perform these functions quickly and realistically.

Two research programs have relied on Gray's theoretical model. The first program is a continuing investigation using an experimental design to explore how people make political tolerance judgments (Marcus, Sullivan, Theiss-Morse, and Wood, 1995; Theiss-Morse, Marcus, and Sullivan, 1993). The second is a continuing program exploring how emotional reactions to candidates shape voters' preferences and their performance as citizens during the campaign period (Marcus, 1988; Marcus and MacKuen, 1993). This second project largely draws on survey research as its source of data.

George E. Marcus and Michael B. MacKuen

Threat, Contemporary Influences, and Political Tolerance Judgments

All learning models are concerned with identifying the conditions under which new information is absorbed to create new response patterns or to modify existing patterns. What kinds of information stimulate learning? When do people modify what they have previously learned? When do they set aside previously learned dispositions to rely instead on newly crafted responses? As we have previously noted, democratic theory requires that citizens be prompted to learn and that they do so in response to the attention-grabbing efforts of those familiar and unfamiliar to them.

Social psychology has long been concerned with issues of attention and persuasion. For the most part, concern has been given to such matters as "primacy" and "recency" (i.e., is it the first message we hear that shapes our views or the most recent message?). Attention has also been given to the content of messages and what constitutes a persuasive appeal (McGuire, 1969) as well as how personality differences might enhance or diminish the impact of a persuasive appeal (McGuire, 1968).

Perhaps simple exposure to a message enhances attention to the matter central to the message (Iyengar and Kinder, 1987). Or perhaps not all persuasive appeals have substantive consequences; maybe only some messages cause attitudes to change (and then perhaps only for a brief time). That is, people in some circumstances, and on some matters, when presented with certain kinds of messages, do pay attention to concurrent circumstances in making a decision.

On the other hand, work in the field of symbolic politics suggests that people give little attention to relevant contemporary facts pertaining to the issue at hand. Instead, they rely on long-standing value orientations without regard to strategic or tactical assessments (Sears, 1990; Sears, Hensler, and Speer, 1979; Sears, Lau, Tyler, and Allen, 1980). Perhaps it is timely to suggest that both views have merit. Perhaps a formulation that combines both will prove superior to either alone. Such a theoretical account would begin by specifying the conditions and the mechanisms by which people *at times* attend to concurrent information to augment their long-standing views.

Within this formulation rest some familiar conceptions. First, the symbolic politics school presumes that in most areas, people already have habits and dispositions to respond in ways previously learned. Second, the attitude change and persuasion schools in social psychology presume that people, under certain circumstances, are influenced by new information contained in persuasive appeals. The trick, of course, is to find a theoretical approach that can identify the kinds of persuasive appeals

50

that work (as well as those that will not be so successful), how attention shifts to successful appeals, and what kinds of information are likely to trigger these processes.

Gray's work suggests that one of the most crucial stimuli that will initiate the process of attending to contemporary information is the perception of threat. Specifically, Gray's model holds that threat is a stimulus for enhanced attention to contemporary information and for enhanced, concentrated, deliberated (rather than automatic) consideration of how to respond. Since threat is identified by the emotional response of increased anxiety, it therefore follows that greater cognitive awareness, fuller consideration, and lessened reliance on habituated responses are dependent on increased emotional reactions of this quite specific range.

Marcus and his colleagues, John L. Sullivan, Elizabeth Theiss-Morse, and Sandy Wood, have conducted a number of studies that use an experimental approach that enables us to explore the extent to which preexisting values and inclinations are influenced by contemporary perceptions of threat. There are too many studies to describe them fully in the brief account that follows. We will summarize some of the findings from one representative study that bear on the immediate question "Is the perception of threat a concurrent or an antecedent factor in shaping political tolerance judgments?" The full report of these studies can be found in Marcus et al. (1995).

One study used adult subjects drawn from the Lincoln, Nebraska, metropolitan area (Marcus, 1991). Some 329 subjects participated in this study.[4] The study consisted of two stages. Subjects were first given a pretest to establish which groups they most disliked. Two weeks later, they were given a posttest that included a scenario about a hypothetical group based on respondents' least-liked group. We used hypothetical groups in order to control the information that people have available when they make a judgment. By using hypothetical groups, we could ensure that current news about actual groups did not contaminate information provided through the experiment. We developed scenarios that defined new groups that emerged, at some point in the near future, from currently familiar groups. Thus, subjects were presented with a scenario describing what was to them a novel group, but one that had a clear lineage to the specific group they had selected as their least-liked group. For example, subjects who chose the Ku Klux Klan as their most disliked group in the pretest read in the

---

4 The number reported here excludes some subjects who did not provide complete information on all measures required for the analyses reported in this section.

posttest a scenario about a hypothetical group called the White Supremacist Faction.[5]

Each scenario described the beliefs held by the hypothetical group. Following this description, common to all the scenarios, were two additional paragraphs that contained the principal experimental manipulations. One paragraph was concerned with the probability of the group's coming to power, and the other was concerned with the violations of the norms of trustworthiness and proper orderly behavior (for a fuller discussion, see Marcus et al., 1995). We included these two factors to determine whether threat perceptions are influenced by the extent of normative violations and/or by changes in the perceived probability of increased power of the target group. Gray's model, unlike rationality-based models, predicts that threat, through increased anxiety, identifies the degree of mismatch between the anticipated sensory stimulus flow concurrent with normal unfolding of plans and contemporary sensory stimuli. Thus, we would expect perceptions of normative violations to be both upsetting and the immediate cause for contemporary reassessment of preexisting dispositions toward the source of the normative violations.

Subjects read one of two normative violations paragraphs that varied the degree to which the group's actions were normatively compliant. A threatening paragraph portrayed the group as uncooperative with the police and devious with regard to their demonstration plans. They were also portrayed as using inflammatory language.[6] This paragraph was designed to invoke perceptions of treachery and belligerence, thereby alerting subjects to the presence of a threat. A reassuring paragraph portrayed the group as cooperative, trustworthy, and peaceful, thereby alerting subjects that the normative threat was minimal. If affective processing is threat monitoring, the threatening paragraph should produce less tolerance than the reassuring paragraph.

What other kind of information might cause people to take immediate notice? Rational choice models, largely derived from economic models of choice, presume that people make choices based on contemporary judgments of utility (Downs, 1957). One necessary aspect of a utility calculation is a judgment of the probability of the event occur-

---

5 Since our definition of tolerance requires a demonstration of forbearance, this design ensures that subjects will be confronted with a group they find objectionable (Sullivan, Piereson, & Marcus, 1982). The texts of the scenarios are available in Marcus et al. (1995). The scenarios differed only in the name of the group and the group's beliefs and specific goals. Subsequent analysis showed no difference in the overall responses by scenario. Thus the variation in responses is due to factors other than the particular target group selected by the respondent.

6 While this paragraph does note that violence occurred, it does not depict the target group engaged in illegal actions or as instigating the violence.

ring. Probability assessments ought to influence how much we seek a desired goal or avoid an unpleasant or noxious event. Considerable effort, with at best mixed results, has gone into the attempt to establish that people do make rational calculations of the sort that rational choice models postulate (Foster, 1984; Key and Cummings, 1966; Page and Shapiro, 1992; Quattrone and Tversky, 1988; Ragsdale, 1991).

Unlike Gray's model, which identifies signs of discrepancy from the expectation of safe execution of uninterrupted plans, rational choice requires that people judge the probability of an event occurring (as well as the expected benefit or cost). The product of the cost–benefit of various choices by their individual probabilities of their occurring generates the utilities that are presumed to be the basis of human judgment (Hastie, 1986). In any case, by including an experimental manipulation of the probability of the hypothetical group gaining power (or remaining weak), we can test the extent to which such information is influential.

To accomplish this test, subjects read one of two probability paragraphs. The paragraphs varied information about the effectiveness of fund-raising, the degree of public responsiveness to the group's appeals, the group's electoral success, and the significance accorded to it by appropriate monitoring organizations. If threat perceptions are based primarily upon a pragmatic assessment of the group's potential for gaining real power, then those who read the high-probability paragraph ought to be less tolerant than those who read the low-probability paragraph.

We randomly alternated the order of presentation of the two sets of paragraphs. Half of the time the probability paragraph preceded the normative violations paragraph, and half of the time it followed the normative violations paragraph. This variation enabled us to see if there was a recency effect.

After reading their scenarios, subjects read an instruction set preceding presentation of the tolerance questions that told them to pay attention to their feelings or to their thoughts. The instruction set was given after the scenarios were read and therefore cannot influence how the subjects processed and stored that information in memory.[7] We discuss the impact of this treatment elsewhere (Marcus et al., 1995). Here we focus only on that portion of our findings that speaks to the relative effects of the two principal variations of contemporary information.

---

7 Previous work has suggested that when subjects are given no instructions with respect to thoughts or feelings, they respond in the same way as if they had been given the affective instruction set (Kuklinski, Riggle, Ottati, Schwarz, & Wyer, 1991). For this reason, we did not add a control group to this already rather complex design.

The tolerance questions made specific mention of the hypothetical group. For example, if the subjects read a scenario about the Christians in Politics, one of the tolerance statements to which they responded was "Members of the Christians in Politics should be allowed to make a public speech." The posttest tolerance scale was created from six questions about the hypothetical group.[8]

Since we had earlier (in the pretest) collected information on the extent of political tolerance of the originally selected least-liked group, as well as their general commitment to democratic norms (two factors we had earlier found to influence tolerance judgments using survey methods; Sullivan et al., 1982), we can assess whether or not either or both of the two experimental manipulations altered political tolerance judgments beyond the impact of the established views of each subject.

In this study, as in all other studies that used that same design, we found a similar overall pattern of findings. We found that the normative violations treatment does influence contemporary tolerance judgments: Reading the threatening paragraph tends to decrease tolerance, while reading the reassuring paragraph tends to increase tolerance ($p = .02$). When people read information about the hypothetical group that depicts the group violating norms of peaceful, orderly behavior, they become more intolerant (a mean of 20.97). When people are reassured about the group's normative behavior, on the other hand, they react with greater tolerance (a mean of 21.24). While this difference is not great, it is replicated in other studies we have conducted (Marcus et al., 1995).

On the other hand, the probability of power manipulation did not have a significant effect on tolerance judgments. Even though the difference is in the correct direction (less tolerance among those who read the higher-probability paragraph), it is statistically insignificant. Moreover, in other studies we have conducted, we have consistently found the probability manipulation to have weak and insignificant effects.

However, the preceding studies do not explore the differential role of the two main mood systems, the Behavioral Approach System and the Behavioral Inhibition System, nor in these studies is mood measured directly. Further, we do not have the ability to measure the dynamic relationships between the two mood systems, standing dispositions, judg-

---

8 The statements that made up the tolerance scale are as follows: Members of the [selected scenario] should be banned from running for public office in the United States. Members of the [selected scenario] should be allowed to teach in public schools. [The selected scenario] should be outlawed. Members of the [selected scenario] should be allowed to make a public speech. The [selected scenario] should have their phones tapped by our government. The [selected scenario] should be allowed to hold public rallies.

ment, learning, and attention. The project described in the next section attempts to advance our understanding on precisely these questions.

Contemporary Influences, Standing Dispositions, and the Role of Emotions

We have completed a project that attempts to verify the unique and distinct effects of the two major mood systems, as proposed by Gray (Marcus and MacKuen, 1993). In this project, we were concerned with testing (1) the assertion that emotional responses are *essential* links in a variety of theoretically specified political circumstances and (2) that the form that those linkages take is properly identified by the hypotheses we have derived from the Gray model. In this project we have measures of the two emotional responses to the mood system, and we apply our attention to three different dependent factors: candidate preference, political learning, and political involvement, all during a presidential campaign.

Applying Gray's model to this group of factors can provide a rigorous test of that model, as well as revealing important dynamic processes that occur within the electorate during a campaign. Let us begin by specifying the relationships we can derive from Gray's model.

First, we expect that increases in anxiety stimulate greater attention to contemporary information and decreased reliance on habitual cues in forming candidate preferences in campaigns. We (Marcus, 1988) and others (Abelson et al., 1982; Page and Brody, 1972; Rahn et al., 1990) have shown that positive affect generated by candidates is a powerful influence on the choices voters make between competing candidates. Indeed, the only other factor that plays a substantial and significant role to rival that of positive affect (what we will call "enthusiasm") is party identification. Clearly, then, a voters' decision about whom to support is a composite judgment shaped by contemporary information contained within the changing levels of enthusiasm and established dispositions contained within partisan identification. Notice that we can derive from Gray's model the prediction that the mood of anxiety should not influence candidate preferences (and, indeed, negative affect does not; data not shown here, but see Marcus, 1988, and Marcus and MacKuen, 1993). That is the case because changes in anxiety alter attention, inhibit ongoing action, and diminish reliance on habit. What role does anxiety play in electoral politics? For if negative moods do not influence candidate preferences, why is there so much reliance on "negative campaigning"?

From Gray's model, we can derive the hypothesis that increased anxiety stimulated within voters by the candidates will *increase* reliance

George E. Marcus and Michael B. MacKuen

on contemporary information (the comparative enthusiasm factor) and *decrease* reliance on established cues and dispositions (partisanship). Traditional models of voting preference introduce a collection of factors thought to influence preference formation. These factors are typically introduced in a multivariate model with the presumption of linear additive effects. Such a model would take the form

$$\text{Candidate preference} = a + b_1 \text{ (enthusiasm)} + b_2 \text{ (anxiety)}$$
$$+ b_3 \text{ (party ID)} + b_4 \text{ (other factor)} + \ldots + e$$

It is worth noting that such a model does not include interaction terms.

When we evaluate this model, we generally find that positive affect has the predominant impact and negative affect has modest or negligible effects (Abelson et al., 1982; Marcus, 1988; Marcus and MacKuen, 1993). Other factors, most commonly party identification, have a substantial impact on candidate preference but generally less than the comparative enthusiasm the candidates generate in the voter (Rahn et al., 1990). Such analyses support the conclusion that contemporary elections are "candidate centered" and that partisan attachments are of declining and decreasing importance (Wattenberg, 1991). This has led to disputes as to when, and if, party identification remains a potent force in shaping voter preferences (Miller, 1991).

Gray's theory enables us to alter the typical specification by properly identifying the theoretical function of anxiety, which takes the form of an interaction. If we rely on habits to make recurring choices, then changes in the environment should be noticed and result in anxiety. Anxiety should then inhibit reliance on the normal, habitual choice. The equation derived from Gray's approach is as follows:

$$\text{Candidate preference} = a + b_1 \text{ (comparative enthusiasm)}$$
$$+ b_2 \text{ (anxiety about one's habitual choice}$$
$$\times \text{ comparative enthusiasm)} + b_3 \text{ (party ID)}$$
$$+ b_4 \text{ (anxiety about one's habitual choice}$$
$$\times \text{ party ID)} + e$$

We specify that anxiety has no direct (i.e., substantive) impact on candidate preferences (hence there is no need to include b_5 [anxiety] in the estimation equation). This proves to be the case empirically, thereby confirming the theoretical claim (data not shown; see earlier citations). Also, we can anticipate on theoretical grounds that the coefficients for each of the two interactions take the following signs:

First, b_2 should be positive. Increased anxiety should *enhance* reliance on the contemporary information contained in comparative enthusiasm generated by the candidates.

Second, b_4 should be negative. Increased anxiety should *reduce* reliance on previous dispositions, in this instance contained in partisan identification.

Gray's model suggests that the ratio between the influence of standing dispositions and the influence of contemporary impression formation depends on the level of anxiety. When anxiety is low or negligible, comparative enthusiasm and partisanship have roughly equivalent influence. In a campaign where little anxiety is generated in the electorate, partisanship would have a major impact on the election outcome. However, when anxiety is high, the ratio between the "standing decision" and reconsideration in light of contemporary information shifts dramatically.

We can make the same point another way. Psychologists often offer two alternative explanations for behavior: behavior as a result of some underlying "trait" (a coherent, enduring, and stable pattern of response) or behavior resulting from some "state" influence (a response that is largely shaped by the immediate environment). Arguments often arise as to whether a trait or state explanation is appropriate or sound. Here we offer a third view. State and trait explanations are warranted *and*, further, both operate simultaneously and interactively. By identifying the attention-shifting role of anxiety, we have gained an important insight into the way affective processes control when we think, what we think, and when we do not reflectively reconsider our political judgments.

The standard, perhaps crucial, concern for democratic theory has been the mixed (at best) evidence that voters make reasoned decisions in the voting booth and that they concentrate on programmatic consequences. For many years, empiricists and normative theorists have been debating how well voters demonstrate the expected characteristics set out by most, if not all, theories of representative democracy (Krouse and Marcus, 1984; Marcus and Hanson, 1993; Thompson, 1970). The typical juxtaposition compares the inattentive, ill-informed voter, who most commonly votes by using traditional cues, that is, partisan identification, with the ideal citizen, who is well informed and who carefully considers the policy and programmatic consequences of voting (Lazarsfeld, Berelson, and Gaudet, 1944).

The National Election Studies (NES) enable us to extend the analysis we have previously reported (Marcus and MacKuen, 1993). In each of three elections, the NES data contain data on voter preferences, emotional responses, and issue placement for the respondents and candidates. By adding issue information, as described subsequently, information of the sort that rational choice theorists have used with only modest success (Rabinowitz and MacDonald, 1989), we can explore how emotionality can be combined with rational choice theories to the mutual benefit of both approaches. The three presidential elections of 1984, 1988, and

1992 offer a rich and varied set of data. In 1984 the incumbent was reelected, and in 1992 the incumbent was defeated. In two of the three elections, in 1984 and 1988, the Republican candidate was elected, while in 1992 the Democratic candidate was elected. The elections seemed to turn on different concerns: taxes in 1984 and 1988 and the economy in 1992. Moral issues seemed to play a greater role in the last two elections than in the first. The 1984 election was a feel-good election; that of 1988 was not. Thus, we have a varied set of elections by which to test whether the anxiety linkage to rationality is robust.

Here we posit an additional interaction effect, this time analyzing national-level data on the presidential election regressing affect and issue distance on vote preference. Drawing on the circumplex model once again, we identify indices of anxiety and enthusiasm for each of the three elections. For the direct effect regression, anxiety is measured as comparative anxiety, with a high score indicating more anxiety toward the Democratic candidate. For the interaction effect, we measure the level of anxiety about the voter's habitual choice (i.e., Democratic identifiers with the Democratic presidential candidate, Republican identifiers with the Republican candidate). The pattern is strong and consistent across all elections. Anxiety and enthusiasm have direct effects on candidate choice (measured so that positive values indicate a democratic choice), but clearly a high level of anxiety about one's habitual choice involves higher reliance on issue evaluation between candidates, greater attention to the candidate's qualities (i.e., enhanced reliance on comparative enthusiasm), and reduced reliance on the standing vote (party identification) (Table 2.1).

We can see this more clearly by graphing the influences of comparative enthusiasm, comparative anxiety, issue distances, and party identification on voter preferences as a percentage of total explained variance. Figures 2.1 and 2.2 display these proportions in two analyses. Figure 2.1 shows the average across the three elections of voters who are calm (obtained by zeroing the interaction terms, i.e., setting total anxiety to 0), and Figure 2.2 shows the situation when they are anxious about the choice before them (i.e., total anxiety set to 1).

What New Insights?

Here we can see more clearly that when the voter is calm (Figure 1), issues play a modest role and emotional cues, along with partisanship, dominate the influences on the voter. For the anxious voter, the matter of choice is considerably different. Figure 2 shows what most democratic theorists would likely describe as properly attentive and, even more significantly, a properly deliberative voter. The anxious voter is *more*

Table 2.1. *Affect Interaction Effect, NES Data, Presidential Elections, 1984–1992*

Variable	1984			1988			1992		
	B	t	Sig T	B	t	Sig T	B	t	Sig T
Comparative anxiety	−.34	−11.2	.000	−.14	−4.6	.000	−.23	−6.5	.000
Comparative enthusiasm	.43	17.2	.000	.48	18.4	.000	.32	9.8	.000
Comparative enthusiasm: own-candidate anxiety	.23	4.1	.000	.08	1.1	.256	.21	3.0	.002
Mean issue distance	.51	5.8	.000	.43	5.1	.000	.22	3.1	.002
Mean issue distance: own-candidate anxiety	.21	2.7	.008	.36	4.1	.000	.28	2.9	.003
Party identification	.36	13.6	.000	.46	19.7	.000	.50	14.8	.000
Party identification: own-candidate anxiety	−.19	−2.9	.004	−.36	−5.1	.000	−.25	−3.0	.002
(Constant)	−.01	−0.2	.812	.05	1.1	.252	.18	5.2	.000

1984 interaction model:	1988 interaction model:	1992 interaction model:
Adjusted R^2 = .73	Adjusted R^2 = .69	Adjusted R^2 = .70
Standard error = .22	Standard error = .22	Standard error = .22
N = 1141	N = 1716	N = 1074

Note: B = "REGNESSION COEFFICIENT"

attentive to the qualities of the candidates, far *more* influenced by which candidate is closer to the voter on the issues of the day, and far *less* influenced by traditional loyalties (partisan cues). These results hold when we extend the data to include the 1980 and 1996 elections (Marcus, Neuman, and MacKuen, 2000).

It is striking, but consistent with our view, that we can gain considerable substantive and theoretical advantage by joining affective and cognitive accounts. The substantive gain is that we have identified dynamic relationships between anxiety and political learning, and between anxiety and concern for and reliance upon issues. These findings enable us to turn from the more dyspeptic portraits of voters (Converse, 1964, 1970; Smith, 1989) to a portrait of voters under the appropriate circumstances; that is when circumstances are novel and/or threatening,

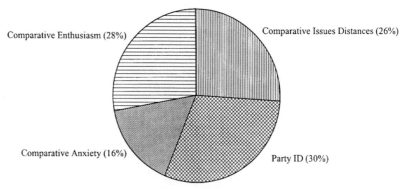

Figure 2.1. Affect interaction model. When voters are calm about their habitual choice: average of the 1984, 1988, and 1992 NES studies.

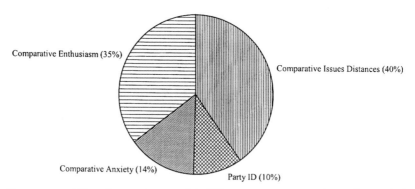

Figure 2.2. Affect interaction model. When voters are anxious about their habitual choices: average of the 1984, 1988, and 1992 NES studies.

voters act much as democratic theorists have long hoped. Our theoretical advantage is that we have identified circumstances in which rational choice theory seems to provide a good account.

If we combine affective intelligence with rational choice theory, as we have here, we find that people seem to be rational because and when their emotional cues motivate them to do the work that rational choice requires. We, like others, have found that emotional responses matter in politics, but that the effects are not singular and are not constant across the campaign period or across voters. We have found that the effects of emotional response are dynamic and modulated by shifting levels of anxiety and enthusiasm.

Moreover, this modulation suggests that the balance between standing decisions, preexisting and preestablished dispositions, and the influence of contemporary events and circumstances is itself dynamic. Dependence on previously learned habits is greatest when anxiety is low. And when anxiety is low, learning and attention to contemporary information are at their nadir. However, when anxiety is high, people break their reliance on habituated patterns of response and, what is important, shift attention to new information so as to consider what choices to make in light of the new and uncertain conditions. This dynamic pattern, of shifting reliance either on previously learned patterns of judgment and action or on contemporary reconsideration in light of attention to new information, is mediated by shifting levels of anxiety and appears to be rational in its consequences.

It may seem unusual to link rationality and emotionality, but there it is. Increased anxiety decreases reliance on standing decisions, increases attention to the sources of anxiety, and increases political learning. Put simply, anxiety stimulates "cognition" (or, more precisely, stimulates the specific kind of reflective, informed reconsideration that democratic theorists demand of democratic citizens).[9] Indeed, in the absence of the effects of increased anxiety, political campaigns would lose an important stimulus to precisely the kinds of democratic faculties that democratic theorists call for: deliberation, the thoughtful reconsideration of the choices before us. Moreover, in the absence of increased enthusiasm, active engagement in the democratic process can be expected to decline. Absent increased anxiety and enthusiasm, political campaigns will be stagnant affairs of habit and dull regularity.

CONCLUSION AND DISCUSSION

In describing the primary results of these two projects, we hope we have provided compelling evidence sufficient to encourage further study of the relationships between emotionality, political thinking, and political action. Not only do we gain an important set of factors that have hitherto been generally set aside, we also gain a better understanding of the emotional reactions that condition the cognitive processes of learning, attention, reflection, and introspection. Integrating a theory of affective intelligence that describes both affective and cognitive processes and their

9 Note that, this pattern reveals an important but inaccurate presumption of democratic theorists. Citizens can display the careful, attentive concern that theorists seem to require of responsible citizens in a democracy, but they do not display these faculties as stable aspects of character (or traits). It is often pointed out that gathering information is time- and energy-consuming. Perhaps paid theorists can display these faculties at most times, but citizens have other demands to meet, and so it seems efficient and rational that they display such faculties when circumstances most demand it.

mutual and cooperative relationships can explain when and how these cognitive faculties are called into play.

In order to make the further progress we have called for, we will need good theory. Merely adding a new collection of variables will not suffice. Too often we rely on the presupposition that anything worth exploring will reveal itself in simple linear effects. As we have shown, important interaction effects reveal themselves when one has a theory that can identify the proper specification. It should not be a surprise to find that emotionality systems have complex, cooperative, and interdependent relationships with cognitive systems. Indeed, it is hard to imagine that an organism as complex as the human brain works in any other way but as a complex, integrated set of systems that intercommunicate and interact in ways that cannot be captured by reducing the focus to cognition or conscious awareness and by searching blindly for simple linear relationships (Gazzaniga, 1985). Moreover, simply acknowledging or conceding that emotions matter will not do, for the systems of emotions are complex, their relationships are dynamic, and their influence on cognitive processes and behavior are also dynamic, compound, and complex.

We often see mention made of emotions. Typically it is asserted that such passions as anger and hostility bear on politics.[10] Yet these references are general, unsystematized, and usually lack formal theoretical specification. Often investigators have ignored the obligation to specify what kinds of emotional expressions they have identified and what typology of emotional expression and response they may have adopted. The domain of emotions has been largely ignored or treated simply and inaccurately as a polar distinction between "likes" and "dislikes" (Marcus, 1991). To the extent that emotionality has been considered and incorporated, it has been treated as a simple valence dimension (Osgood, Suci, and Tannenbaum, 1957). But the treatment of emotions as an adjunctive and subordinate part of cognition cannot accurately encompass the complexity and the independent – though interactive and cooperative – character of affective systems (Marcus, 1991; Marcus and Rahn, 1990). It is not our position that we merely add some measures of affect to our preexisting model of cognition. That strategy will not succeed. It is our position that cognitive processes cannot themselves be understood without an understanding that locates emotionality at the foundation of human personality (Cloninger, 1986; Gray, 1987b; Larsen

10 For example, the classic volume that defines the field of voting behavior, *The American Voter* (Campbell, Converse, Miller, & Stokes, 1960), is replete with explanatory claims that rely on references to emotion, but these are generally unexplicated and rely on commonsense applications without any theoretical specification.

and Ketelaar, 1991; Mayer et al., 1991; Salovey and Mayer, 1990; Watson, Clark, McIntyre, and Hamaker, 1992).

This is hardly a new position. Many of the most important thinkers in the evolution of political theory in the West put sentiment at the center of their work (Hobbes, 1968; Hume, 1739; Smith, 1759,). And, what is more pertinent for those interested in American politics and in democratic politics more generally, the founding fathers all understood the inescapable and essential role that the passions would unavoidably play in the new politics they brought forth (Madison, Hamilton, and Jay, 1961).

However, merely acknowledging the general point that emotions are important and inescapable is not sufficient. Gray's model of emotionality and personality (not detailed previously)[11] provides us with an excellent beginning. This model will certainly not be the definitive explanation of the problems confronting political psychology. We can confidently expect that additional work will lead to important modifications, adjustments, and even falsifications. We hope that the work described in this chapter is sufficient to encourage us to press ahead with a more fully encompassing view of humanity in its engagement in politics and, more broadly, of the human condition.

References

Abelson, Robert P., Donald R. Kinder, Mark D. Peters, and Susan T. Fiske. 1982. "Affective and Semantic Components in Political Personal Perception." *Journal of Personality and Social Psychology.* 42:619–630.

Ax, Albert. 1953. "The Physiological Differentiation between Fear and Anger in Humans." *Psychosomatic Medicine.* 15:433–422.

Batson, C. Daniel, J. Fultz, and P. Schoenrade. 1987. "Distress and Empathy: Two Qualitatively Distinct Vicarious Emotions with Different Motivational Consequences." *Journal of Personality.* 55:19–39.

Beck, Aaron T., Gary Brown, Robert A. Steer, Judy I. Eidelson, and John H. Riskind. 1987. "Differentiating Anxiety and Depression: A Test of the Cognitive Content-Specificity Hypothesis." *Journal of Abnormal Psychology.* 96:179–183.

Campbell, Angus, Philip E. Converse, Warren E. Miller, and Donald E. Stokes. 1960. *The American Voter.* New York: John Wiley and Sons.

Carlson, Michael, Ventura Charlin, and Norman Miller. 1988. "Positive Mood and Helping Behavior: A Test of Six Hypotheses." *Journal of Personality and Social Psychology.* 55:211–229.

Chance, Michael R. 1976. "The Organization of Attention in Groups." In *Methods of Inference from Animal to Human Behavior,* ed. M. v. Cranach. The Hague: Mouton.

11 See Gray (1970, 1973, 1987a) and Zuckerman (1991).

Cloninger, C. Robert. 1986. "A Unified Biosocial Theory of Personality and Its Role in the Development of Anxiety States." *Psychiatric Developments*. 3:167–226.

Converse, Philip E. 1964. "The Nature of Belief Systems in Mass Publics." In *Ideology and Discontent*, ed. D. Apter. New York: Free Press.

　　1970. "Attitudes and Non-Attitudes: Continuation of a Dialogue." In *The Quantitative Analysis of Social Problems*, ed. E. F. Tufte. Reading, MA: Addison-Wesley.

Derryberry, Douglas. 1991. "The Immediate Effects of Positive and Negative Feedback Signals." *Journal of Personality and Social Psychology*. 61: 267–278.

Downs, Anthony. 1957. *An Economic Theory of Democracy*. New York: Harper & Row.

Fiske, Susan T. and Mark Pavelchak. 1985. "Category-Based versus Piecemeal-Based Affective Responses: Developments in Schema-triggered Affect." In *The Handbook of Motivation and Cognition: Foundations of Social Behavior*, ed. R. Sorrentino and E. Higgins. New York: Guilford Press.

Foster, Carroll B. 1984. "The Performance of Rational Voter Models in Recent Presidential Elections." *American Political Science Review*. 78:678–690.

Gazzaniga, Michael. 1985. *The Social Brain: Discovering the Networks of the Mind*. New York: Basic Books.

Gray, Jeffrey. 1970. "The Psychophysiological Basis of Introversion-Extroversion." *Behaviour Research and Therapy*. 8:249–266.

　　1973. "Causal Theories of Personality and How to Test Them." In *Multivariate Analysis and Psychological Theory*, ed. J. R. Joyce. New York: Academic Press.

　　1981. "The Psychophysiology of Anxiety." In *Dimensions of Personality: Papers in Honour of H. J. Eysenck*, ed. R. Lynn. New York: Pergamon Press.

　　1985a. "The Neuropsychology of Anxiety." In *Stress and Anxiety*, ed. C. D. Spielberger. Washington, DC: Hemisphere Publications.

　　1985b. "A Whole and Its Parts: Behaviour, the Brain, Cognition, and Emotion." *Bulletin of the British Psychological Society*. 38:99–112.

　　1987a. "The Neuropsychology of Emotion and Personality." In *Cognitive Neurochemistry*, ed. S. M. Stahl, S. D. Iversen, and E. C. Goodman. Oxford: Oxford University Press.

　　1987b. *The Psychology of Fear and Stress*. 2nd ed. Cambridge, U.K.: Cambridge University Press.

　　1990. "Brain Systems That Mediate Both Emotion and Cognition." *Cognition and Emotion*. 4:269–288.

Hastie, Reid. 1986. "A Primer of Information-Processing Theory for the Political Scientist." In *Political Cognition*, ed. R. Lau and D. Sears. Hillsdale, NJ: Lawrence Erlbaum.

Hobbes, Thomas. 1968. *Leviathan*. London: Penguin Books.

Hume, David. 1739. *A Treatise of Human Nature*. London: Penguin Books.

Iyengar, Shanto and Donald Kinder. 1987. *News That Matters: Television and American Public Opinion*. Chicago: University of Chicago Press.

Key, V. O., Jr. and M. C. Cummings. 1966. *The Responsible Electorate: Rationality in Presidential Voting 1936–1960*. New York: Vintage Books.

Krouse, Richard and George E. Marcus. 1984. "Electoral Studies and Democratic Theory Reconsidered." *Political Behavior*. 6:23–39.

Kuklinski, James, Ellen Riggle, Victor Ottati, Norbert Schwarz, and Robert S. Wyler. 1991. "The Cognitive and Affective Bases of Political Tolerance Judgments." *American Journal of Political Science.* 35(1):1–27.

Lanzetta, John T. and Basil G. Englis. 1989. "Expectations of Cooperation and Competition and Their Effects on Observers' Vicarious Emotional Responses." *Journal of Personality and Social Psychology.* 56:543–554.

Larsen, Randy J. and Timothy Ketelaar. 1991. "Personality and Susceptibility to Positive and Negative Emotional States." *Journal of Personality and Social Psychology.* 61:132–140.

Lazarsfeld, Paul F., Bernard Berelson, and Hazel Gaudet. 1944. *The People's Choice.* New York: Duell, Sloan and Pearce.

Lazarus, Richard. 1982. "Thoughts on the Relations of Emotion and Cognition." *American Psychologist.* 37:1019–1024.

   1984. "On the Primacy of Cognition." *American Psychologist.* 39:124–129.

Lewicki, Pawel. 1986. *Nonconscious Social Information Processing.* New York: Academic Press.

MacLeod, Colin and Andrew Mathews. 1988. "Anxiety and the Allocation of Attention to Threat." *The Quarterly Journal of Experimental Psychology.* 40A:653–670.

Madison, James, Alexander Hamilton, and J. Jay. 1961. *The Federalist Papers.* Cleveland: World Publishing.

Marcus, George E. 1988. "The Structure of Emotional Response: 1984 Presidential Candidates." *American Political Science Review.* 82:735–761.

   1991. "Emotions and Politics: Hot Cognitions and the Rediscovery of Passion." *Social Science Information.* 30:195–232.

Marcus, George E. and Russell Hanson. 1993. *Reconsidering the Democratic Public.* University Park: Pennsylvania State University Press.

Marcus, George E. and Michael MacKuen. 1993. "Anxiety, Enthusiasm and the Vote: The Emotional Underpinnings of Learning and Involvement during Presidential Campaigns." *American Political Science Review.* 87:688–701.

Marcus, George E., Michael MacKuen, and Andrew D. Glassberg. 1989. *The Role of Emotional Response in Presidential Campaign Dynamics: Excitement and Threat.* Paper presented at the annual meeting of the American Political Science Association, Atlanta, Georgia, August 1989.

Marcus, George E., W. Russell Neuman, and Michael MacKuen. 2000. *Affective Intelligence and Political Judgment.* Chicago: University of Chicago Press.

Marcus, George E. and Wendy Rahn. 1990. "Emotions and Democratic Politics." In *Research in Micropolitics*, ed. S. Long. Greenwich, CT: JAI Press.

Marcus, George E., John L. Sullivan, Elizabeth Theiss-Morse, and Sandra Wood. 1995. *With Malice Toward Some: How People Make Civil Liberties Judgments.* New York: Cambridge University Press.

Mayer, John D., Maria DiPaolo, and Peter Salovey. 1990. "Perceiving Affective Content in Ambiguous Visual Stimuli: A Component of Emotional Intelligence." *Journal of Personality Assessment.* 54:772–781.

Mayer, John D. and Yvonne N. Gaschke. 1988. "The Experience and Meta-Experience of Mood." *Journal of Personality and Social Psychology.* 55:102–111.

Mayer, John D., Michelle H. Mamberg, and Alton J. Volanth. 1988. "Cognitive Domains of the Mood System." *Journal of Personality.* 56:453–486.

Mayer, John D., Peter Salovey, Susan Gomberg-Kaufman, and Kathleen Blainey. 1991. "A Broader Conception of Mood Experience." *Journal of Personality and Social Psychology.* 60:100–111.

McGuire, William J. 1968. "Personality and Susceptibility to Social Influence." In *Handbook of Personality Theory and Research*, ed. E. F. Borgatta and W. W. Lambert. Chicago: Rand McNally.

———. 1969. "The Nature of Attitudes and Attitude Change." In *The Handbook of Social Psychology*, ed. G. Lindzey and E. Aronson. Reading, MA: Addison-Wesley.

Miller, Warren E. 1991. "Party Identification, Realignment, and Party Voting: Back to the Basics." *American Political Science Review*. 85:557–568.

Osgood, Charles E., George J. Suci, and Percy H. Tannenbaum. 1957. *The Measurement of Meaning*. Urbana: University of Illinois Press.

Page, Benjamin and Richard A. Brody. 1972. "Policy Voting and the Electoral Process: The Vietnam War Issue." *American Political Science Review*. 66:979–995.

Page, Benjamin and Robert Y. Shapiro. 1992. *The Rational Public*. Chicago: University of Chicago Press.

Pratto, Felicia and Oliver P. John. 1991. "Automatic Vigilance: The Attention-Grabbing Power of Negative Social Information." *Journal of Personality and Social Psychology*. 61:380–391.

Quattrone, George A. and Amos Tversky. 1988. "Contrasting Rational and Psychological Analyses of Political Choice." *American Political Science Review*. 82:719–736.

Rabinowitz, George and Stuart Elaine MacDonald. 1989. "A Directional Theory of Issue Voting." *American Political Science Review*. 83:93–121.

Ragsdale, Lyn. 1991. "Strong Feelings: Emotional Responses to Presidents." *Political Behavior*. 13:33–65.

Rahn, Wendy M., John H. Aldrich, Eugene Borgida, and John L. Sullivan. 1990. "A Social-Cognitive Model of Candidate Appraisal." In *Information and Democratic Processes*, ed. J. Ferejohn and J. Kuklinski. Urbana-Champaign: University of Illinois Press.

Sacks, Colin H. and Daphne B. Bugental. 1987. "Attributions as Moderators of Affective and Behavioral Responses to Social Failure." *Journal of Personality and Social Psychology*. 53:939–947.

Salovey, Peter. 1992. "Mood-Induced Self- Focused Attention." *Journal of Personality and Social Psychology*. 62:699–707.

Salovey, P. and J. D. Mayer. 1990. "Emotional Intelligence." *Imagination, Cognition, and Personality*. 9:185–211.

Schachter, Stanley and Jerome E. Singer. 1962. "Cognitive, Social, and Physiological Determinants of Emotional State." *Psychological Review*. 69:379–399.

Schattschneider, E. E. 1948. *The Struggle for Party Government*. College Park: University of Maryland Press.

———. 1960. *The Semi-Sovereign People*. New York: Holt, Rinehart and Winston.

Schwarz, Norbert and Gerald L. Clore. 1983. "Mood, Misattribution, and Judgments of Well-Being: Informative and Directive Functions of Affective States." *Journal of Personality and Social Psychology*. 45:513–523.

Sears, David O. 1993. "Symbolic Politics: A Socio-Psychological Theory." In *Explorations in Political Psychology*, ed. S. Iyengar and W. McGuire. Durham, NC: Duke University Press.

Sears, David O., Carl Hensler, and Leslie Speer. 1979. "Whites' Opposition to 'Busing': Self-Interest or Symbolic Politics?" *American Political Science Review*. 73:369–385.

Sears, David O., Richard R. Lau, Tom R. Tyler, and Harris M. Allen, Jr. 1980. "Self-Interest vs. Symbolic Politics in Policy Attitudes and Presidential Voting." *American Political Science Review.* 74:670–684.

Seligman, Martin. 1975. *Helplessness: On Depression, Development and Death.* San Francisco: W. H. Freeman.

Smith, Adam. 1759. *The Theory of Moral Sentiments.* Indianapolis: Liberty Fund.

Smith, Eric R. A. N. 1989. *The Unchanging American Voter.* Berkeley and Los Angeles: University of California Press.

Sullivan, John L., James Piereson, and George E. Marcus. 1982. *Political Tolerance and American Democracy.* Chicago: University of Chicago Press.

Theiss-Morse, Elizabeth, George E. Marcus, and John L. Sullivan. 1993. "Passion and Reason in Political Life." In *Reconsidering the Democratic Public,* ed. G. E. Marcus and R. Hanson. University Park: Pennsylvania State University Press.

Thompson, Dennis. 1970. *The Democratic Citizen: Social Science and Democratic Theory in the Twentieth Century.* New York: Cambridge University Press.

Watson, David and Lee Anna Clark. 1991. "Self-versus Peer Ratings of Specific Emotional Traits: Evidence of Convergent and Discriminant Validity." *Journal of Personality and Social Psychology.* 60:927–940.

Watson, David, Lee Anna Clark, Curtis W. McIntyre, and Stacy Hamaker. 1992. "Affect, Personality and Social Activity." *Journal of Personality and Social Psychology.* 63:1011–1025.

Wattenberg, Martin P. 1991. *The Rise of Candidate-Centered Politics.* Cambridge, MA: Harvard University Press.

Zajonc, Robert B. 1980. "Feeling and Thinking: Preferences Need No Inferences." *American Psychologist.* 39:151–175.

1982. "On the Primacy of Affect." *American Psychologist.* 39:117–123.

Zajonc, Robert B. and Hazel Markus. 1984. "Affect and Cognition: The Hard Interface." In *Emotion, Cognition, and Behavior,* ed. C. Izard, J. Kagan, and R. Zajonc. New York: Cambridge University Press.

Zuckerman, Marvin. 1991. *Psychobiology of Personality.* Cambridge: Cambridge University Press.

3

Cognitive Neuroscience, Emotion, and Leadership*

ROGER D. MASTERS

Over the last decade, as advances in cognitive neuroscience have transformed our understanding of the human brain, it has become evident that emotional responses play a central role in learning and memory. At the same time, experimental studies of the way viewers respond to televised images of leaders have confirmed the central role of emotion as a mediating factor in attitude change. By integrating these two lines of research, I propose a new model of emotion and cognition that helps explain many phenomena in contemporary politics. The resulting psychology of leader–follower relations not only points to serious dangers associated with politics in the television age, but suggests practical reforms in our electoral process.

EXPERIMENTAL STUDIES OF THE EFFECTS
OF TELEVISION

It is now generally agreed that television has transformed the political life of industrialized societies because its visual images differ fundamentally from those of print media in their impact. Experimental evidence reveals that seeing a leader on TV elicits emotional responses in viewers (at both a physiological and a conscious level) that can influence attitudes independently of the verbal message. In this process, the leader's facial expressions and nonverbal behavior are often important factors in the viewer's emotional reactions (or "gut reactions"). Thus merely showing the silent images of a leader on television can influence public opinion (for reviews, see Lanzetta et al., 1985; Masters and Sullivan, 1993).

* Acknowledgment. I thank David Dragseth, Baldwin Way, Heather Jones, and Kim Kelly for work in conducting and analyzing the experiment during the 1992 American presidential campaign, and Prof. Denis G. Sullivan for his collaboration in designing this study as well as the earlier research on which it was based.

68

Such emotional responses help to explain why a particularly success-ful TV performance – as in John F. Kennedy's first debate with Richard Nixon in the 1960 campaign – can have a major effect on political events. In this process, viewers are not passive, however: experiments show that the emotional responses and judgments of a leader are dependent on the viewer's partisanship and information, as well as on the image presented on the television screen. In one study, for example, the opinions of viewers without well-defined attitudes were manipulated by seeing either happy or angry silent images of President Ronald Reagan in the background of a set of standard TV news stories; supporters of either party, on the other hand, were not swayed merely by the facial displays (Sullivan and Masters, 1994).

Studies of the emotional responses to leaders can also explore more precisely the difference between habitual television watchers and other citizens. In an experiment during the 1992 election campaign, for example, viewers differed significantly in the extent to which Ross Perot elicited the positive (or "warm") emotions known to be associated with favorable attitudes toward a leader. Perot's nonverbal behavior was par-ticularly effective for men who were not committed to either political party and who watched television frequently; women, partisan men, and those who did not watch television were not as likely to respond emo-tionally to the sight of Perot (Dragseth, 1993).

These effects of television are complex because the human brain simul-taneously processes visual images, matches the images with emotionally evocative memories or established attitudes, and integrates the perceived stimulus with the verbal message and contextual information. Because these processes are highly variable, viewers differ in how they respond to the same situation. Personality, gender, and ethnicity have all been found to have predictable effects, although each seems to influence a dif-ferent component of the experience of watching a leader. To understand how such factors influence the subtle interactions between the images of leaders and the viewers' emotions and political attitudes, it is necessary to transform our model of political psychology.

In 1992, for example, emotional responses to the happy/reassurance displays of George Bush, Dan Quayle, and Patrick Buchannan – the three most ideological Republican leaders – are difficult to explain from the perspective of conventional theories. When watching these leaders, party identification had the opposite effect on the episodic emotions of men and women. Republican women felt *more* warmth when they saw happy/reassuring excerpts of Bush, Quayle, or Buchanan than did Demo-cratic women; in contrast, Republican men reported *less* warmth than Democratic men (see Figure 3.2 later). While a statistical analysis reveals that neither party identification nor gender by itself has a significant relationship to emotional arousal, the interaction of these two variables is highly significant.

Conventional stimulus–response models have led political scientists to view such factors as gender or party identification as variables whose effects are additive. Findings like those just mentioned suggest that some voters may integrate information in entirely different ways, so that frequency of watching television or gender can modify the intensity and even the valence of emotional reactions. In the reactions to Quayle's happy/reassuring excerpt, for example, Democratic women expressed counterempathy, feeling more anger and fear (rather than the usual positive affect) when seeing his facial displays of happiness.

It is impossible to understand such phenomena without reference to the functional organization of the human brain. In recent years, neuroscientists have discovered that the central nervous system has a modular structure in which localized neuronal assemblies process distinct cues in each sensory modality. Because multiple features of a stimulus are processed simultaneously, the brain is seen as a parallel distributed processing system. Often described as "connectionism," this approach paradoxically emphasizes the way global patterns of response emerge from localized events. In this process, the activation of the limbic system, producing episodic emotional arousal, plays a central role in associative learning and memory.

This new model of the brain makes it possible to discover quite precisely how episodic emotional responses to images of leaders contribute to attitude change. Careful analysis of our experimental studies reveals that whereas partisan attachments have a direct effect on emotions, those who watch television frequently differ primarily in their *perceptions* of leaders. Perceptions, in turn, influence emotions and attitudes. These experiments have also shown how the announcer's commentary and other features of television newscasts can shape perceptions, emotional responses, and attitudes. As a result, the effects of television are often hidden or indirect, failing to appear in public opinion polls or other conventional methods of analysis by journalists and social scientists.

COGNITIVE NEUROSCIENCE AND EMOTION: FROM THE TABULA RASA TO THE SELF-ORGANIZING BRAIN

Cognitive neuroscience has revolutionized our knowledge of the way the brain perceives and reacts to social stimuli (for recent surveys, see Gazzaniga, 1985, 1988; Johnson, 1991; Kosslyn and Koenig, 1992). In place of the tabula rasa model of the brain inherited from Locke, neuroscientific research has revealed a modular structure in which specific functional processes are highly localized, giving rise to a parallel distributed processing system in which responses are integrated by the emotional centers of the brain (notably the amygdala and hippocampus). In place of the search for causal relations between stimulus and response, neuroscientists now focus on the brain as a continuously active system of enormous complexity.

There can be little doubt that the human brain, like that of other mammals, has a modular architecture. Hierarchical structures provide simultaneous parallel processing of visual cues (shape, color, motion, spatial location, etc.), auditory cues (pitch, rhythm, phonemic contrast, etc.), and other sensory modalities. When stimuli have sufficient functional importance to the organism, evolutionary processes have resulted in specialized neuronal assemblies that respond to defined cues. Specific pathways have been isolated, enabling the definition of the way that information from the environment is processed by the central nervous system (e.g., Kosslyn and Koenig, 1992: Figure 3.3). Far from being a blank slate, therefore, the brain has inherited the capacity to perceive and process environmental cues, including most particularly the perception of other members of the species.

These pathways are linked to the emotional centers of the brain – the amygdala, hippocampus, and related structures forming the limbic system (MacLean, 1992). What has traditionally been understood as positive and negative reinforcement can now be analyzed as the differential activation of distinct neuronal pathways and structures. As Gray (1987) has suggested, there is a "Behavioral Activation System" – associated with positive affect (the dimension of mood ranging from hope to depression) – integrating a different series of structures from the "Behavioral Inhibition System" entailed in responding to novelty and threat, generating emotions of anxiety and nervousness. The relevance of these two emotional systems to political psychology has been empirically demonstrated on numerous occasions (Abelson et al., 1982; Marcus, 1988; Marcus and MacKuen, 1993).

These findings of cognitive neuroscience are particularly relevant to the way citizens respond to leaders because, as Rolls (1989) has estimated, approximately 10% of the neurons in the inferior temporal lobe are functionally specific to visual processing of faces. Facial recognition seems to be based on "sparse population coding" – that is, a small number of neurons that respond in a particular manner to each known face (Young and Yamane, 1992). Other neurons in the inferior temporal lobe seem specialized in response to dynamic facial cues such as the upward movement of the head (Rolls, 1987, 1989). Since damage to the temporal lobes has been associated with deficits in social behavior (Kling, 1986, 1987), it is plausible to assume that, in some cases, modules or

Roger D. Masters

localized structures may be responsible for quite specific deficits in responses to conspecifics.

Understanding the brain as a modular structure means – paradoxically enough – that perception and cognition entail distributed networks that cannot be entirely reduced to localized events (e.g., Skarda and Freeman, 1990).[1] The traditional stimulus–response model of the brain, based on the metaphor of classical Newtonian physics (Peters and Tajfel, 1972), has therefore been replaced by a radically new approach in which the central nervous system actively changes the stimuli to which it responds:

The idea that perception . . . is caused by the stimulus or can be explained as the sum of responses to stimuli, is no longer acceptable. Our model tells us that perceptual processing is not a passive process of reaction, like a reflex, in which whatever hits the receptors is registered inside the brain. Perception does not begin with causal impact on receptors; it begins within the organism with internally generated (self-organized) neural activity that, by re-afference, lays the ground for processing of future input. In the absence of such activity, receptor stimulation does not lead to any observable changes in the cortex. It is the brain itself that creates the conditions for perceptual processing by generating activity patterns that determine what receptor activity will be accepted and processed. Perception is a self-organized dynamic process of interchange inaugurated by the brain in which the brain fails to respond to irrelevant input, opens itself to the input it accepts, reorganizes itself, and then reaches out to change its input. (Skarda and Freeman, 1990: 279)

This view explains how prior experience can change sensory perceptions by conceptualizing the brain as a nonlinear dynamic system, using deterministic "chaos theory" instead of conventional linear equations or algorithms as a mathematical model (Gleick, 1987; Ruelle, 1991).

In this view, a stable perception or attitude is an emergent "global activity pattern" in the brain that can be modeled mathematically as a "basin of attraction" or "strange attractor."[2] Although this approach

---

1 Although some neuroscientists have properly challenged the assumption that all brain functions can be reduced to sequential processing by a series of specialized modules – the so-called box and arrow models illustrated in Figure 3.1 (e.g., Farah, 1994) – their findings suggest the futility of arguing whether processes are *either* localized *or* distributed. Neuroscientific research needs to consider the extent of distribution as an important *variable* rather than as a theoretical postulate. Empirical evidence of this variability is presented in the text and the Appendix of this chapter.

2 The perception of an odor by the olfactory bulb has therefore been described as follows: "During late inhalation, input to the [olfactory] bulb not only activates the subset of neurons involved in the NCA [neural cell assembly], it excites all bulbar neurons increasing their strength of interaction, priming the entire bulb for an explosive and sudden state change. Receptor input, thus, destabilizes the bulb;

provides a neurological foundation for the concept of the "schema" now widely accepted in political psychology (e.g., Abelson, 1976), it suggests two critical modifications to the usual view of human cognition. First, it is unwarranted to assume that conscious or verbal expressions provide an exhaustive measure of the memories and feelings associated with any given perception or attitude; visual images, for example, may play an important role in the schema of a political party (see the case described in the Appendix). Much of our learning is unconscious or preconscious, and such learning may reflect elements of the basis of attraction of great political relevance.

Second, it is essential to abandon the conventional dichotomy between emotion and cognition. In mammalian brains, the limbic system – the neuronal structures associated with emotion – plays a critical role in formatting and reshaping the distributed patterns that correspond to what political psychologists have called a "schema" or "attitude" (MacLean, 1992). Without the links between the cortex and the hippocampus, amygdala, and other structures modulating emotional arousal, associative learning and memory are destroyed (Mishkin and Appenzeller, 1987; Zola-Morgan and Squire, 1990). Emotion is thus particularly important in the establishment or transformation of the network of neuronal activity or "neuronal cell assembly" that is bound together in a stable perception or attitude (cf. Skarda and Freeman, 1990; Marcus, 1988).

Since the brain is constantly active, the specific pattern of parallel distributed processing associated with any given stimulus thus depends on emotion. But emotional arousal, in turn, depends on the way that parallel distributed processing networks have been shaped and stabilized

it augments interaction over the entire bulb by pushing bulbar neurons far from their initial low energy state. The result is a state change or bifurcation that leads to the emergence of a globally distributed odor specific activity pattern. Upon bifurcation, the bulb converts to a transmitting mode in which bulbar neurons no longer respond to receptor input. In this state, information carried by each neuron is disseminated over the entire bulb and integrated by every neuron in the bulb. These patterns of globally distributed activity, one for each discriminated odor, have been mathematically expressed as a collection of chaotic attractors. These are the patterns that are sent out of the bulb to the cortex and that we suggest are behaviorally relevant for the correlations that are usually associated with learning and memory. Upon exhalation, the bulb returns to its low level chaotic background state in readiness for new interaction with the environment" (Skarda and Freeman, 1990: 279). For the concepts of "bifurcation," "attractors," and "chaotic" states, see the popular introductions to chaos theory by Gleick (1987) or Ruelle (1991). This approach to human thought has broader implications, challenging the dominant paradigms of modern science based on linear algorithms and pointing to the continued relevance of the pattern-matching paradigm of ancient science and philosophy (Masters, 1993).

through the organism's development and life history. Because the same stimulus can even elicit different emotions in the left and right hemispheres of the brain of a single person, as has been shown with a split-brain patient (Gazzaniga, 1985: 74–75), the modular, self-organizing, and dynamic model of the central nervous system forces us to see the perception and response to given environmental stimuli as far more variable than was the case for traditional behaviorist psychology.

Variability in patterns of distributed processing can be illustrated by the way both normal and impaired individuals respond to the faces of political leaders. Many neuroscientists have included this stimulus in their analysis of such phenomena as selective impairments in knowledge of living things and prosopagnosia. In fact, images of leaders are valuable target stimuli in cognitive neuroscience for at least three reasons. First, both recognition of familiar individuals and differential responses to facial displays are characteristic of nonhuman primates as well as humans; such stimuli are meaningful social cues whose evolutionary history can explain the existence of localized modules, such as those in the inferior temporal lobes for facial recognition and display cues. Second, among primates as well as humans, leaders are attention-binding to others in the group (Chance, 1976). When studying human responses, therefore, videotapes of national political leaders are more likely than other stimulus figures to be known, and thereby to elicit meaningful emotional and cognitive responses comparable in normal and cognitively impaired subjects (for a review, see Masters, 1989a: Chap. 2).

A NEUROSCIENTIFIC MODEL OF VIEWERS' RESPONSES TO LEADERS

As applied to the way citizens respond to leaders, a neuroscientific approach to political psychology must begin by specifying the sequence of relationships as individuals perceive relevant events and leaders. First, the *characteristics of the stimulus situation* presented to the viewer need to be defined quite precisely. For example, images of a leader elicit predictable emotional responses in the viewer that depend on the leader's nonverbal displays (Lanzetta et al., 1985). For a single excerpt of a leader, however, both changes in that individual's political status (Masters and Carlotti, 1994) and the channels of communication – for example, image only, sound only, sound plus image – presented to the viewer (Masters et al., 1986) can modify the effect of the stimulus. These effects can differ from one leader to another as a result of individual variations in performance style or facial configuration (e.g., Sullivan and Masters, 1988). Such effects can also be modified if the image is seen in a competitive social context – as when rivals are shown during a political campaign (McHugo et al., 1985, 1991). Finally, viewers' perceptions and emotions are modified by the way television commentators explain or "frame" the events shown on TV (Newton et al., 1987).

Second, *characteristics of viewers*, such as personality, gender, social class, ethnicity, or other attributes that vary within a population, often influence perceptions and responses to a televised event (Masters, 1991). These factors may be understood as predictable ways in which associative learning and memory predispose classes of viewers to integrate their emotional and cognitive responses to sensory cues. For example, there is considerable evidence that men and women differ in their overall patterns of emotional and cognitive processing (Kimura, 1999). When viewers see leaders, however, gender differences need to be distinguished from the effects of personality (Clancy, 1992) or nationality (Warnecke et al., 1992).

Third, *individual political attitudes* – patterns of emotion and cognition that vary within each viewer as the result of prior experience and ongoing information processing – influence the episodic emotions elicited by leaders (Lanzetta et al., 1985; McHugo et al., 1991; Masters and Sullivan, 1993). Within a given category of viewers, such differences in attitude may be associated with diverse patterns of perception, emotion, and attitude change. For example, as data from a 1992 study confirm (see the later discussion), statistically significant interactions between the variables of gender and partisanship have often been found when studying responses to leaders' nonverbal displays (see also Masters, 1989b; Masters and Carlotti, 1994).

Fourth, the *hierarchical structure of the brain* requires a careful distinction between perceptions (or descriptions) of events, episodic emotional responses, and changes in attitude. Independent variables that influence the way viewers respond to leaders may impinge on any one of these levels. Although perceptions strongly influence emotions and emotional responses influence attitudes, the process need not be linear. Hence, as we will see, the experience of watching TV frequently during a campaign seems to influence perceptions of displays (which, in turn, elicit episodic emotions), whereas political attitudes sometimes have direct effects on emotion without influencing perception. Indeed, the mere exposure to a leader can enhance attitude change by direct reinforcement, as well as by processes mediated by emotional arousal.

To depict a process of this complexity, a visual model illustrating the potential causal pathways is highly useful (Figure 3.1). Each column lists factors that have been found to influence viewers in experiments over the last decade. The boldface connecting lines reflect what appear to be the most powerful and consistent relationships, while the thinner lines indicate linkages that have been found to be statistically significant in

Roger D. Masters

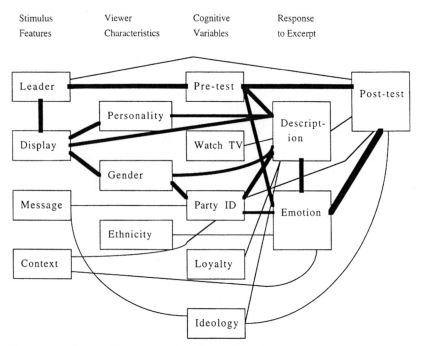

Figure 3.1. A cognitive neuroscientific model of response to TV excerpts of leaders.

one or more studies. Although the list of variables at each of the four stages of emotional and cognitive processing is doubtless incomplete, the overall model shows the complexity required if the perspective of cognitive neuroscience is to replace conventional approaches in political psychology.

THE STRUCTURE OF EMOTIONAL AND COGNITIVE
RESPONSES TO LEADERS

Data from experimental studies over the last decade provide evidence for the complex structure of emotional and cognitive responses depicted in Figure 3.1. In this series of experiments, viewers were presented with recorded excerpts of national leaders exhibiting three basic social and emotional displays (happiness/reassurance, anger/threat, and fear/evasion) that are observed among nonhuman primates, seem to be universal in human societies, and are readily distinguished by contemporary viewers (Masters et al., 1986). In each experiment, subjects were given a pretest questionnaire in which political attitudes and ratings of leaders on the 0–100 "thermometer" scale often used as a summary measure of voter support (e.g., Abelson et al., 1982) were recorded, along with information on age, sex, media exposure – and, in some cases, personality.

During the experiment, subjects observed a series of excerpts, sometimes with the sound and sometimes as a silent image; after each excerpt, subjects first recorded a description of the leader's nonverbal behavior (using unipolar 7-point scales for ratings of such display characteristics as "happy," "angry," "fearful," "comforting," etc.) and then used similar scales to report their own emotional responses or feelings during the excerpt (Lanzetta et al., 1985). Several experiments validated these self-reported emotional responses by recording psychophysiological responses during excerpts and comparing them to the scale scores (McHugo et al., 1985, 1991). After viewing all excerpts, subjects completed a posttest questionnaire, which provided an opportunity to measure thermometer ratings of the leaders after the study and hence to measure attitude changes due to the experience of watching the excerpts.

Studies have varied in the leaders shown, which have included the main rivals for both Republican and Democratic presidential nominations in 1984, 1998, and 1992, as well as the mode of presentation. In some studies, viewers saw all three types of displays for a single leader in the United States (Masters et al., 1986) and France (Masters and Sullivan, 1989); in others, subjects viewed a neutral and a happy/reassuring excerpt of all candidates in an American presidential campaign (Sullivan and Masters, 1988; Masters, 1991; Masters and Carlotti, 1994). And in one experiment, silent nonverbal displays of either happy, angry, or neutral attitudes were inserted in a series of otherwise identical network news stories (Sullivan and Masters, 1994).

The principal results show the importance of both cognition and emotion in the process by which viewers respond to leaders in ordinary experience. Depending on attributes of both the viewer and the politician observed, such cognitive information as the viewer's party allegiance, assessment of the leader, and habits of TV watching are integrated with emotional reactions to specific displays (Masters, 1991; Masters and Sullivan, 1993). In turn, these episodic emotional responses while watching leaders are associated with the attitude changes that can be produced by TV appearances in contemporary political campaigns (e.g., Sullivan and Masters, 1988, 1994).

Given the complex system portrayed in Figure 3.1, it is necessary to analyze each step of information processing carefully in order to discover which functional categories are related to each other. The remarks of two well-known neuroscientists concerning the classic connectionist diagram

of the visual cortex apply as well to Figure 3.1: "There are three important features of the diagram that are worth noting now. First, it is orderly;
everything is not connected to everything else. Second, there is a large
amount of serial processing; in many cases, areas receive input from
lower areas only via intermediate areas. Third, the lines connecting the
areas do not have arrow heads. The reason for this is that virtually every
area that sends information downstream to another area also receives
information from that area" (Kosslyn and Koenig, 1992: 59–60).

To explore such a complex system, it is helpful to focus on the overall
characteristics of data combining numerous experimental studies. No
single stimulus can be used to define the basic system because leaders
vary so much in their performance – and because other features such as
their status, the political context, and the character of the image can
influence the interaction of variables. As a result, findings that occur
for one leader in a particular study could reflect a particularity of the
specific instance.

To facilitate such a comparative analysis, it is useful to construct a
single overall measure that summarizes viewers' responses to each
excerpt. Although the viewers' descriptive ratings and emotional
responses after watching the excerpts were measured on distinct scales
for each emotion, it is possible to compute a net score, subtracting the
two principal "negative" or agonic scales (angry and fearful) from the
two "positive" or hedonic ones. The resulting measure ("net warmth")
provides an overall assessment of the description or emotional response
that reflects the simultaneous activation of the two major limbic systems
described previously.

Across five experimental studies, responses to the neutral display of
each leader can then be subtracted from responses to that leader's display
of happiness/reassurance to provide a measure of the happy/reassuring
display that controls for constants associated with other features of the
leader and his face. When these scores were averaged for entire samples,
to control for variability in the viewer, the difference in descriptive scores
(measuring perceived intensity of the happy/reassuring behavior) is
highly correlated ($r = .90$) with viewers' self-reported positive emotion
elicited by the happy/reassurance cues (Masters, 1990: Figure 3.1). In
other words, controlling for responses to the neutral image of a leader,
descriptions of the intensity of a leader's happy/reassuring display behavior are very closely associated with increased feelings of happiness and
comfort.

It should not, of course, be surprising to realize that perceptions of
nonverbal display behavior are closely related to emotional responses:
the sites in the inferior temporal lobes that process the visual images of
a facial display are located near the limbic system, and the perception,

production, and emotional response to facial expressions are closely related (Schwartz et al., 1976). Hence there is good reason to postulate a strong link between the boxes marked "Description" and "Emotional Response" in Figure 3.1.

To explore the other relationships in Figure 3.1, I will begin with an analysis of data combining responses to the Republican and Democratic presidential candidates in experiments during the 1984, 1988, and 1992 elections. Use of this combined dataset controls for the personal display behavior of the candidates of each party (Reagan and Bush compared to Walter Mondale, George Dukakis, and Bill Clinton), the success of the leader and his party (these campaigns include victories for both parties – and, for the one leader who ran twice, both a successful and an unsuccessful campaign), the status of the leader (all were known presidential candidates, and hence were likely to evoke emotions and cognitions in viewers), and the circumstances of our own experimental studies (samples include both adults and college students at different times during the election campaign and in different locations). Even more important, the combined dataset creates a sample of 263 males and 247 females, comparable in size to some national public opinion polls, thereby making it possible to do many statistical analyses that cannot be performed for a single experiment.

The first task in assessing the system described in Figure 3.1 is to discover how variables are related to each other. To do so, stepwise regression equations were computed for three dependent variables that form a temporal sequence: the viewer's descriptions of the display behavior, self-reported emotional responses during the excerpt, and posttest attitude (measuring the viewer's overall attitude to each leader after seeing a number of candidates on television). This sequence is derived from the experimental procedures: descriptions of each excerpt were recorded before self-reports of episodic emotion, and of course, the posttest thermometer rating of attitude took place minutes after the subjects noted these descriptions and emotional responses.[3] These procedures, in turn, reflect neuroanatomic knowledge of real-time serial processing: the visual processing of nonverbal display behavior associated with perception occurs in the inferior temporal lobes and other sites before neuronal impulses reach the limbic system, and the emotional responses

---

3 A manipulation of the sequence in our experimental instrument confirmed that asking subjects to record their emotional responses *before* they describe each excerpt introduces effects of both gender and sequence of questions (Warnecke, 1991: Chap. 5). Since a questionnaire that introduces such effects is contrary to good experimental procedures, the sequence adopted could be based on methodological grounds as well as on considerations of cognitive neuroscience.

Roger D. Masters

modulated by the limbic systems have a feedback effect on lasting attitudes. In analyzing dependent variables that form such a temporal sequence, for each stage it is necessary to include the prior steps in informational processing. In what follows, results are presented in reverse order, starting with the posttest thermometer ratings that measure the effects of watching leaders on viewers' attitudes.

Viewers' posttest attitudes to the presidential candidates of each party, after watching excerpts of all candidates in the campaign, were analyzed using the following as independent variables: the viewer's pretest thermometer rating of the candidate, agreement on issues with the candidate, rating of the candidate's leadership ability, frequency of reading newspapers, frequency of watching TV, interest in the election, ideology, party identification, partisan loyalty (strength of partisanship), description of the candidate's neutral display, emotional response to the neutral display, difference between the net description of the candidate's neutral and happy/reassuring displays, and the difference in the net warmth of emotional response to the two displays.[4] Then the same procedure was repeated for self-reported emotional responses during each excerpt (dropping posttest thermometer from the equation since it could not have influenced emotional responses that had already taken place) and for viewers' descriptions of each excerpt (dropping the viewer's emotional responses since they depended in part on perceptions of nonverbal behavior).

The stepwise regression equations show that only some variables are significantly correlated with responses at each level. They also reveal, however, that patterns of integration differ for males and females. In what follows, therefore, I will identify the linkages revealed by the stepwise regression equations. Then I will suggest some supplementary evidence of linkages based on analysis of variance, multiple regression

---

4 Although prior studies have typically used multiple regression rather than stepwise regression (e.g., Sullivan and Masters, 1988), critics have often expressed the fear that multicollinearity limits the reliability of our results; using stepwise regression models avoids this problem while permitting an assessment of variables whose relationship to the dependent variable is unknown. In most previous studies, to measure the effects of happy/reassuring display behavior, we have measured the emotional responses to those displays rather than the difference scores between happy/reassuring and neutral excerpts. The procedure used here is appropriate, however, if one is to distinguish between those features elicited by any facial image of a particular leader and that individual's performance of the display itself. This procedure is both theoretically justified, since nonverbal behavior is such a highly evocative system of communicating emotion (Ekman and Oster, 1979), and empirically meaningful: the same independent variables are significant when emotional responses to the happy/reassuring displays or neutral displays are used as the dependent variable.

80

equations for the same variables, or other statistical measures. For these results, relationships are reported only if they are statistically significant (usually $p < .05$ but in no case weaker than $p < .10$).

Posttest Attitudes Toward Leaders

The results for the stepwise regression analysis of posttest thermometer ratings of both the Democratic and Republican candidates in the three elections, computed separately for males and females, are summarized in Table 3.1. Across all campaigns, the main variable predicting posttest attitude – not surprisingly – is pretest thermometer (r^2 between .71 and .78). This finding is far from trivial: the experience of seeing a leader on television has a reinforcing effect, without reference to mediating cognitive or emotional variables. Politicians have good reason to seek to get television coverage.

The second most important variable, as measured by the standardized coefficient (and, for three of the four equations, by order of stepwise entry), is emotional response to the neutral excerpt of the leader. This is true for both males and females when responding to leaders of both parties. Merely seeing a leader elicits feelings that have an independent effect on attitude. The emotions produced by happy/reassuring behavior, as measured by the difference in emotional response to the happy/reassuring and neutral excerpts, are the third most important variable for both male and female posttest attitudes to the Republican candidates and the fourth variable influencing male attitudes to the Democratic candidates.[5] Issue agreement is significant only for women's ratings of Democrats and men's ratings of Republicans – and in each case, it is weaker than the emotional response variables. Apart from pretest attitude, episodic emotions are thus the most important predictor of attitude after watching rival leaders on television.

The four sets of stepwise regression analyses in Table 3.1 confirm earlier reports of multiple regression models on a candidate-by-candidate basis: controlling for the effect of pretest attitude, self-reported emotional responses while watching the excerpts – often, though not always, during the happy/reassuring display – have consistently predicted changes in posttest attitude (Sullivan and Masters, 1988; Masters and Sullivan, 1993). In these earlier studies, while episodic emotions have almost always appeared in regression models for every leader in each

---

5 The absence of this variable from equations explaining female posttest attitudes to Democratic candidates may reflect the weakness of the positive emotion elicited by the happy/reassurance displays of both Mondale and Dukakis (Sullivan and Masters, 1988; Masters and Carlotti, in 1994).

Table 3.1. *Stepwise Regression for Posttest Thermometer Rating After Watching Excerpts of Presidential Candidates in 1984, 1988, and 1992*

FEMALE VIEWERS
(*n* = 248)

Dependent Variable	Republican Candidate			Democratic Candidate		
	Independent Variable	Standardized Coefficient	Adj r^2	Independent Variable	Standardized Coefficient	Adj r^2
Posttest thermometer rating of presidential candidate	Pretest thermometer	.66	.75	Pretest thermometer	.63	.72
	Assessed leadership	.11	.76	Emotion to neutral	.21	.75
	Emotion to neutral	.18	.77	Issue agreement	.15	.76
	Added emotion to happy	.14	.78			
	Watch TV news	−.07	.79			

MALE VIEWERS
(*n* = 263)

Dependent Variable	Republican Candidate			Democratic Candidate		
	Independent Variable	Standardized Coefficient	Adj r^2	Independent Variable	Standardized Coefficient	Adj r^2
Posttest thermometer rating of presidential candidate	Pretest thermometer	.64	.78	Pretest thermometer	.63	.71
	Emotion to neutral	.20	.80	Emotion to neutral	.20	.73
	Added emotion to happy	.15	.82	Assessed leadership	.15	.74
	Probability of voting	.08	.82	Added emotion to happy	.10	.75
	Description of neutral	.09	.83			
	Issue agreement	.12	.84			

Notes: Standardized coefficients are for the last step of the stepwise regression; adjusted r^2 is variance explained after the step on which the variable is entered. Independent variables: pretest thermometer (0–100) at outset; emotion to neutral = net warmth of self-reported episodic emotion during neutral excerpt; added emotion to happy = net warmth during happy/reassuring excerpt minus that during neutral; description of neutral = net descriptive rating of neutral excerpt. For other variables, see Sullivan and Masters (1988).

experiment,[6] such factors as assessments of leadership, issue agreement, probability of voting, or frequency of watching television news (which represent the cognitive variables more typically emphasized in political psychology) have not been consistently significant predictors of attitude change. Emotions while watching leaders thus influence attitude. But what contributes to these feelings in television viewers?

Emotional Response

If episodic emotions while watching a leader on television can influence attitudes, what is it that influences the viewer's feelings? The stepwise regression equations that predict these emotional responses in experiments across all three election campaigns provide an important test of the model presented here. According to the conventional approach in political psychology, one would expect emotions during each excerpt to reflect cognitive variables. In contrast, the perspective of cognitive neuroscience suggests that, in addition to these factors, the perception of the leader's behavior (as measured by average descriptive ratings) should make a distinct contribution to the viewer's emotion.

To assess this possibility, it is necessary to analyze separately the responses to a neutral excerpt of the candidate of each party (Table 3.2a) and those elicited by the leader's happy/reassuring display behavior. The latter is harder to measure because responses to the happy/reassuring excerpt combine effects of facial recognition – as illustrated by watching a neutral excerpt – and those due to the happy/reassuring cues themselves; since cognitive neuroscientists have shown that these features of a facial stimulus are processed by distinct neuronal ensembles (e.g., Rolls, 1989), the specific effect of the expressive display is best measured by using the difference in response to the two excerpts as the dependent variable (Table 3.2b).

Emotions During Neutral Displays. Table 3.2a shows that, for both men and women when responding to neutral excerpts of either the Republican or the Democratic candidate in all three elections, the factor with the highest standardized coefficient influencing emotional response is the viewer's description of the excerpt (standardized coefficients ranging between .42 and .58). Although the order of entry in the stepwise process varies from one equation to another, in all four cases the pretest thermometer is the second strongest predictor of emotional response (standardized coefficients ranging between .25 and .38).

6 The only major exception concerns the responses of black viewers in our 1988 experimental sample (Masters, 1991).

Roger D. Masters

Table 3.2a. *Stepwise Regression for Emotional Response to Neutral Excerpts of Presidential Candidates in 1984, 1988, and 1992*

FEMALE VIEWERS
(n = 248)

	Republican Candidate			Democratic Candidate		
Dependent Variable	Independent Variable	Standardized Coefficient	Adj r^2	Independent Variable	Standardized Coefficient	Adj r^2
Emotional response during neutral excerpt	Pretest thermometer	.35	.35	Description of neutral excerpt	.53	.40
	Description of neutral excerpt	.42	.53	Pretest thermometer	.38	.54
	Issue agreement	.21	.54			

MALE VIEWERS
(n = 262)

	Republican Candidate			Democratic Candidate		
Dependent Variable	Independent Variable	Standardized Coefficient	Adj r^2	Independent Variable	Standardized Coefficient	Adj r^2
Emotional response during neutral excerpt	Issue agreement	.22	.36	Description of neutral excerpt	.58	.46
	Description of neutral excerpt	.45	.54	Pretest thermometer	.25	.57
	Pretest thermometer	.30	.58	Party identification	−.15	.58
	Frequency of watching TV news	−.08	.59			

Notes: Standardized coefficients are for the last step of the stepwise regression; adjusted r^2 is the variance explained after the step on which the variable is entered. Independent variables: pretest thermometer (0–100) at outset; added emotion to happy = net warmth during happy/reassuring excerpt minus that during neutral; description of neutral = net descriptive rating of neutral excerpt. For other variables, see Sullivan and Masters (1988).

To be sure, for men and for women responding to the Republican candidates, other cognitive variables enter the equations; indeed, for men watching Republicans, issue agreement is the first variable to be entered into the stepwise process. When all significant predictors have been accounted for, however, the perception of a leader's display behavior

Table 3.2b. *Stepwise Regression for Added Emotional Response to Happy/Reassuring Excerpts of Presidential Candidates in 1984, 1988, and 1992*

FEMALE VIEWERS
($n = 248$)

	Republican Candidate			Democratic Candidate		
Dependent Variable	Independent Variable	Standardized Coefficient	Adj r^2	Independent Variable	Standardized Coefficient	Adj r^2
Added emotional response to happy/ reassuring (HR) excerpt	Described difference between neutral and HR excerpts	.51	.25	Described difference between neutral and HR excerpts	.39	.16
				Issue agreement	.23	.21
				Ideology	−.16	.23
				Probability of voting	.14	.25

MALE VIEWERS
($n = 262$)

	Republican Candidate			Democratic Candidate		
Dependent Variable	Independent Variable	Standardized Coefficient	Adj r^2	Independent Variable	Standardized Coefficient	Adj r^2
Added emotional response to happy/ reassuring (HR) excerpt	Described difference between neutral and HR excerpts	.58	.34	Described difference between neutral and HR excerpts	.56	.31

Notes: Standardized coefficients are for the last step of the stepwise regression; adjusted r^2 is variance explained after the step on which the variable is entered. Independent variables: pretest thermometer (0–100) at outset; added emotion to happy = net warmth during happy/reassuring excerpt minus that during neutral; description of neutral = net descriptive rating of neutral excerpt. For other variables, see Sullivan and Masters (1988).

remains the most consistent variable influencing emotional responses (although, as is shown by analysis of variance, the viewer's description often interacts with variables like the viewer's party identity, gender, and frequency of watching television news [Dragseth, 1993]). For both parties, the resulting regression equations explain over half of the variance (for female viewers responding to leaders of either party, $r^2 = .54$; for males, $r^2 = .58$ and $.59$).

These findings confirm the political relevance of the neuroscientific evidence that facial images are processed by a pathway from the visual cortex through specialized sites in the inferior temporal lobes and thence to the limbic system, while parallel neuronal pathways link the associative memory centers of the neocortex with the limbic system (Mishkin and Appenzeller, 1987). Such parallel processing is surely the reason for the very strong emotional responses to nonverbal cues even when viewers believe they are attending solely to the verbal message. It also suggests why psychophysiological responses to facial displays would be stronger in the image-only media condition (where no other input reaches the limbic system) than when the same images are seen with sound (McHugo et al., 1985). Finally, these results help to explain why viewers with little or no political information are even more strongly influenced by facial displays than partisans (Sullivan and Masters, 1994): obviously, those with strong party identification have emotional input influenced by verbal memory and cognitive processing in the neocortex that complements the direct responses to the facial cues themselves.

Difference in Emotions During Happy/Reassuring and Neutral Displays. To assess the effect of leaders' display behavior while controlling for emotional responses to the sight of their faces, it is necessary to study the difference between emotions felt during the neutral and happy/reassuring excerpts. In stepwise regression models, only one factor is consistently significant in predicting the added emotional response due to the happy/reassuring cues in the excerpt: the difference between the viewer's net description of the neutral and happy/reassuring displays (Table 3.2b). Only for women's responses to Democratic candidates are any cognitive variables significant – and these have relatively minor effects.[7]

The reason for the apparently weak explanatory value of cognitive variables is probably twofold. First, much of the variation in emotional response to a happy/reassuring cue depends on the specific leader and his mode of performing these expressive displays (Sullivan and Masters,

---

7 It should be added that a multiple regression equation with the same variables shows significant correlations with additional variables: newspaper readership, party identification, assessment of leadership for the Republican candidates, frequency of watching TV news, and party loyalty for the Democratic candidates. These multiple regressions explain proportions of the variance roughly comparable to the stepwise models (for the Republican candidates, $r^2 = .35$; for the Democrats, $r^2 = .14$), suggesting that the influence of the cognitive variables may be mediated by viewers' descriptions of the excerpts.

1988). Since the equations in Tables 3.1 through 3.3 combined different leaders, they average effects due to these differences in performance style. Second, many of the effects of attitude variables on emotion involve interactions between the display seen, the viewer's party or political attitudes, and such factors as gender and frequency of watching TV news (cf. Lanzetta et al., 1985; Masters and Carlotti, 1994). As a result, the effects of independent variables on emotion often reflect nonlinear relationships that can only be revealed by analysis of variance.

The finding that descriptive ratings are the most consistent factors influencing emotional responses to the display component of a televised excerpt is nonetheless of theoretical importance. The stepwise regressions confirm the view, derived from cognitive neuroscience, that the perception of cues has an independent role in modulating the viewer's emotions. But, as neuroscientists emphasize (e.g., Skarda and Freeman, 1990), it would be an error to assume that these perceptions are merely mechanical or reflexive responses to "objective" stimuli.

Emotional responses to televised images of leaders are therefore influenced not only by how we perceive a nonverbal display, but also by many other cognitive factors. This point is all the more telling since, as was noted earlier, if we control for the attitudes or characteristics of viewers, the correlation of the described difference between a leader's happy/-reassuring display and that same individual's neutral excerpt with the corresponding differences in emotion, for leaders across five experimental studies, is .90. But how do viewers differ in the way they perceive leaders and their behavior?

Descriptive Ratings

In these studies, the viewer's perceptions of displays are measured by the net descriptive ratings of each excerpt (ratings of how happy and comforting the leader seemed minus how angry and fearful he was).

Descriptions of Neutral Excerpts. In stepwise regression equations with descriptive ratings of the neutral display as the dependent variable, the most consistent and strongest predictive variable is the difference between the viewer's description of the neutral and happy/reassuring excerpts, which is negatively associated with descriptions of the neutral excerpt in all four equations (Table 3.3a). In contrast, while the pretest thermometer and assessed leadership are each significant in three of the four equations, these cognitive variables are relatively weaker as predictors of descriptive ratings of the neutral excerpts.

This finding contradicts the predictions from the perspective of traditional learning theory, according to which responses to the sight of a

Table 3.3a. *Stepwise Regression for Descriptive Rating of Neutral Excerpts of Presidential Candidates in 1984, 1988, and 1992*

FEMALE VIEWERS
(*n* = 247)

	Republican Candidate			Democratic Candidate		
Dependent Variable	Independent Variable	Standardized Coefficient	Adj r^2	Independent Variable	Standardized Coefficient	Adj r^2
Description of neutral excerpt	Difference between descriptions of neutral and happy/ reassuring displays	−.48	.19	Difference between descriptions of neutral and happy/ reassuring displays	−.49	.28
	Pretest thermometer	.26	.26	Assessed leadership	.31	.10
				Probability of voting	−.12	.37

MALE VIEWERS
(*n* = 262)

	Republican Candidate			Democratic Candidate		
Dependent Variable	Independent Variable	Standardized Coefficient	Adj r^2	Independent Variable	Standardized Coefficient	Adj r^2
Description of neutral excerpt	Difference between descriptions of neutral and happy/ reassuring displays	−.63	.34	Difference between descriptions of neutral and happy/ reassuring displays	−.54	.30
	Pretest thermometer	.23	.44	Assessed leadership	.29	.39
	Assessed leadership	.14	.45			

Notes: Standardized coefficients are for the last step of the stepwise regression; adjusted r^2 is variance explained after the step on which the variable is entered. Independent variables: pretest thermometer (0–100) at outset; added emotion to happy = net warmth during happy/reassuring excerpt minus that during neutral; description of neutral = net descriptive rating of neutral excerpt. For other variables, see Sullivan and Masters (1988).

known leader are closely correlated with such factors as issue agreement or party identification. Instead, it would seem that the viewer's mode of describing expressive displays is itself a highly significant factor in rating the neutral excerpts. That this is not merely a question of conditioned learning when watching leaders is made more plausible by the negative relationship between descriptions of the happy/reassuring cues and descriptions of a neutral excerpt: the more sensitive the viewer is to displays of positive affect, the lower that viewer's ratings of a neutral excerpt. Moreover, if stepwise regression models are computed omitting the difference in the descriptive ratings of the two displays and using only cognitive variables as predictors, the amount of variance falls sharply (from $r^2 = .26$ to .45 to $r^2 = .15$ or less). Such factors as party identification, ideology, frequency of watching television news, probability of voting, and issue agreement do not seem to have any significant influence on perceptions of neutral excerpts of rival leaders.

One possible explanation of this finding is that individuals often differ consistently in their sensitivity to nonverbal display behavior (e.g., Kagan et al., 1987; Kagan, 1988). When watching excerpts of political leaders, individual personality, as measured by the Cloninger TPQ inventory, influences the viewer's descriptive ratings (Masters, 1991; Clancy, 1992). Hence individual attributes like personality may be far more important than cognitive variables as a determinant of the way leaders' nonverbal behavior is described – and this factor may lead to hitherto unexplained differences in emotional response to the same events.

Difference in the Descriptions of the Neutral and Happy/Reassuring Excerpts. The parallel stepwise regression model, predicting viewers' perception of the cues of happiness and reassurance (as measured by the difference in their ratings of the two excerpts), again shows that sensitivity to display behavior is more important than the cognitive variables traditionally studied in political science. Here it is the description of the neutral display that is negatively associated with descriptions of the happy/reassuring cues: not surprisingly, the more positively a viewer perceives the neutral image, the less likely that viewer is to rate additional positive cues in the happy/reassuring excerpt (Table 3.3b). While the pretest thermometer is a significant predictor in three of the four equations – females describing Republican candidates, males describing candidates of both parties – cognitive variables are relatively weak in explaining the way happy/reassuring cues are described. Indeed, when stepwise regressions are computed without the description of the neutral excerpt as an independent variable, the variance explained dwindles almost to zero ($r^2 = .03$ or less).

Table 3.3b. *Stepwise Regression for Difference between Descriptive Rating of Neutral and Happy/Reassuring Excerpts of Presidential Candidates in 1984, 1988, and 1992*

	FEMALE VIEWERS ($n = 248$)					
	Republican Candidate			Democratic Candidate		
Dependent Variable	Independent Variable	Standardized Coefficient	Adj r^2	Independent Variable	Standardized Coefficient	Adj r^2
Difference between descriptions of neutral and happy/ reassuring excerpts	Description of neutral excerpt	−.48	.19	Description of neutral excerpt	−.53	.28
	Pretest thermometer	.24	.25			

	MALE VIEWERS ($n = 262$)					
	Republican Candidate			Democratic Candidate		
Dependent Variable	Independent Variable	Standardized Coefficient	Adj r^2	Independent Variable	Standardized Coefficient	Adj r^2
Difference between neutral and happy/ reassuring excerpts	Description of neutral excerpt	−.64	.34	Description of neutral excerpt	−.53	.28
	Pretest thermometer	.28	.41	Pretest thermometer	.18	.34
	Assessed leadership	.21	.42			
	Issue agreement	−.18	.43			

Notes: Standardized coefficients are for the last step of the stepwise regression; adjusted r^2 is variance explained after the step on which the variable is entered. Independent variables: pretest thermometer (0–100) at outset; added emotion to happy = net warmth during happy/reassuring excerpt minus that during neutral; description of neutral = net descriptive rating of neutral excerpt. For other variables, see Sullivan and Masters (1988).

A potentially relevant gender difference deserves mention. In men's descriptions of happy/reassuring display cues, cognitive variables are more likely to be significant than in the descriptions by women. For Republican candidates, only the pretest thermometer influences women's descriptive ratings, while the pretest thermometer, assessed leadership, and issue agreement have independent effects on men's descriptions. For

Democratic candidates, male viewers' descriptions are influenced by the pretest thermometer as well as by the descriptions of the neutral excerpts, whereas female viewers' descriptions of the happy/reassuring cues are related only to their ratings of neutral excerpts.

This gender difference may be due to a greater sensitivity to some expressive nonverbal cues on the part of women (e.g., Babchuk et al., 1985). In responses to leaders, women who are critical of or neutral toward a leader respond more negatively to that leader's displays of anger/threat than men, whereas women who are supporters are even more positive in their perceptions (Masters, 1989b; Masters and Carlotti, 1994; cf. Figure 3.2). Individual differences in personality and gender may thus enter into responses to leaders at the level of perceptions rather than by directly influencing emotions or attitudes.

These results confirm the political relevance of a model of leader–follower interaction based on cognitive neuroscientific findings. Different sets of cognitive and ascriptive variables seem to influence perceptions and emotional responses to leaders of each party by males or females, reflecting gender differences in the way the brain's parallel processing is integrated (Kimura and Hampson, 1990). As a result, while the stepwise regression equations based on the combined dataset legitimate the model set forth earlier (Figure 3.1), they also point to the need for a more fine-grained mode of analysis. Since we know that nonlinear interactions between multiple variables often characterize emotional and cognitive responses, analysis of variance (ANOVA) techniques are often needed to unravel the interrelations among the variables thus far shown to be significant. Here, it is only possible to summarize briefly the range of results that illustrate the complexity of emotional response.

Attributes of the Viewer

A number of variables that are overall characteristics of each viewer, based on socioeconomic status or individual learning, seem to predict differences in the response pattern to images of leaders. These variables are as follows:

- *Party Identification.* In general, supporters perceive displays as more positive and respond with greater net warmth than critics (Lanzetta et al., 1985; McHugo et al., 1991). This variable can, however, interact with a number of factors, including frequency of watching TV news, partisan loyalty, gender, and the individual leader being seen (e.g., Figure 3.2).
- *Television.* Viewers who watch television news more frequently often respond quite differently from those who do not, but typically

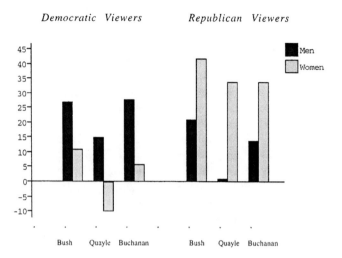

Democratic Viewers   *Republican Viewers*

Mean Difference in Self-Reported Emotions during Happy/Reassuring & Neutral Excerpts

	Bush	Quayle	Buchanan
Democrats			
Men (n = 13)	2.7	1.5	2.8
Women (n = 11)	1.1	-1.0	.6
Republicans			
Men (n = 28)	2.1	0	1.4
Women (n = 14)	4.2	3.4	3.4

*Entries are average "net warmth" of episodic emotion (self-reports of happy and comforting emotions, minus reports of anger and fear) to happy/reassuring excerpt of each leader, minus "net warmth" to a neutral display of same leader. (Scale can range from +12 to -12). In colloquial terms, this measures the extent to which each leader's reassuring behavior "turns on" viewers.

Source: Experiment at Dartmouth College, November 1992 (for methods, see Lanzetta et al., 1985; Sullivan and Masters, 1988) ANOVA: main effects for party identification and gender not significant for any leader. Interaction of party and gender significa Bush (F 3.68, DF 1; p = .0596); Quayle (F 6.35, DF 1; p = .0144); and Buchanan (F3.99, DF 1; p = .0501).

Figure 3.2. Difference in net warmth of emotional response to neutral and happy/reassuring displays of three Republican candidates, 1992.

this variable interacts with party identity, gender, and other variables (Dragseth, 1993).

- *Political Sophistication.* Viewers with weaker cognitive information seem to respond more strongly to nonverbal cues – and to "framing" or verbal cueing by television commentators (Newton et al., 1987).

Type of Viewer

Some variables that influence response patterns are overall ascriptive or sociological characteristics of the viewer; while such factors as personality, gender, and ethnicity obviously influence patterns of associative learning and memory, these effects often emerge even when one controls for cognitive variables. With regard to gender, moreover, there are frequently highly significant interactive effects in which the experience of watching leaders influences males and females in *opposite* directions. Such findings are highly persuasive grounds to abandon the traditional stimulus–response model in favor of the more complex approach depicted in Figure 3.1.

- *Gender*. Much evidence suggests that men and women differ in the way prior attitudes are integrated with the perceived intensity of nonverbal display behavior (Masters, 1989b; Masters and Carlotti, 1994). Hence, in an experimental study of responses to President Bush, Vice-President Quayle, and Patrick Buchanan late in the 1992 campaign, Republican women and Democratic men responded more positively to happy/reassuring cues; conversely, it was Republican men and Democratic women who were the least likely to be responsive (Figure 3.2). While ANOVA shows no main effects for either gender or party identification, the interaction of the two variables is statistically significant for all three leaders. Considering the levels of response, it appears that partisanship has stronger effects in enhancing the positive emotions of Republican women and reducing it among Democratic women; in contrast, party had less of an impact on men.

  These findings can best be explained as the consequence of a tendency toward greater integration of cognitive and emotional cues among women. Gender-based neuroanatomical differences arising from hormonal environments during development (e.g., Kimura and Hampson, 1990) provide a plausible explanation of widely observed differences in male and female cognition (e.g., Gilligan, 1982). Our own studies have repeatedly found statistically significant gender effects, suggesting that men tend to process nonverbal displays and political information in parallel whereas cognitive and emotional cues are more fully integrated in women's responses (Masters, 1989b; Masters and Carlotti, 1994). In some cases, as in the public attitudes generated by Anita Hill's charges against Judge Clarence Thomas, such differences in the way men and women react to the same situation may have enormous political consequences (Febeo, 1993).

- *Personality*. Unlike gender, which can influence perceptions, emotional responses, or attitudes, personality factors seem to have their primary effect only on perceptions; when the viewer's descriptions of a display are controlled for, no residual effects of personality in emotional response or attitude can be found (Clancy, 1992).

Roger D. Masters

- *Ethnic Group.* While few studies provide a rigorous control for the viewer's ethnicity in response to the same set of displays, there is some preliminary evidence that cultural or ethnic background may influence emotional response even among viewers who describe display differences in the same way (Masters, 1991).

Stimulus Features

In addition to the many variables associated with the viewer, the system of emotional response to leaders is, of course, also highly dependent on the stimuli communicated by the media. Among the factors studied to date are:

- *Leader's Performance Style.* Displays that are more homogeneous or more intense elicit much stronger emotional responses than those that are blended or weak (Sullivan and Masters, 1988; McHugo et al., 1991).
- *Type of Display.* As predicted from studies of nonhuman primates, nonverbal behaviors of anger/threat and fear/evasion differ significantly from each other and from happy/reassuring displays (Masters et al., 1986). Both descriptive ratings and emotional responses have the same structure in experiments in France and the United States (Masters and Sullivan, 1989).
- *Leader's Status.* The dominance status of a leader influences the strength of the emotional responses elicited by the same videotape. Hence, when a leader loses power or declines in status, the net warmth of emotions elicited by a happy/reassuring display is also weakened. Interestingly enough, however, this effect interacts strongly with gender, since women integrate the display effects and status effects, whereas the two factors are processed in parallel by men (Masters and Carlotti, 1994).
- *Leader's Nationality.* Some cues associated with leadership seem to be dependent on unconscious patterns of nonverbal behavior that vary from culture to culture. Hence, when a leader's nationality is not known, foreigners elicit more negative emotional responses and judgments than do images of unknown American politicians (Warnecke et al., 1992).
- *Political Context.* In competitive contexts such as electoral campaigns, prior attitudes toward the leader or identification with a political party interact significantly with the display seen or with other variables, whereas when the same or similar excerpts of a single leader are seen alone, these cognitive factors are weaker. Hence the mere fact of political competition activates the partisan

feelings and attitudes in the processing of both nonverbal and verbal information (McHugo et al., 1985, 1991).

- *Production Norms.* In our experiments, little work has been done on such features of the image as distance to the camera (closeups versus long shots), camera angle, setting, and other variables associated with the production of television news; on the contrary, most of our stimuli were standardized for these features as much as possible. Other researchers, however, have found highly significant effects from these cues (for a review, see Kepplinger, 1991).

SUMMARY AND POLICY IMPLICATIONS

The picture that arises from the foregoing analysis may seem at first highly confusing. On reflection, however, the main point is quite simple. Emotions matter greatly in human politics. To be sure, emotions interact with multiple variables in highly complex ways, making it difficult, if not impossible, to trace the exact effects without adopting a new framework of analysis derived from contemporary cognitive neuroscience. When we do so, it becomes apparent that many of the effects of televised images of leaders are emotionally mediated responses of which viewers are dimly if at all conscious.

While these findings have theoretical relevance (cf. Masters, 1993),[8] their practical implications for American politics are especially great. Because television has personalized politics, party attachments are weaker today than a generation ago. This is dangerous because, as our findings confirm, uncommitted voters are so much more susceptible to influence by emotional appeals or nonverbal cues that can be manipulated by media experts. To enhance the role of conscious evaluation of leaders in terms of their policies and parties (rather than easily manipulated cues), it is important to increase the linkage between powerful leaders and such cognitive factors as political party, ideology, and issues.

---

8 Critics of the extreme view of localization have argued that perception of an object or stimulus needs to be understood as a "basin of attraction" in the chaotic, self-organizing processes of the brain (Skarda and Freeman, 1990). If so, instead of viewing localization and distributed processing as *alternative* explanations, we need to think of the extent of integration as itself a variable. Evidence for this interpretation is clearest when meaningful naturalistic stimuli, such as facial images of known political leaders, are presented to normal or functionally impaired subjects. In so doing, while the localization hypothesis can often help explain unusual individual deficits, broader differences in the mode of integrating cognition and emotion – such as those between males and females – show the importance of variations in the way cortical processing is distributed in responses to the same event.

Roger D. Masters

The experimental studies described previously thus underline the widely shared fear that a politics of sound bites and advertisements is more dangerous than longer interviews and debates between known leaders. In the television age, party responsibility may be far more important than ever; otherwise, ambitious politicians can buy media attention and manipulate popular feelings with superficial appeals. With the characteristics of emotional and cognitive response described earlier in mind, three reforms can be suggested that might minimize the dangers of emotion in the age of television.

- First, our system needs a leader of the opposition. The party that does not control the White House should nominate its presidential candidate two years before the next election; for example, the Republicans should have nominated a standard bearer during the 1994 congressional campaign. This would have given their candidate two years to establish a media presence. Since partisanship is to a great extent now incarnated by individual leaders, such a step would strengthen political attachments and thereby provide a measure of protection against the risks of a televised demagogue (who might sway the mass public with appeals that bypass the institutional constraints of our system of checks and balances).
- Second, once named, the leader of the opposition should engage the president in periodic debates. Such events will serve to focus public attention on the substance of the political issues confronting the country. Unlike the carefully crafted advertisements – or equally selective attention of TV newscasts – such debates would provide longer unprogrammed exposure to leaders. Even at the nonverbal level, such debates would provide opportunities for unconscious leakage of cues that give the citizen a broader picture of rival leaders. Such debates would also allow us to reduce the horse-race character of the lengthy primary campaigns, which are enormously costly and breed public skepticism (which, in turn, undermines party attachment and hence increases the reservoir of uncommitted viewers who are more easily manipulated by nonverbal cues).
- Finally, our candidates need public access to television during shorter political campaigns (such as the three-week election periods in Europe). A politics of sound bites and political advertisements provides many opportunities for the kinds of emotional appeals we have demonstrated in the laboratory. A system is needed to give each party's nominees equal opportunities to appear at length on TV. If such opportunities are limited to a brief campaign, the benefits of the privately funded media blitz could be minimized and candidates of both parties freed from the skyrocketing costs of media purchases.

The foregoing proposals will not receive universal assent. It is, however, neither possible nor necessary to show in more detail how such practical reforms might be justified by the theoretical and empirical research described earlier. For present purposes, it should be enough to have shown that the emotions of citizens matter. Moreover, it is hardly controversial to argue that such feelings interact with cognition and judgment in complex ways of which most of us are frequently unaware. An understanding of the way leaders elicit emotional responses from citizens has practical consequences for the political process.

Over the next generation, cognitive neuroscience will continue to make great strides in revealing the way our brains actually work. Political psychology – and the social sciences more broadly – can ignore such research only at their peril: it cannot be assumed that ambitious leaders and their advisors will ignore the power of emotional appeals at a time of radically changing media of communication. Under these circumstances, the failure to revise our theoretical and practical assumptions in the face of changing scientific findings could be fatal to the very survival of constitutional government.

APPENDIX: CATEGORY SPECIFIC SEMANTIC MEMORY
AND PROSOPAGNOSIA

In a recent critique of localization models, Farah (1994) cites several cases in which patients, after bilateral damage to the temporal lobes, exhibit differential impairment of semantic memory concerning living as distinct from nonliving objects. Farah suggests that, in these cases, patients may be responding as a function of the difference between visual information (essential in perceiving living things) and functional information (presumably more salient in response to nonliving things). This categorization fails to consider the salience of nonverbal social signals and emotional displays, which are communicated by both acoustic and visual channels. These cues seem to be processed from birth by specialized modules in the inferior temporal lobes. If so, it is not improbable that – at least insofar as recognizing animals and other humans is concerned – the distinction between visual and semantic information is not the most likely explanation of these deficits in response.

Rather than the presumed module for discriminating living/nonliving entities, the localization seems to be even more specific: a distributed network of specialized neuronal assemblies that respond to the identity and social behavior of other animals. (Lest such a system seem entirely artificial, it is well to wonder why children are so readily taught about human society through the media of stories, pictures, and cartoons describing animals in works ranging from *Peter Rabbit* and *Tom and*

Jerry to *Babar* and *Ninja Turtles*.) Of the cues involved, none is more salient than the face.

That all deficits in responses to living objects need not result from global information processing is well illustrated by prosopagnosics. While Farah speaks of prosopagnosia as the absence of conscious or semantic memory of the face of another, in some instances this deficit may merely reflect the dissociation of left hemispheric verbal functioning from the facial recognition modules in the inferior temporal lobes. To see whether this might be the case, images of known leaders exhibiting different nonverbal displays can provide a valuable probe.

A number of years ago, along with Dr. Mitchell Ross (then at Dartmouth Medical School), I examined a woman who exhibited severe deficits in verbal memory. Among other things, the patient was unable to identify known faces, hesitating extensively despite indications that she remembered the face. To explore the extent of the deficit, we showed the patient a series of photographs of well-known American leaders, some of whom had been president, some vice-president, and some neither. These stimuli provided an opportunity to measure face recognition (could the patient name the leader?), social cognition (could she identify the leader's party and whether that individual had ever been president or vice-president?), and cue response (could she describe non-verbal displays of happiness, anger, or fear?).

The patient could not provide semantic identification of any leader's name, political party, or office held. Although her verbal deficits had been previously attributed to depression, she responded instantly – and accurately – to requests to describe each leader's facial expressions. More striking, when given the opportunity to identify each leader's party by saying "elephant" (for Republican) or "donkey" (for Democrat), and the office with the number "1" (for president), "2" (for vice-president), or "neither," the patient also responded quickly and correctly. In this case, semantic information was accessible only when represented by non-verbal images (animals or numbers) more likely to be stored in the right hemisphere as distinct from lexical information typically found in the left hemisphere.

Depending on the stimulus and the cognitive task, such a patient might be thought to have a complete loss of memory concerning faces when, in fact, there is inability to access semantic codes as distinct from images or simple gestalt perceptions. Whereas Farah suggests a basic distinction between visual and functional semantic memory, here the deficit seems to concern names as distinct from images (since the words "happy" or "angry" describe visual facial cues, whereas "1" stood for the functional role of president of the United States).

While this case is unlike conventional examples of prosopagnosia, it reminds us that an apparently homogeneous category of patients may suffer from varied pathologies. One advantage of the localization hypothesis, insofar as there is evidence for modular organization of a function, is that it can account for so many *varieties* of dissociative deficits. Much the same needs to be said of learning disabilities, since what was once a single category of "dyslexics" has been replaced by a bewildering array of deficits arising from the "disconnection" or damage to particular modules or pathways.[9]

The categories and models invoked by Farah may, of course, explain the cases she cites. What is at issue is the principle of localization and the existence of deficits due to localized damage. Of course, individual cases need to be analyzed with care, since it is not tenable to invent a new localized module to explain each new form of cognitive impairment. For example, I have taught several students who had the specific learning disability of being unable to *see* grammar (when silently reading written language), even though they could instantaneously detect and correct grammatical errors when reading the same sentence out loud or hearing others speak. As this example suggests, it seems hard to deny that some humans suffer from damage to localized neuronal cell assemblies or linkages that can give rise to highly specific disabilities. Such findings call into question the conception of a holistic brain that implicitly informs much of conventional social and political psychology.

References

Abelson, Robert P. (1976). "Script Processing in Attitude Formation and Decision Making." In J. S. Carroll and J. W. Payne, eds., *Cognition and Social Behavior,* pp. 33–45. Hillsdale, NJ: Lawrence Erlbaum Associates.

9 In recent years, many learning disabilities have been observed that seem related to what has been called "disconnection" between localized modules (Denckla, 1986). One student cannot associate acoustic information with spelling (writing "litsen"), whereas another dissociates the written word from its visual form (spelling "lissen" – phonetically correct but without the "t" that gives the word its characteristic visible shape). Without admitting the origin of some deficits in modular damage or dissociation, it would be hard to explain why other learning disabilities include the inability to *see* grammar (in individuals whose spelling of individual words is reliable) or the blockage of all semantic memory during the motor coordinations of handwriting (but not of typing on a computer keyboard).

Abelson, Robert P.; Kinder, Donald R.; Peters, M. D.; and Fiske, Susan T. (1982). "Affective and Semantic Components in Political Person Perception." *Journal of Personality and Social Psychology*, 42:619–630.

Allman, William. (1989). *Apprentices of Wonder*. New York: Bantam Books.

Babchuk, Wayne A.; Hames, R. B.; and Thomason, R. A. (1985). "Sex Differences in the Recognition of Infant Facial Expressions of Emotion: The Primary Caretaker Hypothesis." *Ethology and Sociobiology*, 6:89–102.

Chance, M. R. A. (1976). "The Organization of Attention in Groups." In M. von Cranack, ed., *Methods of Inference from Animal to Human Behavior*, pp. 213–235. The Hague: Mouton.

Clancy, David. (1992). *Paths Not Taken? Personality and an Evolutionary Approach to Politics*. Government Department Honors thesis, Dartmouth College, Hanover, NH.

Denckla, Martha. (1986). "Application of Disconnexion Concepts to Developmental Dyslexia." Geschwind Memorial Lecture, 37th annual meeting of the Orton Dyslexia Society, Philadelphia. Inglewood, Calif.: Audio-Stats Educational Services, Tape #916R-34.

Dragseth, David. (1993). "Are We Still in the Cave?: The Hidden Effect of Watching Television News in the 1992 Presidential Campaign." Unpublished research paper, Department of Government, Dartmouth College, Hanover, NH.

Farah, Martha. (1994). "Neuropsychological Interference with an Interactive Brain: A Critique of the 'Locality' Assumption." *Behavioral and Brain Research*, 17:43–104.

Febeo, Karen. (1993). *Disentangling the Data: Gender Differences in Response to the Anita Hill–Clarence Thomas Hearings*. Senior honors thesis, Department of Government, Dartmouth College, Hanover, NH.

Gazzaniga, Michael. (1985). *The Social Brain*. New York: Basic Books. (1988). *Mind Matters*. Boston: Houghton Mifflin.

Georgopolous, A. P.; Schwartz, A. B.; and Kettner, R. E. (1986). "Neuronal Population Coding of Movement Direction." *Science*, 233:1416–1419.

Gilligan, Carol. (1982). *In a Different Voice*. Cambridge, MA: Harvard University Press.

Gleick, James. (1987). *Chaos*. New York: Viking.

Gray, J. A. (1987). *The Psychology of Fear and Stress*, 2nd ed. Cambridge: Cambridge University Press.

Johnson, George. (1991). *In the Palaces of Memory*. New York: Vintage.

Kagan, Jerome. (1988). "Biological Bases of Childhood Shyness." *Science*, 240:167–171.

Kagan, Jerome; Reznick, J. Steven; and Snidman, Nancy. (1987). "The Physiology and Psychology of Behavioral Inhibition in Children." *Child Development*, 58:1459–1473.

Kepplinger, Hans Mathias. (1991). "The Impact of Presentation Techniques: Theoretical Aspects and Empirical Findings." In Franc Biocca, ed. *Television and Political Advertising*, Vol. 1: *Psychological Processes*, pp. 84–103. Hillsdale, NJ: Lawrence Erlbaum Associates.

Kimura, Doreen (1999). *Sex and Cognition*. Cambridge, MA: MIT Press.

Kimura, Doreen and Hampson, Elizabeth. (1990). "Neural and Hormonal Mechanisms Mediating Sex Differences in Cognition." In *Research Bulletin* #689 (April), Department of Psychology, University of Western Ontario, London, Canada.

Kling, Arthur. (1986). "Neurological Correlates of Social Behavior." In M. Gruter and R. Masters, eds., *Ostracism: A Social and Biological Phenomenon*, pp. 27–38. New York: Elsevier.

(1987). "Brain Mechanisms and Social/Affective Behavior." *Social Science Information*, 26:375–384.

Kosslyn, Stephen M. and Koenig, Olivier. (1992). *Wet Mind: The New Cognitive Neuroscience*. New York: Free Press.

Lanzetta, John T.; Sullivan, Denis G.; Masters, Roger D.; and McHugo, Gregory J. (1985). "Viewers' Emotional and Cognitive Responses to Televised Images of Political Leaders." In Sidney Kraus and Richard Perloff, eds., *Mass Media and Political Thought*, pp. 85–116. Beverly Hills, CA: Sage.

MacLean, Paul. (1992). " A Triangular Brief on the Evolution of the Brain and Law." In M. Gruter and Paul Bohannan, eds., *Law, Biology, and Culture*, 2nd ed., pp. 83–177. New York: Primis–McGraw-Hill.

Marcus, George. (1988). "The Structure of Emotional Appraisal." *American Political Science Review*, 82:737–762.

Marcus, George and MacKuen, Michael. (1993). "Anxiety, Enthusiasm and the Vote: On the Emotional Underpinnings of Learning and Involvement During Presidential Campaigns." *American Political Science Review*, 87:672–685.

Masters, Roger D. (1989a). *The Nature of Politics*. New Haven, CT: Yale University Press.

(1989b). " Gender and Political Cognition." *Politics and the Life Sciences*, 8:3–39.

(1990). "Evolutionary Biology and Political Theory." *American Political Science Review*, 84:195–210.

(1991). "Individual and Cultural Differences in Response to Leaders: Nonverbal Displays." *Journal of Social Issues*, 47:151–165.

(1993). *Beyond Relativism: Science and Human Values*. Hanover, NH: University of New England Press.

Masters, Roger D. and Carlotti, Stephen J., Jr. (1994)."Gender Differences in Response to Political Leaders." In Lee Ellis, ed., *Social Stratification and Socioeconomic Inequality*, Vol. 2, pp. 13–36. Boulder, CO: Praeger.

Masters, Roger D. and Sullivan, Denis G. (1989). "Nonverbal Displays and Political Leadership in France and the United States." *Political Behavior*, 11:121–153.

(1993). "Nonverbal Behavior and Leadership: Emotion and Cognition in Political Attitudes." In Shanto Iyengar and William McGuire, eds., *Explorations in Political Psychology*, pp. 150–182. Durham, NC: Duke University Press.

Masters, Roger D.; Sullivan, D. G.; Lanzetta, J. T.; McHugo, G. J.; and Englis, B. G. (1986). "The Facial Displays of Leaders: Toward an Ethology of Human Politics." *Journal of Social and Biological Structures*, 9: 319–343.

McHugo, Gregory J.; Lanzetta, John T.; and Bush, Laura. (1991). "The Effect of Attitudes on Emotional Reactions to Expressive Displays of Political Leaders." *Journal of Nonverbal Behavior*, 15:19–41.

McHugo, Gregory J.; Sullivan, Denis G.; Masters, Roger D.; and Englis, Basil G. (1985). "Emotional Reactions to Expressive Displays of a Political Leader." *Journal of Personality and Social Psychology*, 49:1512–1529.

Mishkin, Mortimer and Appenzeller, T. 1987. "The Anatomy of Memory." *Scientific American*, 256:80–89.

Newton, James S.; Masters, R. D.; McHugo, G. J.; and Sullivan, D. G. (1987). "Making Up Our Minds: Effects of Network Coverage on Viewer Impressions of Leaders." *Polity*, 20:226–246.

Peters, Richard and Tajfel, Henri. (1972). "Hobbes and Hull: Metaphysicians of Behavior." In M. Cranston and R. S. Peters, eds., *Hobbes and Rousseau*, pp. 165–183. New York: Doubleday Anchor.

Rolls, Edmond T. (1987). "Information Representation, Processing and Storage in the Brain: Analysis at the Single Neuron Level." In J. P. Changeux and M. Konishi, eds., *The Neural and Molecular Bases of Learning*, pp. 503–539. New York: John Wiley & Sons.

(1989). "The Processing of Face Information in the Primate Temporal Lobe." In V. Bruce and M. Burton, eds., *Processing Images of Faces*, pp. 31–62. London: Ablex.

Ruelle, David. (1991). *Chance and Chaos*. Princeton, NJ: Princeton University Press.

Schwartz, Gary E.; Paul L. Fair, Pau L.; Sult, P.; Mandel, M.; and Klerman, G. L. (1976). "Facial Muscle Patterning to Affective Imagery in Depressed and Non-Depressed Subjects." *Science*, 192:489–491.

Skarda, Christine A. and Freeman, W. J. (1990). "Chaos and the New Science of the Brain." *Concepts in Neuroscience*, 1:275–285.

Sullivan, Denis G. and Masters, Roger D. (1988). "'Happy Warriors': Leaders' Facial Displays, Viewers' Emotions, and Political Support." *American Journal of Political Science*, 32:345–368.

(1994). "Nonverbal Cues, Emotions, and Trait Attributions in the Evaluation of Political Leaders: The Contribution of Biopolitics to the Study of Media and Politics." In Albert O. Somit and Steven Peterson, eds., *Research in Biopolitics*, 2:237–274. Greenwich, CT: JAI Press.

Warnecke, A. Michael. (1991). *The Personalization of Politics: An Analysis of Emotion, Cognition, and Nonverbal Cues*. Senior Fellowship thesis, Dartmouth College, Hanover, NH.

Warnecke, A. Michael; Masters, Roger D.; and Kempter, Guido. (1992). "The Roots of Nationalism: Nonverbal Behavior and Xenophobia," *Ethology and Sociobiology*, 13:267–282.

Way, Baldwin M. and Masters, Roger D. (1996)."Political Attitudes: Interactions of Cognition and Affect." *Motivation and Emotion*, 20: 205–236.

Young, Malcolm P. and Yamane, Shigero. (1992). "Sparse Population Coding of Faces in the Inferotemporal Cortex." *Science*, 256: 1327–1331.

Zola-Morgan, Stuart M. and Squire, Larry R. (1990). "The Primate Hippocampal Formation: Evidence for a Time-Limited Role in Memory Storage." *Science*, 250: 288–290.

4

Emotion as Virtue and Vice*

GERALD L. CLORE
LINDA M. ISBELL

"Passion is a sort of fever in the mind, which ever leaves us weaker than it found us." This statement was written by William Penn in 1693. It echoes a theme that has been persistent in Western thought from the Enlightenment to the present: that progress depends on the triumph of reason over emotion. Consistent with that theme is the democratic faith that, guided by rational discourse, an informed people can find liberty and justice. Traditional models of political judgment reflect a similar stance. They generally assume a hypothetical citizen characterized by passionless rationality who is engaged in reasoned action (e.g., Downs, 1957; Ferejohn and Fiorina, 1974; Riker and Ordeshook, 1968). However, there seems to be a growing realization that theories built around idealized decision makers may need revision. Part of the appeal of political psychology is the promise it holds for understanding the contribution of emotion to these processes.

The three excellent chapters on emotion and politics in this volume each address this theme. All three offer powerful and compelling explanations of the phenomena they treat. We found them to be impressive from any standpoint. They each ask crucial and difficult questions about the possible mechanisms of emotional influence. They also do a convincing job of drawing inferences from the cognitive and biological levels all the way to voter behavior. Masters, for example, places his research on the emotional reactions to photographs of political leaders in the context of neuroscience and finds in it practical implications for conducting elections. The chapters are also impressive as works of scholarship. Readers will be particularly rewarded by reading the section of Sears's chapter in which he offers a tutorial concerning recent research on styles of information processing. Equally impressive

* The writing of this chapter was supported by National Science Foundation Grant No. SBR-93-11879 and by National Institute of Mental Health Grant No. MH-50074.

Gerald L. Clore and Linda M. Isbell

is the lucid account given by Marcus and MacKuen of Gray's biological theory of emotion and personality, a theory that is not well known but that is powerful and promises to be influential. In this chapter, our goal is to complement the ideas that have been presented by adding a perspective from recent research on emotion and cognition. Our hope is that ideas from outside of political psychology will serve a heuristic function, affording alternative ways of approaching some of these timeless puzzles.

In the following, we attempt to make four points, which may be summarized as follows:

1. Important as it is, research on how emotion biases cognition is only half of the story. Emotions are also caused by cognitive appraisals of situations with respect to what one values. As such, emotions provide indispensable guides for making sensible choices.
2. The affective cues from irrelevant emotions and moods (or from the presentation of affectively potent faces and symbols) bias political judgment through a process of misattribution when they are seen as part of one's reaction to an issue or a candidate.
3. Emotions affect not only what one thinks about candidates but also how one thinks about them. Negative affective cues may signal that a situation is problematic or threatening and requires systematic analysis (making one difficult to persuade). Conversely, positive affective cues may signal that a situation is benign and that general impressions or heuristic thinking is sufficient (making one easy to persuade).
4. Individual emotions have a counterpart in what might be called "collective emotions." The role of emotions in the cognitive lives of individuals is similar to the role of public demonstrations of feeling in the political life of societies in that both serve to reorder processing priorities.

EMOTIONAL APPRAISAL

Value

With respect to our historical faith in reason, Herbert Simon has argued that reason "is a gun for hire that can be employed in the service of whatever goals we have, good or bad" (1983, p. 7). That is, reason provides only the means; the ends toward which we strive must come from values, which is where emotion comes in. Emotion need not be unreasonable, but it must by definition involve value. Emotions are "affective states," by which we mean states of the organism focused on the goodness or

badness of things. Nothing can be an emotion that is not positive or negative (Clore and Ortony, 1988).

The chapter by Marcus and MacKuen uses the concept of being a partisan to make a related point. To be a partisan is to have an allegiance that affects both one's actions and one's emotions. There is no politics without partisans, and no emotion either. Both require a perspective. For political scientists, a person's perspective depends on party and political ideology, and perhaps on economic, religious, and ethnic identity. For students of emotion, perspective depends on a person's goals, standards, and attitudes. These views are quite compatible. Both political preferences and emotions (as outlined later) are representations of the perceived implications of situations for one's goals, standards, and attitudes.

Although political scientists tend to look to psychology for answers about emotion, in some ways they are better equipped than psychologists to study emotion. Psychologists often fail to consider the larger requirements for emotion – the cognitive and motivational structures within which events are appraised. But political scientists, although they have not focused on values, already understand the importance of complex cognitive structures. They are used to thinking about attitude and belief systems and their role in partisanship.

Cognitive Emotion Theory

From a cognitive perspective, emotions occur when events, actions, and objects take on value by being appraised for their relevance to one's goals, standards, and attitudes. In their cognitive theory of emotion, Ortony, Clore, and Collins (1988) propose that the kind of emotion one feels depends on one's focus of attention. In general, there are three kinds of things that may be attended to: (1) events and their outcomes, (2) actions and their agency, and (3) objects and their attributes. We consider each briefly.

Emotional processing consists of appraising whatever is focused on in terms of one's personal concerns. When focusing on events and their outcomes, one appraises them on the basis of goals. Outcomes can be appraised as desirable or undesirable to the extent that they are perceived to promote or obstruct one's goals. In response to appraisals of desirability or undesirability of sufficient magnitude, one will feel the general affective reaction of being pleased or displeased. In a more differentiated form, this may appear as feeling happy or sad about past outcomes, or feeling hopeful or fearful about the prospect of an outcome.

Alternatively, one may focus not on the outcomes of events, but on someone's actions. Actions can be appraised as praiseworthy or blameworthy to the extent that they exceed or fall short of standards that one sees as applicable. In response to perceptions of praise or blameworthiness of sufficient magnitude, one may feel a general affective reaction of approval or disapproval. In a differentiated form, this may appear as feeling proud or ashamed of one's own actions, or feeling admiration or reproach about the actions of others.

Finally, one may focus on objects and their attributes. Objects can be appraised as appealing or unappealing to the extent that their attributes are consistent with one's attitudes or tastes. In response to perceptions of appealingness, one may feel a general affective reaction of liking or disliking. There appears to be less cognitive differentiation in this branch of emotions, but one may feel a general interest in, attraction to, or love of appealing objects and uninterest in, repulsion at, or disgust of unappealing ones.

The basic idea of Ortony, Clore, and Collins's theory, then, is that specific emotions are differentiated forms of one or more of three kinds of affective reactions (being pleased, approval, liking). These reflect the different possible aspects of situations that can be focused on (events, actions, objects) and the perception that something is relevant to one or more of the cognitive structures concerned with value (goals, standards, attitudes). This is, of course, only one possible account of emotions, but although more detailed than most, the assumptions this theory makes are quite representative of those made by other cognitive accounts (e.g., Roseman, 1984; Smith and Ellsworth, 1985).

Applying this analysis to reactions to political candidates, one might feel emotions related to fear if one anticipated that electing a particular candidate (an event) would result in policies that would obstruct one's personal goals (e.g., instituting new taxes). Alternatively, one might feel emotions related to admiration or reproach about personal or political actions the candidate has engaged in (e.g., sexual harassment). Or one might simply focus on attributes of the candidate as an object (e.g., his style, smile, or demeanor) and feel an emotion related to liking.

Socially Distributed Appraisals

We maintain that emotions are crucial elements in the human information processing system. They arise from appraisal processes and represent the perceived relevance of situations. They reflect one's goals and concerns, and are therefore as important in guiding human behavior as is a rudder in guiding a ship. But it should be noted that every instance of emotion does not involve a new appraisal from the bottom up. We are a social species, and in the broad scheme of things, much of the appraisal process has been left up to the family and the culture within

Emotion as Virtue and Vice

which one develops. Thus, many emotional reactions are adopted from others. Children learn what is good and bad or desirable and undesirable from their parents and peers. Research shows, for example, that when infants are beginning to crawl and encounter new situations, they often engage in social referencing, which involves looking at their caregiver's face to determine whether fear or continued interest is the appropriate reaction (Campos and Barrett, 1984).

In a similar vein, Sears gives a compelling discussion of how attitudes and prejudices are acquired in childhood long before the rationalizations offered by adults for why they feel as they do. Thus, Sears would rightly point out that our conclusions about the crucial guidance function provided by emotions needs to be qualified by the realization that the appraisal is a socially distributed process. One way of thinking about personality development and identity formation is as a sometimes painful process of rejecting the emotional reactions acquired from others and of reappraising situations on the basis of one's own goals, standards, and attitudes. However, it is often the case, as any psychotherapist can attest, that habitual emotional reactions are difficult to change.

The Emotion Cycle

We are focusing in this section on the role of cognitive processes in the appraisal process. The idea is that emotions arise when situations have been appraised as self-relevant in some way. Emotions therefore have cognitive causes in that the appraisal process, although often not available to awareness, is a cognitive process. But most of us do not think about emotions as having anything to do with cognition. Indeed, for some, a cognitive account of emotions may seem an oxymoron. After all, we are usually aware of emotions as bodily reactions or as feelings, which are quite the opposite of thoughts. If anything, our thoughts seem to be the captives of our feelings rather than the sources of feelings.

To accommodate such facts, emotional processes are perhaps best thought of as cyclical. An appraisal of something as good or bad (and as urgent) may make us feel a certain way (which may or may not be expressed), and these feelings, in turn, capture our attention and entrain our thought. This train of thought, now directed toward the emotional topic, may then intensify or diminish our emotion or perhaps give rise to a new emotion. That emotional reaction will then have its own feelings, providing feedback about the nature and importance of the new appraisal, redirecting attention and thought, and so on.

Apparently, one can enter this cycle at any point and exercise influence on the remaining portion. Antidepressant medication, for example, changes the physiological basis of feelings, which then alter the direction of attention and concern, and ultimately reduce the whole cycle of negative affectivity. Similarly, being in a group of sad or happy people may make us alter our facial expression and bodily posture, which can also create relevant feelings. These, in turn, direct thoughts to relevant concerns that may reinforce the feelings, and so on. Hence, the system appears to be cyclical and to have multiple entry points. When stimulated at one point, the entire cycle may be energized, so that peripheral influences such as facial expressions can end up affecting how we think, feel, and act (e.g., Rosenberg and Ekman, 1994; Strack, Martin, and Stepper, 1988).

In the prototypical case, however, emotions start with appraisals, which then affect feelings and attention. However, as in a computer, where most of the information processing that takes place is not visible on the monitor, most of our cognitive processing is also not consciously available. Hence, we need the feedback provided by emotional feelings, which inform us by their quality and intensity about the appraised nature and urgency of emotionally significant events. One consequence is that our feelings are sometimes the first sign that an appraisal has been made, and therefore we can be surprised by our own emotions. This does not change the cognitive nature of emotional causes, but it does mean that our emotions often seem to have a life of their own.

Much of the relevant psychological research focuses on the effects of moods rather than emotions. In our usage, emotions have cognitive causes, but moods may or may not. For example, we may find ourselves in a bad mood simply because we got up on the wrong side of the bed, because we have a hormonal imbalance, or because we are taking drugs. Hence, we can experience affective states that have all the feelings of emotions but that are not emotions proper because they have no object or are not about anything in particular. Such feeling states may nevertheless stimulate the rest of the affective cycle, including mood-consistent attentional and thought patterns that may then become more object-focused affective states or emotions.

Our view, then, is that emotions provide information about the personal significance of situations, information that serves as input to judgments (Schwarz and Clore, 1983) and decisions (Isen and Means, 1983). This information is consciously experienced in a way that captures attention (Niedenthal and Setterlund, 1994) and reorders processing priorities (Simon, 1967) to ensure that urgent and personally important business is attended to first. Without the goals, standards, and attitudes that drive these processes, we would respond in a bland and even-handed way to everything, would accord no special significance to anything, and would be inefficient, undirected, and disordered. Without emotional feelings (providing reliable and valid experiential feedback about the personal meaning and significance of events), we would be highly dysfunctional. Examples of the possible results of disordered affective feedback include the unwise decisions of manic individuals, the crippling fear of the chronically anxious, the inappropriate self-denigration of the depressed, and the lack of sympathy of the psychopath.

The Problem with Emotion

After a long dormant period, emotion is currently receiving a great deal of research attention. Emotion is, of course, a salient aspect of human experience, and that may be sufficient to explain psychologists' interest in the topic, but why might political scientists be interested? How is emotion involved in the processes and problems of specific relevance to politics? Presumably it is the consequences of emotion that are of concern, and more particularly the idea that emotion makes us irrational. Emotion is believed to color our perception, make us short-sighted in our decisions, contaminate our judgment, and keep us from thinking clearly. And if all these things are true, then we may be susceptible to influence by those who would manipulate our emotions for their own ends. These concerns provide ample motivation for the three chapters on emotion in this volume.

The chapters by Masters and Sears focus on emotional contamination of political judgments and decisions – that is, on emotional factors in what voters think. In contrast, the chapter by Marcus and MacKuen focuses on emotional factors in how people think. To these three explanations of emotional influences we add our own proposals about how emotion affects the content and style of political thought and judgment. We begin with judgment or content and then treat processing or style.

EMOTIONAL INFLUENCES ON JUDGMENT

In his chapter, Masters suggests that faces are more powerful affective stimuli than most people realize. The strategic use of pictures of leaders can therefore have a large influence on our reactions and judgment. In fact, when reactions to a picture are entered first in a regression equation, belief and issue measures no longer predict candidate evaluation. This fact, Masters suggests, is especially important because political scientists have tended to look elsewhere for explanations of voter behavior, focusing primarily on political beliefs and issues rather than on emotional reactions. However, seeing the face of a well-known political leader presumably activates not only who the person is but what he stands for. A picture of a political leader is literally worth a thousand words in the sense that it is likely to activate the entire patchwork of political knowledge and belief about the candidate, the candidate's party, liberal or conservative politics, and so on. Hence, a picture of a candidate may provide information that is partially redundant with political beliefs rather than completely independent of them. On the other hand, a single picture surely can elicit more powerful reactions than paragraphs of text, a fact that demands more than merely saying that pictures prime beliefs.

In agreement with Masters, Sears makes a related point, focusing on the power of symbols to evoke emotional reactions. Both suggest that the political preferences that are believed to be based on reasoned judgments may reflect emotional factors of which voters are only dimly aware.

The Affect-as-Information Hypothesis

Social psychologists have recently done considerable research on the role of emotional factors in judgment, and specifically on the conditions under which incidental or irrelevant affect has an influence. Our own position (Schwarz and Clore, 1983) is based on the idea that a primary function of emotion is to provide consciously available information or feedback about largely unconscious appraisals of the personal significance of situations. Emotions provide this information to others through distinctive facial and vocal expressions and to oneself through distinctive thoughts and feelings.

Emotions per se are relatively strong reactions that occur only occasionally, but the appraisal processes that elicit emotions function more or less continuously. Like a computer program that is always running in the background, affective appraisal processes function continuously as we move through the day. We are always alert to the possible relevance of things for our personal goals and concerns, and we generally know without much processing whether we are enjoying ourselves and whether we like something. Just as strong emotions are generally signaled by strong feeling, the ongoing appraisal process also appears to have an experiential output. These weaker affective cues do not capture our attention and change our psychological state the way stronger cues do, but the information they carry is available and is routinely used for making judgments, decisions, and choices.

Many judgments and choices appear to be made simply by asking ourselves "How do I feel about it?" rather than by consulting in a deliberative manner a mental list of pros and cons (Clore, 1992; Schwarz and Clore, 1988). Since such judgments and decisions are based on affective cues that are essentially the same as those of mood and emotion, they are quite susceptible to influence by emotional cues from irrelevant sources. Thus, it is generally difficult to tell which affective cues reflect how one feels about a candidate, for example, and how one feels as a result of a preexisting mood or emotional state. In our view, it is this process of misattribution that is largely responsible for emotional bias in judgment.

The process is illustrated by a well-known experiment (Schwarz and Clore, 1983) in which students responded to a telephone survey that included life satisfaction questions. Half of the subjects were telephoned on the first warm and sunny days of spring and half on several cold and rainy days that followed. Respondents were happier on those first warm and sunny days than on the later cold and rainy days, and they also judged themselves to be more satisfied with their lives. In some cases, however, the interviewer mentioned the weather in order to make salient the true cause of respondents' feelings. When the external cause of their feelings was made apparent by a question about the weather, subjects' life satisfaction ratings became immune to mood effects. That is, for the subjects who attributed their feelings to the weather, the feelings did not seem diagnostic about life satisfaction. The moods of the respondents were still negative on rainy days, so that making the weather salient did not change the intensity of subjects' moods. But it did change the apparent relevance of the associated feelings for answering questions about life satisfaction.

Many of the studies on the effect of emotion on judgment, including the one just described, employ general moods rather than specific emotions. The reason is that the processes are easier to study with moods than with emotions. Both are affective states, but as indicated previously, emotions generally have a specific object and are usually briefer in duration, while moods usually have fewer salient causes and last longer. The importance of this fact is that studies of affectively biased judgment depend on implicit misattributions, and such misattributions are more likely when the true cause of one's state is vague and remote than when it is clear and immediate.

Political Judgment

According to the affect-as-information model, it might not be enough merely to put people in a good mood to make them develop a positive attitude toward a candidate. Affective cues have their influence at the time a judgment is made. Only when one implicitly or explicitly asks oneself "How do I feel about this candidate?" can irrelevant mood cues have an opportunity to be misattributed as part of one's reaction to the candidate. However, a political campaign is a setting in which potential voters are primed to form evaluative impressions of candidates. If candidates are not ruled out on the grounds of party identification or other ideological grounds, voters are likely to consider how they feel about them. This evaluation may simply involve holding the idea of the candidate in mind and noting any evaluative thoughts and feelings that are elicited. But we have only one window on our affective experience, and we tend to process subjective experience holistically. It is therefore difficult to disentangle the positive feelings caused by the candidate's speech from the positive feelings caused by waving flags, patriotic music, and cheering crowds. According to the affect-as-information hypothesis, it is the misattribution of irrelevant affect as a reaction to the candidate's personal qualities or political views that colors judgment.

This approach is also compatible with the proposals made in the chapter by Masters. Masters points out that as one watches television, one must simultaneously process visual images, match the images with emotionally evocative memories and attitudes, and integrate this perception with information from the verbal message and the context. From such a perspective, we assume that one's cautions about emotion arise from the belief that as we integrate these diverse sources of information, it may be impossible to keep the different sources of affective experience straight. There may be multiple sources of affect, but they are experienced as one reaction, with relevant and irrelevant reactions mixed together.

The Relevance of Laboratory Studies

What we have said so far is that under certain conditions, evaluative judgments are based on how one feels in addition to what one knows about an object of judgment. In experimental social psychology this process has generally been studied by inducing moods in research participants, often by showing them humorous or sad films, and then exploring the conditions under which such feelings influence unrelated judgments. The judgments studied have been of life satisfaction, liking for persons described in written passages, consumer products, estimations of risk, attitudes toward political figures, and so on.

These studies may seem far removed from the behavior of voters at election time. Moreover, the emotions are produced by the weather or by having subjects watch emotional films, manipulations that may seem of tangential relevance to the feelings produced by political candidates. Hence, this method of study may require explanation. The goal is to figure out how affective feelings influence judgment. But ordinarily feelings are tightly linked to beliefs and cognitions. We generally feel more positively toward things we have positive information about, and so on. This is not surprising, of course. Failure to feel good about good things and bad about bad things would be a sign of serious disturbance. Indeed, depression is a problem in part because it represents a breakdown of the system whereby feelings are linked to events, so that the person has no accurate feedback about them. But the fact that thoughts and feelings usually move in tandem makes it quite difficult to determine the relative roles played by what we feel versus what we know. Hence, the research paradigm in which the induced affective states are irrelevant allows us to examine the role of feelings by themselves.

It turns out, however, as illustrated in the experiment described earlier examining reactions on sunny and rainy spring days (Schwarz and Clore, 1983), that feelings do not necessarily have any effect by themselves. Moods do not appear to have an automatic effect on judgment. Judgments are influenced only when people make the tacit assumption that their feelings are relevant to the question at hand. Experimental manipulations of the salience of alternative explanations for people's feelings show that people do rely on their feelings as a source of information to guide their judgments, but they are quite sensitive to signs of relevance.

Direct versus Indirect Effects

Social psychologists and political scientists have long assumed that influences on judgment are mediated by changes in beliefs (e.g., Anderson, 1981; Fishbein and Ajzen, 1975). More recently, this same assumption has also been made by social cognition researchers. During the last decade or so, social cognition research has been preoccupied with problems of how information about people is represented, stored, and retrieved (Wyer and Srull, 1989). Similarly, to explain the effects of mood and emotion on judgment, it has generally been assumed that mood influences both how something is represented in memory and what aspect of the representation is retrieved (e.g., Bower, 1981; Isen, 1984). In our view, by contrast, the affective cues of mood and emotion are used directly as evaluative information in addition to being used indirectly as cues to retrieve other information (Clore, 1992).

The difference can be seen by considering how other experiential judgments are made. How, for example, does one answer questions about current experiences such as "How do you like your lunch?" Traditional models of judgment imply that one would proceed by identifying the ingredients in the lunch, looking up the stored liking values for each ingredient, and then integrating these previously established values into a judgment of how much one likes the dish. A more modern social cognition view would have us categorize the dish as, say, lasagna, look up the stored value for lasagna, and then answer accordingly – "I must like my lunch because it is lasagna, and I know I like lasagna." Such an account seems humorously indirect. We assume that, in fact, liking judgments of this kind usually reflect direct information from actually experiencing the food. Similarly, in the domain of political judgments, we contend that voters attend not only to the logic of what candidates say, but also to how they feel about what is said.

Applications of Affect-as-Information Principles

The principles we have discussed represent only a formalization of what is presumably second nature to those engaged in persuasion. Situations ranging from political campaigns to religious conversions can depend heavily on whether participants confuse reactions to the mellifluous voice of a persuader with reactions to the content of what is said. Even romance often depends on the inability (or the disinclination) of individuals to separate their experience of alcohol, soft lights, or music from their experience of the exciting attributes of their partners.

We believe that people routinely consult their feelings when making certain kinds of evaluative judgments and decisions. If this were not the case, advertisers, politicians, and suitors would probably not go to such lengths to elicit feelings in others and encourage their misattribution. Analogous processes may be seen in other contexts. For example, judges are typically seated on raised platforms as they look out over their courtrooms. One consequence is that the experience of looking up to judges physically tends to merge with the experience of looking up to them psychologically as authorities. Similarly, banks always used to be housed in large stone buildings with massive classical columns. A presumably intended consequence was that one's experience of the physical solidity of the building could easily be confused with beliefs about the financial solidity of the bank. Of course, the sense of solidity and the experience of looking up to someone are not emotions, but like emotions, these nonemotional experiences also have informational properties that are integrated into judgments and decisions.

Emotion as Virtue and Vice

It is important to note that our research is not primarily about judgments that are biased by moods or other sources of irrelevant affect. It does focus on judgment bias, but mainly because studying bias is a convenient research strategy. Our goal is not so much to show that people can be led astray by irrelevant emotions as to understand how relevant affective cues inform ordinary human judgment. We assume that the major-

Emotion as Virtue and Vice

ity of the affective cues that people experience are not irrelevant, misattributed sources of bias but appropriate reactions that provide useful information. There is increasing awareness that affect plays a larger role in ordinary judgment than has previously been realized, but in our view this is an adaptive arrangement. We are, therefore, somewhat less pessimistic about the role of affect in information processing than are the other authors.

In our view, the human information processing system, like the democratic system itself, is full of checks and balances in which each part is partially redundant with others and partially distinct. The information provided by feeling is related to but different from the information provided by knowing. Often they are redundant and mutually reinforcing but sometimes they offer conflicting information, as when we are offered what seems like a good deal but still feel uneasy about it. In some situations one's feelings might be more reliable and in others one's logical analysis might be, but experiencing conflicting information is likely to result in further processing, which helps one avoid the pitfalls associated with reliance on a single data source. Of course, we can be fooled into including affective reactions from irrelevant sources in our evaluations, and in some situations we may rely too much on affect. But usually even rapidly made evaluations are based on multiple sources of information from which we demand consistency.

There are, of course, two sides to this issue. Sears, for example, offers a more discouraging view. He suggests that the evaluation of attitude objects is a cumulative process in which, as we receive new information and update our impressions, only the affective import of the information is retained, while the actual content is generally lost. In this way, reactions to attitude objects can become dominated by a person's affective reactions, with minimal informational constraint. This affect is then automatically elicited by the attitude object, so that reasons offered for the reaction must often be constructed and have the status of rationalizations rather than reasons.

EMOTION AND PROCESSING IMPLICATIONS

In addition to influencing what people think about candidates (i.e., cognitive content), emotion influences how people process information (i.e., cognitive style). These processing implications of emotion are the primary focus of the chapter by Marcus and MacKuen. Using Gray's (1971, 1987) theory of emotion, they discuss the emotional factors governing involvement in political campaigns and also emotional factors in whether voters rely on prior attitudes or acquire new information from campaigns.

Gerald L. Clore and Linda M. Isbell

Gray's Theory

Gray offers a neural-behavioral theory in which he suggests that the limbic system is divided into subsystems, of which one concerns reactions to reward and one to punishment. The Behavioral Approach System (BAS) is concerned with reactions to reward, while the Behavioral Inhibition System (BIS) is concerned with reactions to punishment. Evaluations by the BAS produce emotions along a dimension with happiness or enthusiasm at one end and sadness or depression at the other. Reward or anticipation of reward produces happiness and enthusiasm, while withdrawal of reward produces sadness and depression. By contrast, the BIS responds to novelty and threat. Emotions produced by evaluations of the BIS range from calmness and relaxation when incoming stimuli are normal to nervousness and anxiety when they are not. When threat is perceived, attention is redirected to novel or threatening stimuli, which facilitates learning. It is believed that some degree of novelty is required for learning.

Marcus and MacKuen applied Gray's ideas to their research, including their data on voter behavior in the 1988 presidential election. They predicted that increased anxiety should reduce reliance on habitual cues such as party identification and should lead to greater reliance on new information. They compared the power of two variables to predict candidate preference – enthusiasm for the candidates and party identification. Results showed that voter anxiety reduced the impact of partisanship on candidate preference and greatly increased the impact of contemporary emotional reactions (i.e., enthusiasm) to the candidates. As predicted from Gray's model, political learning was stimulated by anxiety, while political interest and involvement in a campaign depended on anticipation of success and enthusiasm. Marcus and MacKuen concluded that dependence on previously learned political habits is high when anxiety is low and that attention to new information is high when anxiety is high, a pattern that appears to be consistent with Gray's theory.

Current Research on Emotion and Processing

From a somewhat different perspective, there is a growing body of evidence, primarily from social psychologists, that positive and negative affective experiences cue different processing styles (see Clore, Schwarz, and Conway, 1994, for a review). These experiences have been studied primarily by inducing positive and negative moods, and the usual finding is that positive affect leads subjects to engage in more heuristic processing. That is, individuals in positive affective states are more likely to use stereotypes, scripts, schemas, and other organizing information and less likely to focus on the details of the available information. Subjects experiencing sad affect are more likely to engage in systematic processing, to be analytical, and to focus on the presented details.

Recent results show, for example, that happy subjects are more likely to (1) recall information consistent with applicable stereotypes and schemas (Bodenhausen, 1993; Forgas and Moylan, 1991), (2) cluster information more in recall (Bless, Hamilton, and Mackie, 1990), (3) make decisions faster and more efficiently (Isen and Means, 1983), (4) engage in more creative problem solving (Isen, 1984), and (5) form more inclusive categories from lists of items (Isen, 1987). Sad subjects, on the other hand, are more likely to (1) discriminate between strong and weak arguments in a persuasive message (Bless, Bohner, Schwarz, and Strack, 1990), (2) estimate correlations more accurately (Sinclair and Mark, 1992), and (3) solve syllogisms better than happy subjects (Melton, 1991).

Such findings suggest that affect influences cognitive processing, perhaps in very fundamental ways. Positive affect is associated with unconstrained, heuristic processing, while sad affect is associated with controlled, systematic processing.

It may be useful to compare the view of emotion inherent in much of this research (affect-as-information processes) and that proposed by Gray and by Marcus and MacKuen. We should note at the outset that it is not at all clear which is the better starting point. The affect-as-information model is useful because it specifies the processes whereby emotional states might have their influence, but the model treats all positive and all negative states the same way. Also, most of the social psychological research on mood and processing has examined only happy and sad moods (but see Bodenhausen, 1993). But Gray's theory distinguishes the effects of sadness and anxiety. This seems likely to be an important step in that negative outcomes signifying the absence of reward (sadness) are likely to be very different from negative outcomes signifying the presence of punishment (fear). It is important to note, however, that Marcus and MacKuen did not compare these two negative emotions (sadness and anxiety) but instead compared the effects of enthusiasm, a positive state, with those of anxiety. Comparing a positive and a negative state rather than two negative states makes the data as relevant to the affect-as-information model as to Gray's theory.

Affect-as-Information Model

According to the affect-as-information model (Schwarz and Clore, 1983), emotional thoughts and feelings routinely provide experiential feedback about appraisal processes. They convey information about the nature and urgency of the personal relevance of appraised situations. Positive affect signals that a situation is safe, and negative affect signals a problem. This cue value of the states is used to explain how positive moods foster a heuristic approach to judgment and decision making, while negative states tend to elicit analytical processing. Thus, affective cues serve as information about a situation and may predispose one to adopt different processing modes.

As applied to information processing in task situations, negative affective states are believed to increase the accessibility of procedural knowledge that was effective in similar affective situations in the past (Schwarz, 1990). Thus, for example, negative affect may be associated with a narrowing of attention (Easterbrook, 1959) and attention directed to acts at a lower level of abstraction (Wenzlaff, Wegner, and Roper, 1988). Sad individuals should be more likely to avoid risks and to engage in systematic, detail-oriented, and resource-dependent processing. In contrast, positive emotions, having been elicited in the past in situations that did not require specific action, may not prime any specific procedure, thereby contributing to greater cognitive flexibility under elated affect. As a result, one might expect happy individuals to be more likely to give novel responses, to engage in heuristic processing, and to take a more global or abstract view.

As in the research on mood and judgment, our general hypothesis is that effects of mood on processing style reflect the informative functions of affective cues. One way to test this interpretation is to undermine the information value of the cues. Subjects who attribute their feelings to an irrelevant source should not interpret them as providing information about the task at hand, and differences in information processing between happy and sad subjects should disappear. To test this hypothesis, Sinclair, Mark, and Clore (1994) report an experiment on mood and persuasion.

Mirroring the original Schwarz and Clore (1983) judgment study, this experiment used naturally occurring variations in the weather as a source of mood. College students were approached on the campus and asked to participate in a survey either on one of the first warm and sunny days in spring or on one of the cold and cloudy days that followed. The results showed that on warm and sunny days participants were in a positive mood, while on cold and cloudy days their moods were more negative. The virtue of this naturalistic procedure is that it is completely nonreactive, and respondents are unlikely to perceive the purpose of the study.

Participants were exposed to either strong or weak arguments in favor of instituting comprehensive university examinations before graduation

(Petty and Cacioppo, 1986). In what has become a standard result in this literature, respondents in sad moods discriminated between strong and weak arguments and were persuaded only by strong ones, while respondents in happy moods did not discriminate between strong and weak arguments and were moderately persuaded by both. However, as in the original Schwarz and Clore (1983) study, for some respondents the weather was made salient as a plausible cause for their feelings, whereas for others it was not. When the feelings were (accurately) attributed to this external source, the effects of mood on persuasion were eliminated.

The results provide support for the general hypothesis that affective feedback provides information about the nature of situations in which one finds oneself (Schwarz, 1990; Schwarz and Clore, 1983). Although a common result in the judgment literature, such attributional effects had not previously been reported in studies examining the processing implications of emotion. According to this cognitive tuning hypothesis, the positive affective cues from pleasant weather informed participants that the situation was benign and that normal heuristic processing was appropriate. As a result, the happy respondents did not distinguish strong from weak arguments, presumably because they did not elaborate them sufficiently. The negative affective cues resulting from unpleasant weather should have alerted respondents that the situation was problematic, eliciting systematic processing and differential responses to strong and weak arguments. In contrast, in the external attribution conditions, there was no interactive effect of mood and argument strength on attitude. When respondents were cued to the weather and its possible influence on their current mood, they no longer employed the momentary affective cues they experienced as a guide for information processing.

To compare Gray's theory to our own, it would be interesting to repeat this experiment but to look at the effects of fear or anxiety in addition to happy versus sad moods. According to Gray, anxious subjects should be alert to new information, an orientation that might also influence their tendency to elaborate persuasive arguments, allowing them to readily distinguish strong and weak arguments. In addition, it is possible that for some tasks, such as persuasion, only the valence of the emotional state is important, while for tasks with greater opportunity for learning, sadness and anxiety would be discriminable. A problem is that anxiety and sadness tend to vary together, so care would be required not to confuse the effects of one with the effects of the other.

Collective Emotion

Emotion is relevant to politics in all the ways that we have touched upon – that is, it influences how persuasive messages are processed, it influences how evaluative judgments are made, and it can, therefore, bias evaluative judgments and presumably electoral choices. Moreover, as Masters points out, peripheral routes to eliciting emotion – facial expressions of the candidates, for example – may influence attitudes in a relatively direct way. All of these microscopic processes are relevant topics for political psychology. But, there is also a larger, more macroscopic way in which emotion and politics are analogous.

At a system level, information processing within individuals and within societies is similar. Both are motivated and characterized by a definite point of view that influences attention, judgment, memory, and processing. Both are part of larger problem-solving and coping processes. Events present opportunities and problems that must be appraised. If the problem is urgent, this must be communicated to the rest of the system. Processing priorities can then be changed and resources directed to new problems. In a similar way, politically important events change what people attend to.

As indicated earlier, Marcus and MacKuen use the concept of being partisan as a link between politics and emotion, and it is one that illuminates the analogy well. One is partisan to the extent that one has some allegiance to a group or an idea. Taking a partisan view involves being biased in the sense that one cares about how things turn out, is motivated to reach certain ends, and will devote effort and attention to relevant concerns.

Individuals have goals, standards, and attitudes with respect to which they appraise and evaluate events, actions, and objects. In society at large, of course, these goals, standards, and attitudes are distributed across people and groups, that is, across polities. Both within the individual and in society at large, the evaluation of an event or action depends on the goals and principles that are activated by the framing of the event or action. The function of emotion within individuals is to provide feedback, to signal when something important has happened, and to motivate the person to mobilize resources to deal with the threat or capitalize on the opportunity that the emotion signals. At the societal level, various disruptions of the status quo – things like the antiwar movement, civil rights demonstrations, parades after Desert Storm, and related events – might be thought of as collective emotions. These events seem to have functions for society similar to those of emotions for individuals. That is, they signal in an attention-getting way that some goal, standard, or attitude has been upheld or thwarted. In this regard, Marcus and MacKuen point out that democratic politics allows citizens the choice of being concerned or disengaged on any given political conflict, but activists and leaders must, when necessary, find ways to attract attention and initiate learning.

Emotion as Virtue and Vice

One function of emotion at both the individual and the collective level is to redirect attention and change the processing agenda. Like an individual's emotions, public outcries, demonstrations, riots, and so on are emotions at the societal level in the sense that they interrupt processing and redirect attention and subsequent processing. The interruption of ongoing processing in order to change the processing agenda is the chief function of emotion, according to Simon (1967), and the same is true, it would seem, of political demonstrations.

References

Anderson, N. H. (1981). *Foundations of Information Integration.* New York: Academic Press.

Bless, H., Bohner, G., Schwarz, N., and Strack, F. (1990). Mood and persuasion: A cognitive response analysis. *Personality and Social Psychology Bulletin, 16,* 331–345.

Bless, H., Hamilton, D. L., and Mackie, D. M. (1990). Mood effects on the organization of person information. Unpublished manuscript.

Bodenhausen, G. V. (1993). Emotions, arousal, and stereotypic judgments: A heuristic model of affect and stereotyping. In D. M. Mackie and D. L. Hamilton (Eds.), *Affect, cognition, and stereotyping: Interactive processes in group perception* (pp. 13–37). San Diego: Academic Press.

Bower, G. H. (1981). Mood and memory. *American Psychologist, 36,* 129–148.

Campos, J. J., and Barrett, K. C. (1984). Toward an understanding of emotions and their development. In C. E. Izard, J. Kagan, and R. B. Zajonc (Eds.), *Emotions, cognition, and behavior* (pp. 229–263). New York: Cambridge University Press.

Clore, G. L. (1985). The cognitive consequences of emotion and feeling. Paper read at the American Psychological Association Meeting, Los Angeles, August.

(1992). Cognitive phenomenology: The role of feelings in the construction of social judgment. In A. Tesser and L. L. Martin (Eds.), *The construction of social judgments* (pp. 133–164). Hillsdale, NJ: Erlbaum.

Clore, G. L., and Ortony, A. (1988). Semantics of the affective lexicon. In V. Hamilton, G. Bower, and N. Frijda (Eds.), *Cognitive science perspectives on emotion and motivation* (pp. 367–398). Amsterdam: Martinus Nijhoff.

Clore, G. L., Schwarz, N., and Conway, M. (1994). Affective causes and consequences of social information processing. In R. S. Wyer and T. Srull (Eds.), *The handbook of social cognition* (2nd ed., pp. 323–417). Hillsdale, NJ: Erlbaum.

Downs, A. (1957). *An economic theory of democracy.* New York: Harper & Row.

Easterbrook, J. A. (1959). The effect of emotion on cue utilization and the organization of behavior. *Psychological Review, 66,* 183–201.

Ferejohn, J. A., and Fiorina, M. P. (1974). The paradox of not voting: A decision theoretic analysis. *American Political Science Review, 68,* 525–536.

Fishbein, M., and Ajzen, I. (1975). *Belief, attitude, intention, and behavior.* Reading, MA: Addison-Wesley.

Forgas, J. P., and Moylan, S. (1991). Affective influences on stereotype judgments. *Cognition and Emotion, 5* (5/6), 379–395.

Gray, J. A. (1971). *The psychology of fear and stress.* London: Weidenfeld & Nicholson.

(1987). *The psychology of fear and stress* (2nd Ed.) Cambridge, UK: Cambridge University Press.

Isen, A. M. (1984). Toward understanding the role of affect in cognition. In R. S. Wyer and T. K. Srull (Eds.), *Handbook of social cognition* (pp. 179–236). Hillsdale, NJ: Erlbaum.

(1987). Positive affect, cognitive processes, and social behavior. In L. Berkowitz (Ed.), *Advances in experimental social psychology* (Vol. 21, pp. 203–253). New York: Academic Press.

Isen, A., and Means, B. (1983). The influence of positive affect on decision-making strategy. *Social Cognition, 2,* 18–31

Keltner, D., Locke, K. D., and Audrain, P. C. (1993). The influence of attributions on the relevance of negative feelings to satisfaction. *Personality and Social Psychology Bulletin, 19,* 21–30.

Melton, R. J. (1991). Effects of induced mood on task performance. Unpublished Ph. D. dissertation, University of Illinois, Urbana-Champaign.

Niedenthal, P. M., and Setterlund, M. (1994). Emotion congruence in perception. *Personality and Social Psychology Bulletin, 20,* 401–411.

Ortony, A., Clore, G. L., and Collins A. (1988). *The cognitive structure of emotions.* New York: Cambridge University Press.

Petty, R., and Cacioppo, J. (1986). *Communication and persuasion: Central and peripheral routes to attitude change.* New York: Springer-Verlag.

Riker, W., and Ordeshook, P. (1968). A theory of the calculus of voting. *American Political Science Review, 62,* 24–42.

Roseman, I. J. (1984). Cognitive determinants of emotion: A structural theory. In P. Shaver (Ed.), *Review of personality and social psychology*: Vol. 5., *Emotions, relationships, and health* (pp. 11–36). Beverly Hills, CA: Sage.

Rosenberg, E. L., and Ekman, P. (1994) Coherence between expressive and experiential systems in emotion. *Cognition and Emotion, 8,* 201–230.

Schwarz, N. (1990). Feelings as information: Informational and motivational functions of affective states. In E.T. Higgins and R. Sorrentino (Eds.), *Handbook of motivation and cognition: Foundations of social behavior* (Vol. 2, pp. 527–561). New York: Guilford.

Schwarz, N., and Clore, G. L. (1983). Mood, misattribution, and judgments of well-being: Informative and directive functions of affective states. *Journal of Personality and Social Psychology, 45,* 513–523.

(1988). How do I feel about it? Informative functions of affective states. In K. Fiedler and J. Forgas (Eds.), *Affect, cognition, and social behavior* (pp. 44–62). Toronto: Hogrefe International.

Simon, H. (1967). Motivational and emotional controls of cognition. *Psychological Review, 74,* 29–39.

(1983). *Reason in human affairs.* Stanford, CA: Stanford University Press, pp. 7–35.

Sinclair, R. C., and Mark, M. M. (1992). The influence of mood state on judgment and action: Effects on persuasion, categorization, social justice, person perception, and judgmental accuracy. In A. Tesser and L. L. Martin (Eds.).,

The construction of social judgments (pp. 163–193). Hillsdale, NJ: Erlbaum.

Sinclair, R. C., Mark, M. M., and Clore, G. L. (1994). Mood-related persuasion depends on misattributions. *Social Cognition*, 12(4), 309–326.

Smith, C. A., and Ellsworth, P. C. (1985). Patterns of cognitive appraisal. *Journal of Personality and Social Psychology*, 48, 813–838.

Strack, F., Martin, L. L., and Stepper, S. (1988). Inhibiting and facilitating conditions of the human smile: A non-obtrusive test of the facial feedback hypothesis. *Journal of Personality and Social Psychology*, 53, 768–777.

Wenzlaff, R. M., Wegner, D. M., and Roper, D. (1988). Depression and mental control: The resurgence of unwanted negative thoughts. *Journal of Personality and Social Psychology*, 55, 882–892.

Wyer, R. S., and Srull, T. K. (1989). *Memory and cognition in its social context.* Hillsdale, NJ: Erlbaum.

Part II   Political Cognition

Introduction

JAMES H. KUKLINSKI

Until the last decade, just about everything we knew about how citizens reach political decisions came from traditional surveys, predominantly the National Election Studies (NES). The NES set the framework for research on public opinion and voting behavior and literally monopolized the research questions scholars asked. Two studies in particular, *The American Voter* and Converse's "The Nature of Mass Belief Systems," set the groundwork for the next three decades of political inquiry.

The well-known conclusions derived from this genre of research have not been particularly uplifting for advocates of democracy. With few exceptions, studies consistently reveal a highly uninformed citizenry.

The survey research that began in the early 1960s and still thrives today has four distinctive characteristics. First, the analysis almost always takes the form of identifying statistical associations among variables. With the passage of time, the statistical models have become more and more sophisticated, but the underlying logic of correlating variables has remained the same. Second, despite the frequent use of terminology to the contrary, this research does not examine the *processes* by which people make political decisions. Survey data simply are not well suited to exploring decision-making dynamics. This is self-evidently true when the data are cross-sectional, but panel studies suffer similar limitations. Identifying structural relationships among variables collected at one point in time or, at best, at two or three points in time falls far short of probing actual thought processes.

Third, the nature of traditional survey data (as opposed to experimental survey data) prevents researchers from examining in detail how people deal with new information and whether and how that new information changes attitudes. Yet this is precisely what most democratic processes are all about. Politicians and the media provide facts and arguments to citizens, who then decide whether to form a preference, change an existing preference, or keep the preference they already hold.

James H. Kuklinski

Finally, those who use survey data necessarily, and usually implicitly, adopt a memory-based model of decision making. When respondents answer questionnaire items, typically right after an election, they draw on their best recollections of what happened during the campaign. In other words, they bring forth information they supposedly stored in memory during the election period. Whether they in fact store specific facts in memory and, if they do, store them accurately are better viewed as empirical questions than as assumptions.

CONCEPTIONS

The three studies included in this part represent research currently being conducted in the area of political cognition. All depart from the traditional survey-based perspective. All draw on an immense literature in social cognition that has accumulated over the last three decades. All identify limitations in the cognitive abilities of ordinary citizens and thus strengths as well as potential problems and weaknesses in the linkage between citizens and elites. The chapters by Lau and Redlawsk and by Taber, Lodge, and Glathar explore the psychological dynamics of voting, while McGraw examines how people react to elected officials' explanations of their behavior in office. Finally, although each of the chapters in this part emphasizes cognitive processes, none of the authors is blind to the importance of feelings and emotions to political decision making.

Lau and Redlawsk pose this question: how do voters form impressions of candidates within a political environment that is constantly evolving and that at best provides fragmentary information at any particular moment in time? Whatever the answer, they argue, it will not come from cross-sectional survey data or even from two- or three-wave panel studies. Instead, researchers must construct methodologies that are commensurate with the nature of political campaigns. In their view, an especially appropriate methodology is a computer-based scrolling technique that emulates the ongoing flow of information of a campaign. A stochastic algorithm determines the probability that any piece of information will appear at any time, and to increase or decrease the chances of particular pieces of information appearing as the "campaign" progresses, this algorithm can be changed. This simulation of an actual campaign context represents a new and highly creative approach to the study of voting behavior, and it affords the authors an opportunity to understand how voters actually go about making their choices during the campaign itself.

The campaign is one-half of the vote choice equation; the other half is the nature of voter decision making. Borrowing from decision theory, Lau and Redlawsk delineate two choice strategies: compensatory and noncompensatory. The former are complex and require the voter to acquire equivalent information about each candidate on a number of attributes, such as party, issue positions, personal characteristics, and the like. Of course, it is the very nature of the campaign context that renders this task difficult. Yet nearly all extant models of voting, the authors assert, assume the use of compensatory strategies. In contrast, noncompensatory strategies do not entail an attribute-by-attribute comparison across the two candidates. Rather, the voter relies on simpler rules, such as elimination-by-aspects. Thus, for example, a voter might eliminate one of the candidates because she does not favor abortion, without pursuing further considerations. The obvious problem is that the voter can easily make suboptimal decisions – rejecting the antiabortion candidate without even realizing that the candidate takes the "right" position on a wide range of other issues.

When will people use compensatory strategies, if at all, and when will they use noncompensatory strategies? Lau and Redlawsk posit two factors that presumably determine the answer to this question. One is task complexity: how many alternatives (candidates) are involved, how much information is there about the candidates, how much control does the voter have over the acquisition of information, and the like? The other is the expertise of the voter: how sophisticated about politics is he or she? In primary elections, where voters often face a half dozen or more choices, individuals overwhelmingly use noncompensatory strategies, including paying attention to only those few candidates who interest them. Indeed, the authors state, in primary elections, noncompensatory strategies are inevitable. In general elections, on the other hand, voters are in a better position to employ compensatory strategies and undertake an intra-attribute search, and they do.

The authors also raise some intriguing questions about the role of memory in political campaigns. As noted earlier, traditional survey research implicitly assumes a memory-based model of voting, whereas the on-line processing model posits that voters forget the specific information that goes into their overall tally. While Lau and Redlawsk do not reject the latter, they note that memory *must* play a role in an environment where information comes to voters in bits and pieces. Their preliminary evidence indicates that the politically sophisticated are markedly more likely than the unsophisticated to use a compensatory strategy in the scrolling condition, which is the authors' simulation of a campaign. Consequently, they find, the sophisticated also do better at remembering the fragmented information they received. This difference does not obtain when people receive static presentations of information, suggesting that voters' abilities interact with the complex environment of campaigns in a way that favors the sophisticated.

Not all aspects of politics are as complex and difficult to master as the political campaign. Sometimes elected officials find themselves face to face with their constituents for the purpose of explaining their behavior. Perhaps a representative has cast a vote that is contrary to the wishes of a large majority of constituents; perhaps a consistently liberal member of Congress has taken a decidedly conservative position on a highly salient piece of legislation; perhaps Congress has passed a bill that will have dire consequences for some social groups in a legislator's district, and they want to know why it passed. In these and similar instances, the official's task is to persuade constituents that he or she deserves their continued support; the individual constituent's task is to decide whether to give it.

McGraw's program of research focuses largely on constituents' response to politicians' accounts of their behavior. In the real world, of course, individuals might not be exposed to the account, pay attention to it, or understand it. McGraw's experimental approach ensures that all three prerequisites – exposure, attention, and understanding – are met. Thus she can validly focus her efforts on determining what people deem legitimate or not legitimate when they listen to elected officials' rationales, their stories or narratives, for their past actions.

McGraw notes that there are four types of accounts: excuses, denials, concessions, and justifications. She limits her analysis to constituents' responses to excuses and justifications. Sometimes officials turn to excuses; they admit that an offense has occurred but deny full or partial responsibility. "I admit that checks were overdrawn at my account at the House of Representatives' Bank, but I, like other members of Congress, had given my administrative assistant responsibility for keeping tabs on my account." On other occasions, they employ justifications and essentially deny the negative or undesirable nature of the event to which their behavior is related. "It's no big deal; overdrawing one's account at the House bank is not like molesting young boys and girls." If successful, excuses should attenuate blame and justifications should reduce the perceived negativity of the event and/or behavior.

Some accounts, McGraw finds in her series of experiments, work better than others. Justifications that appeal to fairness and conscience – "I voted for the tax bill because I believe the distribution of the tax burden is fairer for all of this nation's citizens than under the current tax scheme" or "I had to follow my conscience in voting for the income tax bill, and I did what I thought was in the best interests of the community and nation" – prove to be especially effective. Constituents also accept justifications that point to added benefits resulting from an otherwise unpopular vote. On the whole, excuses do less well, working when the representative identifies mitigating circumstances – "I had to vote for the income tax bill because the previous administration's policies crippled our nation's economy" – but failing miserably when the official pleads ignorance – "I voted for the income tax bill, but it was complicated and I did not foresee that it would result in increased income taxes for so many residents of this district" – or claims a diffusion of responsibility – "the income tax bill was a group decision, passed by a majority of the House of Representatives."

Evaluating politicians' accounts means deciding whether to attribute responsibility to their actions. McGraw finds that people not only attribute responsibility, but they often give credit and assign blame for the same predicament. In other words, constituents apparently recognize the complexity of legislative decision making and thus evaluate events and legislators' accounts of them accordingly. But constituents' hearing the persuasive appeal alone is not sufficient; an appeal has the intended effect only when people find it satisfactory. Acceptance is a crucial step in the blame-management process.

Finally, different kinds of accounts lead to inferences about different dimensions of the legislator's character. When people hear and accept justification of a roll call vote in terms of the legislators' "independent judgment," for example, they attribute traits such as "commands respect" and "not easily influenced." When the legislator couches the justification in terms of the need to think about the country or community as a whole, and constituents find it satisfactory, then they attribute characteristics such as "compassionate," and "not out of touch." The impact of accounts on character attributions is particularly great when officials present normative justifications.

It is only recently that contemporary research on social cognition has begun to return to the role of motives in attitude change. Both Lau and Redlawsk and McGraw assume citizens to be motivated. In the former case, the motivation takes the form of choosing information that will allow them to learn about candidates; in the latter, deciding whether or not to accept public officials' accounts of their past behavior. Taber, Lodge, and Glathar's chapter goes further; as its title, "The Motivated Construction of Political Judgments," suggests, the chapter proposes a theory of political choice that takes motivation as its central concept. In the authors' words, "political reasoning is a motivated process, affected in important ways by goals, expectancies, and prior evaluations."

This work represents yet another development in the on-line processing model that has become identified with the Stony Brook faculty. That model posits that people do not retain the specific information that influences their judgments but instead keep a "running tally" that takes the form of a global, affective evaluation. The authors note that their earlier research (1) treated citizens as passive receptors rather than as active interpreters and rationalizers of information and (2) established too strong a dichotomy between affect and cognition, given that all judgments are affect-laden. On the other hand, they retain the notion of belief formation and change as a constructive process; attitudes are not formed and crystallized once and for all.

Taber, Lodge, and Glathar offer an example that illustrates the need to include motivation in the on-line processing model. John Q. Public holds a highly negative impression of Bill Clinton, perceiving him as untrustworthy and as a tax-and-spender. He then finds out that Clinton, like him, supports the death penalty. The existing on-line processing model predicts that John Q. Public will update his tally for Clinton and evaluate him more positively. Yet he could simply discount the information as discrepant or deem Clinton an insincere and unprincipled politician who will do anything to get reelected. Consequently, John Q. Public's global evaluation might not change or could even become more negative.

Borrowing from various psychologists, the authors set forth two categories of motivational goals: accuracy and maintenance of prior beliefs. When the individual's purpose is to reach an accurate conclusion, he or she will act like an *intuitive scientist*, which entails collecting accurate information, considering all options, and recognizing and eliminating biases. Conversely, the person's goal can be directional. Striving to reach a predetermined conclusion, he or she will then act like an *intuitive lawyer*, who selectively seeks supporting evidence, ignores or misinterprets contrary information, and applies more stringent criteria to incompatible evidence. These two motivational goals, the authors note, have different implications for all stages of information processing, including searching long-term memory, attending to and interpreting additional sources of information, integrating all the evidence available to them, assessing the implications of that evidence, and, finally, reaching a political judgment.

The essential step in this whole process is the individual's choice of a motivational goal. The authors concede that research has not yet adequately identified the conditions under which people choose accuracy versus directional goals. Presumably accuracy will be paramount when people believe their judgment to be consequential for their own lives. Conversely, high personal involvement in the judgment – an individual feels strongly inclined toward a particular candidate, for example – often leads to directional reasoning. One of the key challenges for those working in the motivated reasoning vein will be to enumerate precisely when people engage each of the two goals.

Shavitt and Nelson applaud the preceding authors' incorporation of motivational influences into their work and also their common conception of candidate evaluation as a dynamic process. They then offer their own working model of "attitude reuse versus recomputation," which stems from their research into product evaluation. The model assumes that generating a new attitude (recomputation) when an already formed and accessible one exists is difficult. "It takes motivation, ability, and consideration of the basis for the attitude [why it was formed in the first place], as well as a recognized change in goal contingencies, in order for recomputation to occur." If an already existing attitude has been activated, it also takes a perception that the task is important and relatively simple. Generally speaking, reusing an existing attitude requires less effort than recomputing it.

Interestingly, while both Shavitt and Nelson and Taber, Lodge, and Glathar assert that people will not easily change their attitudes, their reasons for reaching this conclusion differ. The former implicitly assume that people act like intuitive scientists and seek an accurate answer; attitude change comes slowly because of the many steps that must be taken to effect it. Taber and colleagues, in contrast, assume that people often act like intuitive lawyers and seek to confirm an existing attitude; attitudes don't change because people don't want to change them. A juxtaposition of these two perspectives raises an interesting question: do people use the same cognitive processes to evaluate market products and political phenomena, and if not, why not? Specifically, are individuals less motivated to be accurate in their role as citizens than in their role as consumers? If so, does the lesser motivation arise primarily from a basic lack of interest in politics or from the political complexity that Lau and Redlawsk so effectively simulate in their work?

COGNITION AND THE QUALITY OF POLITICAL JUDGMENTS

It has been customary to equate cognition with thinking and reasoning and thus with "good" decision making. If people would only think about politics, so goes a familiar refrain, they would make better choices and judgments than they often do. Of course, defining "better" is itself a formidable task, since a set of agreed-upon criteria do not automatically flow from the term. Leaving that aside, it is crucial to recognize that cognition encompasses more than thinking and reasoning. Many cognitive processes occur unconsciously and/or automatically. For example, categorizing and its product, stereotyping, are routine; people could not make sense of their worlds in the absence of these fundamental processes. Similarly, we constantly make inferences, "filling in the blanks" when all the information is not available.

It has become increasingly evident that many of these routine, ordinary cognitive processes produce suboptimal decisions; "cognition" is not limited to reasoning and deliberation, and it does not necessarily imply solidly grounded and objectively determined outcomes. Even when people undertake deliberative thought, a complex political environment can overwhelm their ability to understand it.

All of the chapters included in this part underline these very points. People are often inclined to support already held convictions, in which case they do not give pro and con evidence an equal hearing, nor do they seek out inconsistent information. This motivation to reinforce directional goals, Taber, Lodge, and Glathar state, is commonplace, and leads to constructed judgments that represent less an evaluation of reality than an endorsement of existing biases. Although Taber, Lodge, and Glathar do not themselves posit such a hypothesis, it is plausible that directional motivation is higher among the politically active and sophisticated, those who otherwise possess the cognitive skills to cope with a complex environment, than among the less sophisticated, whose capacity to deal with political complexity might not be commensurate with their desire to do so. Such a state of affairs, if it exists, should unsettle anyone who cares about citizens' objective analyses of social and economic problems and the platforms candidates offer to rectify them.

As McGraw's work demonstrates, people can and do distinguish weak from strong excuses and justifications when the accounts are put directly before them. In other words, they make proper attributions about legislators' character and responsibility. On the other hand, she observes in her concluding comments, even politicians can become victims of cognitive motivational biases and thus construct poor accounts. They might maintain unrealistically positive views about themselves, overestimate their own effectiveness, or underestimate the ability of their constituents to punish them for questionable behavior. As pressures mount, these failures become more and more likely.

Suppose that most ordinary citizens truly strive to emulate the intuitive scientist; they try to collect all the relevant information, acknowledge their own biases, and thoroughly consider available options, all for the purpose of reaching the best decision. Even then, the political environment rarely lends a helping hand. As Lau and Redlawsk note, information reaches people in bits and pieces over the duration of a presidential campaign; information available today is gone tomorrow. Yet the citizen-as-intuitive-scientist must store it all in memory. At least in primary elections, three or more candidates vie for the voter's inherently limited attention at the same time. The individual's preferred primary candidate fails to make the general election. Issue "discussions" take the form of sound bites rather than prolonged and systematic debates. The result: an understandable use of politically relevant cognitive defaults such as partisanship and non-compensatory decision strategies.

Introduction

Research on political cognition, represented well by the chapters included here, stimulates a question whose time has come: if we can't change the basic nature of human cognition, should we instead try to design institutions that better accommodate what are natural and often automatic mental processes?

5

An Experimental Study of Information Search,
Memory, And Decision Making During a
Political Campaign

RICHARD R. LAU
DAVID P. REDLAWSK

One of the most important questions in political science is "How do voters decide how to vote during a political campaign?" The decision-making process must involve some impression formation of (i.e., data gathering about) the candidates (alternatives) involved and a strategy for choosing amongst them. For a candidate with whom the voter is unfamiliar, the learning process is typically a gradual one. First, the voter will learn a name, a face, perhaps a party (particularly if the election is a primary), and the office for which the candidate is running. The face will convey gender, race, and general age, of course. Later, more detailed information may be learned: a few specific issue stands (Page, 1978), perhaps a general ideology (Levitin and Miller, 1979), and undoubtedly a more refined impression of the candidate's personality (Abelson, Kinder, Peters, and Fiske, 1982; Kinder, 1986; Miller, Wattenberg, and Malanchuk, 1986). The voter will learn what past positions the candidate has held (if any) and how well he or she performed in those positions. As the campaign progresses, information about the likely success of the candidate in this election, campaign strategies the candidate has adopted, and so on will become available (Patterson and McClure, 1976).

Most relevant information about politics is conveyed by the media. During presidential campaigns in the United States, it is almost impossible to *avoid* being exposed to information about the presidential election, although information about lesser offices is harder to come by. With the exception of major headlines or cover pictures that are difficult to avoid if one picks up a newspaper or news magazine, information provided by *print media* is largely under the reader's control; a voter can read in detail, skim, or skip entirely any particular story. On the other hand, unless a voter conscientiously clips and saves stories about an elec-

136

tion (or goes to a library to retrieve those stories, a slightly more likely possibility), there is a dynamic quality to an election campaign in that information available today in the newspapers typically will not be available tomorrow. Information provided by *electronic media* is somewhat less under the voter's control, at least if one chooses to watch the nightly news, for example. You can pay attention or not, but it is difficult to "construct" your own news program from a large menu of options, the way you can when reading a newspaper.[1] On any given evening there are a handful of stories available, and that is all. And as with the print media, what is available today on the news will probably not be available tomorrow.

The point of this discussion is to underline the obvious: any political campaign is a dynamic, continually evolving process, and voters learn about candidates and make their voting decisions in a similarly dynamic, continually evolving information environment. True, many candidates are not new to a particular campaign; we have prior information about and/or impressions of them from previous campaigns, performance in office, or prior public exposure in earlier careers outside of politics, like professional sports or acting. In such cases, the voter has a "store" of prior knowledge about a candidate, some of which can be retrieved from memory, and the voter probably also has some affective evaluation of the candidate at the outset of the campaign. But at some point that familiar candidate *was* new and unfamiliar, and most people learned about him or her as a tabula rasa during the course of a political campaign. Moreover, any campaign provides new information even about old, familiar candidates – frequently new campaign promises, sometimes more refined personality impressions, and, at the very least, "hoopla and horserace" information – and that new information is provided by the same dynamic, continually evolving, largely uncontrollable media environment.

In contrast, how do we political scientists typically study elections and voter decision making? Most commonly, with a static, cross-sectional survey design. The best data we typically have (i.e., the presidential election year National Election Studies [NES]) involve a two-wave panel, with one interview toward the end of the campaign and a follow-up after the election. More frequently, we have only a single interview with each

---

1   The advent of remote controls for television sets and a larger number of channels to choose from with cable TV make this statement less true today than it was a decade ago. Still, the major news organizations cover the same basic stories, and the choice between channels involves whether you want to hear Tom Brokaw or Dan Rather talking about a particular story rather than what particular story you want to hear about.

respondent, in some cases (i.e., the NES off-year election studies) *after* the election and campaign are over. On rare occasions, we have multi-wave panel designs that interview respondents at multiple time points during a campaign (e.g., the Columbia studies of the 1940 and 1948 elections; Patterson and McClure's study of the 1976 election; and the 1980 NES four-wave panel study), but even here we are only taking infrequent snapshots of a continuous process.

It is our contention that the best way to study voter decision making is to study voters *during the course of a political campaign while they are making those decisions.* Taking advantage of modern computer technology and relying on a body of literature from behavioral decision theory, we have developed a new, dynamic process-tracing methodology for studying voter decision making during political campaigns. Our methodology combines features of both the print and electronic media: most of the information about candidates and the campaign is presented in a format that must be read, as is the case with newspapers, but the order of presentation is beyond the voter's control, as is the case with television.

In this chapter we will describe that methodology and the relevant theory that makes it useful. Then we will present a very general theory of how voters make their voting decisions and briefly describe some preliminary evidence for that theory from two experiments that have been conducted using this new methodology. We will then extend our theory by incorporating memory into the general model, derive some hypotheses, and present evidence testing those hypotheses.

BEHAVIORAL DECISION THEORY

Although many studies of decision making take a normative, expectancy-value approach, the field of behavioral decision making has been more concerned with what decision makers actually do than with what they optimally ought to do. In contrast to the comprehensive information search and careful consideration of the consequences associated with every possible alternative dictated by normative theory (e.g., von Neumann and Morgenstern, 1944) and the rational, value-maximizing choice strategy that should be used to make a decision, studies of actual decision making have found that information search is typically far from comprehensive, that few alternatives are actively considered, that the "consideration" given to those alternatives is often cursory at best, and that the method used to actually choose among alternatives is often far less rational than it is optimal (Abelson and Levi, 1985; Dawes, 1988; Einhorn and Hogarth, 1981; Payne, Bettman, and Johnson, 1992). Let us discuss these points in more detail.

An Experimental Study of a Political Campaign

The general behavioral decision-making approach views people as active information processors capable (if sufficiently motivated) of searching their environment for relevant information (Lau and Sears, 1986). Any decision problem presents the decision maker with a choice between $n \geq 2$ alternatives that vary on $m \geq 1$ different attributes or dimensions of judgment. Various *process-tracing* studies examine decision makers as they work their way through that $m \times n$ matrix to reach a decision (Carroll and Johnson, 1990). Studies have shown that while information search by actual decision makers is far from comprehensive, it is also far from random (Jacoby, Jaccard, Kuss, Troutman, and Mazursky, 1987). Indeed, decision makers select information about alternatives in only a few systematic ways (Hogarth, 1981; Payne, 1976, 1982; Payne and Braunstein, 1978; Russo and Dosher, 1983; Svenson, 1979). From this perspective, a key to understanding any decision is observing the *information acquisition process*, because that, in turn, sheds light on the *decision rules* or *choice strategies* that people use to combine the information and make a decision.

Various measures have been devised to describe information acquisition. For present purposes, two general categories of measures are important.

1. *Depth of search* refers to the amount of available information that is considered, including the proportion of all possible alternatives that are considered, the proportion of all possible "attributes" (i.e., different types of information or dimensions of evaluation that are available about any alternative) that are considered, and the proportion of all available information that is examined. The higher the proportions, the "deeper" or more comprehensive the information search, while the lower the proportions, the "shallower" or more cursory the search.

2. *Sequence of search* measures examine the "transitions" that are made from one bit of information to the next. The major question is whether transitions are *intra-attribute,* intercandidate (e.g., examining one candidate's stand on an issue and then another candidate's stand on that same issue), *intracandidate*, interattribute (e.g., examining one attribute about a candidate and then a different attribute about that same candidate), or more random (e.g., interattribute, intercandidate).

All of these measures can be used to infer the decision rules or choice strategies that are employed in making the decision. Choice strategies fall into two major categories.

1. *Compensatory strategies* are fairly complex decision rules in which the good points about an alternative are "traded off against" or

Richard R. Lau and David P. Redlawsk

"compensate for" the bad points about that alternative. Compensatory strategies demand that the same information about each alternative be considered. Hence depth measures that consider the proportion of information that is considered about each alternative, or even more directly the proportion of all attributes considered that are examined for each alternative, are indicative of a compensatory decision strategy. These strategies are cognitively complex because it is difficult to keep track of all the relevant information, particularly if the number of alternatives or number of attributes is relatively large. Normative theories of decision making, and virtually all extant political science models of the vote decision, assume compensatory decision rules (Lau, 1995).

2. *Noncompensatory strategies* are conflict-minimizing decision rules that try to avoid value trade-offs between good and bad points about any alternative (Billings and Marcus, 1983; Hogarth, 1987). That is, the good and bad points about an alternative are not "balanced off" against each other. For example, the "elimination-by-aspects" rule eliminates all alternatives from consideration that do not meet some minimum standard on the most important criteria of evaluation. The problem with noncompensatory strategies is that it is easy to imagine situations in which they lead to suboptimal decisions – for example, when a rejected alternative is superior to the chosen alternative on several criteria that are not even considered.

Decision makers are not restricted to using a single decision rule, of course, and many employ multiple strategies even during the course of a single decision problem. For example, a decision maker might employ a noncompensatory strategy to eliminate several alternatives and then switch to a compensatory strategy when the "decision set" is more manageable.

A DYNAMIC PROCESS-TRACING METHODOLOGY

Most process-tracing studies of decision making have employed a static "information board" technology in which decision makers are presented (on a computer screen, say) with an $m \times n$ matrix of information relevant to some decision (Carroll and Johnson, 1990). The columns of the matrix typically represent different brands of a product, while the rows represent the attributes (price, quality, appearance, etc.) over which the brands differ. By clicking a mouse, the decision maker can "access" any information desired (e.g., the price of brand X), and the researcher can keep track of all information considered, the order in which it is considered, and so on.

An Experimental Study of a Political Campaign

The problem with this standard information board technique is that, while it is a reasonable analog to a consumer choosing between different brands of a particular product on a supermarket shelf, it is a very poor analog to a voter selecting between candidates in a dynamic political campaign. Basically the decision problem represented by a static information board is far more controllable than is the case during a political campaign. On a static information board all information is available all of the time, and it can be considered in any order the decision maker desires; in contrast, there is a dynamic, ongoing, here-today, gone-tomorrow nature to the information available during political campaigns. Moreover, all information on the standard information board is accessible equally easily, while in political campaigns certain types of information (detailed issue stands, say) are much more difficult to come by than other types of information (party affiliation, say).

As an alternative, we have devised a technology by which the different attributes of multiple candidates "scroll" down a computer screen to emulate the ongoing flow of information during a political campaign (see Lau and Redlawsk, 1992, and Redlawsk, 1992, for more details). A simple stochastic algorithm determines the probability that any particular bit of information will appear on the screen at any time. This also makes it possible to vary the probabilities that different kinds of information will appear, thus making certain types of information easier to obtain than others. It is also possible to change those probabilities as the "campaign" progresses, such that certain types of information are easier to obtain at one point in the campaign than at another.[2]

We have constructed a mock presidential campaign as our basic experimental setting. This campaign involves two stages, a "primary campaign" in which six candidates (three from each party) are competing and a "general election" campaign in which only two candidates remain. Before the experiment begins, subjects fill out a fairly standard political attitudes questionnaire, which allows us to determine the normative "correctness" of their subsequent vote choices. Subjects "vote" twice, once in the primary and once in the general election. In the two experiments run to date, we have introduced several experimental

---

2 The probabilities were based on the actual likelihood that the different types of information appeared in the newspapers during different stages of the 1988 presidential campaign. See Lau (1992) for more details. We have also made available certain types of information (poll results, group endorsements) that are *not* specific to a given candidate, but rather that inherently compare several candidates. Although it would be possible to present this information in a standard $m \times n$ matrix (every candidate does or does not get the endorsement of a group), this type of strictly comparative information basically falls outside of the standard candidate-by-attribute matrix.

manipulations after subjects vote in the primary election designed to vary the difficulty of the decision in the general election campaign. After the general election, subjects are asked a series of questions about the candidates and are given an unexpected memory test.

A GENERAL THEORY OF VOTER DECISION MAKING

Elsewhere we have we have begun to develop a general theory of voter decision making (Lau, 1995; Lau and Redlawsk, 1992). We have derived and tested eleven hypotheses from that general model. Although we do not have the space here to describe the theory or those hypotheses in detail, our general model can be illustrated quite simply in Figure 5.1. The subjective nature of any decision task[3] is determined in part by what psychologists call "task demands": how many alternatives are involved, how similar they are, how much information there is about those alternatives, how much control the decision maker has over acquiring that information, how much time there is to make the decision, and so on. The nature of the decision task is also determined by the expertise of the decision maker: in part pure cognitive ability, but mostly past experience with the decision domain (i.e., politics). The subjective nature of the decision problem itself could vary along several dimensions. We have been primarily concerned with the difficulty of the decision, but we could easily imagine the magnitude of the consequences associated with the outcome as another dimension of potential import. Clearly, the more demanding the task, the more subjectively difficult the decision; the more expert the decision maker, the easier the decision.

The subjective nature of the decision task, in turn, affects the ways in which decision makers attempt to gather information and the decision rules they employ to combine that information into a choice. Very easy decision tasks may allow certain information acquisition patterns or decision rules that are not even possible with more difficult or more demanding decision tasks. And political experts may be aware of certain ways of acquiring information or combining it into a choice that novices

---

3 We have found it convenient, for expository purposes, to invoke the hypothetical concept of the "subjective nature of the decision task" that intervenes between task demands and political expertise, on the one hand, and information processing variables, on the other. We have no direct measures of this hypothetical construct (although it would be easy to gather them, which we plan to do in future experiments), but in essence it represents the possibility of an *interaction* between task demands and political expertise – i.e., it represents the possibility that task demands and political expertise do not have simple additive effects on subsequent stages of the model.

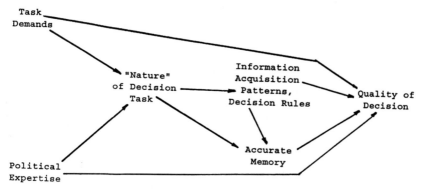

Figure 5.1. Lau–Redlawsk information processing model of voter decision making.

are unfamiliar with. Lau and Redlawsk (1992) report results that are quite consistent with the first part of the model.

Ignoring for the moment the role of memory (which was not included in our initial presentation of this model), all of these factors combined are hypothesized to help explain the quality or normative correctness of the decision reached. Although it is commonsensical to expect that more demanding or more difficult decision tasks should negatively affect the quality of a decision, and that expertise should positively affect decision quality (and, indeed, this is the case), we are most interested in the extent to which different information acquisition patterns and decision rules impinge on decision quality. The data are somewhat less consistent with the second half of our model, in part (we think) because we put less effort into measuring the normative correctness of the vote decision than we did in measuring the earlier concepts in the model, and thus the experiments had less power to detect significant results (but see Lau and Redlawsk, 1997). Nonetheless, we did find evidence that compensatory decision strategies produced better decisions, at least for the subset of subjects we had predicted would be most aided by using them (Lau, 1995; Lau and Redlawsk, 1992), and further, that the use of common political "heuristics" (e.g., party affiliation, group endorsements) improves decision-making quality.

ADDING MEMORY TO THE MODEL

One of the most striking findings from our experiments is the near impossibility of utilizing compensatory decision strategies – at least in a normatively correct manner – in making voting decisions during normal political campaigns. Compensatory decision rules demand that the same information be gathered about each candidate in the choice set. Yet this is nearly impossible during actual political campaigns, at least for all but the simplest and most easily accessible information. That is, if voters only cared about candidates' party affiliations, gender, and race, they could undoubtedly make normatively correct, rational decisions; but the more voters want to know candidates' issue stands or other less easily accessible information, the more difficult it becomes (verging on the impossible) to have all the relevant information at the time the decision must be made.

We did not need our experiments to reach this conclusion. Anyone who knows anything about the nature of modern political campaigns and normal motivation levels of the mass public toward politics, and who realizes what is required to make normatively correct voting decisions, would reach the same conclusion.

There are only two ways the average voter can survive in such a situation, where "survival" in this context means making reasonably correct voting decisions. One is to rely heavily on cognitive schemata in making inferences about candidates based on stereotypic, category-based, *easily accessible* information about the candidates (Conover and Feldman, 1986, 1989; Hamill and Lodge, 1986; Lodge and Hamill, 1986; Popkin, 1991). We have evidence from our experiments that is relevant to this point, but we have yet to analyze it.

The second way is to rely heavily on memory.[4] In an ideal world, the voter would receive all the relevant information about all candidates at once, in a format that could be controlled by the voter, so that information could be processed, learned, and compared in a logical order. In such an ideal world, it would make sense to access information in one of two ways, either intra-attribute, interalternative (where the values or stands that each candidate has on each important attribute are compared one at a time) or intra-alternative, interattribute (where overall impressions of each candidate are formed one at a time by examining each candidate on the same set of attributes).[5] Such systematic information search strategies would minimize cognitive demands on the decision maker because they would minimize the amount of information that would have to be kept in active memory for the comparisons to be made.

---

4 Whether a person knows or cares or can distinguish between veridical memory and a schema-based inference is another question. One of the liabilities of holding schemata is the tendency for the schema to reduce the accuracy of memory for schema-inconsistent information (Hamill and Lodge, 1986).

5 The first is assumed by "additive difference" models of compensatory decision rules, the latter by "linear" models of compensatory decision rules.

An Experimental Study of a Political Campaign

In actual political campaigns, of course, voters do not receive information about candidates in such a controlled setting. If he or she is lucky, the voter might be exposed to all the relevant information about the candidates *some time* during the campaign, but neither simple intra-attribute, interalternative search nor intra-alternative, interattribute search will be possible in all but the most rare or simplified situations. Thus the voter will have to rely heavily on *memory* for information learned at some earlier point in time (say, candidate X's stand on the size of the defense budget) when later information is accessed and learned (candidate Y's stand on that same issue) in order to make the comparison.

This reasoning points to the importance of accurate memory for making normatively correct decisions during political campaigns, and dictates that memory be added to our basic model as a variable potentially mediating the effects of task demands, expertise, information acquisition patterns, and rules on the quality of decisions.[6] Our revised model of voter decision making displayed in Figure 5.1 therefore includes an important role for memory. In the remainder of this chapter, we will develop further this extension of our basic model and provide evidence testing its veracity.

A PROCESS-TRACING STUDY OF MEMORY DURING POLITICAL CAMPAIGNS

Procedure

We have coded memory data only from the second experiment, so our analyses will be limited to it. Half of the subjects for this experiment were defined a priori as political experts – colleagues in the political science department at Rutgers University. The other half of the subjects were defined a priori as nonexperts and were recruited from central New Jersey by several means, with only the prerequisites that they be American citizens, that they not have an advanced degree in political science, and that they not be college students. We make no claims for the representativeness of these subjects, and certainly our nonexperts are

---

6 In truth, we have no way to distinguish between accurate memory and accurate inference, at least for information a voter actually accessed and thus presumably could remember. Because our measure of memory is *recall* rather than *recognition*, however, we expected far fewer schema-based "intrusions" of inaccurate, though schema-consistent, information than would be the case if we relied on recognition memory. Thus we feel reasonably confident that our "memory" measure is in fact tapping memory more than anything else.

much better educated and somewhat more interested in politics than would be those in a random sample.[7]

The procedure for this experiment followed the general format described earlier: subjects first filled out a political attitudes questionnaire, learned about the mock election campaign study, practiced using the computer, "registered" to vote in either the Democratic or Republican primary, "experienced" a primary campaign involving three Democrats and three Republicans, evaluated all six candidates and "voted" for one of the three in their party's primary, "experienced" a general election campaign involving one of the three Democrats and one of the three Republicans, evaluated these two candidates and "voted" for one of them, and finally filled out another questionnaire that included an unexpected memory task of "writing down everything you can remember" about each of the six candidates.

In addition to the a priori assignment of subjects to expert/nonexpert categories, two random manipulations were conducted. First, subjects were randomly assigned either to the dynamic, scrolling format described earlier or to a static, fixed presentation format in which all information was always available. We included such a condition to represent an ideal world for receiving information about candidates during a political campaign in order to contrast it to the more realistic dynamic format. To add to this real versus ideal contrast, subjects in the dynamic condition were under time constraints,[8] while subjects in the static condition were given unlimited time to access information about candidates.

A second manipulation, orthogonal to the first, was introduced at the end of the primary election. The candidate that half of our subjects voted for in the primary election "won" the party's nomination and was thus a candidate in the general election, while the other half of the subjects supported a loser during the primaries and thus experienced a general election campaign in which their party's candidate was one they had rejected

---

7 A balanced sample of male and female subjects was recruited. All of the forty subjects were white, with two claiming Hispanic origins. Subjects ranged in age from twenty-five to seventy-five, with a mean age of forty-one. Fifteen percent were Catholic, 12% Jewish, half Protestant, and 22% atheist or agnostic. The nonexperts had a mean education of just under sixteen years, while all experts had at least a masters degree (and most had a Ph.D). Party identification of subjects was 18% Republican, 58% Democrat, and 24% independent. Nonexperts were paid $10 for their time.

8 The primary and general election campaigns each "lasted" for 12 minutes in the dynamic scrolling condition. Subjects could "exit" from the campaign and vote whenever they wanted, however, and about half of the subjects in the dynamic condition chose to exercise this option before the time expired.

during the primary.[9] These two manipulations varied the task demands facing subjects, with the dynamic scrolling condition and the "rejected candidate" condition being more difficult or demanding than the static presentation format and the "accepted candidate" condition.

Information Processing Measures

We relied on six chief measures of information processing, two reflecting the depth of the information search undertaken (the total amount of time spent searching for information and the number of distinct attributes considered),[10] two concerning the sequence of information search (the proportion of all transitions that were intracandidate and the proportion of all transitions that were intra-attribute), and two reflecting the use of compensatory decision strategies (the variance of the number of distinct attributes considered about each candidate, where high variance would suggest the use of a noncompensatory decision rule; and the proportion of all items considered that were considered about each candidate in the decision set, where a high proportion would suggest the use of a compensatory decision rule).

Memory Measures

As soon as subjects had voted in the general election campaign, they were given a postexperiment questionnaire, which began by asking subjects to "write down everything you can remember learning about the six candidates in this election." The six candidates' names were presented (in random order) followed by ten lines for writing down memories. Each distinct memory was coded (by a general "gist" criterion) as accurate, inaccurate, or unable to code in terms of accuracy.[11] This coding results in three memory measures: the total number of memories

---

9 The opposing candidate for the general election was matched, as much as possible, to the candidate from the subject's party to make the ideological differences between the two as constant as possible. Thus three candidate pairings occurred in the general election: a very liberal Democrat vs. a moderate Republican, a liberal Democrat vs. a conservative Republican, and a moderate Democrat vs. a very conservative Republican.

10 Another common measure is the number of distinct alternatives considered, but every subject save one examined at least something about every candidate, which makes this standard measure useless. These two variables are strongly associated with the presentation format manipulation, which we suspect has more to do with the time limits than with the format itself.

11 A common example of the last would be "I remember liking his position on X."

reported (regardless of their accuracy), the total number of accurate memories reported, and the proportion of all reported memories that are accurate.

In coding the memory data, it became clear that most subjects could not remember much of anything about the four candidates from the primary election who were not involved in the general election. Thus we restrict our analysis of memory to memory about the two candidates involved in the general election campaign. We do consider information that was learned in either the primary or the general election campaigns, however.

Normatively Correct Decision Making

Because our analysis places great emphasis on the normative correctness of the voting decision, it is particularly important that we clearly delineate what we mean by "correct." Elsewhere we describe in detail the steps used to calculate a correct vote (Lau and Redlawsk, 1992; see also Lau and Redlawsk, 1997). For each subject, this multistep process began with the calculation of three independent measures of correctness for each candidate in the election based on issues, group endorsements, and party identification. Each individual issue, group, or party item that could have been accessed by the subject was assigned a weight of 1 if it was accessed in either the primary or general election and a weight of 0 if it was not. Thus, only items that were actually accessed by the subject were used to calculate the three correctness scores. An issue-based score was calculated by comparing where the candidates stood on issues that were accessed to where the subject stood on the same issues using a spatial analysis. A group-based score was calculated by comparing the subject's group likes and dislikes to the endorsements actually accessed, adding a point if a liked group endorsed the candidate, and subtracting a point if a disliked group endorsed the candidate. A party-based score was calculated for each candidate by comparing the subject's party identification to the candidate's party.

Briefly, a subject was considered to have cast a correct vote on any one of these measures if the vote was cast for the candidate closest to the subject on each measure. Since the measures are independent, a subject could be considered correct on some measures and incorrect on others. To determine the overall correctness of the vote, the three independent scores were combined for each subject into a single measure of correctness for the general election. Because we believe that political information processing is, to some degree, mediated by preexisting cognitive constructs, we combined the three measures by weighting them according to the subject's political chronicities, as measured by open-ended

An Experimental Study of a Political Campaign

questions in the preexperiment questionnaire (see Lau, 1986, 1989). On this last weighting, issues count more toward the final determination of correct voting if, in general (i.e., chronically), subjects disproportionately consider issues in candidate evaluation; group endorsements count more if, chronically, subjects disproportionately consider groups in candidate evaluation; and so on. If this final single measure of a correct vote was negative, the subject voted incorrectly. If the result was positive, the subject cast a correct vote. For our analysis, the measure was dichotomized, with those subjects voting correctly assigned a 1 and those voting incorrectly assigned a 0. According to this measure, 37.5% of our subjects voted incorrectly and 62.5% voted correctly.[12]

RESULTS

Effects of Information Processing on Memory

Our analyses are guided by the general model presented in Figure 5.1. The first question this model leads us to ask is whether the memory measures are associated with the six information processing variables. The simple bivariate correlations are presented in Table 5.1. The answer is a clear "yes," albeit with a few deserved caveats. In general, the strongest correlations are between the two depth-of-search variables and the memory measures, and here we must mention the caveats: the two depth measures and the first two memory measures are simple raw counts. It makes sense that the more items a subject considers, the more he or she could possibly remember; thus, to a certain extent, these positive correlations are "built in." The more interesting correlations involve the memory measure listed in the last column of Table 5.1, the proportion of accurate recall. There is no built-in correlation with this variable, and four of the information processing measures correlate significantly with it: the total time spent searching for information, the proportion of intra-attribute search, the variance of the number of items accessed per candidate, and the most direct measure of use of a compensatory decision rule, the percentage of all items considered that were examined for both candidates.

This pattern of correlations may, at first glance, seem somewhat unusual, particularly the correlations between the two measures of type of decision strategy and accuracy of memory. You would think that these

---

12 Eight of the forty subjects came out at exactly 0 on our measure of rationality, so that we could not clearly categorize their vote as correct or incorrect. Because we wanted to isolate incorrect or irrational voting, these subjects were counted as voting correctly.

Table 5.1. *Correlations Between Information Processing Variables and Memory*

	Total Memory	Accurate Memory	% of Accurate Memory
Depth Measures			
Total time searching	.24*	.39***	.30*
No. of distinct attributes	.45***	.27*	.08
Sequence Measures			
% of intracandidate transitions	.19	−.02	−.10
% of intra-attribute transitions	.02	.08	.43**
Decision Strategy			
Variance no. of items per candidate	.16	.59***	.48***
% of items accessed, both candidates	.07	.15	.31*

Note: N = 40. * $p < .05$; ** $p < .01$; *** $p < .001$.

two measures should correlate negatively with each other, and thus we would expect their correlations with memory to have different signs. In fact, however, these two measures of type of decision rule correlate *positively* .23 ($p < .08$) with each other. The reasons for this unexpected positive correlation are the two-stage nature of our political campaign and the fact that our measures of information processing are based on the information learned about the two relevant candidates both during the two-candidate general election *and* during the six-candidate primary campaign. Thus there is no reason that these two indicators must be negatively correlated with each other, as there would be had the measures been based entirely on information searched from a two-candidate election campaign.[13]

The pattern of correlations in the final column of Table 5.1 (and separate analyses reported by Lau and Redlawsk, 1992, which focused on the primary election campaign) suggests two basic findings to us:

1. First, accurate memory is aided by a strategy of reducing the decision set to a manageable number by, for example, limiting your information search during the primary election primarily to the three candidates from your own party. It is very difficult to be systematic at this stage (particularly in the dynamic scrolling condi-

---

13 When we create such a measure based on information searched during the general election campaign only, these two variables correlate −.29 ($p < .03$) with each other.

tion) because so much information about so many candidates is available. Inevitably, a *noncompensatory* decision strategy must be used, which will result in the most information being learned about the most preferred candidate, but also more information being learned about the three candidates from your party than about the other three candidates. In the process of making a decision in the primary election, however, voters can learn what sort of information is most important to them, and concentrate during the more manageable two-candidate general election on learning that important information for the other candidate during the general election.

2. Second, memory is aided by a compensatory decision strategy (at least after the field is reduced to a manageable number – two) based on intra-attribute search.

These two conclusions help explain the pattern of correlations in Table 5.1. Voters who followed this strategy would have a large variance in the number of items accessed about the two candidates because they would access much more information about the candidate from their own party, although not all of this extra information would be of the most useful and important kind. They would also come out reasonably high on the measure of the proportion of accessed items examined for both candidates because they would concentrate their information search during the general election campaign on making sure they had learned the important information about both candidates.

Effects of Experimental Manipulations on Memory

We then turn to see if the experimental manipulations affect memory. The basic analysis is a $2 \times 2 \times 2$ analysis of variance, where the three orthogonal factors vary voter expertise, the format of information presentation, and whether the general election candidate from the subject's party was accepted or rejected by the voter during the primary election. We had predicted that the greater the task demands on the subject, the worse the subject's memory. While the main effects for the two task demand manipulations are not significant, the interaction between the two is $F(1,32) = 3.92$, $p < .03$. As seen in Figure 5.2, it is the combination of the more difficult dynamic, scrolling presentation format and the presence of a rejected candidate from one's own party in the general election campaign that negatively affects the accuracy of recall.

According to our model, the effect of the experimental manipulations on memory should be mediated, at least in part, by the effects of those manipulations on differential information processing – different

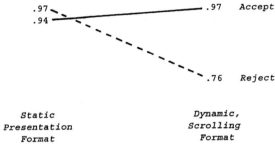

Figure 5.2. Effect of experimental manipulations on accuracy of memory.

information search strategies and/or different decision rules.[14] To determine if this was true, we repeated the basic analysis described earlier, entering the information processing variables as covariates. The covariates are not sufficient to completely eliminate the presentation format by accept/reject interaction, which still approaches significance: $F(1,27) = 2.63$, $p < .06$. As seen in Figure 5.3 (where the means are adjusted for the covariates), the least accurate memory still occurs in the dynamic scrolling presentation format with the reject condition. On the other hand, the difference between this one cell and the other three is reduced substantially, and eta squared for the model more than doubles when the covariates are added, from .24 to .55. Thus the predicted mediation, although not total, would clearly seem to occur.

Effect of Memory on Correct Voting

Finally, we turn to the question of the normative correctness or rationality of the vote decision. As a first cut at this analysis, we conducted a logistic regression in which the probability of a correct vote was a function of the three manipulated experimental variables and their interactions. These results are shown in the first column of Table 5.2. A significant marginal effect of expertise in an unexpected direction (experts are less likely than nonexperts to make correct decisions with the static presentation format in the accept condition) is qualified by a predicted expertise by presentation format interaction: experts make better decisions than nonexperts in the more difficult (and more realistic) dynamic, scrolling format.

14 Although we do not have the space here to describe those effects in detail, suffice it to say that they were substantial. For a more detailed consideration of this question, albeit one that concentrates on the primary election campaign, see Lau and Redlawsk (1992).

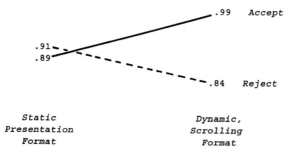

Figure 5.3. Effect of experimental manipulations on accuracy of memory, controlling for differential search strategies and decision rules.

Table 5.2. *Logistic Regression Predicting Correct Voting Decisions*

	Equation 1		Equation 2	
	b	SE	b	SE
Subject expertise	−3.34*	1.51	−.53	.46
Presentation format	−.39	1.56	−.20	.49
Accept/reject	−1.64	1.51	−2.63	1.62
Expertise by format	2.64*	1.55	.33	.46
Expertise by accept/reject	1.39	1.50	.15	.47
Format by accept/reject	−.31	1.50	.06	.44
No. of distinct attributes			−4.14*	2.52
% of intracandidate transitions			−4.21	4.75
% of intra-attribute transitions			−8.83	5.85
Variance no. items per candidate			−2.51	2.78
% of items accessed, both candidates			−1.46	2.80
% of accurate memory			1.15	1.76
Constant	2.41	1.39	7.24*	4.32
−2 log likelihood χ^2	45.70	(33 df)	39.87	(27 df)
% correctly predicted		70%		78%

Note: $N = 40$. * $p < .05$.

Our basic model suggests once again that these experimental manipulation effects should be mediated at least in part by the information search strategies, decision rules, and memory effects that they also influence. To determine if this is the case, we added our measure of accurate memory and five of the information processing variables to the basic equation. These results are shown in the second column of Table 5.2. The interaction effects are now much smaller in absolute terms and much smaller than their standard errors. The coefficients for only two of the mediating variables are larger than their standard errors, but this is due in part to a certain amount of collinearity between them and in part to the small sample size. What is more indicative of the importance of the mediating variables is the increase in the proportion of cases that are correctly classified when they are added to the model, from 70% to almost 78%.

DISCUSSION

In this discussion, we will put our findings into a larger context and mention future directions in which we are planning to go with our dynamic process tracing technique. To begin with, we find the pattern of correlations between the information search and decision strategy variables and accurate memory (reported in Table 5.1) quite intriguing, because they suggest that a compensatory decision strategy based on intraattribute search improves memory. A consideration of the popular associative network model of memory can provide an explanation for this result (Hastie, 1986). Each candidate and each attribute would be represented by different "nodes" in memory. The more time an attribute spends in short-term or active memory, the more likely it is to be recalled. Presumably attributes that are accessed about both candidates would spend more time in active memory because they would require some mental calculation to form the basis for an intercandidate comparison. Thus they should be more likely to be recalled. And once an attribute is recalled about one candidate, it is more likely to be recalled about another candidate (due to spreading activation along the associative network) if a link between the attribute and another candidate exists.

In a larger sense, we are quite impressed with how well the data fit our expanded model depicted in Figure 5.1. Although we found that the experimental manipulations affected both memory and the normative correctness of voting decisions in a predictable manner, much (though certainly not all) of the effects of the manipulations could be explained by differential search strategies and decision rules and by differential accuracy of memory, both of which were also affected by the experimental manipulations. We should stress that we have tried to design experimental manipulations that mirror naturally occurring variants in political campaigns that voters actually face.[15] Some elections involve more candidates, and thus more alternatives, than others; some elections involve candidates who are ideologically similar – and thus more difficult to distinguish – than others; some elections involve a voter's

---

15 The ideal world condition created for the experiment described in this chapter would be an exception to that general rule.

favorite candidate, and some involve two (or more) relatively unattractive candidates; and so on. Thus, by extension, the importance of information search strategies, decision rules, and accurate memory that we have found in our experiments should also apply to actual political campaigns.

These results have much to say to more mainstream political science research. For example, we have suggested that voters may follow very different decision strategies, depending on the number of candidates involved in the election. Voters may make their choices in multi- (i.e., more than two) candidate primaries, or in general election campaigns involving a major third-party candidate, in significantly different ways than is the case with two-candidate elections (see also Bartels, 1988; Kessel, 1992). Our theory provides a cognitive underpinning to any differences that are observed between different types of elections, and could provide insights into how the media might structure information differently to help voters make better voting decisions or how campaign managers might structure their campaign ads differently to present their candidate in the most favorable light.

As another example, there is a growing controversy about whether the basic candidate evaluation process is memory-based or on-line (Kelley and Mirer, 1974; Lodge, McGraw, and Stroh, 1989). Our model certainly suggests that memory is important to the process of making correct choices, but the weight of the evidence in the literature seems to favor the on-line model. We want to note, first, that the process by which voters form impressions of candidates may *not* be the same process by which they choose between them if that is their goal (Fischer and Johnson, 1986). But more important, we think that this controversy is method driven rather than substance driven. That is, the controversy is very relevant to the question of whether likes and dislikes about presidential candidates, reported after the election, accurately reflect the process of candidate evaluation. We think not, and thus are very much on the side of Lodge and his colleagues in this controversy.

But the field is concerned with this question only because of the pre-post election survey design that has so dominated what we have learned about presidential elections. The answer to this question is not the same as the answer to the question of whether memory for events or information learned about candidates during an election campaign is at all important to the voting decision. We think it is, where by "important" we mean "aiding the voter to make the best decision." When information becomes available to decision makers in such a haphazard, uncontrolled way as occurs in all political campaigns, memory *must* play an important role in allowing the voter to make the appropriate comparisons. Thus factors that aid memory – including expertise, cognitive schemata, information acquisition patterns, and decision rules – also play important roles in helping voters make correct decisions.

Turning to future research directions, we have three new types of manipulations planned. So far, all of our candidates have been moderately attractive, well-qualified white males. We are currently running an experiment in which the gender of one of the candidates is manipulated, and we plan to manipulate race and personality in the future. It *is* quite rational to consider candidate factors in making voting decisions, and most voters do. But while our subjects have actively searched for person-related information during the mock campaigns, they have had little reason to distinguish between the candidates on this basis.

Second, we plan to manipulate campaign strategies and/or campaign resources during the course of one of our experiments. At the moment, all candidates have had the same resources and have followed the same basic strategies, in that the probability of certain information being available for access was always identical across candidates. But it would be easy to vary this probability, making *any* information easier to find about some (better-funded) candidates than others or making certain types of information much more readily available about some candidates than others, thus in effect varying campaign strategies. Thus we will be able to study how (or if) voters react to different campaign strategies. For example, do voters strive to "balance out" differential campaign resources by going out of their way to search for information about the less well-funded candidate, thus reducing the effects of differential campaign resources?

Third, as the program is currently set up, voters must actively choose to expose themselves to any information learned during the campaigns, but as we suggest in the introduction to this chapter, during actual presidential campaigns much exposure to relevant information is accidental, that is, unintentional. In our next experiment, we plan to expose all voters to certain bits of information automatically (as "news flashes" and/or as political ads), whether or not they would have chosen to learn that information. A voter may or may not pay attention to these uncontrolled, unchosen exposures, as in a real campaign, but they can be added to the basic experimental technique, and we will then be able to study the differences between actively chosen and haphazardly learned information.

These three avenues for future research by no means exhaust the possibilities and are mentioned here only for illustrative purposes. The information processing perspective is firmly entrenched in psychology and thus is an important perspective in political psychology as well. Behavioral decision theory has had a stronger impact on political psychologists who work in the international relations field than on those whose work concentrates on voting behavior (e.g., Levy, 1992a, 1992b), but it too is becoming firmly a part of political psychology. How much behavioral decision theory (and process-tracing techniques in particular), and the entire information processing paradigm, can contribute to the field of political science is a question for the future.

References

Abelson, Robert P., Donald R. Kinder, Mark Peters, and Susan T. Fiske. (1982). "Affective and Semantic Components in Political Person Perception." *Journal of Personality and Social Psychology*, 42: 619–630.
Abelson, Robert P., and Ariel Levi. (1985). "Decision Making and Decision Theory." In Gardner Lindzey and Elliot Aronson (Eds.), *The Handbook of Social Psychology*, Vol. 1, 3rd ed. (pp. 231–309). New York: Random House.
Bartels, Larry M. (1988). *Presidential Primaries and the Dynamics of Public Choice*. Princeton: Princeton University Press.
Billings, R. S., and Sharon A. Marcus. (1983). "Measures of Compensatory and Noncompensatory Decision Making Strategies: Judgment versus Choice." *Organizational Behavior and Human Performance*, 31: 331–352.
Carroll, John S., and Eric J. Johnson. (1990). *Decision Research: A Field Guide*. Beverly Hills, CA: Sage.
Conover, Pamela J., and Stanley Feldman. (1986). "The Role of Inference in the Perception of Political Candidates." In Richard R. Lau and David O. Sears (Eds.), *Political Cognition: The 19th Annual Carnegie Symposium on Cognition* (pp. 127–158). Hillsdale, NJ: Erlbaum.
  (1989). "Candidate Perception in an Ambiguous World: Campaigns, Cues, and Inference Processes." *American Journal of Political Science*, 33: 912–940.
Dawes, Robyn M. (1988). *Rational Choice in an Uncertain World*. New York: Harcourt Brace Jovanovich.
Einhorn, Hillel J., and Robin M. Hogarth. (1981). "Behavioral Decision Theory: Processes of Judgment and Choice." *Annual Review of Psychology*, 32: 53–88.
Fischer, Greg W., and Eric J. Johnson. (1986). "Behavioral Decision Theory and Political Decision Making." In Richard R. Lau and David O. Sears (Eds.), *Political Cognition: The 19th Annual Carnegie Symposium on Cognition* (pp. 55–65). Hillsdale, NJ: Erlbaum.
Hamill, Ruth, and Milton Lodge. (1986). "Cognitive Consequences of Political Sophistication." In Richard R. Lau and David O. Sears (Eds.), *Political Cognition: The 19th Annual Carnegie Symposium on Cognition* (pp. 69–93). Hillsdale, NJ: Erlbaum.
Hastie, Reid. (1986). "A Primer of Information-Processing Theory for the Political Scientist." In Richard R. Lau and David O. Sears (Eds.), *Political Cognition: The 19th Annual Carnegie Symposium on Cognition* (pp. 11–39). Hillsdale, NJ: Erlbaum.
Hogarth, Robin M. (1981). "Beyond Discrete Biases: Functional and Dysfunctional Aspects of Judgmental Heuristics." *Psychological Bulletin*, 90: 197–217.

Richard R. Lau and David P. Redlawsk

Hogarth, Robin M. (1987). *Judgment and Choice: The Psychology of Decision.* New York: Wiley.

Jacoby, Jacob, James Jaccard, Alfred Kuss, Tracy Troutman, and David Mazursky. (1987). "New Directions in Behavioral Process Research: Implications for Social Psychology." *Journal of Experimental Social Psychology*, 23: 146–175.

Kelley, Stanley, Jr., and Thad W. Mirer. (1974). "The Simple Act of Voting." *American Political Science Review*, 68: 572–591.

Kessel, John. (1992). *Presidential Campaign Politics* (4th ed.). Chicago: Dorsey.

Kinder, Donald R. (1986). "Presidential Character Revisited." In Richard R. Lau and David O. Sears (Eds.), *Political Cognition: The 19th Annual Carnegie Symposium on Cognition* (pp. 233–255). Hillsdale, NJ: Erlbaum.

Lau, Richard R. (1986). "Political Schemata, Candidate Evaluations, and Voting Behavior." In Richard R. Lau and David O. Sears (Eds.), *Political Cognition: The 19th Annual Carnegie Symposium on Cognition* (pp. 95–125). Hillsdale, NJ: Erlbaum.

(1989). "Construct Accessibility and Electoral Choice." *Political Behavior*, 11: 5–32.

(1992). "Searchable Information During an Election Campaign." Unpublished manuscript, Rutgers University.

(1995). "Information Search During an Election Campaign: Introducing a Process Tracing Methodology for Political Scientists." In Milton Lodge and Kathleen McGraw (Eds.), *Political Information Processing* (pp. 179–205). Ann Arbor: University of Michigan Press.

Lau, Richard R., and David P. Redlawsk. (1992). "How Voters Decide: A Process Tracing Study of Decision Making During Political Campaigns." Paper presented at the 88th annual meeting of the American Political Science Association, Chicago, September 1992.

(1997). "Voting Correctly." *American Political Science Review*, 91: 585–598.

Lau, Richard R., and David O. Sears (Eds.). (1986). *Political Cognition: The 19th Annual Carnegie Symposium on Cognition.* Hillsdale, NJ: Erlbaum.

Levitin, Teresa E., and Warren E. Miller. (1979). "Ideological Interpretations of Presidential Elections." *American Political Science Review*, 73: 751–771.

Levy, Jack S. (1992a). "Introduction to Prospect Theory." *Political Psychology*, 13: 171–186.

(1992b). "Prospect Theory and International Relations: Theoretical Applications and Analytical Problems." *Political Psychology*, 13: 283–310.

Lodge, Milton, and Ruth Hamill. (1986). "A Partisan Schema for Political Information Processing." *American Political Science Review*, 80: 505–519.

Lodge, Milton, Kathleen McGraw, and Patrick Stroh. (1989). "An Impression-Driven Model of Candidate Evaluation." *American Political Science Review*, 83: 399–419.

Miller, Arthur H., Martin P. Wattenberg, and Oksana Malanchuk. (1986). "Schematic Assessments of Presidential Candidates." *American Political Science Review*, 80: 521–540.

Page, Benjamin I. (1978). *Choices and Echoes in Presidential Elections.* Chicago: University of Chicago Press.

Patterson, Thomas E., and Robert D. McClure. (1976). *The Unseeing Eye: The Myth of Television Power in National Politics.* New York: Putnam.

An Experimental Study of a Political Campaign

Payne, John W. (1976). "Task Complexity and Contingent Processing in Decision Making: An Information Search and Protocol Analysis." *Organizational Behavior and Human Performance*, 16: 366–387.

———. (1982). "Contingent Decision Behavior." *Psychological Bulletin*, 92: 382–402.

Payne, John W., James R. Bettman, and Eric J. Johnson. (1992). "Behavioral Decision Research: A Constructive Processing Perspective." *Annual Review of Psychology*, 43: 87–131.

Payne, John W., and M. L. Braunstein. (1978). "Risky Choice: An Examination of Information Acquisition Behavior." *Memory and Cognition*, 22: 17–44.

Popkin, Samuel L. (1991). *The Reasoning Voter: Communication and Persuasion in Presidential Campaigns*. Chicago: University of Chicago Press.

Redlawsk, David P. (1992). "Using Hypermedia to Develop a Political Science Simulation." Paper presented at the 25th annual conference of the Association of Small Computer Users in Education (ASCUE), Myrtle Beach, South Carolina.

Russo, J. Edward, and Barbara A. Dosher. (1983). "Strategies for Multiattribute Binary Choice." *Journal of Experimental Psychology: Learning, Memory, and Cognition*, 9: 676–696.

Svenson, O. (1979). "Process Descriptions of Decision Making." *Organizational Behavior and Human Performance*, 23: 86–112.

von Neumann, John, and Oscar Morgenstern. (1944). *Theory of Games and Economic Behavior*. New York: Wiley.

6

Political Accounts and Attribution Processes

KATHLEEN M. MCGRAW*

Whether alcohol was a factor in these incidents, I do not know. In any event, alcohol at best can only be a partial explanation.
(Senator Bob Packwood, November 27, 1992, in response to allegations of sexual misconduct)

As I told the Tower board, I didn't know about any diversion of funds to the Contras. . . . No one kept proper records of meetings or decisions. This led to my failure to recollect whether I approved an arms shipment before or after the fact. I did approve it; I just can't say specifically when.
(President Ronald Reagan, March 4, 1987, speech on his role in the Iran-Contra affair)

I wanted to support Clarence Thomas. The polls in the state clearly favored him. . . . From a political standpoint, I badly wanted to vote for Clarence Thomas. However, my conscience wouldn't let me do it. I thought she [Anita Hill] was telling the truth.
(Senator Harry Reid, October, 16, 1991, after the Senate confirmation vote for Clarence Thomas's nomination to the Supreme Court)

It's no big deal, it's not like molesting young girls and young boys.
(Representative Charles Wilson, March 1992, after it was revealed that he had eighty-one checks overdrawn at the House of Representatives' Bank)

I made the decision. I'm accountable. The buck stops with me.
(Attorney General Janet Reno, April 19, 1993, after the Branch Davidians' deaths in Waco, Texas)

* A number of people provided assistance in various ways with the experiments described in this chapter: Sam Best, Gabor Bruck, Dave Moskowitz, Sandra Moskowitz, Howard Scarrow, Jeff Segal, George Serra, Chuck Taber, and especially, Richard Timpone. I am grateful for their help.

Political Accounts and Attributions

Politicians are frequently called upon to explain their actions because accountability – the principle that elected and appointed public officials are responsible to the people for their actions – is a critical feature of democratic political life. Accordingly, understanding both how public officials respond to accountability pressures and how citizens respond to these verbal "performances"[1] should be of the utmost importance to political researchers. The focus of this chapter is on one aspect of this problem, namely, how political explanations or accounts influence reactions to officials involved in accountability predicaments.

The chapter is organized into four sections. First, the role of attribution processes in social psychological and political research is outlined briefly. I then discuss a number of important conceptual distinctions regarding political accountability. Third, results from a number of studies examining how accounts influence attributions of responsibility and political character are described. In the conclusion, I speculate about a number of factors that might account for why political blame-management strategies frequently fail.

ATTRIBUTION PROCESSES IN SOCIAL AND POLITICAL JUDGMENT

"Attribution theory" in social psychology is actually a collection of diverse theoretical contributions unified by the goal of understanding how the social perceiver uses information to arrive at causal understandings of events, that is, understanding why something happened (see Fiske and Taylor, 1991, for a good recent review). Attribution processes, then, are the means by which individuals make sense of the world around them. Arguably the dominant theoretical perspective in social psychology in the 1960s and 1970s, attribution theory has continued to be influential because it has provided a "hospitably flexible" framework (Jones, 1985) for the understanding of a wide variety of empirical phenomena.

Although much attribution research has been concerned with causal understandings, narrowly defined, the more general notion of "making sense" underlying this theoretical approach implicates other inferential processes. As foreshadowed in the earliest writings on attribution processes (Heider, 1958), it is clear that in making sense of most important social events, people are concerned not only with understanding what

---

1 The theatrical allusion is deliberate, a nod to Erving Goffman's influence on theories of impression management. Goffman defined "performances" as "all the activity of a given participant on a given occasion which serves to influence in any way any of the other participants" (1959, p. 15).

Kathleen M. McGraw

caused the event to occur, but also with attributing *responsibility* for the event. The central meaning of the word "responsible" (in lay understanding) is "answerable, accountable to another for something" (*Oxford English Dictionary*). Because accountability of conduct is a linchpin of the relationship between public officials and the citizens they represent, attributions of responsibility should be a critical and consequential component of citizens' reasoning about political events (Iyengar, 1991).

The importance of citizens' attributions of responsibility for political problems is well supported by the empirical literature on electoral choice and public opinion (e.g., Feldman, 1985; Iyengar, 1987, 1989, 1990, 1991; Kluegel and Smith, 1986; Peffley, 1985; Sniderman, Hagen, and Tetlock, 1986; Thompson, 1980, 1987). The topic deservedly has attracted attention because the evidence indicates that perceptions of responsibility mediate evaluations of political figures (e.g., Abramowitz, Lanoue, and Ramesh, 1988; Feldman, 1985; Iyengar, 1987; Tyler, 1982) and are critical determinants of issue opinions (Iyengar, 1989, 1991). However, the bulk of the empirical literature to this point has been concerned with citizens' attributions of responsibility for broadly defined political and social problems, such as economic conditions, crime, terrorism, and racial inequality. Although valuable, this focus has ignored the question of how citizens' attributions of responsibility for specific or discrete actions of public officials, such as a policy vote or an act of misconduct, are shaped. These discrete actions are important because they constitute much of the "raw material" of citizens' impressions of political actors (Lodge, McGraw, and Stroh, 1989). Indeed, as I've argued elsewhere (McGraw, 1991), a central challenge for models of candidate evaluation and electoral behavior lies in specifying how citizens react to specific behaviors of elected officials and in identifying how these act-specific reactions contribute to more global impressions.

In setting the stage for understanding the role of act-specific attributions in political reasoning, two points must be underscored. The first is that attribution processes are inherently dynamic, constantly under revision as new information – such as accounts – becomes available. Indeed, individuals explain their actions to others in order to influence the answers reached to "why" questions. Account givers have a great deal of creative leeway in constructing accounts in a way that will present themselves in the most positive light. Nowhere is this more evident than in the domain of politics. A central assumption of our research is that politicians are not passive bystanders in the electoral process. Rather, they engage in a variety of strategic behaviors (Jacobson and Kernell, 1983), including trying to influence their constituents' perceptions of political events through explanations of legislative and other activities (Stone, 1989). Accounts are instrumental in shoring up the approval of those to whom they are accountable, and hence are a critical technique in the strategic repertoire of politicians.

The other important issue is that "responsibility" is an elusive concept, with many meanings, encompassing a number of potential judgments (Fincham and Jaspars, 1980; French, 1991; Hamilton and Laurence 1979; Hamilton, 1980; Hart, 1968; Peffley, 1985). There is considerable evidence that people respond to questions about "causality," "responsibility," "blame," and "punishment" in different ways (e.g., Critchlow, 1985; Fincham and Jaspars, 1979; Fincham and Schultz, 1981; McGraw, 1985, 1987). "Attribution of responsibility," as used in this chapter, does not refer to a simple judgment of causality for some event but rather to a broader judgment of moral disapproval (blame) or approval (credit) for some action. This is not to deny that attributions of causality are irrelevant. To the contrary: judgments of moral responsibility of this sort frequently presuppose a judgment of causality (Fincham and Jaspars, 1980; McGraw, 1987). However, the focus in our empirical work (conceptually and operationally) has been on responsibility as a moral rather than a causal judgment.

CONCEPTUAL PARAMETERS IN THE STUDY OF POLITICAL ACCOUNTABILITY

"Political accountability" is a construct that is rich and varied in meaning. At this point, I describe some of the key conceptual parameters in order to stake out the theoretical space our research to this point has occupied, as well as to illustrate the vast potential for other avenues of research in this area.

Timing of Accountability Pressures

The first important parameter concerns *when* accountability pressures are manifested. Goffman, in his theory of "face" (i.e., "the positive social value a person effectively claims for himself," 1959, p. 213), identified two distinct strategies used in "facework." The first, "preventive practices," are those used prior to making a decision, in *anticipation* of an audience's response to some activity, as a means of avoiding criticism and blame. Predecisional accountability was also emphasized by C. Wright Mills when he argued, "Often anticipations of acceptable justifications will control conduct. ('If I did this, what could I say? What could they say?') Decisions may be, wholly or in part, delimited by answers to such queries" (1940, p. 906). In contrast are "corrective practices," which occur *after* a decision has been made or action performed that others find to be inappropriate. Postdecisional accountability of this sort is *reactive*, in response to some audience's actual disapproval or fault-finding with a decision.

The role of predecisional accountability is well established in the congressional literature, where it has been frequently noted that legislators' voting decisions are influenced by their need to eventually justify their decisions to their constituents (Arnold, 1990; Austen-Smith, 1992; Fenno, 1978; Fiorina and Shepsle, 1989; Kingdon, 1981; Mayhew, 1974; Weaver, 1986, 1988). For example, Kingdon (1981) argued that legislators try to anticipate how specific roll-call votes might be used against them and then adjust their votes in order to forestall such electoral problems. In a similar vein, Weaver's (1986, 1988) analysis of "blame-avoidance" strategies is based on the premise that a primary motivation of public officials is to avoid blame, and he describes a number of strategies used by politicians to avoid blame-generating situations (e.g., nonvoting, agenda control, and issue ambiguity). Predecisional accountability also figures strongly in Arnold's (1990) theory of congressional policy making, where he argues that legislators, estimate the probability that their constituents will be able to draw a causal link between a policy vote and some set of outcomes, before choosing between policy alternatives. There is little reason to doubt that legislators, for the most part, cope with the pressures associated with predecisional accountability fairly well, reasonably estimating their constituents' concerns and choosing the optimal – for purposes of electoral security – alternative. Consistent with this presumption, Tetlock's (1992) research leads him to conclude that predecisional accountability usually, but not inevitably, promotes a "forward-looking rationality" and vigilant analysis of options.

In contrast, postdecisional accountability comes into play after a decision has been made and the consequences experienced (psychologically if not concretely) by some constituency or audience. If the consequences are positive or the decision is otherwise positively evaluated, the decision maker will frequently attempt to capitalize through a variety of credit-claiming strategies (Fenno, 1978; Fiorina, 1977; Kingdon, 1981; Mayhew, 1974) or what Schlenker (1980) labeled "acclaiming tactics." If, however, avoidance of a blame-generating situation is not possible – either through a miscalculation of probable consequences, political constraints, an inability to appease diverse constituency groups, or plain bad judgment – and the consequences are negative, subsequent accountability pressures frequently force the decision maker to invoke damage-control tactics to rectify the predicament. I have referred to these "after-the-fact" damage control tactics as "blame-management" strategies (McGraw, 1991); our subsequent research has also been concerned with these postdecisional accounts. In contrast to the vigilant rationality that marks predecisional accountability, Tetlock (1992, p. 345) characterizes postdecisional accountability predicaments as marked by "a defensive search for ways of rationalizing past conduct." This raises the possibility, to which I will return in the chapter's conclusion, that many political accounts may be substantially biased by motivational concerns.

Precipitating Events

Communication theorists generally favor the term "failure event" to denote the specific alleged behavior for which an actor must account (e.g., Cody and McLaughlin, 1990; Schonbach, 1980; although Schonbach, 1990, more recently has used the phrase "account episode"). Impression management theorists in social psychology, on the other hand, have used the term "social predicament," defined as "any event that casts undesired aspersions on the lineage, character, conduct, skills, or motives of an actor" (Schlenker, 1980, p. 125; Tedeschi and Reiss, 1981). Because the latter better corresponds to everyday language and understandings, I adopt that terminology and use "political predicament" to refer to any event linked to a political actor or actors that results in criticism or disapproval from some valued audience (most often constituents, but also the media and other politicians). Political predicaments inevitably occur when an official's actions violate some set of normative expectations. It is the violation of these expectations that leads to criticism and demands for an explanation – "Why did you do X when you should have done Y" or "Why did you do X when you should not have done it?" – which, in turn, forces the politician to provide an account. Political predicaments virtually always involve a violation of role-based expectancies, that is, failure of the representative to do what he or she *should* have done (Hamilton, 1978). Two broad classes of political predicaments exist. The first involves a failure to satisfy the requirements inherent in the representational relationship that exists between the politician and his or her constituents. Representation implies "acting in the interest of the represented, in a manner responsive to them.... The representative must act in such a way that there is no conflict, or if it occurs an explanation is called for" (Pitkin, 1967, pp. 209–210). These violations occur when an official makes a decision, such as voting for some policy that has or could have a negative impact on some constituent group or that violates the cherished values of some segment of the constituency. In either case, the official's decision, made in the course of normal role-related obligations, conflicts with the desires of at least some constituents. Predicaments of this sort, which form the basis of the research described later, have an

Kathleen M. McGraw

important characteristic: namely, that the votes are virtually always verifiable. Denial ("I did not vote for that bill") is rarely a viable blame-management strategy.

Virtually all of the existing empirical and theoretical literature on political accounts – anticipatory and reactive – has similarly been concerned with "explaining the vote" (Kingdon, 1973). The other important type of predicament, in which public officials seem to increasingly find themselves, involves acts of personal misconduct (i.e., corruption and scandal). In contrast to predicaments involving unpopular policy decisions, acts of corruption and scandal occur when officials step beyond the bounds of appropriate (or what perceived as appropriate) behavior. However, empirical research on political explanations for scandalous or corrupt acts, despite the timeliness of the topic, is relatively rare (Chanley, Sullivan, Gonzales, and Kovera, 1994; Gonzales, Kovera, Sullivan, and Chanley, 1995; Riordan, Marlin, and Kellogg, 1983).

Types of Accounts

Distinctions among various types of accounts can be made at two levels. At the first, more general level, the term "account" has been applied to a variety of different linguistic phenomena (see Antaki, 1981, and Fincham, 1992, for discussions). Whereas many researchers have adopted Scott and Lyman's definition of an account as "a statement made by a social actor to explain unanticipated or untoward behavior" (1968, p. 46), others view accounts as "people's explanations, presented in storylike form, for past actions and events that include characterizations of self and key others in plots" (Harvey, Orbuch, and Weber, 1990, p. 192; Harvey, Weber, and Orbuch, 1990; see also Bennett, 1992; Pennington and Hastie, 1986). The central role of explanation is an obvious similarity to both perspectives. There are also important differences. The first perspective views accounts as strategic, relatively simple explanatory statements used to "repair" damaged reputations; these accounts necessarily are provided in an interpersonal context. In contrast, the "storytelling approach" views accounts as complex narrative packages that people use to make sense of social interactions. These narrative accounts are not necessarily linked to interpersonal or conflictual contexts (i.e., the stories we construct for ourselves to make sense of our life experiences).

Politicians undoubtedly make use of both simple explanatory statements and more complex narratives in accounting for predicaments. A reasonable assumption is that more complex and serious predicaments are accompanied by more complex accounts. For example, explaining a policy vote does not require a lengthy narrative; a fairly straightforward explanation should suffice. On the other hand, consider Sen. Edward Kennedy's task in accounting for his involvement in Mary Jo Kopechne's death at Chappaquiddick in 1969: an acceptable account would have had to address, like a short story, where they had been, where they were going, the time delay between the accident and making a police report, and so on. It is also the case that the media "sound bite" practices reduce more complex accounts to briefer statements, so that what most citizens actually are exposed to is a shortened version of the actual account. That practice, of course, raises an interesting philosophical (like the falling tree in the forest) and empirical (in terms of estimating their impact) question, namely, which should be regarded as the real account: that provided by the politician or that reported by the media?

Our own work on accounts has adopted the simpler explanatory statement perspective (as has most recent research on interpersonal accounts, e.g., Chanley et al., 1994; Cody and McLaughlin, 1990; Gonzalez, 1992; Gonzales, Haugen, and Manning, 1994; Gonzales et al., 1995; Gonzalez, Manning, and Haugen, 1992; Gonzales, Pederson, Manning, and Wetter, 1990; McLaughlin, Cody, and French, 1989; Schonbach, 1990; McLaughlin, Cody, and O'Hair, 1983; Sigelman, Sigelman, and Walkosz, 1992; Weiner, Amirkhan, Folkes, and Verette, 1987; Weiner, Figueroa-Munoz, and Kakihara, 1991; Weiner, Graham, Peter, and Zmuidinas, 1991). Within this perspective, a number of typologies of accounts have been proposed (e.g., Goffman, 1971; Schlenker, 1980; Schonbach, 1990; Scott and Lyman, 1968; Snyder, 1985; Snyder and Higgins, 1988; Sykes and Matza, 1957; Tedeschi and Reiss, 1980; Tetlock, 1985). There is widespread agreement that four types of accounts are fundamental. *Concessions* involve an acknowledgment that the negative event occurred and an implicit or explicit assumption of responsibility for the event (e.g., Atty. General Reno's Waco statement at the start of this chapter); concessions also often include expressions of regret, apologies, and even offers of restitution. *Excuses*, like concessions, acknowledge that an offense has occurred but involve a denial of full or partial responsibility. Common political excuses include denial of intent or foreseeability (e.g., Reagan's Iran-Contra excuse), diffusion of responsibility to other actors, and claims of mitigating circumstances (e.g., Packwood's alcoholism excuse). The third account type, *justifications*, are characterized by attempts to deny or minimize the negative or undesirable nature of the event. Justifications can focus on the actual consequences of the act (e.g., Congressman Wilson's questionable justification for his overdrafts) or on normative principles through which the event may be reinterpreted (e.g., Senator Reed's conscience justification). Finally, *denials* or *refusals* are possible, in which the actor does not explain but rather denies his or her involvement in the event. These four

EVENT NEGATIVE?

		YES	NO
ACTOR	YES	CONCESSION	JUSTIFICATION
FULLY RESPONSIBLE?	NO	EXCUSE	DENIAL

Figure 6.1. A typology of accounts.

are generally regarded as superordinate strategies, each of which contains a number of subordinate variants. Schonbach's (1990) typology represents the most elaborate classification scheme, including more than 100 subcategories of accounts.

As summarized in Figure 6.1, the four accounts can be conceptualized within a 2 × 2 framework, based upon how the account giver responds to two key "accusations" about the predicament. If a person finds him- or herself in a predicament, the reproaching audience is really making two accusations: (1) some negative or undesirable event has occurred, and (2) you – the person being criticized – are responsible for the consequences. Thus, the first dimension is concerned with perceptions of the negativity of the event: concessions and excuses acknowledge the negativity of the event, whereas justifications and denials minimize the negative connotations. The second dimension concerns the actor's level of responsibility for the event: concessions and justifications implicitly or explicitly admit responsibility, whereas excuses and denials involve attempts to minimize or deny personal responsibility.

In the research summarized later, we have focused on the two types of accounts that have received the most theoretical attention (following Austin's, 1961, and Scott and Lyman's, 1968, influential papers), and that also appear to be most common in everyday social discourse (Cody and McLaughlin, 1990): excuses and justifications. Bennett (1980) similarly points to excuses and justifications as being the two critical types of political accounts. Excuses and justifications are particularly prominent accounts when explaining controversial policy votes, if only by default. As noted earlier, denial certainly would not be credible when a record of the vote exists. Concessions, by themselves, do not satisfactorily answer the "why" question and therefore also seem to be unlikely strategies in "explaining the vote."

Functions of Accounts

Finally, it should be noted that accounts serve multiple functions (cf. Schlenker and Weigold, 1992; Weiner, Figueroa-Munoz, and Kakihara, 1991, for extended discussions). Although most theorists would agree that accounts are designed to repair damaged reputations, there is some disagreement regarding the relevant audience for realizing that goal. At the risk of gross oversimplification, two goals appear to be central. The first, the *personal identity motive* (Tetlock, 1985), is concerned with the internal audience in that the account giver is primarily concerned with self-enhancement (i.e., decreased depression, increased self-esteem) following the "failure event" (Snyder and Higgins, 1988, best represent this viewpoint). In contrast, the *social identity motive* (Tetlock, 1985) is directed to the external audience in that the account giver is primarily concerned with changing the opinions of those important others who have a negative reaction to the predicament. I have assumed that because electoral security is a dominant motivation for elected officials (Mayhew, 1974), political accounts primarily serve the latter function: accounts are instrumental in maintaining the approval of important constituent groups. This does not mean that accounts do not also provide internal psychological benefits for politicians (see Snyder and Higgins, 1989, for a discussion of President Reagan's "renewed sense of optimism" following his Iran-Contra speech), but these kinds of psychological consequences are obviously less amenable to systematic analysis.

In addition to these "identity" motives, different types of accounts also serve specific functions in terms of their impact on various judgments. Most relevant to the present concerns, an excuse is an attempt by the account giver to challenge perceptions of responsibility for the event, as suggested by the framework in Figure 6.1. This suggests that excuses, if acceptable, should result in a reduction of blame. In contrast, a successful justification serves the function of making the event seem less negative (or even positive); attributions of responsibility are less affected by justifications. (See McGraw, 1991, and McGraw, Best, and Timpone, 1995, for extended discussions of these processes.)

RESEARCH OVERVIEW AND EMPIRICAL RESULTS

The study of accounts in political predicaments can, and should, involve a variety of methodological approaches. In the studies summarized in this chapter, we adopted a "top-down," deductive approach, wherein the

Kathleen M. McGraw

stimulus accounts and research hypotheses evolved out of the conceptual distinctions and typology described earlier. Specifically, we have focused on excuses and justifications, examining their effectiveness in ameliorating the negative consequences resulting from a representative's vote for some policy that has a real or imagined negative impact on some constituency group.[2]

We have also chosen to take advantage of the strengths inherent in the experimental method – that is, the ability to decompose and isolate complex phenomena in order to test cause-and-effect relationships with precision (Kinder and Palfrey, 1992; McGraw, 1996). It can be enormously difficult, if not impossible, to disentangle the effects of a politician's behavior and subsequent explanations in a naturalistic context, making it next to impossible to weigh the independent impact of a politician's words and deeds. Experimentation permits estimation of the independent impact of what the politician says (i.e., the accounts), his or her characteristics, characteristics of the controversial policy, and characteristics of the constituent recipients. Moreover, one of the major goals at the initial stages of this research program is to address hypotheses concerning the effectiveness of political accounts at the micromediational level (e.g., their impact on responsibility and character attributions), a purpose for which experimentation is particularly well suited.

Of course, other methodological approaches are possible and have yielded valuable insights (e.g., intensive case studies [Fenno, 1978] and systematic interviews [Kingdon, 1973] with members of Congress, content analyses of political rhetoric [Sigelman and Walkosz, 1992], and formal modeling [Austen-Smith, 1992; Denzau, Riker, and Shepsle, 1985]). External validation of experimental results ultimately requires corresponding research in the real world. In addition to the top-down experimental approach of the studies described here, research in progress utilizes a bottom-up, inductive approach wherein our goal is to docu-

2 The focus of the studies to this point has been on representatives rather than on other types of politicians, such as executives or appointed officials, for a number of reasons. First, there is a long scholarly tradition concerning explanations as an important strategic device in the congressional repertoire. Moreover, accountability is a critical concept in theories of representation. Finally, a recent experiment by Sigelman, Sigelman, and Walkosz (1992) indicates that citizens react differently to the same explanation, depending on whether the official is a legislator or an executive, suggesting that people may have role-specific expectations about appropriate accounts. Nevertheless, the basic theoretical framework advocated here and elsewhere should be applicable to politicians regardless of their specific role.

ment and clarify, through extensive content analyses, the nature, prevalence, and impact of accounts provided in real, high-stakes political predicaments (e.g., the House Bank scandal).

Five experiments have been conducted since the initially published studies in this research program (McGraw, 1990, 1991). Each experiment has a common procedural core: (1) college student subjects are told to imagine that the official described in fairly detailed, written scenarios is their elected representative in Congress; (2) the representative is described as having voted for some controversial or unpopular policy, also explained in detail; (3) in response to disgruntled constituents, a media question, or a challenger's criticism, the representative is forced to account for his decision; the accounts themselves are systematically manipulated, so that a number of different accounts accompany each predicament; and (4) the subjects react to the various components of the predicament (i.e., the representative, the policy, and the account). The key dependent variables in each study were satisfaction with the account; attributions of credit and blame; character perceptions; and thermometer evaluations of the policy and the representative. The wording and response formats for the dependent variables are provided in Appendix A.

Of course, each of the five experiments were designed to examine specific theoretical questions. Although consideration of these issues is beyond the scope of this chapter, each experiment will be briefly described in order to illustrate its purpose and to provide the reader with identifying labels (capitalized) for the analyses to follow. (Details of each experiment, including the account expressions, are provided in Appendix B.) Two of the experiments drew on Fenno's (1978) "home style" interviews as the source of the accounts, and they were designed to test empirically some of Fenno's intuitions about their effectiveness. The first, the DELEGATE-TRUSTEE study, examined the impact of accounts that typified those two well-known representational styles, in which the official explained that the decision was based either on the expressed preferences of constituents or on his independent judgment (McGraw, Timpone, and Bruck, 1991; see also Sigelman, Sigelman, and Walkosz, 1992). The second, "home style" experiment was designed to explore the implications of INCONSISTENCY between a representative's previously established reputation and a provided explanation (McGraw, Timpone, and Bruck, 1993). Fenno speculated that "the credibility of any given explanation probably depends less on the content of the explanation itself than on its compatibility with some previously established perceptions of the explainer 'as a person'" (1978, p. 149). This hypothesis, that explanations that are inconsistent with an established impression can be politically damaging, was supported by the experimental results.

The third experiment varied the initial impression of the representative (positive, negative, or neutral) in order to determine whether PRIOR SUPPORT cushions representatives from political fallout when voting for unpopular policies or providing poor explanations (McGraw and Timpone, 1994a). The fourth experiment, CONSTITUENT IMPACT, varied the consequences of the targeted policy (changes in education funding), so that some gained and some lost educational funding as a result of the bill's passage (McGraw, Best, and Timpone, 1995). The final experiment varied the GENDER of the politician, as well as gender connotations of the policy and explanation, in order to examine the role of gender stereotypes in the blame-management process (McGraw and Timpone, 1994b).

Before I describe the results of these experiments as they pertain to the impact of the accounts on attributional processes, a brief outline of our conceptualization of how accounts work is in order. (These points are developed in more detail in McGraw, Timpone, and Bruck, 1993, and in McGraw and Hubbard, 1996.) Accounts can profitably be conceptualized as a type of persuasive communication because politicians provide accounts in order to *persuade* their constituents that they deserve continued support, despite the occasional mishap. Accordingly, citizens' reactions to accounts can be understood in terms of the series of steps outlined in McGuire's (1985) chain of responses necessary for successful persuasive communication, including the following: (1) constituents must be exposed to the account; (2) they must pay attention to it; (3) they must understand it; (4) and they must accept the account as legitimate and credible. This fourth step, acceptance, is critical because a person must be satisfied with the account for it to have its desired ameliorative impact. If the explanation is accepted (considered satisfactory), the persuasive communication should be successful and attitudes toward the official accordingly modified. Accordingly, satisfaction with political accounts is a critical component of our model of account effectiveness.

Satisfaction with the Experimental Accounts

As Cody and McLaughlin (1990) make clear in their recent review, the evidence regarding the issue of which of the four types of accounts are more or less effective is decidedly mixed, with seemingly all possible orderings of effectiveness resulting, orderings that appear to vary widely with the context (e.g., interpersonal, legal, and organizational). Moreover, all four account types – concessions, excuses, justifications, and denials – have effective and ineffective variants.

Political Accounts and Attributions

Table 6.1. *Satisfaction with Accounts*

Delegate-Trustee Experiment ($p < .01$)
    Delegate justification: .79
    Trustee justification: .68

Inconsistency Experiment (ns)
    Individualistic conscience justification: .66
    Communitarian conscience justification: .64

Gender Experiment (ns)
    Fairness justification: .52
    Conscience justification: .56

Constituent Support Experiment ($p < .001$)
    Mitigating circumstances excuses: .47
    Benefits justifications: .43
    Normative justifications: .41
    Comparative justifications: .39
    Diffusion of responsibility excuses: .30
    Plea of ignorance excuse: .21

Constituent Impact Experiment ($p < .001$)
    Benefits justification: .43
    Normative justification: .42
    Mitigating circumstances excuse: .40
    Party loyalty: .35
    Worse-case comparison justification: .33
    Diffusion of responsibility excuse: .22

Note: See Appendix B for the complete wording of the accounts. Satisfaction ranges from o to 1, with higher values reflecting more satisfaction. The midpoint of the scale is .5, so that values lower than the midpoint indicate *dis*satisfaction. The p-values for each experiment indicate the level of statistical significance of the differences among the means (ns = not significant, $p > .05$).

Table 6.1 summarizes the levels of satisfaction with the various political justifications and excuses expressed in our experiments.[3] It is clear that some accounts work better than others and that some accounts fail miserably, at least in explaining controversial policy votes. Four general

---

3 Because the data have been recoded to a common o to 1 scale, the mean ratings can be compared across experiments. However, this should be done cautiously, as the various parameters of the predicament, such as characteristics of the policy and the representative, both of which influence account satisfaction, vary widely across the five experiments. The means in Table 6.1 are main effects, independent of the impact of the various manipulations included in each study. See the original write-ups of these studies for elaboration of various contingency effects on satisfaction.

Kathleen M. McGraw

conclusions regarding the effectiveness of these types of excuses and justifications in explaining controversial policy decisions can be offered (these conclusions are also supported by the earlier studies: McGraw, 1990, 1991). First, justifications appealing to normative principles – ethical standards like fairness and conscience, as well as appeals relevant to appropriate representational roles – are consistently among the most effective accounts. Second, among justifications challenging the objective consequences of the unpopular policy, those pointing to additional benefits tend to be more acceptable than those that involve abstract comparisons. Third, among the excuses, claims of mitigating circumstances (e.g., the economy, the previous administration) are relatively effective, no doubt reflecting people's understanding that real political decisions are not made in a vacuum but are constrained by external circumstances. Finally, the excuses involving diffusion of responsibility or a plea of ignorance are consistently poor accounts.

I would hasten to add that these four conclusions, although apparently robust in regard to explanation of policy decisions, may not hold for other types of political predicaments. For example, I suspect that Senator Packwood's explanation alluding to problems with alcohol – an excuse claiming mitigating circumstances, which as a "type" was generally effective in explaining policy votes – did not satisfy most of his constituents. It is undoubtedly the case that very different types of accounts are constructed for different types of political predicaments, and that acceptance of those accounts depends upon a number of situational and psychological factors (see McGraw and Hubbard, 1996, and Sigelman, Sigelman, and Walkosz, 1992, for more detailed discussions).

Attribution of Responsibility: Credit and Blame

Attributions of responsibility for actions invoking normative expectations are usually conceptualized as two distinct judgments that operate in different valence contexts: *blame* for expectation violations and other negative outcomes, *credit* for satisfaction of expectations and positive outcomes. Measurement strategies typically reflect an either/or view of these judgments, such that only one or the other attribution can occur. "Blame" is obviously important in the context of political predicaments, as evidenced by the labels given to the various strategies politicians use to cope with predicaments (e.g., blame management [McGraw, 1991] and blame avoidance [Weaver, 1986, 1988]). Interestingly, little (if any) research in social or political psychology has considered the possibility that both responsibility judgments – credit and blame – can occur for a single event. To the extent that political predicaments are complex, multifaceted events, it is possible that citizens can see both good and bad points in the same situation and attribute credit and blame to an actor simultaneously. For example, an individual may disapprove of a representative's policy vote (and attribute blame) but at the same time admire how the representative accounts for the decision (and attribute credit).

Subjects in our experiments were provided with the opportunity to assign either credit or blame, or to assign both credit and blame to the representative, after learning of the policy decision and account. The resulting data indicate that a substantial percentage prefer to attribute both credit and blame, with an average (across the five studies) of 44.5% of the subjects choosing that response option. This suggests that future researchers should take into account the possibility that subjects' attributions of responsibility for multifaceted predicaments may be considerably more complex than previous theories and research have assumed.

Politicians presumably utilize blame-management strategies in order to shape their constituents' perceptions of responsibility for political events. In line with a persuasive communication perspective on this process, revisions of these attributional judgments are necessarily contingent upon acceptance of (satisfaction with) the account. Of course, attributions of credit and blame should also be a function of other characteristics of the predicament, most obviously, in the present context, evaluations of the controversial policy decision. In order to examine the impact of account satisfaction on attributions of credit and blame, the following model was estimated for the data in each experiment:

$$Y = \beta_0 + \beta_1 \text{ Account Satisfaction} + \beta_2 \text{ Policy Evaluation} + \beta_{i \ldots n} \text{ Accounts}$$

where the dependent variable was alternately attributions of credit and blame,[4] and the predictors the satisfaction ratings, the thermometer ratings of the controversial policy, and dummy-coded terms reflecting the direct impact of the accounts (with the number of terms in each model varying, depending upon the number of accounts manipulated within each experiment). The results are summarized in Table 6.2.

There are two important points to be made about the data summarized in Table 6.2. First, there is little evidence that the accounts themselves had a direct impact on attributions of credit and blame, as the direct effects were uniformly weak. Rather, satisfaction with the account provided was critical, consistent with the view that the impact of the

4 The dependent variables are continuous, based on the follow-up "magnitude" questions (see Appendix A). Those who thought the representative only deserved blame were given a credit score of 0; those who thought the representative only deserved credit were given a blame score of 0.

Table 6.2. *Predicting Attributions of Credit and Blame*

	Experiment				
	Delegate/ Trustee	Inconsistency	Constituent Support	Constituent Impact	Gender
DV = CREDIT					
Account Satisfaction	.37*** (.11)	.61*** (.07)	.44*** (.05)	.52*** (.07)	.23* (.11)
Policy Evaluation	.65*** (.11)	.38*** (.07)	.49*** (.04)	.35*** (.07)	−.12 (.14)
Adjusted R^2 (n)	.49*** (75)	.50*** (204)	.33*** (768)	.31*** (322)	.01 (181)
DV = BLAME					
Account Satisfaction	−.46*** (.15)	−.57*** (.08)	−.49*** (.05)	−.49*** (.07)	−.19 (.11)
Policy Evaluation	−.41*** (.15)	−.28*** (.08)	−.45*** (.04)	−.12* (.07)	−.13 (.14)
Adjusted R^2 (n)	.29*** (75)	.38*** (204)	.30*** (768)	.24*** (322)	.03 (181)

Note: The entries are unstandardized regression coefficients, with standard errors in parentheses. All variables were recoded to range from o to 1. The equations also included dummy-coded terms estimating the direct effects of the accounts. These were by and large not significant (all p-values except one >.05), so those coefficients were omitted.

* $p < .05$; ** $p < .01$; *** $p < .001$.

"persuasive appeal" on these judgments is necessarily contingent upon acceptance of the message. Second, the magnitude of the satisfaction effects was uniformly large and, in the case of blame, consistently larger than the impact due to evaluations of the policy. In short, what politicians say (their explanations) has at least as much impact as what they do (their votes) in shaping attributions of responsibility for controversial policy decisions (see McGraw, Best, and Timpone, 1995, for an extended discussion).

Subsequent analyses (not reported in tabular form) of the two studies that included both excuses and justifications (i.e., the CONSTITUENT IMPACT and PRIOR SUPPORT studies) reveal moderate support for the proposition that satisfaction with excuses has a stronger influence on attributions of blame than satisfaction with justifications. Recall that this asymmetrical influence due to account type should occur because excuses explicitly challenge assignment of responsibility, whereas justifications challenge views about the negativity of the event. Separate within-account estimations of the impact of account satisfaction and policy evaluations on assignment of blame indicate that the regression estimates for satisfaction were consistently larger in the excuse conditions than in the justification conditions.[5] Thus, construction of an effective excuse – with the caveat that many excuses are inherently poor accounts – can be a particularly effective strategy in realizing the political goal of minimizing attributions of blame.

Attribution of Political Character

In the service of reaching a meaningful understanding of another's behavior, attribution processes also manifest themselves in perceptions of dispositional, or personality, characteristics (Jones and Davis, 1965). Social psychological research indicates that the attribution of person-ality traits is frequently spontaneous, occurring at encoding without explicit intent or conscious awareness (Uleman, 1987, 1989; Winter and Uleman, 1984; Winter, Uleman, and Cunniff, 1985) and not requiring much in the way of allocation of cognitive resources (Gilbert, Krull, and Pelham, 1988; Gilbert, Pelham, and Krull, 1988). Personality traits are a critical component of social impressions, dominating the content of such impressions relative to other types of information such as physical characteristics and behavioral information (Park, 1986). Surprisingly, as Harvey, Weber, and Orbuch (1990) note, there has been little consideration in the account literature of whether and how accounts influence attributions of trait characteristics. The work of Weiner and his colleagues (1987) is an exception. Those researchers demonstrated that "good" excuses lead to more positive trait perceptions, particularly along personality dimensions most relevant to the predicament context.

Given the prominence of trait attributions in everyday social interaction, it is not surprising that political scientists have also sought to understand how such attributions (usually referred to in the political literature as "judgments of candidate character") are implicated in the evaluation of political candidates (Kinder, 1986; Kinder, Peters, Abelson, and Fiske, 1980; Lau, 1986, 1989; Markus, 1982; Miller, Wattenberg, and Malanchuk, 1986; Rahn, Aldrich, Borgida, and Sullivan, 1991; Stoker, 1993; Sullivan, Aldrich, Borgida, and Rahn, 1990). Four personality dimensions are particularly prominent in politics – leadership, competence, integrity, and empathy – and research indicates that these dimensions are both distinct and consequential in terms of their

---

5 The unstandardized regression coefficients for the excuses and justifications (collapsing across the specific variants) in each study were: for the CONSTITUENT SUPPORT study, .65 for excuses and .42 for justifications; for the CONSTITUENT IMPACT study, .53 for excuses and .43 for justifications.

impact on political evaluations (Kinder, 1986; Miller, Wattenberg, and Malanchuk, 1986). From a blame-management perspective, these character perceptions should play a pivotal role. Officials are concerned not only with minimizing blame for some unpopular decision, but also with persuading their constituents that they are competent and responsive leaders deserving of continued support. In other words, politicians need to convince their constituents that they are of admirable character.

An important question concerns how citizens respond to the "particular and often distinctive things they know about particular leaders" (Kinder, 1986, p. 253) in making character assessments. These judgments no doubt reflect stereotypic beliefs the individual holds about politicians in general, as well as specific information learned about a particular politician. The critical issue involves understanding how citizens respond to new information – such as a legislative vote or an act of misconduct as well as the accompanying accounts – in appraising and revising perceptions of political character. Two plausible hypotheses suggest themselves. The first is that accounts have an impact analogous to a "halo effect" (Cooper, 1981) such that acceptable accounts result in more positive evaluations along all character dimensions, and in a corresponding across-the-board fashion, unacceptable accounts result in more negative character attributions.

The alternative hypothesis, which is congruent with a persuasive communication perspective as well as with Weiner et al.'s (1987) results, suggests that accounts convey dimension-specific information. For example, referring back to the accounts provided at the outset of this chapter, the dimension-specific hypothesis suggests that acceptance of Senator Reid's "conscience" justification for his vote against Justice Thomas would be particularly likely to strengthen perceptions of his moral integrity (with a less striking impact, or no impact, on attributions of competence, leadership, or empathy). According to the same logic, dissatisfaction with Reagan's plea of ignorance regarding the sale of arms to Iran should have weakened perceptions of his competence and mental capabilities, but not necessarily an impact on the other trait dimensions. Note that both the halo-effect and dimension-specific hypotheses imply that citizens are responsive to new information, and that they revise their impressions as new raw material becomes available (Lodge, McGraw, and Stroh, 1989). However, the dimension-specific hypothesis suggests that citizens use evidence, like accounts, to revise their impressions along the most relevant trait dimensions, consistent with Kinder's (1986) claim that the four components of political character are distinct. In contrast, the halo-effect hypothesis suggests that citizens revise their impressions along all dimensions in an upward or downward fashion, suggesting a lack of differentiation among the various components.

The four dimensions of political character – competence, leadership, integrity, and empathy – were assessed in each experiment, based on the National Election Studies (NES) multitrait item questions. These data were analyzed by multivariate analyses of variance (MANOVA), incorporating the independent variables manipulated in each study (most important, the account) and the four trait judgments analyzed as the repeated measure variable. Support for the halo-effect hypothesis would be manifested by a statistically significant main effect for the manipulated account but no interaction between the account and trait dimension factors (meaning that the accounts had a similar impact, positive or negative, on all of the four traits), whereas support for the dimension-specific hypothesis requires a statistically significant Account × Trait Dimension interaction (meaning that the impact of the accounts, positive or negative, varied for the particular trait judgments). The results from the five experiments are summarized in Figures 6.2 through 6.6.

The character trait data summarized in the figures are presented primarily to illustrate a couple of key points; discussion of the details of those results will be kept (mercifully) to a minimum. First and

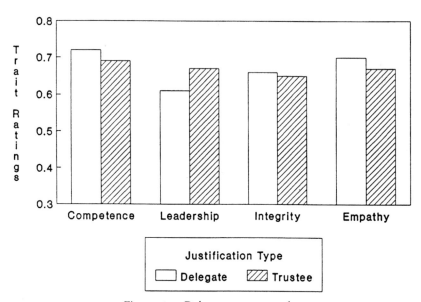

Figure 6.2. Delegate-trustee study.

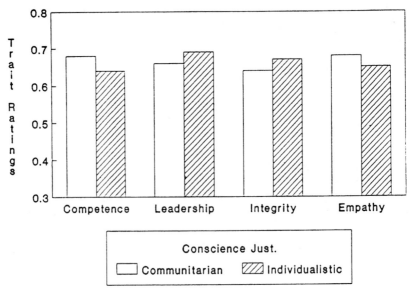

Figure 6.3. Inconsistency study.

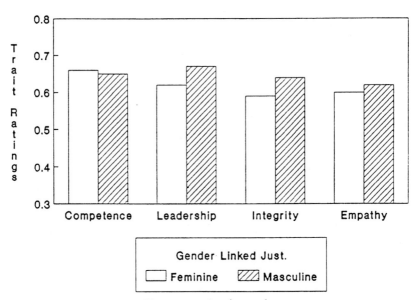

Figure 6.4. Gender study.

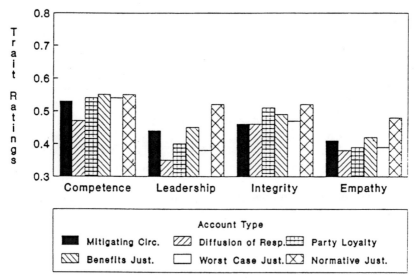

Figure 6.5. Constituent impact study.

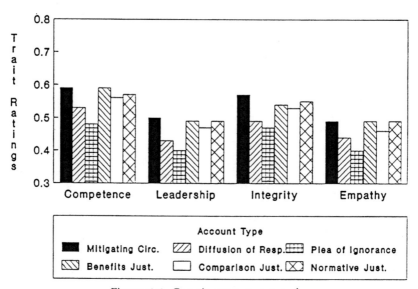

Figure 6.6. Constituent support study.

foremost, the results from four of the five experiments lend support for the dimension-specific hypothesis, as the Account × Trait Dimension interaction effects were significant; the exception is the PRIOR SUPPORT study.[6]

The accounts in three of the experiments (Delegate-Trustee, Inconsistency, and Gender; Figures 6.2–6.4) had a common conceptual basis in that all three compared the impact of two normative justifications, one of which implied independence and strength (i.e., the trustee justification and the two individualistic conscience appeals, which were judged to be male-stereotypic in the GENDER study), the other attentiveness to constituent concerns (i.e., the delegate justification, communitarian conscience appeal, and "fairness for all" justification, judged to be female-stereotypic). The "independent judgment" justifications consistently enhanced attributions of leadership (composed of the traits "commands respect," [not] "easily influenced," [not] "weak," and "inspiring"). In contrast, in two of the three cases, the more "communitarian," socially responsive justifications (the delegate justification, Figure 6.1, and the communitarian conscience appeal, Figure 6.2) increased attributions of empathy (composed of the traits "compassionate," [not] "out of touch," "really cares"). Interestingly, there was also a trend for those same "responsive" justifications to lead to more positive perceptions of competence ("intelligent," "hard-working," and "qualified"), perhaps because most citizens prefer their political leaders to be responsive to their needs rather than exerting independent judgment (McGraw, Timpone, and Bruck, 1993; Sigelman, Sigelman, and Walkosz, 1992). All in all, the data from the three "normative justification" experiments indicate that character trait inferences are influenced by accounts, particularly along the character dimensions most relevant to the qualities implied by the account.

The fourth study revealing a dimension-specificity effect, the CONSTITUENT IMPACT study (Figure 6.5), included both excuses and justifications. The important result from that study also involves the impact of the normative justifications. Those accounts consistently had a positive impact on all four trait dimensions, but that impact was particularly striking – when considered in comparison with the other five accounts –

---

6 The Account × Trait Dimension interaction effects from each MANOVA: for the DELEGATE-TRUSTEE experiment, $F[3,234] = 3.47$, $p = .017$; for the Inconsistency experiment, $F[3,609] = 4.52$, $p = .004$; for the CONSTITUENT IMPACT experiment, $F[18,1104] = 2.41$, $p < .001$; for the GENDER experiment, $F[3,771] = 3.09$, $p = .005$. None of these interactions was qualified by higher-order interactions, meaning that the effects were not dependent upon the other manipulated factors in the experiments.

on the dimensions of leadership and empathy, complementing the data from the three other experiments.

The PRIOR SUPPORT study (where the initial impression of the representative was manipulated by presenting information designed to result in a positive or negative first impression) was the only one where the impact of the accounts on the trait attributions was halo-like (actually, a more apt description is "devil-like"). As is evident from Figure 6, the pattern of influence of the six accounts was identical across the four trait dimensions, with the two poor excuses – diffusion of responsibility and a plea of ignorance – resulting in significantly more negative trait judgments than the other four accounts. The reasons for the discrepancy between this study and the other four are not entirely clear. It is not the case that having an established impression of a politician (experimentally manufactured in this study) eliminated the influence of accounts on character attributions, as the poor accounts did have a significant negative impact. Rather, the data suggest that once impressions are "crystallized," the impact of accounts, particularly in a positive direction, is weaker and more diffuse than in a context where impressions are still relatively weak.

Intriguingly, none of the effects described earlier were dependent on satisfaction with the accounts. That is, although account satisfaction consistently had a significant positive association with all of the character attributions, the tendency to attribute strong leadership qualities to an official who presents a "delegate-like" justification (for example) was not moderated by satisfaction with that account – those who were satisfied and those who were dissatisfied judged the representative to possess leadership qualities.[7] This is, of course, in sharp contrast to the responsibility data presented earlier, where account satisfaction was the critical determinant of attributions of credit and blame. It appears that some accounts, in themselves, lead to certain character attributions that are not dependent upon context or satisfaction with the provided account. This conclusion is consistent with the social psychological literature indicating that trait attribution is frequently a spontaneous cognitive process.

Summary

The results of the five experiments indicate that accounts have a systematic influence on attributions of responsibility and character. Four

---

7 To be precise, inclusion of satisfaction in the statistical models yields a main effect for account satisfaction but no significant interactions involving satisfaction. The Account × Trait Dimension interactions, described in footnote 6 remain statistically significant.

patterns were clear in these data. First, people were willing to make both positive (credit) and negative (blame) attributions of responsibility for a single predicament. Second, these attributions were substantially influenced not directly by the account itself, but rather by satisfaction with the account, indicating that acceptance of the persuasive appeal is a critical step in the blame-management process. Third, the accounts generally influenced attributions of political character in a dimension-specific manner: different accounts led to inferences about different dimensions of political character. The impact of accounts on character attributions was particularly prominent when normative justifications were provided.

Finally, the accounts were consequential for the overall evaluations of the politicians in these experiments in a variety of ways (see the original papers for elaboration). First, the attributions – both responsibility and trait – were generally important determinants of these evaluations of the politician, consistent with the political literature concerning the impact of these variables. Second, these evaluations were significantly enhanced when the account was satisfactory. That is, account satisfaction has both direct and indirect (through its impact on attributions of responsibility and other judgments) consequences for evaluations of political actors, indicating that citizens' acceptance or rejection of political accounts is a critical input to their impressions of their elected officials.

DIRECTIONS FOR THE FUTURE: GOALS AND BLAME-MANAGEMENT FAILURES

In a recent review, Schlenker and Weigold noted that "as social psychology has matured as a discipline, it has increasingly endorsed a more dynamic, purposeful, and strategic view of human nature" (1992, p. 134; see also Fiske, 1992). An optimistic view of political psychology is that it will follow along the same path, self-conscious in its recognition that the ever-evolving relationships between political leaders and their constituents are the result of dynamic, goal-driven processes. Politicians engage in a variety of strategic activities in order to shape and influence their constituents' perceptions of political events (Jacobson and Kernell, 1983; Stone, 1989). Citizens' attributions and perceptions, in turn, are also a function of the goals, values, and motivations they bring to the political arena (Lane, 1986; Lau, 1990). Understanding the role accounts play in this multimotive, dynamic process is important because accounts lie at its intersection. That is, their expression is a function of the political and personal goals of the politician, whereas their acceptance is a function of the goals and values of the constituent audience.

Political Accounts and Attributions

As I hope was evident from the delineation of some of the important parameters of political accountability at the outset of this chapter (pre- and postdecisional accountability, role-related vs. ethical predicaments, simple vs. complex narrative accounts, internal vs. external "identity" goals), a number of important issues in this process remain to be examined. At this juncture, let me elaborate on one important "unknown" particularly relevant to understanding blame management as a goal-driven process: the goals politicians bring to the blame game, and their success and failure in attaining those goals. It is patently obvious that politicians are motivated in part by a desire for electoral security (Arnold, 1990; Fenno, 1978; Mayhew, 1974) or, as Kingdon (1981) prefers, "satisfying constituents."[8] But how is this goal – to be liked, positively evaluated, and eventually reelected – translated into specific self-presentational concerns? A number of important questions are at issue here: How do politicians want to be perceived? How do they translate those goals into specific communication strategies? How successful are politicians in achieving their self-presentational character goals? How do politicians accommodate occasionally conflicting goals (e.g., to be truthful ["I made a mistake"] and to convey an impression of strong leadership)?

It is also evident that many accounts, political and otherwise, are unsuccessful. Blame-management strategies often succeed, but they also can fail spectacularly. For example, less than one-quarter of the American public reported being satisfied with the most common explanations that were provided by members of Congress to account for their overdraft checks (Hugick, 1992). To paraphrase Art Linkletter, "politicians say the darndest things!" How can theoretical perspectives characterizing politicians as rational, strategic actors be reconciled with their all-too-common tendency to construct poor accounts? As a way of beginning to address this discrepancy, the distinction between pre- and postdecisional accountability is crucial. Although, as Tetlock (1992) notes, predecisional accountability tends to promote a vigilant, rational analysis of options, "postdecisional accountability – far from encouraging complex, self-critical thought – actually exacerbates many judgmental biases and defects of the cognitive miser" (1992, p. 346). In other words, the likelihood of failure to cope with accountability pressures increases once a predicament has occurred and damage control tactics are necessary.

A number of cognitive motivational biases may be operative when politicians fail to satisfy their goals by constructing unacceptable

---

8 Gaining influence or power within government and enacting good public policy are the two other major goals discussed by congressional theorists (Arnold, 1990; Fenno, 1978; Kingdon, 1981).

Kathleen M. McGraw

accounts (see Ginzel, Kramer, and Sutton, 1992, for an insightful discussion of this issue in the realm of business management). For example,
politicians, like most people, may maintain unrealistically positive views
about themselves (Taylor, 1989; Taylor and Brown, 1988). As a result
of an overly positive self-image, politicians may overestimate the strength
of their reputation in the eyes of their constituents and, as a result, underestimate their constituents' disapproval. In addition, illusions of control
lead people to overestimate their own instrumentality (Langer, 1975),
perhaps leading some politicians to believe, unrealistically, that they can
successfully manage the postpredicament fallout. Finally, negative stereotypes about antagonistic audiences (i.e., hostile constituents, challengers,
and the media) may lead politicians to underestimate and otherwise
devalue the capabilities – "They'll believe anything" – of those receiving
the accounts (Brewer, 1979).

In addition to these psychological factors, a number of external situational forces can contribute to the failure of the blame-management
process. For example, many predicaments are characterized by anxiety
and time pressures to respond, both of which undermine decision quality
(Janis and Mann, 1977). Organizational routines, or standard operating
procedures (March and Simon, 1958) for handling problems, such as
reliance on staff members to deal with predicaments, may also result in
poor accounts if those routines are not sufficiently well established or
not sufficiently responsive to changing public views about accountability and acceptable behavior (Ginzel, Kramer, and Sutton, 1992). Finally,
if a politician's constituents are diverse and heterogeneous, the task of
accounting is even more complex because the interests and concerns of
those "multiple audiences" (Fleming and Darley, 1991) create a communication dilemma: it may be impossible to construct an account that
is acceptable to all audiences. And in attempting to construct accounts
that satisfy all, the result may be an account that satisfies none.

APPENDIX A: MEASUREMENT OF VARIABLES

1. *Account Satisfaction*: How satisfied are you with Cong. _____'s
   explanation of his/her vote?
2. *Attributions of Credit and Blame*: Do you think Cong. _____ is
   deserving of credit for his/her decision to vote for _____, or do you
   think he/she is deserving of blame, or do you think he/she is deserving of both credit and blame? (Follow-up question assessing magnitude anchored "not much at all" and "a great deal.")
3. *Trait Attributions*: Listed here are several characteristics frequently
   used to describe politicians. Please indicate the extent to which you
   agree that each describes Cong. _____, based on what you know

about him/her. (An explicit "don't know" option is provided.) The fourteen traits and resulting scales are given in parentheses:
a. Intelligent, hard-working, and not qualified (competence)
b. Commands respect, easily influenced, weak, and inspiring (leadership)
c. Moral, dishonest, lies to public, and decent (integrity)
d. Compassionate, out of touch, really cares (empathy)
4. *Thermometer Rating of Representative* (following description of scale): Based on what you know about Cong. _____, please indicate your own feelings toward him/her using the feeling thermometer.
5. *Thermometer Rating of Policy*: Based on what you know about _____, please indicate your feelings toward it using the feeling thermometer.

APPENDIX B: SUMMARY OF FIVE EXPERIMENTS

1. Delegate-Trustee Study

Controversial Vote: Housing Programs Authorization Bill
Accounts (from Fenno, 1978): "This was a difficult decision to make. I read my mail carefully, and I talked to people as much as I could . . ."

1. *Trustee Justification*: "I listen to you, believe me. But if I were sitting where you are, I think I would want a man in Congress who will exercise his best judgment on the facts when he has them all. I had all the facts on this housing bill, and I believe the bill will benefit the community. In the end, I used my own judgment as to what is in your best interests."
2. *Delegate Justification*: "I sought out what you the people thought about housing programs. I'm here to represent you, and the feedback I got from my constituents was that the benefits associated with this bill are greater than the disadvantages. I owe it to my constituents to vote according to their feelings, and that is what I did."

2. Inconsistency Study

Controversial Vote: Voted in favor of reprimand (least severe punishment) of Rep. Barney Frank. (Stimulus materials based on the Frank ethics hearings in 1989.)
Accounts (from Fenno, 1978): "I know that many of my friends, in and out of Congress, are displeased with me. I know that some of my longtime supporters will no longer support me . . ."

1. *Individualistic Conscience Appeal*: "But to base this decision on politics and public opinion would violate my own conscience, as to what I feel is the proper course of action. I know this vote may damage my political career. But that pales into insignificance when weighted against my duty to vote as my conscience dictates. Therefore I voted my conscience, against the acknowledged wishes of many of my constituents."

2. *Communitarian Conscience Appeal*: "But I know the people of my district. I am one of you and the issue is our conscience as a community. I imagined how the people of this district would vote if they were in my shoes. We are a compassionate, forgiving people. I have voted as I believe this community would vote, in a compassionate and forgiving manner."

Other Manipulation: Reputation of the representative varied along the "individualistic-communitarian" dimension.

3. Prior Support Study

Controversial Vote: Policy to increase personal income taxes.
Accounts:

1. *Past Mitigating Circumstances*: "I had to vote for the income tax bill because the previous administration's policies crippled our nation's economy; drastic measures had to be taken."

2. *Present Mitigating Circumstances*: "I had to vote for the income tax bill because of the poor shape of the nation's economy; drastic measures had to be taken."

3. *Horizontal Diffusion of Responsibility*: "Although I voted for the income tax bill, I think that it is important to remember that it was a group decision; the bill was passed by a majority of the House of Representatives."

4. *Vertical Diffusion of Responsibility*: "Although I voted for the income tax bill, I think that it is important to remember that its ultimate passage will be due to the President signing it into law."

5. *Plea of Ignorance*: "I voted for the income tax bill, but it was complicated and I did not foresee that it would result in increased income taxes for so many residents of this district."

6. *Present Benefits*: "Although the bill will result in increased income taxes, I think that it is important to remember that the increased revenue brings important benefits to this district."

7. *Future Benefits*: "Although the bill will result in increased income taxes, I think that it is important to remember that the increased

revenue will result in greater economic efficiency that will help this community."

8. *Comparison to Past Circumstances*: "Although the bill will result in increased income taxes, I think that it is important to remember that the tax rates are still generally lower than what they have been in the past."

9. *Comparison to Others*: "Although the bill will result in increased income taxes, I think that it is important to remember that the bill had even more serious consequences in other districts in the nation."

10. *Comparison to Worse Case*: "Although the bill will result in increased income taxes, it could have been a lot worse. Other proposals would have raised taxes even more."

11. *Fairness Justification*: "I voted for the tax bill because I believe the distribution of the tax burden is fairer for all of this nation's citizens than under the current tax scheme."

12. *Conscience Justification*: "I had to follow my conscience in voting for the income tax bill, and therefore I did what I thought was in the best interests of the community and the nation."

Other Manipulation: Reputation of the representative varied (positive, negative, or no prior).

4. Constituent Impact Study

Controversial Vote: Education bill
Accounts: "These kinds of decisions are always difficult . . ."

1. *Mitigating Circumstances*: I didn't feel that I had a choice on this one because a change was necessary. The failure of this nation's previous education policies requires drastic solutions such as those included in the education bill."

2. *Vertical (downward) Diffusion of Responsibility*: ". . . and very complicated. Unfortunately, my staff failed to provide me with complete information about the likely consequences of the bill, and therefore I wasn't made fully aware of all its possible ramifications."

3. *Party Loyalty*: "I agree with the leaders of my party that the passage of this bill is in the nation's best interests, and I voted accordingly."

4. *Normative Justification*: "I voted for the education bill because I believe that under the new allocation criteria the distribution of education funds is fairer, going to those who need the funding the most. I followed my conscience and did what I thought was the right thing to do."

5. *Worse-Case Comparison*: "This education bill could have been a lot worse. For example, other versions of the bill were considered that would have resulted in more serious cuts in funding for this district."

Other Manipulation: Consequences of education bill varied.

5. Gender Study

Controversial Policy: Either foreign sanctions or child care.
Account:

1. *Female-Stereotypic*: "This was not an easy decision to make, but in the end I had to weigh the options and felt that this was the fairest alternative for *everyone* involved."
2. *Male-Stereotypic*: "This was not an easy decision to make, but in the end, while I realize this is not an universally accepted position, I looked at the alternatives and had to do what *I* thought was best for the nation."

Other Manipulation: Sex of the representative.

References

Abramowitz, Alan I., David Lanoue, and Subha Ramesh. 1988. "Economic Conditions, Causal Attributions, and Political Evaluations in the 1984 Presidential Election." *Journal of Politics* 50:848–863.

Antaki, Charles. 1981. *The Psychology of Ordinary Explanations of Social Behaviour*. London: Academic Press.

Arnold, R. Douglas. 1990. *The Logic of Congressional Action*. New Haven, CT: Yale University Press.

Austen-Smith, David. 1992. "Explaining the Vote: Constituency Constraints on Sophisticated Voting." *American Journal of Political Science* 31:68–95.

Austin, John L. 1961. "A Plea for Excuses." In J. D. Urmson and G. Warnock (eds.), *Philosophical Papers*. Oxford: Clarendon Press.

Bennett, W. Lance. 1980. "The Paradox of Public Discourse: A Framework for the Analysis of Political Accounts." *Journal of Politics* 42:792–817.

1992. "Legal Fictions: Telling Stories and Doing Justice." In Margaret L. McLaughlin, Michael J. Cody, and Stephen J. Read (eds.), *Explaining One's Self to Others: Reason-Giving in a Social Context*. Hillsdale, NJ: Erlbaum.

Brewer, Marilyn B. 1979. "In-Group Bias in the Minimal Intergroup Situation: A Cognitive-Motivational Analysis." *Psychological Bulletin* 86:307–324.

Chanley, Virginia, John L. Sullivan, Marti Hope Gonzales, and Margaret Bull Kovera. 1994. "Lust and Avarice in Politics: Damage Control by Four Politicians Accused of Wrongdoing (or, Politics as Usual)." *American Politics Quarterly* 22:297–333.

Cody, Michael J., and Margaret L. McLaughlin. 1990. "Interpersonal Accounting." In Howard Giles and Peter Robinson (eds.), *Handbook of Language and Social Psychology.* New York: Wiley.

Cooper, W. H. 1981. "Ubiquitous Halo." *Psychological Bulletin* 90:218–244.

Critchlow, Barbara. 1985. "The Blame in the Bottle: Attributions about Drunken Behavior." *Personality and Social Psychology Bulletin* 11:351–363.

Denzau, Arthur, William H. Riker, and Kenneth Shepsle. 1985. "Farguharson and Fenno: Sophisticated Voting and Homestyle." *American Political Science Review* 79:1117–1134.

Feldman, Stanley. 1985. "Economic Self-Interest and the Vote: Evidence and Meaning." In Heinz Eulau and Michael Lewis-Beck (eds.), *Economic Conditions and Electoral Outcomes: The United States and Western Europe.* New York: Agathon Press.

Fenno, Richard. 1978. *Home Style: House Members in their Districts.* Boston: Little, Brown.

Fincham, Frank D. 1992. "The Account Episode in Close Relationships." In Margaret L. McLaughlin, Michael J. Cody, and Stephen J. Read (eds.), *Explaining One's Self to Others: Reason-Giving in a Social Context.* Hillsdale, NJ: Erlbaum.

Fincham, Frank D., and Jos M. Jaspars. 1979. "Attribution of Responsibility to Self and Others in Children and Adults." *Journal of Personality and Social Psychology* 37:1589–1602.

   1980. "Attribution of Responsibility: From Man the Scientist to Man as Lawyer." In Leonard Berkowitz (ed.), *Advances in Experimental Social Psychology* (Vol. 13). New York: Academic Press.

Fincham, Frank D., and Thomas R. Shulz. 1981. "Intervening Causation and the Mitigation of Responsibility for Harm." *British Journal of Social and Clinical Psychology* 20:113–120.

Fiorina, Morris P. 1977. *Congress: Keystone of the Washington Establishment.* New Haven, CT: Yale University Press.

Fiorina, Morris P., and Kenneth A. Shepsle. 1989. "Is Negative Voting an Artifact?" *American Journal of Political Science* 33:423–439.

Fiske, Susan T. 1992. "Thinking Is for Doing: Portraits of Social Cognition from Daguerreotype to Laserphoto." *Journal of Personality and Social Psychology* 63:877–889.

Fiske, Susan T., and Shelley E. Taylor. 1991. *Social Cognition.* New York: McGraw-Hill.

Fleming, John H., and John M. Darley. 1991. "Mixed Messages: The Multiple Audience Problem and Strategic Communication." *Social Cognition* 9:25–46.

French, Peter A. 1991. *The Spectrum of Responsibility.* New York: St. Martin's Press.

Garment, Suzanne. 1991. *Scandal: The Culture of Mistrust in American Politics.* New York: Random House.

Gilbert, Daniel T., D. S. Krull, and Brett W. Pelham. 1988. "Of Thoughts Unspoken: Social Inference and the Self-Regulation of Behavior." *Journal of Personality and Social Psychology* 55:685–694.

Gilbert, Daniel T., Brett W. Pelham, and D. S. Krull. 1988. "On Cognitive Busyness: When Person Perceivers Meet Persons Perceived." *Journal of Personality and Social Psychology* 54:733–739.

Giles, Howard, and W. Peter Robinson (eds.). 1990. *Handbook of Language and Social Psychology*. New York: Wiley.

Ginzel, Linda E., Roderick M. Kramer, and Robert I. Sutton. 1992. "Organizational Impression Management as a Reciprocal Influence Process: The Neglected Role of the Organizational Audience." *Research in Organizational Behavior* 15:227–266.

Goffman, Erving. 1959. *The Presentation of Self in Everyday Life*. Garden City, NY: Doubleday Anchor.

1971. *Relations in Public: Microstudies of the Public Order*. New York: Basic Books.

Gonzales, Marti Hope. 1992. "A Thousand Pardons: The Effectiveness of Verbal Remedial Tactics." *Journal of Language and Social Psychology* 11:133–151.

Gonzales, Marti Hope, Julie A. Haugen, and D. J. Manning. 1994. "Victims as 'Narrative Critics': Factors Influencing Rejoinders and Evaluative Responses to Offenders' Accounts." *Personality and Social Psychology Bulletin* 20:691–704.

Gonzales, Marti Hope, Margaret Bull Kovera, John L. Sullivan, and Virginia Chanley. 1995. "Private Reactions to Public Transgressions: Predictors of Evaluative Responses to Allegations of Political Misconduct." *Personality and Social Psychology Bulletin* 21:136–148.

Gonzales, Marti Hope, Debra J. Manning, and Julie A. Haugen. 1992. "Explaining Our Sins: Factors Influencing Offender Accounts and Anticipated Victim Responses." *Journal of Personality and Social Psychology* 62:958–971.

Gonzales, Marti Hope, Julie Haugen Pederson, Debra J. Manning, and David W. Wetter. 1990. "Pardon My Gaffe: Effects of Sex, Status, and Consequence Severity on Accounts." *Journal of Personality and Social Psychology* 58:610–621.

Hamilton, V. Lee. 1978. "Who Is Responsible? Toward a Social Psychology of Responsibility Attributions." *Social Psychology* 41:316–328.

1980. "Intuitive Psychologist or Intuitive Lawyer? Alternative Models of the Attribution Process." *Journal of Personality and Social Psychology* 39(5):767–772.

Hamilton, V. L., and Laurence, Rotkin. 1979. "The Capital Punishment Debate: Public Perceptions of Crime and Punishment." *Journal of Applied Social Psychology* 9(4):350–376.

Hart, H. L. A. 1968. *Punishment and Responsibility*. Oxford: Oxford University Press.

Harvey, John H., Terri L. Orbuch, and Ann L. Weber. 1990. "A Social Psychological Model of Account-Making in Response to Severe Stress." *Journal of Language and Social Psychology* 9:191–207.

Harvey, John H., Ann L. Weber, and Terri L. Orbuch. 1990. *Interpersonal Accounts: A Social Psychological Perspective*. Oxford: Basil Blackwell.

Hastie, Reid, and Nancy Pennington. 1991. "Cognitive and Social Processes in Decision Making." In Lauren B. Resnick, John M. Levine, and Stephanie D. Teasley (eds.), *Perspectives on Socially Shared Cognition*. Washington, DC: American Psychological Association.

Heider, Fritz. 1958. *The Psychology of Interpersonal Relations*. New York: Wiley.

Hugick, Larry. 1992. "The 'Rubbergate' Scandal." *The Gallup Poll Monthly*. March, pp. 2–4.

Iyengar, Shanto. 1987. "Television News and Citizens' Explanations for National Affairs." *American Political Science Review* 81:815–832.

1989. "How Citizens Think about National Issues: A Matter of Responsibility." *American Journal of Political Science* 33:878–900.

1990. "Framing Responsibility for Political Issues: The Case of Poverty." *Political Behavior* 12:19–40.

1991. *Is Anyone Responsible? How Television Frames Political Issues.* Chicago: University of Chicago Press.

Jacobson, Gary C., and Samuel Kernell. 1983. *Strategy and Choice in Congressional Elections.* New Haven, CT: Yale University Press.

Janis, Irving L., and Leon Mann. 1977. *Decision-Making: A Psychological Analysis of Conflict.* New York: Free Press.

Jones, Edward E. 1985. "Major Developments in Social Psychology During the Past Five Decades." In Gardner Lindzey and Eliot Aronson (eds.), *Handbook of Social Psychology.* New York: Random House.

Jones, Edward E., and Keith E. Davis. 1965. "From Acts to Dispositions: The Attribution Process in Person Perception." In Leon Berkowitz (ed.), *Advances in Experimental Social Psychology* (Vol. 2). New York: Academic Press.

Kelman, Harold C., and Lee H. Hamilton. 1972. "Assignment of Responsibility in the Case of Lt. Calley: Preliminary Report of a National Survey." *Journal of Social Issues* 28:177–212.

Kinder, Donald R. 1986. "Presidential Character Revisited." In Richard R. Lau and David O. Sears (eds.), *Political Cognition.* Hillsdale, NJ: Erlbaum.

Kinder, Donald R., and Thomas R. Palfrey. 1992. "On Behalf of an Experimental Political Science." In Donald R. Kinder and Thomas R. Palfrey (eds.), *Experimental Foundations of Political Science.* Ann Arbor: University of Michigan Press.

Kinder, Donald R., Mark D. Peters, Robert P. Abelson, and Susan T. Fiske. 1980. "Presidential Prototypes." *Political Behavior* 2:315–337.

Kingdon, John W. 1981. *Congressman's Voting Decisions* (2d ed.). New York: Harper and Row.

Kleugel, James R., and Eliot R. Smith. 1986. *Beliefs about Inequality: Americans' Views of What Is and What Ought to Be.* New York: Aldine de Gruyter.

Lane, Robert E. 1986. "What Are People Trying to Do with Their Schemata?: The Question of Purpose." In Richard R. Lau and David O. Sears (eds.), *Political Cognition.* Hillsdale, NJ: Erlbaum.

Langer, Ellen J. 1975. "The Illusion of Control." *Journal of Personality and Social Psychology* 32:311–328.

Lau, Richard R. 1986. "Political Schemata, Candidate Evaluations, and Voting Behavior." In Richard R. Lau and David O. Sears (eds.), *Political Cognition.* Hillsdale, NJ: Erlbaum.

1989. "Construct Accessibility and Electoral Choice." *Political Behavior* 11:5–32.

1990. "Political Motivation and Political Cognition." In E. Tory Higgins and Richard M. Sorrentino (eds.), *Handbook of Motivation and Social Cognition: Foundations of Social Behavior* (Vol. 2). New York: Guilford Press.

Levine, John M., Lauren B. Resnick, and E. Tory Higgins. 1993. "Social Foundations of Cognition." *Annual Review of Psychology* 44:585–612.

Kathleen M. McGraw

Lodge, Milton, Kathleen M. McGraw, and Patrick Stroh. 1989. "An Impression-Driven Model of Candidate Evaluation." *American Political Science Review* 83:399–419.

March, James G., and G. A. Simon. 1958. Organizations. New York: Wiley.

Markus, Gregory B. 1982. "Political Attitudes in an Election Year: A Report of the 1980 NES Panel Study." *American Political Science Review* 76:538–560.

Mayhew, David. 1974. *Congress: The Electoral Connection.* New Haven, CT: Yale University Press.

McGraw, Kathleen M. 1985. "Subjective Probabilities and Moral Judgments." *Journal of Experimental Social Psychology* 21: 501–518.

1987. "Guilt Following Transgression: An Attribution of Responsibility Approach." *Journal of Personality and Social Psychology* 53:247–256.

1990. "Avoiding Blame: An Experimental Investigation of Political Excuses and Justifications." *British Journal of Political Science* 20:119–142.

1991. "Managing Blame: An Experimental Investigation into the Effectiveness of Political Accounts." *American Political Science Review* 85:1133–1158.

1996. "Political Methodology: Research Design and Experimental Methods." In Robert E. Goodin and Hans-Dieter Klingemann (eds.), *A New Handbook of Political Science.* New York: Oxford University Press.

McGraw, Kathleen M., Samuel Best, and Richard Timpone. 1995. " 'What They Say or What They Do?' The Impact of Elite Explanation and Policy Outcomes on Public Opinion." *American Journal of Political Science* 39:53–74.

McGraw, Kathleen M., and Clark Hubbard. 1996. "Some of the People Some of the Time: Individual Differences in Acceptance of Political Accounts." In Diana C. Mutz, Paul M. Sniderman, and Richard Brody (eds.), *Political Persuasion and Attitude Change.* Ann Arbor: University of Michigan Press.

McGraw, Kathleen M., and Richard Timpone. 1994a. "Managing Blame with a Cushion of Support." Unpublished manuscript, SUNY at Stony Brook.

1994b. "Blame-Management Strategies and Gender Stereotypes." Unpublished manuscript, SUNY at Stony Brook.

McGraw, Kathleen M., Richard Timpone, and Gabor Bruck. 1991. "Justifying Controversial Political Decisions: *Home Style* in the Laboratory." Presented at the annual meeting of the Midwest Political Science Association, Chicago.

1993. "Justifying Controversial Political Decisions: *Home Style* in the Laboratory." *Political Behavior* 15:289–308.

McGuire, William J. 1985. "Attitudes and Attitude Change." In G. Lindzey and E. Aronson (eds.), *The Handbook of Social Psychology* (Vol. 2). New York: Random House.

McLaughlin, Margaret L., Michael J. Cody, and Kathryn French. 1989. "Account-Giving and Attribution of Responsibility: Impressions of Traffic Offenders." In Michael J. Cody and Margaret L. McLaughlin (eds.), *The Psychology of Tactical Communication.* Clevedon: Multilingual Matters.

McLaughlin, Margaret L., Michael J. Cody, and H. D. O'Hair. 1983. "The Management of Failure Events: Some Contextual Determinants of Accounting Behavior." *Human Communication Research* 9:208–224.

McLaughlin, Margaret L., Michael J. Cody, and Stephen J. Read (eds.). 1992. *Explaining One's Self to Others: Reason-Giving in a Social Context.* Hillsdale, NJ: Erlbaum.

Miller, Arthur H., Martin P. Wattenberg, and Oksana Malanchuk. 1986. "Schematic Assessments of Presidential Candidates." *American Political Science Review* 80:521–540.

Mills, C. Wright. 1940. "Situated Action and Vocabularies of Motive." *American Sociological Review* 5:904–913.

Park, Bernadette. 1986. "A Method for Studying the Development of Impressions of Real People." *Journal of Personality and Social Psychology* 51:907–917.

Peffley, Mark. 1985. "The Voter as Juror: Attributing Responsibility for National Outcomes." In Heinz Eulau and Michael Lewis-Beck (eds.), *Economic Conditions and Electoral Outcomes: The United States and Western Europe.* New York: Agathon Press.

Pennington, Nancy, and Reid Hastie. 1986. "Evidence Evaluation in Complex Decision Making." *Journal of Personality and Social Psychology* 51: 242–258.

Peters, John G., and Susan Welch. 1978. "Political Corruption in America: A Search for Definitions and a Theory, or If Political Corruption Is in the Mainstream of American Politics Why Is It Not in the Mainstream of American Politics Research?" *American Political Science Review* 72:974–984.

Pitkin, Hanna F. 1967. *The Concept of Representation.* Berkeley: University of California Press.

Rahn, Wendy, John H. Aldrich, Eugene Borgida, and John L. Sullivan. 1991. "A Social-Cognitive Model of Candidate Appraisal." In John A. Ferejohn and James H. Kuklinski (eds.), *Information and Democratic Processes.* Urbana: University of Illinois Press.

Read, Stephen J. 1992. "Constructing Accounts: The Role of Explanatory Coherence." In Margaret L. McLaughlin, Michael J. Cody, and Stephen J. Read (eds.), *Explaining One's Self to Others: Reason-Giving in a Social Context.* Hillsdale, NJ: Erlbaum.

Resnick, Lauren B., John M. Levine, and Stephanie D. Teasley (eds.). 1991. *Perspectives on Socially Shared Cognition.* Washington, DC: American Psychological Association.

Riordan, Catherine A., N. A. Marlin, and R. T. Kellogg. 1983. "The Effectiveness of Accounts Following Transgression." *Social Psychology Quarterly* 46:213–219.

Ross, Lee. 1977. "The Intuitive Psychologist and His Shortcomings: Distortions in the Attribution Process." In Leonard Berkowitz (ed.), *Advances in Experimental Social Psychology* (Vol. 10). New York: Academic Press.

Schlenker, Barry R. 1980. *Impression Management.* Monterey, CA: Brooks/Cole.

Schlenker, Barry R., and Michael F. Weigold. 1992. "Interpersonal Processes Involving Impression Regulation and Management." *Annual Review of Psychology* 43:133–168.

Schonbach, Peter. 1980. "A Category System for Account Phases." *European Journal of Social Psychology* 10:195–200.

——— 1990. *Account Episodes: The Management or Escalation of Conflict.* Cambridge, UK: Cambridge University Press.

Scott, Marvin B., and Stanford M. Lyman. 1968. "Accounts." *American Sociological Review* 33:46–62.

Sigelman, Lee, Carol K. Sigelman, and Barbara Walkosz. 1992. "The Public and the Paradox of Leadership: An Experimental Analysis." *American Journal of Political Science* 36:366–385.

Sigelman, Lee, and Barbara Walkosz. 1992. "Letters to the Editor as a Public Opinion Barometer: The Martin Luther King Holiday Vote in Arizona." *Social Science Quarterly* 73:938–946.

Sniderman, P. M., M. G. Hagen, and P. E. Tetlock. 1986. "Reasoning Chains: Causal Models of Policy Reasoning in Mass Publics." *British Journal of Political Science* 16:405–430.

Snyder, C. R. 1985. "The Excuse: An Amazing Grace?" In Barry R. Schlenker (ed.), *The Self and Social Life*. New York: McGraw-Hill.

Snyder, C. R., and Raymond L. Higgins. 1988. "Excuses: Their Effective Role in the Negotiation of Reality." *Psychological Bulletin* 104:23–35.

Snyder, C. R., and Raymond L. Higgins. 1989. "Reality Negotiation and Excuse-Making: President Reagan's 4 March 1987 Iran Arms Scandal Speech and Other Literature." In Michael J. Cody and Margaret L. McLaughlin (eds.), *The Psychology of Tactical Communication*. Clevedon: Multilingual Matters.

Stoker, Laura. 1993. "Judging Presidential Character: The Demise of Gary Hart." *Political Behavior* 15:193–223.

Stone, Deborah. 1989. "Causal Stories and the Formation of Policy Agendas." *Political Science Quarterly* 104:23–35.

Sullivan, John L., John H. Aldrich, Eugene Borgida, and Wendy Rahn. 1990. "Candidate Appraisal and Human Nature: Man and Superman in the 1984 Election." *Political Psychology* 11:459–484.

Sykes, G. M., and D. Matza. 1957. "Techniques of Neutralization: A Theory of Delinquency." *American Sociological Review* 22:664–670.

Taylor, Shelley E. 1989. *Positive Illusions: Creative Self-Deception and the Healthy Mind*. New York: Basic Books.

Taylor, Shelley E., and J. D. Brown. 1988. "Illusion and Well-Being: A Social Psychological Perspective on Mental Health." *Psychological Bulletin* 103:193–210.

Tedeschi, James T., and Harry Reiss. 1981. "Predicaments and Verbal Tactics of Impression Management." In Charles Antaki (ed.), *Ordinary Language Explanations of Social Behavior*. London: Academic Press.

Tetlock, Philip E. 1985. "Toward an Intuitive Politician Model of Attribution Processes." In Barry Schlenker (ed.), *The Self and Social Life*. New York: McGraw-Hill.

    1992. "The Impact of Accountability on Judgment and Choice: Toward a Social Contingency Model." *Advances in Experimental Social Psychology* 25:331–376.

Thompson, Dennis F. 1980. "Moral Responsibility of Public Officials: The Problems of Many Hands." *American Political Science Review* 74:905–916.

    1987. *Political Ethics and Public Office*. Cambridge, MA: Harvard University Press.

Thompson, Dennis F. 1993. "Mediated Corruption: The Case of the Keating Five." *American Political Science Review* 87:369–399.

Tyler, Tom R. 1982. "Personalization in Attributing Responsibility for National Problems to the President." *Political Behavior* 4:379–399.

Uleman, James S. 1987. "Consciousness and Control: The Case of Spontaneous Trait Inferences." *Personality and Social Psychology Bulletin* 13:337–354.

    1989. "A Framework for Thinking Intentionally about Unintended Thoughts." In J. S. Uleman and J. A. Bargh (eds.), *Unintended Thought*. New York: Guilford Press.

Weaver, R. Kent. 1986. "The Politics of Blame Avoidance." *Journal of Public Policy* 6:371–398.

Weaver, R. Kent. 1988. *Automatic Government: The Politics of Indexation.* Washington, DC: The Brookings Institution.

Weiner, Bernard, James Amirkhan, Valerie S. Folkes, and Julie A. Verette. 1987. "An Attributional Analysis of Excuse Giving: Studies of a Naive Theory of Emotion." *Journal of Personality and Social Psychology* 52:316–324.

Weiner, Bernard, Alice Figueroa-Munoz, and Craig Kakihara. 1991. "The Goals of Excuses and Communication Strategies Related to Causal Perceptions." *Personality and Social Psychology Bulletin* 17:4–14.

Weiner, Bernard, Sandra Graham, Orli Peter, and Mary Zmuidinas. 1991. "Public Confession and Forgiveness." *Journal of Personality* 59:281–312.

Winter, Lorraine, and James S. Uleman. 1984. "When Are Social Inferences Made? Evidence for the Spontaneity of Trait Inferences." *Journal of Personality and Social Psychology* 47:237–252.

Winter, Lorraine, James S. Uleman, and C. Cunniff. 1985. "How Automatic Are Social Judgments?" *Journal of Personality and Social Psychology* 49: 904–917.

7

The Motivated Construction of
Political Judgments*

CHARLES S. TABER
MILTON LODGE
JILL GLATHAR

By one point of view, little remains to be said about voting behavior. A variety of models predict electoral behavior rather accurately, both at the individual and at the aggregate level. But from another point of view, forecasting vote outcomes is not enough. Twenty-seven years ago, Kelley and Mirer (1974: 572) observed that "Our ability to predict how voters will vote is far more solidly based than our ability to explain why they vote as they do." This deficiency, which remains true today, stems from the black box nature of virtually all models of electoral choice, which are based on some form of information processing but are silent about the mechanisms that turn inputs into outputs.

Political psychologists have taken note of the deficiencies of black box models of electoral choice, focusing instead on providing plausible explanations of voting behavior (Boynton and Lodge, 1994; Einhorn, Komorita, and Rosen, 1972; Herstein, 1981; Lodge, McGraw, and Stroh, 1989; Ottati and Wyer, 1990; Rahn, Aldrich, Borgida, and Sullivan, 1990; Taber and Steenbergen, 1995). But this work, our own included, has two key weaknesses. First, we have focused too heavily on the content and structure of beliefs and have paid too little attention to cognitive process. We treat people as passive receptors of information rather than as active, motivated reasoners who interpret information, make inferences, and often choose suboptimally. Second, we have established much too strong a dichotomy between affect and cognition. All social stimuli are affect-laden; indeed, many political choices can result from simple like–dislike judgments (Sniderman, Brody, and Tetlock, 1991). Political reasoning is a motivated process, affected in important ways

* This research was funded by the National Science Foundation under Grant SES-931351.

by goals, expectancies, and prior evaluations (Kunda, 1990; Pratkanis, 1989).

Consider the judgment task citizens face in an election campaign as candidates, image managers, and partisans all attempt to manipulate their impressions and attitudes. Following any political debate, for example, the political allies and campaign staff of each candidate will "spin" a favorable interpretation of the debate in an effort to manage the impact of information on public opinion. Political campaigns are extended attempts at persuasion, including direct personal appeals by the candidates and sophisticated advertising designed by media experts to sway public opinion. But their success varies. What makes some messages more persuasive than others and some people more persuadable? More generally, what factors and processes mediate the impact of political information on individual citizens? Some political and media analysts believe that the public are slaves to media manipulation, while others assert that only certain citizens will be affected and only under special circumstances.

The study of persuasion has a long history in social psychology (see, e.g., Kiesler, Collins, and Miller, 1969; McGuire, 1969). A variety of factors that affect the persuasiveness of a message have been identified in experiments, including various characteristics of the information source, of the message itself, and of the audience (Eagly and Chaiken, 1984; Petty and Cacioppo, 1986). But surprisingly little of this research has found its way into models of political information processing, which remain generally unable to address the basic questions that interest us here: Why do some attitudes persevere in the face of the concerted efforts of expert persuaders, while others seem to fluctuate daily and at the slightest pretext? How do prior opinions and impressions affect the interpretation of new information? And why is counterattitudinal evidence sometimes accepted, though more often rejected out of hand? Unfortunately, from a theoretical perspective, academic research on attitude change provides little more consensus than do media pundits, with one line of research suggesting that attitudes are quite malleable (Eagly and Chaiken, 1984; Petty and Cacioppo, 1986) and another finding strong resistance to persuasive appeals (Wilson and Hodges, 1992).

A plausible explanation for these conflicting results and, we believe, the most promising direction for research on political information processing, derives from the combination of *constructed judgment* and *motivated reasoning*. In this chapter, we will explore recent work on the construction of judgments and the role of motivation in political attitude change. To continue our spin doctor example, the effectiveness of political persuasion rests in large part on the cognitive and motivational processes by which individual citizens process the affect-laden political information presented to them. After briefly reviewing the constructivist view of attitude formation and a simple model of the role of memory structures in this process, we will turn to our main interest in this chapter: the interplay between cognitive processing and motivational bias.

THE CONSTRUCTION OF POLITICAL ATTITUDES

Perhaps the most basic assumption of research on political attitudes and beliefs has been that they exist as crystallized objects in memory. When piqued by experience (or properly phrased survey questions), these attitudes pop into consciousness, fully formed, to guide political behavior (or survey responses). In this theory, the mind is little more than a storage device, with the explicit implication that, once formed and stored, attitudes are reasonably stable and enduring.

While some attitudes are no doubt crystallized, recent research has cast doubt on the traditional theory. The expression of attitudes appears to be very sensitive to a host of extraneous factors – question wording, question sequence, and interviewer characteristics, for example (Bishop, Oldendick, and Tuchfarber, 1978, 1982, 1985) – suggesting that some attitudes are constructed at the time of expression rather than simply being retrieved from memory. In contrast with the traditional "file drawer" view of memory and attitudes, many theorists now argue that the formation and expression of beliefs about people, places, and things is a constructive process (Martin and Tesser, 1992), that there is no single attitude toward an object, but rather multiple considerations whereby the expression of an attitude is dependent on the most salient schematas then available in conscious memory (Boynton and Lodge, 1992; Feldman, 1995; Zaller, 1992; Zanna, 1990).

The basic tenets of the attitude-as-construction argument (Wilson and Hodges, 1992) are:

- People often construct their attitudes rather than simply report the contents of a mental file.
- When people construct their attitudes they have a large data base to draw from, including their behavior, their moods, and a multitude of (often conflicting) beliefs about the attitude object.
- People rarely use the entire data base, instead constructing their attitude from a subset of the data.
- The data people use are influenced by both the social context and the kind of introspection in which they engage. As a result, many attitudes are unstable, momentarily affected by whatever internal or external cues are activated by the situational context.

The Construction of Political Judgments

- The context and the content of people's introspections can lead to consequential changes in attitudes, changes that may be nonoptimal.

Note the qualifiers "often," "sometimes," and "rarely." Given that many citizens do not have the time, energy, information, or motivation to think long and hard enough about most political issues to build crystallized attitudes, their evaluations of things political are often constructed from whatever considerations are available at the time a question is asked or a political decision is made. Currently available memory may not contain the same considerations that weighed heavily on earlier judgments but will reflect what is now salient or plausible, which may depend on immediate contextual cues – for example, the interpretations of media analysts or spin doctors.

Of course, this does not mean that memory is unstructured. Knowledge is built on conceptual associations bundled in memory as schematas, scripts, cases, or frames, which guide inferential reasoning (Bartlett, 1932; Minsky, 1975; Rumelhart and Ortony, 1977; Schank and Abelson, 1977). To illustrate this point, consider again the political spin example. Sophisticated citizens have undoubtedly seen enough political debates to have a basic mental "script" to form expectations and guide their interpretations. This script, derived from experience with prior debates, may contain a mental image of politicians in suits smiling thinly at each other, knowledge of various debate formats (e.g., the classic thesis/rebuttal format or the more recent media question format), expectations about the types of issues that will be discussed or ignored, and some knowledge of postdebate spin doctoring, in which the various analyses of who "won" the debate should not be taken at face value. If political sophisticates in fact have such a knowledge structure crystallized in memory, it will provide a rich source of inferences about the debate, allowing them to establish expectations and interpretations. In addition, it may affect the persuasiveness of both debate and postdebate messages. Of course, other knowledge structures may be active at the time of the debate, including at least partial candidate schemata and more general partisan schemata, all of which may be highly affect-laden. These other knowledge structures may also influence the persuasiveness of partisan appeals or political spin.

In short, many political attitudes appear to be constructed on the spot from the interaction between currently active knowledge structures and information from the environment. Moreover, inferential processes, based on the connections among bits of knowledge and biased by the motivational considerations stored with these knowledge bundles, actively affect the construction of attitudes and judgments in a process Robert Abelson (1963) called "hot cognition."

Charles S. Taber, Milton Lodge, and Jill Glathar

A SIMPLE ASSOCIATIVE MODEL OF ON-LINE CANDIDATE EVALUATION

The associative model proposes that the evaluation of political candidates (and other political objects) is constructed from a relatively simple node-link semantic memory architecture and a still simpler heuristic that tallies up the affective weight of each association in working memory into a global impression (Lodge and Stroh, 1993). This model depicts thinking and reasoning in terms of "elementary information processes" operating on two basic memory structures – a long-term memory and a working memory (Ericsson and Simon, 1984; Sanford, 1986).

"Working memory" is the site of conscious processing. Information must be retrieved from the long-term store and shifted to working memory to be recalled and to affect the processing of new information, including the construction of political attitudes or the production of responses to political surveys. But working memory is transitory and of limited capacity and can only accommodate serial processing (Simon, 1957, 1981). It is the bottleneck of cognition. Decision makers – both elites and ordinary folk – are "bounded rationalists" because of their limited capacity to process information in real time (Simon, 1985).

"Long-term memory," on the other hand, is relatively permanent and unlimited and may be capable of parallel processing. We represent long-term memory as a network of associated nodes, pieces of which may be activated and drawn into working memory for conscious processing. Knowledge of candidates, their traits, issue positions, or abstract concepts that label them may be bundled as configurations of linked nodes. For example, the network fragment depicted in Figure 7.1 associates Clinton with taxes, Democrats, and a lack of sincerity.

In most semantic network models, nodes carry only the cognitive value of the concept they symbolize; that is, they can only represent "cold cognition" (see Taber and Timpone, 1996). But our model posits that each node, in addition to its cognitive content, has an "affective tag" attached to it representing the positive or negative feelings for the node concept. This affective tag can vary with strength of feeling. Figure 7.1 depicts someone with moderately negative affect for Clinton, moderately positive affect for sincerity, and very negative affect for taxes.

"Activation," which spreads along the links in an associative network, represents the degree to which a node has been "energized" as the result of hearing, seeing, or thinking about its concept. Highly activated nodes have the potential to be moved into WM, where information may be consciously processed. Activation spreads among the linked nodes according to three simple rules. First, according to the "exposure rule," external stimuli always activate their matching nodes in long-term

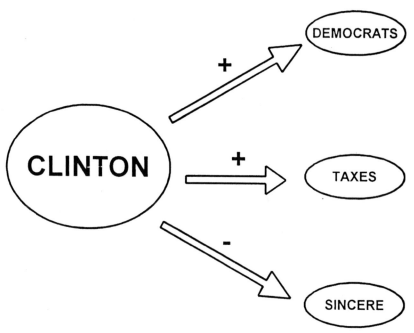

Figure 7.1. A fragment of associative memory.

memory. Second, the "fan rule" asserts that activated nodes spread activation to directly connected nodes, with the amount of activation spread being a function of the strengths of the nodes and links. Finally, activation "decays" very quickly.

At any given moment, memories are differentially accessible because nodes in LTM vary in their node strengths. In Figure 7.1, for example, the nodes CLINTON and SINCERE have greater strength than TAXES, so at this time point, they are more sensitive to activation and hence recall. Following Anderson's (1983) lead, node strength is treated in this model as a function of the number of times the node concept has been thought about in the past (that is, brought into working memory), less a decay factor.

The links connecting nodes, which represent associative beliefs, vary also according to their "implicational relations" (the direction, positive or negative, of the connection between the indicated nodes) and "belief strengths." Both the direction and the strength of beliefs are important in how the information stored in long-term memory affects processing. The more strongly an individual believes that one concept is related to another, the greater the probability that any activation that reaches one of the nodes will spread to the other. Like node strength, belief strength is thought to be a function of frequency of activation less a decay factor.

Once the activated fragments of long-term memory (i.e., considerations) have been brought into working memory, the nature of their associative relations (i.e., their linkages) affects how they are applied to interpret new information, generate evaluations, and guide behavior. And the evaluative implications of the connections drawn among the considerations in working memory as attitudes and beliefs are constructed will determine the direction of their associative relations (positive, negative, or neutral) if they are transferred to long-term memory. For example, the headline "Bill Clinton Proposes New Taxes" may be placed in working memory, interpreted on the basis of the node/link fragments that become activated by thinking about Bill Clinton and about Taxes, and eventually transferred back to long-term memory as a new belief with a positive relation linking Clinton and Taxes.

The on-line (OL) model holds that people form evaluations spontaneously upon exposure to information about a candidate and then immediately integrate the affective charge into a running evaluative tally for the candidate (i.e., the affective tag for the candidate node). Once the evaluative tally has been updated, the actual information may be forgotten, though it need not be. In other words, the information may not be stored in LTM in the candidate schema, though its evaluative impact will alter the candidate's affective tag. OL processing seems to be a pervasive heuristic when one's goal is to form an impression, especially when cognitive resources or motivation to process are low.

This model contrasts sharply with the memory-based (MB) model of candidate evaluation that dominates the political science literature. MB processing suggests that people store information as they are exposed to it, and only later generate evaluations of candidates (or other objects) on the basis of whatever information they can recall at the time an evaluation is called for (for a comparison of OL and MB processing, see Rahn, Aldrich, and Borgida, 1994). Though people certainly do engage in MB processing under some conditions (e.g., when resources, time, and motivation are high, a fairly rare occurrence, we think, for routine political information processing), MB models cannot account for two related puzzles. The first is the "paradox of the ill-informed voter": our discipline's most successful predictive models of vote choice assume a level of informational and procedural sophistication that we know voters do not possess. The second is the "paradox of the forgetful voter": most voters (as well as most experimental subjects) can recount little of the information they were exposed to in a political campaign, yet their evaluations of the candidates reflect the impact of this forgotten information (Graber, 1984; Lodge, Steenbergen, and Brau, 1995).

Both the MB and OL models can be accommodated within the simple associative model we have outlined, as both models rely completely on the exchange of information between long-term and working memory, though the sequence of that exchange differs. The OL model suggests that affective tags for political candidates or other important memory objects are updated on the fly as associations move into and out of working memory, while in the MB model impressions are not formed during initial processing, but are generated later from the mix of information and affect recovered from long-term memory when the citizen is asked for an evaluation. Both are undoubtedly accurate descriptions of information processing some of the time (Sanbonmatsu and Fazio, 1990).

Though most discussion of the OL model has focused on the OL-MB debate described previously, the OL tally is important to our understanding of political behavior for another reason. In addition to providing a summary evaluation of political candidates, OL tallies attached to memory representations of political candidates, parties, important issues, and events serve as affective cues for subsequent information processing. They set the direction and strength of initial motivational goals and can lead to directional bias in judgment processes. They are the source of hot cognition.

Just as campaigns unfold over time, impressions evolve continually as new information is evaluated and integrated into an overall summary impression. Once a judgment is formed (and retrieved when reactivated), it influences subsequent information processing. The simple OL model portrays this as an *anchoring and adjustment process* whereby (depending on various individual and contextual factors) information is turned into evidence on being evaluated in terms of its positive or negative relevance to one's current belief (McGraw, Lodge, and Stroh, 1990). This conversion of information into evidence is a constructive process in that it relies solely on the information selectively drawn from structures in long-term memory and from the external world (e.g., from media coverage of politics or from a highly motivated citizen's active search for information on some important political issue). The adjusted belief then becomes the anchor for subsequent information processing. Following Norman Anderson's lead (1982, 1991), we posit that the revision of impressions is based on an averaging rather than an additive process. A characteristic of averaging models is that they show a curvilinear impact of new information on judgment, what may be called a "discount function," whereby information evaluated early in a sequence has greater impact on the evaluation than would the same information presented later in the sequence. In our model, owing much to Hogarth and Einhorn's (1992) "belief adjustment model," the variable effects of information on judgment can be characterized as a conflict between adaptation and inertia, between the strength of one's anchoring opinion and the impact of new evidence. Beliefs, evaluations, and impressions therefore tend toward inertia, as new information – whether negative or positive – counts less over the course of information flow, hence the oft-noted "perseverance of beliefs" in the face of new, incongruent information (Rothbart 1981).

MOTIVATED POLITICAL REASONING

Despite its advantages, the current version of the OL model fails to explain processing beyond the integration of affect into a global assessment. Though it can account for the finding that information sequence is important, it does not provide a psychologically reasonable account of how the individual converts this information into judgments, or for why some pieces of information have more impact on judgments than others. It does not explain what forces organize information processing. The long and the short of it: our simple model does not treat citizens as active information processors who think about, rationalize, construct, and reconstruct their political worlds based on both prior and new information. The evaluative tally provides a powerful affective cue for the processing of political information, but it is only the beginning of the story.

An illustration should clarify our goal. Consider a hypothetical citizen – John Q. Public (JQP) – making judgments about presidential candidates. JQP has a negative impression of Bill Clinton based on the perceptions that Clinton is untrustworthy and would increase taxes. JQP is aware of his negative evaluation of Clinton, indexed in the OL tally, but the justifications for these feelings may have been forgotten, though if he considered them important at the time of processing, he may have linked them to his representation of Clinton in long-term memory. What will JQP, who strongly supports capital punishment, do on learning of Clinton's support of the death penalty? The OL model predicts that he will update his tally for Clinton, revising his evaluation toward a more positive impression.

But this obviously is not the only possible, or even the most likely, outcome. On the contrary, JQP's evaluation may become more negative or remain unchanged, depending on how he incorporates the new information into his judgment process. The potentially favorable information that Clinton supports the death penalty may be discounted for a variety of reasons. For example, JQP may perceive this support as opportunistic, designed only to capture votes. Or he may discount the importance of the issue and consider Clinton to be out of touch with the electorate. Both of these lines of reasoning allow JQP to retain his prior impression in the face of discrepant information; neither reaction would be predicted from any simple associative model. Our goal in this chapter is to explore the influence of such motivational forces on cognitive information processing. Ultimately, we want to modify the simple model to account for motivated reasoning, including the types of processing illustrated in this example.

Though it has rarely been dealt with explicitly, motivation is not a novel concept for political science. *The American Voter* (Campbell, Converse, Miller, and Stokes, 1960) demonstrated that partisanship acts as a heuristic for guiding many political beliefs. Lazersfeld, Berelson, and Gaudet (1944) also found that individuals tend to talk about politics and interact with people who hold similar political beliefs. Underlying these findings is the notion of consistency in that individuals feel more comfortable when encountering information that is compatible with their opinions. When confronted with dissimilar information, the individual may experience "cognitive dissonance" (Festinger, 1957), which pressures the citizen to reconcile discrepant information and perceptions. Even the Downsian notion of an "economic man" making judgments and decisions to maximize the probability of obtaining a particular set of outcomes is based on a theory of motivation – economic man is motivated to be accurate and complete in information processing.

While these theories speak to but do not directly address the role of motivation in information processing, there has been considerable work in psychology that focuses on the role of motivation in human reasoning. A long-standing debate between researchers who stress the importance of affect and those who stress cold cognittion has dominated this literature. The notion that affect influences attitudes (Festinger, 1957) and attributions (Heider, 1958) is based on the hypothesis that individuals tend to process information in a way that allows them to preserve their prior beliefs and affect; that is, existing beliefs and affect guide the processing of new information, with pressure to discount discrepant stimuli. The alternative position in this debate (Miller and Ross, 1975; Nisbett and Ross, 1980) draws on the cognitive mechanisms underlying processing, proposing that individuals make self-serving judgments "not because they [want] to, but because these conclusions [seem] more plausible, given their prior beliefs and expectancies" (Kunda, 1990: 480). Returning to our earlier example, JQP might maintain his dislike of Clinton in the face of discrepant information by (1) discounting the validity of the new information simply because it does not conform to expectation or (2) building a plausible argument about Clinton's opportunism based on a straightforward retrieval of prior beliefs about Clinton's insincerity or about "unprincipled politicians" more generally. The former is classic dissonance reduction involving the direct impact of motivation on the final judgment, while the latter is a purely cognitive interpretation.

Following a recent trend in psychology (e.g., Kunda, 1990), we propose a union of these theoretical positions. Motivational goals alter the cognitive processing of information whereby prior beliefs and affect come to influence the integration of new information. Other researchers have addressed this notion in attempts to identify the direct effects of motivation on cognitive mechanisms (Baumeister and Newman, 1994; Kunda, 1990). In this view, motivation affects reasoning by biasing (or eliminating bias from) the cognitive processing of information. The rest of this chapter begins to specify processes of motivated political reasoning, describing a model in which an individual with the purpose of constructing a judgment acts upon various motivational goals when cognitively integrating new and old information.

MOTIVATIONAL GOALS

Motivation is typically defined as a *drive* to do something or as a *reason* behind thoughts and behavior. Clearly distinguishing motivational goals is difficult, for there may be many possible reasons underlying any one thought or action. However, motivational goals generally fall into two categories: at one end of the continuum is the desire to arrive at an accurate conclusion, and at the other is the desire to maintain prior beliefs (Baumeister and Newman, 1994; Kruglanski, 1980; Kunda, 1990). In Baumeister and Newman's (1994) illustrative analogies, accuracy goals, which motivate a more "objective" cognitive processing of information, are likened to an *intuitive scientist,* while directional goals, which strive to support a predetermined conclusion, are metaphorically like an *intuitive lawyer.* The intuitive scientist seeks no one particular solution or outcome, but rather makes an effort to recognize and eliminate biases, interpret information correctly, and consider all possible options. The intuitive scientist aims to reach the best decision by seeking thoroughness in the collection of evidence, setting decision rules and criteria before knowing the evidence, emphasizing the detection of bias during the assessment of evidence, and adjusting or recomputing decisions to correct for any remaining bias or distortion. In contrast, an intuitive lawyer – essentially an agent of predisposition – may ignore or devalue contrary information, bias the perception of credibility, or overlook important factors. Intuitive lawyers selectively seek evidence that will be favorable, assess the implications of evidence in a way that is carefully critical of disagreeable implications while failing to subject supporting evidence to equally critical scrutiny, and postpone setting decision rules or criteria until they can assign greater weight to factors that provide a more favorable assessment.

We have then two broad categories of motivation that impact cognitive processes in very different ways. Accuracy goals should lead people to use more deliberate, conscious, and explicit information processing strategies that involve more cognitive effort (Baumeister and Newman, 1994). This may include an increased effort to recall information (McAllister, Mitchell, and Beach, 1979), an attempt consciously to override such biases as primacy effects, use of stereotypes, incorrect assessment of probabilities (Kruglanski and Freund, 1983), and a reduction in the fundamental attribution error (Tetlock, 1985). All of this comes from spending time and effort consciously evaluating more information more deeply (Tetlock and Kim, 1987).

While cognitive processing directed by accuracy goals may eliminate some of the biases that frequently lead to erroneous conclusions, it requires more effort than decision makers will typically expend for most everyday decisions (Kinder and Sears, 1985; Markus and Zajonc, 1985; Payne, Bettman, and Johnson, 1992). Directional goals, on the other hand, place fewer demands on cognitive resources, as processing focuses on updating judgments with new information in such a way that the new conclusion confirms prior beliefs or expectations. This may be achieved through skewing the information sampled from memory or from the environment, devaluing disconfirming information, or forming counterarguments to offset discrepant ideas (Lord, Ross, and Lepper, 1979). However, as stated previously, people cannot simply believe whatever they want to; they would like their conclusions to appear rational to dispassionate observers (Darley and Gross, 1983). In short, they feel some pressure to maintain an "illusion of objectivity" (Pyszczynski and Greenberg, 1987).

Our argument, with a heavy debt to Kunda (1990) and Baumeister and Newman (1994), is that motivational goals impact the cognitive processing of information. Each stage of processing, from initial exposure to final conclusion, is affected by goals, although in slightly different ways, the details of which we discuss subsequently. We begin with the question of how motivational goals are established and then progress through aspects of gathering evidence, assessing and reassessing the evidence, and integrating information leading to the construction of judgments.

Charles S. Taber, Milton Lodge, and Jill Glathar

ESTABLISHING GOALS

It may be impossible for researchers and individual decision makers to identify precisely all the motivational goals underlying thought or action. Rather than attempt this feat, we as researchers strive to identify conditions under which differing types of goals are more likely to occur. For example, individuals who expect to be personally affected by their political decisions may be more likely to engage in accuracy-based processing. On the other hand, such individuals may be motivated by directional goals to deny the necessity of personally undesirable policies, as in ignoring the necessity to reduce spending to cut the budget deficit.

The conditions under which people tend to use accuracy goals remain largely unknown. One clearly identifiable factor contributing to the impact of accuracy goals is accountability. Tetlock (1985) found that when individuals are told that they will have to discuss their judgments publicly, they tend to process information in a more even-handed manner, as best they can "scientifically," in order to find the most defensible position. More generally, we assume that accuracy goals are paramount when people believe that their judgment will have real consequences for their lives; the greater the perceived importance of the judgment, the greater the potency of the accuracy goal. Most assuredly, individuals do not engage in this process routinely, for as we will see, it can be extremely taxing cognitively. In politics, accuracy goals may be most likely to affect electoral judgment processes when the election is believed to have great importance for the voter, as in a "realigning" election or one believed to have direct economic consequences for the voter.

Substantially more research has focused on directional goals, attempting to establish conditions under which individuals process information to support a desired conclusion. The primary identifiable source of directional reasoning is high personal involvement in the judgment (Kunda, 1990). For instance, people with a lot of self-interest invested in a candidate are less likely to believe reports of dubious character, particularly if the reports originate from the opposition. More likely, they will counterargue or discount contrary evidence. Involvement may also include strong prior beliefs or affect. In fact, the strength of the directional goal is believed to be proportional to the strength of the prior belief/affect.

Evidence of the activation of directional goals among highly involved people comes from the work of Chaiken, Liberman, and Eagly (1989) and Petty and Cacioppo (1986), where, in response to counterattitudinal information, highly involved individuals formed more counterarguments to the presented message than did people with low involvement.

The Construction of Political Judgments

Likewise, Howard-Pitney, Borgida, and Omoto (1986) found that individuals with strong feelings about an issue can identify more arguments related to their position, list more thoughts related to their own argument, and list more unfavorable thoughts concerning opposing positions than people with low involvement.

Whether drawn from long-term memory or from contextual information, motivational goals have far-reaching consequences for subsequent processing. Once they are engaged, accuracy and directional goals affect how people gather and assess evidence and construct judgments. This impact of motivation on cognitive processing determines the persuasiveness of a message and the perseverence of prior attitudes.

GATHERING EVIDENCE

Once goals have been established, the impact on cognitive processing is immediate. Individuals will first seek information to use in making their judgments, primarily through a search of long-term memory. The mechanisms of gathering evidence that are influenced by goals include the amount of time spent searching, the variable attention paid to different pieces of information during the search, and the selection of information for retrieval to working memory. For intuitive scientists, who seek accurate conclusions, the optimal strategy is to ensure that all relevant information gets a fair hearing, whereas intuitive lawyers, who want to reach a desired conclusion, will search for evidence favorable to that conclusion.

The careful management of the information search is the most important way to regulate what evidence is brought to bear on a judgment. Those motivated to be accurate are likely to seek out a great deal of information. Kruglanski and Freund (1983), for example, find that subjects who expect that their judgments will be made public consider a wider range of information and are less susceptible to bias. Tetlock (1985) has found in a variety of studies that simply encouraging people to process information more thoroughly leads them to look at more information and produce more accurate conclusions. Moreover, intuitive scientists may self-consciously try to balance the views they attend to during the search for evidence (Kruglanski, 1980; Kruglanski and Ajzen, 1983; Neuberg, 1989; Neuberg and Fiske, 1987). For example, Lord, Lepper, and Preston (1984) found that people could reduce bias in judgment simply by considering an opposing argument. Of course, a point we return to in the conclusion is that well-meant efforts to overcome bias do not guarantee optimal, accurate conclusions: many studies demonstrate that greater attention and effort can backfire (Nisbett, Zukier, and Lemley, 1981; Tetlock and Boettger, 1989).

Those motivated to support preconviction, on the other hand, will not pay equal attention to pro and con evidence and generally do not seek out inconsistent information. Since they seek to defend one position rather than be evenhanded, they need not spend time and cognitive effort in searching for evidence that will challenge their goal. Kunda (1990) argues that most (if not all) research on the effects of directional goals on reasoning can be interpreted in terms of biased memory search and subsequent judgments constructed on the basis of that biased sample of evidence. Most of the evidence for biased memory search comes from dissonance research, in which motivational goals are triggered when people behave counter to their prior attitudes. Linder, Cooper, and Jones's (1967) study on attitudes toward limits on free speech is a case in point. They found less opposition to limits on free speech when subjects had been induced to endorse such a law. If we assume that subjects in such studies are motivated to construct attitudes consistent with their behavior, we can explain their shift in position as the result of a directionally biased search of long-term memory, in which counterbehavioral beliefs are filtered out or discounted. "The constraints imposed by prior beliefs on attitude change imply that prior beliefs were accessed in the process of constructing current ones, and the directional shift in attitudes implies that only a biased subset of the relevant prior beliefs were accessed" (Kunda, 1990: 484).

Further evidence for biased memory search can be found in studies of changes in people's self-concepts or perceptions of their past behavior. Sanitioso, Kunda, and Fong (1990), for example, asked subjects to provide autobiographical memories illustrating their position on the extraversion-introversion scale. In keeping with a biased memory search, those who were led to see introversion as a desirable trait produced more introverted memories, produced them first, and produced them faster. Other studies have found that when people are told that specific behaviors are bad for their health, they report engaging in them less frequently (Ross, McFarland, and Fletcher, 1981; Sherman and Kunda, 1989). The implications for motivated reasoning seem clear: the information about health risks presented to these subjects established a directional goal, which biased their retrieval of behavioral examples from long-term memory.

Beyond memory search, people may also attend selectively to other sources of information relevant to the decision (e.g., Abelson et al., 1968). For example, people may actively seek out new information from the environment that will support their prior views (McGuire, 1969). Sweeney and Gruber (1984) found that Americans who supported Nixon tended to ignore the extensive news coverage of the Watergate scandal, in contrast to those who disliked him. Thus, by simply using the remote

The Construction of Political Judgments

control, people can selectively expose themselves to supportive information and avoid that which may challenge their views. The overall experimental support for this notion is mixed, however, and suggests that the relationship between one's prior attitude and the selective search for consistent information is not straightforward. It appears that people who have publicly committed themselves to a position will seek out new evidence in support of their attitude, while those without a prior expressed attitude may not be motivated enough to bother (Frey, 1986). Other research supports the selective exposure hypothesis only for people experiencing moderate dissonance: low levels of dissonance do not create the necessary motivation to search actively for new information, while high levels of dissonance make attitude change likely (Sweeney and Gruber, 1984).

Selective attention, wherein one looks longer and harder at the consistent than at the inconsistent information that is presented, finds a great deal of experimental support (Brock and Balloun, 1967; Jecker, 1964), though this too must be qualified. Olson and Zanna (1979), for example, find that some people are naturally inclined to play down inconsistent information (repressors), while others force themselves to attend to discrepant evidence (sensitizers). Others have found that directionally motivated people pay attention only to the discrepant information that they judge to be weak, thereby allowing them to think themselves evenhanded, though they can easily refute the weak inconsistent evidence to which they attend (Kleinhesselink and Edwards, 1975).

Finally, people also selectively interpret the information they are exposed to in order to maintain their prior attitude. Fazio and Williams (1986), for example, found that people's perceptions of who "won" the 1984 presidential and vice presidential debates were strongly colored by their prior opinions about the candidates. Similarly, support for one side or the other in the Arab–Israeli conflict appeared to distort perceptions of the fairness of media coverage of the Beirut massacre (Vallone, Ross, and Lepper, 1985). These and other studies suggest that strong prior attitudes – memory objects with strong evaluative tags – mold interpretations of new information. Presumably, objects about which no such crystallized attitudes exist will not trigger this process of selective interpretation.

ASSESSING AND REASSESSING THE EVIDENCE

Although the step from evidence to implication is automatic, the reassessment of these implications may be more under the control of motivation, as people decide whether to accept implications at face value or modify them. In evaluating candidates or constructing judgments of

213

other political objects, accuracy goals again lead to a more evenhanded treatment of the evidence, while directional goals bias the evaluation process to reach the desired conclusion. Intuitive scientists must consider how well each bit of evidence justifies its implication, which was derived automatically. In trying to make an accurate judgment, they must work to adjust for biases and distortion. The problem is that because these implications have been drawn automatically, they will seem self-evident, even to those motivated to be accurate.

People with directional goals, on the other hand, not only rely on a biased subset of memory but also differentially evaluate the evidence they do have in working memory at the time of judgment. They may not be able to avoid finding some disagreeable evidence, but this evidence will be susceptible to discounting. People may, for example, subjectively interpret probability estimates to match their expectations (Kunda, 1990), improperly apply base rate information to undermine evidence they don't like and enhance what they do like (Ginosar and Trope, 1987), or misapply the law of large numbers (Sanitioso and Kunda, 1991). Strong partisans, for example, tend to overestimate the probability that their candidate will win, even when the evidence suggests otherwise. Within the bounds imposed by the desire to appear impartial, people seem free to manipulate the laws of probability and statistical inference to serve directional goals.

There is now considerable evidence that people heavily bias judgment processes in forming beliefs about themselves and about others. For example, people – not only politicians – typically take credit for successes while blaming others for their failures (Pyszczynski and Greenberg, 1987). Tesser (1986) has argued that many people actively maintain positive self-images by selectively comparing their performances with those of others. When threatened by the superior performances of similar others, subjects often reduce the self-relevance of the task. In other words, they maintain their positive self-image by altering their self-schema so that a particular skill or task is no longer as important as was originally thought. A host of studies also show biased judgment processes when people evaluate others. For example, when people depend on another person for some important outcome – they are to go on a date, perhaps – they tend to see them more positively than others on whom they do not depend (Berscheid, Graziano, Monson, and Dermer, 1976; Neuberg and Fiske, 1987). Presumably, these subjects were responding to a directional motivation to like those on whom they depend. This sort of biased judgment may account, in part, for the tendency to view top political leaders more positively during crises, especially foreign crises. Citizens may "rally round the flag" because they depend on their elected officials to deal effectively with an external problem.

More compelling evidence for motivated bias in weighing evidence comes from a study by Lord, Ross, and Lepper (1979), who presented two apparently scientific studies on the effectiveness of capital punishment in deterring crime to experimental subjects known to be either for or against the death penalty. As expected, subjects were far more skeptical about the evidence and methods used in the counterattitudinal study. They selected criticisms based on apparently scientific reasons (e.g., insufficient sample size or lack of adequate control), corroborating the notion that people feel pressure to use rational arguments, though their directional goals drive their conclusions. Moreover, their attitudes became significantly more polarized after exposure to and evaluation of the conflicting evidence. This strengthening of prior attitudes is a consequence of the assimilation of supportive evidence and successful counterarguments for contrary evidence. Similarly, Liberman and Chaiken (1992) found female coffee drinkers to be more critical than noncoffee drinkers of research reports linking consumption of coffee to a serious fibrocystic disease. Several other studies show similar results, though using different attitude objects (Kassarjian and Cohen, 1965; Kunda, 1987; Pyszczynski, Greenberg, and Holt, 1985; Sherman and Kunda, 1989). Taken together, these studies support the idea that people not only bias the considerations they attend to or draw from memory, but also bias the assessment of the implications of that evidence. They tend to accept the evidence and arguments that support the position they want to believe and devalue or counterargue the contrary evidence.

INTEGRATION AND JUDGMENT

In the final stage of constructing a judgment, the evidence must be integrated into a coherent evaluation or choice, a process that is also susceptible to motivated bias. Of course, the evidence gathered and assessed in earlier information processing stages may clearly point to one conclusion, in which case integration and judgment are straightforward. But where the evidence conflicts with one's prior beliefs and is ambiguous, the integration of evidence into a summary evaluation is more easily affected by biased motivation.

When one is faced with conflicting evidence, accuracy goals require that the evidence be weighed carefully and evenhandedly before being combined into a summary judgment. Moreover, the intuitive scientist must maintain objectivity by self-consciously establishing rules, procedures, and standards for judgment in advance of collecting and evaluating the evidence. When evaluating performance, for example, those motivated to be accurate may set particular criteria for the evaluation in advance, so that the standards themselves will not be biased by the evidence (Harkness, DeBono, and Borgida, 1985). More generally, accuracy-based processing is more likely to lead people to weigh the evidence fairly and form a final judgment that reflects the overall weight of the evidence.

Intuitive lawyers, on the other hand, would like to have the evidence in hand before establishing criteria for judgment. This enables them to pick standards and rules that favor their desired conclusion, given the evidence. Schaller (1992), for example, found that directionally motivated subjects followed reasonable rules of correlational inference only when the rules favored their desired conclusion. They ignored confounding third variables unless considering them would help them make their case. As we have pointed out, they may also counterargue contrary evidence, reducing or even reversing its weight in the final judgment. These arguments can take two basic forms: the discounting of contrary evidence or the bolstering of supportive evidence. Lord, Ross, and Lepper (1979) found evidence of such counterarguing in the study described earlier. For example, our hypothetical citizen JQP, after processing the information that Clinton supports capital punishment, may want to justify his negative judgment of Clinton by seeking and constructing arguments that fit this new information into a negative view of Clinton (e.g., by constructing the counterargument that Clinton was just seeking electoral advantage rather than expressing a real pro–death penalty conviction).

SKETCH OF A MODEL OF MOTIVATED POLITICAL JUDGMENT

How can we build these motivational processes onto the simple associational architecture described earlier? In this section we propose the skeleton of such a model with preliminary suggestions for integrating directionally motivated processes like counterarguing and bolstering. Following recent trends in cognitive science, we need to go beyond simple node–link associations, employing larger memory structures and introducing biases into the memory search mechanism. Node–link *structures* for particular objects – prominent politicians, major issues, and so on – may exist in long-term memory and may be treated as chunks (Bartlett, 1932; Minsky, 1975; Rumelhart and Ortony, 1977; Schank and Abelson, 1977). JQP had a schema for capital punishment, for example, which contained a lot of information that we now posit could be treated as a single unit in processing. That is, chunks can be drawn into working memory as singular units, where they occupy only *one* slot, though all the knowledge contained within the chunk is accessible. Most important for this chapter, we suggest a mechanism for biased memory search. Activation spreads through the network, as in the simpler model, but directional goals reduce the liklihood that countermotivational considerations will be retrieved into working memory to affect subsequent processing.

We suggest that initial directional goals are a straightforward function of the affective tags attached to the objects in long-term memory that are invoked in the initial stages of processing a new piece of information. People "know" immediately how they feel about a given stimulus object (e.g., Clinton) by simply retrieving their OL tally for that object (Lodge and Taber, 2000). In other words, hot cognition emerges from the *automatic* retrieval of a memory object's affective tally when one thinks about that object. This includes both the direction and the strength of affect toward the object. When reading about Bill Clinton and the death penalty, JQP immediately knows he strongly dislikes Clinton and supports the death penalty. This instantiates the directional goal of maintaining his dislike for Clinton, which will permeate subsequent processing. Accuracy goals, we posit, are always present to some extent, producing the desire, referred to earlier, to appear rational to a dispassionate observer. From this perspective, all reasoning is conflicted to some extent – the stronger one's prior beliefs the weaker the struggle, since strong directional goals may overwhelm relatively weak accuracy goals. On the other hand, accuracy goals may be enhanced by the salience of new information as cued by environmental signals or when recalled information suggests that the judgment may have consequences for one's life.

People motivated to engage in deeper processing by strong accuracy goals or by having their directional goals challenged must construct a fuller understanding of the available information for the judgment. Those who are directionally motivated will build this fuller understanding through a biased search of memory. Long-term memory search relies on spreading activation across links to nodes related to the key objects. But memories and knowledge that are evaluatively consistent with the directional goal have a better chance of being transferred to working memory, where they can affect the construction of the judgment. So, for example, JQP would construct a representation of the information contained in the headline by selectively sifting through knowledge that becomes energized when activation is applied at the Clinton and Death Penalty nodes. His understanding would be an elaboration of the basic information that (1) he dislikes Clinton, (2) he supports the death penalty, and (3) Clinton apparently supports the death penalty, and reasoning would be guided by the goal to retain beliefs 1 and 2 (prior beliefs). This elaboration process relies on continued long-term memory search, cued by the current motivated goals. JQP might key one of these searches on the belief that Clinton is an insincere politician (which might have emerged earlier as part of his understanding of Clinton), and this might activate knowledge about "dishonest politicians" doing "anything" for votes. Finally, this might suggest a line of argument that will bolster his prior convictions and directly undermine the discrepant new information. Moreover, this argument reflects poorly on Clinton and, if accepted by JQP, will worsen his evaluative tally for Clinton.

We can think of three mechanisms to produce biased memory search. First, as suggested earlier, objects in long-term memory that are evaluatively inconsistent may have a reduced chance of being recalled to working memory. Directional goals may bias the spread of activation by favoring linked objects that serve these goals. For example, JQP, who has a directional goal to dislike Clinton, may experience more spreading activation to long-term memory objects that have negative implicational relations for Clinton. These might be positively evaluated objects that are negatively related to Clinton (perhaps "the right to life" for JQP) or negatively evaluated objects that are positively associated with Clinton (e.g., taxes). Like all processes in long-term *biased spreading activation* all would be unconscious. Second, the product of unbiased spreading activation might be subjected to *evaluative review in working memory* immediately upon recall. That is, strong directional goals might cause evaluatively inconsistent objects in working memory to be rejected before they can affect subsequent processing. Memories that reflect well on Clinton (e.g., his apparent intelligence) would be consciously discounted and perhaps eliminated from JQP's working memory during initial processing. Third, some of what appears to be biased memory search may result from *biased encoding*. Over time, judgments compiled in working memory and transferred to long-term memory according to an established set of predispositions would produce bias in the contents of long-term memory. JQP, for example, undoubtedly has a biased representation of Clinton stored in long-term memory, which any search keyed on Clinton should reveal.

Though the process of constructing counterarguments and deeper judgments that reconcile discrepant information may increase the probability that the information will be encoded and stored with the Clinton schema (making it available for future memory searches), it may not be encoded, and if encoded it may be forgotten quickly. In other words, the OL model still allows for the possibility that such arguments can affect the evaluative tally and then be forgotten.

CONCLUSION

We have suggested a simple model of the phases of political decision making (Baumeister and Newman, 1994) and an underlying model of associative memory and information processes (Anderson, 1983). The modified OL model described in the previous section provides the process details behind the more general stepwise model.

Step 1: Defining the Problem/Establishing Goals. Something in the environment raises a question or problem. If the problem is salient, goals are established and the judgment process begins. Directional goals emerge spontaneously as the affective tags associated with elements of the problem represented in long-term memory are brought into working memory (hot cognition). Accuracy goals are always present, perhaps because they make adaptive sense. Accuracy goals are strengthened when one believes the judgment will have personal consequences; directional goals are similarly enhanced by high personal involvement and the strength of prior attitudes.

Step 2: Gathering Evidence. Sometimes one is a passive, exposure-driven witness to information, as may be the case when one watches the evening news with one eye open (Zaller, 1992), but at other times the same person may be more active, searching long-term memory for relevant information, seeking information from newspapers or the local library (!), or asking friends for their opinions. More active processing will occur when motivation is strong. Accuracy goals provoke deeper, broader, and more evenhanded search as the intuitive scientist seeks the truth; directional goals lead to biased search as the intuitive lawyer builds a case. This stage of processing relies on memory processes, including spreading activation through long-term memory and biased memory search caused by directional goals.

Step 3: Assessing Implications. One becomes immediately aware of the implications of each piece of evidence drawn in step 2. This is an automatic process of spreading activation, as associations and the implications of messages spontaneously "pop" into one's mind without conscious effort or design (Uleman and Bargh, 1989).

Step 4: Reassessing Implications. Here one consciously reassesses the automatic implications generated in step 3. Intuitive scientists, for example, may actively try to correct for biases that may have emerged during automatic retrieval of implications from long-term memory. Intuitive lawyers, on the other hand, may actively discount or counterargue any inconvenient implications drawn in step 3.

Step 5: Integrating the Evidence. At some point, the evidence and its implications must be drawn together into a summary judgment. If the evidence and implications conflict or are ambiguous, this may not be easy. When motivated to be accurate, people try to weigh all the evidence carefully and even-handedly before reaching a summary judgment. Directional goals, by contrast, lead people to continue the process, begun in step 4, of discounting and counterarguing contrary evidence and bolstering supporting evidence. Many models have been suggested for integrating considerations into a summary judgment (Taber and Steenbergen, 1995). Though virtually all put this step last, people may reach preliminary conclusions at earlier points in the overall judgment process. Moreover, this five-step model suggests an ideal ordering of processes, rather than a necessary ordering.

Kelley and Mirer (1974) were right: it is far easier to predict votes than to explain them. The latter requires us to open the decision-making black box and confront information processing in some detail. Two themes from recent social and cognitive psychology provide the basic insights of this chapter: political judgments are *constructed* from considerations drawn from memory or context, and they are *motivated*. Until we account for the motivated construction of political judgments, we will never be able to explain adequately why some attitudes persevere, while others fluctuate wildly; why counterattitudinal evidence may temper one's prior judgment but more often will bolster it; and why political spin sometimes has the intended consequences but may also provoke counterarguments and attitude polarization. Without delving into detail, we will not explain why people vote as they do.

References

Abelson, Robert P. (1963). "Computer Simulation of 'Hot' Cognition." In Silvan S. Tomkins and Samuel Messick (Eds.), *Computer Simulation of Personality*. New York: Wiley.
Abelson, Robert P., Elliot Aronson, William J. McGuire, Theodore M. Newcomb, Milton J. Rosenberg, and Percy H. Tannenbaum (1968). *Theories of Cognitive Consistency: A Sourcebook*. Chicago: Rand McNally.
Anderson, John A. (1983). *The Architecture of Cognition*. Cambridge, MA: Harvard University Press.
Anderson, Norman H. (1982). *Methods of Information Integration Theory*. New York: Academic Press.
  (1991). *Contributions to Information Integration Theory*. Hillsdale, NJ: Lawrence Erlbaum.
Bartlett, Frederick A. (1932). *Remembering: A Study in Experimental and Social Psychology*. New York: Cambridge University Press.

Baumeister, Roy F., and Leonard S. Newman (1994). "Self-Regulation of Cognitive Inference and Decision Processes." *Personality and Social Psychology Bulletin* 20(1): 3–19.

Bersheid, Ellen, William Graziano, Thomas Monson, and Marshall Dermer (1976). "Outcome Dependency: Attention, Attribution, and Attraction." *Journal of Personality and Social Psychology* 34: 978–989.

Bishop, George, Robert W. Oldendick, and Alfred J. Tuchfarber (1978). "Effects of Question Wording and Format on Attitude Consistency." *Public Opinion Quarterly*, 42: 81–92.

(1982). "Political Information Processing: Question Order and Context Effects." *Political Behavior*, 4: 177–200.

(1985). "The Importance of Replicating a Failure: Order Effects on Abortion Items." *Public Opinion Quarterly*, 49: 105–114.

Boynton, G. Robert, and Milton Lodge (1992). "A Cognitive Model of Forming Impressions of Candidates." Paper presented at the annual meeting of the Midwest Political Science Association, Chicago.

(1994). "Voter's Images of Candidates." In Arthur Miller and Bruce Gronbeck (Eds.), *Presidential Campaigns and American Self Images*. Boulder, CO: Westview Press.

Brock, Timothy C., and Joseph L. Balloun (1967). "Behavioral Receptivity to Dissonant Information." *Journal of Personality and Social Psychology* 6: 413–428.

Campbell, Angus, Philip Converse, Warren Miller, and Donald Stokes (1960). *The American Voter*. New York: Wiley.

Chaiken, Shelly, Akiva Liberman, and Alice H. Eagly (1989). "Heuristic and Systematic Information Processing Within and Beyond the Persuasion Context." In James S. Uleman and John A. Bargh (Eds.), *Unintended Thought*. New York: Guilford Press.

Darley, John M., and Paget H. Gross (1983). "A Hypothesis-Confirming Bias in Labeling Effects." *Journal of Personality and Social Psychology* 44: 20–33.

Eagly, Alice H., and Shelly Chaiken (1984). "Cognitive Theories of Persuasion." In Leonard Berkowitz (Ed.), *Advances in Experimental Social Psychology* (Vol. 17). New York: Academic Press.

Ericsson, Andres K., and Herbert A. Simon (1984). *Protocol Analysis: Verbal Reports as Data*. Cambridge, MA: MIT Press.

Einhorn, Hillel J., Stephen S. Komorita, and Benson Rosen (1972). "Multidimensional Models for the Evaluation of Political Candidates." *Journal of Experimental Social Psychology* 8: 58–73.

Fazio, Russell H., and Carol J. Williams (1986). "Attitude Accessibility as a Moderator of the Attitude–Perception and Attitude–Behavior Relations: An Investigation of the 1984 Presidential Election." *Journal of Personality and Social Psychology* 51: 505–514.

Feldman, Stanley (1995). "Answering Survey Questions: The Measurement and Meaning of Public Opinion." In Milton Lodge and Kathleen M. McGraw (Eds.), *Political Judgment: Structure and Process*. Ann Arbor: University of Michigan Press.

Festinger, Leon (1957). *A Theory of Cognitive Dissonance*. Stanford, CA: Stanford University Press.

Frey, Dieter (1986). "Recent Research on Selective Exposure." In Leonard Berkowitz (Ed.), *Advances in Experimental Social Psychology* (Vol. 19). New York: Academic Press.

Ginosar, Zvi, and Yaacov Trope (1987). "Problem Solving in Judgment Under Uncertainty." *Journal of Personality and Social Psychology* 52: 464–474.

Graber, Doris (1984). *Processing the News: How People Tame the Information Flow.* New York: Longman.

Harkness, Allan R., Kenneth G. DeBono, and Eugene Borgida (1985). "Personal Involvement and Strategies for Making Contingency Judgments: A Stake in the Dating Game Makes a Difference." *Journal of Personality and Social Psychology* 49: 22–32.

Heider, Fritz (1958). *The Psychology of Interpersonal Relations.* New York: Wiley.

Herstein, John A. (1981). "Keeping the Voter's Limits in Mind: A Cognitive Process Analysis of Decision Making in Voting." *Journal of Personality and Social Psychology* 40: 843–861.

Hogarth, Robin M., and Hillel J. Einhorn (1992). "Order Effects in Belief Updating: The Belief Adjustment Model." *Cognitive Psychology* 24: 1–55.

Howard-Pitney, Beth, Eugene Borgida, and Allen M. Omoto (1986). "Personal Involvement: An Examination of Processing Differences." *Social Cognition* 4: 39–57.

Jecker, Jon D. (1964). "The Cognitive Effects of Conflict and Dissonance." In Leon Festinger (Ed.), *Conflict, Decision, and Dissonance.* Palo Alto, CA: Stanford University Press.

Kassarjian, Harold H., and Joel B. Cohen (1965). "Cognitive Dissonance and Consumer Behavior." *California Management Review* 8: 55–64.

Kelley, Stanley, and Thaddeus Mirer (1974). "The Simple Act of Voting." *American Political Science Review* 61: 572–591.

Kiesler, Charles A., Barry E. Collins, and Norman Miller (1969). *Attitude Change: A Critical Analysis of Theoretical Approaches.* New York: Wiley.

Kinder, Donald R., and David O. Sears (1985). "Public Opinion and Political Action." In Gardner Lindzey and Elliot Aronson (Eds.), *The Handbook of Social Psychology* (3rd Ed., Vol. 2). Reading, MA: Addison-Wesley.

Kleinhesselink, Randall R., and Richard E. Edwards (1975). "Seeking and Avoiding Belief-Discrepant Information as a Function of Its Perceived Refutability." *Journal of Personality and Social Psychology* 31: 787–790.

Kruglanski, Arie W. (1980). "Lay Epistemology Process and Contents." *Psychological Review* 87: 70–87.

Kruglanski, Arie W., and Icek Ajzen (1983). "Bias and Error in Human Judgment." *European Journal of Social Psychology* 13: 1–44.

Kruglanski, Arie W., and Tallie Freund (1983). "The Freezing and Unfreezing of Lay Inferences: Effects on Impressional Primacy, Ethnic Stereotyping, and Numerical Anchoring." *Journal of Experimental Social Psychology* 19: 448–468.

Kunda, Ziva (1987). "Motivation and Inference: Self-Serving Generation and Evaluation of Evidence." *Journal of Personality and Social Psychology* 53: 636–647.

(1990). "The Case for Motivated Reasoning." *Psychological Bulletin* 108(3): 480–498.

Lazarsfeld, Paul, Bernard Berelson, and Hazel Gaudet (1944). *The People's Choice.* New York: Columbia University Press.

Liberman, Akiva, and Shelly Chaiken (1992). "Defensive Processing of Personally Relevant Health Messages." *Personality and Social Psychology Bulletin* 18: 669–679.

Linder, Darwyn E., Joel Cooper, and Edward E. Jones (1967). "Decision Freedom as a Determinant of the Role of Incentive Magnitude in Attitude Change." *Journal of Personality and Social Psychology* 6: 245–254.

Lodge, Milton, Kathleen M. McGraw, and Patrick Stroh (1989). "An Impression-Driven Model of Candidate Evaluation." *American Political Science Review* 83: 399–419.

Lodge, Milton, Marco Steenbergen, and Shawn Brau (1995). "The Responsive Voter: Campaign Information and the Dynamics of Candidate Evaluation." *American Political Science Review* 89: 309–326.

Lodge, Milton, and Patrick Stroh (1993). "Inside the Mental Voting Booth: An Impression-Driven Model." In Shanto Iyengar and William McGuire (Eds.), *Explorations in Political Psychology*. Durham, NC: Duke University Press.

Lodge, Milton, and Charles S. Taber (2000). "Three Steps Toward a Theory of Motivated Political Reasoning." In Arthur Lupia, Matthew McCubbins, and Samuel Popkin (Eds.), *Elements of Political Reason: Understanding and Expanding the Limits of Rationality*. New York: Cambridge University Press.

Lord, Charles G., Mark R. Lepper, and Elizabeth Preston (1984). "Considering the Opposite: A Corrective Strategy for Social Judgment." *Journal of Personality and Social Psychology* 47: 1231–1243.

Lord, Charles G., Lee Ross, and Mark R. Lepper (1979). "Biased Assimilation and Attitude Polarization: The Effects of Prior Theories on Subsequently Considered Evidence." *Journal of Personality and Social Psychology* 27: 2098–2109.

Markus, Hazel, and Robert B. Zajonc (1985). "The Cognitive Perspective in Social Psychology." In Gardner Lindzey and Elliot Aronson (Eds.), *The Handbook of Social Psychology* (Vol. 1). New York: Random House.

Martin, Lawrence, and Abraham Tesser (1992). *Construction of Social Judgments*. Hillsdale, NJ: Lawrence Erlbaum.

McAllister, Daniel W., Terence R. Mitchell, and Lee R. Beach (1979). "The Contingency Model for the Selection of Decision Strategies: An Empirical Test of the Effects of Significance, Accountability, and Reversibility." *Organizational Behavior and Human Performance* 24: 228–244.

McGraw, Kathleen M., Milton Lodge, and Patrick Stroh (1990). "On-Line Processing in Candidate Evaluation: The Effects of Issue Order, Issue Importance, and Sophistication." *Political Behavior* 12: 41–58.

McGuire, William J. (1969). "Nature of Attitudes and Attitude Change." In Gardner Lindzey and Elliot Aronson (Eds.), *The Handbook of Social Psychology* (2nd Ed., Vol. 3). Reading, MA: Addison-Wesley.

Miller, D. T., and M. Ross (1975). "Self-Serving Biases in the Attribution of Causality: Fact or Fiction?" *Psychological Bulletin* 82: 213–225.

Minsky, Marvin (1975). "A Framework for Representing Knowledge." In Patrick H. Winston (Ed.), *The Psychology of Computer Vision*. New York: McGraw-Hill.

Neuberg, Steven L. (1989). "The Goal of Forming Accurate Impressions During Social Interactions: Attenuating the Impact of Negative Expectancies." *Journal of Personality and Social Psychology* 56: 374–386.

Neuberg, Steven L., and Susan T. Fiske (1987). "Motivational Influences on Impression Formation: Dependence, Accuracy-Driven Attention, and Individuating Information." *Journal of Personality and Social Psychology* 53: 431–444.

Nisbett, Richard E., and Lee Ross (1980). *Human Inference: Strategies and Shortcomings of Social Judgment.* Englewood Cliffs, NJ: Prentice-Hall.

Nisbett, Richard E., Henry Zukier, and Ronald E. Lemley (1981). "The Dilution Effect: Nondiagnostic Information Weakens the Implications of Diagnostic Information." *Cognitive Psychology* 13(2): 248–277.

Olson, James M., and Mark P. Zanna (1979). "A New Look at Selective Exposure." *Journal of Experimental Social Psychology* 15: 1–15.

Ottati, Victor C., and Robert S. Wyer (1990). "The Cognitive Mediators of Political Choice: Toward a Comprehensive Model of Political Information Processing." In John A. Ferejohn and James H. Kuklinski (Eds.), *Information and Democratic Processes.* Urbana: University of Illinois Press.

Payne, John W., James R. Bettman, and Eric J. Johnson (1992). "Behavioral Decision Research: A Constructive Processing Perspective." *Annual Review of Psychology* 43: 87–131.

Petty, Richard E., and John T. Cacioppo (1986). "The Elaboration Likelihood Model of Persuasion." In Leonard Berkowitz (Ed.), *Advances in Experimental Social Psychology* (Vol. 19). New York: Academic Press.

Pratkanis, Anthony (1989). "The Cognitive Structure of Attitudes." In Anthony Pratkanis, Steven Breckler, and Anthony Greenwald (Eds.), *Attitude Structure and Function.* Hillsdale, NJ: Lawrene Erlbaum.

Pyszczynski, Tom, and Jeff Greenberg (1987). "Toward an Integration of Cognitive and Motivational Perspectives on Social Inference: A Biased Hypothesis-Testing Model." In Leonard Berkowitz (Ed.), *Advances in Social Psychology* (Vol. 20). New York: Academic Press.

Pyszczynski, Tom, Jeff Greenberg, and Kathleen Holt (1985). "Maintaining Consistency Between Self-Serving Beliefs and Available Data: A Bias in Information Evaluation." *Personality and Social Psychology Bulletin* 11: 179–190.

Rahn, Wendy M., John H. Aldrich, and Eugene Borgida (1994). "Individual and Contextual Variations in Political Candidate Appraisal." *American Political Science Review* 88: 193–199.

Rahn, Wendy M., John H. Aldrich, Eugene Borgida, and John Sullivan (1990). "A Social-Cognitive Model of Candidate Appraisal." In John A. Ferejohn and James H. Kuklinski (Eds.), *Information and Democratic Processes.* Urbana: University of Illinois Press.

Ross, Michael, Cathy McFarland, and Garth J. Fletcher (1981). "The Effect of Attitude on Recall of Personal Histories." *Journal of Personality and Social Psychology* 10: 627–634.

Rothbart, Myron (1981). "Memory Processes and Social Beliefs." In David L. Hamilton (Ed.), *Cognitive Processes in Stereotyping and Intergroup Behavior.* Hillsdale, NJ: Lawrence Erlbaum.

Rumelhart, David E., and Andrew Ortony (1977). "The Representation of Knowledge in Memory." In Richard C. Anderson, Paul J. Spiro, and William E. Montague (Eds.), *Schooling and the Acquisition of Knowledge.* Hillsdale, NJ: Lawrence Erlbaum.

Sanbonmatsu, David M., and Russell H. Fazio (1990). "The Role of Attitudes in Memory-Based Decision Making." *Journal of Personality and Social Psychology* 59(4): 614–622.

Sanford, Anthony (1986). *The Mind of Man: Models of Human Understanding.* New Haven, CT: Yale University Press.

Sanitioso, Rasyid, and Ziva Kunda (1991). "Ducking the Collection of Costly Evidence: Motivated Use of Statistical Heuristics." *Journal of Behavioral Decision Making* 4(3): 161–176.

Sanitioso, Rasyid, Ziva Kunda, and Geoffrey T. Fong (1990). "Motivated Recruitment of Autobiographical Memory." *Journal of Personality and Social Psychology* 59: 229–241.

Schaller, Mark (1992). "In-Group Favoritism and Statistical Reasoning in Social Inferences: Implications for Formation and Maintenance of Group Stereotypes." *Journal of Personality and Social Psychology* 63: 61–74.

Schank, Roger C., and Robert P. Abelson (1977). *Scripts, Plans, Goals, and Understanding*. Hillsdale, NJ: Lawrence Erlbaum.

Sherman, B. R., and Ziva Kunda (1989). "Motivated Evaluation of Scientific Evidence." Paper presented at the annual meeting of the American Psychological Society, Arlington, Virginia. Reported in Kunda (1990).

Simon, Herbert A. (1957). *Models of Man*. New York: Wiley.
  (1981). *The Science of the Artifical* (2nd Ed.). Cambridge, MA: MIT Press.
  (1985). "Human Nature in Politics: The Dialogue of Psychology with Political Science." *American Political Science Review*, 79: 293–304.

Sniderman, Paul M., Richard A. Brody, and Philip E. Tetlock (1991). *Reasoning and Choice: Explorations in Political Psychology*. Cambridge: Cambridge University Press.

Sweeney, Paul D., and Kathy L. Gruber (1984). "Selective Exposure: Voter Information Preferences and the Watergate Affair." *Journal of Personality and Social Psychology* 46: 1208–1221.

Taber, Charles S., and Marco R. Steenbergen (1995). "Computational Experiments in Electoral Behavior." In Milton Lodge and Kathleen M. McGraw (Eds.), *Political Judgment: Structure and Process*. Ann Arbor: University of Michigan Press.

Taber, Charles S., and Richard J. Timpone (1996). *Computational Modeling* (Sage University Paper Series on Quantitative Applications in the Social Sciences, 07–113). Newbury Park, CA: Sage.

Tesser, Abraham (1986). "Some Effects of Self-Evaluation Maintenance on Cognition and Action." In Richard M. Sorrentino and E. Tory Higgins (Eds.), *The Handbook of Motivation and Cognition: Foundations of Social Behavior*. New York: Guilford Press.

Tetlock, Philip E. (1985). "Accountability: A Social Check on the Fundamental Attribution Error." *Social Psychology Quarterly* 48: 227–238.

Tetlock, Philip E., and Richard Boettger (1989). "Accountability: A Social Magnifier of the Dilution Effect." *Journal of Personality and Social Psychology* 57: 388–398.

Tetlock, Philip E., and Jae I. Kim (1987). "Accountability and Judgment Processes in a Personality Prediction Task." *Journal of Personality and Social Psychology* 52: 700–709.

Uleman, James S., and John A. Bargh (Eds.) (1989). *Unintended Thought*. New York: Guilford Press.

Vallone, Robert P., Lee Ross, and Mark R. Lepper (1985). "The Hostile Media Phenomenon: Biased Perception and Perceptions of Media Bias in Coverage of the Beirut Massacre." *Journal of Personality and Social Psychology* 49: 577–585.

Wilson, Timothy, and Sara Hodges (1992). "Attitudes as Temporary Constructs." In Lawrence Martin and Abraham Tesser (Eds.), *Construction of Social Judgments*. Hillsdale, NJ: Lawrence Erlbaum.

Zaller, John R. (1992). *The Nature and Origins of Mass Opinion*. Cambridge, UK: Cambridge University Press.

Zanna, Mark (1990). "Attitude Function: Is It Related to Attitude Structure?" *Advances in Consumer Research* 17: 98–100.

8

Commentary: On the Dynamic and
Goal-Oriented Nature of (Candidate)
Evaluations

SHARON SHAVITT
MICHELLE R. NELSON

The three preceding chapters offer important conceptual and methodological insights for the study of candidate evaluation. Moreover, they
provide information relevant to social evaluation processes in general,
regardless of the nature of the target being evaluated. In this chapter, we
shall offer some comments and ideas elicited by these chapters. These
comments emerge from our own perspective as researchers interested in
evaluation processes primarily in the context of consumer advertising
campaigns. Thus, we seek not to evaluate the chapters in light of the
literature on political psychology or political science, but instead to offer
some integrative observations regarding the relation between the present
formulations and those used in the study of consumer judgments, as well
as the study of social judgments more generally.

OVERVIEW OF CHAPTERS

The chapter by Lau and Redlawsk approaches the issue of candidate evaluation from the perspective of behavioral decision theories (e.g., Abelson
and Levi, 1985; Einhorn and Hogarth, 1981; Slovic, Fischhoff, and
Lichtenstein, 1977). These are models that focus primarily on choice
processes and for which choice decisions are often the central dependent
variables. In contrast, the chapters by Taber, Lodge, and Glathar and
by McGraw approach candidate evaluation primarily from the perspective of attitude models such as information processing theory (McGuire,
1968, 1972) that focus on appraisals of individual targets. For these types
of models, absolute judgments are typically the dependent variables of
interest.

Perhaps these approaches all succeed because candidate judgments
can be effectively conceptualized both as absolute judgments and

ultimately, in the voting booth, as choice situations. Indeed, we observe the same research distinctions in other social judgment domains including consumer psychology, where some models focus on factors that influence evaluations of individual brands (e.g., Fishbein and Ajzen, 1975; Petty and Cacioppo, 1983) and other models focus on choices between brands (see Bettman, Johnson, and Payne, 1991, and Meyer and Kahn, 1991, for reviews).

Lau and Redlawsk's work draws attention to the fact that the information environment in which candidate judgments take place is highly complex. Their research reminds us that citizens are busy people with things to do. Even the most motivated citizens are functioning in a media environment that is a blooming, buzzing confusion of messages, issues, and candidates.

The fact that Lau and Redlawsk have been able to simulate many of the complexities of the typical campaign information environment in an experimental context is a valuable contribution in itself. Moreover, their work provides an important demonstration of the impact of this dynamic environment on people's information processing strategies and, in turn, on the quality of the decisions they make. Lau and Redlawsk's work highlights the need for more attention to how the information environment drives candidate choice processes.

Taber, Lodge, and Glathar outline a dynamic "constructive" theory of candidate evaluation in which candidate judgments are continually brought into working memory for updating and revision. The authors describe their refinement of the Stony Brook model (Lodge, 1993; Lodge, McGraw, and Stroh, 1989; Lodge and Stroh, 1992) – a model that was already impressively integrative before it was broadened to consider processes of motivated reasoning. The model that the authors present provides a unifying framework for conceptualizing ongoing evaluation processes, drawing as it does on models of categorization, memory, evaluation, and now motivation. Moreover, its focus on specific cognitive underpinnings gives this model the power to make precise predictions about candidate evaluations.

Finally, McGraw's program of research draws upon attribution theories and persuasion models to investigate the effects of political accounts (politicians' explanations for their actions) on constituents. McGraw provides a cogent conceptualization of accounts as persuasive messages and analyzes the impact of these accounts using a multistage persuasion model, information processing theory (McGuire, 1968, 1972).

One of the most useful aspects of this research is that it distinguishes between the effects of political accounts on attributions of responsibility, on perceptions of distinct dimensions of political character, on satisfaction with the accounts (i.e., their persuasiveness), and on global evaluations of politicians. In differentiating these effects, McGraw's work provides insight into the processes by which constituents are influenced by officials' accounts.

COMMON THEMES

Although these chapters deal with substantively different aspects of candidate judgments, some common issues emerge across them. First, all three chapters address the importance of accounting for *motivational influences* on the candidate evaluation process.

As noted earlier, Taber, Lodge, and Glathar broaden the Stony Brook model to address the impact of motivation on political cognition. Their approach focuses on how motivation affects reasoning at every stage of information processing, including information retrieval, interpretation, and evaluation. Basing their motivational typology on the work of Kunda (1990) and Kruglanski (1980), Taber et al. examine "accuracy goals" and "directional goals" as potential biases in the reception and processing of political information (see also Chaiken, Liberman, and Eagly, 1989, and Petty and Cacioppo, 1986, for reviews of how these goals impact attitude-formation processes). In the model that Taber et al. present, the motivated political perceiver acts to forestall a change in his or her attitudes. The model describes the mechanisms by which accuracy goals and directional goals are likely to function to preserve prior political beliefs. We shall return to this issue later.

Lau and Redlawsk conceptualize citizens as purposeful and strategic in their selection of candidate information to be processed. Although they recognize that voters are often exposed to political information in an uncontrolled and haphazard manner, Lau and Redlawsk focus on what voters actively choose to learn about candidates. Their results suggest that the information-search and decision strategies that voters use may depend upon their election decision goals (i.e., selecting a candidate in a primary campaign versus in a general election).

Finally, McGraw considers the motivations driving both politicians and their constituent audiences in "blame-management" episodes. In particular, McGraw recognizes that political accounts serve a *social identity function* in that they are designed to obtain or maintain social support among important constituencies. Her view of political accounts is grounded within the broad scope of strategic activities in which politicians engage in order to shape constituent opinions.

Another common theme emerging across these chapters is the need to approach candidate evaluation as a *dynamic process*. Indeed, a variety of recent psychological studies suggest that the expression of attitudes and other social judgments is quite malleable and easily influenced by

229

salient and often temporary internal or external cues (see Martin and Tesser, 1992; Wilson and Hodges, 1992; see also Shavitt and Fazio, 1991, for evidence regarding the malleability of consumer judgments; but see Wilson, Lindsey, and Schooler, 1999, for detailed consideration of the possibility that explicit expressions of attitudes exaggerate the ease with which people change their habitual implicit attitudes).

As noted earlier, Taber et al. take a constructivist view of candidate evaluation, noting that for many citizens "political attitudes appear to be constructed on the spot from currently active knowledge structures." The authors' work focuses on the crucial fact that candidate evaluations reported by voters in one context need not be based on the same considerations or information underlying their evaluations in another context. Their model describes the cognitive mechanisms by which candidate evaluations are brought into working memory, compared to currently salient information, and, if appropriate, updated.

McGraw's research on political accounts focuses on the ongoing goal-driven relationship between politicians and their constituents. Her analysis underscores the fact that "attribution processes are inherently dynamic, constantly under revision as new information – such as accounts – becomes available." McGraw's studies demonstrate that citizens are indeed responsive to new information in updating and revising their perceptions of specific dimensions of a politician's character.

Lau and Redlawsk's work focuses on the ever-changing information environment often faced by voters. As the authors point out, most studies of voter decision making utilize static survey designs that cannot fully address the real-world decision processes used by voters. The dynamic process-tracing methodology they develop emphasizes the changing nature of the media information environment and enables continuous monitoring of evaluative responses to that information.

All of the foregoing chapters highlight the need for techniques that capture the dynamic nature of candidate evaluations. The importance of theory and methods that provide insight into this ongoing evaluation process cannot be overstated. We turn now to some questions raised in addressing the dynamic, goal-oriented nature of candidate evaluation.

QUESTIONS TO CONSIDER

As Taber et al. point out, the notion of attitudes as static and enduring has been the traditional view in the attitude literature. In deviating from this assumption, a variety of new questions need to be considered. One of the key questions is, *What are the conditions that will prompt a voter to reevaluate his or her existing attitude?*

Dynamic and Goal-Oriented Evaluations

Previous research in social psychology has suggested that people sometimes retrieve an existing attitude and reapply it (e.g., Srull, 1989), even in situations that merit a new judgment (Lingle and Ostrom, 1979). Other research has suggested that people sometimes compute a new judgment of an issue or a candidate even though they already possess a relevant attitude toward it (e.g., Krosnick and Schuman, 1988; Tourangeau and Rasinski, 1988). Is there any regularity to when each strategy is used?

What will be the role of motives in prompting the reevaluation of attitudes? It is particularly important to consider motivational influences on these evaluation processes. Because attitudes are formed in the service of particular goals or functions (see Katz, 1960; Kelman, 1958, 1961; Smith, Bruner, and White, 1956), these goals should also influence the likelihood that an attitude will be updated or changed when making a subsequent judgment.

Another important and related issue concerns how individual attributes or considerations will be weighed when evaluating (or reevaluating) a candidate. *Will there be differences in the weights assigned to individual attributes? And will those weights change when reevaluation occurs?* The weights assigned to candidate attributes are likely to vary across attributes and across evaluation occasions. One reason this may happen is that the goals or purposes underlying the evaluation may change from the time an initial attitude is formed until the opportunity to reevaluate comes along.

When one turns to the domain of product evaluation, one sees how easily this can happen. Picture your evaluation of restaurants in your community: When taking a visiting colleague out to dinner, your primary goal may be to create a positive social impression and have a pleasant social interaction (this is related to the social identity goal that McGraw describes). In this case, your evaluation will be based on such attributes as a restaurant's ambience, the quality of its food, and the professionalism of its staff.

In contrast, when going out for lunch in the middle of a busy day, your goal may be to obtain a quick meal at the lowest possible cost (in terms of time and money). In this case, your evaluation will be based on speed of service, low price, and *adequacy* of the food (i.e., is it edible?).

As this illustrates, the attributes that enter into an evaluation may vary, depending on the purpose or goal one has in mind when making that evaluation. Moreover, the weights assigned to these attributes may vary (e.g., the weight assigned to food quality would likely be much lower in the second scenario). As a result, one's evaluation of a restaurant would likely be computed quite differently in these two contexts (see Shavitt, Swan, Lowrey, and Wanke, 1994).

Similarly, in the political domain, voters' decisions may be driven by a variety of motives. Indeed, election campaigns often attempt to frame voting decisions in terms of particular goals. A presidential campaign that suggests that you "ask yourself, are you better off now than you were four years ago?" would likely make salient different goals than a political campaign that urges you to "vote your conscience."

The goals that are salient in evaluating a politician may vary across evaluation occasions as a function of such campaign slogans, as well as media reports and other contextual stimuli. Thus, the reevaluation of one's candidate tally may be driven by different motives than were prior evaluations of the candidate. This makes it likely that some considerations and attributes of the candidate will receive greater or lesser weight in a reevaluation than they did in the initial attitude.

A WORKING MODEL

Kim and Shavitt (1993) outlined a working model of "attitude reuse versus recomputation" that attempts to address some of these issues concerning reevaluation processes (see Figure 8.1). It shares with several other processing models the view of individuals as "cognitive misers" (Taylor and Fiske, 1981). For that reason, the model is set up with the assumption that it is fairly difficult to trigger the generation of a new attitude (recomputation) when an already formed and accessible one exists. It takes motivation, ability, and consideration of the basis for the attitude, as well as a recognized change in goal contingencies, in order for recomputation to occur. The model consists of several stages or decision points that direct the individual away from the more effortful path leading to recomputation and toward the less effortful path of reusing an existing attitude. These stages can be thought of as defenses not only against the task of recomputing the attitude, but also against changes in related attitudes that may be necessitated by the recomputation.

As noted earlier, the model proposed by Taber et al. also assumes that attitudes will resist recomputation. Interestingly, however, their model puts greater emphasis on the ego-defensive motive underlying this resistance. Perhaps this is a reflection of the different attitudinal domains (political vs. consumer) for which the two models were developed. Changing one's key political beliefs would likely be more ego-threatening than changing one's product evaluations.

Cognitive Effort

As with Taber et al.'s model, Kim and Shavitt (1993) highlight the role of judgment importance in motivating attitude recomputation: if an

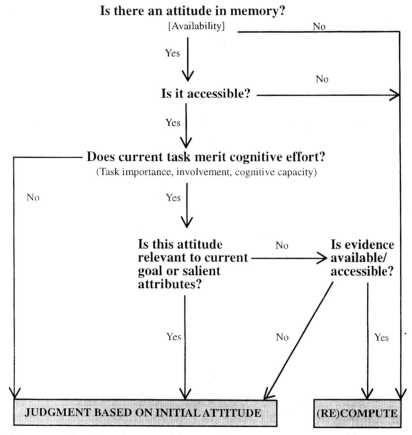

Figure 8.1. Flowchart for attitude reuse versus recomputation. Source: Kim and Shavitt, 1993. Reprinted by permission.

already existing attitude has been activated, it would be especially likely to guide one's subsequent judgment if that judgment is not considered particularly important. Reconsideration of the attitude would take effort. Thus, whether any further processing occurs (as opposed to opting out at this point and reapplying one's existing attitude) depends on the perceived importance of the judgment task, including the level of involvement or personal relevance associated with the task.

Cognitive capacity will also play an important role. In capacity-limited situations – such as the dynamic, scrolling presentation format used by Lau and Redlawsk or the complex real-world media environment to which voters are often exposed – one would expect attitudes more often to be reused without reconsideration, regardless of task importance. For example, studies have shown that social stereotypes function to preserve cognitive resources (Macrae, Milne, and Bodenhausen, 1994), and thus are more likely to guide evaluations of members of a stereotyped group when processing is constrained by time limits or task complexity (e.g., Bodenhausen and Lichtenstein, 1987; Bodenhausen and Wyer, 1985; Jamieson and Zanna, 1989; Kruglanski and Freund, 1983).

Attitude Relevance

In our view, the perceived relevance of the attitude for current goals is one of the most important factors in prompting recomputation. If task importance and cognitive capacity are sufficiently high to motivate recomputation of the attitude, then one proceeds to assess whether there is a need to do so, that is, whether one's initial evaluation is sufficiently relevant for current purposes. The model proposes a number of factors that can influence this judgment of relevance.

The relevance judgment is based on information that one can access about the beliefs on which the initial attitude was based (e.g., beliefs about the attributes or benefits of the target) or about the goals that were salient when the attitude was formed. This does not necessarily mean detailed information about the content of one's beliefs (e.g., Wood, 1982; Wood, Kallgren, and Priesler, 1985), but more likely a summary "tag" describing the criterion for the initial attitude (e.g., *I liked the restaurant because of the food* or *I liked the candidate because of his views on the environment*).

A judgment of relevance is made along a continuum, not as a yes/no judgment. When a certain threshold is surpassed, the initial basis for the attitude is likely to be rejected as insufficiently relevant for one's current goals (e.g., *I liked that candidate when he last ran for office, but I was younger then and cared more about the environment than about my taxes*). Again, the perceived importance of the judgment will play a key role in determining the height of the threshold. The more important the judgment, the lower the threshold. The lower the threshold, the more likely one will be to reject the basis for the initial attitude and, thus, to reject the initial attitude itself as insufficiently relevant to one's current goals.

A variety of other factors can also affect the relevance judgment, including the salience of concepts that may influence how one interprets the basis for one's existing attitude. For example, let's say that an initial attitude toward a restaurant was based on its food quality. Now one needs to decide whether to take an important visitor to this restaurant, so one's new goal is to judge whether the restaurant would make a good impression. Whether food quality will be perceived as relevant to the new social identity goal will depend on whether such concepts as "gourmet" are salient. If such concepts are salient in the judgment context, then the initial restaurant attitude (based on food quality) will likely be reused to evaluate the restaurant. Otherwise, one may look for relevant evidence with which to recompute the evaluation.

As Zanna and Rempel (1988) and Wood (1982) have pointed out, people are not always able to access the informational basis for their initial attitude (e.g., *I agreed with that tax policy, but I can't remember why*). In such cases, one may be reluctant to base a current judgment about the topic on the existing attitude because the relevance of that attitude cannot be determined. Instead, one may seek evidence on which to base a recomputation that is specific to one's current goals.

Evidence Availability/Accessibility

If one perceives the need for more evidence, one will consider new information that one is exposed to or seeks and/or existing knowledge in memory that one can retrieve. Whether a piece of information will be perceived as evidence that is specific to one's current goals is a relevance type of judgment, and is determined by the same factors that affect the judgments of relevance discussed earlier.

Assuming one has evidence that is perceived to be relevant, how will that evidence be dealt with? The answer may depend on why the additional evidence is being sought. If it is because the informational basis of the initial attitude is not accessible, and thus the relevance of that attitude cannot be established, then the directional goal processes reviewed by Taber et al. will likely bias the search for and interpretation of evidence. That is, the perception of new evidence will be filtered through the initial attitude, leading to the selective interpretation processes that have been described by Fazio (1989). Also, any evidence retrieved from memory will be subject to known biases of retrieval and reconstruction. Overall, then, these directional biases will lead to *assimilation* of the new judgment to the initial attitude. McGraw points to similar processes in describing how a politician's previously established reputation can bias the evaluation of accounts offered by that politician.

On the other hand, if additional evidence is being sought because the basis for the initial attitude has been accessed and judged to be irrelevant to one's current goal, then the processes described by Martin (1986) and by Tourangeau and Rasinski (1988) may apply. That is, in evaluating the evidence, one will consciously adjust for the presumed influence of the existing evaluation. This could lead to *contrast* of the new judgment away from the initial attitude.

Sharon Shavitt and Michelle R. Nelson

(Re)computation of Attitude

Recomputing an attitude does not necessarily mean abandoning the existing attitude (see Wilson et al., 1999). But recomputation may involve an adjustment or updating of that attitude. The valence of the new judgment may be similar to or very different from that of the initial attitude.

Recomputation may occur through different processes, depending on the earlier decision points. The new judgment could be formed systematically and deliberatively, or through more peripheral or heuristic processes (Chaiken, 1987; Petty and Cacioppo, 1986), depending in part on the perceived relevance of the initial attitude and the perceived importance of the judgment task (i.e., the degree to which they surpassed the threshold to prompt recomputation). The greater the perceived relevance, importance, and so on of the attitude, the more effort and deliberation will go into the recomputation.

Reuse of Attitude

Reapplication of one's initial attitude may also occur through different processes. Reuse of the attitude may be relatively automatic and effortless, as when the new judgment task is not perceived to be important and the existing attitude is accessed and used without evaluating its relevance. Alternatively, reuse of the attitude may be a fairly deliberate decision made upon comparing that attitude to the new situation and evaluating its relevance to current needs. In some cases, the evidence needed to perform a recomputation may be sought but not found, and the decision to reuse the initial attitude may then follow.

CONCLUSIONS AND IMPLICATIONS

This working model is presented in an attempt to raise issues that reinforce or complement the important points addressed in the previous chapters. In describing the model here, we hope to stimulate research that sheds additional light on the dynamic, goal-oriented nature of candidate evaluations.

Unfortunately, our model does leave some important issues unresolved. For instance, it fails to address the information-driven nature of the candidate evaluation process. As the three foregoing chapters illustrate, candidate evaluations (or reevaluations) are often prompted by information encountered in the media (facts about candidates, political accounts, or other coverage). In contrast, the approach we have outlined here attempts to model situations in which the need to make a judgment or decision (e.g., in response to a pollster, in the voting booth) serves as the prompt to (re)evaluation. More work is needed to broaden this approach to contexts in which new information is encountered that may call into question one's initial candidate evaluation.

On the other hand, the model offers a number of important implications for studying the reevaluation of candidate judgments. For example, it suggests that the decision to reuse an initial candidate evaluation when making subsequent judgments or decisions may not be less effortful than the decision to reevaluate (recompute). Also, when the judgment is deemed important, highly accessible attitudes may not necessarily be reused unless the basis for the attitude is accessible and is judged to be relevant to current goals.

Finally, the model suggests that the goals or attributes made salient by the judgment context can have important effects at a number of points in the candidate evaluation process, facilitating access to existing attitudes in memory, affecting judgments of the relevance of those attitudes for meeting current goals, and influencing the access to and interpretation of additional evidence during the recomputation of candidate evaluations.

References

Abelson, R., and A. Levi (1985). "Decision Making and Decision Theory." In G. Lindzey and E. Aronson (Eds.), *The Handbook of Social Psychology* (Vol. 1, 3rd ed., pp. 231–309). New York: Random House.

Bettman, J. R., E. J. Johnson, and J. W. Payne (1991). "Consumer Decision Making." In T. S. Robertson and H. H. Kassarjian (Eds.), *Handbook of Consumer Behavior* (pp. 50–84). Englewood Cliffs, NJ: Prentice-Hall.

Bodenhausen, G. V., and M. Lichtenstein (1987). "Social Stereotypes and Information-Processing Strategies: The Impact of Task Complexity." *Journal of Personality and Social Psychology* 52: 871–880.

Bodenhausen, G. V., and R. S. Wyer (1985). "Effects of Stereotypes on Decision Making and Information-Processing Strategy." *Journal of Personality and Social Psychology* 48: 267–282.

Chaiken, S. (1987). "The Heuristic Model of Persuasion." In M. P. Zanna, J. M. Olson, and C. P. Herman (Eds.), *Social Influence: The Ontario Symposium* (Vol. 5, pp. 3–39). Hillsdale, NJ: Erlbaum.

Chaiken, S., A. Liberman, and A. H. Eagly (1989). "Heuristic and Systematic Information Processing within the Persuasion Context." In J. S. Uleman and J. A. Bargh (Eds.), *Unintended Thought* (pp. 212–252). New York: Guilford Press.

Einhorn, H. J., and R. M. Hogarth (1981). "Behavioral Decision Theory: Processes of Judgment and Choice." *Annual Review of Psychology* 32: 53–88.

Fazio, R. H. (1989). "On the Power and Functionality of Attitudes: The Role of Attitude Accessibility." In A. R. Pratkanis, S. J. Breckler, and A. G. Greenwald (Eds.), *Attitude Structure and Function* (pp. 153–179). Hillsdale, NJ: Erlbaum.

Fishbein, M., and I. Ajzen (1975). *Belief, Attitude, Intention and Behavior: An Introduction to Theory and Research.* Reading, MA: Addison-Wesley.

Jamieson, D. W., and M. P. Zanna (1989). "Need for Structure in Attitude Formation and Expression." In A. R. Pratkanis, S. J. Breckler, and A. G. Greenwald (Eds.), *Attitude Structure and Function* (pp. 383–406). Hillsdale, NJ: Erlbaum.

Katz, D. (1960). "The Functional Approach to the Study of Attitudes." *Public Opinion Quarterly* 24(2): 163–204.

Kelman, H. C. (1958). "Compliance, Identification, and Internalization: Three Processes of Attitude Change." *Journal of Conflict Resolution* 2, 51–60.

(1961). "Processes of Opinion Change." *Public Opinion Quarterly* 25: 57–78.

Kim, K., and S. Shavitt (1993). "Toward a Model of Attitude Reuse and Recomputation." In K. Finlay, A. A. Mitchell, and F. C. Cummins (Eds.), *Proceedings of the Society for Consumer Psychology, American Psychological Association* (pp. 105–110). Clemson, SC: CtC Press.

Krosnick, J. A., and H. Schuman (1988). "Attitude Intensity, Importance, and Certainty and Susceptibility to Response Effects." *Journal of Personality and Social Psychology* 65: 940–952.

Kruglanski, A. W. (1980). "Lay Epistemology Process and Contents." *Psychological Review* 87: 70–87.

Kruglanski, A. W., and T. Freund (1983). "The Freezing and Unfreezing of Lay References: Effects on Impressional Primacy, Ethnic Stereotyping, and Numerical Anchoring." *Journal of Experimental Social Psychology* 19: 448–468.

Kunda, Z. (1990). "The Case for Motivated Reasoning." *Psychological Bulletin* 108(3): 480–498.

Lingle, J. H., and T. M. Ostrom (1979). "Retrieval Selectivity in Memory-Based Impression Judgments." *Journal of Personality and Social Psychology* 37: 180–194.

Lodge, M. (1993). "Toward a Procedural Model of Candidate Evaluation." In M. L. Lodge and K. M. McGraw (Eds.), *Political Judgment: Structure and Process* (pp. 111–139). Ann Arbor: University of Michigan Press.

Lodge, M., K. McGraw, and P. Stroh (1989). "An Impression-Driven Model of Candidate Evaluation." *American Political Science Review* 83: 399–419.

Lodge, M., and P. Stroh (1992). "Inside the Mental Voting Booth: An Impression-Driven Process Model of Candidate Evaluation." In S. Iyengar and W. J. McGuire (Eds.), *Explorations in Political Psychology. Duke Studies in Political Psychology* (pp. 225–263). Durham, NC: Duke University Press.

Macrae, N. C., and A. B. Milne (1994). "Stereotypes as Energy-Saving Devices: A Peek Inside the Cognitive Toolbox." *Journal of Personality and Social Psychology* 66(1): 37–47.

Macrae, C. N., A. B. Milne, and G. V. Bodenhausen (1994). "Stereotypes as Energy-Saving Devices: A Peek Inside the Cognitive Tool Box." *Journal of Personality and Social Psychology* 66(1): 37–47.

Martin, L. (1986). "Set/Reset: Use and Disuse of Concepts in Impression Formation." *Journal of Personality and Social Psychology* 51: 493–504.

Martin, L., and A. Tesser (1992). *Construction of Social Judgments.* Hillsdale, NJ: Erlbaum.

McGuire, W. J. (1968). "Personality and Attitude Change: An Information-Processing Theory." In A. G. Greenwald, T. C. Brock, and T. M. Ostrom (Eds.), *Psychological Foundations of Attitudes* (pp. 171–196). New York: Academic Press.

Dynamic and Goal-Oriented Evaluations

(1972). "Attitude Change: An Information-Processing Paradigm." In C. G. McClintock (Ed.), *Experimental Social Psychology* (pp. 108–141). New York: Holt, Rinehart and Winston.

Meyer, R. J., and B. E. Kahn (1991). "Probabilistic Models of Consumer Choice Behavior." In T. S. Robertson and H. H. Kassarjian (Eds.), *Handbook of Consumer Behavior* (pp. 85–123). Englewood Cliffs, NJ: Prentice-Hall.

Petty, R. E., and J. T. Cacioppo (1983). "Central and Peripheral Routes to Persuasion: Application to Advertising." In L. Percy and A. G. Woodside (Eds.), *Advertising and Consumer Psychology* (pp. 3–23). Lexington, MA: Lexington Books.

(1986). *Communication and Persuasion: Central and Peripheral Routes to Attitude Change.* New York: Springer-Verlag.

Shavitt, S., and R. H. Fazio (1991). "Effects of Attribute Salience on the Consistency Between Attitudes and Behavior Predictions." *Personality and Social Psychology Bulletin* 17: 507–516.

Shavitt, S., S. Swan, T. M. Lowrey, and M. Wanke (1994). "The Interaction of Endorser Attractiveness and Involvement in Persuasion Depends on the Goal That Guides Message Processing." *Journal of Consumer Psychology* 3(2): 137–162.

Slovic, P., B. Fischoff, and S. Lichtenstein (1977). "Behavioral Decision Theory." *Annual Review of Psychology* 28: 1–39.

Smith, M. B., J. S. Bruner, and R. W. White (1956). *Opinions and Personality.* New York: Wiley.

Srull, T. K. (1989). "Advertising and Product Evaluation: The Relation Between Consumer Memory and Judgment." In P. Cafferata and A. Tybout (Eds.), *Cognitive and Affective Responses to Advertising* (pp. 121–134). Lexington, MA: Heath.

Taylor, S. E., and S. T. Fiske (1981). "Getting Inside the Head: Methodologies for Process Analysis in Attribution and Social Cognition." In J. H. Harvey, W. Ickes, and R. F. Kidd (Eds.), *New Directions in Attribution Research* (Vol. 3, pp. 459–524). Hillsdale, NJ: Erlbaum.

Tourangeau, R., and K. A. Rasinski (1988). "Cognitive Processes Underlying Context Effects in Attitude Measurement." *Psychological Bulletin* 103: 299–314.

Wilson, T., and S. Hodges (1992). "Attitudes as Temporary Constructs." In L. Martin and A. Tesser (Eds.), *Construction of Social Judgements* (pp. 37–65). Hillsdale, NJ: Erlbaum.

Wilson, T., S. Lindsey, and T. Y. Schooler (1999). A model of dual attitudes. *Psychological Review* 107(1): 101–126.

Wood, W. (1982). "Retrieval of Attitude-Relevant Information from Memory: Effects on Susceptibility to Persuasion and on Intrinsic Motivation." *Journal of Personality and Social Psychology* 42: 798–810.

Wood, W., C. A. Kallgren, and R. M. Priesler (1985). "Access to Attitude-Relevant Information in Memory as a Determinant of Persuasion: The Role of Message Attributes." *Journal of Experimental Social Psychology* 21: 73–85.

Zanna, M. P., and J. K. Rempel (1988). "Attitudes: A New Look at an Old Concept." In D. Bar-Tal and A. W. Kruglanski (Eds.), *The Social Psychology of Knowledge* (pp. 315–334). Cambridge, UK: Cambridge University Press.

Part III Political Attitudes and Perceptions

Introduction

The study of attitudes is the bread and butter of public opinion research. It has a history traceable at least to the Lazarsfeld-led Columbia studies conducted during the 1940s and early 1950s. A decade after the last of the Columbia studies was published, Converse crystallized what continues to be a strongly debated question: just how real and meaningful are ordinary citizens' attitudes?

Converse reported compelling evidence that the majority of people lacked stable or consistent attitudes. Their expressed policy preferences changed randomly over time and reflected almost no liberal-conservative coherence across issue domains. In Converse's view, most citizens could not, or at least did not, engage issues of public policy.

Although several scholars raised serious challenges to Converse's portrayal, only recently has anyone proposed a new and fundamentally different conception of attitudes and attitude formation. In his 1992 publication *The Nature and Origins of Mass Opinion*, John Zaller adopts a social constructionist perspective that had gained some prominence in social psychology. For any given policy domain, he argues, people hold more than one relevant consideration; what an individual's preference will be at any given time depends on which considerations prevail, which in turn depends on the social cues that the individual happens to receive. Thus, for example, a taxpayer might initially oppose increased school funding because high property taxes come to mind but then later support it because another consideration, low teachers' salaries, say, gains her attention. In a word, the taxpayer is ambivalent, and thus her expressed attitude at any point in time depends on whether she is cued to think principally about the pro or con considerations.

CONCEPTIONS

The three chapters that follow push the discussion of political attitudes even further. Sniderman, Tetlock, and Elms use creative experimental

243

survey data to demonstrate that, contrary to the ambivalence thesis, attitudes look quite real when both situational and predispositional factors are taken into account; thus they challenge the validity of Zaller's social constructionist perspective. In Diamond's view, the crucial task is to move beyond "point placement" measures of attitudes, which nearly all researchers (including Zaller and Sniderman) use but which do not comport with how ordinary citizens think about issues. Diamond proposes a latitude model that demarcates the policy options and issue positions individuals reject from those they accept or feel noncommital about. Finally, Hochschild recommends that scholars incorporate perceptions into attitude research. People "see" their worlds, and what they "see" reflects and also influences their values and attitudes. More important, perceptions can interact with values and attitudes to shape people's policy preferences in ways that traditional attitude research has not explored.

Sniderman et al. begin by noting that the Zaller view of political attitudes represents a marked departure from existing conceptions. Even Converse, they argue, did not say that most of the people, most of the time "just make it up as they go along." And in striking contrast to Converse, who saw the basic problem as a lack of thought, and thus too few ideas, Zaller sees the problem as people having too many ideas (considerations), which push their attitudes in all directions. In the authors' words, because citizens believe everything, they believe nothing.

Two central factors in the Zaller model are the individual's predispositions, principally ideology, and the context or situation. In the real world, the context consists of available social and political cues; in survey research, question wording and ordering serve as a proxy for these cues. A situational change thus implies, in the first case, a redistribution of existing cues or the emergence of new ones and, in the second case, a rewording and/or reordering of the survey questions. Sniderman et al. argue that the social construction perspective places context and predisposition at odds: the more influential the former, the less influential the latter. This follows logically in that reliance on ideology implies attitude consistency, while reliance on cues or considerations implies attitude flip-flopping. The Zaller model, by giving center stage to ambivalence, emphasizes context and simultaneously attenuates ideology.

The authors propose an alternative, which they call "cognitive combinatorics". On this view, attitudes are a product of both situation and predisposition. These two factors can influence attitudes additively or interactively. What distinguishes the Sniderman et al. model is that when one factor strongly influences attitudes, the other need not be weak. Indeed, Sniderman et al. argue, the two factors normally should complement rather than be at odds with each other. In their words, "a bigot will respond more negatively to African Americans in some situations than others; but in all situations where there is any choice, a bigot will respond more negatively to African Americans than a person who is racially tolerant."

Before examining some experimental survey data of their own, the authors take stock of the evidence that Zaller provides. In their impressively thorough critique, Sniderman et al. first note that, despite a growing awareness among scholars of the need to do so, Zaller does not correct for measurement error. Putting that aside, Zaller's test-retest correlations show a marked stability in attitudes over time, a finding that does not comport with his thesis. Conversely, since the same question wording is used in over-time measurement, responses should be nearly identical; they are not. In other words, the modest across-time correlations damage Zaller on two fronts. Finally, Sniderman et al. criticize Zaller's (and Zaller and Feldman's) "stop and think" experiments, which entail first reading a question about an issue and then interrupting the respondent before he answers and asking what considerations come to mind. This extraordinary request, say Sniderman et al., discombobulates people and thus itself increases the variability in their answers.

The authors' own evidence takes the form of two exceptionally creative experiments embedded in their 1991 Politics and Race Study. In the Probable Cause experiment, respondents consider a situation in which the police see two young men walking near a house where drugs are known to be sold. A randomly selected half of the respondents are told that the young men are well dressed and well behaved. The other half are told that the men are using foul language. Everyone is told that the police searched them and then everyone is asked to evaluate the police action. The authors find the following: (1) there is a modest relationship between the young men's demeanor – well behaved or using foul language – and judgments about the police conduct; (2) people who favor more law and order support the search more than those who do not; and (3) the situational (men's demeanor) and predispositional (support for law and order) factors additively influence reactions to the police action. In either situation, advocates of law and order more strongly condone the police search; and the search receives more support from both the low and high law-and-order groups when the young men are using foul language.

The Helping Hand experiment takes the complementarity argument a step further by showing that people's predispositions, in this case their ideologies, can interact with the situational cue. Conservatives express an especially high level of support for a hypothetical poverty program when they are told that the program is designed to help people who have shown that they want to work their way out of their own problems; this is mostly the case among sophisticated conservatives. On the other hand, liberals express their highest support when the program is described as intended to help blacks and other minorities; again, this interaction between situation and predisposition is strongest among the most politically aware. In the authors' view, the evidence overwhelmingly shows that people consistently and systematically use their political priors and then update by using the current information about the situation described to them. Attitudes, in short, do not randomly flip-flop.

Despite the sharp differences in conclusions, Sniderman et al. and Zaller share one important premise: point placement measures are the most useful method to reveal the true nature of political attitudes. Such measures dominate survey research. People are given 7- or 10-point scales and asked to identify their single most preferred position on them. The underlying assumption is that the item taps a single dimension.

Diamond swims upstream and proposes that political scientists consider an alternative to the point placement form: latitude measures. Such measures stem from latitude theory, which has roots in work that psychologists Sherif and Hovland introduced three decades ago. The idea is to study attitudes in terms of three regions, or latitudes: a latitude of acceptance, a latitude of noncommitment, and a latitude of rejection. As the three regions imply, an individual might find one or more options acceptable, be indifferent to others, and deem yet others totally unacceptable. Of the three regions, the latitude of rejection is key. It allows for negative political thinking, which, Diamond asserts, is common to decision making. Indeed, people will be more stable in their determinations of what is unacceptable and unreasonable than in their choice of optimal points.

More generally, latitude judgments require less effort from citizens. Rather than wasting time trying to distinguish an optimal from a nearly optimal point, the individual respondent simply places each option into one of three categories: good, bad, or indifferent. Most significantly, these determinations are largely affect-driven. To classify something as bad, especially, is to express a feeling about what is not desirable; and most people know what they don't like.

The two defining characteristics of the latitude of rejection are its width and its placement. On a 7-point scale, for example, one individual's rejection zone might include 4, 5, 6, and 7, while another's might include only 6 and 7. Or one individual's might include 6 and 7, while another's might include 1 and 2. In the first case, width differs; in the second, placement. Neither the width nor the placement is written in stone; to the contrary, they presumably will vary, for any given individual, over time and across circumstances. It is this variability, in fact, that renders the latitude of rejection so important to politics. Political operatives will work to narrow the latitude of rejection on their side of the issue and widen it on the other side.

Diamond offers many illustrative examples. In 1988, George Bush successfully widened the latitude of rejection on the issue of flag burning. He did so by convincing the majority of the electorate that any form of desecration to the flag was unpatriotic and thus intolerable. Whereas cries for maintaining civil liberties had previously kept many people noncommittal, they now defined anything that even hinted of disrespect as an affront to the country.

A more provocative example takes the form of a hypothetical debate on some issue between two candidates. Two citizens, A and B, each begin with a latitude structure, that is, each initially accepts some positions on a 7-point liberal–conservative dimension, remains noncommittal on others, and rejects the remainder. A's initial structure differs from B's. The two citizens then encounter a conservative argument, and both shift their structure 1 point in a conservative direction. They then hear a relatively persuasive liberal argument, which again leads the two citizens to change what they will accept, reject, and remain noncommittal about. What happens is that both citizens' noncommittal regions grow larger. When the two arguments are maximally convincing, neither voter will reject either candidate for taking any stance on the dimension. Consequently, what had been an issue becomes a nonissue in the campaign, and other, less debated issues become the basis for choosing a candidate. All of this assumes that each candidate argues on his or her own behalf. If, on the other hand, each candidate tries to convince voters that they should reject the opponent, the overall effect often can be gridlock and thus a bias toward the status quo.

Latitude theory also affords a novel perspective on citizen–elite linkages. As long as a politician works within the citizenry's latitude of noncommitment, he or she can maneuver with considerable freedom. This is not, of course, because most citizens find the politician's positions acceptable; rather, they are indifferent. If the politician unwittingly enters what is a consensual region of rejection, however, public outcry can be swift and widespread. Diamond illustrates his point with the Clinton administration's attempt to appoint Zoe Baird as attorney general early in his first term. A point placement model, in contrast, predicts that opposition to an official's changing policy stances will occur incrementally as the official moves further and further from the median voter's position.

After considering some additional implications that follow from adoption of a latitude perspective, Diamond reviews some of his earlier empirical work. The major obstacle is that people often don't support, tolerate, and reject options on a dimension in any kind of systematic

James H. Kuklinski

order. Thus, an individual's latitude of rejection could include options both to the left and to the right of his noncommittal region (assuming a liberal–conservative dimension). That the responses do not form any kind of Guttman scale (harder to easier, liberal to conservative, etc.) renders latitude measurement problematic. In his defense, Diamond notes that this problem also plagues point placement measurements that assume a dimension. The difference is that point placement measures essentially mask the problem.

While Diamond proposes a fundamentally different approach to the measure of political attitudes, Hochschild recommends the front-and-center addition of a heretofore neglected element: people's perceptions of facts. In her view, such perceptions probably shape a whole range of political attitudes, including particular policy preferences. "Where you stand depends on what you see."

What makes perceptions of facts so crucial to the study of political attitudes is that people grossly misperceive the world. It is well known, for example, that more than half of all Americans widely overestimate the proportion of blacks in the populace. Other evidence shows that people also get the facts about welfare wrong – and firmly believe they have them right. For example, even though about 1% of the national budget goes to Aid to Families with Dependent Children (AFDC) payments, many citizens "see" a government that spends 20% or more of its annual budget on AFDC payments.

Hochschild offers numerous examples of how perceptions of facts could induce some attitudes rather than others. Similarly, she illustrates how the same attitude can interact with different perceptions to produce divergent reactions toward the society as a whole. Take two people who both subscribe strongly to individualism and the work ethic. One over-estimates his income and concludes that it is above the national average; the other underestimates and "sees" her income as below the national average. The consequence: despite a common adherence to basic principles like individualism, one person feels gratified and thus embraces society, while the other feels bitter and thus castigates it. Hochschild believes that the United States harbors more of the latter than the former, which leads to a politics of resentment. The more general point is that a focus on attitudes alone would not detect a dynamic that potentially could help to explain much about American politics.

There is also the matter of metaperceptions: people's perceptions of others' perceptions. Citizens often are influenced by their perceptions of what others think. The collective result is that the distribution of opinion on an issue tends to move in tandem over time with people's perceptions of how many other people fall on one or the other side of

248

an issue. Perceptions feed attitudes, which then appear to influence perceptions, and so on.

The O. J. Simpson trial did more than any other event in recent times to dramatize how differently blacks and whites see the same world. Hochschild presents a sophisticated portrayal of this phenomenon. In fact, she reports, black and white Americans share the ideology of the American Dream. Overwhelming majorities of all Americans, black and white alike, support self-reliance, getting a good education, trying to get ahead through hard work, and equality of opportunity over equality of results. No "two worlds" phenomenon here. But ask about perceptions of how successful the country has been in establishing a more equitable society, and the phenomenon jumps out. Twice as many whites as blacks feel the nation has been making progress in achieving racial equality; indeed, the ratio has been increasing since the 1960s.

Middle-class black Americans have most strongly felt this discrepancy between values and perceptions. On the one hand, they believe strongly in the elements of the American Creed; on the other, they see themselves as worse off than they really are. The result: a declining faith, over time, in the American Dream accompanied by growing bitterness and declining faith in white Americans' desire to achieve racial equality. In this case, then, values and perceptions interact to generate attitudes.

Clearly, the introduction of perceptions into the study of political attitudes complicates an already challenging area of study. As Hochschild correctly observes, we know little about the causal relationships among values, attitudes, perceptions, and policy prescriptions; these relationships most likely are complex and, as a research matter, difficult to disentangle. Suppose that (mis)perceptions influence attitudes, which in turn then influence (mis)perceptions. One plausible and interesting implication is that attitudes will stabilize, such that even the availability of correct factual information will not readily change them.

Each of the chapters just discussed makes a compelling case for a particular point of view. What, in combination, do they tell us about the study of political attitudes? Most obviously, it's a complicated, if not bewildering, business. It has been more than three decades since Converse wrote. Despite, and perhaps because of, a proliferation of research since then, we still have not found an agreed-upon answer to his fundamental question: do real attitudes exist? Why? Part of the problem, just as it is with respect to the study of emotions, stems from political scientists' (inevitable) use of extant psychological perspectives. Anyone who has followed the psychological literature knows that these perspectives change. When Converse wrote, social constructionist views of attitudes had not gained prominence among social psychologists. By the time

Zaller was completing *The Nature and Origins of Mass Opinion*, some influential psychologists had begun to rethink the nature of attitudes. The idea that people constructed survey responses on the spot has a certain intuitive appeal. It also comports with and gains support from an experimental methodology that manipulates question wording and ordering (although Sniderman et al. demonstrate that survey experiments can also generate data in support of more traditional views). By the time that Sniderman et al. completed their critique of Zaller, many psychologists had already begun to recoil from the social constructionist perspective.

This is not to say that one perspective is inherently better than the other, or that students of public opinion blindly grab whatever psychological theory happens to be popular at the moment. They are much smarter than that. But no one who borrows from another discipline, and most political scientists do, is immune to its currents.

Introducing factual perceptions has great potential to contribute to ongoing discussions about the nature of political attitudes. People probably misperceive social and economic facts for a reason: to reinforce their existing attitudes. This very statement implies that attitudes exist. It also implies that attitudes should stabilize over time, since people's perceptions of facts, such as the proportion of the population that is black, presumably do not change randomly (at least within bounds). This said, it is equally plausible that people answer survey questions about facts from "the seats of their pants," just as Zaller says they do questions about attitudes.

The basic problem, of course, is that we cannot directly observe attitudes and perceptions. They are not physical "things," to be viewed, say, by a high-technology scanner. Researchers must ask people to express their thoughts and attitudes, which by definition represents an intrusion. "Pure," uncontaminated attitudes, if they ever existed at all, are then no longer pure. What then to do? The best answer is precisely what scholars have done: discern whether the attitudes, as survey instruments measure them, randomly or systematically change over time and context; determine whether these attitudes covary with other factors in predictable ways; see if people change their attitudes when confronted with arguments against their expressed positions; and so forth. But there would seem to be limits to how far scholars can go, within a survey context, and still claim validity for their survey measures. Where these limits are is not self-evident. Thus Zaller believes his stop-and-think experiment to be a legitimate measure of what he calls "considerations"; Sniderman et al. think otherwise and indeed argue that the experiment literally interrupts respondents' thought processes and thus invalidates the answers they give right after the experiment. And from Diamond's perspective, scholars should rethink the point measure enterprise in its totality. Scholars are using the wrong playing field.

So who is right? Future research undoubtedly will supply answers, which the scholarly community will judge. Someone almost certainly will speak to the Zaller–Sniderman disagreement. Hochschild has already offered preliminary evidence that the study of perceptions has much to offer scholars who investigate attitudes. Since Diamond proffers a fundamental change, from point to latitude measurement, he will probably find resistance from the scholarly community. Changes of the size that Diamond proposes do not come easily. Yet these kinds of changes, when made, can lead to powerful insights. Diamond himself provides some counterintuitive examples.

All of this research, too, will entail collecting measures that require some form and some level of intrusion. Intrusion by definition changes the very phenomenon one wants to understand. Thus it seems safe to predict that scholars will continue to debate the nature and meaningfulness of political attitudes well into the foreseeable future.

As they continue this debate, Kuklinski and Jerit recommend in their commentary, that scholars might want to shift some of their efforts from additional empirical analysis to a discussion of the logic of political attitudes in large-scale representative democracies. There are inherent limits on how well grounded citizens' opinions and preferences can be in modern societies, and those limits presumably tell us something about how to construe and think about political attitudes.

ATTITUDES AND THE QUALITY OF POLITICAL JUDGMENTS

Increasingly, or so it seems, reported national polls are becoming a primary vehicle by which citizens express their collective voice. To be sure, individual representatives still listen to the voices of their constituents; yet it cannot be denied that national polls can and do create momentum or stop it in its tracks. The dramatic decline in support for the Clinton health care plan, and its subsequent demise in Congress, are good evidence of the latter. But is the collective public voice grounded in some evaluation of reality or do polls and surveys send elected officials what looks like a strong but is in fact a noisy and ill-grounded signal?

The chapters in this part report evidence on both sides. Sniderman et al.'s findings show that people indeed do have meaningful attitudes. Their preferences and evaluations vary systematically with their ideologies and the situations they are given. Overall, liberals act like liberals and conservatives like conservatives. Moreover, people use situational information as they should: the more negative the information, the more negative the evaluation of the situation. And in at least one case, conservatives respond especially strongly to positive information, specifically that a government program is designed to help poor people who are trying to help themselves. In the authors' concluding paragraph they state, "if citizens acted only on the basis of their political attitudes, they would be blind to the present; if they acted only on the basis of their immediate circumstances, they would be blind to the past. They must, if they are to judge coherently, take account of both, and our results show they do."

The compelling experimental evidence that Sniderman et al. present, then, reveals a citizenry making reasonably well-grounded judgments. The authors would not propose that citizens' decisions are always error-free. To the contrary, the correlations they present throughout their chapter are modest, suggesting that there is considerable slippage in linking ideology to political evaluation. And it is equally obvious that some people, the less educated in particular, are often oblivious to changing circumstances. Nonetheless, the overall verdict is positive, especially when compared to the Zaller findings to which the authors are responding.

But people's attitudes and policy preferences, even when they exist, can still be problematic. Take the case of people forming their attitudes on the basis of faulty factual information, which is precisely where Hochschild's research is heading. On the kinds of facts that presumably shape and reinforce values and attitudes – the percentage of the population that is black, one's family income vis-à-vis the average national income – perceptions badly distort reality. Many overestimate the black proportion of the population, which, Hochschild suggests, might be increasing whites' sense of threat and thus reducing support for a racial policy. At least a third of all poor blacks see themselves doing better than they are, causing them to hold more positive attitudes toward the political system than they might otherwise. At this juncture, statements about relationships among values, attitudes, and perceptions are speculative. Nonetheless, it seems reasonable to assume that grossly wrong perceptions influence people's attitudes. If so, there could be a considerable bias in the collective attitudes that polls routinely support.

It is important to emphasize what Hochschild brings to the study of attitudes. That citizens are *un*informed is now an axiom of political science. But the more serious problem might be not an uninformed electorate but a badly *mis*informed one.

Let us suppose, for the moment, that Diamond's plea for latitude measures of opinions and attitudes is on the mark. Conceivably, conclusions about the quality of individual judgments could then be even more positive than those that Sniderman et al. reach. Intuitively, we would expect people to do reasonably well in deciding what is not acceptable. Unfortunately, we do not yet have good evidence one way or the other. And as Diamond demonstrates, if people do in fact think in terms of latitudes, the collective consequences are not always desirable.

Latitude measures raise yet another issue. Even if they revealed a citizenry that keeps its public officials accountable by saying "no," it is not at all obvious what to make of such behavior. One interpretation, which Diamond would endorse, is that citizens do considerably better than political scientists believe; point placement models impose an unrealistic standard that few people can meet. On the other hand, critics might argue that latitude measures inevitably will support more optimistic conclusions precisely because they demand less of citizens; relaxing standards to gain positive results serves no purpose. Unfortunately, there are no obvious criteria by which to choose one perspective over the other; measurement decisions are imbued with normative prescriptions of what people should do and assumptions about what they can do in their role as citizens.

Taken singly, all the chapters in this part reach well-founded conclusions or at least offer reasoned speculations. What to say more generally is not self-evident, except that the authors agree that attitudes exist. In one case, the authors present empirical evidence in support of this proposition; in the other two cases, they assume it to be true. Beyond this, however, the authors do not send a single message about the quality of political judgments. Conceivably there will never be one.

9

Public Opinion and Democratic Politics: The Problem of Nonattitudes and the Social Construction of Political Judgment*

PAUL M. SNIDERMAN
PHILIP E. TETLOCK
LAUREL ELMS

The study of public opinion, although at one level preoccupied with the transient issues and political personalities of the day, takes its direction at a deeper level from a recurring consideration of a small number of enduring themes integral to the understanding of democratic politics. We want to take this opportunity to engage perhaps the most fundamental of these themes – the competence of ordinary citizens to discharge the responsibilities expected of them in modern democratic politics.

There is, of course, a distinguished literature deeply skeptical of the ordinary citizen's understanding of public affairs. But our concern here is not with the classic essays of Walter Lippman or Graham Wallas, notable and enduringly instructive as they are. Rather, we are concerned with more recent studies that purport to demonstrate that ordinary citizens lack attitudes on the important issues of the day.

Our concern is both normative and empirical. Democratic ideals cannot be reduced to issues of fact. But ideals, whether ethical or political, are subject to evaluation, and their evaluation cannot be indifferent to matters of fact. No one can be under an obligation to do what he or she does not have a capacity to do, and it cannot make sense to hold out as an ideal of conduct a standard of behavior that citizens cannot reach. The more imperfect ordinary citizens' understanding of political ideas, the less capable they are of grounded judgment, the more crabbed a creditable conception of democratic citizenship must be.

* Data collection was supported by the National Science Foundation (Grant No. SES 8508937). We want also to thank the Survey Research Center and the Institute for Personality and Social Research, both of the University of California, Berkeley, for invaluable assistance.

Problems of Political Judgment

The portrait of the citizen painted by public opinion analysts has never been a flattering one. Beginning with the Columbia studies of Lazarsfeld and his colleagues,[1] a classic theme in the study of public opinion has been ordinary citizens' minimal level of attention to public affairs and knowledge of them, not to mention the minimal levels of constraint and stability in their political preferences (Converse, 1964). This portrait has been challenged from time to time,[2] but the challenges have been buried under an avalanche of demonstrations that levels of public information, comprehension, and consistency have remained low over the last four decades (e.g., Delli, Carpini, and Keeter, 1989, 1991; Smith, 1989; Sniderman, 1993). It has come to be taken for granted, thanks very much to the consistency and decisiveness of research on the public's level of political awareness, that ordinary citizens are not deeply engaged by public affairs, that they do not devote a major effort to organizing and coordinating their views on issues of public policy, and that their judgments about the major issues of the day, supposing that they have troubled to form any, often are ill-considered, superficial, and ephemeral.

The heart of the modern critique of citizen reasoning has concentrated on the problem of nonattitudes. There is surely merit in the suggestion that people, pummeled with question after question about issue after issue, sometimes will come up with "top-of-the-head" responses.[3] Every experienced survey researcher is aware that ordinary citizens sometimes are at a loss when asked their view about public policy, that the "positions" they take are sometimes improvised, and that, in trying to recall their attitudes toward matters of public concern, they often do so imperfectly. But the original argument (Converse, 1964, 1970), which claimed only that on some issues, because they are so abstract or peripheral, many people fail to form an attitude, has recently been transformed into the radically different claim that "most people, on most issues, do not 'really think' any particular thing"[4]; that "*most* people really aren't sure what their opinions are on *most* political matters"[5]; indeed, that most of the people, most of the time, just "make it up as they go along."[6]

This is an extraordinary assertion. It is one thing to acknowledge that ordinary citizens, from time to time, will construct a judgment on the spot about an issue they think and care little about. It is quite another thing to

1 Lazarsfeld, Berelson, and Gaudet, 1944; Berelson, Lazarsfeld, and McPhee, 1954.
2 Nie, Verba, and Petrocik, 1979.
3 The phrase belongs to Taylor and Fiske, 1978.   4 Zaller, 1994, p. 194.
5 Zaller, 1992, p. 76; italics added for emphasis.
6 "Making It Up as You Go Along" is the title of Chapter 5 in Zaller's *The Nature and Origins of Mass Opinion* (1992).

contend that ordinary citizens do not know where they stand on the issues of the day *as the rule and not as the exception*. If this is true, then it is necessary to scale back radically any presumption of citizen competence in democratic politics; it is also necessary to reconsider fundamentally any notion of a responsibility of political leaders to consult and take account of the judgments of citizens at large. If this is accurate, it is hard to understand in what sense public officials have a duty in a democratic polity to take account of their constituents' views. For the expanded version of the nonattitudes hypothesis amounts to an argument that citizens are not capable of exercising judgment on public affairs. They cannot manage the task of judgment, moreover, not just in the strong sense of determining what should be done, but even in the weak sense of determining what they think should be done. If those responsible for government know that whether the public approves or disapproves of a line of public policy hinges crucially on accidents of question wording, such leaders can hardly be said to have a duty to attend to what citizens think about a matter of public policy before making a determination about it. Indeed, if it is true that citizens are just making it up as they go along, then political leaders may even have an obligation to discount what the public thinks that it thinks, since if the questions had varied even slightly, the answers could well have varied markedly.

There is, therefore, much at stake in understanding the dynamics of public judgment. We proceed in four steps. First, we detail the expanded version of the nonattitudes argument. Second, we identify the specific response model underlying it. Third, we evaluate the evidence advanced in its favor. Finally, taking advantage of the new methods we have developed to integrate the classical public opinion interview with complex experimental designs, we examine directly the interplay of issue framing and political predispositions.

THE EXPANDED VERSION OF THE NONATTITUDES CLAIM

What does it mean to say that citizens, in taking a position on a matter of public concern, have made a genuine determination of where they stand and may, therefore, be said to hold a true attitude about the issue? To be committed to the view that people hold attitudes, it is argued, is to be committed to the "file drawer" model. On the file drawer model:

When people are asked how they feel about something, such as legalized abortion, their Uncle Harry, or anchovies on a pizza, presumably they consult a mental file containing their evaluation. They look for the file marked *abortion*, or *Uncle Harry*, or *anchovies*, and report the evaluation it contains.[7]

7 Wilson and Hodges, 1992, p. 38, cited by Zaller, 1992, p. 35.

By contrast, it is argued that attitudes are socially constructed and that rather than people reporting the contents of files they have retrieved, they instead figure out where they stand on the spot.

But what does it mean to say that citizens figure out, on the spot, where they stand on public issues? Citizens, the argument runs, lack organized, rehearsed, internally consistent political attitudes. Instead, they "fill up their minds with large stores of only partially consistent ideas, arguments, and considerations."[8] Their view of any given matter is, in consequence, confused and contradictory.[9] They "possess numerous, frequently inconsistent considerations relating to each issue."[10] And just as far as they have reasons to favor and to oppose any given course of action, they are capable of standing on opposing sides of most issues.[11]

Why do most citizens stand on both sides of most issues? It is not because they have failed to attend to public issues. Indeed, the difficulty is precisely that they have been paying attention, and

in an environment that carries roughly evenly balanced communications on both sides of issues, people are likely to internalize many contradictory arguments, which is to say, they are likely to form considerations that induce them both to favor and to oppose the same issues.[12]

As in most serious matters, the claim being made is not absolute but a matter of degree. The contention is not that "every member of the public is ambivalent on every issue," or that "everyone is ambivalent to the same degree,"[13] but that nonambivalence is "unusual."[14] Most people, on most political issues, are ambivalent, able to draw on those favorable to a proposal for public action and those unfavorable to it. But if most people have reasons for saying yes and for saying no, how on any particular occasion do one or two considerations in favor of saying yes or no happen to wind up at the "top of the head"?

8 Zaller, 1992, p. 36. 9 Zaller, 1992, p. 95. 10 Zaller, 1992, p. 54.
11 Zaller, 1992, p. 54. 12 Zaller, 1992, p. 59. 13 Zaller, 1992, p. 93.
14 Zaller, 1992, p. 94. Zaller thus also turns Festinger on his head. Cognitive consistency theorists disagree among themselves over how much inconsistency typically exists within belief systems. Maximalists (such as McGuire, 1968) portray belief systems as tightly integrated. People may sometimes be slow to recognize contradictions, but they do typically put their mental house in order (e.g., work on the Socratic effect). Minimalists (such as Abelson, 1968) invoke the loose-linkage metaphor for characterizing belief systems. People often hold a lot of contradictory beliefs and preferences but fail to recognize the contradictions (and hence experience no dissonance). In the Ambivalence Deduction, Zaller seems to posit a level of tolerance for inconsistency that surpasses even the loosest of the loose-linkage models within the cognitive consistency tradition. Cognitive consistency – the tendency to organize one's beliefs and preferences into evaluatively harmonious gestalts – is, on Zaller's account, conspicuous by its absence.

From a social construction point of view, social cues are the crucial factor. Which particular considerations people attend to is a function of where their attention is directed just before they answer; and where their attention is directed just before they answer is a function of their immediate circumstances, particularly the specific wording of the questions put to them. Just so far as their attention is directed to the positive considerations they hold on a given matter of public policy, people will be inclined to give a thumbs up, but just so far as their attention is directed to the negative considerations they also hold about it, they will be inclined to give a thumbs down. In Zaller's words:

> Which of a person's attitudes is expressed at different times depends on which has been made most immediately salient by chance and the details of questionnaire construction, especially the order and framing of questions.[15]

The result: lacking genuine attitudes to stabilize their judgments, most people can and will flip-flop on most issues, taking first one side and then the other as a function even of minor variations in the wording of a question. We therefore call this the "flip-flop model."

It has not always been appreciated that Zaller intends his argument to depart radically from, rather than to extend, previous work, although he himself is strikingly frank about his aims, declaring that his claim of ambivalence, for example, "both contradicts the dominant theories of mass political attitudes, those of Converse and Achen, and violates common sense notions of public opinion."[16] Nor, in making this claim, is he exaggerating. The flip-flop model turns the original nonattitudes model on its head. Converse's claim is that, having no real thoughts about some issues, yet being unwilling to acknowledge they have given issues little thought, citizens sometimes conjure up an opinion on the spot, choosing a position on a random basis, precisely in order to conceal the fact that they have failed to form one. Absence of thought, randomness of response, and impression management are the three keys to Converse's classic account of the dynamics of nonattitudes. By contrast, on the new version, the difficulty is not that people have too few ideas but that they have too many, going in all directions rather than pointing in none. As Zaller and Feldman put it, "most people possess opposing considerations on most issues that might lead them to decide the issue either way."[17] Furthermore, the position citizens take on any given occasion, rather than randomly chosen, is the product of immediate cues in the form of particular wordings and orderings of questions. The net result: believing everything, citizens believe nothing – the positions they

---

15 Zaller, 1992, p. 93.   16 Zaller, 1992, p. 92.
17 Zaller and Feldman, 1992, p. 585.

take, they take for the moment, and for no better reason than the fortuitous wording of the question put to them.[18]

In order to understand questions of cause and effect, we want to move from the general claims that are being advanced to the specific response models that have been delineated.

RESPONSE MODELS

The Nature and Origins of Mass Opinion is multifaceted and develops two quite different response models. One of these – the political awareness-predisposition model – is very far from controversial, and indeed, draws on the now standard account of political reasoning. Figure 9.1 represents the core of the model schematically.

Before commenting on substance, a word about terminology. The term "attitude" has an idiosyncratic use in the model, but once its usage is specified, there should be no problem, serious or slight. By an "attitude," Zaller has in mind a response, positive or negative, to a specific issue or candidate; by a "predisposition," a readiness systematically to respond positively or negatively to a class of issue-objects. In this usage, then, attitudes are the preferences that respondents express about particular courses of public action: "opinions," in the ordinary usage; whereas predispositions refer to underlying consistencies in response to political choices: their "attitudes," in the ordinary usage. So defined, opinions about an issue like job programs for blacks are examples of attitudes; ideological sets, liberal and conservative, are examples of predispositions.

Terminology in place, the awareness-predisposition model makes two points. First, the beliefs and preferences that citizens express about specific political choices are not conjured up on the spot. On the contrary, they are grounded in organized predispositions to respond consistently, either positively or negatively, favorably or unfavorably, to political objects, whether issues or candidates.[19] Second, the influence of predispositions on attitudes is conditional on political awareness: the better

---

18 There is a contrasting thread in Zaller's argument, his analysis of political predispositions, prominent in the second part of his book and difficult to reconcile with the nonattitudes argument of the first part. The more important political predispositions (e.g., liberalism-conservatism) as a basis for issue positions, the more predictable people's positions on issues – hence the weaker Zaller's nonattitudes argument. Moreover, the more important the role of political predispositions, the more consistent people's intermediate beliefs and evaluations – hence the weaker his ambivalence deduction.

19 See Campbell, 1963.

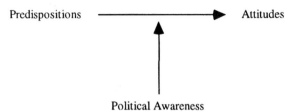

Figure 9.1. The political awareness–political predisposition model.

people's grasp of political issues and ideas, the stronger the connection between their stands on a specific issue and their broader orientation to politics.[20] So expressed, the sophistication-interaction hypothesis has become standard fare in the static analysis of political reasoning (e.g., Sniderman, Brody, and Tetlock, 1991). Zaller's contribution has been to apply the sophistication-interaction hypothesis to the dynamics as well as the statics of political reasoning. The pivotal question, from a dynamic point of view, is the differential responsiveness of citizens to political messages over time. Setting details to one side, the political sophistication mediator summarizes differences among citizens, over time, in the degree of their exposure to and understanding of the stream of political messages. Properly interpreted, the sophistication mediator supplies a mechanism to account for both the convergence of the politically sophisticated on a common position over time (the one-sided message case) and their divergence toward opposing positions (the two-sided message case).

Dealing with the problem not of attitude change over time, but of attitude construction on any given occasion, Zaller advances a rather different, and at some levels conflicting, model. Figure 9.2 displays this second model schematically. Again, let us begin with terminology. Following Kelley (1983), Zaller defines a "consideration" as "any reason that might induce an individual to decide a political issue one way or the other."[21] For any given issue, any given person is likely to have considerations that are positive, inclining him to favor a particular course of public action, but likely also to have considerations that are negative, inclining him to oppose it. To signal its status, this claim is given a special title, the "Ambivalence Deduction." Although not given precise expression, the Ambivalence Deduction carries the implication that on most matters, most people have enough considerations that are negative and

20 Assuming, obviously, a logical connection between the two.
21 Zaller, 1992, p. 40.

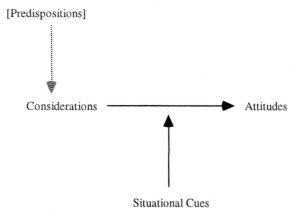

[Predispositions]

Considerations ⟶ Attitudes

Situational Cues

Figure 9.2. The "considerations" model of attitude construction.

enough that are positive to make it likely that, given even a slight push, they can say yes as well as no, no as well as yes.

Given this premise, the key claim of the second model is this. Over a series of trials, the same individual will sometimes favor a proposed course of public action and sometimes oppose it – hence our character-ization of this as the flip-flop model. Whether a person favors or opposes a proposed course of action on any particular occasion depends on the one or two considerations that, on that occasion, come to the top of her head. It does not, however, depend on the particular content of the con-sideration but rather on its affective direction. If the momentarily salient considerations are positive, she will favor the course of action; if nega-tive, she will oppose it. But – and this is the crucial point – whether the momentarily salient considerations are positive or negative is not, as Converse hypothesized, randomly determined. Although Zaller agrees that there is an element of chance, his distinctive claim is that which con-siderations are salient on any given occasion depends on where a person's attention was directed, on that occasion, by the wording of the question. If the wording directed her attention to the positive considerations she holds, she will respond positively; if to the negative considerations, she will respond negatively.

A social construction view extends naturally to a nonattitudes account of question-wording effects. As a legion of experimental studies have demonstrated, the responses people express can vary as a function of variations in question wording, ordering, and formatting.[22] The point of

22 For the classic work on the subject, see Schuman and Presser, 1981.

Figure 9.2 is to make explicit the intervening mechanism: the same person will favor completely opposing positions on an issue just so far as different considerations are called to his or her attention by the wording of the question. He or she will favor foreign aid or oppose it, support government assistance for blacks or criticize it, merely because, owing to the accidents of question wording, considerations on one side of the issue are momentarily more accessible than those on the other.

On this view, people change their positions, but not because they have changed their minds. On the contrary, because they don't have to change their minds, they can change their positions readily. Since, by hypothesis, most people walk about with considerations on both sides of most issues, which side they take on any particular occasion hinges on which considerations are called to their attention. And whether they happen to think of reasons for saying yes or saying no hinges on the accidents of question wording and ordering. Hence their capacity to flip-flop from one side of an issue to the other.

The thesis that political attitudes are situationally contingent, like any thesis, can be deployed in degrees. Zaller, it must be admitted, offers an extreme version, declaring rhetorically that citizens, rather than having views about matters of public importance, are simply "making it up as they go along." We shall instead concentrate on a more moderate interpretation, namely, that the differential accessibility of positive or negative considerations on any given occasion tends to be significantly – but not exclusively – a function of (typically semantic) cues encountered on that occasion. Hence the causal arrow, from predispositions to considerations, in Figure 9.2.

Yet, even on a moderate interpretation, the cue model of attitude construction makes its point not so much by the kind of factor it accentuates – situational cues in the form of question-wording effects – but rather by the kind of factor it omits (in its extreme version) or downplays (in its moderate version) – predispositions in the form of underlying tendencies to respond consistently positively or negatively to political objects.[23] Hence, the causal arrow from predispositions to considerations in Figure 9.2 is dashed.

To argue that political attitudes are socially constructed is distinctively to contend that the positions people take on political issues or candidates on any given occasion, at most, are shallowly rooted in deeper lying predispositions that are enduring over time and consistent across situations. After all, the point of Zaller's interpretation is to emphasize the probability that, on any given occasion, the same person could as

---

23 The inclusion of situational cues, as we shall show, is as compatible with a combinatorial as with a constructionist account.

easily vote thumbs up as thumbs down: and whether he does the one or the other on any given occasion hinges on the particular considerations that come to the top of his head as a function of situational cues on a particular occasion.

From a social construction perspective, then, situational (or transient) and dispositional (or enduring) factors are at odds: the more important the former, the less important the latter. We want to develop, for the purpose of contrast, an interpretation grounded in cognitive combinatorics. This interpretation takes as its fundamental premise that responses, on any given occasion, tend to be a product of both situational and dispositional factors. People, on this second view, rely on both external and internal cues in generating responses to attitude surveys, not on one or the other. The positions they take, on any given occasion, may be a function of their overall attitudes in additive combination with the definition of the situation on that occasion; alternatively, they may be a multiplicative function of their overall attitude and their definition of that situation in light of their overall attitude. From this vantage point, the research challenge is to identify (a) the conditions under which different combinatorial principles apply and (b) the mediating mechanisms that produce distinctive combinatorial patterns.

To sharpen the contrast between social constructionist and cognitive combinatorial alternatives, let us specify a quartet of hypotheses. First, it follows from Zaller's theory of the survey response that the role of dispositional factors must be minimal; otherwise, people would respond consistently at different points in time and in different situations, which is precisely what a social construction account contends they do not do. It does not follow that the contribution of dispositional factors, even on a social construction account, is zero: only that their influence is minimal. By contrast, on a combinatorial hypothesis, even when responses to political issues are under the influence of question-wording variations, it need not be true that the influence of dispositional factors is minimal, and indeed, even when the influence of question-wording variations is strong, the influence of dispositional factors need not be weak.

If the impact of dispositional factors is not minimal, as we believe, then it is necessary to specify the nature of their joint impact with situational factors. Zaller maintains, by contrast, that citizens' ideas about political issues, rather than being organized and coherent, characteristically are a miscellany of positive and negative considerations, with any given citizen able, on any given occasion, to draw on considerations either favoring or opposing any given course of public action. Any given individual is about as likely as any other, it follows, to change sides on any given occasion. On a combinatorial hypothesis, too, any given individual will behave differently in relevantly different circumstances. What distinguishes a combinatorial from a social construction point of view is the further contention that, even when people behave differently in one situation than in another, they tend to respond the same way relative to one another. A bigot will respond more negatively to African Americans in some situations than in others: but in all situations where there is any choice, a bigot will respond more negatively to African Americans than a person who is racially tolerant. We call this "the rank order invariance" hypothesis.

If it is further granted that some people are systematically more likely to be subject to the influence of situational cues than others, then from Zaller's perspective, those who are most influenceable should be those whose relevant dispositions are least consistent. The reasoning is straightforward. Other things being equal, the likelihood of a positive or negative consideration being accessible on any given occasion is a function of the ratio of positive to negative considerations on hand. It follows that, in situations that direct attention to positive considerations, those whose views of the matter are most mixed are the ones most likely to have positive considerations to draw on; and in situations that direct attention to negative considerations, they are also the ones most likely to have *them* to draw on. If so, the impact of situational cues should be curvilinear: decreasing as people approach either pole of a dispositional continuum, increasing as they approach its midpoint. We call this the "curvilinear-ambivalence" hypothesis.

We are broadly skeptical of the general claim that situational and dispositional factors are at odds with one another. But we are specifically dubious of the curvilinear-ambivalence hypothesis. Unless there is a zero order relation between the weight given a specific situational cue and the relevant political predisposition, their impact should be complementary, with the influence of situational cues approximately equal at any point along a dispositional continuum. For convenience we call this the "additivity" hypothesis.

Against the inclination to view behavior as a product of either situational or predispositional factors, if the relation between the two is linear and additive, their joint impact is complementary. So we believe it to be, more often than not. To get a clearer view of the logic of the problem, however, it is useful to consider alternative forms of the functional relation between the two. Situational and dispositional factors may be complementary in the weak sense of both mattering. They may be complementary in the strong sense that one matters because the other matters. Having set out the weak claim, in the form of the additivity hypothesis, we now set out the strong claim, in the form of the interaction hypothesis.

For clarity, it will be helpful to revert for a moment to standard terminology, referring to predispositions as attitudes. An attitude, standardly conceived, represents a systematic tendency to respond consistently to a social or political object, with individuals reliably differing from one another depending on how positive or negative their attitude happens to be. Equivalently, following Bruner (1951) and Postman, Bruner, and Walk (1951), an attitude may be regarded as a perceptual hypothesis, that is, as a prejudgment about the favorability or unfavorability of a social or political object. On this interpretation, large question-wording effects do *not* signal weak attitudinal effects: question-wording effects occur precisely because people *do* have attitudes. In Bruner and Postman's vocabulary, "the stronger a perceptual hypothesis, the greater its likelihood of arousal in a given situation."[24] We call this the "interaction" hypothesis and shall test it in several versions.

Having sketched both the constructionist response model of nonattitudes and hypotheses specifying alternative interrelations of situational and predispositional factors, we now turn to the task of analysis.

TAKING STOCK: THE EVIDENCE ON HAND

Before examining our own studies, we want to evaluate the evidence supposed to establish the validity of the expanded version of the nonattitudes argument. A portion of the evidence is familiar, consisting of so-called stability coefficients. If citizens have genuine attitudes, the argument runs, then their positions on issues should be stable over time. On the assumption that nothing in the external world has changed in the interval, when people are asked their position on an issue a second time, their answers should be the same as the first ones. On the other hand, if they have not formed a genuine view about the issue, there is no reason why they should give the same answer the second time as the first. They should instead say the first thing that comes to mind. And, if this is so, the correlation of their positions on the same issue over time should be approximately zero.

Judged by this standard, Zaller's results fail on two counts. First, his analysis doesn't take account of the obvious alternative explanation. Since the time of Converse's seminal study, the standard rejoinder to a nonattitudes claim has been that the problem is not the absence of an attitude on the part of respondents, but the unreliability of the measures deployed to assess their attitudes (e.g., Achen, 1975). Zaller, however, doesn't correct for measurement error, which is puzzling considering how standardized arguments and counterarguments over nonattitudes have

---

24 We owe this quote to Campbell, 1963, p. 112.

become.[25] Worse, even in the absence of any compensating correction for measurement error, Zaller's turnover tables and test-retest correlations, rather than showing the absence of a relation over time, show marked stability over time. This is not, it should be emphasized, merely *our* reading of the results. Zaller concurs. His results, he acknowledges,[26] fall short of confirming his claims. But since it is quite clear that all the other evidence on over-time attitudinal stability, including Converse's, does not confirm Zaller's drastically expanded version of the nonattitudes problem, it is not obvious what evidentiary support it can claim.

No less vexing, the logic of Zaller's argument on question-wording effects suggests a prediction opposite to the prediction Zaller suggests. He argues that, lacking attitudes to stabilize their responses, respondents should be inclined to give different responses at different points in time. He also argues that the response they give on a particular occasion is a product of the particular wording of the question on that occasion. By design, the same wording is used in over-time measurement; otherwise, it would be logically impossible to tell whether a different response was an indication of a change in attitude or merely a change in wording. But since, according to Zaller's question-wording theory of the survey response, the response at any one point in time is a product of the particular wording of the question at that point in time, and since the wording of the question is the same at all points in time, according to Zaller's own question-wording argument, the response should not differ at different points in time, as he predicts, but be the same at all points in time, which is neither what he predicts nor what he claims to observe.[27]

---

25 The absence of an explicit correction for measurement error is harder to understand since at one point he declares that "response instability consists almost exclusively of chance variation around a largely stable central tendency," which seems to invoke precisely the kind of underlying, organizing response disposition, set within a measurement error framework, that the concept of attitude is intended to denote. See Zaller, 1992, p. 65.

26 See Zaller, 1992, p. 57.

27 On any given occasion, any specific consideration may be activated, i.e., come to the top of the head. But on every occasion, the proportion of positive and negative considerations is constant; that is, after all, the point of the Ambivalence Deduction. Since (i) what counts in determining a response is not the specific content of a consideration, but whether it is positive or negative, Zaller, following Kelly (1983), takes account not of the particular content of a consideration, but just of the number, or proportion, of positive to negative considerations; (ii) the proportion of positive and negative considerations is approximately constant over time; (iii) the probability on any given occasion of activating a positive or negative consideration is a function of the particular wording of a question; and (iv) the wording of the question is exactly constant over time; therefore, on Zaller's

A more original line of argument offered in behalf of the view that people construct their political attitudes is based on the "stop-and-think" experiments. In these experiments, interviewers read a question about a political issue in the usual way but

without waiting for the respondent to answer, they ask the respondent to discuss particular phrases and ideas in the question.[28]

For example, on the question of whether government services in areas such as education and health care should be decreased or increased,

respondents to this survey were not permitted to give an immediate answer to the question. Instead, the interviewer continued:

Before telling me how you feel about this, could you tell me what kinds of things come to mind when you think about *cutting government services*? (Any others?)

The interviewer wrote down respondents' remarks verbatim, and then asked:

Now, what comes to mind when you think about increases in government services? (Any others?)[29]

Using this procedure, Zaller finds that, depending on the issue, between one-third and one-half of the respondents in the stop-and-think experiments expressed more than one conflicting consideration[30] and also that the stability of issue positions was markedly lower when respondents were interrupted before being allowed to make their choice and were asked first to discuss key ideas and phrases.

Both findings – the increase in "conflicting" considerations and the decrease in stability – are said to support the nonattitudes claim.[31] Neither does. Consider the ambivalence finding. It is necessary to distinguish between the position that citizens take on an issue and the reasons they are capable of giving for taking a position on it, whether their own or others'. The two are not the same. You may have a definite position on an issue, yet without any difficulty may be able to cite, if asked, reasons not only for taking your side of the issue but also for taking the other. A person may unequivocally oppose affirmative action but be able, if asked, to mention reasons for supporting it, or the other way around. It does not follow that, because she is knowledgeable about reasons both for

argument, the response should be the same over time. It is, moreover, not open to Zaller to argue that it should be different, at different points in time, since the process is random. That is Converse's position, and Zaller explicitly rejects it. He must, moreover, reject it, since he wants to claim that nonattitudes are the rule, not the exception, and it is impossible to sustain an empirical claim that the responses of most people on most matters of public concern are randomly generated.

28 Zaller, 1992, pp. 55–56.   29 Zaller, 1992, p. 53, italics in the original.
30 Zaller, 1992, Table 4.2, p. 61.   31 Zaller, 1992, Table 5.3, p. 88.

supporting and for opposing affirmative action that she is internally conflicted, uncertain of her position, just making it up as she goes along. On
the contrary, the more politically sophisticated she is, the more likely she
simultaneously will be able to cite considerations on opposing sides of the
issue *and* to possess a definite and stable attitude toward it (cf. Baron,
1994; Tetlock, Peterson, and Lerner, 1996).

There is a deeper difficulty with the stop-and-think procedure. People
are asked their position on an issue. But before they are able to answer,
they are stopped in their tracks. Their train of thought is interrupted.
They are asked, instead of answering, to report on whatever ideas
or associations the specific wording of a question calls to mind. Only
then, having reported on whatever happened to come to their minds –
which, but for this extraordinary request, might well not have come
to their minds – are they allowed to give a response to the original
question. Think about the consequences of interrupting in this way a
person's train of thought. Suppose people really do have positions on
an issue like welfare. But before they can give it, they are interrupted,
then distracted by reporting a swirl of ideas. Surely, they risk being
sidetracked. And the result? Using the stop-and-think procedure, Zaller
finds precisely what other investigators using similar techniques find –
namely, that interrupting and distracting people discombobulates them,
making their answers more variable across time and circumstance (e.g.,
Wilson, 1990).[32]

The expanded version of the nonattitudes hypothesis, on the evidence
to this point, is very far from having been sustained. But for an argument not to have been shown to be true is not the same as its having
been shown to be false. We therefore turn to a direct examination of the
impact of predispositional and situational factors.

THE PROBABLE CAUSE EXPERIMENT

To explore how judgments about public issues can be jointly grounded
in the specific features of particular situations and in deeper lying political predispositions, we conducted the Probable Cause experiment. All
respondents are asked to consider a situation "where the police see two
young men . . . walking very near a house where the police know drugs
are being sold." Everyone is told that the police subsequently search them

---

32 It is still harder to understand Zaller's reliance on the stop-and-think procedure
given that he places himself in the camp of Wilson and his colleagues. Wilson has
made use of just such a procedure, but in order to demonstrate that asking people
why they believe a particular thing *changes* their attitude toward it at least tem-
porarily, thereby weakening attitude–behavior consistency.

and find they are carrying drugs. However, for a randomly selected half of the respondents, the young men are characterized as "well dressed and well behaved." In contrast, the other half are told that the young men "are using foul language." All respondents are then asked whether the police search was reasonable.

This is, we submit, a near-paradigmatic example of an issue-framing experiment. Respondents are asked to take a position on an issue of public concern, with a relevant feature of the issue deliberately varied to alter the probability that they will take one rather than the other side of the issue. In weighing the impact of both situational cues and political predispositions in shaping political attitudes, let us begin by considering the "minimal impact" hypothesis.

According to the minimal impact hypothesis, the judgments that citizens make about specific matters of public interest, rather than being grounded in consistently organized attitudes, are instead socially constructed, with the same people ready to favor or oppose a course of public action as a function of often minimally varied wordings or orderings of questions. By design, however, the Probable Cause experiment varies not a peripheral but an immediately relevant consideration in judging the propriety of police conduct – namely, the demeanor of the suspects. Their demeanor surely should make a difference to judgments about the propriety of police conduct. If the suspects were using foul language rather than being well dressed and well behaved, then, of course, respondents should be more likely to believe that the police search was reasonable.

A nearly taken-for-granted premise of Zaller's question-wording argument is that question-wording effects are in some straightforward sense very large – large enough, certainly, to outweigh the effect of an underlying attitude. This is an argument that has considerable plausibility, especially to those who have not had the opportunity to examine question-wording experiments on their own. The difficulty is that there is, properly considered, virtually no straightforward sense in which the relative contribution of so-called question-wording effects and of attitudes can be responsibly compared. But considering the relative paucity of information in the public domain, we think it is important to convey a sense of the order of magnitude of question-wording and attitudinal effects. Therefore, the various methodological pitfalls notwithstanding, we shall give a ballpark sense of orders of magnitude by looking at the impact of both kinds of effects expressed in terms of correlation coefficients.

Table 9.1, accordingly, begins by reporting the correlation between the demeanor of the suspects – whether they were using foul language or well dressed and well behaved – and judgments about the police conduct

Paul M. Sniderman, Philip E. Tetlock, and Laurel Elms

Table 9.1. *Correlations between Level of Agreement That the Drug Search Was Reasonable, Question-Wording Variation, and Predispositional Factors*

		Level of Agreement That the Drug Search Was Reasonable	
Queston-Wording Variable	Suspects: using foul language/ well dressed	.14	(N = 1710)
Predispositional Factors	Law and order	.34	(N = 967)
	Traditionalism	.26	(N = 1693)
	Conventionality	.23	(N = 1684)
	Ideological self-identification	.21	(N = 1682)

– whether their search was reasonable or not. As the results make plain, the demeanor of the suspects makes a significant difference, but – and this is the key point – the difference it makes is far from vast: expressed in terms of a correlation coefficient, .14.

The impact of this particular variation in question wording is manifestly modest, and one may wonder whether this particular illustration of a variation in question wording is atypical. We recognize that in one sense the size of question-wording effects is arbitrary. Effects of any desired size can be evoked: it is only necessary to maximize the semantic contrast between alternative wordings of a question. Nevertheless, from a social construction perspective, people construct their responses on the spot by relying on cues of the moment. If political attitudes are indeed so constructed, question-wording effects should typically be pronounced. In our study of race and American politics, there were thirty-eight question-wording experiments. Taking the absolute value of the standard correlation coefficient as a measure of the magnitude of the impact of alternative issue frames, the mean was .11 and the range was from .01 to .37.[33] In terms of the size of the impact of question-wording effects, then, the results of the Probable Cause experiment thus offer a typical illustration of the impact of question-wording effects.

33 Nor can it be argued that the focus of this particular study, race, is responsible for the modest size of question-wording effects. Comparable calculations of question-wording effects from other studies we have done in examining attitudes toward quite different subjects are comparable in size.

In weighing the difference that the demeanor of the suspects makes – whether, that is, they are using foul language or are well dressed and well behaved – it is also necessary to consider the role of predispositional factors. A number of such factors are potentially relevant. For example, the more importance people attach to maintaining respect for authority or preserving traditional ideas of right and wrong, the more likely they should be to believe that the police conduct was proper. Table 9.1 accordingly reports the impact, summarized in terms of correlations, between judgments about whether the police search was reasonable and an array of potentially relevant predispositions, including commitment to law and order, support for traditional values, conventionality, and ideological self-identification.[34] These correlations range from the mid .2's to the mid .3's, with the size of the smallest significantly larger than that of the question-wording variation and the size of the largest significantly larger still.

In our view, very little should be made of the absolute size of coefficients summarizing the impact of situational and predispositional factors in any specific circumstance. Which matters more, and which less, is a function of the specific phenomena selected for analysis, the terms of analysis, and the apparatus deployed to carry out the analysis.[35] Comparison of the size of coefficients, however, is instructive in the context of a claim that political attitudes are socially constructed. For to say that people decide their position on the spot is to say that they rely not on a predisposition, but on cues of the moment. Against this claim for the decisiveness of cues of the moment, over the range of variation characteristic of public opinion studies, two points are worth remarking. First, in our experience, question-wording effects rarely approach the influence that dispositional factors exercise commonly. Second, and more important by far, it does not follow from a finding of a question-wording effect that predispositional factors are not at work, let alone that the influence of the latter is swamped by that of the former – the minimal impact hypothesis.

This "horse race" approach is of limited value, however. Whether situational or dispositional factors account for more hinges on what one specifically wishes to account for and how one operationally wants to

34 The measures are described in Appendix B.
35 Funder and Ozer, 1983. We want to emphasize the potential for endless wrangling over effect sizes. One can easily set up studies in which question-wording manipulations are so heavy-handed that situational causes swamp individual differences. Or one can select highly partisan elite samples in which individual difference effects swamp those of anemic situational manipulations. Our point is simply that, given the evidence Zaller cites and the evidence we have collected over the years, individual differences in political attitudes generally account for as much or more of the variance as do question-framing and wording manipulations.

Paul M. Sniderman, Philip E. Tetlock, and Laurel Elms

go about accounting for it. We offer a comparison of their relative impact only to illustrate the weakness of the claim that situational factors characteristically have primacy. The more important question to address, however, is not whether predispositional or situational factors count for more, but how the two types of factors operate together.

In the spirit of Zaller's argument, situational factors should count for more the more capable people are of calling up considerations on both sides of an issue; conversely, situational factors should count for less, the more one-sided are people's orientations. To illustrate this argument, imagine that citizens are arrayed in terms of the importance they attach to law and order as a value, as shown in Figure 9.3. The further to the right they are, the higher the probability that an argument in favor of supporting the police will come to mind; the further to the left they are, the higher the probability that an argument in favor of supporting the rights of defendants will come to mind; the closer they are to the midpoint, the higher the probability that arguments on opposing sides of the issue will come to mind. It then follows, on Zaller's argument, that responsiveness to a situational cue such as the suspects' demeanor in the Probable Cause experiment should be curvilinear: heightened as one approaches the midpoint, diminished as one moves to the poles.

Figure 9.3 describes the prediction of curvilinearity following from the ambivalence hypothesis. Figure 9.4 presents a series of actual results from

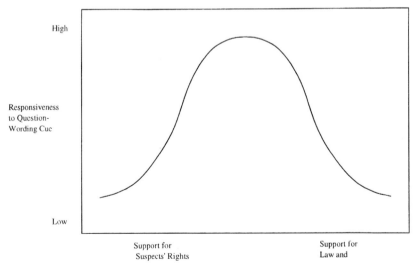

Figure 9.3. Ambivalence model: hypothesized responsiveness to a situational cue as a function of commitment to law and order.

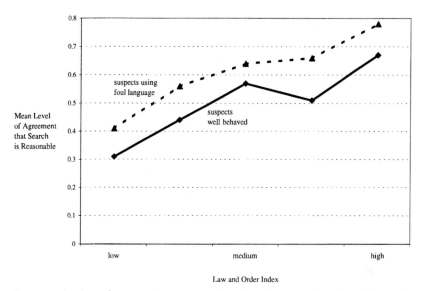

Figure 9.4A. Actual responsiveness to a situational cue as a function of commitment to law and order.

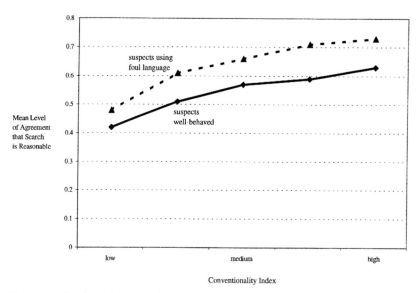

Figure 9.4B. Actual responsiveness to a situational cue as a function of conventionality.

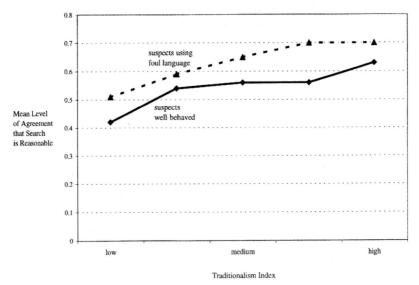

Figure 9.4C. Actual responsiveness to a situational cue as a function of commitment to traditional values.

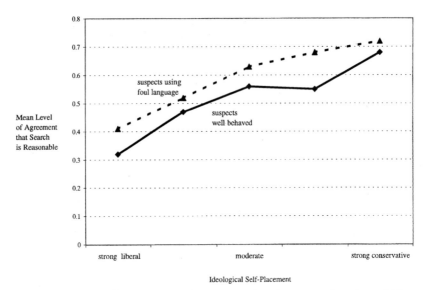

Figure 9.4D. Actual responsiveness to a situational cue as a function of ideological self-identification.

the Probable Cause experiment. As testimony of robustness, a number of dispositional factors are examined, and the likelihood of agreeing that the police search is reasonable is plotted as a function of each. To illustrate the role of predispositional factors, consider commitment to law and order as a value. We do this by taking account of the importance that respondents attach to strengthening law and order; by observing whether, in the case of a suspect arrested for a serious crime, they believe he should be permitted to remain silent or required to answer all questions; and, finally, by noting whether, in dealing with serious street crime, they believe it is more important to protect the rights of suspects even if a guilty person sometimes goes free or to stop such crimes and make the streets safe even if a suspect's rights are sometimes violated.

How are judgments about whether the police have behaved reasonably on a particular occasion influenced by both people's broader orientations and the features of the actual situation? In the case of the Probable Cause experiment, does the demeanor of the suspects matter more, as the attitude construction model suggests, for those whose responses to issues of order are most mixed and matter less for those whose responses are most one-sided, whatever side they happen to favor?

Figure 9.4A summarizes the joint impact of a predispositional factor, in the form of a commitment to law and order, and a situational cue, in the form of information about the suspects' demeanor. The upper line summarizes judgments about the reasonableness of searches of suspects using foul language; the lower line judgments about searches of well-dressed and well-behaved suspects. The greater the distance between the two lines, the greater the importance of the situational cue. If the ambivalence curvilinearity hypothesis is correct, then the lines should diverge nearer the midpoint of the underlying dispositional continuum and converge nearer the poles. Looking at Figure 9.4A, we see that (1) both lines rise monotonically from left to right, indicating that respondents are more likely to find the police search reasonable the more importance they attach to law and order as a value and (2) the two lines rise in approximately parallel fashion: a given increase in commitment to law and order as a value goes along with an approximately comparable increase in approval of police conduct in both situations. Figures 9.4B through 9.4D, which present equivalent analyses of the joint effect of the suspects' demeanor and conventionality, commitment to traditional values, and ideological self-identification, respectively, report comparable results.

All of these results are at odds with the hypothesis that situational cues have the greatest impact on those whose underlying orientations are the least one-sided. No doubt, there are specialized circumstances in which the "ambivalence-curvilinearity" hypothesis applies, but the results of the Probable Cause experiment suggest two points.

The first concerns the meaning of a "midpoint" attitude. From a social construction perspective, if people are arrayed along an attitudinal continuum, those who fall midway between the two poles are the most ambivalent. The term "ambivalence" is intended, of course, to suggest that those midway between the poles are conflicted, divided in their own minds over the proper course of action, caught in a mental tug-of-war. Without denying that ambivalence exists, and sometimes translates into moderate or midrange responses to attitude scales, our results suggest that, as a rule, political attitudes should be thought of by analogy to tastes. Imagine arraying people as a function of how much they like ice cream. The closer a person is to the top of the order, the more he likes ice cream; the closer to the bottom, the less. And the person in between? She is not conflicted, ambivalent, uncertain about whether she likes ice cream or not: the point is that she likes it more than some, less than others. So, too, with political orientations. To fall near the middle of an attitudinal distribution is not to lack an attitude but to have one of median intensity.

The second point concerns the joint impact of situational and predispositional factors. The ambivalence-curvilinearity hypothesis offers an avenue for conceding that, even from a social construction perspective, both may matter. But the hypothesis retains the spirit of the social construction perspective, predicting that if people are making use of situational cues in arriving at their judgments, they do not have established predispositions to guide their responses, and vice versa. The results of the Probable Cause experiment suggest instead that the influence of predispositional and situational factors, rather than being mutually exclusive, is complementary. Any given individual, depending on the particular circumstances, may be more likely to approve of the conduct of the police or less; however, in any given set of circumstances, the individual who is more predisposed in general to favor law and order than one who is less predisposed is more likely to approve of the conduct of the police in carrying out the search. So far as this is true, the influence of predispositional and situational factors should be additive, not antagonistic.

THE HELPING HAND EXPERIMENT

To claim that the impact of situational and predispositional factors is additive is a weak version of the hypothesis that their influence is complementary. We now consider a strong version.

A political attitude, standardly conceived, represents a perceptual hypothesis: an organized readiness to adopt a particular perspective on a public issue. The more liberal a person's outlook on politics, the more consistently he or she should support a broad set of proposals for government assistance for the disadvantaged; conversely, the more conservative a person's outlook, the more consistently he or she should oppose them. But it does not follow from this that a liberal is equally likely to support every conceivable proposal to assist the disadvantaged and that a conservative is equally likely to oppose every conceivable proposal to assist the disadvantaged, still less that either is equally likely to support any particular proposal in every conceivable set of circumstances. It will make a difference – indeed, from the perspective of any normative theory of political reasoning, it ought to make a difference – (1) what the government specifically is proposing to do (not every form of assistance is equally meritorious); (2) who exactly the government is proposing to assist (not everyone who is not well off is equally badly off); and (3) why the people to be helped may distinctively merit help or not (not every person who may benefit from government assistance has an equally strong claim to merit it). All of these considerations may matter in the determinations citizens make about whether to support a specific proposal to assist some who are disadvantaged. The interesting issue is how, exactly, they may matter. On Zaller's argument, if people are attending to considerations like who is to be helped, or how they are to be helped, or why they are to be helped, considerations that vary from case to case, they are not responding on the basis of an attitude they have formed in advance. By contrast, we suggest that not only may citizens' responses to a specific policy proposal be affected both by these considerations and by a general attitude, but also that the importance of these particular considerations may depend on their general attitude. After all, considerations like who is to be helped by a particular program, or what they may either have done or failed to do in their own behalf to qualify for help, represent subarguments for or against particular proposals for public action. But these arguments need not be evaluated in a vacuum. How far they are seen to be compelling can depend on the perspective from which they are viewed.

On this interactive hypothesis, predispositions facilitate responses to dispositionally consonant situational cues. The more pronounced, organized, and developed citizens' political predispositions are, the more likely they are to recognize and respond to cues consonant with them: the more liberal they are, the more likely they are to recognize and respond to considerations relevant to a liberal; the more conservative, the more likely they are to recognize and respond to considerations relevant to a conservative. Responsiveness to a dispositionally consonant situational cue, it follows, should be a curvilinear function of a person's location on a dispositional continuum. The ambivalence hypothesis also suggests a curvilinear function, but its form is convex, with those nearest the midpoint the most responsive and those closest to the poles least responsive. By contrast, the "cue weighting" hypothesis predicts a curvilinear function concave in form, with those closest to the poles the most responsive and those nearest the midpoint the least responsive.

Moreover, to take the argument a step further, the steepness of this concave function, rather than being a constant, should be a function of political awareness and sophistication. The argument is a familiar one. Other things being equal, the likelihood of citizens understanding the messages to which they are exposed is a function of their level of political awareness. If so, the more politically sophisticated liberals are, the more likely they should be to respond to messages consonant with liberal views; the more politically sophisticated conservatives are, the more likely they should be to respond to messages consonant with conservative views.

Figure 9.5 maps this two-part expectation. Responsiveness to a dispositionally consonant situational cue is represented as a function both of the intensity of the predisposition and of the level of political sophistication. The function is concave, since responsiveness increases with intensity, with the degree of concavity a function of political awareness,

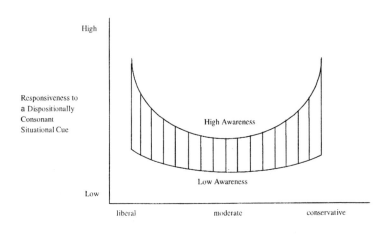

Figure 9.5. Model of the cue weighting hypothesis: ideology by cue by sophistication.

the thatched area between the two curves mapping the greater responsiveness of the more politically aware at the poles of the underlying predisposition.

We test the reasoning underlying Figure 9.5 through the "Helping Hand" experiment. Very briefly, all respondents are told about a program designed to help people "who have problems with poverty." Taking advantage of computer-assisted interviewing, we inform one-half of the respondents that the programs are intended to help people, "many of whom are blacks and minorities," while the other half are told that they are intended to help "new immigrants from Europe." Independently, however, we inform one-half of the respondents that the programs are designed to help "people who have shown that they want to work their way out of their own problems" and the other half that they are designed to help "people who have had trouble hanging on to jobs." We assume that conservatives are likely to attach more importance than liberals to people showing that they want to work their way out of their own problems than liberals, and conversely, that liberals are likely to attach more importance than conservatives to helping blacks and minorities.

In the Helping Hand experiment, then, liberals and conservatives are each presented with a cue consonant with their position. Taking advantage of experimental randomization, Table 9.2 estimates the extent to which the judgments that citizens make about a proposal to assist the disadvantaged are a function of their political predispositions (in the form of their ideological self-identification); the availability of a cue consonant with their political orientation (in the upper panel, whether they are making an effort to help themselves or not; in the lower panel, whether the group to be helped is black or white); and, finally, their level of political awareness (taking years of education as a proxy for political awareness).

The upper panel of Table 2 focuses on the condition in which a cue consonant with a conservative orientation is randomly presented; the lower panel, on the condition in which a cue consonant with a liberal position is randomly presented. Column 1 tests for the predicted two-way interaction (political predisposition × consonant cue; column 2, for the predicted three-way interaction (political predisposition × consonant cue × education). Both are significant. The more pronounced citizens' ideological orientations, the greater the weight they place on a specific piece of information consonant with their orientation and bearing on the political judgment they are asked to make; and, no less important, the more politically aware they are, the more likely this is true. In a word, political attitudes, rather than working at cross-purposes with situational cues, help citizens get the point of them, and the better they are at political reasoning, the more likely this is to be true.

Paul M. Sniderman, Philip E. Tetlock, and Laurel Elms

Table 9.2. *Situational and Dispositional Sources of Support for Poverty Programs*

Conservative Cue	Disposition–Situation Interaction	Disposition–Situation–Awareness Interaction
Beneficiaries help themselves[1]	.017	.074
	(.030)	(.126)
Ideological self-placement	.049	.113
	(.043)	(.100)
Effort of beneficiaries × ideology	−.112*	
	(−.330)	
Education		.319**
		(.260)
Effort of beneficiaries × ideology × education		−.098**
		(−.476)

Liberal Cue	Disposition–Situation Interaction	Disposition–Situation–Awareness Interaction
Beneficiaries black[2]	−.142	−.103
	(−.240)	(−.175)
Ideological self-placement	−.129	−.097
	(−.113)	(−.085)
Race of beneficiaries × ideology	.153**	
	(.438)	
Education		−.088
		(−.072)
Race of beneficiaries × ideology × education		.084**
		(.402)

Notes: Weighted $N = 1676$.
Standardized beta coefficients in parentheses.
* $p \leq .05$; ** $p \leq .01$.
[1] This is a randomized variable taking two values: beneficiaries of the program either "have shown that they want to work their way out of their own problems" or "have had trouble hanging on to jobs."
[2] This is a randomized variable taking two values: beneficiaries of the program are either "blacks and minorities" or "new immigrants from Europe."

REPRISE

There are two quite different reasons to grapple with the problem of political attitudes and political judgment. The narrower reason is to understand better the dynamics of public opinion interviews; the broader one is to understand better the quality of citizens' judgments in liberal democracies. These two reasons, though different in character, are not in conflict. On the contrary, it is not possible to respond to the normative issue of what citizens may have a right, or even a responsibility, to do without addressing the empirical issue of what they are capable of doing.

It has again become fashionable to suggest that citizens are incapable of judgment on matters of public interest. This skepticism now takes the form of a general claim that political attitudes are socially constructed. Though available in a number of formulations, this general claim consists of two crucial claims. The first is that "most people possess opposing considerations on most issues that might lead them to decide the issue either way."[36] The second is that most people, on most issues, will just as readily take one side of an issue as the other, depending "on which has been made most immediately salient by chance and the details of questionnaire construction, especially the order and framing of questions."[37] The first we have called the "flip-flop claim"; the second, the "ambivalence claim."

There is, so far as we can see, no evidence in favor of the flip-flop claim. Neither the results of the question-wording experiments nor those of over-time stability calculations remotely approach the strength required to sustain the suggestion that most citizens could, on any given occasion, just as easily line up on one side of most issues as on the other. Nor is the flip-flop claim, applied to real issues, self-evidently plausible. Who really supposes that on issues like affirmative action or welfare or crime citizens have no genuine attitudes, that "most people, on most issues, do not 'really think' any particular thing,"[38] that they are simply making it up as they go along?

The second claim, the ambivalence claim, is, to borrow a metaphor, the turtle on which all the other explanatory turtles stand. However, it suffers from two kinds of difficulties: the first methodological, the second conceptual. The empirical difficulty is that the strongest evidence for it derives from the stop-and-think experiment, but the stop-and-think experiment is the weakest link methodologically. The experiment has two drawbacks. First, it confuses the position people have on an issue with the reasons they may, on request, come up with for taking a position on the issue, theirs or others'. Second, it purports to show that responses to issues are unstable and contradictory. What it actually shows is that respondents, not surprisingly, are less likely to remember their accustomed response if their customary train of thought is interrupted.

36 Zaller and Feldman, 1992, p. 585.
37 Zaller, 1992, p. 93.   38 Zaller, 1994, p. 194.

Quite apart from methodological problems, Zaller's argument suffers from a deeper conceptual problem. As we have seen, he proposes two models of attitudes, not one, and though the first is predicated on the proposition that people do not have political predispositions organizing and making coherent their beliefs about and their responses to specific issues, the second takes as its central premise that they do. It is very far from obvious how it is possible to argue at the same time that people lack organized, coherent dispositions to respond consistently (either positively or negatively) to political objects and that they have such dispositions. The conflict is less obvious because, in Zaller's treatment, the two models are taken up seriatim. This separation, in addition to obscuring the tension between them, has the further unfortunate effect of framing the analysis in either-or terms, suggesting that a difference in responses to a question as a function of the wording of the question is, in itself, proof of the absence of a genuine underlying attitude. In turn, treating dispositional and question-wording effects as mutually exclusive leads to the extreme suggestion that most citizens, on most issues, can and will flip-flop, taking first one side and then the other merely as a function of seemingly minor variations in the wording of a question.

By contrast, we concentrate on assessing *simultaneously* the impact of predispositional and situational factors. When the influence of both is assessed simultaneously and not seriatim, a different picture emerges. It turns out to be emphatically not the case that if respondents attend to situational cues, they do not act on the basis of attitudinal priors. On the contrary, they tend to make use of all the information at hand, viewing the specific choice they are asked to make in the light of their political priors plus taking account of its distinctive features. Nor is there a tug-of-war between their predispositions and the distinguishing features of a specific choice they are asked to make on a given occasion. The two are complementary. But they may be complementary in two different ways, one we have illustrated with the Probable Cause experiment, the other with the Helping Hand experiment.

In the Probable Cause experiment, the response to question-wording effects is uniform. Liberals are as likely as conservatives to take the use of foul language in a public place as a violation of acceptable standards. If question-wording effects are uniform, the impact of predispositional and situational factors is additive. The person who is most committed to law and order as a value is even more likely to believe the police had probable cause for a drug search if the suspects were using foul language rather than being well dressed and well behaved. But then, so too is the person most supportive of the rights of crime suspects. Each reacts the same way relative to the other. Both adjust their response the same way relative to the situation. In the Helping Hand experiment, by contrast, their response to specific features of a situation is itself a function of their general pre-dispositions. The liberal is more likely to favor government assistance for the disadvantaged than the conservative and still more likely to do so if those to be assisted are black; the conservative is more likely to oppose government assistance and still more likely to do so if those to be helped have not shown that they will make the effort to help themselves. The rela-tion between predisposition and question wording is interactive. But in either case, whether in the Probable Cause or the Helping Hand experi-ment, citizens make use of all the information at hand.

The expanded version of the nonattitudes thesis claims that most cit-izens do not know what they think about most issues and, lacking genuine attitudes to stabilize their judgments, flip-flop from one side of an issue to the opposite as a function of situational cues in the form of question-wording effects. We have examined question-wording effects in two conditions: when the weight attached to the cue is independent of people's political predispositions and when it is dependent. The flip-flop model fails in both conditions. In both, citizens make their best estimate of the right course of action based on their political priors, updated by current information about the specific decision they are being asked to make. In the first condition, the relation between the two is additive; in the second, interactive. If the situational cue is orthogonal to the attitudinal predisposition, then the effect of the cue is complementary. It increases by an approximately constant amount the probability, at any point along the underlying dispositional continuum, of a response consonant with it. If the weight of the cue is related to a person's loca-tion along the underlying dispositional continuum, then the effect is interactive. Consonant cues reinforce people's underlying disposition, and do so more strongly the stronger the disposition. In neither condi-tion, then, do citizens simply flip-flop from one side of an issue to the opposite under the control of situational cues in the form of question-wording effects.

In making a determination as to how a specific problem, given a par-ticular set of circumstances, should be dealt with at a given time, citi-zens need to make use of two kinds of information. The first is their general views about how problems of this type should be dealt with; the second is the information they have on hand about the particular fea-tures of the specific problem they wish to resolve. So, in the Probable Cause experiment, in determining whether the police conduct on a par-ticular occasion was or was not reasonable, citizens can, and should, draw both on their attitudes toward law and order in general and on the information they have on the demeanor of the suspects on this particu-lar occasion. Analogously, in the Helping Hand experiment, in judging whether a particular government program is or is not deserving of support, citizens can, and should, draw both on their attitudes toward government assistance in general and on the information they have on the distinctive features of the specific program they are being asked to evaluate – who is to be helped, what kind of help they are to get, and what they may have done to deserve help. Indeed, as a general principle, if citizens are to make judgments about actual matters of public policy approximately rationally, they need to take account of their political priors updated by information on the distinctive features of the specific problem and the course of public action before them. If citizens acted only on the basis of their political attitudes, they would be blind to the present; if they acted only on the basis of their immediate circumstances, they would be blind to the past. They must, if they are to be approximately rational, take account of both, and our results show they do. It is accordingly an irony worth observing when citizens are judged not to know what they think because they are paying attention to what they are specifically being asked to think about.

APPENDIX A: SAMPLE DESCRIPTION

We shall rely on data from a national telephone survey – the Race and American Values Study – to explore these issues. The survey, funded by the National Science Foundation, was carried out on a nationwide random-digit telephone sample designed by the Survey Research Center of the University of California, Berkeley. The target population for the study was all English-speaking adults, eighteen years of age or older, residing in households with telephones, within the forty-eight contiguous states. An unusually large number of interviews, 2223, were completed, with a 65.3% response rate.

Because the telephone interviews, which the Survey Research Center of the University of California also conducted, were computer-assisted, we were able to randomize many elements of the questionnaire, including some items discussed in this chapter. The interviewing was implemented using the CASES software developed by the Computer-Assisted Survey Methods Program of the University of California, Berkeley.

The sample of telephone numbers for this survey was generated using a new stratified two-phase procedure that produced a high proportion of households in the sample, yet did not require the replacement methodology of the two-stage Mitofsky–Waksberg method. A discussion of the sampling methodology used for this study can be found in R. J. Casady and J. M. Lepkowski, "Optimal Allocation for Stratified Telephone Survey Designs," *Proceedings of the Section on Survey Research Methods*, American Statistical Association (1991). The sampling was carried out in the following steps:

1. The area code and prefix combinations on the AT&T Bellcore tape were ordered geographically, and a large first-phase sample of those combinations was selected with systematic random sampling. Four-digit random numbers were appended to the area code and prefix combinations to generate complete telephone numbers.

2. The selected first-phase telephone numbers were compared with a tape created by Donnelley Marketing Services, which gives the number of listed residential telephone numbers in each series of 100 numbers – that is, how many residential telephone numbers in phone directories begin with the same eight digits. Based on this information, the selected telephone numbers were placed into two strata – telephone numbers from series with no residential listings and telephone numbers from series with at least one listing.

3. From the stratified pool of first-phase selections, a second-phase sample was drawn. Many replicate samples of telephone numbers were drawn from the stratum containing telephone numbers from series of numbers with at least one residential listing; a random sample of telephone numbers was also drawn from the other stratum, but with a smaller sampling fraction. This method of disproportionate sampling resulted in the selection of a second-phase sample in which approximately half of the selected telephone numbers turned out to be households. The difference in selection probabilities between the two strata is compensated for by using weights. Only four cases were completed from the zero-listing stratum, but they receive weights of 10.3 relative to cases in the main sample.

4. A small supplementary sample of telephone numbers from new prefixes was also drawn to compensate for the fact that the major sampling work just described was carried out several months before the beginning of this study. A new Bellcore tape was obtained, and 761 area code and prefix combinations that had not appeared on the older tape were identified. A sample of 102 such prefixes was selected at random, and four-digit random numbers were appended to each selected prefix to generate the supplementary sample. Of those 102 numbers, 6 turned out to be households, and interviews were completed at 5 of them. Those completed cases receive weights of 3.0 relative to cases in the main sample.

In addition to the weighting adjustments for selection probabilities already mentioned, the weight used for analysis incorporated adjustments for number of telephone lines and number of eligible adults in the household. The final weight also included poststratification adjustments for gender, race, age, and education. The variance of the weight is .45 for all cases; it is .42 for whites alone.

APPENDIX B: MEASURES

Commitment to Law and Order

This measure is an additive index of three items: the rating (from 0 to 10) of the importance of "strengthening law and order"; whether someone arrested for a serious crime "should have to answer all questions" or "should be permitted to remain silent"; and whether "In dealing with serious street crime like hold-ups or robbery . . . it's more important to 'Protect the rights of suspects even if a guilty person sometimes goes free' or 'Stop such crimes and make the street safe even if suspects' rights are sometimes violated.'"

Commitment to Traditional Values

This measure is an additive index of six items rated from 0 to 10: "preserving the traditional ideas of right and wrong"; "respect for authority"; "following God's will"; "improving standards of politeness in everyday behavior"; "strengthening law and order"; and "maintaining respect for America's power in the world."

Conventionality

This measure is an additive combination of six items: the ratings of three values – the importance of "preserving traditional ideas of right and wrong"; "respect for authority"; and "improving politeness" – all on a scale from 0 to 10 and of three questions on the qualities respondents think a child should have – "independence OR respect for elders?", "obedience OR self-reliance?", and "curiosity OR good manners?"

Black Work Ethic Index

This index draws on a larger measure of stereotypes, where respondents were asked to judge how well a number of descriptors describe "most blacks," and combines responses to a quartet of stereotypes: "dependable," "lazy," "hardworking," and "irresponsible."

Ideological Self-Identification

A 7-point measure, in branching format, running from strong liberal to strong conservative.

References

Abelson, Robert P. 1968. "Discussion: Minimalist vs. Maximalist Positions on Cognitive Structure." In Robert P. Abelson, Elliot Aronson, William J. McGuire, Theodore M. Newcomb, Milton J. Rosenberg, and Percy H. Tannenbaum, eds., *Theories of Cognitive Consistency: A Sourcebook.* Chicago: Rand McNally and Company, pp. 526–528.

Achen, Christopher. 1975. "Mass Political Attitudes and the Survey Response." *American Political Science Review* 69: 1218–1231.

Baron, Jonathan. 1994. *Thinking and Deciding.* 2nd ed. New York: Cambridge University Press.

Berelson, Bernard, Paul F. Lazarsfeld, and William N. McPhee. 1954. *Voting: A Study of Opinion Formation in a Presidential Campaign.* Chicago: University of Chicago Press.

Bishop, George F., Alfred J. Tuchfarber, and Robert W. Oldendick. 1978. "Change in the Structure of American Political Attitudes: The Nagging Question of Question Wording." *American Journal of Political Science* 22: 250–269.

Bruner, Jerome S. 1951. "Personality Dynamics and the Process of Perceiving." In R. R. Blake and G. U. Ramsey, eds., *Perception: An Approach to Personality.* New York: Ronald Press, pp. 121–147.

Campbell, Donald T. 1963. "Social Attitudes and Other Acquired Behavioral Dispositions." In Sigmund Koch, ed., *Psychology: Study of a Science.* New York: McGraw-Hill, vol. 6, 94–172.

Converse, Philip E. 1964. "The Nature of Belief Systems in Mass Publics." In David Apter, ed., *Ideology and Discontent.* New York: Free Press, 206–261.

Converse, Philip E. 1970. "Attitudes and Non-Attitudes: Continuation of a Dialogue." In Edward R. Tufte, ed., *The Quantitative Analysis of Social Problems.* Reading, Mass: Addison-Wesley, 168–190.

Delli Carpini, Michael X., and Scott Keeter. 1989. "Political Knowledge of the U.S. Public: Results from a National Survey." Paper presented at the annual meeting of the American Association for Public Opinion Research, St. Petersburg, Florida.

Delli Carpini, Michael X., and Scott Keeter. 1991. "Stability and Change in the U.S. Public's Knowledge of Politics." *Public Opinion Quarterly* 55: 583–612.

Funder, David C., and Daniel J. Ozer. 1983. "Behavior as a Function of the Situation." *Journal of Personality and Social Psychology* 44: 107–112.

Hyman, Herbert. 1969. "Social Psychology and Race Relations." In I. Katz and Patricia Gurin, eds., *Race and the Social Sciences.* New York: Basic Books, pp. 3–48.

Kelley, Stanley, Jr. 1983. *Interpreting Elections.* Princeton: Princeton University Press.

Kinder, Donald, and L. M. Sanders. 1990. "Mimicking Political Debate with Survey Questions: The Case of White Opinion on Affirmative Action for Blacks." *Social Cognition* 8: 73–103.

Lazarsfeld, Paul F., Bernard Berelson, and Hazel Gaudet. 1944. *The People's Choice: How the Voter Makes Up His Mind in a Presidential Campaign.* New York: Duell, Sloan and Pierce.

Lewin, Kurt. 1935. *A Dynamic Theory of Personality: Selected Papers.* New York: McGraw-Hill.

McGuire, William J. 1968. "Theory of the Structure of Human Thought." In Robert P. Abelson, Elliot Aronson, William J. McGuire, Theodore M. Newcomb, Milton J. Rosenberg, and Percy H. Tannenbaum, eds., *Theories of Cognitive Consistency: A Sourcebook.* Chicago: Rand McNally and Company, pp. 140–162.

Nie, Norman H., Sidney Verba, and John R. Petrocik. 1979. *The Changing American Voter.* Cambridge: Harvard University Press.

Postman, L., J. S. Bruner, and R. D. Walk. 1951. "The Perception of Error." *British Journal of Psychology* 42:1–10.

Schuman, Howard, and Stanley Presser. 1981. *Questions and Answers in Attitude Surveys: Experiments on Question Form, Wording, and Context.* New York: Academic Press.

Smith, Eric R. A. N. 1989. *The Unchanging American Voter.* Berkeley: University of California Press.

Sniderman, Paul M. 1993. "The New Look in Public Opinion Research." In Ada W. Finifter, ed., *Political Science: The State of the Discipline II.* Washington, D.C.: The American Political Science Association, pp. 219–245.

Sniderman, Paul M., Richard A. Brody, and Philip E. Tetlock. 1991. *Reasoning and Choice: Explorations in Political Psychology.* New York: Cambridge University Press.

Sniderman, Paul M., and Thomas Piazza. 1993. *The Scar of Race.* Cambridge: Harvard University Press.

Sniderman, Paul M., Philip E. Tetlock, and Edward G. Carmines. 1993. *Prejudice, Politics and the American Dilemma.* Stanford: Stanford University Press.

Taylor, Shelly E., and Susan Fiske. 1978. "Salience, Attention, and Attribution: Top of the Head Phenomena." In L. Berkowitz, ed., *Advances in Experimental Social Psychology.* New York: Academic Press, vol. 11, pp. 249–288.

Tetlock, Philip E., Randall S. Peterson, and Jennifer S. Lerner. 1996. "Revising the Value Pluralism Model of Ideological Reasoning: Incorporating Social Content and Context Postulates." In Clive Seligman, James M. Olson, and Mark P. Zanna, eds., *The Psychology of Values.* Hillsdale, NJ: Erlbaum, 25–51.

Tourangeau, Roger, and Kenneth A. Rasinski. 1988. "Cognitive Processes Underlying Context Effects in Attitude Measurement." *Psychological Bulletin* 103: 299–314.

Wilson, Timothy D. 1990. "Self-Persuasion Via Self-Reflection." In James M. Olson and Mark P. Zanna, eds., *Self-Inference Processes: The Ontario Symposium.* Hillsdale, NJ: Erlbaum, pp. 43–67.

Wilson, Timony D., and Sara D. Hodges. 1992. "Attitudes as Temporary Constructions." In Leonard L. Martin and Abraham Tesser, eds., *The Construction of Social Judgments.* Hillsdale, NJ: Erlbaum, 37–65.

Zaller, John. 1992. *The Nature and Origins of Mass Opinion.* New York: Cambridge University Press.

——— 1994. "Elite Leadership of Mass Opinion: New Evidence from the Gulf War." In W. Lance Bennett and David L. Paletz, eds., *Taken by Storm: The Media, Public Opinion, and U.S. Foreign Policy in the Gulf War.* Chicago: University of Chicago Press, 186–209.

Zaller, John, and Stanley Feldman. 1992. "A Simple Theory of the Survey Response: Answering Questions versus Revealing Preferences." *American Journal of Political Science* 36: 579–616.

10

Implications of a Latitude-Theory Model of Citizen Attitudes for Political Campaigning, Debate, and Representation

GREGORY ANDRADE DIAMOND

Political public opinion can be expressed either positively or negatively. A positively expressed attitude endorses a particular policy from among a range of options for a given issue. Favoring a reduction in defense spending or a prohibition of late-term abortions are both positively expressed attitudes. A negatively expressed attitude on an issue indicates what one does *not* want to happen and is difficult to portray as crisply. With respect to defense spending, for example, one might feel: "No increase is needed; any more than a slight increase would be damaging; drastic cuts are also unreasonable; even some moderate cuts are worrisome." Here one rules out disliked positions and is left with a set of options ranging from inoffensive at worst to desirable at best. Politicians retain some latitude to endorse policies from within this range of non-objectionable options without alienating the voter.

Whatever virtue negatively expressed attitudes may have – such as more accurately reflecting the way people think about many issues – they are messy, disturbingly provisional, and difficult to summarize across persons. Academic and political observers have avoided them; while recognizing that negative *information* may play strong roles in determining political attitudes (Lau, 1982), they construct the attitudes themselves as positively expressed. Elsewhere (Diamond and Cobb, 1996), I argue that modeling political attitudes in this unwieldy, imprecise, negatively expressed fashion greatly aids our understanding of real voters' conceptions of real candidates. This chapter explores some of the counterintuitive implications of this negatively expressed political opinion – based

Jim Kuklinski first suggested that I explore the implications of latitude theory for theories of representation, and I gratefully acknowledge his and Michael Cobb's help in puzzling them out. The responsibility for these ideas, and particularly for any errors, remains solely mine.

on a theory of attitudes presented later – for understanding political campaigning, political debate, and our normative models of political representation.

THE PSYCHOLOGICAL STRUCTURE OF ATTITUDES

Diamond and Cobb (1996) argue that the standard model of political attitudes – that people endorse ideal points on political dimensions and oppose other points along these dimensions as a function of their distance from the ideal – is so pervasive and unquestioned that it does not really have a name; we rectify that situation by calling it the "point placement model." This model implies a positive approach to political cognition. It also implies that, aside from the costs of acquiring and processing information (Downs, 1957), political debate and information about candidate placements are unambiguously useful, since they improve the individual's ability to place herself on an ideological dimension, to place candidates on that dimension, and to calculate the differences between them. And if attitudes can be conceived of as points on a line, we may subsequently add or average them to reach conclusions about individuals or populations. If one relies on the point placement model, it is hard to imagine how these assumptions could be wrong.

This model's hold is so strong that one can explain seeming departures from its predicted effects mainly by arguing that when it does not apply, one is not in fact dealing with an attitude after all. Thus, Converse (1964) argues that most of the population does not have attitudes, but rather "nonattitudes," and that many of those who do have attitudes simply learn who or what they should prefer from their local opinion leader, memorizing it as they might the name of the capital of a foreign country. Or one might hold that attitudes do exist for various people, but only on certain issues that they happen to find centrally important (Converse, 1970; Judd and Krosnick, 1982). Or one can argue that most expressed attitudes are ad hoc and ephemeral constructions (Zaller, 1992). In all these cases, if one is constrained by the point placement metaphor, one can only respond to situations in which people do not seem to have stable ideal points by claiming that they therefore do not, in fact *must* not, have "real" attitudes. Since the process of political cognition seems to be fairly arduous, if one accepts the point placement assumption, theorists consider the instability of most mass political attitudes to be unsurprising.

An Alternative Model of Attitudes

The point placement model does have at least one historical alternative, found in the "social judgment theory" of Muzafer Sherif and Carl

Hovland (1961). This theory comprises (1) a model of attitude *structure* and (2) a model of attitude *change* based on assimilation of and contrasts between persuasive communications and individuals' own positions. This chapter is concerned only with Sherif and Hovland's structural model, which, for reasons expressed later, will be identified specifically as "latitude theory" as distinct from the "assimilation and contrast model" of attitude change.

Latitude theory accepts that one or more given dimensions underlie the policy choices that people make, although it depends less on their clear understanding of those dimensions. It breaks from point placement models in putting little or no emphasis on respondents' "optimally preferred point" on those dimensions.[1] Instead, it introduces three theoretical constructs: the "latitude of acceptance," the "latitude of noncommitment," and the "latitude of rejection." The boundary between the first two of these latitudes demarcates what one actively likes from what one is indifferent to, and the boundary between the last two separates what one is indifferent to from what one actively dislikes. People are assumed to be essentially equivocal when choosing among proposals within a given latitude. Figure 10.1 contrasts the standard and latitude-based models of attitudes.

Using latitude theory, a reasonable description of an individual's attitude on a given dimension would include the location of the points demarcating each of these latitudes. While more complex for the theorist to describe, this attitude model assumes less effort on the part of the individual, since it assumes only simple affective responses (many of which will be neutral) to various points arrayed along a dimension rather than determination of the maximum positive affective value across all of the points. (See Diamond and Cobb, 1994 and 1996, for an extensive comparison of the relative advantages of the latitude and point placement models.)

Latitude theory relaxes many of the assumptions undergirding the point placement model. It does not assume that people generate and calibrate an issues dimension, but simply that they react to specific proposals that the theorist can then place along a dimension as she sees fit. It does not assume that people put forth the mostly wasted effort of distinguishing among neutral or among repugnant alternatives, or that they bother determining which of an appealing set of propositions is precisely

---

1 Sherif and Hovland had people indicate their most and least preferred points on dimensions, but this played no important part in their structural theory. The model presented here exaggerates theirs slightly to highlight the differences between the latitude and point placement approaches, but its most severe assumptions can be relaxed without compromising this argument.

<u>Standard</u>   <u>Latitude-based</u>

X (ideal point)   R A A N N R R

| | | | | | | | | | | | | | | | | |

+0 +2 +4 +2 +0 -2 -4   -4 +4 +4 +0 +0 -4 -4
L   C   L   C

Attitude described   Attitude described by location
solely by ideal   of boundaries between
preference point [X]   latitudes of non commitment
along the liberal [L]   [N],rejection [R], and
to conservative [C]   acceptance [A] on the [L] to
dimension   [C] dimension.

Numbers beneath each scale indicate the degree of support for
proposals at given points along an ideological dimension, from +4
(highest) to -4 (lowest).

Figure 10.1. Two models of attitudes along an ideological dimension of opinion.

optimal rather than sufficiently good. All that matters is the assignment of a person or proposal to one of the three basic affective classes – good, bad, and indifferent. Information about individuals' preferences is not conveyed by their ideal points on a dimension, but instead by shifting boundaries between what is desirable and what is tolerable on that issue, and between what is tolerable and what is intolerable.

This last point is one of the few aspects of latitude theory's structural model that did receive serious research attention during the 1960s. Sherif and colleagues (Sherif and Hovland, 1961; Sherif, Sherif, and Nebergall, 1965) argued that the latitude of acceptance has a relatively fixed width. People are willing to endorse a range of options covering a consistent proportion of a political dimension, even if the location of the range they endorse may change over time. What does vary is the dimension of the latitude of rejection, which either encroaches upon or cedes territory to the latitude of noncommitment.[2] The width of the latitude of rejection is an important individual difference variable within subjects over time and circumstance, between subjects, and across populations. While

2 Conceptually, one could as easily represent the latitude of noncommitment as taking territory from or yielding it to the latitude of rejection. But since assigning something to the latitude of rejection means an active affective response to it rather than what may be a passive reaction, it seems more reasonable to write as if this latitude is the one that expands or shrinks – although we may sometimes talk about a "growing ambivalence." While the language used in this chapter presumes that the latitude of acceptance is in fact of stable width, the ideas expressed here would in general survive (with some recasting) were this found not to be reliably true.

people's ideal policy preferences for various issues may not change over time, the width of their latitude of rejection may.[3]

Latitude theory provides a strong foundation for a model of negative political thinking in which people judge whether policies or candidates are clearly unacceptable in one of various ways. While the proposition is untested, it seems likely that the determination that certain positions are *unreasonable* will be more stable and considered than the determination that they are *optimal*. If we assume that (especially the least sophisticated) citizens determine their political attitudes by working from the outside of the political dimensions inward, we may be able to escape the problems presented by Converse and by Zaller. Lau (1982) has shown that people attend more to negative than to positive political information; Tversky (1972) has shown that an early stage of the decision-making process involves shucking off undesirable options before distinguishing among one's optimal preferences. Such an analysis also easily accommodates the symbolic role of political labels ("racist," "socialist," "anti-American") that may help especially less sophisticated voters avoid what they might expect to be offensive ideological objects with little effort while they navigate through the political landscape. Latitude theory extends these theories by applying them to the development of political opinions.

Latitude Theory: Old Wine in Old Wineskins?

Before applying latitude theory to questions of representation and political debate, I must address a question that is logically extraneous but practically important. Sherif and Hovland introduced social judgment theory over forty years ago. It has had limited and declining influence since that time and is now moribund. Researchers might understandably be dubious about its reclamation. Why now or at all?

Researchers' level of concern, of course, should depend on why the theory was initially discredited. A review of the literature yields a

---

3 This distinguishes latitude theory from the work of Stimson (1991), who applies concepts similar to the latitudes of acceptance/noncommitment – he combines the two – and rejection to his study of the "public mood," emphasizing the importance of a boundary between them. Stimson assumes the latitude of acceptance/noncommitment to be of fixed width, shifting over time along an ideological dimension, while latitude theory considers the variability of such latitudes over persons and time to be a critically important variable. Stimson also adheres to traditional survey measurement tools in pursuing these notions, while I have argued (Diamond and Cobb, 1996) that these tools are inappropriate for the task. I am grateful to Michael Cobb for both raising this problem and helping to resolve it.

surprising finding: latitude theory itself never *was* discredited. Almost all of the intellectual debate over social judgment theory in major psychological journals during the 1960s and early 1970s addressed predictions of the assimilation and contrast model of attitude change (Atkins, Deaux, and Bieri, 1967; Eagly and Manis, 1966; Eagly and Telaak, 1972; Ostrom, 1966; Powell, 1966). This is understandable; the assimilation and contrast model yielded crisp predictions that challenged the dominant psychological balance theories of the day. The underlying structural model yielded relatively few predictions by itself, aside from its challenge to the theoretical and methodological convenience of point placement models. In textbooks on attitudes from this time that address social judgment theory at all (e.g., Fishbein and Ajzen, 1975; Oskamp, 1977; Triandis, 1971), discussion of the assimilation and contrast predictions predominated, and the structural model itself received brief, and generally kind, mention.

Latitude theory was not influential by the time that affect, especially as related to cognitive structure (Fiske, 1982; Mandler, 1982; Zajonc, 1980), reemerged as a major topic in social psychology. This is unfortunate, since the structural model of attitudes maps nicely onto a social cognitive model that would attach negative and positive affect to items found within the latitudes of rejection and acceptance, respectively.

A final reason for the failure of latitude theory in the court of professional opinion may be its methodological unwieldiness. Experimental work based on latitude theory demands procedures that have much in common with Thurstone scaling (although some differences are noted in Diamond and Cobb, 1996), in that consensual ratings of the placement of various policies on an underlying dimension should be obtained so as to provide a stable metric against which expansion and contraction of the various latitudes may be gauged. One may well question the study of individuals' latitudes using consensus ratings of a policy's scale placement, since individuals may order alternatives idiosyncratically. The best answer to this objection may simply be the present lack of a workable alternative. Since moderate positions on issues may derive from "contamination" of a "pure" ideological dimension by a competing one – as when one's stance on Medicare funding for abortions is determined not only by opinions on abortion but also by opinions on government entitlements – the task becomes nearly impossible.

Nevertheless, far from being discredited, latitude theory remains a viable challenge to point prediction models. The next sections of this chapter will examine its applicability to various aspects of mass–elite interaction: campaigning, political debate, and governmental representation.

IMPLICATIONS FOR POLITICAL CAMPAIGNING

The point prediction model does little to explain why negative attitudes should be relatively powerful, or indeed why candidates should try to slant ads in either a negative or a positive direction. Latitude theory, by contrast, takes advantage of the notion that people perceive negative information more readily than positive information. The catch phrase of political operatives – "we want to drive up the opponents' negatives" – is not readily represented with traditional Likert policy scales, where the only two things that can move are the individual's own placement and the candidates' placements, all of which are at least somewhat resistant to persuasive appeals.[4]

Latitude theory suggests two additional manipulable variables: the width and placement to the latitude of rejection. It even suggests an optimal strategy for political operatives: even if neither one's own nor one's opponent's positions are generally accepted by voters, one wants to narrow the latitude of rejection on the side of the issue where one differs from the median voter and widen the latitude of rejection on the side of the issue where one's opponent falls. As shown in Figure 10.2, this can work even if one's position is no closer to (or, in fact, further away from) that of the median voter. By convincing voters that the liberal position is *reasonable*, even if not desirable, and that anything *more* conservative than the median voter's position is undesirable, Candidate 1 is able to capitalize on this issue without being closer to the median voter. Note that these shifts in voter preference would not necessarily show up in measures of candidate placements.

In 1988, George Bush successfully used this strategy, adjusting the latitudes of acceptance and/or noncommitment so that his position was contained and his opponent's position was excluded, when he successfully defined the only tolerable positions on "values" issues such as the mandatory Pledge of Allegiance as close to the "flag-waving" one he endorsed. By concentrating his efforts on making the civil libertarian stances on such issues appear actively unpatriotic, he was able to move responses to them from toleration (however grudging) to spirited rejection. His use of the

---

4 Naturally, sometimes it is possible to change voters' minds on an issue, or to convince them that oneself or one's opponent stands differently from where they thought, but relying on such strategies is a poor gamble. A better strategy has been to highlight the salience of issues on which one is believed to be closer to voters' preferences than is one's opponent. This is well and good, but the fact remains that one must at some point (often at an opponent's instigation) address issues on which one is vulnerable. This is where the tactics suggested by latitude theory are especially useful.

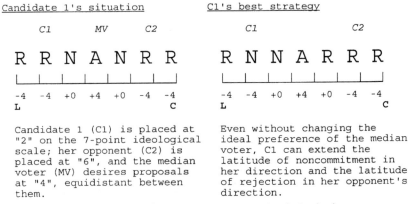

Figure 10.2. Optimal campaign strategy using latitude theory.

Willie Horton issue had a similar effect. While it is not clear that voters would necessarily find the idea of prison furlough plans a priori intolerable, what *was* intolerable to voters was the end result of allowing someone to escape such a program and commit violent acts. Michael Dukakis was unable to transform the issue into one about means (e.g., "Is Bush arguing that *all* furlough programs should be eliminated because of the possibility of tragedy?") and was thus unable to make his position appear reasonable (even if slightly unappealing).

This analysis also helps explain why moralistic/values issues are so useful to politicians: they more readily afford absolutist reasoning. On issues that many voters find confusing (e.g., industry bailouts, high-technology industrial policy), there is little concern about "compromise with the devil." The debate is over the best means to achieve desired ends, and even positions that one does not favor will not seem morally wrong. Lacking expertise, voters may not be sure of exactly where they fall on these issues, so it's hard for a politician to portray the opponent's position as in the latitude of rejection except by successfully attaching to it some symbolic blemish (e.g., 'socialism," "greedy businessmen").

On moral issues, by contrast, all people can claim expertise. Thus, they have wider latitudes of rejection. For many voters (however hypocritical), the only acceptable amount of extramarital sexual activity is none; likewise for drug use, lying, check bouncing, and so on. It is likely that voters are most comfortable with the ability to frame issues in ways that generate easy assignment to latitudes of acceptance and rejection. This is why, in 1992, the complex issue of congressional fiduciary responsibility was reduced to the easy issue of check kiting (with a wide latitude of rejection encompassing the behavior of representatives who had any checks on the list of those with overdrafts; Dimock and Jacobson, 1995) and perhaps also why the powerful ecological impetus behind society's complex "jobs versus environment" debate gets channeled into tough public service campaigns against the clearly unacceptable but much less consequential activity of littering.

While Figure 2 shows the advantages of getting voters to tolerate one's position on an issue even if they don't support it, it may be somewhat limited. Clearly, one way of moving voters' reactions to one's positions from rejection to noncommitment is by *persuading* them that they should do so, but this is hardly the only way. Confusing voters with statistics generated by think tanks or public relations firms hired to obfuscate (Greider, 1992), convincing them that an issue is highly technical and best left to experts, and other such maneuvers may effectively keep an issue from counting against a candidate even if voters retain some sense of unease. It may be that fostering a sense of resignation, impotence, or cynicism also leaves voters less likely to reject one's policy stances. The question of how and when voters develop sufficient confidence to conclude definitively that a candidate's stance is wrong is wide open for research. I expand on this notion, applying it to debates over political proposals, in the next section.

IMPLICATIONS FOR POLITICAL DEBATE

It has been almost axiomatic that political debate, by making voters more aware of the political issues of the day and increasing the likelihood of their having informed and well-considered opinions on those issues, has a beneficial effect both on the citizens in a democratic system and on society as a whole (Pateman, 1970; "debate" here is not meant to refer only to formal candidate debates, but to policy-related political discourse in general). Decisions that are qualitatively better, or at least more representative, would be expected to arise from a culture in which major conflicting policy viewpoints are aired. Certainly exceptions to this might be possible – demagogic, specious, or venal arguments might be used to sway voters in certain cases – but if debate proceeds on a high plane, the presumable salutary effect is clear. This philosophical presumption underlies all but the most biased editorial pages.

Latitude theory, however, suggests some counterintuitive and distressing hypotheses about our normative models of political debate. Consider the schematic diagram in Figure 10.3a. This figure depicts a dimension of opinions towards Issue X that can be divided for the sake of clarity into seven sections. Moderate Mr. A's reactions to proposals expressed on this dimension are displayed above it. A will be attracted to any proposal on Issue X that he sees as falling into region 4 and will be repelled

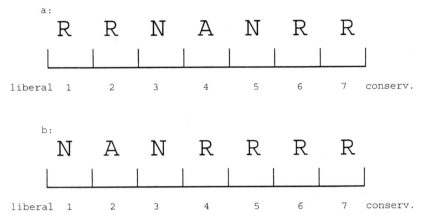

Figure 10.3. Initial orientations of Mr. A and Ms. B on issue X.

by proposals falling into regions 1, 2, 6, and 7. Proposals falling into regions 3 and 5 will not influence his vote.

Contrast A's latitude pattern with that of Ms. B (Figure 10.3b). B is much more liberal than A, being attracted to proposals that fall into region 2, repelled by anything in regions 4 to 7, and unaffected by proposals in regions 1 and 3. Combining their patterns, we find that proposals in 2 and 4 will attract one voter and repel the other, proposals in 3 won't affect either (except by comparison to other proposals), proposals in 1 and 5 will repel one and not affect the other, and proposals in 6 and 7 will repel both.

At this point, we can make one of two provisional assumptions about an empirical matter: is it easier for a politician to make her own argument seem reasonable or to make an opponent's argument seem unreasonable? We will explore both possibilities in this section, but in deference to the skill with which politicians produce letters defusing the anger of outraged constituents, let's assume first that making oneself seem reasonable is easier.

Now assume that both A and B encounter a conservative argument on Issue X that is strong enough to shrink their latitude of rejection by one unit. We will assume that no countervailing liberal argument is presented, and further, that the argument is simply one that argues that a conservative approach is reasonable rather than that a liberal approach is necessarily bad. The effects may be found in Figures 10.4a and 10.4b. Now the only proposal sure to repel both voters is one falling in region 7. Proposals in regions 1, 2, 5, and 6 will repel one and won't affect the other; proposals in regions 3 and 4 will attract one and won't affect the other.

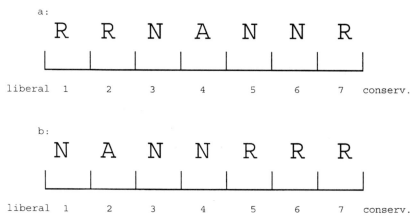

Figure 10.4. Orientations of A and B after initial persuasive conservative message (assumption: easier to make oneself seem reasonable).

What if A and B now hear a reasonable liberal argument on the issue that has comparable effects? Figure 10.5 depicts the consequences. Mr. A, while attracted by the most moderate proposals, will now tolerate all but the most radical ones. Ms. B will tolerate or endorse proposals ranging over half of the political spectrum, although the effect on her has been less than the effect on A. The stronger the arguments on both sides become, the more the latitude of rejection gives way to the latitude of noncommitment. At the limit of maximally reasonable arguments on both sides, neither voter will reject a candidate on the basis of his or her taking *any* policy stance on Issue X. (Either could still be attracted by an argument that fell into their latitude of acceptance, but one may wonder whether their latitudes of acceptance would *really* remain at a stable width under such conditions. The implications of the theory do not depend on this being so.)

Now, recall two things. First, politics tends to proceed in a negative way, with people ruling out what they can't abide. Second, each issue exists in the political context of other issues (W, Y, Z) that might affect voters. Given this, what happens to the impact of Issue X upon voters' decisions? In essence, it falls out of the voting equation. Since there is no way that a candidate can go wrong with respect to X after all sides of the debate have come to appear reasonable, X ceases to determine votes. Voters will instead make their decisions on the basis of the less often debated issues W, Y, and Z. Contrary to the implications of the point placement model relied on by Downs (1957), more and better information may lead to a worse outcome.

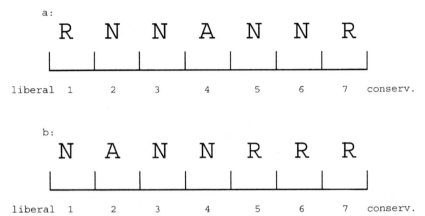

Figure 10.5. New orientations of A and B after subsequent persuasive liberal message (assumption: easier to make oneself seem reasonable).

What happens if we make the opposite assumption, that it is easier to lead people to *reject* opponents' proposals than to lead them to tolerate one's own? The implications of this possibility are depicted in Figures 10.6 and 10.7. By undermining tolerance of opposing proposals, this tactic creates a situation in which only "perfect" proposals – those that one actively endorses – are acceptable. In situations where a majority of a population endorses a given proposal, this will not have much of an effect, but in such situations political debate is hardly necessary. In situations where a divergence of opinion exists such that neither camp can impose its view on the other, this is a recipe for gridlock, as it fosters an environment where at every point along the dimension the impetus for rejection of a proposal will outweigh that for acceptance. This clearly becomes useful for those who are attempting to block change. As political reform proposals across the dimension are seen as increasingly repugnant, the status quo becomes a more reasonable alternative by default ("Better the devil you know . . ."). Voters may become cynical about the inability of the political process to deliver workable proposals and withdraw from the political process. Again, voters are more likely to disregard the issue, given the high likelihood that no candidate escapes their latitude of rejection. The abortive 1994 debate over health care reform may be a good example of what happens when voters are persuaded that all available alternatives are bad.

We should not assume that either the effect portrayed in Figure 10.5 or that portrayed in Figure 10.7 is entirely dominant. These may be complementary rather than competing phenomena, and different political

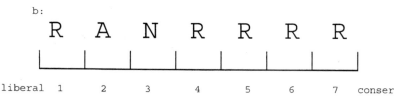

Figure 10.6. Orientations of A and B after initial persuasive conservative message (assumption: easier to make one's opponent seem unreasonable).

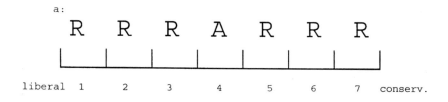

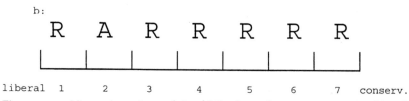

Figure 10.7. New orientations of A and B after subsequent persuasive liberal message (assumption: easier to make one's opponent seem unreasonable).

tactics likely yield different results. Let us distinguish the attempt to make one's positions seem reasonable – call this "soft-soaping" – from the attempt to make one's opponent's positions seem unreasonable – call this "rock-throwing." Soft-soaping should prove especially useful to politicians who want to neutralize a given issue or to gain leeway from the public to innovate in policy formation. It should be a favored tool, then, of those in power, as well as those endorsing antipopulist proposals that thrive when the public remains disengaged. Rock throwing should be favored by those out of power and those who want to freeze the policy-making process by making all alternatives seem comparably bad. (When considering prospects of comparable positive value, people tend to avoid risk and stand pat; Tversky and Kahneman, 1986.) Importantly, these tools may have their effects even if no voters' optimal point preferences are moved at all. Traditional modes of assessing political opinion might miss all of the action.

Soft-soaping and rock throwing may also be differently afforded by different types of political issues. "Character issues," moral issues, and issues that appeal to our worst instincts of chauvinism and intolerance may lend themselves most readily to a widening of latitudes of rejection via rock-throwing debate. As will be noted in the next section, complex issues and ones requiring special expertise may be especially liable to soft-soaping.

IMPLICATIONS FOR POLITICAL REPRESENTATION

Latitude theory probes many assumptions regarding representation, including those about how a government best represents the will of a society, the strength of the tie between public opinion and government action, and the forms such a bond takes.

Who Gets Represented?

Downs (1957) presented the classic argument of why political parties in a two-party system must converge on a central ideological point. Any party that finds itself further from the median voter on an issue is at a disadvantage, being by definition further away from more than 50% of the voters on the relevant ideological dimension. This should lead to a bidding war as both parties try to converge on the public's consensus "ideal point."

Downs's argument depends on a point placement assumption: parties are driven to reduce the aggregate distance between themselves and voters on a variety of issues. Analyzing the ideological dimension from the perspective of latitude theory suggests alternative possibilities, however, as depicted in Figure 10.8. If, for the majority of the public, policies covering a wide expanse of the middle ground of an ideological dimension are considered tolerable, then the centripetal force that Downs argues should operate on a party is negligible for that issue. Given an equivocal public composed of negative voters, little is to be gained by moving to the median voter's position. Note that the equivocal public posited here may be composed entirely of people with strong feelings

Latitude-Theory Model of Citizen Attitudes

a) <u>Downs's model</u>:

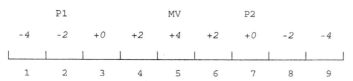

Italicized numbers indicate degree of approval for each position
along dimension. While Party 2 is advantaged at present, each
party would benefit from shifting position toward that of the
median voter. P1 = Party 1; P2 = Party 2; MV = Median Voter.

b) <u>Equivocal electorate</u>:

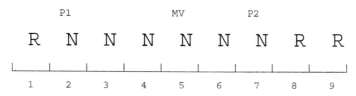

Neither party suffers from staying put or would gain from
moderating. (Absence of an aggregate latitude of acceptance
indicates a lack of societal consensus for a particular policy.)

c) <u>Polarized electorate</u>:

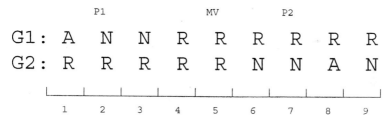

The first line represents the attitudes of Group 1 (G1), the base
of Party 1. The second line represents the attitudes of Group 2
(G2), the base of Party 2. Neither party can gain support by
moving toward the median voter. Either would lose support by
doing so. Each could gain support by moving further away from
the median voter, in the direction of its political base.

Figure 10.8. Models of the impetus toward parties' moderation.

about the issue at hand, but those feelings may involve rejection of one
or the other end of the ideological dimension rather than endorsement
of a single ideological position.

If, on the other hand, a society is *polarized* on a given issue, such that half
(or, more likely, half of those having strong opinions) are bunched at one

303

side of the dimension and half are at the other, then a moderate position will neither attract nor placate anybody. In either of these cases, parties cannot succeed by attempting to appeal to the median voter.

Beyond this, those voters who have the widest latitudes of rejection should be disproportionately influential in the political system, especially given the assumption that the total area belonging to the latitude of rejection and the politically inert latitude of noncommitment remains fairly constant. While the tolerance literature, for example, has sought out people's mean attitudes regarding treatment of disliked groups, there may be little reason to believe that the ideal preferences that most people express on the tolerance dimension are consequential. Consider the case in which a small portion of society is extremely intolerant of a given group. Even if most of the balance of society does not desire ill treatment of that group, their willingness to *tolerate* others' expressions of intolerance, for example by failing to make efforts to protect that group a political priority, may allow the intolerant few to translate their preferences into action. (And, in fact, even in a moderate society in which most people are unsupportive of either political extreme, differences in the *toleration* of actions at the two extremes may affect the room they have to flourish.) The point placement model would measure the aggregate inclinations of individuals toward intolerant actions, but unlike latitude theory, it does not account for the consequences of Burke's famous dictum, "all that is necessary for the triumph of evil is for men of good will to do nothing."

The Strength of Ties between Mass Opinion and Government Policy

Consider two societies, in both of which optimal positions regarding tax policy are clustered at a central, moderate level. In one, latitudes of noncommitment are narrow and latitudes of rejection are wide; in the other, latitudes of noncommitment are wide. The regime of the latter society has much more room to maneuver regarding tax policy than does that of the former, a finding opaque to traditional tools of public opinion analysis.[5] (Complete information spatial voting models [Enelow and

5 It might be argued that these societies *would* in fact be distinguishable by current techniques through the use of a strength or importance measure. Aside from the aesthetic distastefulness of a solution that requires asking people separate intensity and placement questions in order to understand their attitude structure, it is not clear that such questioning would lead to desired results. Some issues, such as the federal budget deficit or the "war on drugs," may be subjectively important to voters without their having a good sense of what should be done about them. This

Hinich, 1984], by contrast, predict that in either case candidates should and do converge on the equilibrium point at the center of the set of voter-ideal points, and therefore would predict no changes in a regime's ability to maneuver.)

Even in a society such as the latter, however, the limits to such freedom may arise suddenly. Latitude theory suggests an alternative to customary models of mass–elite interaction, which might be called the "electrified fence model." Within broad bounds, on many issues a politician may feel complete freedom to maneuver with impunity. But this is not because the public necessarily supports her actions, but rather because she is operating within the public's aggregate latitude of noncommitment. Upon encountering a point marking the beginning of a consensual latitude of rejection, she may suddenly encounter a catastrophic avalanche of protest that could not previously have been predicted from a point placement perspective, which would predict that opposition to a politician's actions should increase gradually as she moves away from the median voter's position. The abortive appointment of Zoe Baird as U.S. attorney general at the start of the Clinton administration may have been such a situation. Here, of course, it was not an issue stance that people rejected, but a perceived moral stance that people should not necessarily be disqualified from public office for breaking a law – *any* law. Little evidence in the years preceding the Baird appointment suggested that the public took official wrongdoing quite so seriously. (More on the special status of moral issues under latitude theory is found later in this chapter.)

Another example of this model in action is U.S. involvement in Somalia. Public opinion on U.S. intervention went from diffuse to sharply focused and negative as soon as the media broadcast pictures of an American soldier's corpse being dragged through the streets. What is it that changed overnight? To some extent, public estimates of the cost of participating in intervention may have changed, although it is hard to believe that the public had had no notion of what sending troops into a

would lead to strong professions of subjective importance coupled with wide latitudes of noncommitment. Such issues may thus be both important and politically inconsequential; as a practical matter, deft politicians with a variety of ideological stances might be able to avoid offending a group of voters professing concern about the problem. Alternatively, such complex problems would seem to be especially ripe for symbolic, even demagogic, approaches that represent them as simple and readily solvable by persons of good character. This should be especially evident when voters feel threatened by the prospect that candidates will not act to solve a social problem. It may be a mere coincidence that Diamond and Cobb (1994) found the experience of such "threats of omission" to be strikingly common among Perot voters in the 1992 election.

civil war implied. Some might argue that the salience of intervention in Somalia changed, but this begs the question: why did *this* event capture the public's attention, and whipsaw public opinion, when the death of American soldiers overseas is not all that unusual? One supplement to the previously presented hypotheses, from a latitude perspective, is that while the public is willing to tolerate some American casualties in what they perceive as a reasonable cause, it has absolutely no tolerance for being publicly humiliated on the international stage. Short of crossing this line, the government had ample room to respond to the famine in Somalia in a variety of ways. Once the humiliating images were aired, however, the administration found itself suddenly and firmly mired in the public's latitude of rejection.

This model suggests that governments have more leeway in policy implementation than most theories of public opinion suggest. To the extent that addressing social problems requires approaches that won't garner general public support in advance (e.g., tax increases, benefit cuts), this message is a relatively hopeful one: citizens need not be "converted" before change can occur, but need only be willing – or made willing – to reserve judgment. A successful leader need not convince citizens that her position is right, but simply that it is *not unreasonable*. Craven "government by poll" is less necessary than is commonly supposed; politicians may safely take a longer view without panicking at every jag of public opinion.[6]

While this conclusion may reassure those who decry governments' pandering to voters instead of making tough choices, it should unsettle those who place a high premium on representation. The argument that governments *need* not persuade citizens on issues is often made by elite theorists who portray mass opinion as inconsequential (Schattschneider, 1960); that is emphatically not my message. Masses can and do constrain elite initiatives – but only when they have the ability and motivation to do so. And when they do so, it is usually in a cybernetic fashion, whacking politicians on the head when they go a pledge too far. While political theorists have made categorical assertions about how much governments need to represent popular will, it is likely both that the practical need to do so varies over instances and that leaders do a fair job of distinguishing between when it is and when it isn't necessary.

---

6 Oddly, the main reason politicians might nevertheless *have* to pay attention to every jag of public opinion is that reporters and critics represent them as consequential. While reports do occasionally inform the public that fluctuations in presidential polling results before the conventions don't matter much, the widespread belief that they do matter may lead to a self-fulfilling prophecy.

When Will People Feel Represented?

If people don't think about politics in a positive way, it stands to reason that in deciding whether they are being well represented, they do not concern themselves primarily with whether the specific proposals they favor have been enacted. This creates a normative problem for latitude theory: what *is* good representation if people think about issues negatively?

The answers to this question aren't very reassuring. First of all, as noted in the previous example of Somalia policy, people continue to care about desired political ends even if they have only hazy ideas about preferred means to those ends. That is to say, people have a wide latitude of rejection when it comes to the preferred results of policies even if they have a wide latitude of noncommitment when it comes to the choice of policies themselves. This means that in determining whether they feel represented, people take a consequentialist approach to analyzing political leaders: did they deliver the goods?[7] The public is also quite willing to judge politicians with the benefit of hindsight and quick to believe that the consequences of actions were more predictable than was in fact the case (Fischhoff, 1980). Given this, latitude theory could be taken to imply that politicians should not worry too much about representation so long as the public does not actively reject their policies. If things go well, the public will feel that it was well represented.

One issue may be an exception to this conclusion. As noted previously, people may feel confident about making judgments about issues regarding morality and values, perhaps because these are closer to ends than to means. Politicians recognize that they can appeal to voters concerned about values issues largely through symbolic action. On the issue of crime, voters may feel represented by a politician who pledges to "get tough on criminals" through even symbolic and ineffectual means, such as the rarely enforced federal death penalty, without worrying about whether these are the specific means that they would choose from a menu. On the other hand, voters are more clearly represented in their rejection of specific means, such as, for example, drug decriminalization as a method of taking the money out of illegal trafficking, relieving prison overcrowding, and freeing up police resources. Feeling represented by an official may entail a combination of general support for desired ends and specific opposition to undesired means – a combination that leaves politicians room for both innovation and demagoguery.

---

7 For those familiar with Lawrence Kohlberg's (1981) hierarchy of moral reasoning, this is quite low on the hierarchy.

Gregory Andrade Diamond

EMPIRICAL EXPLORATIONS OF LATITUDE THEORY

Following the earlier failure of social judgment theory to catch on within political science, empirical research on the implications of latitude theory is just beginning. Diamond and Cobb (1996) report results of a survey of 486 voters in Champaign, Illinois, taken during the week before the 1992 presidential election. Using a split ballot format, they compared the standard National Election Studies (NES)-style approach to measuring candidate–respondent congruity with an approach based on latitude theory. They compiled a list of seven concrete policy proposals for each of three issue domains and had respondents indicate approval, neutrality, or disapproval for each option. They then had respondents indicate whether they thought each option was very, somewhat, not very, or not at all likely in the event of the election of each of the three presidential candidates. Policies toward which respondents were neutral were assumed to fall into their latitudes of noncommitment. Policies that respondents rejected but felt were likely given a candidate's election, and that they favored but felt were unlikely given a candidate's election, were both counted as being in the candidate's latitude of rejection. (Comparable analyses involving latitudes of acceptance were reported in Cobb and Diamond, 1995.) While in the point placement (NES-style) form vote intention was predicted as a function of distance from each candidate on each of the three issues using 7-point scales, the latitude-based form totted up the number of policy proposals for each issue on which the candidate's stance fell into the latitude of rejection.

The results solidly supported the assumptions of latitude theory. Across the three issues, explaining the votes for each candidate on the basis of either distance from or threat felt by each one, the latitude models did a consistently better job of explaining voting intentions. The story of what it was that voters feared from each candidate on each issue was consistent and compelling. Candidates who voted against Bush saw him as stagnant: while there was little fear that he would support policies that they didn't desire, there was great concern that he would not support policies that they wanted. Voters were roughly equally afraid that Bush and Clinton would support policies that they disliked, but were only about half as concerned that Clinton would fail to take actions they desired. The latitude-based analysis reinforces the popular view that the 1992 election was about change.

Problems with Empirical Research in Latitude Theory

The process of preparation for these studies did suggest some serious practical problems with research on latitude theory. The pattern of subjects' endorsement or tolerance of proposals was far from the ideal. In some cases, subjects vacillated among support, toleration, and rejection of proposals arrayed in order across an ideological dimension without apparent rhyme or reason. Some of this may be attributed to nonattitudes or inadequate formation of the dimension, but some of it simply demonstrates a problem that has been around at least since Thurstone scaling: people disagree on how items are rated and ranked along ideological dimensions, in part because they may bring their own idiosyncratic dimensions to bear. (Note that this is as much of a problem for point placement approaches that assume that the ideological scales people generate match what the researcher has in mind.) Short of restricting oneself solely to idiographic research on public opinion, little can be done to solve this problem except to note that it clouds empirical results.

Sherif, Sherif, and Nebergall (1965) avoided this problem in a dubious manner, creating a range of nine options that constituted a de facto Likert scale ranging from "the election of the Republican[s] to the election of the Democrat[s] is . . . absolutely essential. . . . [Our] interests would be better served if the . . . Republicans . . . were elected." This offers an impoverished view of latitude theory in which the latitude of acceptance operates simply as a confidence interval around one's introspective judgment of one's opinion. (In the preceding example, one might tolerate the view that electing Republicans is essential, endorse each view from its being "important" to "slightly better than not," and so on.) Latitude theory should mean much more than this. Applying it to one's own degree of affect offers some improvement on Likert scales, but its greatest contribution lies in how people think about policy options, even if it is problematic to place those options on an ideological dimension in a way all would find reasonable.

CONCLUSIONS

Latitude theory is especially compelling for political science because it suggests that the psychological "action" in a dynamic political culture will not be at the *means* of opinion distributions – means change slowly and are likely "lagging indicators" of political change – but at the boundaries of what becomes desirable, acceptable, conceivable, or impossible. Time after time during the 1980s, for example, liberals lamented the lack of "political space" to promote various arguments. While means of opinions on certain issues may have changed between the mid-1960s and that time, what changed more profoundly was the growing admissibility into the political mainstream of ideas that had gotten Goldwater branded as extreme in 1964 and the displacement of what were

Gregory Andrade Diamond

previously topics of mainstream debate (e.g., socialized medicine, marijuana legalization) to the periphery.[8]

Fundamentally, latitude theory points us to a novel model of the relationship between masses and elites. Rather than masses determining the positions elites will take (either directly through their opinions and votes or indirectly through their parties or interest groups; Miller and Stokes, 1963) and rather than elites substantially determining masses' positions on issues (Zaller, 1992), latitude theory suggests a third alternative: masses have a strong effect on the political system, but it is a *negative* effect, *constraining* the options available to elites. (See Kingdon, 1993, 78, for a different pathway to this same conclusion.) To the extent that leaders do not venture outside the confines of "safe" policies – within which there may be ample room for maneuvering – masses will *appear* not to be influencing policy. When elites venture outside the confines of the generally acceptable, however, mass public opinion can arise as if from nowhere to put them in their places. Knowing this, smart elites venture beyond safe pastures only with great caution.

Politics is often depicted as a game of either tug-of-war (in which politicians attempt to rope the median voter and yank him closer to their preferred point) or king of the hill (in which politicians attempt to bestride the highest point of voters' preference functions and push other competitors away from it). Both metaphors depend on an implicit model of ideal preference points. The lens of latitude theory shows that political attitudes and the tactics aimed at influencing popular opinion are more complex and intricate than this. We might do well to abandon these simplistic metaphors; politics, after all, is not child's play.

---

8 A comparison of proposals regarding welfare policy through the 1980s and 1990s suggests not only changes in point preferences, but a softening of opposition to notions such as wholesale replacement of the social welfare system by privatized charitable donations and taking away children of the poor to raise them in orphanages. While aggressive pursuit of these and other changes may have hit the electrified fence by the end of 1995, that pundits continue to broach these proposals suggests that political support for such drastic measures may soon no longer scare off voters, even if they don't (yet?) endorse them. That is to say, as a leading indicator of possible future changes, what would have been considered outlandishly conservative proposals were still, in the mid-1990s, moving from the public's latitude of rejection to noncommitment. The advent of gay rights over this period, as cultural proscriptions toward positive and realistic portrayals of gays and lesbians in the media softened over the decade, may reflect a similar shift in the opposite ideological direction.

References

Atkins, A., K. Deaux, and J. Bieri. (1967) Latitude of acceptance and attitude change: Empirical evidence for a reformulation. *Journal of Personality and Social Psychology*, 6, 1, 47–54.

Cobb, M. D. and G. A. Diamond. (1995) "Optimal choices, fear, or hope? Latitude theory and Presidential voting in 1992." Paper presented at the American Political Science Association meeting, Chicago, September 1995.

Converse, P. (1964) The nature of belief systems in mass publics. In D. Apter (ed.), *Ideology and discontent*. New York: Free Press.

(1970) Attitudes and non-attitudes: Continuation of a dialogue. In E. R. Tufte (ed.), *The quantitative analysis of social problems*. Reading, MA: Addison-Wesley.

Diamond, G. A. and M. D. Cobb. (1994) "The candidate as catastrophe: Threat perception and issue voting in the 1992 Presidential election." Paper presented at the Midwest Political Science Association meeting, Chicago, April 1994.

(1996) The candidate as catastrophe: Latitude theory and the problems of political persuasion. In D. Mutz, P. Sniderman, and R. Brody, *Political persuasion and attitude change*. Ann Arbor: University of Michigan Press.

Dimock, M. A. and G. C. Jacobson (1995) Checks and choices: The House Bank scandal's impact on voters in 1992. *Journal of Politics*, 57, 1143–1159.

Downs, A. (1957) *An economic theory of democracy*. New York: Harper and Row.

Eagly, A. and M. Manis. (1966) Evaluation of message and communicator as a function of involvement. *Journal of Personality and Social Psychology*, 3, 4, 483–485.

Eagly, A. and K. Telaak. (1972) Width of the latitude of acceptance as a determinant of attitude change. *Journal of Personality and Social Psychology*, 23, 3, 388–397.

Enelow, J. and M. Hinich. (1984) *The spatial theory of voting: An introduction*. New York: Cambridge University Press.

Fischhoff, B. (1980) For those condemned to study the past: Reflections on historical judgment. In R. A. Schweder and D. W. Fiske (eds.), *New directions for methodology of behavioral science: Fallible judgments in behavioral research*. San Francisco: Jossey-Bass.

Fishbein, M. and Ajzen, I. (1975) *Belief, attitude, intention and behavior: An introduction to theory and research*. Reading, MA: Addison-Wesley.

Fiske, S. (1982) Schema-triggered affect: Applications to social perception. In M. Clark and S. Fiske, *Affect and cognition: The 17th annual Carnegie Symposium on cognition*. Hillsdale, NJ: Erlbaum.

Greider, W. (1992) *Who will tell the people?: The betrayal of American democracy*. New York: Simon and Schuster.

Judd, C. and J. Krosnick. (1982) Attitude centrality, organization and measurement. *Journal of Personality and Social Psychology*, 42, 436–447.

Kingdon, J. W. (1993) Politicians, self-interest, and ideas. In G. Marcus and R. Hanson, eds, *Reconsidering the democratic public*. University Park: Pennsylvania State University Press.

Kohlberg, L. (1981) *The philosophy of moral development.* New York: Harper and Row.

Lau, R. (1982) Negativity in political perceptions. *Political Behavior,* 4, 353–378.

Mandler, G. (1982) The structure of value: Accounting for taste. In M. Clark and S. Fiske, *Affect and cognition: The 17th annual Carnegie Symposium on cognition.* Hillsdale, NJ: Erlbaum.

Miller, W. E. and D. E. Stokes. (1963) Constituency influence in Congress. *American Political Science Review,* 57, 45–57.

Oskamp, S. (1977) *Attitudes and opinion.* Englewood Cliffs, NJ: Prentice-Hall.

Ostrom, T. (1966) Perspective as an intervening construct in the judgment of attitude statements. *Journal of Personality and Social Psychology,* 3, 2, 135–144.

Pateman, C. (1970) *Participation and democratic theory.* New York: Cambridge University Press.

Powell, F. (1966) Latitudes of acceptance and rejection and the belief–disbelief dimension. *Journal of Personality and Social Psychology,* 4, 4, 453–457.

Schattschneider, E. E. (1960) *The semi-sovereign people: A realist's view of democracy in America.* New York: Holt, Rinehart and Winston.

Sherif, C. W., M. Sherif, and R. Nebergall. (1965) *Attitude and attitude change: The social judgment-involvement approach.* Philadelphia: W. B. Saunders.

Sherif, M. and C. Hovland. (1961) *Social judgment: Assimilation and contrast effects in communication and attitude change.* New Haven: Yale University Press.

Stimson, J. A. (1991) *Public opinion in America: Moods, cycles and swings.* Boulder, CO: Westview Press.

Triandis, H. (1971) *Attitude and attitude change.* New York: Wiley.

Tversky, A. (1972) Elimination by aspects: A theory of choice. *Psychological Review,* 79, 281–299.

Tversky, A. and D. Kahneman. (1986) Rational choice and the framing of decision. *Journal of Business,* 59, Part 2, S251–S278.

Zajonc, R. (1980) Feeling and thinking: Preferences need no inferences. *American Psychologist,* 35, 2, 151–175.

Zaller, J. (1992) *The nature and origin of mass opinion.* Cambridge, UK: Cambridge University Press.

II

Where You Stand Depends on What You See: Connections among Values, Perceptions of Fact, and Political Prescriptions

JENNIFER L. HOCHSCHILD

> We must note particularly...the insertion between man and his environment of a pseudo-environment. To that pseudo-environment his behavior is a response. ... The analyst of public opinion must begin then, by recognizing the triangular relationship between the scene of action, the human picture of that scene, and the human response to that picture working itself out upon the scene of action.
>
> Walter Lippmann[1]

> One good solid murder of a baby or a rape-murder of a 7-year-old girl will outweigh a ton of statistics.
>
> Lawrence Friedman, explaining popular perceptions of a rising crime rate[2]

Including values as a central component of the study of public opinion was long overdue, and therefore their appearance in this volume is a cause for celebration. Of course, if values are defined broadly enough, public opinion researchers have been studying values for decades, if not centuries. Alexis de Tocqueville sampled the American public in the 1830s and analyzed Americans' distinctive values both as independent and as dependent variables. So did James Bryce a few decades later and Hector St. John de Crèvecoeur a few decades earlier. Scholars using qualitative interviews and ethnographic techniques to explore values succeeded Europeans with notepads around the turn of the twentieth century (Hochschild, 1981; Lane, 1962; Lynd and Lynd, 1929; Warner, 1949), and they, in turn, were succeeded by survey researchers measuring the origins of authoritarianism or the importance of family ties in

---

1 Lippmann, 1961: 15, 16. My thanks to Kristi Andersen of Syracuse University for this quotation.
2 Golden, 1996: 26.

Jennifer L. Hochschild

partisan identification (Adorno et al., 1950; Niemi and Weisberg, 1993, sections II and III).

Acknowledging venerable ancestry, however, does nothing to diminish the claim that the study of citizens' values has recently moved into maturity. The array of values under serious investigation has expanded beyond Rokeach's grid or Maslow's hierarchy into a manageably sized set of core concepts. Those concepts – egalitarianism, individualism, humanitarianism, religious fundamentalism, postmaterialism, ethnocentrism – are themselves being defined more rigorously and compared more systematically than in earlier eras (for example, see Sears, Sidanius, and Bobo, 2000). Values are being asked to do more explanatory work on more issues than ever before, and they are responding in provocative ways.

The study of the role of values in public opinion is becoming broader as well as deeper. Surveyors are now able to compare values held by citizens of different nations, and they are using those comparisons to defend claims ranging from universal cultural transformation to sharp ethnic differences within putative nation-states (Abramson and Inglehart, 1994; Gibson and Duch, 1993; Hofrichter, 1993; McIntosh and MacIver, 1992). Cross-national comparisons of values, and of their causes and effects, allow us to get a handle on the old question of American exceptionalism, as well as on new questions of cultural capital and the consequences of collective identification.

The new studies of values make a methodological contribution almost as great as their substantive ones. One must be as adept at interpreting political philosophy as at performing regression coefficients to understand the content and effect of values in citizens' belief systems. That fact destroys, because it demonstrates the evident silliness of, methodological disputes between science and philosophy, interpretation and explanation, qualitative and quantitative methods. One must get one's philosophy right to do interesting science about values; one must get one's science right to make empirical contributions to democratic theory and practice. That is probably true for most interesting questions of politics, but it is a fortiori true for the study of values in public opinion so that students of this topic can show the way for other social scientists.

WHAT NOT TO DO IN STUDYING VALUES

I want to note four dangers facing the study of values before exploring the edges of yet another new frontier that the study of values opens up. First, we must take care not to allow the study of values to be subsumed by the study of ideology, especially the traditional liberal–conservative

314

dimension. That dimension is itself deeply problematic conceptually and often has little leverage politically. Social conservatives, who want the government to enforce traditional norms of morality through legislation and exhortation, have little in common with libertarians, who are not much concerned about traditional norms of morality and who want as little governmental intervention in people's lives as possible. Yet both are called "conservatives" in common parlance. Similarly, "liberals" may all share egalitarian convictions and a belief that government should act to promote equality, but they vehemently disagree with one another over, for example, whether to promote universal policies of family support or to target assistance to the poorest or most discriminated against. When Robert Kennedy was assassinated in 1968, many of his supporters turned next to George Wallace; H. Ross Perot's supporters in 1992 were about evenly divided between George Bush and Bill Clinton as their second choice for president. As Greg Markus demonstrates in this volume, liberals are individualists when individualism is defined as autonomy, and conservatives are individualists when individualism is defined as self-reliance.

In short, one can distinguish between liberals and conservatives philosophically only by adding many qualifiers, and one can make few predictions about how individuals' attitudes will be arrayed or how political disputes will be resolved by labeling one set of views or contenders "liberal" and the other "conservative." Students of the role of values in public opinion know all of this; frustration with the liberal–conservative dimension is largely why they turned to the study of values to begin with. But the dimension has such a powerful hold on American linguistic norms and such deep roots in the academic study of public opinion that it will be equally hard to relinquish it or to incorporate it into work on values without letting it take over.

A second danger in studying values is that the researcher will be tempted to move directly from determining that individuals share a given value to presuming that they share a given attitude or policy prescription. That is, one might presume that individualists will oppose affirmative action and egalitarians will support it. But an egalitarian like Randall Kennedy (1997) or Orlando Patterson (1973) may oppose affirmative action because it perpetuates an employer's tendency to think in terms of hierarchical racial categories rather than to see people as potentially equal separate persons. Or an individualist may support affirmative action programs because they are the only way to ensure that people with certain ascriptive traits get the chance to show what they can really do (Rosenfeld, 1991).

There are actually two dangers here. One is that researchers will unwarrantedly infer respondents' attitudes or policy prescriptions from

315

their values. The other danger is that researchers will actually do the work to determine how prescriptions relate to values, but then assume that if the respondent's policy preferences do not fit his or her value in a way that makes sense to the researcher, the respondent's attitudes are "unconstrained" (in a new usage of this term). After climbing out of the hole caused by the assumption that views should be arrayed along a single ideological dimension (such as liberalism–conservatism), one may fall into the nearby trap of assuming that specific policy positions should map neatly onto general values.

This danger arises at the level of societies as well as of individuals. It would be a mistake, for example, to assume that because Americans are more individualistic than the French, they have a less robust social welfare state. That conclusion depends on a narrow definition of social welfare. For example, if one includes a free system of lightly tracked public education through age eighteen (and an almost free system of somewhat more heavily tracked higher education) in one's definition of a social welfare state – a system that is well suited to a highly individualistic and success-oriented society – the United States is not a welfare laggard at all. Thus societies with different value emphases may have similar, or at least comparable, policy outcomes. Conversely, societies with similar value emphases may have highly disparate policy outcomes; Great Britain and the United States are almost equally individualistic, but out of that shared normative base they have developed very different health care systems (Jacobs, 1993).

A third potential pitfall for the study of values lies in defining the relationship between values and self-interest. Some define the relationship as antithetical: altruism is contrasted with self-protection or adversary democracy is posed against unitary (or communitarian) democracy (Mansbridge, 1980, 1990; Monroe, 1996). Others define self-interest as one among other values; in this volume, Stoker defines partial judgments as more self-interested than impartial judgments, but they are no less values. Others, such as Feldman and Steenbergen in this volume, define the degree to which one is self-interested or empathetic as a feeling rather than a value, so self-interest is neither posed against nor included within the category of "values."

All of these choices are conceptually defensible, and all can do real work in an analysis of public opinion. The dangers come when analysts are imprecise about how they relate values to interests, when they are unwarrantedly imperialistic or timid, or when they choose a definition tendentiously. The dangers of imprecision are sufficiently obvious to need no further discussion. The dangers of imperialism would occur, for example, if a researcher redefined the value of altruism into (perhaps genetically driven) self-interest over a long period, thereby losing an interesting distinction in the service of an ideological claim.[3] That problem would be compounded if a researcher who responds that altruism or love really does exist is pushed into seeking the pure Kantian altruist (or the perfect parent!), who cannot admit any self-interested motives and still be considered altruistic or loving.

The other problem that occurs frequently in the context of relating interests to values lies in submerged valuations masquerading as definitions. The category of "self-interested" is elided with "selfish"; alternatively, respondents exhibiting empathy are made to seem naive or hypocritical. The clearest example of this phenomenon that I know of, with perhaps the greatest political justification, is the claim that African Americans cannot be racist. By definition, in this view, racism is necessarily associated with dominance; thus in the United States only whites, or the mainstream society, can be racist. If proponents of this claim were truly concerned with definitional exactness, they could easily distinguish between institutional racism, which can only be enacted by the dominant race, and individual racism, which may be expressed by anyone. But their concern is not definitional precision; it is rather to link the pejorative connotation of "racist" with whites and to proclaim blacks' innocence. One may sympathize with the anger behind this elision, but from the perspective of the study of values in public opinion, building a sharp value judgment into a definition seems mistaken.

A final danger in the study of values in public opinion is the temptation of product differentiation. The best analysts of public attitudes have always examined values under one or another rubric. That fact does not undermine the importance of the new attentiveness to values, so it should be built on rather than downplayed. Conversely, students of values should not dismiss the old focuses on party identification, childhood socialization, or demographic characteristics in their eagerness to broach new frontiers. This point is more than an exhortation to be comprehensive; as I argue later with regard to demographics, one may sometimes be unable to analyze values properly without embedding them in other characteristics of the population being studied.

WHAT TO ADD TO THE STUDY OF VALUES

Having just argued for methodological expertise ranging from philosophy to statistics, and for adding the study of values to the plethora of old concerns rather than allowing it to substitute for them, I will now compound my unreasonableness by seeking to persuade students of

---

3 Gary Becker (1981) comes close to that view in his analysis of the economic worth of children to their parents.

values in public opinion to add an additional element to their analyses. That element is respondents' perceptions of facts.

The rest of this chapter focuses on what we know about citizens' perceptions of facts (not very much) and what we need to learn (a lot). But I want first to set the stage with a few observations about why we should care.

Various people should care about citizens' perceptions of facts for varied reasons. Psychologists have a long tradition of distinguishing beliefs from values, attitudes, opinions, preferences, emotions, causal attributions, and so on and seeking to tease out the relations among those forms of mentation. That is a worthy enterprise, but not mine. Behavioral students of public opinion have an equally long tradition of seeking to explain why some citizens hold certain values, attitudes, causal attributions, and so on, whereas other citizens hold other values, attitudes, and so on. That is the chief enterprise of most contributors to this volume, but in the end it also is not mine. Political actors seek to change people's values, attitudes, and so on or to galvanize people who already hold the "right" values and attitudes into political action, that too is not my agenda.

I wish to focus on the political, policy, and normative implications of the fact that people's perceptions of fact are frequently wrong, and wrong in particularly patterned ways. Let us start with a simple but not trivial example: most Anglo-Americans estimate the number of black and Latino-Americans to be at least twice the actual number in the American population. It makes good sense to oppose a strong program of affirmative action in that case, because if half of the population are potential beneficiaries of "special preferences," you are quite likely to lose your job or promotion to them. Now suppose that whites suddenly learned that only 12% of the population is black and 10% is Latino (and a disproportionate number of them are children, and thus are not competitors for coveted jobs). Might those newly educated whites now be more willing to say, "I still don't like affirmative action but it is not the threat that I thought it was, so I guess I can live with it"? Probably not. None of us are that logical, and opposition to affirmative action has many more causes than an arithmetic calculation of its threat to one's own position. But that hypothetical example suggests the reason for my interest in this topic.

To what degree are citizens' political attitudes and policy preferences based on, or at least supported by, mistaken perceptions of fact? How much credence should we grant to such political and policy views? How firmly can we assert that people act in their own interests if they do not know facts that might be crucial to their deciding what is in their interest? How much effort should be devoted, and by whom, to helping

318

people get the facts right before they make judgments about what should be done in the political arena? How malleable are people's values on the one hand, and policy preferences or political attitudes on the other, if somehow they do learn to correct their perceptual mistakes? May we legitimately evaluate the quality of the democratic process partly in terms of how well informed citizens were when they elected political leaders or responded to referendum offerings? Should factually oriented decision makers be granted more authority than others?

These are ultimately unanswerable questions because they involve deep and inherently contestable normative positions, because we cannot conduct experiments with individual voters or the democratic process, and because they focus on only one piece of an enormously complicated structure of political decision making. Nevertheless, they are important questions, and I want to draw our attention to their importance by focusing on an aspect of public opinion that is poorly developed compared with the study of attitudes or even of values.

MISPERCEPTIONS OF SOCIAL FACTS

Social scientists have pointed out for a long time that many Americans do not know basic political facts such as the name of the vice president or the meaning of the Bill of Rights.[4] That phenomenon is important politically and normatively. But it does not in itself speak to the role of values in shaping public opinion; one can be a strong individualist and support freedom of speech even for expounders of disliked opinions without being able to identify the First Amendment.

Some perceptions of fact do, however, matter for our interpretation of values and for our understanding of how general values connect with particular political attitudes and policy preferences:

4 In 1952, 1989, and 1994, at least one-fourth of Americans could not correctly name the vice president (Delli Carpini and Keeter, 1991: 591; *The Polling Report*, 1994: 4). A *Washington Post* columnist noted, however, that although "40 percent of the adult population is not familiar with . . . who . . . is the vice president," after all, "the vice president . . . doesn't know the names of 40 percent of the adult population, either" (Weingarten, 1996). Ridiculous though that riposte is, it does remind us that analysts need to consider the value of a particular piece of political knowledge from the citizen's perspective before decrying ignorance of it.

In addition to the other publications cited in this chapter, Sniderman et al. (1991, chap. 9), Zaller (1992, Appendix), Lindeman (1996), Bennett (1996), Graber (1996), Delli Carpini and Keeter (1996), and Kuklinski et al. (1997) all demonstrate the resurgence of interest in what people know and how they use that knowledge politically. Most of these studies focus on knowledge about political events, persons, or structures rather than on the kinds of contextual or social facts on which I am focusing here.

- "The average American thinks America is 32 percent black, 21 percent Hispanic and 18 percent Jewish" (Gallup and Newport, 1990: 2; see also *Washington Post* et al., 1995: table 1.1).
- Over half of Americans think that the nation is at least 30% black, and a seventh of Americans think that the nation is at least half black.[5]
- Americans systematically overestimate the rate of unemployment likely to occur in the near future, although they are no more likely to overestimate than to underestimate the upcoming rate of inflation (Dua and Smyth, 1993: 568, 571).
- Almost three-fourths of Americans believe that most new immigrants come into the country illegally (Espenshade and Hempstead, 1996: 21).
- A quarter of Americans thought that at least 40% of Americans were poor at a point when the poverty rate had been hovering around 13% for several years (*Los Angeles Times*, 1985: ques. 81).
- A fifth of Americans think that "the government spends the most money these days" on foreign aid (actually about 2% of the budget), and another fifth thinks the same about welfare for the poor (about 3% of the budget) (*Los Angeles Times* Poll, 1995: ques. 33; see also Donelan, Blendon, and Hill, 1994: figure 2, table 1; Program on International Policy Attitudes, 1995: 6).
- In October 1995, about half of Americans believed that "the federal budget deficit . . . has gone up every year . . . since Bill Clinton became president" (*New York Times*/CBS News Poll, 1995, ques. 9).
- Residents of communities around Atlanta are more likely to name the job-rich areas as having the fewest job openings rather than as having the most, despite widespread local publicity about the need for workers in some areas and the excess of unemployed adults in others (Ihlanfeldt, 1995: table 3).
- In 1985, "almost a third of the Jews in one northern California region said that they did not think non-Jews would vote for a Jew for Congress. At the time they said this, *all three* of their elected Representatives in that area were Jewish" (the author describes this as the "Jewish Foreboding Complex"; Raab, 1988: 47, italics in original).
- Ninety-five percent of the residents of a school district who were slated to lose money in a state educational finance reform knew that their district would lose. But only 53% of the residents of a district that was slated to get more money knew that their district would win (Tedin, 1994: 641).

---

5 A quarter think the nation is at least 30% Latino and 40% think the nation is at least 20% Jewish. An additional 10–15% gave no estimate in each case (Nadeau et al., 1993: 335).

Where You Stand Depends on What You See

These findings are more than fodder for either conservatives who proclaim, pace V. O. Key (1966: 7), that voters really are fools, or liberals who deplore the vacuity of the American educational system and public media. They are crucial for understanding how people make political judgments and how the polity responds to those judgments. Colloquially, "where you stand depends on what you see"; more formally, I hypothesize that perceptions of fact help to shape values, help to transform general values into particular views, and perhaps are shaped in turn by values or policy preferences and political attitudes.

These mutually caused interrelationships have important implications for the polity as a whole, as well as for individuals' political stances. Those implications stem from the fact of systematic distortions in the overall pattern of factual mistakes. People are on balance excessively *pessimistic* about the public arena in the sense that they exaggerate the prevalence of political or social phenomena that they dislike. They are simultaneously excessively *optimistic* much of the time about the private arena in the sense that they exaggerate their own well-being compared with that of others, or they do not draw unhappy conclusions for their own lives from the negative views they hold about the political arena. Although there is no logical or cognitive reason why they should, these countervailing sets of misperceptions perhaps balance each other out and help to create a polity that is more stable than political actors of many different persuasions either expect it to be or think it should be. They also raise the question of just what value to place on democratic processes of choice.

VALUES, FACTS, AND PRESCRIPTIONS IN THE MINDS OF INDIVIDUAL CITIZENS

Connecting Values and Perceptions of Fact

How much one finds that perceptions of fact shape values – or vice versa – depends in part on how one defines values.[6] If they are defined as deep-seated predispositions or fundamental constructs that stem from

---

6 It is also surprisingly difficult to define "facts." Here I focus on items of information that do *not* have three chief characteristics. First, their content does not vary, depending on what people think of them (e.g., per capita income, not whether the president is popular). Second, they are social facts rather than, say, physical, historical, or institutional facts (e.g., the rate of unemployment rather than the direction from which the sun rises, the date of the Civil War, or the number of justices on the Supreme Court). Third, they are not values or preferences or causal beliefs masquerading as statements of truth (e.g., blacks are disproportionately poor because of white racism or because of lack of motivation).

childhood socialization, community ties, or searing personal experiences, a long line of psychological research tells us that values are more likely to create than to be created by perceptions (Festinger et al., 1956; citations in note 25 of Nadeau and Niemi, 1995; Sniderman et al., 1991). Conversely, if values are defined as "broad statements of principle – often mutually contradictory – about how to prioritize interests" (Mark Lindeman, Columbia University, personal communication), they will be operationalized and measured differently by the researcher, will function differently in the respondent's mental processes, and probably will be more amenable to change through changes in perceptions.

How might perceptions of fact shape values? For this to be possible, we must think of values as relatively broad statements of principle that help one to make sense of the world but that are amenable to change if confronted with a competing principle or a challenge from the external world. Consider, for example, the trajectory of middle-class African Americans over the past thirty years. Until recently, they believed as firmly as did poor blacks and whites in the ideology of the American dream. Blacks endorse "self-reliance" almost as strongly as do whites. Seventy percent of black and 80% of white Californians agree that "trying to get ahead" is very important in "making someone a true American" (Citrin et al., 1990: 1132). As many blacks as whites (up to 90%) agree that a good education, ambition, and hard work are crucial to getting ahead; more blacks than whites add ability to the list (General Social Survey, 1987: vars. 507C–F). Middle-class as well as poor blacks share these values.

And yet compared with whites and poor African Americans, well-off African Americans are increasingly angry about the past practice, and pessimistic about the future practice, of the American dream. In the 1960s, to cite only one example, blacks with less than a high school education were more likely than blacks with at least some college education to agree that "most white people . . . want to keep blacks down"; by the 1980s, the reverse was the case, mainly because middle-class African Americans had become much more embittered about whites' racial motivations (Hochschild, 1995: chap. 4).

Among the factors that explain affluent blacks' increasing alienation, the one I wish to focus on here is perceptions. About 20% of middle-class blacks mistakenly describe their family incomes as below average, compared with about 5% of middle-class whites (calculations from General Social Survey: var. 149, 1972–1982; var. 188, 1983–1991). Middle-class blacks are one and a half times *more* likely than all other Americans to agree that "the percentage of blacks living in poverty has been increasing from year to year." They also overestimate the proportion of the poor who are black at a much higher rate than do all other

Where You Stand Depends on What You See

Americans (*Los Angeles Times*, 1985: ques. 83, 85). Affluent blacks see
more racial discrimination, are more likely to see an increase in racism,
and see more effects of racial discrimination in their own lives than do
poor blacks (Hochschild, 1995: chap. 4).

This combination of shared values, divergent perceptions of fact, different descriptions of American society, and the ensuing conflicts in policy
prescriptions is so frustrating that it is driving many blacks to question
their underlying values. Thus by 1994, middle-class African Americans
demonstrated much more nationalism than they had even five years earlier
and more than they had in any survey of the 1960s. A year later, fewer
blacks than whites (56–63%) agreed that racial integration has been good
for society. More blacks than whites opted for "building strong institutions within the black community" (rather than emphasizing "integration
and opportunity," which was whites' preferred choice) as the best means
for "improving the situation for blacks in America" (Dawson, 1994: 7;
Hart/Teeter, 1995). It is hard to know who would be more surprised by
that result – Rev. Martin Luther King, Jr., or Sheriff Bull Connor.

In short, perceptions of facts that people care passionately about –
some of which are demonstrably wrong, as in middle-class blacks' views
about black poverty – are leading to a change in values. Belief in the
American dream may not be disappearing in the black middle class, but
it is taking second place to a belief in black nationalism, which, if it need
not contradict the ideology of the dream, at least heads one in a different direction in the current American political configuration.

Another plausible trajectory goes in the opposite direction: values
(understood now as fundamental constructs from which other political
views stem) will combine with relevant perceptions of fact, and thereby
lead to political attitudes and policy prescriptions. This is the more
straightforward logic, and more the province of political scientists than
of psychologists. For example, one analysis of the 1995 *Washington Post*
survey shows that both political party identification and perception of
blacks' opportunities to get ahead (as compared with whites' opportunities) are both significant determinants of whites' attitudes toward affirmative action (Sanders, 1996: table 8; see also Delli Carpini and Keeter,
1996, and Zaller, 1992).

So far, I have discussed two possibilities – that perceptions might shape
values and the two together generate policy prescriptions, and that values
and perceptions, independently derived, might jointly shape policy preferences. Either is a reasonable starting point for a positivistically oriented
survey researcher, since both presume that perceptions of fact are cognitions about the way the world really is. But consider now a third possibility – that values shape perceptions of fact. This is the fundamental
claim of postmodernist, gendered, and Afrocentric perspectives.

323

Some survey evidence suggests that people who feel threatened by a group or a political situation are more likely to make factual mistakes than people who do not feel so threatened. "In Quebec, respondents who believe that the situation of the French language is bad are ... much less likely to be accurate" in their estimate of the size of the French-speaking population of Quebec. Similarly, in the mid-1980s, those who believed that the civil war in Nicaragua threatened the United States made more mistakes about which side the United States supported than did people who did not worry much about Nicaragua. People who fear that Latino immigrants will cause an increase in crime overestimate the number of Latinos in the United States more than those without such fears (Nadeau and Niemi, 1995: 338–339). Men with a high school education are twice as likely as men with a college education to see themselves as a likely victim of burglary or robbery during the coming year, even though they had not been victimized at a greater rate in the previous year (Dominitz and Manski, 1995: 13; the pattern does not hold for women). Thus values (in this set of examples, a very high premium on personal or group-based security in an apparently dangerous world) may under some circumstances affect one's understanding of "empirical" facts.

Connecting Perceptions to Political Attitudes and Policy Prescriptions

Public education systems in democratic polities are built on the premise that "ye shall know the truth and the truth shall set ye free." It turns out, according to the small amount of research that has been conducted on the subject, that knowing the truth often sets people, if not free, then at least in a liberal direction. In the abstract, I see no reason why this should be the case; people as frequently become more conservative as more liberal when they gain the knowledge or wisdom that presumably comes with higher education and advancing age. But the survey data are consistent. Knowledge of more facts or more accurate knowledge of facts either has no connection with political attitudes and policy prescriptions or is associated with more liberal views.

In lieu of clear hypotheses about why these findings should obtain, let me present some findings. A 1995 survey of racial attitudes found that 40–70% of whites mistakenly think that the average African American is as well off as or better off than the average white American in terms of income, jobs, housing, access to health care, education, and the risk of losing a job (*Washington Post* et al., 1995: sections 1, 5). Compared with whites who make the fewest mistakes, whites who make the most mistakes on these points are

- more likely to believe that Congress should limit affirmative action;
- more likely to believe that the government should not spend more to help low-income minorities;
- more likely to favor major spending cuts in the food stamp program, legal aid for the poor, and federal aid for cities; and
- more likely to oppose major spending cuts in Medicaid and federal aid for student loans.[7]

With the exception of opposition to cuts in Medicaid, and possibly opposition to cuts in student loans, the least well informed are more conservative than the most well informed. The groups were similarly inclined toward cuts in five other arenas of government spending, so it is not the case that better information necessarily implies more liberalism. But in this case at least, it almost never implies more conservatism.

One might argue that understanding facts about African Americans is so closely connected to policy views about their treatment that this association between perceptions and prescriptions is almost tautologous. Other evidence reinforces the possibility that the link between perceptions and prescriptions is especially close in the racial arena because the issue of race is so volatile in American politics. Compare whites who (mistakenly) perceive most welfare recipients to be black with whites who (correctly) perceive most recipients to be white. The former are more likely to agree that most welfare recipients could get along without aid; the latter are more likely to agree that recipients really need help. Blacks return the compliment; those who see the welfare population as predominantly white are especially likely to say that recipients can get along without government aid.[8]

But we need not fear a tautologous link between perceptions and prescriptions when we consider perceptions of more neutral facts and/or prescriptions about policies that are not closely related to those facts. And in these circumstances also, ignorance is relative conservatism or political disengagement, if not bliss. Americans who do not know which political party controls the House of Representatives are less likely than those who do to endorse greater government spending on child care,

7 Whites who make the most mistakes are the 42% who misperceive blacks' positions on five or six of the six measures of well-being. Whites who make the fewest mistakes are the 25% who correctly perceive blacks' positions on five or six of the six measures of well-being.
8 Personal communication from Kathleen Frankovic, CBS News, Jan. 10, 1995. Data are from *New York Times*/CBS Poll, Dec. 6–9, 1994b. Some of the cell sizes are very small, so these results are only tentative.

social security, and aid to the poor.[9] "The proportion saying that one of the lessons of the Holocaust was that 'firm steps need to be taken to protect the rights of minorities' rose from 29 percent among those scoring zero on a five-item World War II knowledge scale to 77 percent for those with two correct answers, to 83 percent for those with three or more answers correct" (Smith, 1995: 52). Those who rank low on a scale of political knowledge are more likely than those who rank high to believe that members of Congress who had overdrafts in the congressional bank should be voted out of office and less likely to vote in national elections (Popkin and Dimock, 1999).[10]

There are at least two possible, and contradictory, interpretations of these findings. One might argue that people who are less knowledgeable about how the political world works are more fearful and defensive, so they hold highly personalistic, or even narrow, policy views designed mostly to fend off potential dangers. Alternatively, one might argue that people who are more knowledgeable about how the political world works have attained that knowledge through attention to the predominantly liberal media and publicly visible political elites, and they parrot the policy views of those journalists and elites as well as their facts.[11]

Luckily, I need not take a position on the competing explanations here. My point is the narrower one of showing that there apparently is a pat-

---

9 Personal correspondence from Eric Uslaner of the University of Maryland, Oct. 7, 1994. These results obtain with controls for respondents' income, education, gender, marital and parental statuses, party identification, ideology, and attitudes toward the federal government's role in the economy. Data are from the 1992 National Election Studies. All three findings are statistically significant at least $p < .05$. These results apparently conflict with Althaus's (1996) conclusion that well-informed respondents are more economically conservative than are poorly informed respondents (although he too finds that the well-informed are more socially liberal). I leave for another day the resolution of this contradiction.

10 The political knowledge scale was based on the ability to identify Dan Quayle (or Al Gore), Tom Foley (or Newt Gingrich), and William Rehnquist (depending on the year of the survey), to identify the majority party in the House and Senate, and to identify whether the president, Congress, or the Supreme Court nominated judges and engaged in constitutional adjudication. Data are from the 1992–1996 National Election Studies. Results reported in the text controlled for respondents' ideology, political interest and exposure, education, age, and income. All results are significant at least $p < .05$.

11 Popkin roughly accepted the first view at a conference on Citizen Competence and the Design of Democratic Institutions (Feb. 10–11, 1995, Washington, DC). The second paraphrases responses to his analysis as presented at that conference.

terned association between factual knowledge and policy prescriptions.[12]
How that association connects with underlying values, and how a
change in one element of the triad would affect the others (e.g., do people
who hold egalitarian and democratic values seek out political knowledge, or does the possession of political knowledge make one more
inclined to be egalitarian and democratic, or . . . ?), remains to be
discovered.

Adding Demographic Characteristics to the Mix

I argued earlier that in our eagerness to study the new issues of values
and perceptions, we should not ignore the old issue of demographics.
After all, not only does where you stand perhaps depend on what you
see, but also what you see sometimes depends on who you are.

Consider the example of sexual harassment. In a 1995 survey of
almost 50,000 military personnel, about twice as many women as
men thought sexual harassment was occurring more often in the military compared with a few years ago; conversely, more men than women
reported that its incidence was declining (Office of Assistant Secretary
of Defense, 1996: 9). Or anti-Semitism: in 1978, 8% of respondents to
a Harris survey thought anti-Semitism was rising and 21% thought it
was declining. Among Jewish respondents, however, the figures were
exactly reversed (Smith, 1994: 11, 18). Or poverty: poor men are *less*
likely to overestimate the number of Americans living in poverty than
are nonpoor men (especially blacks) (*Los Angeles Times*, 1985: ques.
81). Or racial discrimination: an endless series of polls show that most
African Americans think discrimination is rampant and arguably rising,
whereas most whites perceive racial discrimination to be unusual
and declining. To cite only two examples: only a handful of whites
but fully a quarter of blacks think that more than half of whites share
the attitudes of the Ku Klux Klan. Over half of blacks but only a
quarter of whites think our nation is moving toward two separate and
unequal societies (Hochschild, 1995: chap. 3). For all of these issues,
perceptions of fact vary in ways whose explanation must begin
(although should not end) with demographic characteristics of the
respondents.

Ascriptive characteristics affect citizens' understanding of values as
well as their perceptions of facts. Many basic values do not themselves

12 "Apparently" because one careful analysis of the relationship between mistakes
in estimates of the size of the black population and various policy views found
"one theoretically explicable finding, . . . several mystifying findings, . . . and a
great many non-findings" (Highton and Wolfinger, 1992: 12).

vary much with demography: whites as well as blacks oppose racial discrimination; men as well as women oppose sexual harassment; non-Jews endorse anti-Semitism no more than do Jews. But the definition of what counts as a violation of that value does vary with demography. The military survey referred to earlier asked respondents which of twenty-five items of gender-related behavior they had experienced. They were then asked if the items they had checked constituted sexual harassment. Although 78% of women and 38% of men checked one or more items, two-thirds of the women but only one-fourth of the men considered their experiences to have been sexual harassment (Office of Assistant Secretary of Defense, 1996: 4). Similarly, African Americans are much more likely than white Americans to interpret a wide variety of behaviors as evidence of racism. Those behaviors range from the ready availability of lethal drugs in inner-city neighborhoods to being left out of a meeting in one's place of business (Hochschild, 1995: 106, 114–117). Thus citizens' race or gender affects not only their perceptions of the frequency and trajectory of political phenomena, but also their construal of values that are apparently shared by all (and that are linked to perceptions, attitudes, and prescriptions in complicated ways).

Let us return for a moment to those links between perceptions of fact, values, and policy prescriptions discussed earlier and examine them through the filter of demographic characteristics. I reported earlier that whites dramatically overestimate the fraction of the population that is black or Latino. So do blacks and Latinos – even more so. (Asians estimate a *lower* proportion of the population to be Asian than do the other three groups; whites are in the middle of the estimates of the size of the white population; *Washington Post* et al., 1995: table 1.1.) Although these factual mistakes presumably stem from many different bases – residential and school segregation, lower educational levels among the African American and Latino populations, and others – my interest here is in the political meaning rather than the individual causes of these mis-estimates. Blacks' overestimate of the number of African Americans in the United States is likely to mean something very different to them than whites' overestimate of the number of African Americans means to *them*. Blacks are inappropriately gratified, whites inappropriately threatened. More precisely – adding values to the mix of demographics and perceptions – individualistic blacks may be inappropriately pleased because, with so many others like themselves, some who work hard enough are sure to succeed; individualistic whites may be inappropriately concerned because, with so many blacks seeking to benefit "unfairly" from affirmative action, people like themselves have almost no chance to succeed no matter how hard they work.[13] Alternatively, nationalist or collectivist blacks may be inappropriately frustrated because they perceive the disparity between their race's proportion of the population and the proportion of the nation's wealth and power to be even greater than it really is. Nationalist or collectivist whites feel even more threatened by the encroaching hordes than they are already inclined to do.

Once again, this is all hypothetical; my point is not the particular argument but rather the claim that we must attend to the connections among demographic traits, perceptions, and values in order to understand where citizens' policy preferences and political attitudes come from and where they seek to take the polity.[14]

THE POLITICAL PATTERNING OF VALUES, PERCEPTIONS OF FACT, AND POLICY PRESCRIPTIONS

To this point, I have discussed connections among values, perceptions of fact, and prescriptions at the individual level – either individuals in the abstract or individuals with particular races, genders, or religions.[15] I want to turn now to the overall pattern in misperceptions of fact, again more in order to raise issues worth exploration than to provide sharp hypotheses or dispositive evidence (never mind conclusions).

We have seen that citizens incline toward pessimism when they make factual mistakes about the public world in the sense that they misperceive in ways that work against their preferences. (The main exception

13 Fewer than 10% of whites claim to have lost a job or promotion due to affirmative action. Nevertheless, up to two-thirds believe it likely that a white person will suffer such a loss; one-third think affirmative action programs frequently "deprive someone . . . of their rights," and two-tenths think "blacks have more of a chance to get good jobs and education than whites" (General Social Survey, 1990–1991: var. 399; *Los Angeles Times*, 1991: ques. 50, 71, 76). A combination of individualistic values and overestimations of the number of blacks might explain these apparently inconsistent views.

14 One survey includes ascriptively relevant questions about both perceptions of facts – which gender takes more responsibility for child care, do women have equal job influence, and so on – and values, such as whether gender equality should obtain. Since both men and women were surveyed, analyzing this data set in terms of the issues raised here would be very fruitful (Kane and Macaulay, 1993).

15 An intermediate set of issues, between the individual and societywide levels of analysis, is the role of social networks in shaping values, perceptions of facts, and political attitudes or policy preferences. A huge literature examines the ways in which people's values and attitudes are influenced by their communities, chosen or otherwise. But as far as I know, few studies analyze how social ties shape "knowledge." For a fascinating beginning, see Turner (1993).

is African Americans' and Latinos' greater than usual overestimation of their own group's share of the population.) Let me focus this discussion by adding one more to the list of pessimistic misperceptions. Consider the second epigram with which this chapter begins: "One good solid murder of a baby or a rape-murder of a 7-year-old girl will outweigh a ton of statistics." This rather cold-blooded comment – which may, incidentally, help to explain why Americans are not very sympathetic to university professors – came in response to a journalist's query about why people rank crime as one of the nation's greatest problems despite the fact that the crime rate is plummeting. In 1993, 9% of the population ranked crime at the top of the nation's list of problems, but in 1994, 37% did so. In 1989, over 80% of respondents to a *National Law Journal* survey thought crime was worsening in the United States, and 34% described themselves as "truly desperate" about it (Golden, 1996). In 1997, two-thirds of Americans agreed that crime was worsening (Yankelovich Partners, 1997). This when the murder rate had been declining steadily for a decade and other, less visible crime rates had been dropping by 10% a year or more in most areas of the country.

Again, one could pursue many explanations, but my interest lies in another direction – the fact that even in the 1989 "truly desperate" poll, almost two-thirds of the respondents said the crime problem *in their neighborhood* was stable or improving. This is an absolutely common finding in survey after survey. Most Americans think Congress is doing a bad job but their own representative is fine (*New York Times*/CBS News Poll, 1994a: 5–9; "Public Opinion and Demographic Report," 1994: 84–85). Nine-tenths think crime is rising in the nation, but only half think it is rising in their community. Teachers in *all* Chicago schools see students in their own school as "basically good kids" or "the quiet, sweet ones" but fear the gangs and students at "really tough schools" elsewhere in the city (Hess, 1987: 31; "My Town, the Nation," 1992: 95). Only 20% of blacks think race relations are "generally good" across the United States, but three times as many are satisfied with their own community. A slight majority of both races predict "a lot of racial prejudice and discrimination in America," but only one-fourth of whites and one-third of blacks say the same for their community (*New York Times*/CBS News Poll, 1992: vars. 19, 20, 29, 30). Although two-thirds of African Americans think the police in most big cities are unfair to blacks, a plurality (45%) think their local police are racially fair (Holmes, 1991). Although everyone outside large public housing projects, and many inside them, deplore their filth, crime, and disrepair, a surprising number of residents resist moving out of their own project even to purportedly better surroundings (Lee, 1981). Citizens think public schools across the nation are adequate, public schools in their community are pretty good, and the school that their oldest child attends is very good (Hochschild and Scott, 1998). Even residents of Harlem and the South Bronx, who deplore their neighborhood and almost all of the city services they encounter, claim that the rest of New York City has deteriorated more than their own neighborhood (Louis Harris and Associates, 1979: 3–6).

"The denial of personal disadvantage" is an even more focused, and surprising, manifestation of the same bias toward personal optimism. Most community college students in one study saw themselves as suffering more discrimination than either "men as a group" or "women as a group." Nevertheless, most thought their "chance for a successful life" was at least as good as others'. (Responses did not vary by ethnicity [Crosby et al., 1989: 88–93; see also Clayton and Crosby, 1992].) In 1984 fewer than three in ten African Americans claimed that members of their race were "better off economically than one year ago," and yet over half agreed that their own family was "better off financially than one year ago" (Jackson et al., 1994: tables 8.2, 8.4, 8.5). In every year since 1972, over seven in ten Americans have claimed that their family's income is average or above average – which is not logically possible if "average" is the median and not remotely plausible if "average" is the mean. Most distressingly, even 30% or more of blacks in the lowest third of the black distribution of income – that is, people whose income is less than one-third of the national median – claim that their family income is average or above average.[16]

Psychologists explain these anomalous views by the need to believe that one controls one's own life. After all, "crime can't be seen as being too bad in respondents' neighborhoods; the schools must be good and the health care fine. If not, people might be forced to ask themselves why they haven't moved" (quoted in Holmes, 1991: 6). That comment reflects the views of a person who could afford to move if he chose to; many people cannot. So I would look for alternative or additional explanations of this odd phenomenon if I were seeking to explain it – but I am not. Once again, my interest lies less in finding explanations than in drawing out political implications. What does it mean that people make factual mistakes *against* their own preferences when they think of the public arena but *in support of* their own preferences when they think about their own lives?

At the level of individual psychology, this pattern probably indicates the common impulse to believe that we are exceptions to the general rule.

---

16 More poor whites make the same mistake, but the gap between their income and the median family income is only half as great. Calculations from General Social Survey: var. 149, 1972–1982; var. 188, 1983–1991.

(As Garrison Keillor notes, in the ideal town, all the women are strong, all the men are good-looking, and all the children are above average.) At a methodological level, it reminds us that collective phenomena are not simply aggregations of individual phenomena. (In other words, it is possible for some people to be correct in asserting that members of Congress in general are crooks and charlatans but that their own member is admirable. But it is not possible for all people to be correct in that assertion.)

At the political level, this set of countervailing mistakes may explain some of the disparity between political rhetoric and political action in the United States. Politicians and advocates make loud claims about the need to eliminate "pork" in the federal budget, to protect our borders from encroaching Communist – now immigrant – hordes, to punish racist policemen and corporate officials, and so on. They do so partly because they are rewarded with reelection if they are politicians or with contributions and activism if they are advocates. That is, they engage in this rhetoric because it is what the public wants to hear, and the public wants to hear it because the rhetoric fits people's perceptions of the facts about the cold cruel social world out there.

Politicians and activists, however, seldom act in accordance with this rhetoric. The disparity between talk and action has, of course, many causes, of which the pattern of public perceptions is only a small piece. Nevertheless, the failure of politicians of both parties to slash the federal budget or to take the steps really needed to curtail illegal immigration, to pick only two examples, may occur partly because citizens do not *actually* want radical change. People perceive their own lives and circumstances to be relatively better than those of others, and perhaps even absolutely satisfying, so they have a deep underlying conservatism about change that will disrupt their perceived status quo. Even middle-class African Americans, who are deeply and increasingly furious about individual and structural racism as they see it, increasingly work in integrated settings and express gratification at their own personal trajectories (Hochschild 1995: 57–59, 93–98). So maybe they too would quail before really substantial political change.

Thus balanced misperceptions of fact may provide yet another answer to the old question "Why no socialism in the United States?" (Louis Hartz would remind us to add, "why no fascism either?") "The country is in bad shape, but I and mine are doing pretty well" – that is not a recipe for big political swings either to the right or to the left. It is also not a recipe for a type of democratic practice that Rousseau would approve, or even Thomas Jefferson.

Where You Stand Depends on What You See

PERCEPTIONS OF FACTS AND DEMOCRATIC THEORY

Inserting the study of factual perceptions into the traditional study of opinions and the newer study of values could fill both theoretical and substantive holes. Theoretically, we know surprisingly little about the relationships among the three elements. Do people, or when do people, follow the "schooling model" – learn new facts, which change the ways in which they apply deep values to particular policy questions? Do they, or when do they, follow the "psychological model" – hold values or experience emotions that lead them to perceive or even invent certain facts, which in turn reinforce their extant policy views? Do they, or when do they, follow the "conversion model" – learn new facts, which undermine their old values and change their attitudes or policy preferences? How do one's social position or ascriptive traits affect factual perceptions and the use to which those perceptions are put? We know surprisingly little about these basic analytic questions.

Substantively, understanding what people think they know and how they use that "knowledge" would tell us a lot about political choices. People overestimate some facts and underestimate others; they are aware of some institutions and events and unaware of others. Most important, there may well be systematic biases in what people "know" and do not "know." They apparently overestimate threats to the polity, and simultaneously overestimate their own advantages. They may mistake current circumstances for long-term trends or inevitable facts of nature. They are more aware of individuals than of institutions, and of institutions than of processes.

Furthermore, perceptions of fact may relate systematically to political attitudes. The scanty evidence available suggests that people who are more knowledgeable hold more liberal policy views; would that finding hold up under closer scrutiny? Are people who are more knowledgeable also more liberal in their values? If so, then some politicians and policy activists have an incentive to conduct informational campaigns, and others do not. But the millions of dollars spent by conservative think tanks suggest that conservatives do not believe that information leads to liberalism, and they may well be right – at least some of the time.

In response to an earlier version of this chapter, Michael Walzer observed that citizens' misinformation or lack of information is the "dirty secret of democratic theory," and that theorists of democracy must attend to its extent and implications more than they have done so far. I concur. How can we justify making policy choices or choosing political leaders based on democratically expressed preferences if those preferences themselves arguably stem from large and biased mistakes?

Jennifer L. Hochschild

I have two sets of answers to this question, one at the general level of theory and one at the more specific level of institutional design. A democratic theorist might well argue – many have – that people have a right to choose their leaders or their political direction regardless of what they know or believe. Political choice is part of what it means to be a free person, and a "free government," as the framers put it, is in part a democratically chosen government. A more strategically inclined political theorist might argue that despite misinformation, people still know their own interests and can articulate their own values better than anyone else can, so they have the right to act on those interests and values in the political arena. Conversely, the political regime will be more stable, or at least less likely to go radically wrong, if it responds to revealed preferences than if it seeks to determine or shape "real" interests.

A second set of answers, all variants on the theme of the hidden hand of interest aggregation, are more common to thoughtful students of public opinion than to democratic theorists. First, individual citizens make "good enough" choices of policy direction or political leaders based on tiny, superficial, but appropriate cues – which party supports the candidate or proposition, what a neighbor or coworker believes, a slogan on a bumper sticker or a tag line on a political advertisement. These cues are designed to evoke associations within the voter between the candidate (or proposition) and a broad range of values and preferences, and they mostly succeed. Thus people vote intelligibly and appropriately despite their misinformation (Althaus, 1995, efficiently summarizes, and critiques, the literature on heuristic information processing).

The other common "hidden hand" argument operates at the aggregate rather than the individual level. Perhaps most voters choose candidates or propositions randomly or mistakenly, but these errors cancel each other out. A few voters *are* politically knowledgeable – either in general or about a particular issue or person – and their choices provide the margin of victory or defeat. Thus the whole process produces a result based on links between values, correct information, and policy preferences, even if only a very few people hold correct information. (Delli Carpini and Keeter, 1996: chap.1, nicely summarize this literature.)

A different way to respond to the "dirty secret of democratic theory" is to focus on the particular institutions that transform democratic choice into governing rules. Here the implicit assumption that I have made heretofore, that referenda and candidates are analytically identical for my purposes in this chapter, breaks down. The analysis implies skepticism, at best, about referenda, because they place the greatest demands on citizens' knowledge and on their ability to intelligibly connect knowledge to values and policy preferences. The number of referenda in bien-

334

nial national elections increased from forty-one in 1986 to ninety (across twenty states) in 1996; in the 1996 election, their subjects ranged from the legality of affirmative action in California to an initiative in Nevada that would have eliminated sales tax on the sale of airplane parts and equipment (Public Affairs Research Institute of New Jersey, 1996). Press coverage of most propositions is scanty to nonexistent (Lascher, 1997). And even extremely well-informed voters cannot make meaningful decisions about a flood of detailed policy proposals that are mostly put before them arbitrarily.

The argument in this chapter seems to imply that governance should be left not to the most participatory forum but rather to the least – that is, to nonpartisan experts. Our nation's history of leaving major decisions to "the best and the brightest," however, suggests that expertise and brilliance alone do not warrant great faith with regard to matters of deep public import (Halberstam, 1972; McNamara, 1995). Perhaps the model of the European civil service, with neutral experts in staff roles but elected leaders in decision-making roles, best instantiates the normative imperative of weighing values and preferences at least as heavily as knowledge.

The analysis of this chapter also suggests skepticism in allowing advocates of particular positions to be heavily involved in making policy decisions. Advocates are usually very knowledgeable about their issue. But their perceptions are likely to be very selective and possibly even more biased than the perceptions of ordinary citizens. We do not have a strong enough empirical base to judge the relative weights of greater knowledge, more passionate values, deeper misperceptions, and more sharply honed policy views of advocates compared with the views held by ordinary citizens, but I suspect that with further study we would not conclude that advocates' merits outweigh their defects as decision makers in a democratic society.

That leaves us with two kinds of decision makers, judges and elected representatives. In arenas such as school desegregation, congressional redistricting, support for free speech, and school finance reform, judges have mostly made better decisions from the perspective of enhancing individuals' life chances and the possibilities of democratic decision making than have elected officials or any other set of actors. Perhaps the categories of this analysis help us to understand why. Judges become highly knowledgeable about particular issues through attention to competing advocates; they (one hopes) see their role as fostering the deep values of individual rights, constitutional balances, and democratic procedures; and they must provide public reasons for the policy decisions that they enunciate. In most cases, judicial decisions can be overruled by a court that finds those reasons insufficient or wrong, so there is an individual and institutional incentive to arrive at the best possible answer. (Rebell and Block, 1982, and Melnick, 1994, provide broad comparisons of judicial and legislation decision making.)

Judges have, of course, a great defect as decision makers; they are only indirectly tied to democratic processes as we conventionally understand them. And history shows plenty of cases in which judges' decisions have harmed democratic practices. That leaves us with elected representatives. Politicians may get elected by pandering to, and even helping to create, the misperceptions and poorly grounded attitudes and policy preferences of citizens. But, again one hopes, they make decisions based at least partly on substantive knowledge about the policy problem at hand and on commitment to the public good. They certainly have more opportunity and more institutional supports than any other political actor for combining their own and their constituents' values with reasonably unbiased factual knowledge, thereby producing good policy choices.[17]

Perhaps "ye shall know the truth, and the truth shall set ye free." But another aphorism holds that "books give not wisdom where none was before." Finding out what people know, what they think they know, and how their knowledge connects to their values and views will help us to decide which, if either, of these ancient insights is correct. At that point, we can gain a slightly new purchase on the perennial question of "why (and how) democracy?"

References

Abramson, Paul and Ronald Inglehart (1994) "The Structure of Values on Five Continents," paper presented at the World Congress of the International Political Science Association, Berlin, Aug. 21–25.

Adorno, T. W., Else Frenkel-Brunswik, Daniel Levinson, and R. Nevitt Sanford (1950) *The Authoritarian Personality*. New York: Norton.

Althaus, Scott (1995) "The Practical Limits of Information Shortcuts: Public Opinion, Political Equality, and the Social Distribution of Knowledge." Paper presented at the annual meeting of the Midwest Political Science Association, Chicago.

(1996) "Opinion Polls, Information Effects, and Political Equality: Exploring Ideological Biases in Collective Opinion." *Political Communication* 13: 3–21.

Becker, Gary (1981) *A Treatise on the Family*. Cambridge MA: Harvard University Press.

Bennett, Stephen (1996) "'Know-Nothings' Revisited Again." *Political Behavior* 15: 219–233.

17 I am here, readers will note, re-creating part of Madison's justification for representative government in *The Federalist Papers*. See also Kateb (1981).

Citrin, Jack, Beth Reingold, and Donald Green (1990) "American Identity and the Politics of Ethnic Change." *Journal of Politics* 52: 1124–1154.

Clayton, Susan and Faye Crosby (1992) *Justice, Gender, and Affirmative Action.* Ann Arbor: University of Michigan Press.

Crosby, Faye, Ann Pufall, Rebecca Clair Snyder, Marion O'Connell, and Peg Whalen (1989) "The Denial of Personal Disadvantage Among You, Me, and All the Other Ostriches." In Mary Crawford and Margaret Gentry, ed., *Gender and Thought.* New York: Springer-Verlag. 9–99.

Dawson, Michael (1994) "African American Political Discontent." *Polling Report* 10, No. 8: 1, 6.

Delli Carpini, Michael and Scott Keeter (1991) "Stability and Change in the U.S. Public's Knowledge of Politics." *Public Opinion Quarterly* 55: 583–612.

(1996) *What Americans Know About Politics and Why It Matters.* New Haven CT: Yale University Press.

Dominitz, Jeff and Charles Manski (1995) "Perceptions of Economic Vulnerability: First Evidence from the Survey of Economic Expectations." Madison: University of Wisconsin, Institute for Research on Poverty.

Donelan, Karen, Robert Blendon, and Craig Hill (1995) "What Does the Public Know About Entitlements?" Paper presented at the annual meeting of the American Association for Public Opinion Research, May 18–21.

Dua, Pami and David Smyth (1993) "Survey Evidence on Excessive Public Pessimism about the Future Behavior of Unemployment." *Public Opinion Quarterly* 57: 566–574.

Espenshade, Thomas and Katherine Hempstead (1996) "Contemporary American Attitudes Toward U.S. Immigration." *International Migration Review* 30: 535–570.

Festinger, Leon, H. W. Riecken, and S. Schacter (1956) *When Prophecy Fails: A Social and Psychological Study of a Modern Group That Predicted the Destruction of the World.* New York: Harper & Row.

Gallup, George Jr. and Frank Newport (1990) "Americans Ignorant of Basic Census Facts." *Gallup Poll Monthly,* No. 294: 2–5.

General Social Survey (various years), directed by James Davis and Tom Smith (Chicago: National Opinion Research Center). Unpublished tabulations in possession of the author.

Gibson, James and Raymond Duch (1993) "Support for Rights in Western Europe and the Soviet Union: An Analysis of the Beliefs of Mass Publics." In Frederick Weil, ed., *Research on Democracy and Society: Democratization in Eastern and Western Europe,* vol. 1. Greenwich, CT: JAI Press: 241–263.

Golden, Tim (1996) "Crime Rates May Be Down, But the Problem Stays Hot with Politicians and Voters." *New York Times,* Sept. 22: 26.

Graber, Doris (1996) "Wrong Questions, Wrong Answers: Measuring Political Knowledge." Paper presented at the annual meeting of the Midwest Political Science Association, Chicago.

Halberstam, David (1972) *The Best and the Brightest.* New York: Random House.

Hart/Teeter, *Wall Street Journal* /NBC News (1995).

Hess, Fred (1987) "A Comprehensive Analysis of the Dropout Phenomenon in an Urban School System." Paper presented at the annual meeting of the American Educational Research Association, Washington, DC.

Highton, Benjamin and Raymond Wolfinger (1992) "Estimating the Size of Minority Groups," memo to Board of Overseers, National Election Studies, Jan. 24.

Hochschild, Jennifer (1981) *What's Fair? American Beliefs about Distributive Justice.* Cambridge, MA: Harvard University Press.

(1995) *Facing Up to the American Dream: Race, Class, and the Soul of the Nation.* Princeton, NJ: Princeton University Press.

Hochschild, Jennifer and Bridget Scott (1998) "Poll Trends: Attitudes Toward Governance of Public Education." *Public Opinion Quarterly* 62, No 1: 79–120.

Hofrichter, Jurgen. (1993). "Acceptance of Basic Values of Democracy in the European Community." Paper presented at the conference on "Basic Values of Democracy" sponsored by Federal Center for Political Education of the Federal Republic of Germany and the Center for Civic Education, U.S.A., in Herrsching, Germany.

Holmes, Steven (1991) "When Grass Looks Greener on This Side of the Fence." *New York Times,* Apr. 21: E6.

Ihlanfeldt, Keith (1995) "Information on the Spatial Distribution of Job Opportunities within Metropolitan Areas." Unpublished paper, Georgia State University, College of Business Administration, Atlanta, GA.

Jackson, John S., Ronald E. Brown, Michael Dawson, K. Tate, and S. J. Hatchett (1994) *The 1984–1988 National Black Election Panel Study [NBES]: A Sourcebook.* Ann Arbor: University of Michigan, Institute for Social Research.

Jacobs, Lawrence (1993) *The Health of Nations: Public Opinion and the Making of American and British Health Policy.* Ithaca, NY: Cornell University Press.

Kane, Emily and Laura Macaulay (1993) "Interviewer Gender and Gender Attitudes." *Public Opinion Quarterly* 57: 1–28.

Kateb, George (1981) "The Moral Distinctiveness of Representative Democracy." *Ethics* 91, No. 3: 357–374.

Kennedy, Randall (1997) *Race, Crime, and the Law.* New York: Pantheon Books.

Key, V. O. (1966) *The Responsible Electorate.* Cambridge, MA: Harvard University Press.

Kuklinski, James, Paul Quirk, David Schwieder, and Robert Rich (1997) "Misinformation and the Currency of Citizenship." Paper presented at the annual meeting of the Midwest Political Science Association, Chicago.

Lane, Robert (1962) *Political Ideology: Why the American Common Man Believes What He Does.* New York: Free Press.

Lascher, Edward (1997) "Press Coverage of Propositions Is Sparse in California." IGS *Public Affairs Reporter* 38, No. 2: 9–10.

Lee, Jessica (1981) "Life at Cabrini Green." In *Equality: America's Unfinished Business,* Chicago: Gannett Newspaper Company. Washington, DC: Gannett News Service: 4–5.

Lindeman, Mark (1996) "Studying Informed Preferences: Measures, Models, and Mysteries." Paper presented at the annual meeting of the Midwest Political Science Association, Chicago.

Lippmann, Walter (1961 [orig. 1922]) *Public Opinion.* New York: Macmillan.

Los Angeles Times (1985) The Poverty Poll, Poll #96, Apr. 19–26.

(1991) Race Relations and Judge Thomas' Nomination, Poll #259, Sept. 21–25.

(1995) National Issues, Survey #352, Jan. 19–22.

Louis Harris and Associates (1979) *A Survey of Residents' Perceptions of Neighborhood Services in the Southeast Bronx and Central Harlem.* Report for Community Service Society of New York.

Lynd, Robert and Helen Lynd (1929) *Middletown: A Study in Contemporary American Culture.* New York: Harcourt, Brace.

Madison, James, Alexander Hamilton, and John Jay (1961 [1788]) *The Federalist,* Jacob Cooke, ed. Middletown, CT: Wesleyan University Press.

Mansbridge, Jane (1980) *Beyond Adversary Democracy.* Chicago: University of Chicago Press.

Mansbridge, Jane, ed. (1990) *Beyond Self Interest.* Chicago: University of Chicago Press.

McIntosh, Mary and Martha MacIver (1992) "Coping with Freedom and Uncertainty: Public Opinion in Hungary, Poland, and Czechoslovakia, 1989–92." *International Journal of Public Opinion Research* 4: 375–391.

McNamera, Robert (1995). *In Retrospect: The Tragedy and Lessons of Vietnam.* New York: Times Books.

Melnick, R. Shep (1994) *Between the Lines: Interpreting Welfare Rights.* Washington, DC: Brookings Institution.

Monroe, Kristen (1996) *The Heart of Altruism: Perceptions of a Common Humanity.* Princeton, NJ: Princeton University Press.

"My Town, the Nation" (1992) *Public Perspective.* 3, No. 5: 94–96.

Nadeau, Richard, and Richard G. Niemi (1995). "The Process of Answering Factual Knowledge Questions." *Public Opinion Quarterly* 59: 323–346.

Nadeau, Richard, Richard Niemi, and Jeffrey Levine (1993) "Innumeracy About Minority Populations." *Public Opinion Quarterly* 57: 332–247.

New York Times/CBS News Poll (1992), untitled, May 6–8.

　(1994a), untitled, Oct. 29–Nov. 1.

　(1994b), untitled, Dec. 6–9.

　(1995), untitled, Oct. 22–25.

Niemi, Richard and Herbert Weisberg (1993) *Classics in Voting Behavior.* Washington, DC: Congressional Quarterly Press.

Office of Assistant Secretary of Defense, Public Affairs (1996) *1995 Sexual Harassment Survey.* Washington, DC: U.S. Department of Defense.

Patterson, Orlando (1973) "The Moral Crisis of the Black American." *Public Interest* 23: 43–69.

The Polling Report (1994) "The Incredible Shrinking Vice President." 10, No. 19: 4.

Popkin, Samuel and Michael Dimock (1999) "Political Knowledge and Citizen Competence." In Stephen Elkin and Karol Soltan, eds., *Citizen Competence and Democratic Institutions.* University Park: Pennsylvania State University Press: 117–146.

Program on International Policy Attitudes (1995) "Americans and Foreign Aid: A Study of American Public Attitudes." College Park, MD: University of Maryland, School of Public Affairs.

Public Affairs Research Institute of New Jersey (1996) "Citizen Initiative Ballot Questions, 1991 Through 1995." Princeton: Public Affairs Research Institute of New Jersey.

"Public Opinion and Demographic Report" (1994) *Public Perspective* 5, No. 2: 82–104.

Raab, Earl (1988) "High Anxiety." *Present Tense* 15 (Jan.–Feb.): 46–49.

Rebell, Michael and Arthur Block (1982) *Educational Policy Making and the Courts*. Chicago: University of Chicago Press.

Rosenfeld, Michel (1991) *Affirmative Action and Justice: A Philosophical and Constitutional Inquiry*. New Haven, CT: Yale University Press.

Sanders, Lynn (1996) "Integrated Interviews, Alternative Models: How Differently Whites Think When They Discuss Politics with Blacks." Unpublished paper, Chicago: University of Chicago, Department of Political Science.

Sears, David O., James Sidanius, and Lawrence Bobo (2000). *Racialized Politics: The Debate about Racism in America*. Chicago: University of Chicago Press.

Smith, Tom (1994) *Anti-Semitism in Contemporary America*. New York: American Jewish Committee.

(1995) "World War II and the Lessons of History." *The Public Perspective*, 6, No. 5: 51–53.

Sniderman, Paul, Richard Brody, and Philip Tetlock (1991) *Reasoning and Choice: Explorations in Political Psychology*. New York: Cambridge University Press.

Tedin, Kent (1994) "Self-Interest, Symbolic Values, and the Financial Equalization of the Public Schools." *Journal of Politics* 56: 628–649.

Turner, Patricia (1993) *I Heard It Through the Grapevine: Rumor in African-American Culture*. Berkeley: University of California Press.

Warner, W. Lloyd (1949) *Democracy in Jonesville: A Study in Quality and Inequality*. New York: Harper & Row.

Washington Post/ Kaiser Family Foundation/ Harvard University Survey Project (1995) *The Four Americas: Government and Social Policy Through the Eyes of America's Multi-racial and Multi-ethnic Society*. Menlo Park, CA: Kaiser Family Foundation.

Weingarten, Gene (1996) "Read It and Veep." *Washington Post*, Feb. 4: F1.

Yankelovich Partners (1997) "Fear of Crime." *The Polling Report*, 13, No. 12: June 16: 3.

Zaller, John (1992) *The Nature and Origins of Mass Opinion*. New York: Cambridge University Press.

12

Commentary: The Meaning of "Attitude" in Representative Democracies

JAMES H. KUKLINSKI
JENNIFER JERIT

Two of the chapters in this part continue the debate over the true nature of citizens' attitudes. The third asks how accurately people perceive social and political reality and what difference it makes, a question that will take on increasing importance in the political behavior literature. All chapters speak to citizen competence, a self-evidently important topic.

In commenting on the three chapters and on related works, we emphasize intuitive appeal more and data analysis less than scholars usually do. Our discussion is divided into two main sections and proceeds as follows. In the first, we briefly revisit Converse's "Attitudes and Non-Attitudes: Continuation of a Dialogue" (1970) and Zaller's *The Nature and Origins of Mass Opinion* (1992). We then offer a hypothetical case of three citizens faced with evaluating the now-defeated Clinton health care proposal. What, we ask, would Converse and Zaller conclude about the existence or nonexistence of attitudes in the three cases? Do some conclusions make more sense than others? Where does the Sniderman et al. study fit in?

In the second part of the chapter, we suggest stepping away from the attitude versus nonattitude distinction and considering instead the extent to which citizens' decisions are well grounded. Although not an especially new idea, it takes us down two infrequently traveled paths: one leads to Hochschild and the role of perceptions, the other to Diamond and a latitude conception of attitudes. A fundamental question underlies our discussion: what can we realistically expect from citizens in a large, modern society such as ours?

We thank Peter Nardulli and Paul Quirk for comments on an earlier draft of this chapter.

ATTITUDES AND NONATTITUDES REVISITED

It is Converse (1964, 1970), of course, who initially raised the problem of nonattitudes in survey research. The preponderance of attention has been on his black-white model, which Converse used to show that many interviewees' responses to a set of survey items followed a random pattern over time. Not only did time 1 responses poorly predict time 2 responses, they did no better at predicting time 2 than time 3 responses. Responses were most unstable of all on the question of whether the federal government should "leave things like electric power and housing for private businessmen to handle."

One might ask whether we should expect stable responses on this item, given the dual reference to housing and electric power. Conceivably, many people's feelings about the private sector's providing housing differed from their feelings toward its providing electricity. How individuals responded at any point in time, therefore, would depend on how they handled the dual referents. Putting that aside, what we want to underline here is the discussion that follows Converse's presentation of the black-white model results. It consists of the repeated message that inattention, lack of information, and lack of engagement are the stuff of nonattitudes. With characteristic clarity, Converse (1970, p. 177) puts it this way: "*Attitudes take practice....* When such practice has not occurred, the state to be measured is non-existent."

Converse did not precisely delineate at what level of practice a nonattitude becomes an attitude. All the patterns in Figure 12.1 comport with his discussion. Line A depicts a continuum from nonattitude to attitude, such that someone in the middle has "some" attitude. Lines B and C depict a jump from nonattitude to attitude as the level of practice increases. What distinguishes these latter two lines from each other is the amount of practice that is required for the jump from one category to the other. Most researchers, including Converse himself, have forgone the idea of more or less attitude (for one thing, it's clumsy to discuss) and used the two-category (attitudes versus nonattitudes) distinction. We will return to this point later.

Nor did Converse have data on people's knowledge about and cognitive engagement in the particular political topics the survey asked about. So he made two assumptions: first, although many people lack knowledge and thus real attitudes about an issue, they nonetheless will answer the survey question; and, second, if people lack real attitudes, then their responses across time will be unstable. On the basis of these and a few other assumptions, he estimated that 80% lacked a true attitude about abstract issues such as private versus government provision of housing and electricity. People performed better on other issues, especially race.

"Attitude" in Representative Democracies

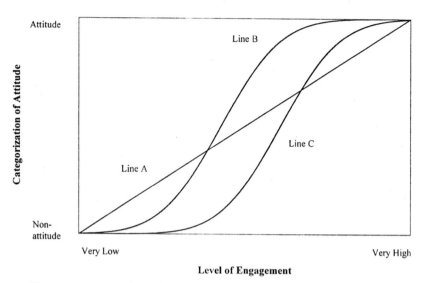

Figure 12.1. Hypothetical relationships between practice and attitudes.

Converse also distinguished the ambivalent from those with no attitudes. Unlike the latter, the ambivalent hold true attitudes; at the least, they hold "zero-attitudes" (1970, p. 180). They are fully engaged with the general issue, but internal conflict among a set of constituent attitudes precludes their reaching a final determination. When asked general survey questions, they tend to "resolve" the conflict by placing themselves at the middle. To Converse, then, ambivalence and nonattitudes represent qualitatively different states. The ambivalent legitimately belong at the middle of a scale ranging from strongly pro to strongly con; those with nonattitudes do not belong on the scale at all. Thus, two types of people fall at the middle of the scale: the ambivalent and those who are truly indifferent.

Finally, Converse apparently assumed that it was possible for sizable segments of the American citizenry to hold true attitudes across a range of issues. For a lot of people to hold attitudes on a lot of issues, however, requires a level of motivation and attention to politics that most individuals are not wont to give. What is possible in principle is unlikely in practice. At best, we find "issue publics" who center on a single issue.

Ambivalence plays an even more central albeit a very different role in Zaller's perspective on political attitudes. Most people, Zaller argues, are ambivalent about political issues. To be sure, the most politically aware – defined in general, not issue-specific, terms – are less likely to

343

experience ambivalence, but even they are not immune to it. This ambivalence arises because a variety of considerations come to mind when an individual ponders a political issue. Some considerations push the respondent to answer in one direction, others in the opposite direction. In the real world of politics, it is the configuration of elite messages that determines the mix and relative salience of an individual's considerations.

Although he makes statements that suggest otherwise, Zaller apparently views true political attitudes as largely nonexistent. This is most evident from the kinds of literature he cites to support his considerations model. First is the work of Wilson and his colleagues (Wilson and Hodges, 1991; Wilson et al., 1989a, 1989b), who stirred considerable controversy in their field by arguing that nearly all attitudes measured in surveys are on-the-spot constructions. Second is Kahneman and Tversky's well-known research on framing (Kahneman and Tversky, 1982; Tversky and Kahneman, 1982). In an unusually large number of studies spanning more than two decades, the authors revealed, again and again, that people change their judgments as a function of how a situation is framed. Saying that 10% are unemployed, for instance, generates different responses than saying that 90% are employed.

Converse and Zaller differ, then, on at least two crucial points. First, whereas Converse sees a relatively small proportion of the population as ambivalent, Zaller sees nearly everyone as so. Second, whereas Converse believes that, in principle, a greater proportion of the American electorate could hold true attitudes, Zaller apparently does not. These differences, it is crucial to emphasize, arise principally because the two authors define their central terms differently, not because the data lead them in different directions.

To see more concretely how Converse and Zaller differ, consider the following hypothetical although realistic situation. It is 1994 and Congress is considering a national health care proposal that President Bill Clinton introduced. Smith pays literally no attention to politics. He does not even know that Congress is debating national health care. Jackson knows there is a Clinton health proposal "out there," but that's it. In contrast, Jones has been vigilantly following the debate. Her employer covers her insurance, but she realizes that many other people cannot get adequate health care under the current system. She sees national health care as a potentially good solution.

A survey researcher interviews Smith, Jackson, and Jones three times throughout the health care debate. Among the questions asked each time is the following: "Do you favor or oppose the Clinton health care plan now being debated in Congress?"

Suppose Smith, oblivious to the debate in Washington but wanting to please the interviewer, answers "yes," "no," and "yes" the three times he is asked the question. Jackson, who is strongly anti-Clinton, answers "no" all three times despite his complete ignorance about the health plan itself. Jones answers "yes," "yes," and "no." She answers "no" the third time because she recently heard arguments that a national health care plan would restrict, if not eliminate, her choice of doctors. This is something she had not thought about before. Although she still sees the merits of national health care, Jones cannot accept the thought of losing her freedom to choose physicians and facilities. What conclusions would – and should – we reach about our three citizens' attitudes? And how would Converse's and Zaller's answers differ, if at all?

One can answer the latter question from two perspectives. The first is to assume that Converse and Zaller know nothing other than the pattern of responses over time. The second is to assume that they know everything included in the three citizens' profiles. Let's take them in order.

Knowing only the stability of responses, both Converse and Zaller presumably would attribute nonattitudes to Smith on the first question ("yes," "no," "yes") and true attitudes to Jackson ("no," "no," "no"). They might not agree on Jones ("yes," "yes," "no"). Whereas Zaller would interpret the responses as evidence of nonattitudes, Converse might leave open the possibility of real attitude change (since the only change came at the third point in time).

On the other hand, suppose that Converse and Zaller know all there is to know about the three hypothetical citizens. On the basis of his definition of an attitude, Converse seemingly would attribute nonattitudes to Smith and Jackson and true attitudes to Jones. Smith and Jackson show no evidence of "practice," to use Converse's term, but Jones does. Assuming that our interpretation of Zaller is correct, he would attribute nonattitudes to everyone.

What can we extract from all of this? First, by no means are stability and true attitudes perfectly correlated. That Jackson responds consistently, despite his ignorance about the policy initiative, removes any doubt. This is not news. Converse never construed stability to be a perfect measure of true attitudes. More generally, some people will express the same answer across time either as a matter of luck or on a basis that has little to do with the particular issue (although one arguably might believe that Jackson's disliking Clinton is a good enough reason to oppose the plan). Similarly, some individuals who meet Converse's practice criterion will not display perfectly stable attitudes across time. People such as Jones can be fully engaged in a particular policy debate and respond to arguments as they arise.

This leads to the second and far more crucial point. Jones paid close attention to the debate. She thought about the wisdom of a national health care plan. Then she heard arguments about a likely loss of choice and reacted to them. Assuming that the researcher knows these things about the three individuals, the question is this: does it feel intuitively right to put Jones in the same nonattitude category as Smith and Jackson? From Converse's perspective, as we've already noted, Jones meets the practice criterion and thus holds a true attitude. To Zaller, Jones is yet another example of someone constructing an answer on the spot, using whatever comes to mind. In short, Converse would not put Jones in the same category as the two others; Zaller would.

Almost never, of course, do survey researchers have the respondent profiles that we presented here. That is the point: even with rather complete profiles of their respondents, Converse and Zaller would not reach the same conclusion about the nature of Jones's attitude. They begin with different premises and define some of the same terms (notably, ambivalence) differently. Which conclusion one prefers, then, depends wholly on which set of assumptions and definitions one prefers.

We believe that Sniderman et al. would be in Converse's corner with respect to Jones if her full profile were put before them. Concluding that Jones held a true attitude, we think, would feel intuitively right. However, they too lack the kind of in-depth data about their respondents that we provided in the hypothetical example and thus seek an answer in additional data. The empirical evidence they report challenges Zaller's constructed-on-the-spot conception of attitudes. In short, their story goes like this. When one asks liberals and conservatives about African Americans under different circumstances, they respond in ways that reflect those circumstances. By itself, this finding could be construed as support for Zaller's position; different considerations lead to different preferences. However, liberals also consistently take more liberal positions across all the situations that interviewers primed respondents to think about. This systematic pattern does not reflect top-of-the-head responses. To the contrary, it reflects the existence of true attitudes, without which people could not respond to changing conditions in intelligible and understandable ways (also see Kuklinski and Hurley, 1994, 1996).

Sniderman et al. set forth a compelling argument for the existence of true attitudes among ordinary citizens. But as we just said, Zaller could still argue to the contrary, noting the variability in responses across situations. Liberals and conservatives might remain on the proper ideological side of each other, but both groups, as the considerations model predicts, change their positions when given differently worded survey questions. Moreover, Sniderman et al. do not look at changes in responses to the same item across time, which is the crux of Zaller's empirical evidence.

"Attitude" in Representative Democracies

Nonetheless, Sniderman et al.'s important study brings the discussion of attitudes versus nonattitudes to a new level. The question it raises is this: must *any* change in people's responses arising from a change in question wording (a surrogate for elite messages) be taken as evidence of nonattitudes? That is, even if people respond to different contexts in seemingly logical ways, must the researcher by definition construe the change in their responses as evidence in support of the top-of-the-head model? Sniderman et al. answer no, of course, and argue strongly that an affirmative answer does not make sense. In their view, the systematic patterns they report could not exist in the absence of true attitudes.

Sniderman et al.'s chapter not only brings a new perspective to bear, it also shifts some of the burden of proof to those who advocate the top-of-the-head model. How do they reconcile the Sniderman et al. conclusions with their own? Do they feel they need to? More generally, how might the continuing attitude versus nonattitude dialogue most fruitfully proceed?

The participants themselves must answer the last question. However, we recommend separating the purely conceptual issues from the attendant and quite separate problems of measuring political attitudes in surveys. A fundamental need is for each principal to explicate what he considers, conceptually, to be the necessary and sufficient conditions for a true political attitude. Converse explicitly stated his: the individual must be appropriately informed about and mentally engaged in the issue. Unfortunately, as we noted earlier, researchers subsequently focused their attention almost exclusively on Converse's instability findings and lost sight of what he offered as the necessary and sufficient conditions for the existence of a true attitude.[1] As we also noted earlier, even Converse did not specify precisely what it takes for a nonattitude to become an attitude; perhaps no one can. In any event, despite the outstanding work in the area, others have not been as explicit as Converse. Explicating the conditions will help to illuminate where authors agree and where they do not, quite independently of the data. It might also identify new directions for empirical analysis.

THE GROUNDING OF POLITICAL ATTITUDES

The preceding prescription, for better or worse, takes the attitudes versus nonattitudes distinction as given. An alternative is to change the terms of discourse and ask how well grounded citizens' "attitudes" (or

[1] There is a fine but real distinction between a definition of a political attitude and a statement of the necessary and sufficient conditions. Psychologists' efforts to define an attitude have generated numerous definitions and little consensus, which should stand as a lesson for political scientists.

347

"decisions" or "preferences") are. By "well grounded," we mean simply the extent to which people reach their political judgments on the basis of concrete, meaningful information.

Thinking in terms of grounding accomplishes two purposes. First, it eliminates the dichotomous, attitude versus nonattitude language that leads to polarized, yes–no conclusions. Second, the term "grounding" raises what is perhaps the most fundamental question of all: how well grounded can citizens' political attitudes be in a modern representative democracy like the United States?

It will be useful, at the outset, to distinguish between general political attitudes, as measured, say, by the National Election Studies' standard-of-living question, and attitudes toward specific policies being debated in Congress (e.g., the North American Free Trade Agreement [NAFTA], the Clinton health care bill). These two types of attitudes are and necessarily must be grounded differently.

Much of the research effort, including Converse's, has focused on general attitudes: should the government see to it that everyone has a job and a good standard of living? Should the government try to improve the social and economic positions of blacks and other minorities? Should the government provide more or fewer services? Although the Sniderman et al. items are more complex and innovative, they also measure general attitudes (toward specifically defined situations). A primary question has been whether an underlying liberal–conservative ideology motivates these attitudes. Converse, of course, showed that people do not use or understand the liberal–conservative ideology that structures elite discourse. His conclusion has been the orthodoxy for four decades, although the evidence reported by Sniderman et al. seems to say otherwise.

To be well grounded in general political attitudes requires more than a working knowledge of ideology. We also expect that people will hold reasonably correct views of the social world, since those views serve as the most essential data that an individual can possess. It is here that the study of beliefs and perceptions becomes important. The study of perceptions has lagged far behind the study of attitudes, yet, as Hochschild convincingly argues, how people see their worlds almost certainly shapes their attitudes (and vice versa). She shows that people do not perceive their social worlds accurately. In particular, white Americans grossly overestimate what percentage of the total population is African American. (In Kuklinski et al.'s words [2000], the problem is that people are misinformed, not uninformed.[2]) It is likely that these overestimates

---

2 During the course of measuring the accuracy of citizens' welfare factual beliefs, Kuklinski et al. (2000) asked a nonrandom sample of political scientists the same questions. The political scientists did only slightly better than the average citizen.

shape people's ideological leanings as well as some of their domain-specific attitudes.

Simply examining the interrelationships among a set of attitudes cannot reveal the kind of misperception that Hochschild reports in her chapter; a distorted view of societal conditions could be shaping them all. If the purpose is to ascertain the validity of people's attitudes, the study of perceptions – a glaring void in the political attitudes literature – necessarily must become an integral part of it. Hochschild has taken a big step in the right direction.

Let's turn now to policy-specific attitudes, which pollsters routinely report during the heat of a congressional policy debate. Scholars and practitioners alike would like to know how well grounded such policy-specific preferences are. But by what criteria does one make such a judgment?

We have already discussed one criterion: the accuracy of people's perceptions of the social world. When people evaluate a proposal to limit welfare to two years, for example, do they start with a correct portrayal of who is on welfare and for how long? Do they come close to knowing what the average annual welfare benefit is? Unfortunately, politicians and the media disseminate such factual information sparsely – so sparsely, in fact, that political scientists often fail to know the right answers.[3]

Citizens receive most of their information in the form of political arguments. The core of these arguments typically consists of simplistic predictions: "If NAFTA passes, you will lose your job"; "If NAFTA does not pass, you will lose your job." In the abstract, we prefer that people know the arguments on both sides of a policy debate. That said, it is not self-evident that knowing such predictions renders better grounded preferences. When citizens form attitudes on the basis of elite arguments, they do little more than put more faith in one side than in the other. That is what Jones did when she reacted to predictions about the loss of choice in health care.

Consider, in contrast, small-town citizens deciding whether or not to build a new school. They make their decision on the basis of tangible evidence. They see that the existing school is overcrowded; that continuing to use it will require costly repairs; and that the property on which the new school would be built is easily accessible. They participate in a deliberative process. After the school is built, they observe problems directly. In short, they "see" and "get their hands on" concrete information.

---

3 We use the terms interchangeably, knowing that each term warrants a unique definition. Doing so facilitates our discussion and does not change our argument.

James H. Kuklinski and Jennifer Jerit

What does the general lack of concrete information about national policy imply for citizens' policy-specific attitudes? At a minimum, it implies that even the relatively well informed often form preferences on the basis of little concrete information. That the relatively well informed display more stability in their attitudes than the less informed is important to know; it does not mean that either set of attitudes stands on a strong foundation.

Diamond offers what, on its surface, might be a way out of this conundrum. People's attitudes might not be well grounded, but citizens supposedly know what is and is not acceptable to them. In other words, scholars have been conceiving attitudes improperly, especially in light of the citizens' plight. People might not be able to offer politicians point-specific indicators of their preferences, but they can tell their elected officials what is off limits. And this is "all the attitude" they need.

Diamond offers a compelling case for his perspective. Anyone who reads his chapter will find much that rings true. And he offers a set of implications that helps to clarify what are anomalous political phenomena from the currently dominant perspective. To use latitudes of acceptance, however, requires that individuals know a lot about a range of policy options. Rarely is that the case. Indeed, we have been arguing that in lieu of a heroic search for information, it cannot be the case.

Zaller's top-down view of representative democracy and his related considerations model thus appear to be right on the money with respect to policy-specific attitudes. If citizens must rely on politicians and the media for their information, and if that information takes the form of argument and unsubstantiated prediction, then grounding will necessarily be thin. And the considerations that come to people's minds as a result of elite arguments indeed will vary over time. We want them to; the alternative is that people not listen at all. If the alternatives are Jones and Smith, we take Jones.

But this still leaves the nagging question: do people possess true attitudes or, to use our suggested terminology, well-grounded attitudes? In ending, we suggest that this is not quite the right question. The question we need to ask precedes this one and includes a crucial conditional: *in light of the inherent limitations that citizens face*, what should we construe as a reasonably well-grounded attitude? At least with respect to policy proposals, can there be such a thing?

We don't have final answers. We do believe that studies of citizen performance should recognize that the very nature of representative democracy fosters a citizenry whose attitudes toward policy will be poorly grounded. When evaluating citizen performance, then, we might want to take the preceding conditional into account and thus rethink the standards we use to judge that performance. This is not a plea to lower standards; it is a plea to make them more realistic.

References

Converse, P. E. 1964. "The Nature of Belief Systems in Mass Publics." In D. Apter, ed., *Ideology and Discontent*. New York: Free Press.
——— 1970. "Attitudes and Non-Attitudes: Continuation of a Dialogue." In E. R. Tufte, ed., *The Quantitative Analysis of Social Problems*. Reading, MA: Addison-Wesley.
Kahneman, D., P. Slovic, and A. Tversky, eds. 1982. *Judgment Under Uncertainty: Heuristics and Biases*. New York: Cambridge University Press.
Kuklinski, J. H., P. J. Quirk, J. Jerit, D. Schwieder, and R. Rich. 2000. "Misinformation and the Currency of Democratic Citizenship." *Journal of Politics* 62: 791–816.
Kuklinski, J. H., and N. L. Hurley. 1994. "On Hearing and Interpreting Political Messages: A Cautionary Tale of Citizen Cue-taking." *Journal of Politics* 56: 729–751.
——— 1996. "It's a Matter of Interpretation." In D. M. Mutz, P. M. Sniderman, and R. Brody, eds., *Political Persuasion and Attitude Change*. Ann Arbor: University of Michigan Press.
Tversky, A., and D. Kahneman. 1982. "The Framing of Decisions and the Psychology of Choice." In R. Hogarth, ed., *Question Framing and Response Consistency*. San Francisco: Jossey-Bass.
Wilson, T., D. S. Dunn, D. Kraft, and D. Lisle. 1989a. "Introspection, Attitude Change, and Attitude–Behavior Consistency: The Disruptive Effects of Explaining Why We Feel the Way We Do." In L. Berkowitz, ed., *Advances in Social Psychology*, Vol. 19. Orlando, FL: Academic Press.
Wilson, T., D. Kraft, and D. S. Dunn. 1989b. "The Disruptive Effects of Explaining Attitudes: The Moderating Effect of Knowledge About an Attitude Object." *Journal of Experimental Social Psychology* 25: 379–400.
Wilson, T., and S. Hodges. 1991. "Attitudes as Temporary Constructions." In A. Tesser and L. Martin, eds., *The Construction of Social Judgment*. Hillsdale, NJ: Erlbaum.
Zaller, J. R. 1992. *The Nature and Origins of Mass Opinion*. New York: Cambridge University Press.

Part IV   Political Values

Introduction

JAMES H. KUKLINSKI

The study of values has been cyclical. It reached its nadir in the early 1970s, fell from prominence following a barrage of criticisms, and now once again is gaining momentum. Most of the criticisms focused on two aspects of the values research. First, scholars disagreed on which values were fundamental, leaving them open to the the argument that if they cannot agree, they probably do not know what values are. Second, and closely related, researchers measured values in a variety of ways, from open-ended questions to simple lists to rank orderings. As a result, exchanges often dwelled on what became narrow questions about measurement.

The recent revival of values is readily explainable: they are so basic to human thought that they simply cannot be ignored. Not everyone holds political attitudes, but presumably everyone has ideas about right and wrong, good and bad, how people should conduct their lives, and the like. One obvious question for political scientists is, to what extent, and how, do people use their values to reach political judgments? Two of the chapters in this part address this question, using data collected for just this purpose. One introduces a value – humanitarianism – that is central to judgments about welfare policy. This value, the authors show, helps to explain why most Americans endorse the welfare state even though they openly criticize the policies that undergird it. The other chapter challenges what is perhaps the most cherished and widespread assumption in American political thought: individualism is a value to which nearly all Americans subscribe. The reported evidence reveals not only that support for some aspects of individualism is low overall, but also that support varies markedly across social groups.

The third chapter takes the discussion in a different direction. Here the focus is not political values, as traditionally defined, but political value judgments. The change in terminology is not trivial; whereas political values are statements of what the person qua individual wants and deems important, political value judgments make claims about what *anyone* would want or what *we*, the community, would want. Political value judgments demand public justification; personal values do not.

The study of values simultaneously engages psychology and philosophy, the former to understand how and how much values influence political choices, the latter because values are by definition normative. Not surprisingly, then, the three chapters included in this part, as well as the two commentaries (one by a psychologist, the other by a political philosopher), have a much stronger philosophical-psychological bent than any of the other chapters in this volume.

CONCEPTIONS

Feldman and Steenbergen begin with a puzzle: Americans ideologically oppose the idea of a welfare state, yet endorse it in practice. How, the authors ask, can so many people be so suspicious of the welfare state while at the same time supporting its specific policies?

Might the answer be egalitarianism? Research has shown, after all, that it produces support for welfare policies. No, Feldman and Steenbergen conclude. Only a small portion of Americans endorse egalitarianism, defined as support for equal outcomes. Moreover, in-depth interviews have shown that supporters of welfare rarely justify their support in terms of egalitarianism. And finally, if egalitarianism were the driving force, people would not reject redistributive policies as overwhelmingly as they do.

In the authors' view, the answer lies elsewhere, in the form of humanitarianism. Humanitarianism is the belief that one has a responsibility to help others, to come to their assistance in time of need. The "humanitarian sensibility," Feldman and Steenbergen note, has long been a part of American rhetoric and writing but has not been part of empirical research.

Humanitarianism differs fundamentally from better known values such as egalitarianism and limited government. The former, unlike the latter, is relational. It defines a relationship between an individual and other members of society. Thus, for example, forgiveness is a relational value, while broad-mindedness is not. Forgiving requires a relationship, but one can be broad-minded even in isolation.

Because relational values entail some kind of relationship between an individual and others, they evoke an affective response, whereas nonrelational values do not. If one cares for those in distress, then he will feel sympathy for them; he will also feel morally wrong and thus guilty if he neglects them.

Feldman and Steenbergen use data they themselves collected to test the effects of humanitarianism as well as those of three traditional values – egalitarianism, limited government, and economic individualism – on support for welfare policy. Because humanitarianism is a relational value and the others are not, the authors hypothesize that the former's relationship to policy preferences will differ from the others. After completing an impressive set of validity checks, they first show that, contrary to their hypothesis, both egalitarianism and humanitarianism are strongly related to support for general spending on social welfare programs. However, the referents in the survey questions are broad – spending on the poor, on welfare, on food stamps, and so on. Such global descriptions, the authors argue, don't allow researchers to make inferences about which principles are associated with egalitarianism and which with humanitarianism.

They next consider how the four values influence responses to two other more specific survey items. The first explicitly refers to paying taxes and therefore emphasizes redistribution. The second refers only to helping the needy; its emphasis is on providing a safety net. Feldman and Steenbergen's analysis shows that egalitarianism is strongly related to responses to the redistributive item and not at all to the safety net item. Humanitarianism, on the other hand, is associated with responses to both items. And whereas support for egalitarianism is strongly related to support for government intervention generally, humanitarianism is, at best, marginally related.

Finally, the authors consider how people judge the fairness of their own tax burden. They find that humanitarianism scores are strongly related to dissatisfaction with personal taxes, while egalitarianism is not related at all. In other words, people apparently see the welfare component of their taxes going to assist the disadvantaged rather than as a mechanism of redistribution. Those who hold little sympathy for the plight of the disadvantaged express much dissatisfaction with their own taxes, while the sympathetic do not. In contrast, strong opponents of egalitarianism are just as likely as strong supporters to describe their own taxes as fair.

Overall, then, when Feldman and Steenbergen turn to finely tuned measures of welfare support, they find empirical support for their hypothesis. It is people's sympathy for the poor that motivates them to support the welfare state.

Whereas Feldman and Steenbergen introduce a new value into their empirical research, Markus revisits an old and revered one: American individualism. If scholars were to choose one value to describe American society, most would choose this one. Indeed, Markus cites author after author who refers to individualism as the most fundamental of

American values. He also notes that most of the writings have not offered systematic empirical evidence. All the literature notwithstanding, one cannot confidently say whether the supposedly widespread individualism is real or a product of a well perpetuated myth.

Markus conducts his analysis using data included in a 1989 American National Election Studies (ANES) Pilot Survey (seven of the items were also used in the 1990 ANES Survey). The survey items tap three distinct aspects of individualism: individual autonomy, self-reliance, and limited government. The first refers to independence of thinking; the second to the idea that people should take care of themselves, especially economically; and the third to the notion that government should limit its activities to basic protections.

Markus's first finding – an important one – is that respondents are much more likely to answer the value questions than they are routinely to answer the ideological self-identification item included in the ANES and other surveys. Apparently people relate more easily to basic values than to the liberal versus conservative understanding that pervades national politics. Markus devotes most of the remainder of his chapter to his second result: contrary to conventional wisdom, Americans vary considerably in their support of individualism. In fact, a majority *rejects* the individualistic principle on four of his seven items. For example, only three in ten respondents agree that "the less government the better." Only 20% endorse the idea that "poor people are poor because they don't work hard enough."

The demographic correlates of individualism underline the distinctiveness of the three elements that Markus identifies. African Americans and Latinos express considerably less support than whites for the idea of limited government. Females, the young, the less educated, and the less well-to-do reject limiting the scope of government more than men, the well educated, and the well-to-do. All this said, it should be duly noted that three-fourths of *all* respondents decline to endorse a limited government.

A similar overall distribution exists on the autonomy scale, and, again, whites display discernibly more support than African Americans and Latinos. The most dramatic difference is educational: the college educated are four times more likely than those with less than a high school education to take the pro-autonomy position. Education also best predicts support for self-reliance, with the highly educated having the lowest average scores on the scale. Finally, partisanship (Democrat–Republican) and ideology (liberal–conservative) are strongly linked to support for a limited government.

It is one thing to hold or reject basic values; it is quite another to use them to evaluate political phenomena. Markus finds that people do indeed draw on them when evaluating policy and political leaders. Interestingly, the different components of individualism tend to come into play in different domains: limited government on welfare spending, autonomy on civil liberties, and self-reliance on affirmative action. Apparently people not only employ values, they do so in highly selective ways.

The preceding two studies tie values closely to the person who holds them. Stoker, on the other hand, begins with the premise that political debate and controversy emerge interpersonally. Her conception of values, which she labels "political value judgments," reflects that premise. Whereas scholars normally construe values as "what is good for *me*, the individual," Stoker proposes that values should be viewed as either making objective claims about worth – what would *anyone* deem valuable? – or expressing intersubjective evaluations – "what is good for *us*?" In other words, political value judgments require that individuals detach (at least to some degree) their own desires and preferences from judgments about values.

If people's evaluations of political objects emerge from political value judgments, an empirical question that Stoker addresses later, then scholars need to know how such judgments are justified. This requires, in turn, analytical schemes to map the justifications. Drawing heavily on work in political philosophy, Stoker offers two schemes. The first is consequentialist/nonconsequentialist. Consequential judgments evaluate the consequences of policy for the entire collectivity once it is implemented. Values drive the assessment: will the consequences be good or bad? As the question implies, consequential reasoning requires prospective judgments, that is, predictions about the future. Nonconsequential judgments focus on the constitutive features of a policy (often the process). Principles are central. Was the process right? Did the participants follow proper procedures? Nonconsequential reasons are found concurrently or retrospectively. Thus, for example, a consequentialist ponders the future deterrence consequences of the death penalty, while a nonconsequentialist worries, right now, whether taking a human life is morally acceptable. Stoker hypothesizes that people vary systematically in their tendency to use one or the other justificatory considerations.

Stoker's second scheme is partial/impartial. Partial judgments refer to what is happening to me or my group, impartial judgments to all the people or each person. Although self-interest obviously motivates the former, partial justifications require some kind of universalizing move: "my action is justified because every individual should have the right to express himself." As this statement implies, the universalizing move ties self-interest to questions of fairness. Stoker speculates that people rarely articulate partial arguments (except, perhaps, in court proceedings) and that others give the arguments little weight in any case.

Stoker acknowledges the challenge of applying her schemes empirically. People and governments face a variety of problems. There are a multiplicity of things to which people can attribute value. In short, the world is complex. Thus, trying to apply her schemes deductively is destined to fail. Rather, the researcher should begin by examining specific cases, with particular goals and particular conflicts that arise in each context. The initial empirical research, in other words, necessarily must be inductive.

Following her own advice, Stoker offers two empirically based illustrations. The first looks at public opinion on affirmative action. The point of departure is the Supreme Court decisions on affirmative action. Stoker notes that in the area of employment, the Court has supported preferential treatment only in cases where a particular business or governmental unit has been found to be engaging in discriminatory practices. The Court justifies its decisions in these specific cases by invoking a principle of compensatory justice: preferential treatment policies should be used to remedy wrongs where instances of racial discrimination have been identified (but, again, not to remedy the effects of supposed societal discrimination).

To ascertain whether people think in compensatory justice terms as the Supreme Court has defined them, Stoker designed an ingenious experiment that was incorporated into a national survey of racial attitudes. One-third of the sample were simply asked whether they thought large companies should be required to give a certain number of jobs to blacks. A second group received much the same question, except that the reference was to large companies where blacks are underrepresented. The final third of the sample were asked whether companies with discriminatory employment policies should be required to give a certain number of jobs to blacks. People overwhelmingly oppose the requirement in the first two conditions but become much more supportive in the third – discrimination – condition. What people deem justifiable, Stoker concludes, is context-contingent; only in the presence of overt discrimination do large segments of the population, whites and black alike, support compensatory action. This finding of context specificity underlines Stoker's earlier call for inductive research that investigates individual cases in detail.

In her second study, Stoker asks why some citizens support, and others oppose, public policies that restrict or prohibit certain activities that people would otherwise engage in. Why, in short, do people vary in their attitudes toward social control? Stoker frames the problem in terms of liberalism, asking how a liberal (as defined classically) would decide when government intervention is justifiable. First, there must be a judgment that some conduct is immoral or morally wrong. If so, a liberal must still ask where the control over the decision belongs. Generally, liberals give great weight to individual autonomy, which they must balance against the importance of limiting the objectionable act. Finally, whether an act deemed wrong is justifiably subject to government intervention depends still further on the perceived nature of the harm – is it to oneself, to others, or to society at large?

Stoker proposes a general model that "specifies a process of judgment that is sensitive to the specific mode of conduct under investigation." In other words, while general, the model allows the influence of the three factors – moral judgment of the conduct, concern for individual autonomy, and perception of the nature of the harm – to vary across social policies (abortion, homosexuality, pornography, and euthanasia). In addition, the model includes an interaction between moral judgment and individual autonomy on the hypothesis that whether people's support for autonomy influences their attitudes toward social control depends on how immoral they believe the conduct to be.

As she did in the affirmative action experiment, Stoker finds that people evoke principles in a contingent, context-specific fashion. When people judge practices as unobjectionable, they do not even consider issues of individual autonomy. This holds true across all four policy domains. When an action is deemed morally wrong, however, both moral judgments of the conduct and questions of autonomy come into play. How much weight people give to the two factors – morality and autonomy – depends on the policy being judged. On homosexuality and pornography, opposition to government intervention remains firm regardless of how immoral they judge the conduct to be. Conversely, on abortion and euthanasia, moral judgments trump considerations of autonomy. While assessments of harm to society affect opinions on all four policy domains, their importance varies across them. Perceived harm to oneself influences opinions on homosexuality and euthanasia but not on abortion and pornography.

This study underlines two of Stoker's principal arguments. First, she shows that concepts from political philosophy, in this case liberalism, can indeed frame and inform empirical research. Second, no amount of deduction could have predicted the variability in reactions to the different policy domains; inductive research had to discover it. An obvious implication follows: building a general theory that includes context-specific contingencies will be a long, arduous endeavor, not impossible but painstakingly slow. Stoker recognizes and acknowledges this implication.

Each of the three studies presents evidence that people use their values to evaluate political phenomena. This stands in striking contrast to nearly four decades of research that has documented how *little* people draw on their political ideologies; indeed, from Converse on, the general theme has been people's inability to grasp the meaning of the liberal–conservative dimension. It seemingly would follow that much is to be gained from shifting the focus from ideology to basic political values. Presumably it is more profitable to study what people do than what they don't do. Values offer a more realistic accounting than ideology of how people go about evaluating politics.

Unfortunately, the study of values has its own potential shortcomings. Scholars have refused to abandon the study of ideological use among the general citizenry for a reason: liberal–conservative thought pervades national politics. If elites dance to an ideological tune, it makes sense to determine whether ordinary citizens can sing the song. In other words, ideological thinking is a natural standard by which to judge citizen performance. Values might be also, but the connection to elite rhetoric and behavior is not as self-evident. In his commentary, Rasinski, himself a student of values, cautions against a wholesale abandonment of economic and ideological models.

Ideological studies have another advantage: nearly everyone agrees on the concept and its measurement. The ANES, for better or worse, measures political ideology on a 7-point scale that is now the standard. Students of values do not enjoy such a luxury. Researchers adopt the same concepts but measure them differently. Markus, for example, identifies three elements of individualism. Important as this delineation is, chances are that not everyone who studies individualism in the future will employ it. Rasinski summarizes some of his own earlier work in which he identified an egalitarianism dimension. It reflects "the notions of human need, government responsibility for the well-being of citizens, and compassion for others." Human need and compassion for others? This sounds awfully close to Feldman and Steenbergen's conception of humanitarianism.

On the other hand, one might argue that it would be premature to agree on a set of values and their measurement. On this view, it is the very lack of closure that enriches the study of values. Take Feldman and Steenbergen's introduction of humanitarianism, for example. That people's sympathy for the plight of the downtrodden influences welfare attitudes quite independently of their thoughts about egalitarianism is intuitively satisfying and an undeniably important discovery. Agreement on a single set of values might have precluded it.

Rasinski's own work of the last 15 years is very much in the Markus–Feldman and Steenbergen mode. Whereas the latter examine the direct effects of values on policy choices, Rasinski uses as his dependent variable the application of fairness judgments to government policies:

how do citizens' values influence what they judge to be fair or unfair? He suggests that conceptions of social justice may bridge the gap between values and policy preferences, and thus recommends that researchers include fairness judgments as a mediating factor in their future work.

Rasinski also points to the complexity of the value construct. Are values to be considered attributes of a collective, representing some shared norm, or ideas located within individuals?

Markus and Feldman and Steenbergen adopt the second perspective, while Stoker emphasizes their collective, interpersonal nature. Rasinski recommends that the two perspectives be incorporated simultaneously. None of the three studies reported subsequently fully meets this (demanding) standard.

In political philosopher Orlie's eyes, if the purpose is to understand politics, then Stoker's approach to the study of values is preferable to that of the others. Values and opinions must be viewed as contestable and alterable through public deliberation. Markus and Feldman and Steenbergen measure personal preferences, she asserts, which are not properly public opinions. The one becomes the other only when people publicly justify their views. In measuring personal values and preferences as they do, survey researchers (presumably not limited to Markus and Feldman and Steenbergen) unwittingly adopt a political theory that endorses "thoughtless assertion." Mainstream public opinion research does not deal with the truly political.

Orlie contrasts Stoker's emphasis on public deliberation with Feldman and Steenbergen's emphasis on feelings, as incorporated in the concept of humanitarianism. Just what kind of citizen is he who is impelled by feelings, she asks? Her answer: a passive being who feels a sense of individual and collective inefficacy. What this type of citizen has to offer is reaction, not action. What Orlie does not ask is, just what kind of citizen is he who lacks feelings altogether?

Feldman and Steenbergen begin their chapter with a puzzle; Orlie poses one of her own: how do we explain the current dismantling of the welfare system in light of the pervasiveness of humanitarianism among American citizens? The answer, she believes, lies with the very fact that the values and preferences survey researchers measure *are* personal. They are not the outcome of interpersonal interaction. Not feeling bound to each other, and confronted with a crisis, we dismiss those individuals who are inessential to our lives. "Humanitarian feelings are perfectly compatible with reticence to help others who request our aid or with resentment of those who require it. In other words, those who express unqualified humanitarianism may constrict or contradict those expressions in practice, perhaps without even recognizing it."

Markus's study of individualism affords Orlie an opportunity to explore her theme further. Markus asks whether valuing independence and simultaneously supporting an activist government might not cause some psychological dissonance. Tocqueville, Orlie asserts, not only helps us to understand this apparent contradiction, but also identifies a political danger that lies behind it.

As Tocqueville saw it, the commitment to individualism disposes citizens to isolate themselves from the mass of others and withdraw into family and friends. Consequently, any particular citizen becomes reticent to respond to those in need or ask others for help. In lieu of interpersonal relationships, people increasingly look to government to help them. As government grows and serves more and more functions, individuals become even less inclined to form associations and more disinclined toward interpersonal relationships. An individualistic culture (which Orlie sees as an overbearing ideology) dictates a certain set of political institutions. Survey researchers unwittingly perpetuate these structures when they ask about personal values and preferences.

Markus's point, however, is that the presumed dominance of individualism simply is not today's reality. The majority of Americans reject many of individualism's basic tenets. As the nation becomes even more racially and ethnically diverse, support for individualism conceivably will dwindle even more. Whether institutions will change to accommodate a different set of values is the unanswered question. Those who work in the Markus and Feldman and Steenbergen mode will seek an empirically grounded answer. On the other hand, Stoker and especially Orlie will continue to believe that the study of the truly political lies elsewhere.

VALUES AND THE QUALITY OF POLITICAL JUDGMENTS

Nothing could be more satisfying to democrats than to find that people evaluate candidates and public policies in terms of their values. Values are people's normative views of life, and when they use them correctly to make political choices, they have made the penultimate connection between their personal lives and politics.

The crucial term here is "correctly." Suppose that an individual strongly opposes egalitarianism *and* equally strongly endorses humanitarianism. Suppose, moreover, that Congress is deliberating a policy proposal (as it did) that would allow welfare mothers and children to continue to receive Aid to Families with Dependent Children (AFDC) for two years, after which they become fully responsible for their own well-being. In light of the values the individual holds, what would be the correct position to take? Should he favor the policy or oppose it (assuming that he is familiar with it)? Once the individual has made a choice, is it good and correct by definition? Suppose that a second individual endorses the same values with the same intensity but chooses the opposite option. Are both choices correct? Or, if the values of the citizenry are overwhelmingly in a pro-humanitarian direction yet that same citizenry supports deep welfare cuts, what should we make of this collective decision?

The very strength of the study of values – people actually use them – also poses two challenges. First, individuals hold more than one value; sometimes their values come into conflict, sometimes they do not. In any event, there are no obvious standards that say how much weight people should give to each of the values. To be sure, scholars can estimate the relative influence of a set of values on policy preferences, as Markus, Stoker, and Feldman and Steenbergen all effectively do, but this does not address the issue of standards. Second, it is not always self-evident which values should translate into which policy preferences. Feldman and Steenbergen's fine-tuned analysis, for example, finds that humanitarianism and egalitarianism vary as a function of how the policy is described. Descriptively, this finding is valuable; which of the associations is the most desirable is not at all self-evident.

Focusing exclusively on political ideology and partisan identification, as scholars often do, avoids both problems. We know what the liberal and conservative stances are on issues and policies and thus easily can ascertain whether citizens choose in accordance with their self-proclaimed ideologies and party loyalties. The stronger the relationships between the two political orientations and policy preferences, as measured on a liberal–conservative scale, the better. It is that simple. Unrealistically simple, perhaps, but simple.

If a purpose of research on values is to evaluate the quality of political judgments, and surely it must be, scholars might seek to begin to offer standards by which to make such evaluations. All three authors implicitly offer what seem to be some reasonable criteria that, it is hoped, will become more explicit in the future.

If one adopts the stronger position that Orlie and Stoker take, then the task of setting standards in the spirit just suggested is beside the point. As long as values and preferences remain "private," as these two scholars define the term, they are substandard by definition. Good political judgments can only emerge from a deliberative process that is largely absent from contemporary American politics. But if the process is currently absent, what are students of public opinion to do? Abandoning the whole enterprise is not likely.

13

Social Welfare Attitudes and the Humanitarian Sensibility

STANLEY FELDMAN
MARCO STEENBERGEN

Some thirty years ago, Free and Cantril invoked the image of a psychological pathology to describe the state of American public opinion on matters of social welfare policy. In their words, public opinion displayed a "schizoid combination of operational liberalism with ideological conservatism" (Free and Cantril, 1967: 37). While many Americans expressed opposition to an expansive government and upheld the view that people should take care of their own problems, a large portion of these same Americans also indicated support for social welfare policies. Thus, while ideological backing for the *idea* of a welfare state was generally lacking, endorsement of the welfare state in practice – that is, at the level of policies – was strong.

More than thirty years later we still find much the same pattern in American public opinion. Numerous studies suggest that a majority of Americans favor many social welfare programs. Reviews of survey evidence show consistently high support for Social Security (Shapiro and Smith, 1985) and spending efforts by the government to reduce unemployment (Shapiro et al., 1987a). Government guarantees for jobs are met with less enthusiasm, although support for such policies is by no means lacking (Shapiro et al., 1987a). Even in the controversial domain of public assistance, support for a range of government programs has generally been high, indicating a general willingness of the American public to come to the assistance of the poor (Shapiro et al., 1987b; Weaver et al., 1995).

To be sure, welfare support in the United States is not as high as it is in countries with more developed welfare states (Smith, 1987). Moreover, public opinion toward the welfare state has shown considerable fluctuation and has on occasion been quite negative toward social welfare policies (see Cook and Barrett, 1992; Shapiro and Young, 1989; Stimson, 1991). However, the bottom line is that "in general, over the years the public has supported programs to help the needy . . . and this support does not appear to have diminished" (Cook and Barrett, 1992: 27), not even in the Reagan–Bush era (see Shapiro and Young, 1989). Even in the aftermath of welfare reform, surveys in 1996 and 1997 found that two-thirds of the U.S. public believed that the federal government did *not* make enough effort to serve the needs of the poor at the same time that a majority felt that the reforms ended a system that kept poor people in poverty (*The Public Perspective* 1998: 34–35).

This evidence of public support for social welfare policies is accompanied by serious misgivings about the welfare state. Survey evidence continues to show that Americans are quite *unwilling* to accept the welfare state in principle (McClosky and Zaller, 1984). The idea that government should play a role in socioeconomic affairs is met with a great deal of suspicion, as is the idea that the poor should be taken care of by society (see Sniderman and Brody, 1977). There also is some evidence that many Americans view the welfare state as unjust, believing that welfare recipients are unduly advantaged at the expense of the middle class (Jennings, 1989).

We are left, then, with a puzzle. If Americans are so suspicious of the welfare state and its philosophical underpinnings, why do so many champion its policies? That is, why does a clear majority of Americans support social welfare programs, including programs to assist the poor? In addressing these questions, researchers have typically focused on three core values of American political culture: egalitarianism, economic individualism, and limited government. In this chapter we will argue that these values cannot adequately explain welfare support in the United States. We will propose an alternative value-based framework that emphasizes the solidaristic ties between people. An empirical analysis of survey data on welfare support will show the utility of this alternative approach.

CURRENT VALUE-BASED EXPLANATIONS OF WELFARE SUPPORT

A popular explanation of welfare support in political science is to attribute attitudes toward welfare policies to a limited set of core values of American political culture. From this perspective, people will be more or less supportive of social welfare policies, depending on their endorsement of the values of egalitarianism, economic individualism, and (to some extent) limited government. McClosky and Zaller (1984: 265) provide a most eloquent summary of this theory of welfare support:

[T]he impetus toward welfare capitalism stems in great part from the democratic and egalitarian aspects of the [American] ethos. Yet other elements in the American creed – in particular, traditional notions of individualism, self-help, minimal government, and economic independence from the government – have functioned as a counter force to the growth of the welfare state and to the principle of government responsibility for individual well-being. We believe that the forms taken by the American welfare state and the attitudes Americans exhibit toward it can be accounted for only if these disparate cultural influences are given adequate consideration.

This emphasis on cultural values is reminiscent of earlier work in history and political science that sought to explain why the welfare state developed to a lesser extent in the United States than in Europe. For example, Rimlinger (1971) argued that the emphasis on individualism in the United States provided a major obstacle for the development of the American welfare state. In a similar vein, King (1973) faulted the value of limited government for the slow and incomplete development (by European standards) of social welfare policies in the United States.

Such attempts to attribute the structure of American social policy to the particular configuration of values in this country have always been problematic. As Krieger (1963) has pointed out, there have been welfare policies for most of the history of the United States, and these policies often have defined an extensive socioeconomic role for the government, in spite of Americans' resentment against an invasive state. More recently, Skocpol (1992) has shown that the United States was ahead of other nations in the implementation of many welfare policies, even if these other nations endorsed values that were much more favorable toward the development of a welfare state. These findings about the American welfare state are an anomaly from the perspective of value-based welfare theory as it is currently defined and show how incomplete this theory is.

This incompleteness extends into the domain of public welfare attitudes. In our view, the most important contribution that an emphasis on egalitarianism, economic individualism, and limited government can make is in accounting for the conflicting welfare attitudes that Americans hold. As Feldman and Zaller (1992) point out, it is understandable that Americans have ambivalent opinions about the welfare state, given a political culture that is itself torn between various ideological forces. One cannot expect fully consistent opinions in the mass public, that is, a reconciliation of operational and ideological reasoning, if the cultural foundations for such consistency are lacking.

The question remains, however, why Americans support social welfare policies as much as they do. In answering this question, current value-based explanations of welfare support do not take us very far. To be sure, analyses of mass survey data often show effects of egalitarianism and economic individualism, with the former producing support for social welfare policies and the latter opposition (Feldman, 1987; Kluegel and Smith, 1986). However, these effects beg more questions than they answer.

First, if egalitarianism generates welfare support, it can do so only for a small portion of the American public. Americans are not particularly supportive of the principle that outcomes should be equalized and indeed often reject it outright (see Gans, 1988; Kluegel and Smith, 1986; Lane, 1962; McClosky and Zaller, 1984; Verba and Orren, 1985). Thus, we continue to have a puzzle: why are so many Americans in favor of the welfare state when so few endorse egalitarian norms?

A second problem with the egalitarianism argument is that it does not appear to underlie people's reasoning about the welfare state. In-depth interviews with supporters of social welfare policies have typically found them grappling with the problem of reconciling their pro-welfare attitudes with economic individualism (see Hochschild, 1981; Reinarman, 1987). It is telling that these respondents have hardly ever resolved the conflict between attitudes and values by appealing to an egalitarian principle. On the contrary, the in-depth interviews often reveal that people do not seek equality but just a "fairer" distribution of resources (Hochschild, 1981). From a somewhat different methodological angle, Feldman and Zaller (1992) also found that supporters of the welfare state rarely justify their attitudes in terms of egalitarianism. Apparently, support for the welfare state does not depend on the ability to verbalize egalitarian values, even if surveys show a correlation between such support and egalitarianism.[1]

Finally, egalitarianism cannot account for the *nature* of the welfare support that we find in the United States. If egalitarianism truly were the driving force behind welfare attitudes, we would expect Americans to express support for precisely those policies that they tend to reject, namely, redistributive policies. These policies are logically most closely related to egalitarianism, while the link between egalitarianism and policies like Social Security and assistance to the poor is much more tenuous. The latter policies do not necessarily contribute to the goal of equality, yet they receive the widest support from the American public.

In conclusion, current value-based explanations of welfare support have severe limitations. While they can account for the conflicting feelings that Americans have about the welfare state, it is much less clear that they can also account for the fact that Americans tend to be

1 We have to keep in mind, of course, that people may not always be aware of the true motivations for their opinions (Nisbett and Wilson, 1977). In-depth interviews and open-ended questions about reasons for supporting the welfare state may therefore be somewhat misleading.

quite supportive of social welfare policies (despite all their misgivings). Hence it is time to consider alternative explanations of welfare support.

AN ALTERNATIVE VALUE-BASED APPROACH

It is not necessary to move away from a value-based approach in order to construct a more successful explanation of welfare support; we need only extend its scope. One of the major limitations of existing value-based explanations of the welfare state and public welfare attitudes is that they provide an incomplete characterization of the American political culture. Although egalitarianism, economic individualism, and limited government are undeniably important elements of the American political and social creed, they do not exhaust it. Among the neglected aspects of American political culture is the presence of an (at times strong) humanitarian sentiment (Katz and Hass, 1988).

Humanitarianism and the American Ethos

Humanitarianism, which we will for now define as the belief that people have responsibilities toward their fellow human beings and should come to the assistance of others in need, has always been an important element in American society. It was perhaps most visible in the antislavery movement, which, according to the historian Haskell (1985a, 1985b), is best interpreted as the outgrowth of a "humanitarian sensibility." Haskell (1985a: 342) argued that the antislavery movement reflected "changes the market wrought in *perception* or *cognitive style*." Capitalism instilled in people the sense that their actions had consequences, however remote, and that they were fully responsible for those consequences. As a result, "the very possibility of feeling obliged to go to the aid of a suffering stranger . . . was enormously heightened by the emergence of a form of life that made attention to the remote consequences of one's acts (or omissions) an emblem of civilization itself" (Haskell, 1985b: 562).

This humanitarian sensibility not only played a role in the issue of slavery but has also pervaded important segments of American economic thought. As Krieger (1963) points out, economic thought in the United States has generally been composed of both scientific and ethical arguments. With respect to the latter, it has not been just the ethic of self-reliance that has been prominent. On the contrary, as the work of Matthew and Henry Carey illustrates, economists have also been greatly concerned with the condition of human need, and often they have appealed to human generosity and the norm that the wealthy should help the poor (see Spiegel, 1960). It is important to note that these humanitarian appeals were not considered to be antagonistic to economic individualism. Rather, they reflected a belief that human beings sometimes need help, despite their own efforts to move ahead. Interestingly, this belief also comes through in many of the justifications that survey respondents now give for their support of social welfare policy (see Feldman and Zaller, 1992).

Humanitarianism could also be used as a descriptive label for many of the behaviors that Wuthnow (1991) reported in his *Acts of Compassion*. The case studies in voluntarism that he presents bear witness to the presence of a strong sense of caring for others in at least certain segments of American society. It should again be noted that this sense of caring exists against the backdrop of strong individualistic beliefs and is not considered to be inconsistent with them.

Clearly, then, humanitarianism is an important, albeit often neglected, element of American (political) culture. What is more, it has a great deal of relevance for social welfare policies. It should not be surprising that Feldman and Zaller's (1992) respondents often justified their pro-welfare attitudes in humanitarian terms, for historically there is a strong link between humanitarianism and poverty relief. This link goes back at least to the Roman Empire, when attempts to help the poor were often founded on *humanitas*, the Latin word for sympathy for the weak (see Hands 1968; Morris 1986).

Given the historical link between humanitarianism and poverty relief, we want to make a strong case for the inclusion of this value in studies of public welfare attitudes.[2] Doing so makes sense not only because humanitarianism is part of American political culture, but also because it fits much more easily in the capitalist order than egalitarianism (see Haskell, 1985a, 1985b). As such, it may help us better understand support for social welfare policies within the confines of a capitalist economic system.

Relational Values

Our emphasis on humanitarianism, however, is more than just the addition of another value to existing value-based explanations of welfare

2 De Swaan (1988) has argued against an understanding of the welfare state in humanitarian terms. He claims that humanitarianism is characterized by a sense of personal responsibility for other people's well-being. However, the welfare state does not provide citizens with a chance to be personally involved with the care of others, since poverty relief is considered to be the task of the state and not of citizens. We believe that this analysis is incomplete, as it does not permit efficiency considerations. Humanitarians may prefer to help the poor themselves but may nonetheless opt for a welfare state because this is a more efficient means to combat poverty. For a more elaborate discussion of this point, see Steenbergen (1994).

support. Humanitarianism exemplifies a class of values that is quite distinct from egalitarianism, economic individualism, or limited government. It is important to consider the properties of this class of values, which we will refer to as "relational" values.

We distinguish relational values from nonrelational values. The key to this distinction is whether a relationship is implied by the value or not. A relational value defines a clear relationship between an individual and other members of society (cf. Lau, 1989).[3] Usually this relationship is of a conative nature: it defines a desired action that is targeted to some person or group. In other cases, the relationship may place greater emphasis on an affective bond. In either case, however, the critical point is the relationship between two or more actors. To put it differently, relational values give content to a relationship; if the relationship is not defined, it makes no sense to describe a relational value.

Nonrelational values do not specify such a relationship between individuals. These values come in two varieties. First, whether a relationship exists or not may be irrelevant for a value (relational irrelevance). Second, the value may actually deny a relationship between people (relational denial). Values of this second type are clearly the opposite of relational values.

We can illustrate our distinction between relational and nonrelational values with two examples from Rokeach's (1973) value scale. First, consider forgiveness. This value by definition specifies a relationship between the value holder and other individuals, since forgiving is the act of pardoning others for their behavior. If someone holds this value, it means that he desires to be forgiving in his relationship with others (regardless of who these others are). Thus, forgiveness is a relational value.

Next, consider broad-mindedness – the desire to be open-minded. This is a nonrelational value. Broad-mindedness does not necessarily entail a relationship with others; it is a quality that can be aspired to by any individual, even one who lives in complete isolation. Thus, while broad-mindedness may apply to the lifestyles of certain groups, it does not depend on a relationship to these groups. On the contrary, people can aspire to broad-mindedness with respect to abstract philosophies that are dissociated from any particular living individual or group. In this sense broad-mindedness is relationship irrelevant.

---

3 By emphasizing "others" it is possible to reconcile our distinction between relational and nonrelational values with Kluckhohn's (1959; Kluckhohn and Strodtbeck 1961) claim that all values are relational. We agree that values should not be viewed as entities but as a relationship between a person and an object. Our distinction addresses whether this object is a person or not.

It should be noted that the distinction between relational and nonrelational values is comparable to one version of the distinction between social and personal values. Group psychologists, for example, have defined social values in terms of interpersonal situations (Levine and Moreland, 1989; McClintock and Keil, 1983; also see Gordon, 1975), implying that personal values pertain to a person's own situation.

We prefer our terminology over the social-personal value distinction, primarily because the latter carries multiple meanings in psychology and is therefore somewhat ambiguous. Indeed, there exists another version of the distinction between social and personal values that is orthogonal to our value classification. A number of studies have made a distinction between values that take the self as a referent versus values that emphasize society as a whole (Morris, 1956; Mueller and Wornhoff, 1990; Rokeach, 1973; Wojciszke, 1989). For example, personal independence entails a desired state for oneself (e.g., "I want to be independent"), whereas social independence refers to a desired end state for society (e.g., "people should try to be independent"). In our view, both relational and nonrelational values can be framed in personal and social terms. For example, forgiveness could be advocated for oneself (e.g., " I want to be forgiving") and for society (e.g., "people should be forgiving"). A similar argument can be made with respect to a nonrelational value such as broad-mindedness. It is important to keep these shifts in referents separate from shifts in the content of values, whence our introduction of the more novel terminology of relational and nonrelational values.

Having developed the links between our value typology and other typologies, it is now possible to make a distinction between humanitarianism, on the one hand, and egalitarianism, economic individualism, and limited government, on the other. Humanitarianism clearly is a relational value: it implies a sense of caring for other people's well-being and a belief that one should help others in need (Katz and Hass, 1988; *Random House Webster's College Dictionary*, 1992). Without question, a relationship is implied in these orientations. When a sense of caring is emphasized, an affective bond between people is postulated. When people are expected to help each other, a conative link is established as well. Without one or both of these links, the value of humanitarianism becomes meaningless.

By contrast, egalitarianism, limited government, and economic individualism are nonrelational values. The first two of these values exemplify relation irrelevance, whereas the last one exemplifies relation denial. Egalitarianism postulates that opportunities and outcomes should be equal in society, while limited government expresses the ideal of a minimalist state. Neither of these values refers to a relationship between two or more persons, at least not a relationship of an affective or a behavioral nature. On the contrary, what these values do is describe a preferred end state of society, not a desired type of social relationship.

The story is a little different with respect to economic individualism. Clearly, this value defines an ideal for social relationships, but this ideal turns out to be a rejection of the idea that people are interdependent. That is, economic individualism does not postulate a behavioral or affective link between two or more people, for in essence everyone should take care of his or her own problems. Hence economic individualism denies the existence of a relationship between people and should be classified as a nonrelational value.[4]

From this analysis, it should be quite evident that humanitarianism is distinct from egalitarianism, limited government, and economic individualism. This distinctiveness has important ramifications, since we believe that relational values operate differently from nonrelational values. The key to the differential operation of relational and nonrelational values is that the former require persons to take into account their relationship with others. The fact that relationships are quintessential to relational values implies that holders of these values are aware of others and their situation. In applications of relational values, this awareness becomes targeted to the specific individual or group that is under consideration.

If relational values entail the consideration of specific others, one of the consequences should be that sympathetic responses are easily evoked, for sympathy is an affective response to the situation of others. In the case of nonrelational values, affective responses such as sympathy should be much less prevalent because those values do not sensitize a person to the plight of others: they can be specified as abstract norms that are dissociated from social relationships. Thus, one prediction is that humanitarianism is more closely associated with sympathy for the poor than is egalitarianism. As a consequence, humanitarianism should provide a powerful basis for welfare support precisely because it sensitizes people to the plight of others.

Another implication of relational values is that they tend to specify a moral relationship between the holder and a target (Lau, 1989). In the case of humanitarianism, for example, the moral expectation is that the humanitarian comes to the assistance of others in need. The moral nature of many relational values may well mean that not living up to those values in specific situations produces guilt – if the values have the

---

4 This characterization of economic individualism is consistent with psychological research that has excluded individualism from the category of relationship values (Lau, 1989).

self as a referent (Rokeach, 1973). This can be a powerful motivation of behavior and may also predict why humanitarians may support social welfare policies as a mechanism to assist the poor. However, we will not test this proposition explicitly in this chapter.

Relational Values, Nonrelational Values, and Welfare Support

Our discussion so far suggests that relational values such as humanitarianism can provide a basis for welfare support alternative to nonrelational values like egalitarianism. Thus, not considering relational values in studies of social welfare attitudes may well produce model misspecification. This is only part of the story, for humanitarianism and egalitarianism not only provide separate bases of welfare support, they should not even be highly collinear. Moreover, the type of welfare support that these values produce is also distinct.

If humanitarianism and egalitarianism were highly correlated, we would add little to our understanding of welfare support by considering them simultaneously. However, while it is reasonable to expect some relationship between them, egalitarianism and humanitarianism should be far from redundant predictors. According to our conceptualization, egalitarianism is a rule or norm that people may internalize from any number of socialization sources. Humanitarianism, on the other hand, is typically conceptualized as a more affective orientation, associated with feelings of sympathy and empathy. While it is certainly possible that people may be put in situations in which they develop both humanitarianism and egalitarianism (or do not), the extent to which this happens is an empirical question. We expect, at best, a modest correlation between these two dimensions.

Humanitarianism and egalitarianism should also have very different effects on attitudes toward social welfare policies. Consider two broad categories of welfare policies: redistributional policies and safety-net policies. While there may not be a crystal clear distinction between these two categories in practice, in general it is plausible (and almost tautological) to expect egalitarianism to predispose people favorably toward redistribution. Moreover, programs that may be needed to serve the goal of egalitarianism should require the government to intervene in the economy in a substantial and ongoing way because of the tendency of capitalist economies to produce unequal outcomes.

Humanitarianism should not be strongly associated with support for redistributive or regulatory programs but should result in considerable support for assistance to the poor (in the form of a social "safety net") by the very nature of the emotions it arouses. At the same time, it is not obvious that egalitarianism is a necessary or even a sufficient determinant of support for assistance programs since the redistributive component of these programs is minimal and of secondary importance. In sum, humanitarianism and egalitarianism should produce support for very different types of social welfare programs.

DATA AND MEASURES

Few existing survey data have the required level of detail to assess the impact of relational and nonrelational values on a variety of social policies that differ in their scope and underlying philosophy. We therefore collected our own data through a local survey sample that was administered by telephone in the New York metropolitan area early in 1992. We interviewed a total of 294 people from Nassau and Suffolk counties, Long Island, and from Brooklyn and Queens County in New York City,[5] with an overall response rate of 38%.[6] Because the sample was selected from one metropolitan area, no claims about the generalizability of the results are made. Nonetheless, the results can provide important clues about public welfare attitudes and orientations in the American public at large, especially since our sample – drawn from both the central city and surrounding suburbs – has a great deal of variance in key demographics and ideological characteristics.

The survey was constructed to meet three goals. First, it covers welfare attitudes at a more detailed level, not just asking respondents about their preferred spending levels for social programs but also asking them questions about the *structure* that certain programs should take. For example, for several domains we assessed general support for a program and the extent to which respondents would like to see redistributive elements enter the policy.

---

5 The sample is about equally split in terms of gender (50.3% female), is predominantly white (80%), moderate to conservative in ideology (24% liberals), and predominantly Democratic (32%) in party identification. Although no stratified sampling technique was used to select respondents who receive welfare benefits, 29% of the sample reported that they had received some form of welfare (mostly Social Security and unemployment benefits). Financially, the sample is well off (20% report incomes over $70,000), but the sample also includes a fair number of low-income respondents (13% have incomes below $15,000). About 25% of the respondents reported that they completed at least four years of college, making for a rather well-educated sample. Finally, the sample consisted mainly of respondents from the two Long Island counties (57.5%).

6 The response rate is low, in particular, because of the difficulty of getting respondents in Brooklyn and Queens. The number of refusals in these areas was rather large and refusal conversions generally lacked success. It is not clear in what ways these refusal patterns may have biased our results, but caution is clearly warranted.

Second, we asked questions on both the affective and cognitive mediators of welfare attitudes. Thus, beliefs about the welfare state were combined with emotional responses to poverty and people on welfare. Since previous research on affect and cognition has demonstrated the relative independence of these factors (see Abelson et al., 1982; Conover and Feldman, 1986; Ottati et al., 1992) – although not specifically for welfare attitudes – it is important to consider them in combination.

Finally, the survey measured both relational and nonrelational values. Specifically, scales for egalitarianism, individualism, limited government, and humanitarianism were included to provide information about the relative importance of these determinants of welfare attitudes. This again gives us insight into cognitive, as well as affective components of public opinion.

Since a humanitarianism measure was constructed for this study, we will use a second data set to check the scale characteristics of this new measure. The 1995 National Election Studies (NES) pilot study included seven of the eight humanitarianism items that were created for the New York area survey. These questions were included in a random half of the pilot study (n = 247). If we obtain similar scale properties from the national data, we will have greater confidence in the basic characteristics of the humanitarianism measure.

For the measurement of egalitarianism we adopted a fairly typical set of questions, drawn primarily from earlier NES surveys (see Feldman, 1987) and from the work of Kluegel and Smith (1986). The questions are all 5-point Likert-type agree–disagree items. The set of questions are balanced so that in half of the "cases" agree indicates support for egalitarianism while in the other half it reflects opposition. Table 13.1 provides the wording of each of the egalitarianism items, as well as the marginal distributions for these items.

What is striking about the egalitarianism questions is the degree of polarization in the American public that they reflect. On most of the items, about equal numbers of people agree and disagree with the statement. In addition, the distribution of the items illustrates how ambiguous Americans really are when it comes to equality. A majority of Americans (53.2%) views inequality as a major problem in the United States (item 1), and close to a majority (49.5%) do not agree that economic differences are justified (item 4). In addition, many Americans see some value in equality: 54.3% believes that greater equality will cause fewer problems for the country (item 2), while 69.4% feel that it will allow more people to have better lives (item 5). But Americans also seem to believe that it is not possible to do anything about inequality. Fully 81.1% of the respondents agreed that incomes "cannot be made

Table 13.1. *Frequency Distributions for Egalitarianism Questions*

	Strongly Agree	Somewhat Agree	Neutral	Somewhat Disagree	Strongly Disagree
1. One of the biggest problems in this country is that we don't give everyone an equal chance.	23.5	29.7	5.5	23.9	17.4
2. If wealth were more equal in this country we would have many fewer problems.	24.9	29.4	6.8	20.8	18.1
3. We have gone too far in pushing equality in this country.	11.7	20.7	6.6	26.6	34.5
4. All in all, I think economic differences in this country are justified.	12.8	27.0	10.7	26.0	23.5
5. More equality of income would allow most people to live better.	32.3	37.1	7.9	13.7	8.9
6. Incomes should be more equal because every family's needs for food, housing, and so on are the same.	16.9	25.9	5.9	29.3	22.1
7. This country would be better off if we worried less about how equal people are.	16.0	26.8	5.9	23.0	28.2
8. Incomes cannot be made more equal since people's abilities and talents are unequal.	44.5	36.6	2.8	14.1	2.1

more equal since people's abilities and talents are unequal" (item 8), suggesting a meritocratric principle for the distribution of wealth that no one can really interfere with. It is, then, not at all surprising that only about half of the people (42.8%) feel that incomes should be made more equal because of the basic correspondence of people's needs (item 6).

When the endorsement of humanitarian principles is considered, a different picture emerges (Table 13.2). Americans say that they are quite willing to go out of their way to help others and that they deem the well-

Social Welfare Attitudes

Table 13.2. *Frequency Distributions for Humanitarianism Questions*

	Strongly Agree	Somewhat Agree	Neutral	Somewhat Disagree	Strongly Disagree
1. One should always find ways to help others less fortunate than oneself.	53.4 (49.8)	42.9 (43.7)	2.4 (.0)	1.0 (4.1)	0.3 (2.0)
2. It is better not to be too kind to people because kindness will only be abused.	7.9 (10.9)	23.4 (18.6)	5.5 (.0)	29.9 (29.6)	33.3 (40.5)
3. The dignity and welfare of people should be the most important concern in any society.	43.0 (51.4)	37.5 (34.4)	6.5 (.0)	8.5 (9.7)	4.4 (4.1)
4. People tend to pay more attention to the well-being of others than they should.	5.8 (6.5)	15.8 (14.2)	4.5 (.8)	44.0 (46.6)	29.9 (31.6)
5. All people who are unable to provide for their basic needs should be helped by others.	31.7 (39.7)	54.6 (42.1)	5.7 (.4)	8.2 (14.2)	2.7 (2.8)
6. One of the problems of today's society is that we are often too kind to people who don't deserve it.	14.5	26.9	7.2	28.6	22.8
7. A person should always be concerned about the well-being of others.	47.8 (55.5)	41.3 (35.6)	4.4 (.0)	4.8 (6.5)	1.7 (2.0)
8. I believe it is best not to get involved in taking care of other people's needs.	8.7 (8.5)	24.1 (30.4)	8.4 (.4)	34.3 (31.2)	24.5 (27.9)

Note: The first set of frequencies for each item is from the 1992 New York Metropolitan Area Survey. The second set of frequencies, in parentheses, is from the 1995 National Election Studies Pilot Study.

being of others to be of the utmost importance.[7] Support for humanitarianism tapers off only when reference is made to negative qualities of the recipients of their benevolence – for instance, an inclination to abuse

---

7 We should keep in mind, of course, that there are limitations to the interpretation of frequency distributions of survey questions. It is, for example, possible that social desirability effects may have increased the frequency of humanitarian responses.

kindness (item 2) or the lack of desert (item 6). Even in these cases, however, there remains remarkably high support for a humanitarian orientation. As can be seen in the second set of frequencies in Table 13.2 (those in parentheses), there is a striking similarity between the distributions from the New York sample and those from the 1995 NES Pilot Study. The substantial support for humanitarianism we see in these data is not, therefore, a function of an odd local sample. If anything, there is a bit more humanitarian sentiment in the national data.

The ambivalent status of egalitarianism and the greater support for humanitarianism provide an interesting match to the nature of the American welfare state. Given the considerable conflict over equality, it may be more than coincidental that redistribution is not a very prevalent feature of the American welfare state (cf. Plattner, 1979). On the other hand, the prevalence of humanitarian sentiments makes it very plausible that there is basic support for a safety-net type of welfare state in this country. At a macroscopic and admittedly impressionistic level, then, there seem to be important links between nonrelational values (egalitarianism), relational values (humanitarianism), and the welfare state. Whether such links also emerge at the individual level is still an open question, one to which we will turn next.

RESULTS

The humanitarianism and egalitarianism items have very similar scale characteristics in the New York area sample. The mean interitem correlation is .27 for egalitarianism and .23 for humanitarianism. This produces reliability estimates (coefficient alpha) of .75 for egalitarianism and .69 for humanitarianism. The internal consistency of the humanitarianism items is significantly higher in the NES pilot study. The mean interitem correlation is .33, yielding a reliability estimate of .80. As we expected, the two egalitarianism and humanitarianism scales are only modestly related; the simple correlation is .23 in the New York sample. Since coefficient alpha is a lower bound for reliability (Greene and Carmines, 1980), the true correlation between egalitarianism and humanitarianism should be in the range of .23 to .31. The correlation between the humanitarianism scale and a similar egalitarianism scale in the NES data is .21. At best, these two dimensions are far from redundant.

The distinctiveness of egalitarianism and humanitarianism can also be established by examining the predictors of each dimension. Although our New York area survey was not developed with the goal of explaining these predispositions, we can get an initial indication of the types of variables that influence each. The top part of Table 13.3 shows the correla-

Table 13.3. *Correlations of Humanitarianism and Egalitarianism*

	Egalitarianism			Humanitarianism		
	All	High School[a]	College[b]	All	High School	College
Empathy	.04	−.01	.07	.23*	.24*	.22
Race	.25*	.37*	.17*	−.07	.03	−.13
Gender	.12*	.01	.15*	.08	.11	.08
Income	−.18*	−.16	−.17*	.14*	.10	.14
Age	−.16*	−.23*	−.15*	−.01	.02	−.02
Government benefits	.04	−.12	.09	−.06	−.03	−.06
Unemployed	.01	.05	−.01	−.06	−.02	−.07
Church attendance	−.14*	−.09	−.17*	.09	−.02	.15*
Education	−.11			.13*		
Economic individualism	−.30*	−.19	−.35*	−.11	.00	−.18*
Limited government	−.38*	−.14	−.43*	−.04	.07	−.09*
Party identification	.24*	.29*	.22*	.16*	.14	.17*
Ideology	.24*	.21*	.25*	.11*	.12	.12

* $p < .05$.
[a] Correlations for those with no more than a high school degree.
[b] Correlations for those with at least some college education.

tions of egalitarianism and humanitarianism with a series of exogenous variables.

There is a great deal of theory and research in psychology that links orientations like our humanitarianism scale to empathy (see Batson, 1991; Eisenberg, 1986; Hoffman, 1989). Given all of this research, we would doubt the validity of the humanitarianism scale if there were no relationship with empathy. On the other hand, there is no reason to believe that empathy should be related to the value of egalitarianism. We included eight questions in our survey to measure the trait of empathy.[8] These questions were drawn from a much longer scale developed by Mehrabian and Epstein (1972). Although our eight-item scale produces a coefficient alpha of only .51, there is a great deal of evidence that the scale the questions were drawn from is a valid measure of individual differences in empathy (see Bryant, 1987). As shown in Table 13.3, the empathy and humanitarianism scales are correlated at $r = .23$, while

8 See the Appendix for details of question wording.

there is no correlation at all between empathy and egalitarianism. The relative unreliability of the empathy measure makes it very likely that the true correlation is substantially higher than the value we estimate here. We also find small, but statistically significant, relationships between income, education, and humanitarianism.

What sort of people should be more egalitarian? Although Hochschild (1981) shows that poor people are not necessarily strong supporters of equality, it is reasonable to expect that minorities and the poor will be more egalitarian than whites and the wealthy (see Kluegel and Smith, 1986). The results in Table 13.3 support these expectations. The correlation of egalitarianism with race (nonwhite/white) is .25, somewhat larger than the correlation with income (–.18). In addition, younger people are somewhat more egalitarian than older people. It seems likely that the egalitarian environment of the 1960s and 1970s had a lasting effect on people socialized in those years, leading them to be more supportive of equality than the previous generations. Finally, increasing attendance at religious services is negatively related to egalitarianism.

These correlations indicate that humanitarianism and egalitarianism have very different relationships with a range of predictor variables. We can take advantage of these results to examine more closely the connection between these two predispositions. Does the modest correlation between them suggest that there might be some direct relationship between them? For example, perhaps increasing humanitarianism leads people to be more supportive of egalitarian principles. If we assume that empathy has a direct effect on humanitarianism but not egalitarianism, while age and race have direct effects only on egalitarianism, we can specify a pair of regression equations in which each dimension is allowed to influence the other and estimate the two equations via two-stage least squares analysis. As in any analysis of this sort, the estimates are only as good as the assumptions used to specify the equations. Therefore, these results should be viewed cautiously.

The estimates of these two regressions, shown in Table 13.4, suggest that there is *no* direct connection between humanitarianism and egalitarianism. The correlation between them appears to be spurious, the result of influences common to both. Otherwise, the regressions are in line with the simple correlations. Empathy is the only significant predictor of humanitarianism, while race and age are significantly related to egalitarianism. In addition, Catholics appear to be somewhat less egalitarian than members of other religious groups.

We can further illustrate how humanitarianism and egalitarianism differ by looking at their relationships with other values and political orientations. As shown in the bottom half of Table 13.3, egalitarianism is significantly related to party identification, ideology, and measures of

Table 13.4. *Predictors of Egalitarianism and Humanitarianism*

	Egalitarianism	Humanitarianism
Humanitarianism	.11	
	(.27)	
Egalitarianism		−.09
		(.25)
Age	−.0021*	
	(.0007)	
Income	−.0006	.0008
	(.0005)	(.0005)
Education	−.008	.004
	(.005)	(.006)
Race (nonwhite)	.11*	
	(.03)	
Gender (female)	.05	.05
	(.03)	(.03)
Receive gov't benefits	.04	−.02
	(.03)	(.03)
Unemployed	−.03	−.02
	(.03)	(.04)
Church attendance (per month)	−.011	.012
	(.007)	(.007)
Religion		
Catholic	−.12*	−.07
	(.04)	(.06)
Protestant	−.07	−.03
	(.04)	(.06)
Jewish	−.06	−.02
	(.04)	(.06)
Other	−.07	−.08
	(.05)	(.05)
Empathy		.28*
		(.09)
R^2	.23	.08

* $p < .05$. Entries are unstandardized regression coefficients, with standard errors in parentheses. The equations were estimated via two-stage least squares analysis.

economic individualism and belief in limited government (see the Appendix). Humanitarianism has much weaker correlations with all of these variables, especially the values of economic individualism and limited government. This is consistent with our assumption that egalitarianism is a nonrelational value, tied to other dimensions of this type. Humanitarianism, a relational value, is virtually unrelated to values like economic individualism, and limited government. Moreover, these results are not simply a function of low correlations due to unsophisticated respondents. Although the relationships between egalitarianism, economic individualism, and limited government do get stronger with increasing education (see Table 13.3), the correlations between humanitarianism, economic individualism, and limited government are still weak, even among people with more than a high school education. In contrast, it is interesting to note that the relationship between humanitarianism and empathy is completely unaffected by education.

These results are also important from a political perspective. As we might expect from the long history of political debate over equality (Verba and Orren, 1985), this value is associated with traditional lines of political conflict in the United States: party, ideology, individualism, and limited government. Humanitarianism is distributed almost independently of these same political forces. Those who oppose big government score as high in humanitarianism as those who favor government action. Liberals and conservatives barely differ on this dimension (a result that is consistent with the NES pilot study data). To the extent that humanitarianism is a basis of support for social welfare, it has little to do with traditional partisan and ideological cleavages.

Cognitive and Affective Reactions to Poverty

Poverty exists. How do people react to it? One strategy is to explain *why* some people are poor. They could be responsible for their own situation or structural barriers could prevent them from achieving economic success. This type of reaction involves a cognitive appraisal of the causes of poverty. People could also react to poverty emotionally or affectively. Specifically, they could feel sympathy for the poor and disadvantaged. Egalitarianism, a nonrelational value, should operate largely through cognitive processes. Humanitarianism, a relational value, is more likely to prompt affective reactions to the poor.

In order to test these hypotheses, our survey included two sets of questions. The first, drawn from Feagin (1975) and Kluegel and Smith (1986), presented the respondents with six possible reasons for poverty and asked them to judge how important each one is. Three of the items attributed responsibility to the poor themselves: lack of effort, loose morals and drunkenness, and lack of ambition and desire to get ahead. The other three items involved social barriers to success: the failure of society to provide good schools for Americans, the failure of private industries to provide enough jobs, and being taken advantage of by rich people. The second set of questions was designed to measure positive emotions toward the poor and homeless. Specifically, the questions first asked respondents to think about the homeless and report whether they feel sympathetic toward them, concerned about them, and worried about them. The same three questions were then asked about families in poverty.

Three separate summated scales were constructed to measure societal causes of poverty, individual causes of poverty, and emotional reactions to the poor and homeless. The three scales are almost uncorrelated with each other; the largest correlation is $-.17$, between sympathetic emotions and individualistic explanations of poverty. This is consistent with previous research that has found these two explanations of poverty to be largely independent (Kluegel and Smith, 1986) and emotions often to be uncorrelated with cognitions (Abelson et al., 1982; Conover and Feldman, 1986; Ottati et al., 1992).

In order to examine the connections between these reactions to poverty and egalitarianism and humanitarianism, a series of partial correlations were computed. Specifically, partial correlations were computed between the causes of poverty and emotional reactions scales and humanitarianism, egalitarianism, economic individualism, belief in limited government, party identification, ideological self-identification, race (nonwhite/white), gender, education (years), income (thousands of dollars), and age. In each case, the partial correlation between one of the three reactions to poverty measures and each of the other variables holds all other variables (except for the other poverty measures) constant. We use partial correlations here rather than regression in order to avoid making strong claims about the casual relationships between these values, on the one hand, and affective and cognitive reactions to poverty, on the other hand. The results are presented in Table 13.5.

Looking first at the correlations for social causes of poverty, the most prominent coefficient is for egalitarianism. Increasing egalitarianism is strongly associated with attributions of poverty to social factors. The correlation with humanitarianism is much smaller and, somewhat surprisingly, in the opposite direction (although it is not statistically significant). The picture is somewhat different for individualistic explanations of poverty. Increases in both egalitarianism and humanitarianism are associated with a decrease in individualistic explanations of poverty.

The results for egalitarianism tell a consistent story. The more people believe in equality, the more likely they are to hold society, but not the poor themselves, responsible for poverty. Thus, as we expected, egalitarianism is strongly related to people's understanding of the causes of poverty. However, a different pattern is evident for humanitarianism. People high in humanitarianism do not hold either the individual or society responsible for poverty. Refusing to blame the poor themselves, those high in humanitarianism do not see society to be the culprit. Are the poor simply unfortunate?

Table 13.5. *Partial Correlations of Affective and Cognitive Reactions to Poverty*

	Explanations of Poverty		
	Structural	Individual	Affect
Humanitarianism	−.09	−.17*	.28*
Egalitarianism	.30*	−.21*	.12*
Economic individualism	−.09	.06	−.16*
Limited government	−.11	−.07	−.10
Ideology (liberal)	−.06	−.16*	.07
Party identification (Democrat)	−.04	−.12*	−.00
Race (nonwhite)	.20*	.10	−.05
Gender (female)	−.08	.04	.10
Education	−.12*	−.11	.02
Income	−.12*	−.13*	−.00
Age	−.06	.01	−.05

* $p < .05$. Entries are partial correlations, holding constant all other variables in the list.

While egalitarianism has a much more pronounced correlation with the assignment of blame for poverty, humanitarianism is more strongly linked to sympathy for the poor and homeless. Increases in both predispositions are associated with greater feelings of sympathy, but it is clearly humanitarianism that has the larger partial correlation; its coefficient is almost twice the size of the coefficient for egalitarianism. The relatively weak relationship of humanitarianism with beliefs about poverty is thus balanced by its correlation with affective reactions to the disadvantaged. The negative relationship between humanitarianism and individualistic explanations of poverty is at least partially understandable as a reflection of the sympathy for the poor with which humanitarianism is associated.

Sources of Support for Social Welfare Policy

Having demonstrated that humanitarianism and egalitarianism are distinct dimensions, we now turn our attention to their influence on attitudes toward social welfare programs. Does this distinctiveness characterize the effects of these two predispositions on the public's attitudes toward welfare state policies? Our earlier discussion suggested that humanitarianism should be related to support for the basic principle of aid for the disadvantaged, while egalitarianism should come into play when redistributive elements become prominent. We begin our analysis where most studies do: accounting for variation in support for spending on social programs. We asked our respondents whether they thought spending on the poor, on welfare, on food stamps, for unmarried women with young children, on health care for the poor, and on shelters for the homeless should be greatly increased, somewhat increased, kept the same, somewhat decreased, or greatly decreased. Responses to these six questions correlated highly, and a scale constructed from them has an estimated reliability (coefficient alpha) of .81.

Table 13.6 shows the results of regressing the spending scale and the six individual questions on humanitarianism, egalitarianism, economic individualism, belief in limited government, party identification, ideological self-identification, a measure of racial stereotyping,[9] race (nonwhite/white), gender, education (years), income (thousands of dollars), and age. In all the following analyses, the dependent variables and all of the independent variables were rescaled to range from 0 to 1 (except where noted).

If we were to stop at this point, it would be easy to conclude that humanitarianism and egalitarianism are simply alternative sources of support for social welfare programs. Their coefficients in the overall spending equation are statistically and substantively significant and roughly equal in size. There is some interesting variation in the size of the coefficients across the separate questions, especially for the humanitarianism scale. It appears that humanitarianism has a more pronounced effect on preferences for spending on health care for the poor and shelters for the homeless as well as on general preferences on spending for the poor. The coefficients are smallest for AFDC and food stamps – the programs most associated with the label "welfare."

Besides humanitarianism and egalitarianism, economic individualism and belief in limited government are both significant influences on support for greater social welfare spending in total, although the coefficients rarely reach statistical significance in the equations for each spending question. Increases in both of these values are associated with greater opposition to social welfare spending. A good indication of the impact of humanitarianism and egalitarianism is the size of their estimated coefficients in comparison to economic individualism and limited government. Although the latter two are often advanced as explanations of attitudes toward social welfare policy, their effects are much smaller – on average about half or less – than the effects of both humanitarianism and egalitarianism.

While the social spending items we have just considered are common in studies of public opinion toward social welfare, they are limited in what it can tell us about the *nature* of support for welfare programs. The

9 See the Appendix for question wording.

Table 13.6. *Predictors of Support for Social Welfare Spending*

	More Government Spending For:						Spending Scale
	Poor	Welfare	Fd Stamps	AFDC	Health Care	Shelters	
Humanitarianism	.20*	.16*	.12	.11	.21*	.19*	.17*
	(.055)	(.070)	(.067)	(.074)	(.057)	(.073)	(.042)
Egalitarianism	.23*	.23*	.23*	.29*	.15*	.20*	.22*
	(.067)	(.085)	(.081)	(.089)	(.069)	(.088)	(.052)
Economic individualism	-.12	-.03	-.08	-.05	-.18*	-.14	-.10*
	(.064)	(.082)	(.078)	(.086)	(.067)	(.086)	(.050)
Limited government	-.09*	-.04	-.05	-.07	-.13*	-.11*	-.08*
	(.037)	(.047)	(.045)	(.049)	(.038)	(.049)	(.029)
Racial stereotyping	-.16*	-.16	-.28	.01	-.07	-.03	-.12
	(.081)	(.105)	(.100)	(.111)	(.086)	(.109)	(.064)
Ideology	-.02	.04	.10*	.07	.03	.04	.04
	(.042)	(.054)	(.051)	(.056)	(.044)	(.055)	(.032)
Party identification	.07	.13*	.03	-.00	.06	.03	.05
	(.043)	(.054)	(.052)	(.057)	(.045)	(.057)	(.033)
Race	.07*	.05	.02	-.03	.01	.04	.03
	(.030)	(.038)	(.036)	(.041)	(.031)	(.040)	(.024)
Gender	-.00	-.03	-.05	-.05	-.00	.02	-.02
	(.025)	(.030)	(.029)	(.033)	(.025)	(.032)	(.019)
Education	-.0124	.0089	.0072	-.0081	-.0027	-.0032	-.0017
	(.0050)	(.0064)	(.0061)	(.0067)	(.0052)	(.0066)	(.0039)
Income	-.0003	-.0009	-.0007	-.0001	-.0003	-.0004	-.005
	(.0004)	(.0005)	(.0005)	(.0005)	(.0004)	(.0006)	(.0003)
Age	-.0009	.0008	-.0000	-.0019*	.0001	-.0024*	-.0007
	(.0007)	(.0009)	(.0009)	(.0009)	(.0007)	(.0009)	(.0006)
R^2	.31	.18	.19	.14	.25	.20	.34

* $p < .05$. Entries are unstandardized regression coefficients, with standard errors in parentheses.

Table 13.7. *Predictors of Support for Social Welfare Policy*

	No Welfare	Tax the Rich	Social Security	
			Nursing Home Care	Increase Taxes
Humanitarianism	−.26*	.24*	.19*	.25*
	(.099)	(.091)	(.071)	(.090)
Egalitarianism	.15	.35*	−.07	.24*
	(.120)	(.109)	(.087)	(.109)
Economic	.29*	−.33*	−.02	.01
individualism	(.116)	(.105)	(.085)	(.106)
Limited	.26*	−.01	−.15*	−.01
government	(.067)	(.061)	(.049)	(.061)
Racial	.14	−.03		
stereotyping	(.149)	(.135)		
Ideology	−.04	−.04	−.01	.03
	(.075)	(.069)	(.055)	(.069)
Party	−.06	.08	−.03	.00
identification	(.077)	(.070)	(.056)	(.071)
Race	−.05	.01	.07	−.02
	(.05)	(.049)	(.040)	(.050)
Gender	−.00	−.09*	−.01	−.09*
	(.044)	(.039)	(.032)	(.040)
Education	−.0008	−.0175*	−.0179*	−.0205*
	(.0090)	(.0082)	(.0066)	(.0083)
Income	−.0002	−.0003	.0001	.0004
	(.0007)	(.0007)	(.0005)	(.0007)
Age	−.0004	.0008	.0013	.0007
	(.0012)	(.0012)	(.0009)	(.0012)
R^2	.14	.19	.11	.10

* $p < .05$. Entries are unstandardized regression coefficients, with standard errors in parentheses.

referents are broad and carry little information about the desired types of social welfare programs that the public wants. What *principles* of social welfare are associated with humanitarianism and egalitarianism? We asked our respondents to react to two statements to tap general beliefs about social welfare policy: (1) "All except the old and handicapped should have to take care of themselves without social welfare benefits" and (2) "Taxing those with high incomes to help the poor is only fair." Columns 1 and 2 of Table 13.7 show the regressions of responses to these two questions on the set of predictor variables.

Three variables are strongly related to responses on the "no welfare" statement: humanitarianism, economic individualism, and limited government. All have roughly equal effects in the expected direction. What is most interesting is that egalitarianism has *no* significant effect in this equation. In fact, the sign of the coefficient is wrong, although this should not be taken very seriously since we cannot reject the null hypothesis. The story is very different for the "tax the rich" statement. Egalitarianism now joins humanitarianism and economic individualism as substantial predictors of responses to this statement. Even though the focus of both statements is the provision of aid to the poor, the framing of the statements leads to very different patterns of results. We have just seen that egalitarianism is strongly related to support for government spending on social welfare. But it is not at all related to feelings about people having to take care of themselves without social welfare benefits. As soon as the issue is placed in more redistributive terms – taxing the rich to help the poor – egalitarianism becomes a pronounced factor again.

This same pattern can be seen in a pair of questions that ask about government assistance for the elderly: (1) "To what extent are you in favor of expanding Medicare to pay nursing home care and long hospital stays for the elderly?" and (2) "To what extent are you in favor of increased taxes to pay for long term care for the elderly?" As can be seen in Table 13.7, when the issue is framed simply in terms of expanding Medicare coverage, there is a significant effect of humanitarianism but no effect of egalitarianism at all. As soon as we include the prospect of raising taxes to pay for this, we again begin to observe the influence of egalitarianism.

Thus, as expected, the relationship of egalitarianism to support for social welfare policy appears to depend on the presence of a redistributive element to the policy being evaluated. In the two cases we've considered here, taxes provide the redistributive frame. In the two questions that deal simply with the provision of benefits to the needy, we get clear evidence of the effects of humanitarianism but *not* egalitarianism.

Government Responsibilities

The questions that we have looked at to this point have focused on the provision of social welfare benefits to people in need. But they have not dealt directly with the issue of the *scope* of the government's involvement in the economy. Since we are arguing that there is a connection between humanitarianism and safety-net policies and between egalitarianism and redistributional policies, we should find that the latter is a better predictor of a more general role of the government in the economy. On the other hand, there is no reason to believe that humanitarianism should be related to support for economic policies that go beyond those necessary to provide temporary assistance to the disadvantaged. A set of

Social Welfare Attitudes

Table 13.8. *Predictors of Government Responsibilities*

	Standard of Living		Reduce Income Differences		Regulate Businesses	
Humanitarianism	.15	.21*	−.08	.04	−.01	.09
	(.082)	(.081)	(.100)	(.103)	(.096)	(.098)
Egalitarianism	.32*		.67*		.53*	
	(.099)		(.122)		(.120)	
Economic individualism	−.15	−.22*	−.01	−.15	.01	−.10
	(.096)	(.095)	(.117)	(.120)	(.113)	(.115)
Limited government	−.17*	−.21*	−.04	−.14*	−.08	−.15*
	(.055)	(.054)	(.068)	(.068)	(.065)	(.066)
Racial stereotyping	.11	.07	−.04	−.11	−.04	−.10
	(.123)	(.124)	(.150)	(.158)	(.145)	(.149)
Ideology	.05	.063	.02	.05	−.04	−.02
	(.062)	(.064)	(.076)	(.080)	(.074)	(.076)
Party identification	.12	.141*	.12	.17*	.06	.09
	(.064)	(.065)	(.078)	(.082)	(.075)	(.077)
Race	.01	.043	.07	.13*	.03	.08
	(.045)	(.045)	(.055)	(.056)	(.053)	(.054)
Gender	.03	.03	−.01	.00	.08	.09
	(.036)	(.037)	(.044)	(.047)	(.043)	(.045)
Education	−.0233*	−.0244*	−.0292*	−.0316*	.0104	.0085
	(.0075)	(.0076)	(.0091)	(.0096)	(.0088)	(.0091)
Income	−.0005	−.0007	−.0014	−.0019*	−.0003	−.0007
	(.0006)	(.0006)	(.0008)	(.0008)	(.0007)	(.0008)
Age	−.0006	−.0011	.0008	−.0001	−.0017	−.0024
	(.0011)	(.0011)	(.0013)	(.0014)	(.0013)	(.0013)
R^2	.28	.25	.28	.20	.17	.10

* $p < .05$. Entries are unstandardized regression coefficients, with standard errors in parentheses.

three items included on the survey allows us to probe these relationships. The introduction to the questions was: "People have different ideas about the responsibilities of government. For each of the following please tell me if you think it should definitely be the government's responsibility, probably be the government's responsibility, probably not be the government's responsibility, or definitely not be the government's responsibility." The three questions were: (1) "Providing a decent standard of living for the unemployed?" (2) "Reducing income differences between the rich and poor?" and (3) "Regulating business?" Responses to these questions were regressed on the same set of predictors used in the previous analyses. The estimates are shown in Table 13.8.

While it may border on the tautological to find that egalitarianism is strongly associated with support for government responsibility to reduce income differences, large coefficients appear for providing a decent standard of living and regulating business as well. Egalitarianism does more than just lead to support for higher taxes on the wealthy. Increasing levels of egalitarianism are associated with support for greater government intervention in the economy – even beyond that necessary to provide assistance to people. In contrast, humanitarianism has only a marginal effect on the desire for government to provide a decent standard of living for the unemployed. Even if we exclude the egalitarianism scale from the "reduce income differences" equation, humanitarianism shows no effect at all, nor does it have any influence on regulating businesses.

The distinctive effects of egalitarianism and humanitarianism on social welfare attitudes are clearly shown in these results. Egalitarianism is associated with a desire for an active government to eliminate barriers to equal opportunity, tax the wealthy, guarantee a decent standard of living, and regulate business. Humanitarianism is associated with sympathy for the disadvantaged and support for social welfare benefits for the poor and elderly. Yet it is not at all related to policies to redistribute income or regulate the economy.

Satisfaction with Taxes

Although egalitarianism appears to be activated by the redistributive frame of taxes, it is worth considering how people understand the *current function* of taxes in the U.S. welfare state. Specifically, how do people judge the fairness of their *own* tax burden? This question provides another basis for examining the roles of egalitarianism and humanitarianism in generating support for social welfare policies. The relationship between these two values and dissatisfaction with personal taxes provides evidence of the extent to which people see the social welfare component of their taxes going to assist the disadvantaged as opposed to being used as a mechanism of redistribution. Specifically, if people believe that the function of their taxes is to redistribute income, those with a stronger belief in egalitarianism should be less dissatisfied with their taxes than those opposed to the principle. On the other hand, if the perceived end of taxation is to provide assistance to those in need, we should find dissatisfaction with taxes to vary inversely with humanitarianism.

We asked our respondents a standard question about their personal tax burden: "Do you consider the amount of income taxes that you have to pay as much too high, somewhat too high, about right, somewhat too low, or much too low?" Not surprisingly, only a handful of people thought that they were paying too little in taxes. We therefore combined these few people with those who thought their taxes were about right.

The result is a 3-point measure of dissatisfaction with taxes (high scores indicate greater dissatisfaction).

Due to the ordinal nature of the dependent variable, probit estimation was used to examine the determinants of dissatisfaction with taxes. Since we are interested in making inferences about the perceived redistributive and humanitarian purposes of taxes, it is dissatisfaction with taxes among the relatively affluent that is most relevant. We therefore present the probit estimates for the sample as a whole and then separately for those above and below the median income in our sample (approximately $37,000). To complete the specification of these equations, we also include responses to questions on trust in government and government waste.[10] The results are shown in Table 13.9.

Regardless of income level, we find that scores on the humanitarian-ism scale are significantly related (inversely) to dissatisfaction with personal taxes. This relationship is just as strong for those above the median income as for those below. Perhaps more surprisingly, we find no effect at all of egalitarianism. Even among the relatively wealthy, increasing levels of egalitarianism do not mitigate complaints about taxes. If these results are replicable, it therefore appears that Americans see their tax dollars as a means of assisting those in need and not as a mechanism of redistribution. Discontent with taxes thus decreases as people become more committed to humanitarian goals but not to egalitarian ends.

It is also interesting to note that there is no discernible effect of economic individualism on dissatisfaction with taxes, and belief in limited government has an effect only for those below the median income level. These findings reinforce the conclusion that dissatisfaction with taxes is based not on an ideological opposition to taxation, but on a lack of support for the goal of government assistance. It is particularly notable that, besides humanitarianism, the only other predictor of dissatisfaction with taxes among people above the median income level is gender (women are more dissatisfied than men).

CONCLUSIONS

The overwhelming majority of discussions and empirical studies of attitudes toward social welfare policy have relied on a traditional set of values to account for the variance in those attitudes. Egalitarianism,

10 Trust in government: How much of the time do you think we can trust the government in Washington to do what is right – just about always, most of the time, only some of the time, or hardly ever? Government waste: Do you think that people in government waste a lot of the money we pay in taxes, waste some of it, or don't waste very much of it?

Table 13.9. *Predictors of Opposition to Taxes By Income Level*

	All	Below Median	Above Median
Humanitarianism	−.91*	−.99*	−1.12*
	(.341)	(.498)	(.493)
Egalitarianism	.00	.49	−.07
	(.409)	(.659)	(.549)
Economic	−.38	−.78	.02
individualism	(.398)	(.663)	(.525)
Limited	.25	.73*	−.04
government	(.227)	(.350)	(.312)
Racial	.25	1.08	−.72
stereotyping	(.518)	(.760)	(.753)
Trust in	−.80*	−1.67*	−.15
government	(.321)	(.513)	(.434)
Government	.08	.006	.15
waste	(.141)	(.205)	(.206)
Party	.35	.70	−.07
identification	(.264)	(.395)	(.376)
Ideology	.17	.31	−.07
	(.259)	(.382)	(.373)
Race	.17	−.12	.19
	(.187)	(.278)	(.279)
Gender	.40*	.13	.49*
	(.150)	(.234)	(.210)
Age	−.0045	−.0064	−.0029
	(.0044)	(.0060)	(.0078)
Education	−.0083	−.0357	.0224
	(.0315)	(.0534)	(.0411)
Income	.0020		
	(.0025)		
N	271	127	144

* $p < .05$. Entries are maximum likelihood probit coeffients, with standard errors in parentheses.

individualism, and limited government have frequently been identified as bases of political conflict in the United States. While we do not dispute the relevance of these values for understanding public opinion, the dimension we have labeled humanitarianism may be a key overlooked factor in the origins of social welfare attitudes. The effects of nonrelational values like egalitarianism and individualism are typically seen in cognitive terms: what sorts of social mechanisms and outcomes are desirable? What has been missing (but see Conover, 1988) is the affective or emotional component: how do I feel about the disadvantaged?

Our analysis has shown that egalitarianism and humanitarianism are distinct dimensions. They are only modestly correlated, and there appears to be little or no necessary connection between them. More important, their effects on public opinion are dramatically different. Although both are associated with support for greater spending on social welfare, their distinctive effects become clear once we focus on different types of programs and the justification for those programs. Feeling sympathy for the plight of the poor and disadvantaged, those high in humanitarianism support policies to provide direct assistance. That support does not extend to programs to involve the government more deeply in the ongoing operation of the economy. Those high in egalitarianism perceive structural problems in society. The solution to these problems is not just to provide temporary assistance to people, but to intervene where necessary to deal with the structural issues. This may require the use of taxation, the regulation of business and markets, and ultimately the redistribution of income and wealth.

It is also important to note that while egalitarianism is related to traditional American value conflicts as well as to ideology and partisanship, humanitarianism is virtually orthogonal to these debates. The issues of progressive taxation, regulation, and redistribution are therefore a part of the familiar partisan-ideological conflict. However, the humanitarian basis of support for direct assistance for the needy is not a part of this partisan debate. According to our analysis, variation in humanitarianism is almost nonideological. Support for basic social programs must be understood apart from the conventional political terms we are used to. This is consistent with research by Wuthnow (1991), who finds that the willingness to volunteer time to help others is virtually unrelated to the belief in individualism.

We believe that students of the American polity may have been too narrow in their consideration of the various social forces and values that have shaped political debate. More specifically, they have unjustly neglected a critical element that has entered the creation of the American welfare state: humanitarianism. As a relational value, humanitarianism captures a set of ideals and sentiments that almost naturally lead to a safety-net type of social welfare state. The basic valuation of human life and the sense of obligation to help the poor, for example, find a natural expression in the assistance to the poor that is the hallmark of the welfare state, even in a society with a market economy. Thus, a consideration of a third dimension in people's social orientations, along with egalitarianism and individualism, can, at least at face value, help account for the characteristic nature of the American welfare state. It can also help us better understand why the public can, to this day, support government efforts to assist the poor at the same time that other values lead to a continuing suspicion of many public assistance programs.

APPENDIX

Empathy

5-point Likert items (1 = strongly agree, 5 = strongly disagree)

1. I tend to get emotionally involved with a friends' problems. (L)*
2. I am able to remain calm even though those around me worry. (H)
3. I am able to make decisions without being influenced by people's feelings. (H)
4. It is hard for me to see how some things upset people so much. (H)
5. I cannot continue to feel okay if people around me are depressed. (L)
6. When a friend starts to talk about his or her problems, I try to steer the conversation to something else. (H)
7. I often find that I can remain cool in spite of the excitement around me. (H)
8. I become very involved when I watch a movie. (L)

Economic Individualism

5-point Likert items (1 = strongly agree, 5 = strongly disagree)

1. Hard work offers little guarantee of success. (H)
2. Most people who don't get ahead should not blame the system; they really have only themselves to blame. (L)
3. Even if people are ambitious, they often cannot succeed. (H)
4. If people work hard, they almost always get what they want. (L)
5. When people fail at one thing after another, it usually means that they are lazy and lack self-discipline. (L)
6. Getting ahead in the world is mostly a matter of getting the breaks. (H)

Racial Stereotyping

Now I will read you a few words that people sometimes use to describe blacks. Of course, no word fits absolutely everybody, but as I read each

---

* The symbol L indicates that lower scale values (i.e., greater agreement with a statement) indicate a greater possession of the trait. For reversed items, the symbol H (stronger disagreement with a statement) indicates that low scale values are indicative of great trait possession.

one, please tell me, using a number from 1 to 10, how well you think it describes blacks as a group. If you think it a very good description of most blacks, give it a 10. If you feel it's a very inaccurate description of most blacks, give it a 0. You should fee free to use any number between 0 and 10 that you think is appropriate. If you are not sure whether a word describes blacks well or not you can use the number 5.

1. The first word is: hardworking.
2. Aggressive or violent
3. Good neighbors
4. Irresponsible

Limited Government

Forced choice items:

1. ONE, **the less government the better**[†] or, TWO, there are more things that government should be doing.
2. ONE, we need a stronger government to handle today's complex economic problems or, TWO, **the free market economy can handle these problems without government being involved.**
3. ONE, **the main reason that government has gotten bigger over the years is because it has gotten involved in things that people should do for themselves** or, TWO, government has gotten bigger because the problems we face have gotten bigger.

References

Abelson, Robert P., Donald R. Kinder, Mark D. Peters, and Susan F. Fiske. 1982. "Affective and Semantic Components in Political Person Perception." *Journal of Personality and Social Psychology* 42:619–630.

Batson, C. Daniel. 1991. *The Altruism Question: Toward a Social-Psychological Answer.* Hillsdale, NJ: Elrbaum.

Bryant, Brenda K. 1987. "Critique of Comparable Questionnaire Methods in Use to Assess Empathy in Children and Adults." In Nancy Eisenberg and Janet Strayer (eds.), *Empathy and Its Development.* New York: Cambridge University Press.

Conover, Pamela J. 1988. "So Who Cares? Sympathy and Politics." Paper presented at the annual meeting of the Midwest Political Science Association, Chicago.

[†] Boldface indicates the response consistent with a predilection for limited government.

Conover, Pamela J. and Stanley Feldman. 1986. "Emotional Responses to the Economy: I'm Mad as Hell and I'm Not Going to Take It Anymore." *American Journal of Political Science* 30:50–78.

Cook, Fay Lomax and Edith J. Barrett. 1992. *Support for the American Welfare State: The Views of Congress and the Public.* New York: Columbia University Press.

De Swaan, Abram. 1988. In *Care of the State: Health Care, Education and Welfare in Europe and the United States in the Modern Era.* Cambridge: Polity Press.

Eisenberg, Nancy. 1986. *Altruistic Emotion, Cognition, and Behavior.* Hillsdale, NJ: Erlbaum.

Feagin, Joe R. 1975. *Subordinating the Poor: Welfare and American Beliefs.* Englewood Cliffs, NJ: Prentice-Hall.

Feldman, Stanley. 1987. "Structure and Consistency in Public Opinions: The Role of Core Beliefs and Values." *American Journal of Political Science* 31:416–440.

Feldman, Stanley and John Zaller. 1992. "The Political Culture of Ambivalence: Ideological Responses to the Welfare State." *American Journal of Political Science* 36:268–307.

Free, Lloyd A. and Hadley Cantril. 1967. *The Political Beliefs of Americans: A Study of Public Opinion.* New Brunswick, NJ: Rutgers University Press.

Gans, Herbert J. 1988. *Middle American Individualism: The Future of Liberal Democracy.* New York: Free Press.

Gordon, Leonard V. 1975. *The Measurement of Interpersonal Values.* Chicago: Science Research Associates.

Greene, Vernon L. and Edward G. Carmines. 1980. "Assessing the Reliability of Linear Composites." In Karl F. Schuessler (ed.), *Sociological Methodology 1980.* San Francisco: Jossey-Bass.

Hands, Arthur R. 1968. *Charities and Social Aid in Greece and Rome.* Ithaca, NY: Cornell University Press.

Haskell, Thomas L. 1985a. "Capitalism and the Origins of the Humanitarian Sensibility, Part 1." *American Historical Review* 90:339–361.

   1985b. "Capitalism and the Origins of the Humanitarian Sensibility, Part 2." *American Historical Review* 90:547–566.

Hochschild, Jennifer L. 1981. *What Is Fair? American Beliefs About Distributive Justice.* Cambridge, MA: Harvard University Press.

Jennings, M. Kent. 1989. "Perceptions of Social Injustice." In M. Kent Jennings, Jan W. Van Deth, Samuel H. Barnes, Dieter Fuchs, Felix J. Heunks, Ronald Ingelhart, Max Kaase, Mans-Dieter Klingetmann, and Jacques J. A. Thomassen (eds.), *Continuities in Political Action: A Longitudinal Study of Political Orientations in Three Western Democracies.* Berlin: De Gruyter.

Katz, Irwin and R. Glen Hass. 1988. "Racial Ambivalence and American Value Conflict: Correlational and Priming Studies of Dual Cognitive Structures." *Journal of Personality and Social Psychology* 55:893–905.

King, Anthony. 1973. "Ideas, Institutions and the Policies of Governments: A Comparative Analysis, Part III." *British Journal of Political Science* 3:409–423.

Kluckhohn, Clyde. 1959. *Three Lectures.* Toronto: University of Toronto Press.

Kluckhohn, Florence Rockwood and Fred L. Strodtbeck. 1961. *Variations in Value Orientations.* Evanston, IL: Row, Peterson.

Kluegel, James R. and Eliot R. Smith. 1986. *Beliefs About Inequality: Americans' Views of What Is and What Ought to Be.* New York: Aldine De Gruyter.

Krieger, Leonard. 1963. "The Idea of the Welfare State in Europe and the United States." *Journal of the History of Ideas* 24:553–568.

Lane, Robert E. 1962. *Political Ideology: Why the American Common Man Believes What He Does.* New York: Free Press of Glencoe.

Lau, Sing. 1989. "Religious Schema and Values." *International Journal of Psychology* 74:137–156.

Levine, John M. and Richard L. Moreland. 1989. "Social Values and Multiple Outcome Comparisons." In Nancy Eisenberg, Janusz Reykowski, and Ervin Staub (eds.), *Social and Moral Values: Individual and Societal Perspectives.* Hillsdale, NJ: Erlbaum.

McClintock, Charles G. and Linda J. Keil. 1983. "Social Values: Their Definition, Their Development, and Their Impact Upon Human Decision Making in Settings of Outcome Interdependence." In Herbert H. Blumberg, A. Paul Hare, Valerie Kent, and Martin F. Davies (eds.), *Small Groups and Social Interaction.* Chichester, UK: Wiley.

McClosky, Herbert and John Zaller. 1984. *The American Ethos: Public Attitudes Toward Capitalism and Democracy.* Cambridge, MA: Harvard University Press.

Mehrabian, Albert and Norman Epstein. 1972. "A Measure of Emotional Empathy." *Journal of Personality* 40:525–543.

Morris, Charles. 1956. *Varieties of Human Value.* Chicago: University of Chicago Press.

Morris, Robert. 1986. *Rethinking Social Welfare: Why Care for the Stranger.* New York: Longman.

Mueller, Daniel J. and Steven A. Wornhoff. 1990. "Distinguishing Personal and Social Values." *Educational And Psychological Measurement* 50:691–699.

Nisbett, Richard E. and Timothy D. Wilson. 1977. "Telling More Than We Can Know: Verbal Reports on Mental Processes." *Psychological Review* 84:231–259.

Ottati, Victor C., Marco R. Steenbergen, and Ellen Riggle. 1992. "The Cognitive and Affective Components of Political Attitudes: Measuring the Determinants of Candidate Evaluation." *Political Behavior* 14:424–442.

Plattner, Marc F. 1979. "The Welfare State vs. the Redistributive State." *Public Interest* 55:28–48.

Public Perspective, The. 1998. "American Opinion in the 1990s." *The Public Perspective* 5:34–35.

Random House Websteis College Dictionary. New York: Random House.

Reinarman, Craig. 1987. *American States of Mind: Visions of Capitalism and Democracy Among Private and Public Workers.* New Haven, CT: Yale University Press.

Rimlinger, Gaston V. 1971. *Welfare Policy and Industrialization in Europe, America, and Russia.* New York: Wiley.

Rokeach, Milton. 1973. *The Nature of Human Values.* New York: Free Press.

Shapiro, Robert Y., Kelly D. Patterson, Judith Russell, and John T. Young. 1987a. "Employment and Social Welfare." *Public Opinion Quarterly* 51:268–281. 1987b. "Public Assistance." *Public Opinion Quarterly* 51:120–130.

Shapiro, Robert Y. and Tom W. Smith. 1985. "Social Security." *Public Opinion Quarterly* 49:561–572.

Shapiro, Robert Y. and John T. Young. 1989. "Public Opinion and the Welfare State: The United States in Comparative Perspective." *Political Science Quarterly* 104:59–89.

Skocpol, Theda. 1992. *Protecting Soldiers and Mothers: The Political Origins of Social Policy in the United States*. Cambridge, MA: Harvard University Press.

Smith, Tom W. 1987. "The Welfare State in Cross-National Perspective." *Public Opinion Quarterly* 51:404–421.

Sniderman, Paul M. and Richard A. Brody. 1977. "Coping: The Ethic of Self-Reliance." *American Journal of Political Science* 21:501–521.

Spiegel, Henry William. 1960. *The Rise of American Economic Thought*. Philadelphia: Chilton.

Steenbergen, Marco R. 1994. "Citizens, the State and Social Welfare: The Citizenship Bases of Public Welfare Attitudes in the United States." Dissertation, State University of New York, Stony Brook.

Stimson, James A. 1991. *Public Opinion in America: Moods, Cycles, and Swings*. Boulder, CO: Westview Press.

Verba, Sidney and Gary R. Orren. 1985. *Equality in America: The View from the Top*. Cambridge, MA: Harvard University Press.

Weaver, R. Kent, Robert Y. Shapiro, and Lawrence R. Jacobs. 1995. "Trends: Welfare." *Public Opinion Quarterly* 59:606–627.

Wojciszke, Bogdan. 1989. "The System of Personal Values and Behavior." In Nancy Eisenberg, Janusz Reykowski, and Ervin Staub (eds.), *Social and Moral Values: Individual and Societal Perspectives*. Hillsdale, NJ: Erlbaum.

Wuthnow, Robert. 1991. *Acts of Compassion: Caring for Others and Helping Ourselves*. Princeton, NJ: Princeton University Press.

14

American Individualism Reconsidered

GREGORY B. MARKUS

INTRODUCTION

Forty years of research in political psychology indicates that most Americans most of the time do not deduce their issue attitudes or assessments of political leaders from enduring ideological principles such as liberalism, conservatism, libertarianism, or socialism (Converse, 1964; Kinder, 1983; Neuman, 1986). That this is bad news is not at all self-evident (Barber, 1988; Marcus, 1988), and more than one author has praised the American public for its practical, nonideological approach to politics (e.g., Bell, 1960; Dionne, 1991, ch. 13; Lipset, 1960). Even if citizens are generally nonideological, however, even if they may tend to favor "whatever works," one is still left with the question: "works in terms of *what?*" That is, what standards or criteria do Americans employ when deciding whether one policy or candidate works better than another?

Borrowing from their colleagues in economics, the rational-choice school of political science would have us believe that the primary (some would claim the *only*) criterion that matters in making political judgments is self-interest (see, e.g., Downs, 1957; Riker and Ordeshook, 1973). Of course, the definition of what constitutes self-interest can be (and has been) stretched to explain pretty much anything – donating anonymously to a charity, bearing and raising children, even volunteering for dangerous combat duty. Whether such theorizing adds appreciably to our understanding of political life is a topic I won't pursue here, other than to observe that just as political science is embracing the rational-choice approach, no few economists (including at least two Nobel Prize-winning ones) are raising questions about the wisdom of relying so relentlessly upon a paradigm that, while it certainly has much to offer, clearly fails to account for – or even to offer a way to account for – many important aspects of individual and market behavior (Anderson, Arrow, and Pines, 1988; Elster, 1989; Sen, 1977).

Self-interest in its commonsense meaning is of limited use as a guide for thinking about many public issues. I cannot imagine trying to make sense of the civil rights, antiwar, environmental, or women's movements solely in terms of models of rational self-interested behavior. Debates about abortion, gay rights, endangered species, aid to Somalia, or the U.S. role in Bosnia are just a few examples from recent news that are similarly comprehensible only if one takes into account personal and public ethics, along with considerations of self-interest. Even opinions on issues that are seemingly more readily amenable to calculations of individual utility maximization – such as what priority to give to reducing the federal budget deficit and how best to do it or how to reform the nation's health care system – turn out to involve citizens' concerns about "what's fair?" at least as much as "what's in it for me?"

Public opinion polls and focus group interviews during the 1992 presidential campaign, for example, consistently showed that many Americans were attracted to Ross Perot's candidacy in part because of his belief that it was morally wrong for one generation to saddle the next with a multi-trillion-dollar national debt. In a similar vein, a 1993 national survey of public opinion on health care policy found that more than 80% of Americans supported major reform of the current system even though most believed they would not benefit personally from such reform (Toner, 1993). And in a study that shines as an exemplar of social science at its best, Martin Gilens (1999) demonstrated that Americans' deep ambivalence toward welfare policy is explained not by their narrow calculations of self-interest but instead by their perception that most recipients of "welfare as we knew it" were undeserving of support – perceptions that were created in no small degree by racially distorted coverage of poverty and welfare in the mass media.

The point, which anywhere other than among political scientists would be so self-evident as not to warrant mention, is that citizens' political beliefs and judgments do not always and everywhere turn on matters of "self-interest," at least not in any reasonably limited sense of the term. To quote Stoker (1992, p. 370), often citizens "are not merely trying to figure out what or who they like or what it is they want, they are also trying to figure out what or who is good or what is right." To quote Gilens (1999, p. 3), when ordinary Americans evaluate government policy, "the question foremost in their minds is 'what policy is best,' not 'what policy is best for me.'"

If political science has relied far too uncritically upon the model of *Homo economicus*, so has it leaned much too heavily upon the concept of *Homo ideologicus*. For many years, empirical examinations of the structure of popular political attitudes and beliefs were organized almost exclusively around the concept of the liberal–conservative continuum.

Respondents' replies to open- and closed-ended survey items were ransacked for indications that the citizens could supply some meaningful content to that continuum when asked to do so or could make use of it, more or less, to interpret the political world. All in all, nearly a half century's accumulation of evidence points unswervingly to the conclusion that for most Americans most of the time, political thinking is not structured, facilitated, or informed by such a construct – except perhaps to the extent that individuals are conditioned to associate certain emotional responses with the tags "liberal" and "conservative" (see Feldman and Conover, 1981; Kinder, 1983; Luskin, 1987).

The widespread absence of ideological thinking within the electorate has been explained by reference to the casual attention that most citizens devote to politics, the availability of a generally satisfactory and far simpler alternative interpretive and predispositional scheme (viz., partisan labels), the natural cognitive limitations of a large fraction of the public, and so on. At least as important, however, is the fact that even interested, informed, and intelligent citizens often find a single left–right continuum to be of limited utility in trying to understand a good deal of contemporary American policy debate. In American politics, at least, the labels "liberal" and "conservative" have been stretched across so many different positions in so many disparate policy domains as to be scarcely recognizable or intelligible, even to the most politically sophisticated.

In light of the generally uninspiring results of research on the role of ideology in guiding public political beliefs and judgments, Kinder (1983, p. 401), echoing Rokeach (1973), speculated that one of the more important "roots of political beliefs" may be the cultural values that characterize a particular society. Values, according to Kinder, are "general and enduring standards" that "are usually accorded a more central position than are attitudes" in individuals' cognitive belief systems (p. 406). After reviewing evidence from a series of cross-cultural investigations, Hazel Markus and Shinobu Kitayama (1991, p. 224) concluded that "the very nature of individual experience, including cognition, emotion, and motivation," is powerfully influenced by the cultural milieu in which people are embedded socially. Other recent cross-national studies lend empirical support to the hypothesis that political beliefs and preferences in particular are influenced by cultural values (Inglehart, 1990; Triandis, 1989; Triandis, Bontempo, and Villareal, 1988).

Regarding the United States, perhaps no core cultural value has received more attention over the years in both scholarly and popular literature than has individualism. Ever since Alexis de Tocqueville visited the United States more than 150 years ago, political observers have been fascinated by what they have perceived to be the enduring centrality of individualistic values to the American ethos. The consensus among these observers, whether they be critics or celebrants, is that most Americans cleave to the ideals of personal autonomy, self-reliance, and freedom from the unwelcome constraints of government (see, e.g., Boorstin, 1953; Devine, 1972; Hartz, 1955). Miller (1967, p. 75) wrote: "In America today, no doctrine is more highly praised than individualism." Dolbeare and Medcalf (1988: 14) echoed that sentiment: "Probably no country in the world has as deep a cultural commitment to individualism as the United States." According to Morone (1990, p. 324), individualism is "among the most potent and persistent myths of American political life." For Sears and Funk (1991, p. 77), individualism is "the most fundamental of American values."

There is broad agreement, moreover, that individualistic values powerfully shape, and delimit, the workings and outputs of government. As Lerner (1957, p. 626) put it:

The American emphasis . . . is individualist and atomist. It gives rise, for example, to such a characteristic popular myth as the feeling that the social services undertaken by government are a rape of the public treasury by incompetents who have fallen behind in the battle of life and that all collective effort is a betrayal of the laws of life.

Sniderman and Brody (1977, pp. 520–521) concurred. Not only did they find evidence in the 1972 National Election Studies survey data that "the notion of self reliance appears to be an important aspect of the American political culture," they further concluded that the prevalence of this value "is a major restraint on the production of political demand." According to Wills (1987), Ronald Reagan won two overwhelming electoral victories (and helped set up George Bush for a third Republican triumph) in part by championing individualism and by making "the individualist fantasy" all the more believable by believing in it so thoroughly himself.

Despite – or perhaps because of – its robustness, individualism has been under attack on a number of fronts lately. Sociologists, historians, and clinicians decry the damage to American culture and mental health that has been inflicted by materialistic and narcissistic excesses of modern life (Etzioni, 1993; Lasch, 1979, 1991). Political theorists argue that a declining sense of community endangers collective action in pursuit of (even) such goals as equality of legal rights and economic opportunity (Barber, 1984; Sandel, 1982; Walzer, 1983). Some feminist scholars criticize what they interpret to be antifeminist strains beneath the surface of individualist values (Fox-Genovese, 1991; Gilligan, 1982; Nedelsky, 1989). Others, most notably Bellah and his coauthors of *Habits of the Heart* (1985), are deeply concerned that the eclipse of communitarian values by purely individualistic interests leaves Americans morally impoverished and ultimately unsatisfied (see also MacIntyre, 1981; Taylor, 1985; Wolfe, 1989). The American ethos of individualism has even been implicated as the culprit responsible for the country's "depressing, brutal, ugly, unhealthy and spiritually degrading" man-made landscape (Kunstler, 1993, p. 10).

Although much has been written about the alleged centrality of individualism to American society and politics, we are only just beginning to accumulate systematic empirical evidence on the extent to which ordinary Americans actually subscribe to individualist principles or rely upon those principles when thinking about political issues and leaders. The available evidence tends to support the proposition that many Americans possess reasonably identifiable and stable core values involving some central tenets of individualism (Conover, Crewe, and Searing, 1991; Feldman, 1988; Gans, 1988; McClosky and Zaller, 1984; Sniderman and Brody, 1977). Moreover, citizens' values are linked to their articulated opinions about such issues as social welfare (Feldman, 1983, 1988; Feldman and Zaller, 1992; Gilens, 1999), racial affirmative action (Kinder and Sanders, 1990; Sniderman and Piazza, 1993), and even foreign affairs (Hurwitz and Peffley, 1987).

Markus and Kitayama (1991) made the case that, in contrast to Japanese culture, Western culture – and that of the United States in particular – tends to "stress attending to the self, the appreciation of one's difference from others, and the importance of asserting the self" (p. 224). Those cultural differences were manifested in data obtained from a variety of laboratory studies of cognitions, emotions, and motivations of individuals from Eastern versus Western cultures. Blanket assertions about "Western culture" must be handled with care, lest they unravel. Markus and Kitayama emphasized that the cultural distinctions to which they referred should be regarded only as "general tendencies that may emerge when the members of the culture are considered as a whole." They continued: "The prototypical American view of the self, for example, may prove to be most characteristic of White, middle-class men with a Western European ethnic background. It may be somewhat less descriptive of women in general, or of men and women from other ethnic groups or social classes" (p. 225).

In a more explicitly political vein, Smith (1993: pp. 549–550) reminded us that there are "multiple traditions in America." The Tocquevillean story of an American democracy grounded in an unusually individualistic culture is deceptively incomplete:

It is centered on relationships among a minority of Americans (white men, largely of northern European ancestry) analyzed via reference to categories derived from the hierarchy of political and economic statuses men have held in Europe.... Although liberal democratic ideas and practices have been more potent in

Gregory B. Markus

America than elsewhere, American politics is best seen as expressing the interaction of multiple political traditions ... which have collectively comprised American political culture, without any one constituting it as a whole.

This point is particularly relevant to the present study, one purpose of which is to assess the degree of *variation* in the American public's responses to survey items intended to tap certain basic principles of individualism.

Acquiring a clearer understanding of the place of individualistic values in contemporary American culture is of more than purely academic interest. A number of emerging public policy controversies rub uncomfortably against key tenets of individualism. For example, state and local governments across the United States are considering – or have already enacted – legislation imposing substantial restrictions on everyday actions of individuals and businesses in the name of environmental protection (house painting, landscaping, and air conditioning, for example). At the same time, legislatures grapple with such issues as abortion rights, welfare reform, gun control, school prayer, and assisted suicide – issues that test the balancing of individual liberty and government authority on behalf of the public good. Before he became U.S. secretary of labor, Robert Reich wrote a book in which he outlined how prevailing policy debates about the future of the American economy take place within the framework of "our culture's tales," in particular the persistent myths about the "Triumphant Individual" (1987, p. 146).

In a democracy, public policy is not conceived and implemented in a vacuum; it reflects public values. We have much to learn about what those basic values are in the United States, how consensually they are held, and the degree to which citizens' policy judgments are informed by their value orientations. In a nutshell, the story that motivates the research presented here is as follows. First, because of its prominence in Western culture, most Americans presumably possess relatively stable and readily cognitively accessible beliefs about aspects of the "individualist myth." Second, whatever the central tendencies of the American public, there may well be substantial diversity in the degree to which population subgroups support individualistic values. Third, variation in support for aspects of individualism can help to account for coincident variation in attitudes toward policy proposals and political leaders.

MEASURING INDIVIDUALISTIC VALUES

To bring evidence to bear on this story, I obtained approval to include a series of forced-choice items in the 1989 American National Election Studies (ANES) Pilot Survey. A forced-choice format was employed because some research suggests that, compared with agree-disagree formats, forced-choice items encourage more thoughtful responses and are less prone to response-set bias (Petty, Rennier, and Cacioppo, 1987). Seven of these items were also included in the 1990 ANES Survey. Most of the findings described in this report are based on the pooled responses from both surveys.[1]

The survey items were intended to tap three distinct aspects of individualism: individual autonomy, self-reliance, and limited government. These different faces of individualism are featured in the works of a number of contemporary philosophers, historians, and social scientists, including (to name just a few) Lukes (1973), Nozick (1974), Kateb (1984), Ketcham (1987), Rosenblum (1987), Gans (1988), Crittenden (1992), and Ellis (1993).

Very briefly, "autonomy" refers to the notion that an individual's thoughts and actions should be determined not by agents or causes outside of one's control but rather by individual reflection and tastes. As Nedelsky (1989: 8) put it, "The image of humans as self-determining creatures ... remains one of the most powerful dimensions of liberal thought. For all of us raised in liberal societies, our deep attachment to freedom takes its meaning and value from the presupposition of our self-determining, self-making nature: that is what freedom is for, the exercise of that capacity."

"Self-reliance" is a nineteenth-century term popularized by Ralph Waldo Emerson, but it is commonly understood today. It refers to the idea that individuals should take care of their own well-being, particularly (but not only) their economic condition. Self-reliance ought not be confused with mere selfishness. Emerson, Thoreau, and other shapers of American political thought upheld self-reliance not at all on materialistic grounds; indeed, nothing was valued less by them than mere "acquisitiveness." Rather, the champions of self-reliance claimed that its practice was essential to the development of the whole person; it developed character, it promoted a proper appreciation of nature, and it fostered an understanding that the meaning of life transcended material wealth (see, e.g., Diggins, 1984; Richardson, 1995).

By "limited government," I am evoking the belief that, as opposed to pursuing some allegedly ephemeral conception of the "public interest," the purpose of government is strictly to protect life, liberty, and property, and thereby provide a framework within which individuals may pursue their private interests.

---

1 The marginal distributions of responses to the individualism items differed negligibly between the 1989 and 1990 surveys.

Gregory B. Markus

FINDINGS

A Nation of "Rugged Individualists"?

Table 14.1 displays the distributions of responses to seven survey items, grouped according to the particular aspects of individualism the items were intended to tap. Two general points about Table 14.1 are noteworthy. First, few individuals declined to choose one of the two response alternatives presented to them in any given item. This contrasts with results that routinely obtain when respondents are asked to describe their ideological self-identifications in terms of a labeled liberal–conservative continuum – where nonresponse rates of one-third or higher are not uncommon (see, e.g., Markus, 1982). Second, contrary to the common assertion that an overwhelming majority of Americans support individualistic principles, a surprising amount of variation occurred in responses to these items. Indeed, on four of the seven items, a clear majority rejected the individualistic response, and on a fifth, opinion was evenly divided. On only two of the seven items did a majority prefer the individualist alternative.

When asked to choose between the assertion that "we need a strong government to handle today's complex economic problems" and the claim that "the free market can handle these problems without government being involved," 72% opted for the former view and only 22% preferred the latter. (Six percent declined to choose either statement.) Only three in ten respondents maintained that "the less government, the better," while more than twice as many supported the alternative view that "there are more things that government should be doing." By a comparable margin, survey participants rejected the claim that the main reason government has gotten bigger "is because it has gotten involved in things that people should do for themselves" in favor of the position that government has grown "because the problems we face have gotten bigger."[2]

On one of the two items intended to gauge support for the ideal of self-reliance, only 20% of respondents agreed with the proposition that "most poor people are poor because they don't work hard enough," whereas 70% associated themselves with the belief that poor people are poor "because of circumstances beyond their control." And with regard to one of the two "autonomy" items, survey participants were evenly divided as to whether it is more important when raising children "to encourage them to be independent-minded" or "to teach them obedience and respect for authorities."

---

2 Very similar results were obtained when the three "limited government" items were repeated in the 1992 ANES.

408

American Individualism Reconsidered

Table 14.1. *Response Distributions for the Individualism Items*

"Next, I am going to ask you to choose which of two statements I read comes closer to your own opinion. You might agree to some extent with both, but we want to know which one is closer to your views." ["Individualism" response is in boldface.]

I. Limited Government
ONE, we need a strong government to handle today's complex economic problems; or TWO, the free market can handle these problems without government being involved.

Strong government	72%	(1151)
Both, depends (volunteered)	3	(43)
Free market	22	(350)
DK	4	(61)

ONE, the less government the better; or TWO, there are more things that government should be doing?

Less government	30%	(483)
Both, depends (volunteered)	4	(64)
More things government should do	63	(1019)
DK	3	(43)

ONE, the main reason that government has gotten bigger over the years is because it has gotten involved in things that people should do for themselves; or TWO, government has gotten bigger because the problems we face have gotten bigger.

Gotten involved in things	30%	(490)
Both, depends (volunteered)	3	(52)
Problems we face are bigger	65	(1044)
DK	2	(25)

II. Self-Reliance
ONE, people should take care of themselves and their families and let others do the same; or TWO, people should care less about their own success and more about the needs of society.

Take care of self	58%	(932)
Both, depends (volunteered)	7	(112)
Care more about society	34	(551)
DK	1	(14)

ONE, most poor people are poor because they don't work hard enough; or TWO, they are poor because of circumstances beyond their control.

Don't work hard	20%	(319)
Both, depends (volunteered)	8	(132)
Beyond their control	70	(1130)
DK	2	(25)

(continued)

409

Table 14.1 *(continued)*

III. Individual Autonomy		

ONE, it is better to fit in with the people around you; or TWO, it is better to conduct yourself according to your own standards, even if that makes you stand out.

Fit in	18%	(286)
Both, depends (volunteered)	1	(18)
Own standards	81	(1301)
DK	*	(8)

When raising children, which is more important: ONE to encourage them to be independent-minded and think for themselves; or TWO, to teach them obedience and respect for authorities?

Independent-minded	43%	(689)
Both, depends (volunteered)	14	(227)
Obedience	43	(688)
DK	*	(6)

DK = don't know.
* Less than 1%.
Source: 1989 and 1990 ANES.

Unambiguous support for individualistic values was evident on two of the seven items. By better than a four to one margin, respondents said they believed "it is better to conduct yourself according to your own standards, even if that makes you stand out" than it is "to fit in with the people around you." Also, 58% agreed that "people should take care of themselves and their families and let others do the same," compared with 34% who preferred the idea that "people should care less about their own success and more about the needs of society."

Five additional items intended to tap individualistic values (not shown in Table 14.1) were included in the 1989 survey ($N = 614$). On four of the five items, majorities once again rejected (often overwhelmingly) the individualistic position in favor of the cooperative, egalitarian, or communitarian one. Three out of four respondents in 1989 believed that "the government should try to ensure that all Americans have such things as jobs, health care, and housing" rather than that "the government should not be involved in this." Fifty-nine percent took the position that "government regulation of big businesses is necessary to protect the public," compared with 34% who favored the alternative that "government regulation does more harm than good." By a margin of 51% to 40%, respondents agreed that "it is more important to be a cooperative person who works well with others" than it is "to be a self-reliant person able to take care of oneself." And a nearly two to one majority rejected the view that "there is too much restriction and regulation of personal opinion and behavior" (32%) in favor of the proposition that "there is too little respect for traditional authorities, such as religious leaders and government officials" (60%). Only one of the five additional items generated majority support for a conventionally individualist viewpoint: 59% favored the laissez-faire idea that "society is better off when businesses are free to make as much money as they can," while 36% agreed with the proposition that "businesses should be prohibited from earning excessive profits."

Policy Preferences

When participants in the 1989 ANES were presented with a set of forced-choice items that referred to specific policy applications of individualistic principles in such domains as environmental protection, public safety, mandatory national service, and rent control, the results were much the same: on all six items, majorities rejected the individualistic positions (see Table 14.2). For example, nearly two out of three respondents favored mandatory seat belt and motorcycle helmet laws, nearly nine out of ten favored mandatory recycling, 56% thought that government limits on rents and home prices is a good idea, and 55% agreed with the concept of requiring some form of national service for all young adults.

Individualism Subscale Construction

Table 14.3 reports the gamma coefficient values for the bivariate relationships among the seven "principles" items.[3] A visual examination of the coefficient matrix reveals the fairly high associations (for survey data) among the items expected to tap a hypothesized dimension of individualism and also the much weaker correlations across dimensions. The distinctiveness of the three aspects of individualism was also manifested in the results of a rotated principal-components analysis (shown in Table 14.4) as well as in a separate LISREL confirmatory factor analysis (not

3 Gamma is a "weak association" measure that yields values similar to the tetrachoric *r* (for details, see Weisberg, 1974). Weak association measures are often preferred when exploring the scalability of binary items that have skewed marginals or that are expected to conform to a particular scaling model, e.g., Guttman or Rasch scales (see Andrich, 1988). Pearson correlation coefficients (a "strong" measure of association) were also computed and examined. Although specific numerical results varied somewhat, depending upon the choice of measure of association, the overall conclusions did not. "Don't know" and "depends" responses were excluded when the values reported in Table 14.3 were calculated.

Table 14.2. *Marginals for the Specific Applications Items*

Now, here are some questions about how much say the government should have in regulating things that individuals and businesses do. ["Individualism" response is in boldface.]

In the interests of public safety, should the government require the use of seatbelts in automobiles or helmets for motorcycle riders OR should those decisions be left up to individuals?

Government require	64%	(314)
Both, depends (volunteered)	2	(11)
Left to individuals	33	(161)
DK	1	(7)

Generally speaking, are government limits on rents and home prices a bad idea or a good idea?

Bad idea	37%	(182)
Both, depends (volunteered)	1	(7)
Good idea	56	(274)
DK	6	(29)

Would you favor or oppose a law requiring school children to recite the Pledge of Allegiance daily?

Favor	69%	(337)
Both, depends (volunteered)	1	(4)
Oppose	28	(138)
DK	2	(11)

If people want to smoke marijuana in their own homes, is that basically their business OR should it be illegal?

Basically their business	32%	(158)
Both, depends (volunteered)	1	(5)
Should be illegal	66	(323)
DK	1	(6)

Would you favor or oppose a law requiring that all young adults serve their country by spending some time in the military, the Peace Corps, or in some other kind of national service?

Favor	55%	(269)
Both, depends (volunteered)	0	(0)
Oppose	43	(213)
DK	2	(9)

Would you favor or oppose a law requiring people to recycle newspaper, glass, and other recyclable waste in order to reduce the trash problem?

Favor	89%	(438)
Both, depends (volunteered)	0	(0)
Oppose	10	(52)
DK	1	(3)

DK = don't know.
* Less than 1%.
Source: 1989 ANES.

Table 14.3. *Bivariate Relations Among "Principles of Individualism" Items*[a]

1. The less government the better						
2. Government gotten involved in things	.72					
3. Free market can handle problems without gov't	.80	.73				
4. People should take care of themselves	.18	.14	.10			
5. Poor people don't work hard enough	.28	.21	.21	.33		
6. Conduct self according to own standards	.28	.30	.28	−.21	−.08	
7. Teach children to be independent-minded	.21	.16	.20	−.03	.08	.40
	Var 1	Var 2	Var 3	Var 4	Var 5	Var 6

[a] Entries are gamma coefficients. Response codes were reflected when necessary, so that for all items the nonindividualist response is "low" and the individualist response is "high."
Source: 1989 and 1990 ANES.

Table 14.4. *Rotated Principal Components Analysis of Individualism Items*

	Limited Gov't	Autonomy	Self-Reliance	Communality
Free market can handle problems	.78	.03	−.02	.62
The less government the better	.77	.07	−.10	.61
Government gotten involved in things	.75	.04	−.04	.56
Conduct self according to own standards	.12	.70	.21	.54
Teach children to be independent-minded	.01	.80	−.15	.66
People should take care of themselves	−.05	.16	.71	.53
Poor people don't work hard enough	−.07	−.12	.74	.57
Cumulative % of total variance	25.6	42.2	58.4	

shown; see Markus, 1990, for details). The LISREL goodness of fit coefficient between the hypothesized three-dimensional factor structure and the empirically obtained patterns of association was .994.

Although the individualism items were included in the 1989 and 1990 surveys, with one exception it is not possible to say anything about the temporal reliability of item responses because the two surveys involved different samples of individuals. The one exception involves an item from the self-reliance subscale ("poor people don't work hard enough" versus "circumstances beyond their control"). This item was (inadvertently?)

posed to the same respondents in two waves of the 1989 ANES Pilot Study. The test-retest correlation (Pearson *r*) for that item is .55, a fairly impressive value by survey research standards.

Based on the results reported previously, three additive individualism subscales were created: a three-item limited government scale, a two-item self-reliance scale, and a two-item individual autonomy scale.[4] As the relationships among the items (as displayed in Table 14.3) suggest, correlations between respondents' scores on the limited government subscale and on the self-reliance and autonomy subscales were modestly positive (Kendall's τ = .11 and .09, respectively). The correlation between the latter two subscales was actually slightly negative (Kendall's τ = –.04). In the past, such weak (and even inverse) correlations among expressions of support for various dimensions of individualism might well have been taken as evidence of ideological "innocence" or inconsistency. Those correlations are, however, entirely compatible with sophisticated understandings of individualism – which is not to say that many Americans are politically sophisticated, but only that the combinations of viewpoints they express in surveys are not self-evidently incoherent. Nedelsky (1989), for instance, argued that the "traditional American conception of autonomy" presents a false choice between discovering and living in accordance with one's own values and beliefs, on the one hand, and social embeddedness and collective responsibility for citizens' welfare, on the other. Although there is certainly "a real and enduring tension between the individual and collective," she continued, "the collective is not simply a potential threat to individuals, but is constitutive of them, and thus is a source of their autonomy as well as a danger to it" (p. 21). One does not, and cannot, develop a sense of self and personal values in isolation but only in connection with, and with the support of, others (see also Guisinger and Blatt, 1994).

Similarly, Crittenden (1992, p. 74) insisted that "autonomy need not entail a rejection of society's values or an isolation from the presence or influence of others." Autonomy implies a process through which individuals come to discover their own ways of life; it does not presuppose any particular content to the choices individuals may make. There is no logical or normative reason why an autonomous individual cannot also be deeply concerned about social justice and community. Indeed, citizens who value autonomy most highly may well be the ones best equipped to resist the daily bombardment of cultural messages urging them to "look

4 For purposes of scale construction, "don't know" and "depends" responses were scored as midway between the two available responses for an item. Item scoring was reflected when necessary so that higher values indicated agreement with the individualistic response alternative.

out for Number One." Autonomous citizens may thus be among the strongest champions of the belief that people should "care about the needs of society" – which is precisely what the present study finds.

Demographic Correlates of Individualism

Limited Government. Table 14.5 displays the marginal distribution for the limited government subscale and also shows how scores on that subscale varied by race, age, level of formal education, family income, and sex. Overall, three out of four respondents were located in the lowest

Table 14.5. *Demographic Differences in Limited Government Subscale Score Distributions (Row Percentages)*

	Low	2	3	4	High	N
Race						
White	45	22	3	14	15	1270
Black	68	23	3	6	1	189
Hispanic	70	17	2	10	1	93
Age						
18–29	61	22	2	10	6	349
30–39	54	21	2	12	11	398
40–49	41	26	2	13	18	269
50–59	43	19	5	16	17	196
60–69	47	23	6	11	13	187
70 up	42	24	7	16	12	194
Education						
<High school	50	27	4	12	5	335
High school	56	22	3	10	9	554
Some college	46	22	2	12	18	343
College graduate	43	19	3	16	19	345
Annual income						
<$10,000	58	24	3	11	4	234
$10K–14,999	51	29	2	10	8	177
$15K–19,999	58	19	2	11	11	132
$20K–29,999	50	26	3	12	10	404
$30K–39,999	46	21	2	16	16	204
$40K–49,999	41	19	2	16	22	229
$50,000 up	40	20	3	16	21	92
Sex						
Male	42	21	2	18	17	670
Female	55	23	4	9	9	923
Total	50	22	3	13	12	1593

two categories of the limited government subscale, which means that those individuals rejected the limited government response option on each of the three items constituting the scale. African Americans and Latinos were significantly less likely than whites were to endorse the idea of limited government, as measured by the survey items in this study: 45% of whites scored at the low end of the limited government scale, compared with 68% of blacks and 70% of Latinos. Responses to one of the component items of the limited government subscale make the point concretely: more than one in three white respondents favored the idea of "the less government the better" over the alternative that "there are more things that government should be doing"; only one in ten black or Latino respondents did. With regard to other demographic variables, the results shown in Table 14.4 indicate that younger Americans, the less educated, the less well-to-do, and females were more consistent in rejecting tenets of limited government than were older citizens, the more highly educated, those with higher incomes, and males.

Self-Reliance. The marginal distribution for the self-reliance subscale (shown in Table 14.6) was comparatively more balanced, but here, too, the center of gravity was toward the low end of the scale. Demographic differences with regard to scores on the self-reliance subscale are less evident. A significant relationship between education and support for the self-reliance norm obtained, however, with the most highly educated having the *lowest* average scores on the self-reliance scale. For example, two out of three respondents with less than a high school education said that "people should take care of themselves" rather than "care more about the needs of society"; in contrast, fewer than half of the respondents with a college degree took that position.

Autonomy. Of the three individualism subscales, only for the two-item autonomy scale did more respondents endorse the pro-individualism response options than reject them. Demographic differences were particularly dramatic with respect to support of the principle of individual autonomy, as shown in Table 14.7. Forty percent of white respondents preferred the pro-autonomy alternative on both relevant survey items, compared with 26% of African Americans and 19% of Latinos. Substantial age- and income-related variations in scores on the autonomy subscale were also apparent. Largest of all, however, were the differences across education levels. Only 16% of respondents with less than a high school education took the pro-autonomy position on the two survey items; the comparable percentages were 31% for those with a high school diploma, 46% among respondents having some college education, and 59% among college degree holders.

Table 14.6. *Demographic Differences in Self-Reliance Subscale Score Distributions (Row Percentages)*

	Low	2	3	4	High	N
Race						
White	26	8	46	6	15	1271
Black	27	8	52	4	10	191
Hispanic	31	4	49	6	9	96
Age						
18–29	28	6	48	4	14	351
30–39	32	6	44	3	15	397
40–49	30	9	43	4	15	268
50–59	22	10	45	8	14	196
60–69	22	10	50	6	12	190
70 up	18	8	49	11	15	197
Education						
<High school	19	6	54	6	15	336
High school	24	9	48	6	12	558
Some college	31	7	41	4	18	346
College graduate	33	9	40	6	12	343
Annual income						
<$10,000	21	6	56	5	13	237
$10K–14,999	31	7	50	5	8	179
$15K–19,999	27	10	44	8	11	134
$20K–29,999	29	8	44	4	16	406
$30K–39,999	28	6	42	5	19	203
$40K–49,999	28	9	46	5	12	227
$50,000 up	25	6	41	5	23	93
Sex						
Male	26	6	48	5	16	675
Female	27	9	45	6	12	924
Total	26	8	46	5	14	1599

Summary of Demographic Analyses. The preceding demographic analyses underscore the distinctiveness of the different strands of individualism as interpreted by ordinary Americans. Respondents with less than a high school education possessed the *lowest* average scores on the limited government and autonomy scales yet were among the *strongest* proponents of self-reliance. The baby boom generation (persons aged forty to forty-nine) were simultaneously the *most ardent* proponents of individual autonomy and the age group with the *lowest* average score on the self-reliance scale. White respondents were significantly *more* likely than African American or Latino respondents to express support for

Table 14.7. *Demographic Differences in Autonomy Subscale Score Distributions (Row Percentages)*

	Low	2	3	4	High	N
Race						
White	9	2	36	13	40	1281
Black	17	4	43	10	26	191
Hispanic	24	7	42	7	19	95
Age						
18–29	8	2	36	12	42	353
30–39	8	2	35	11	44	399
40–49	7	2	33	11	47	272
50–59	12	2	42	13	30	197
60–69	16	3	38	17	25	189
70 up	18	6	44	13	20	198
Education						
<High school	24	5	47	8	16	336
High school	11	2	43	14	31	557
Some college	5	2	34	13	46	348
College graduate	3	1	22	14	59	351
Annual income						
<$10,000	20	5	44	9	22	237
$10K–14,999	16	3	47	7	26	178
$15K–19,999	16	2	31	13	38	134
$20K–29,999	8	3	40	13	38	410
$30K–39,999	7	1	34	12	46	202
$40K–49,999	5	1	32	14	48	231
$50,000 up	5	1	28	12	54	93
Sex						
Male	10	2	37	12	39	675
Female	11	3	38	12	36	933
Total	10	3	37	12	37	1608

Source: 1989 and 1990 ANES.

principles of limited government and individual autonomy, but the three subgroups were virtually *indistinguishable* in terms of their average scores on the self-reliance scale. The regularities in the ways that demographically classified groups are distinguished by their particular mixes of beliefs about individualism bolster the claim that low overall correlations among autonomy, self-reliance, and limited government subscales are not necessarily evidence of attitudinal incoherence. As Hochschild (1993, p. 189) put it in a slightly different context, "there are systematic ways in which citizens are [seemingly] not consistent."

American Individualism Reconsidered

Partisan and Liberal–Conservative Differences in Individualism

Endorsement of individualistic principles in the 1989–1990 survey covaried with respondents' stated party identifications and liberal–conservative self-identifications, as shown in Table 14.8. Democrats were much less likely than Republicans to favor the idea of limited government: two out of three strong Democrats rejected the limited government response alternative on all three relevant survey items, compared with only 37% of strong Republicans. A preference for bigger, more activist government also declined steadily as one moved from left to right along an ideological self-placement continuum: 58% of self-declared extreme liberals preferred the big-government response option on all three survey items, compared with only 26% of self-declared extreme conservatives.

Correlations between party identification and the other two individualism subscales (self-reliance and autonomy) were statistically significant but not particularly impressive substantively. Relationships between left–right self-placement and the latter two subscales were quite strong, however. *Conservatives* were much more likely than liberals to endorse the ideal of self-reliance. With regard to the autonomy subscale, though, it was self-declared *liberals* who scored highest: two out of three extreme liberals endorsed the pro-autonomy position on both relevant survey items, compared with only 28% of extreme conservatives.

Relationships between Individualism and Policy Preferences

This study has shown that the degree to which ordinary Americans endorse key tenets of individualism varies demographically and also with respect to partisan attachment and ideological orientation. What remains to be determined are the practical consequences of this variation in support for individualistic values. For instance, to what extent does one's degree of support for individualistic values covary with one's position on salient political and social issues?[5]

As Table 14.9 demonstrates, there are indeed such connections. Respondents' scores on the three individualism subscales correlated

---

5 Linkages between abstract values and policy attitudes are almost certainly bidi-rectional to some extent, with personal observations and assessments of real-world issue controversies influencing underlying value orientations as well as vice versa. Survey data, particularly of the cross-sectional or short-term panel sort, are limited in their power to untangle the causal interplay of values and attitudes. The purpose of the analysis presented here is not to establish definitively what causes what, but rather to determine whether there is *any* connection between expressions of pro- or anti-individualistic sentiments, on the one hand, and positions on specific policy controversies, on the other.

Table 14.8. *Variation in Individualism Subscales by Party Identification and Liberal–Conservative Self-Placement (Row Percentages)*

1. Limited Government	Low	2	3	4	High	N
Party ID						
Strong Democrat	68	18	2	9	3	290
Democrat	56	24	3	12	6	286
Leaning Democrat	58	24	1	10	7	197
Independent	42	24	4	17	13	163
Leaning Republican	37	25	2	14	21	202
Republican	40	25	3	12	20	232
Strong Republican	37	18	4	17	24	195
Liberal–conservative placement						
Extremely liberal	58	33	0	8	0	24
Liberal	57	23	4	12	3	94
Slightly liberal	57	17	1	14	11	142
Moderate	52	23	3	12	9	375
Slightly conservative	40	21	1	16	22	230
Conservative	32	19	4	14	30	188
Extremely conservative	26	21	8	16	29	38
2. Self-Reliance	**Low**	**2**	**3**	**4**	**High**	**N**
Party ID						
Strong Democrat	33	8	44	4	11	293
Democrat	27	6	50	4	12	285
Leaning Democrat	35	8	43	2	12	197
Independent	26	10	43	7	14	166
Leaning Republican	23	7	46	9	15	203
Republican	25	8	44	4	19	233
Strong Republican	17	10	47	8	18	194
Liberal–conservative placement						
Extremely liberal	33	8	44	4	11	293
Liberal	27	6	50	4	12	285
Slightly liberal	35	8	43	2	12	197
Moderate	26	10	43	7	14	166
Slightly conservative	23	7	46	9	15	203
Conservative	25	8	44	4	19	233
Extremely conservative	17	10	47	8	18	194

3. Autonomy	Low	2	3	4	High	N
Party ID						
Strong Democrat	12	2	38	9	39	292
Democrat	14	2	38	11	35	288
Leaning Democrat	11	2	30	9	48	198
Independent	8	5	39	16	32	166
Leaning Republican	11	1	36	16	36	205
Republican	8	3	36	14	40	235
Strong Republican	8	3	43	13	33	196
Liberal–conservative placement						
Extremely liberal	8	0	21	4	67	24
Liberal	6	2	19	7	65	95
Slightly liberal	2	0	31	11	56	144
Moderate	11	2	38	11	39	379
Slightly conservative	5	1	32	14	47	234
Conservative	7	3	42	16	32	188
Extremely conservative	12	2	50	8	28	40

Source: Pooled 1989 and 1990 ANES.

significantly with their policy preferences, as measured by a broad range of items in the 1989 and 1990 ANES referring to affirmative action, social welfare, and civil liberties issues. Moreover, the correlations between individualism subscales and issue attitudes were frequently as large as, or larger than, the correlations between issue attitudes and either party identification or liberal–conservative self-placement. Bear in mind, also, that whereas the vast majority of survey participants responded to the individualism subscale items, nearly one-third of the combined 1989 and 1990 samples declined to place themselves along a labeled liberal–conservative continuum. So although the correlations of many expressed policy attitudes with ideological location were fairly robust, those correlations pertain strictly to a decidedly unrepresentative subset of the total sample.

Correlation coefficients are useful for scanning across a large array of items, but they fail to convey intuitively the substantive significance of many of the relationships between individualist orientations and issue attitudes. Table 14.10 is intended to communicate that sense of substantive importance more straightforwardly. As that table shows, beliefs about the principle of limited government were strongly related to attitudes about the scope and scale of government activism across a range

Gregory B. Markus

Table 14.9. *Correlations of Liberal–Conservative Self-Placement, Party Identification, and Individualism Subscales with Policy Preferences*[a]

	Lib–Cons Placement	Party ID	Limited Gov't	Self-Reliance	Autonomy
I. Race affirmative action					
Cut budget assistance to blacks	.29	.27	.21	.20	
Govt should help blacks (disagr.)	.30	.20	.21	.24	
Oppose affirmative hiring	.19	.20	.23	.12	.12
Oppose university quotas	.19	.17	.19	.11	
Should expect no favors (disagr.)	−.22	−.12		−.25	.12
II. Social welfare					
Cut Social Security budget	.14	.22	.23		.11
Cut food stamps budget	.26	.21	.18	.21	
Cut homelessness budget	.23	.20	.29	.26	
Gov't should see to jobs (disagr.)	.31	.27	.30	.20	
More government services	−.32	−.28	−.34	−.18	
III. Civil liberties					
Women's place is in home	.26		.11		−.26
Abortion pro-choice	−.28				.27
Favor school prayer		.16			−.20
Oppose mandatory national svc					.13

[a] Correlations (Pearson product-moment) greater than .10 are shown. All correlations shown are statistically significant at the .01 level.
Source: Pooled 1989 and 1990 ANES.

of specific domains, including social welfare spending and affirmative action policies targeting minorities and women. Respondents' scores on the autonomy subscale correlated primarily with survey items dealing with civil liberties issues. Beliefs about the value of self-reliance were most clearly linked to attitudes on welfare spending issues and to whether one believes that government should "make every effort to improve the social and economic position of blacks" or if, instead, blacks "should help themselves."

Individualism and Evaluations of Political Leaders

Respondents' evaluations of well-known political figures also varied significantly as a function of their scores on two of the three individualism

Table 14.10. *Relationships between Individualism Subscales and Policy Preferences*

Limited Government Score	% Favoring Increased Budget For:				% Gov't Should See to Job and Living Standard	% Favor Gov't Help to Women
	Aid to Blacks	Social Security	Food Stamps	Home-less		
Low	33	69	22	76	40	88
2	22	61	16	69	31	85
3	10	52	7	50	28	76
4	19	53	9	54	18	69
High	10	37	6	35	9	40

Autonomy Score	% Abortion Should Be a Matter of Personal Choice	% Women Should Have Equal Role in Business/Govt	% Oppose Organized School Prayer	% Oppose Mandatory Nat'l Service
Low	29	49	53	32
2	26	57	63	46
3	30	61	61	47
4	33	68	62	53
High	54	82	73	55

Self-Reliance Score	% Blacks Should Help Themselves	% Favor Cut Food Stamps Budget	% Not Raise Homeless Budget	% Gov't Should Not See to Job and Living Standard
Low	36	15	20	37
2	38	23	29	43
3	49	26	33	50
4	62	35	46	67
High	70	47	57	64

subscales, as shown in Table 14.11. Average ratings of Republican presidents George Bush and Ronald Reagan increase steadily as one moves from respondents at the low end of the limited government subscale to those at the high end. In contrast, feeling thermometer ratings of civil rights leader and Democratic presidential candidate Jesse Jackson varied inversely with expressed support for the principle of limited government. Comparable relationships obtained between respondents' scores on the self-reliance subscale and their feeling thermometer ratings of each of the three politicians. Feeling thermometer scores for Reagan, Bush, and Jackson did not vary significantly as a function of respondents' locations on the autonomy subscale, however.

Table 14.11. *Mean Feeling Thermometer Ratings of
Political Leaders as a Function of Respondent's
Position on Individualism Subscales*[a]

Limited Government score	George Bush	Ronald Reagan	Jesse Jackson
Low	56.7	57.1	53.1
2	62.2	60.2	49.2
3	70.6	67.8	44.4
4	63.0	68.2	48.0
High	75.6	78.0	34.6
Grand mean	61.6	62.1	48.9
N	587	591	573

Self-Reliance Score	George Bush	Ronald Reagan	Jesse Jackson
Low	57.0	56.6	56.2
2	52.9	59.5	52.8
3	61.3	61.3	47.6
4	63.2	62.1	41.6
High	70.4	72.2	43.5
Grand mean	61.3	61.9	49.0
N	590	594	576

Autonomy Score	George Bush	Ronald Reagan	Jesse Jackson
Low	61.3	60.5	53.0
2	76.8	68.2	54.2
3	63.4	63.6	47.0
4	59.6	63.3	47.6
High	59.2	59.8	50.5
Grand mean	61.5	62.0	49.1
N	595	599	581

[a] *F*-test on differences of feeling thermometer means across
categories of the limited government and self-reliance subscales is statistically significant at $\alpha < .01$ for all three
political leaders. Differences are not statistically significant
with respect to the autonomy subscale.

Multivariate Analyses

In view of the covariation among the individualism subscales and partisan and ideological self-identifications, I conducted a series of multiple
regressions in which respondents' opinions on representative policy items

from the three policy domains of social welfare, civil liberties, and racial affirmative action were regressed on their scores on the three individualism subscales while simultaneously taking into account their liberal–conservative self-placement and party identification.[6] Race was included as an additional control variable in the regressions for racial issue attitudes.[7] Feeling thermometer scores for George Bush, Ronald Reagan, and Jesse Jackson were also utilized as the criterion variables. To facilitate comparisons among coefficients, all independent variables were rescaled to the 0,1 interval.

Table 14.12 displays the results of the regression analyses. To reduce visual clutter, the table reports only coefficients that indicated for a regressor an estimated maximum direct effect equal to at least 10% of the range of the criterion variable (for the policy items) or five degrees (for the feeling thermometer ratings).[8]

Several features of Table 14.12 merit attention. First, the three individualism subscales were important predictors of a broad range of policy preferences and evaluations of political leaders, even when ideological self-identification and partisanship were taken into account. Second, the different components of individualism tended to come into play in distinct issue domains: beliefs about limited government were linked principally to welfare spending items, autonomy to civil liberties issues, and self-reliance to affirmative action policy preferences (and, secondarily, to social welfare views). Third, although ideological self-placement was the most potent predictor of issue attitudes in 8 of 15 instances, one of the individualism subscales possessed the largest coefficient in the other five instances – outperforming party identification consistently.[9] Fourth,

6 To minimize the loss of cases, respondents who did not provide an ideological self-identification were classified at the midpoint of that scale. In the end, it made little difference to the analytical results whether those cases were included in or excluded from the regressions. Regression equations were estimated by ordinary least squares. I am under no illusion that these regressions are estimating unknown population parameters for a fully specified model. Rather, I employ the regression results as a useful device for describing the empirical patterns in the data set at hand. See Achen (1982) for an elaboration of this perspective on regression analysis – a referral that does not imply that Achen necessarily endorses anything I have done in the present study.

7 The race variable takes on the values: 1 = African American respondent, 0 = otherwise.

8 All reported coefficients attained nominal statistical significance at the .05 level.

9 The prominence of liberal–conservative self-identification in these regressions seems to run counter to the prevailing view that ideological predispositions play a minor role at best in helping citizens structure and interpret political information. It should be borne in mind, however, that one-third of the individuals who were surveyed were unable to place themselves along a labeled seven-category liberal–conservative

either the self-reliance or autonomy subscale (or both) was a significant predictor of feelings toward Bush, Reagan, and Jackson; the third sub-scale (limited government) evidently shares its predictive power with other included variables. In sum, the evidence suggests that citizens' beliefs about key elements of individualism are strongly connected with the judgments they make in the real political world.

CONCLUSIONS

As Fowler (1991, p. 11) observed, rampant individualism is both the favorite theme and the constant complaint of American political intellec-tuals. This study has found that Americans are hardly the pathological individualists they are often made out to be, however. Clear majorities of survey respondents explicitly rejected characterizations of government as overbearing and intrusive, voicing instead a preference for stronger, more effective government to deal with problems that "have gotten bigger" and increasingly "complex" in recent years. While most Americans value self-reliance and the work ethic, they have also apparently concluded that hard work alone is no guarantee of success in a world in which unemployment and economic recession are increasingly the result of distant forces and circumstances beyond individual control. And although eight out of ten respondents said it is better to be true to one's own standards than it is "to fit in with the people around you," opinion was evenly divided on whether it is more important to encourage children to "think for them-selves" or to teach them "obedience and respect for authorities."

The portrait of America as a nation of rugged individualists is thus incompatible with the empirical evidence. It would be equally erroneous to conclude that Americans today are predominantly communitarian in their impulses, however. As Gans (1988) has argued, "middle Ameri-cans" favor government action, particularly in economic spheres, mainly to enhance the personal control they have over their own futures and to broaden the array of choices they have available to themselves:

Although the advocates of entrepreneurial . . . individualism may not like to hear it, popular individualism does not preach the values of risk-taking. Most middle Americans hold jobs rather than pursue careers, and many people can lose these jobs quickly in an economic crisis. . . . No wonder, then, that people shun needless risks and would like government to protect them from unexpected problems. (p. 3)

continuum. For the remaining two-thirds, moreover, it can be argued that, unlike party identification or individualist value orientations, ideological self-labeling is less a determinant of one's policy or political candidate preferences than it is an out-growth of them. See Bem (1972) in this regard.

Table 14.12. *Multiple Regression Estimates of Policy Preferences and Feelings Toward Political Figures as a Function of Individualism Subscales, Ideological Self-Placement, and Party Identification*

Dependent Variable	Range	Autonomy	Self-Reliance	Limited Gov't	Lib-Con Self-Place	(Repub.) Party ID	R^2	N
Social Welfare								
Cut Social Security budget	1–3			.25		.25	.09	1527
Cut homelessness budget	1–3		.38	.34	.24		.15	1510
More gov't services	1–7		−.47	−1.01	−1.31	−.63	.18	1288
Get ahead on own	1–7		.71	.97	1.48	.70	.17	1332
Favor rent control	1–5	−.78		−1.46			.09	469
Civil Liberties								
Women's place is in home	1–7	−1.50		.52	1.65		.11	555
Pro-abortion	1–4	.80			−1.20		.11	1519
No mandatory drug testing	1–4	.67			−1.06		.07	559
Favor school prayer	1–4	−.45			.52		.05	1500
Racial Issues								
Cut budget for aid to blacks	1–3		−.29		.48	.21	.21[a]	1491
Gov't should not help blacks	1–5		.70			.71	.20[a]	355
No racial college quotas	1–5	.50	.40	.44	.85		.15[a]	1432
No special favors (disagree)	1–5		−.83		−.72		.15[a]	1523
Feelings for political figures								
George Bush F-T score	0–100	−9.95	5.82		10.53	41.63	.37	569
Ronald Reagan F-T score	0–100	−7.38			20.90	44.86	.37	573
Jesse Jackson F-T score	0–100		−9.23		−16.78	−17.75	.22[a]	554

[a] Includes race as a control variable.

By the same token, an expressed preference for teaching children "obedience and respect for authorities" as well as "to be independent-minded and think for themselves" may not reflect a principled effort at balancing autonomy with community so much as it reflects worry over such things as rising rates of crime and unwed motherhood – external forces that threaten one's sense of control over the future.

If the central tendency of popular American political culture tilts toward individualism – albeit a decidedly nonideological version – there is nonetheless evidence in the survey data of what Bellah et al. (1985) have described as a "second language" of community. The litmus test of communitarian thinking, according to Dietz (1993, pp. 182–183), is whether or not individuals "are willing to sacrifice or restrict other political goods – liberties foremost among them – in the pursuit of a 'moral community.'" Will they "sacrifice personal interests or rights for the common good?" The answer to that question appears to be yes, at least up to a point. By better than two to one, survey respondents endorsed mandatory daily recitation of the Pledge of Allegiance in schools; more than eight out of ten favored setting aside time during school for prayer; 55% would support a law requiring all young adults to "serve their country by spending some time in the military, the Peace Corps, or in some other kind of national service"; nearly nine out of ten wanted mandatory recycling.

This blending of individualistic and communitarian impulses was not a property of the aggregated "American public" alone. It was found at the individual level as well. Unalloyed endorsement or rejection of individualist value statements was quite rare among the survey participants. Of the 1621 respondents, only 19 (1.2%) selected the individualistic alternative on all seven items constituting the individualism subscales. By the way, all nineteen were white, seventeen had attended college or had college degrees (89%), and fourteen (74%) were males. At the other end of the spectrum were thirty respondents (1.9%) who rejected the individualistic option on all seven items. This group was 30% nonwhite and 60% female, and only 14% had gone beyond high school.

The preceding statistics highlight another problem with sweeping generalizations about America's "rampant individualism," namely, that popular endorsement of individualistic principles varied significantly across subpopulations. Demographic analyses also underscored the empirical as well as conceptual distinctiveness of the different strands of individualism as interpreted by ordinary Americans.

All of this would be interesting intellectually but of marginal practical consequence if the political values that citizens expressed floated untethered from their positions on issues of the day, as some earlier studies claimed (e.g., McClosky, 1964; Prothro and Grigg, 1960). The present investigation revealed significant linkages between values and both policy preferences and assessments of political leaders, however. The diverse, pragmatic, and ambivalent nature of their beliefs about individualism thus helps us to understand Americans' diverse, pragmatic, and ambivalent approach to political affairs.

References

Achen, Christopher H. (1982) *Interpreting and Using Regression.* Beverly Hills, Calif.: Sage.

Anderson, Philip W., Kenneth J. Arrow, and David Pines, eds. (1988) *The Economy as an Evolving Complex System.* Redwood City, Calif.: Addison-Wesley.

Andrich, David (1988) *Rasch Models for Measurement.* Beverly Hills, Calif.: Sage.

Barber, Benjamin (1984) *Strong Democracy.* Berkeley: University of California Press.

(1988) *The Conquest of Politics.* Princeton, N.J.: Princeton University Press.

Bell, Daniel (1960) *The End of Ideology.* Glencoe, Ill.: Free Press.

Bellah, Robert N., Richard Madsen, William M. Sullivan, Ann Swidler, and Steven M. Tipton (1985) *Habits of the Heart.* Berkeley: University of California Press.

Bem, Darryl J. (1972) "Self-Perception Theory." In Leonard Berkowitz (ed.), *Advances in Experimental Social Psychology*, Vol. 6. New York: Academic Press, 1–62.

Boorstin, Daniel J. (1953) *The Genius of American Politics.* Chicago: University of Chicago Press.

Conover, Pamela Johnston, Ivor M. Crewe, and Donald D. Searing (1991) "The Nature of Citizenship in the United States and Great Britain: Empirical Comments on Theoretical Themes," *Journal of Political Science*, 53: 800–832.

Converse, Philip E. (1964) "The Nature of Belief Systems in Mass Publics." In David E. Apter (ed.), *Ideology and Discontent.* New York: Free Press, pp. 206–261.

Crittenden, Jack (1992) *Beyond Individualism: Reconstituting the Liberal Self.* New York: Oxford University Press.

Devine, Donald J. (1972) *The Political Culture of the United States.* Boston: Little, Brown.

Dietz, Mary G. (1993) "In Search of a Citizen Ethic." In George E. Marcus and Russell L. Hanson (eds.), *Reconsidering the Democratic Public.* University Park: Pennsylvania State University Press, pp. 173–185.

Diggins, John P. (1984) *The Lost Soul of American Politics.* New York: Basic Books.

Dionne, E. J., Jr. (1991) *Why Americans Hate Politics.* New York: Simon & Schuster.

Dolbeare, Kenneth M., and Linda J. Medcalf (1988) *American Ideologies Today.* New York: Random House.

Downs, Anthony (1957) *An Economic Theory of Democracy.* New York: Harper & Row.

Ellis, Richard E. (1993) *American Political Cultures*. New York: Oxford University Press.

Elster, Jon (1989) *Solomonic Judgments: Studies in the Limitations of Rationality*. New York: Cambridge University Press.

Etzioni, Amitai (1993) *The Spirit of Community*. New York: Crown Publishers.

Feldman, Stanley (1983) "Economic Individualism and American Public Opinion," *American Politics Quarterly*, 11: 3–30.

(1988) "Structure and Consistency in Public Opinion: Evidence and Meaning," *American Journal of Political Science*, 32: 416–440.

Feldman, Stanley, and Pamela J. Conover (1981) "The Origins and Meanings of Liberal/Conservative Self-Identifications," *American Journal of Political Science*, 25: 617–645.

Feldman, Stanley, and John Zaller (1992) "The Political Culture of Ambivalence: Ideological Responses to the Welfare State," *American Journal of Political Science*, 36: 268–307.

Fowler, Robert B. (1991) *The Dance with Community*. Lawrence: University Press of Kansas.

Fox-Genovese, Elizabeth (1991) *Feminism without Illusions: A Critique of Individualism*. Chapel Hill: University of North Carolina Press.

Gans, Herbert J. (1988) *Middle American Individualism*. New York: Free Press.

Gilens, Martin (1999) *Why Americans Hate Welfare*. Chicago: University of Chicago Press.

Gilligan, Carol (1982) *In a Different Voice*. Cambridge, Mass.: Harvard University Press.

Guisinger, Shan, and Sidney J. Blatt (1994) "Individuality and Relatedness: Evolution of a Fundamental Dialectic," *American Psychologist*, 49: 104–111.

Hartz, Louis (1955) *The Liberal Tradition in America*. New York: Harcourt.

Hochschild, Jennifer L. (1993) "Disjunction and Ambivalence in Citizens' Political Outlooks." In George E. Marcus and Russell L. Hanson (eds.), *Reconsidering the Democratic Public*. University Park: Pennsylvania State University Press, pp. 187–210.

Hurwitz, Jon, and Mark Peffley (1987) "How Are Foreign Policy Attitudes Structured? A Hierarchical Model," *American Political Science Review*, 81: 1099–1130.

Inglehart, Ronald (1990) *Culture Shift*. Princeton, N.J.: Princeton University Press.

Kateb, George (1984) "Democratic Individuality and the Claims of Politics," *Political Theory*, 12: 331–360.

Ketcham, Ralph (1987) *Individualism and Public Life*. Oxford: Basil Blackwell.

Kinder, Donald R. (1983) "Diversity and Complexity in American Public Opinion." In Ada Finifter (ed.), *Political Science: The State of the Discipline*. Washington, D.C.: American Political Science Association, pp. 389–428.

Kinder, Donald R., and Lynn M. Sanders (1990) "Mimicking Political Debate with Survey Questions: The Case of White Opinion on Affirmative Action for Blacks," *Social Cognition*, 8: 73–103.

Kunstler, James H. (1993) *The Geography of Nowhere*. New York: Simon & Schuster.

Lasch, Christopher (1979) *The Culture of Narcissism*. New York: Norton.

(1991) *The True and Only Heaven*. New York: Norton.

Lerner, Max (1957) *America as a Civilization*. New York: Simon & Schuster.

Lipset, Seymour Martin (1960) *Political Man*. Garden City, N.Y.: Doubleday.

Lukes, Steven (1973) *Individualism*. Oxford: Basil Blackwell.

Luskin, Robert C. (1987) "Measuring Political Sophistication," *American Journal of Political Science*, 31: 856–899.

MacIntyre, Alasdair (1981) *After Virtue*. South Bend, Ind.: University of Notre Dame Press.

Marcus, George E. (1988) "Democratic Theories and the Study of Public Opinion," *Polity*, 21: 25–44.

Markus, Gregory B. (1982) "Political Attitudes During an Election Year: A Report on the 1980 NES Panel Study," *American Political Science Review*, 76: 538–560.

(1990) "Measuring popular individualism." Memo to ANES Board of Overseers. Ann Arbor, Mich.: Institute for Social Research.

Markus, Hazel Rose, and Shinobu Kitayama (1991) "Culture and Self: Implications for Cognition, Emotion, and Motivation," *Psychological Review*, 98: 224–253.

McClosky, Herbert (1964) "Consensus and Ideology in American Politics," *American Political Science Review*, 58: 361–382.

McClosky, Herbert, and John Zaller (1984) *The American Ethos*. Cambridge, Mass.: Harvard University Press.

Miller, David L. (1967) *Individualism*. Austin: University of Texas Press.

Morone, James (1990) *The Democratic Wish*. New York: Basic Books.

Nedelsky, Jennifer (1989) "Reconceiving Autonomy: Sources, Thoughts and Possibilities," *Yale Journal of Law and Feminism*, 1: 7–36.

Neuman, W. Russell (1986) *The Paradox of Mass Politics*. Cambridge, Mass.: Harvard University Press.

Nozick, Robert (1974) *Anarchy, State, and Utopia*. New York: Basic Books.

Petty, Richard E., Greg A. Rennier, and John T. Cacioppo (1987) "Assertion versus Interrogation Format in Opinion Surveys: Questions Enhance Thoughtful Responding," *Public Opinion Quarterly*, 51: 481–494.

Prothro, James W., and Charles W. Grigg (1960) "Fundamental Principles of Democracy: Bases of Agreement and Disagreement," *Journal of Politics*, 22: 276–294.

Reich, Robert B. (1987) *Tales of a New America*. New York: Times Books.

Richardson, Robert D., Jr. (1995) *Emerson: The Mind on Fire*. Berkeley: University of California Press.

Riker, William H., and Peter C. Ordeshook (1973) *An Introduction to Positive Political Theory*. Englewood Cliffs, N.J.: Prentice-Hall.

Rokeach, Milton (1973) *The Nature of Human Values*. New York: Free Press.

Rosenblum, Nancy (1987) *Another Liberalism*. Cambridge, Mass.: Harvard University Press.

Sandel, Michael (1982) *Liberalism and the Limits of Justice*. Cambridge, UK: Cambridge University Press.

Sears, David O., and Carolyn L. Funk (1991) "The Role of Self-Interest in Social and Political Attitudes." In Mark P. Zanna (ed.), *Advances in Experimental Social Psychology*, Vol. 24. San Diego: Academic Press, pp. 1–91.

Sen, Amartya S. (1977) "Rational Fools: A Critique of the Behavioral Foundations of Economic Theory," *Philosophy and Public Affairs*, 6(4): 317–344.

Smith, Rogers M. (1993) "Beyond Tocqueville, Myrdal, and Hartz: The Multiple Traditions in America," *American Political Science Review*, 87: 549–566.

Gregory B. Markus

Sniderman, Paul M., and Richard A. Brody (1977) "Coping: The Ethic of Self-Reliance," *American Journal of Political Science*, 21: 501–521.

Sniderman, Paul M., and Thomas Piazza (1993) *The Scar of Race.* Cambridge, Mass.: Belknap Press.

Stoker, Laura (1992) "Interests and Ethics in Politics," *American Political Science Review*, 86(2): 369–380.

Taylor, Charles (1985) *Philosophy and the Human Sciences.* Cambridge, UK: Cambridge University Press.

Toner, Robin (1993) "Poll on Changes in Health Care Finds Support Amid Skepticism," *New York Times*, Sept. 22, p. A1.

Triandis, Harry C. (1989) "The Self and Social Behavior in Differing Cultural Contexts," *Psychological Review*, 96: 506–520.

Triandis, Harry C., Robert Bontempo, and Marcelo J. Villareal (1988) "Individualism and Collectivism: Cross-Cultural Perspectives on Self–Group Relationships," *Journal of Personality and Social Psychology*, 54: 323–338.

Walzer, Michael (1983) *Spheres of Justice.* New York: Basic Books.

Weisberg, Herbert F. (1974) "Models of Statistical Relationships," *American Political Science Review*, 68: 1638–1655.

Wills, Garry (1987) *Reagan's America: Innocents at Home.* New York: Doubleday.

Wolfe, Alan (1989) *Whose Keeper?* Berkeley: University of California Press.

15

Political Value Judgments

LAURA STOKER

Even the most casual observation of American politics reveals it to be the site of ever-present contests over what government *ought* to be doing and promoting. Some of these contests are about the best way to achieve consensually valued ends. Others are about the very purposes of government actions and policies themselves. Some engender bitter conflict and define political enemies. Others find people united behind a shared sense of purpose but divided about how exactly to proceed. Some engage material interests directly and concretely. Others do so only indirectly and indeterminately. My purpose in this chapter is to outline and illustrate an approach to studying public opinion that tries to illuminate this normative terrain.

This approach assumes that citizens evaluate public policies by bringing moral criteria to bear – in effect, asking questions like "Is this a *good* policy" or "What, in this case, is *right*?" Accordingly, one job facing public opinion analysts is to understand how citizens come to answer, and to disagree about, such questions. In their efforts to do so, I recommend that public opinion analysts think about political *value judgments* rather than about political *values* per se.

I first define and illustrate what I mean by political value judgments and develop two different ways of thinking about the kinds of considerations that underlie them. The focus here is on conceptual issues – on what political value judgments might consist of and how they might differ from one another. Next, I briefly present findings from two

I would like to acknowledge the research support I received from the Survey Research Center at the University of California at Berkeley and from the Center for Advanced Study in the Behavioral Sciences (NSF Grant SES-9022192). I also wish to thank Gordon Adams, Jim Kuklinski, Margaret Levi, Melissa Orlie, Sam Popkin, Charles Stein, Nate Teske, and John Zaller for reading and commenting on an earlier draft of this chapter and Kathleen Much for providing editorial assistance.

empirical studies that illustrate this approach to studying public opinion. One demonstrates the importance of concerns about compensatory justice to the public's views on affirmative action. The second explores opinions on policies of social control (policies regulating abortion, euthanasia, pornography, and homosexuality) by estimating a model representing liberalism's contentions about when such policies are justifiable. Finally, I situate my arguments about political value judgments within the context of existing research on public opinion and political psychology.

POLITICAL VALUE JUDGMENTS

What I call "political value judgments" are judgments made in politics about what is *valuable* or *of value* – to anyone or to us – often expressed as claims about what is "good" or "bad," "right" or "wrong."[1] These might be judgments made about objects of any kind, for example people (as in "Clinton is a good president"), actions (as in "Storming the Branch Davidian complex in Waco was wrong"), or policies (as in "Allowing gays to serve in the military is the right thing to do"). Because good and bad or right and wrong are verdicts offered in the language of morality or ethics, we might speak of such claims as moral instead of political judgments. Or we might follow commonsense notions of morality by conceiving of value judgments about people and their conduct as moral and value judgments about public policies or the actions of governments as political. Such distinctions will be useful at times. I construe political value judgments broadly, however, and recognize both kinds of value judgments as entering into political conflicts.

Value judgments either assert objective claims about value – about what *anyone* must acknowledge to be of value – or express intersubjective contentions – about some *we* must acknowledge to be of value. In this they are unlike purely subjective desires or personal preferences that identify what a person qua individual wants or values ("what *I* value"). Of course, value judgments are the judgments of a subject, and in this sense they too are subjective judgments; it is some person who says or believes, for example, that "abortion is wrong." But they purport to characterize the object of judgment rather than simply to reveal something about the subject; they "resist being reduced to claims about the

1 Conceptually, value judgments are not limited to judgments that are expressed in the language of good and bad, or right and wrong. Thus, for example, "he's a despicable man" would still count as a value judgment even though it doesn't contain the requisite locutions. Nevertheless, the concreteness of this linguistic simplification is useful, and I rely upon it here.

434

subject of the sort that if I think abortion is murder this is a proposition about me" (Modood, 1984, 237). As such, value judgments admit of a degree of detachment between the contention about value and the contingencies of personal desire; the judgment ostensibly cannot be simply traced to who I am or what, by my particular history and place in society, I have come to value.[2]

This detachment can be traced to the kinds of reasons that sustain preferences and value judgments. Preferences can be explained by reasons that are articulated in subjective biographical terms, whereas value judgments must be supported by reasons that justify in objective or intersubjective terms. If I ask you "Why do you like X?" you can explain your preference by telling me a personal story, a story about yourself. If, however, I ask you "Why do you judge X right?" then you must justify your judgment by telling me an impersonal story, a story compelling to anyone or, at least, compelling to us.

Justifications describe morally relevant characteristics of the policy or action being judged. They both define what we (or anyone) ought to pay attention to when evaluating the policy or action – for example, that some person is being harmed, some value is being advanced, or some principle is being instantiated – and enjoin a conclusion. Philosophers commonly distinguish between consequentialist and nonconsequentialist justifications, and between partial and impartial justifications. The distinction between consequentialist and nonconsequentialist justifications centers on whether values or principles are invoked, whereas the distinction between partial and impartial justifications centers on whether the justifier's own interests are invoked.

From a consequentialist perspective, the goodness of a policy depends on the goodness of the policy's consequences, as indexed for important

---

2 Another way to put the distinction is to say that preferences express what one desires, and value judgments claim to identify what is desirable (for anyone or for us). The desires–desirable contrast was regularly drawn in early work on values. Kluckhohn's (1951) influential definition of values centered on the phrase "conceptions of the desirable" (see Spates, 1983); more recently, Meddin (1975) used this contrast to define what he called the "normative-appetitive struggle"; and Williams (1979), in his review of work on values, argued that "[v]ery broad definitions tend to equate 'value' with preference, desire, liking, or satisfaction – thus passing over the most distinctive feature of valuing, that is, the partial autonomy of criteria of desirability from desire or wish" (p. 19, reference excluded). This is not to say that people are simply recognizing value that (somehow) inheres in the objects of their judgment or that their judgments are undistorted by their personal circumstances. The contrast here is defined from the perspective of the individual doing the judging. Moreover, in practice, people may (or may not) desire what they judge desirable.

intrinsic values[3] considered with respect to the entire collectivity. When reasoning consequentially, judging the value of different policy options requires considering the states of affairs each option will engender and asking such questions as "In which state are people collectively best off?" (invoking the value of personal welfare), "Which state maximizes the freedom provided to individuals?" (invoking the value of individual freedom), and "Which state best advances the goal of equality?" (invoking some version of the value of equality).[4] Rokeach's (1973) famous list of "terminal" or intrinsic values included a world at peace, a world of beauty, equality, family security, freedom, national security, a comfortable life, an exciting life, a sense of accomplishment, happiness, inner harmony, mature love, pleasure, salvation, self-respect, social recognition, true friendship, and wisdom. Disagreement may arise over which values ought to count in the assessment of "good" and how values are to be weighed when in conflict.

"Nonconsequentialist justifications" refer to rules (absolute directives) or principles (prima facie directives) defining what an actor (whether an individual or a government) should or should not *do*.[5] These are typically claims about rights, duties, or obligations, of which the following are illustrative:

Sher (1983)
Acts which are right:
  Acts which discharge promises
  Acts which repay debts
  Acts which punish the guilty
  Acts which reward the deserving
  Acts which compensate the victims of wrongdoing

3 Something valued intrinsically is an end "in itself," something "worth having, achieving, choosing, desiring, experiencing, bringing into existence, or sustaining in existence, for its own sake" (Edwards, 1979, 17). In contrast, something is valued extrinsically or instrumentally if its value is found in its production of something else of value.
4 Notice that some of these values have individual referents and others collective referents. Individuals can be categorized as more or less well off or as more or less free to pursue their own goals and plans, whereas societies can be described as more or less egalitarian. An unspoiled natural environment is another example of the latter. The consequentialist will worry about the attainment of both kinds of values in society as a whole. This distinguishes consequentialist concerns from rational-choice, personal-utility-maximizing concerns.
5 Following common usage, we might also refer to some of these prescriptions as "absolute" or "prima facie norms," especially if they refer to modes of individual conduct as opposed to things that governments or public policies might do.

Gert (1988)
    Don't kill
    Don't cause pain
    Don't disable
    Don't deprive of freedom
    Don't deprive of pleasure
    Don't deceive
    Keep your promises
    Don't cheat
    Obey the law
    Do your duty

Nonconsequentialist codes of duty and obligation derive from particular premises about personhood, nature, society, human life, or even the afterlife – about who we are and what kind of world we inhabit. People are viewed as unique individuals with their own goals and preferences (which yields rights), yet also bound to particular others through their social roles and relationships (which yields obligations) and to all others by virtue of their common humanity (which yields duties).

Controversies over the death penalty illustrate the differences between consequentialist and nonconsequentialist justification. From a consequentialist perspective, one might worry about the deterrence consequences of the death penalty (with an eye toward the reduction of crime, which would enhance human welfare) or the beneficial consequences of the death penalty for the families of the victims. From a nonconsequentialist perspective, by contrast, one might focus on whether it is ever morally acceptable to take a human life or on the justice of punishment: on whether the punishment fits the crime.

When distinguishing impartial from partial justification, what is at issue is the agent's relationship to those whose interests are alleged to be harmed, protected, or advanced by the action or policy under consideration. Impartial justifications manifest a concern with *all* people or with *each* person, as in "This would be good for the community as a whole" or "This would be fair to each person involved."[6] By contrast, partial

6 Consequentialists make claims of the first sort; what matters is whether policies produce states of affairs that advance values for the citizenry as a whole, without giving any special weight to the particular claims made by individuals or subgroups. Nonconsequentialists make claims of the second sort. Protecting a given right, for example, means protecting each or any person's right; "the citizenry as a whole" is disaggregated into sets of unique persons, each of whom has rights. Both count as impartial in the sense being developed here. Note that to call a judgment "impartial" in this sense does not imply that the policy or action being judged treats all people alike or that it distributes equal shares of some good. Nor does it mean

justifications refer to what is happening to *me* or to *my group*, as in "This would require a heavy sacrifice on my part," or "This is not what I prefer," or "This would set back the interests of my group."

Like these examples, partial justifications make some essential reference to the self. The justification does not simply stop there, however; it must make some sort of universalizing move: My sacrifice is unacceptable because no person should have to so sacrifice;[7] my ability to act on my preference should be preserved, along with the ability of others to do so too; my group should not be so adversely affected, nor should any other such group. To count as a justification, then, it is not enough simply to make such claims as "This doesn't help me." The interest bearer must, as Nagel (1991) put it, offer a "general argument which one would be willing to recognize if someone else offered it" (p. 76). These kinds of arguments join contentions about self-interest or group interest with nonconsequentialist principles of right.

In illustration, consider the following arguments articulated in Senate subcommittee hearings on proposed amendments to the Clean Air Act:[8]

Partial: (New York State Attorney General, Robert Abrams) New York's people and environment are among the primary victims of acid rain pollution. Over the years, it has contributed to thousands of premature deaths, destroyed our lakes, damaged crops, forests, buildings and statues and shrouded our cities and countryside in a poisonous haze. Halting acid rain has been among the highest environmental priorities in New York for nearly 10 years. . . . But action in New York is not enough. We are located near the end of an air pollution pipeline that brings millions of tons of acid rain, air toxics and smog from other states. This is a national problem that demands a Federal solution.

Partial: (Mr. Benjamin Y. Cooper, Senior Vice President, Printing Industries of America) I appear here today as a representative for the numerous small businesses who are members of the Clean Air Working Group. . . . [W]e fear stringent and technologically infeasible regulations under this legislative proposal. . . . Small operators have neither the technical capabilities nor the human resources to devote to complying with these requirements.

Impartial: (Mr. Richard E. Ayres, Chairman, National Clean Air Coalition) Air pollution shortens lives, increases medical costs, diminishes human productivity, cuts crop yields. . . . The American people want clean air. Survey after survey con-

---

that, in order to be impartial, any argument on behalf of the policy must actually refer to each person or to all of the people in a given community. For example, I argue impartially if I say that a given policy is wrong because it sets back the interests or violates the basic rights of a particular person or set of people that the policy happens to target – whether children, gays, businesspeople, women, and so on.

7 Or put intersubjectively, "because no American should have to so sacrifice."

8 All quotes are taken from the *Congressional Digest*, March 1990, pp. 74–95.

firms their desire, and their willingness to pay for it. The time has come for action – comprehensive, aggressive, ambitious actions – to clean up our skies and remove the public health threat of air pollution.

Impartial: (Ms. Regina McLaurin, President, National Parking Association) NPA opposes these measures because they would drain people, jobs and economic vitality out of our central cities, while ultimately doing nothing to curb overall pollution.

Some of these arguments refer to the general consequences of the proposed policy for the nation as a whole (e.g., it "would drain people, jobs, and economic vitality out of our central cities") or to what air pollution means for the American people as individuals (e.g., it "shortens lives"). Alongside these impartial viewpoints are partial arguments that speak directly to what the policy/problem means for oneself or for a group to which one is particularly tied (as in Abrams's concern for New York State or Cooper's concern for small businesses).

The partial–impartial distinction reminds us that questions of right are not just concerned with what all persons have in common or with what is happening to people or society writ large. They are also concerned with what is happening to individuals qua individuals and to individuals as people who are tied to particular others and groups in a socially differentiated society. As such, efforts to protect one's own preferences, for example, or to preserve distinctive aspects of one's particular group subculture, although indeed self- or group-interested, may also be defended as "right."

In sum, justifications invoke values, principles, and interests in the course of explaining why a policy is good or bad, right or wrong. They identify (ostensibly) morally valuable or reprehensible characteristics of what the policy does or produces. If citizens' opinions on a public policy reflect their sense of the policy's goodness or rightness, then one project for public opinion analysts is to study the justificatory basis of citizens' views. Understanding political value judgments requires understanding the justifications that underlie and sustain them.

In what follows, I present two examples of this kind of work. The first demonstrates that citizens' support for affirmative action in the workplace depends on the circumstances in which those programs are implemented. This result, I argue, reflects the application of one principle, compensatory justice, to the question of when affirmative action programs are justifiable. The second example concerns opinions on the government regulation of homosexuality, abortion, pornography, and euthanasia. I develop an explanatory model based on classic liberal ideas about the circumstances under which governments might justifiably restrict individual liberties. Both of these examples suggest that citizens evaluate public policies by bringing moral criteria to bear.

Laura Stoker

COMPENSATORY JUSTICE AND PUBLIC OPINION ON AFFIRMATIVE ACTION IN THE WORKPLACE

The Supreme Court's Compensatory Justice Rationale

Since passage of the Civil Rights Act of 1964, the Supreme Court has regularly confronted the issue of affirmative action programs for blacks and other minorities.[9] Despite the numerous points of controversy that have arisen, many of which remain unsettled, some points of consensus have emerged. In the area of employment, the Supreme Court has clearly rejected preferential treatment policies introduced either to compensate blacks for disadvantages rooted in historical practices of discrimination in American society or to promote racial balance in the workforce. Instead, the Court has judged such policies legitimate only when they are implemented by a particular business or governmental unit in response to a finding that the unit itself had been engaging in discriminatory hiring practices. Thus, for example, in *Wygant v. Jackson Board of Education*, Justice Lewis F. Powell wrote: "This Court never has held that societal discrimination alone is sufficient to justify a racial classification. Rather, the Court has insisted upon some showing of prior discrimination by the government unit involved before allowing limited use of racial classifications in order to remedy such discrimination" (1985 476 US 267, 274). Controversy exists, of course, about how to recognize discrimination.[10]

The Court rests its case here on an argument about compensatory justice: When it has been established that a given company or govern-

9 Rosenfeld (1991) contains a useful summary and analysis of the cases from the 1970s through 1988. Dansicker (1991) discusses several important subsequent cases in the context of an analysis of the failed 1990 civil rights legislation and the 1991 Civil Rights Act.

10 The Supreme Court has developed two lines of analysis on this issue, one involving circumstances of discriminatory intent ("disparate treatment" cases) and one involving circumstances of disparate racial impact, with or without intent ("disparate impact" cases; see Maikovich and Brown, 1989, chapter 3, for a straightforward rendition of the basic issues here). Not surprisingly, disparate impact cases are more controversial and less settled in law. In *Wards Cove Packing Company v. Antonio* (1989 490 US 642), for example, the Court introduced a more stringent standard for establishing a prima facie case of discrimination in disparate impact cases than that which had been established in an important early case, *Griggs v. Duke Power Co.* (1971 401 US 424). This was one of the major issues of controversy addressed in the (failed) 1990 civil rights legislation and in the 1991 Civil Rights Act. That act reaffirmed the *Griggs* standard. See Dansicker (1991).

mental unit has wrongfully discriminated against blacks, then justice demands that its discriminatory hiring practices be dismantled and that compensatory or remedial actions be undertaken. Implementing race-conscious hiring policies in such circumstances is just, the Court argues, if it can be shown that they are narrowly tailored to the particular case at hand, and thus yield an appropriate form and level of compensation for the discriminatory practices that were in place. Prior findings as to the existence and nature of the discriminatory hiring practices, as Justice Sandra Day O'Connor put it in a 1988 opinion, are "necessary to define both the scope of the injury and the extent of the remedy necessary to cure its effects" and "also serve to assure all citizens that the deviation from the norm of equal treatment of all racial and ethnic groups is a temporary matter, a measure taken in the service of the goal of equality itself" (*Richmond v. J. A. Croson Co.*, 1988 488 US, 497 and 510). In such cases, affirmative action policies then serve the "focused goal of remedying wrongs worked by specific instances of racial discrimination" rather than "the remedying of the effects of 'societal discrimination,' an amorphous concept of injury that may be ageless in its reach to the past" (ibid, 469).[11] According to the compensatory logic, as one observer put it, it is "black *qua* victim and not black *qua* black person" that is significant (Simon, 1977, 41).[12]

The key elements of the compensatory justice situation consist of a wrongdoer, a wrong, a victim, and an act of compensation. The logic is straightforward. Some actor acts wrongly toward some person. That wrong act creates both a victim (the wronged person) and an obligation

---

11 Here, Justice O'Connor is partially quoting from Justice Powell's opinion in the *University of California Regents v. Baake* case (1978 438 US 265).

12 Compensatory or remedial justice requires reparation or restitution to victims. One problematic issue that remains here focuses on the question of whether preferential treatment policies are acceptable only if they compensate "actual victims" or whether they may apply to the entire "class of victims" (e.g., blacks) affected by the discriminatory practice (see, e.g., Groarke, 1990). This continues to be debated by the Court (e.g., see Justice Antonin Scalia's separate opinion in *Richmond v. J. A. Croson Co.* 1988 488 US 469), but in *Sheet Metal Workers v. EEOC* the Court explicitly rejected the argument that Title VII, Section 706(g), of the 1964 Civil Rights Act "authorizes a district court to award preferential relief only to the actual victims of unlawful discrimination" and concluded that it "does not prohibit a court from ordering, in appropriate circumstances, affirmative race-conscious relief as a remedy for past discrimination. Specifically, we hold that such relief may be appropriate where an employer or a labor union has engaged in persistent or egregious discrimination, or where necessary to dissipate the lingering effects of pervasive discrimination" (1985 478 US 421, 444–445, opinion delivered by Justice William J. Brennan).

of compensation on the part of the wrongdoer. The wrongdoer is obligated to respond by compensating the victim to an appropriate (or just or fair) extent.[13] In the United States, some efforts to compensate the victims of discrimination reflect this logic quite directly; cases in which those who have been subject to intentional discrimination are deemed by the Court to be due compensation by the discriminator ("disparate treatment" cases; see footnote 10). Others depart from the logic in one or another way, and to the extent that they do so, they become more controversial.

In the ordinary cases of affirmative action in hiring that the Court has judged legitimate (and those that I will be concerned with here, in the sense that they are represented by the survey questions I will be analyzing), some but not all aspects of the paradigmatic compensatory justice logic are in place. They represent the standard logic in that they are cases where the compensatory policy arises in response to a previous wrong, where the nature or extent of the compensation must be appropriate to the nature or extent of the wrong, and where compensation is (arguably) both owed and to be provided by the wrongdoer. Moreover, in the case of affirmative action, where the wrong is discrimination that both violates the principle of equal treatment and undermines the principle of equal opportunity, the remedy involves measures that, as O'Connor put it in the opinion quoted earlier, are "taken in the service of the goal of equality itself."

They depart from the standard logic, however, in two ways. First, compensation goes to members of the class of people that the "actual victims" represent, not to the actual victims themselves, who are usually not identifiable (see footnote 12). Second, the compensatory policy often extracts costs (effort, financial resources, and so on) not only from the wrongdoer, but from other "innocent" people as well – those not falling into the relevant class. This occurs because the wrongdoer and victim are not involved in a simple dyadic exchange; instead, the wrongdoer is in a position to distribute goods (jobs, promotions) to members of different classes of people, and the distributive process is zero sum: when some gain, others necessarily lose.

One important point follows directly. People could affirm the general rationale of compensatory justice as it applies to the paradigmatic case but not as it applies to the case of affirmative action as I have described it. This is one way to think of some of the debates that have taken place among Supreme Court justices and may be true of the positions taken

---

13 See Frankel-Paul (1991) for a discussion of the general compensatory logic.

by ordinary people as well. More generally, this means that while we can think of the compensatory justice rationale as lending support to the contention that affirmative action policies are morally justifiable, that is not to say that there are no moral reasons that weigh against that conclusion. Yet the compensatory justice rationale is of significance to the Supreme Court's thinking about affirmative action and, as we will soon see, to that of ordinary citizens as well.

Survey Research on Affirmative Action

Questions about compensatory justice are relational and backward-looking: rightness is defined in relation to a previous wrong. Whether or not a compensatory action or policy is right (or just) depends on whether or not it can be described as an appropriate response to the wrong that it is designed to compensate. Because of this, judgments about compensatory justice are also context-specific. What is judged just compensation in one context may be judged unjust in another. Or what is judged to be an appropriate or just level of compensation for the victim of one wrong may be judged to be an utterly inappropriate or unfair level of compensation for the victim of a different wrong.

Accordingly, if people care about considerations of compensatory justice, then we would expect their opinions about affirmative action programs to be sensitive to the context in which those programs are implemented. If those programs are introduced in a context where nondiscriminatory hiring has been taking place, in an attempt to compensate blacks for the historical and societywide practices of discrimination to which they have been subject, their justice would be assessed one way. (Here the Court would be likely to say that they are unjust and illegal.) If they are introduced in a context where discriminatory hiring has been taking place, in an effort to dismantle those practices and to compensate those subject to discrimination, their justice would be assessed another way. (Here the Court would be likely to say that they are just and legal.) Thus, if compensatory justice considerations are relevant to opinions on this issue, the question that needs to be asked is not whether people, in some general sense, favor or oppose affirmative action in hiring for blacks. The right question is: "Under what circumstances, if any, would they lend them their support?"

This, however, is not a question that previous researchers have asked. As far as I can tell, virtually all of the questions on affirmative action that pollsters and academic survey researchers have posed have either generalized over the kinds of contexts that the Court has deemed so significant or have ignored those contexts altogether. The first case is illustrated by the following questions:[14]

(Caddell/Cambridge Survey Research): Some large corporations are required to practice what is called affirmative action. This sometimes requires employers to give special preference to minorities or women when hiring. Do you approve or disapprove of affirmative action?

(Gallup): The U.S. Supreme Court has ruled that employers may sometimes favor women and members of minorities over better qualified men and whites in hiring and promoting, to achieve better balance in their work forces. Do you approve or disapprove of this decision?

The critical words in these questions are "some" and "sometimes." "*Some* corporations are *sometimes* required to implement preferential hiring programs" says the first. "The U.S. Supreme Court has ruled that employers may *sometimes* favor women and members of minorities over better qualified men and whites in hiring and promoting" says the second. These questions treat the contexts in which affirmative action programs are implemented as irrelevant to the question of what the public thinks of them – those affirmative action policies that some corporations sometimes are legally required to implement.

What makes these questions problematic is not that they simplify reality, as any survey question must do. Rather, the problem is in the nature of the simplifications that they introduce. If we are interested in knowing what the public thinks about affirmative action programs that are implemented in circumstances that the Court has deemed legitimate, then we should be asking affirmative action questions that aptly situate the programs in those circumstances. If we want to know how the public would respond to affirmative action programs that are or might be found in circumstances that fail to meet the conditions that the Court has identified, then we should ask questions about the use of affirmative action in those circumstances too. Either way, questions that generalize across or ignore the contexts in which affirmative action programs are implemented may (and, as we will see, do) yield results that misrepresent the level of public support for affirmative action programs that, as the Court puts it, serve as "narrowly tailored" remedial responses to wrongful

14 The second case, where the affirmative action opinion question makes no reference to context at all, is illustrated by the formulation used by the American National Election Studies (NES): "Some people say that because of past discrimination against blacks, preference in hiring and promotion should be given to blacks. Others say preferential hiring and promotion of blacks is wrong [Form A: because it discriminates against whites; Form B: because it gives blacks advantages they haven't earned]. What about your opinion – are you for or against preferential hiring and promotion of blacks?"

practices of discrimination. If people take considerations of compensatory justice into account when they evaluate affirmative action policies, then they will pay attention to the circumstances under which those policies are implemented – and we researchers should too.

In order to evaluate this issue empirically, an experiment was introduced into a survey on race and politics carried out by the Survey Research Center at the University of California, Berkeley.[15] The survey posed three different versions of an affirmative action policy question, each one administered to a random third of the respondents. The first version was a standard, context-free question:

Question 1: No Context

Do you think that large companies should be required to give a certain number of jobs to blacks, or should the government stay out of this?

The distribution of responses to this question parallels that typically found in opinion surveys; whites overwhelmingly oppose preferential treatment of blacks in hiring (see Figure 15.1a). Answers to the second and third versions of the question, however, tell a different story.

The second and third versions of the question each introduce contextual information. The second version simply identifies a circumstance where blacks are underrepresented in the company, whereas the third version identifies a circumstance where the company is engaging in discriminatory hiring practices:

Question 2: Underrepresentation Context

There are some large companies where blacks are under-represented. . . . Do you think these large companies should be required to give a certain number of jobs to blacks, or should the government stay out of this?

Question 3: Discrimination Context

There are some large companies with employment policies that discriminate against blacks. . . . Do you think these large companies should be required to give a certain number of jobs to blacks, or should the government stay out of this?

When the company is described as one where blacks are underrepresented, white opinion remains overwhelmingly opposed to affirmative action (Figure 15.1b). The portrait of opinion changes, however, once that policy is presented as a response to identified conditions of

---

15 The study was run under the direction of Principal Investigators Paul Sniderman of Stanford University, Philip Tetlock of the University of California(UC)-Berkeley, and Thomas Piazza of the UC-Berkeley Survey Research Center. A random digital dial sample of 2223 people were interviewed by telephone between February and November 1991, with a response rate of 65.3%.

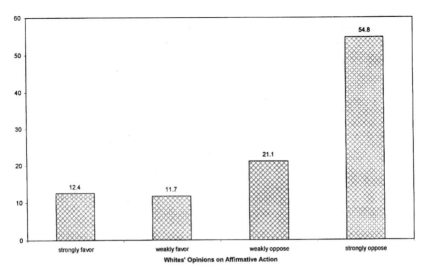

Figure 15.1a. No context.

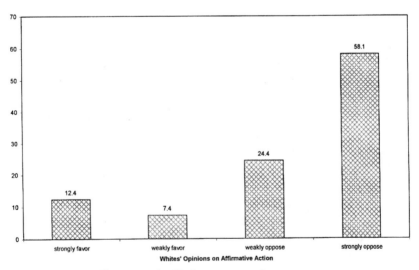

Figure 15.1b. Underrepresentation context.

discrimination. Rather than revealing overwhelming opposition to the policy, opinion becomes polarized (Figure 15.1c). Those opposing affirmative action policies still outnumber those who express support, but the distribution shifts dramatically in the direction of greater support,

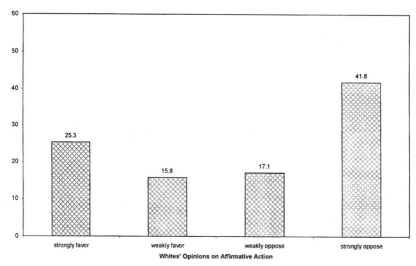

Figure 15.1c. Discrimination context.

with those expressing strong opinions outweighing those expressing weak opinions on both sides of the issue.

The conventional wisdom about public opinion on affirmative action is that the public, or at least the white public, is overwhelmingly and invariably opposed to race-conscious hiring policies. This, indeed, is what poll after poll and survey after survey has appeared to document. But this conclusion is based on responses to survey questions that either generalize across the circumstances in which affirmative action programs are or might be implemented or that leave out any mention of those circumstances altogether. We reach a different conclusion about where the public stands when we ask about affirmative action programs that are situated in circumstances that the Supreme Court has deemed legitimate – those in which it can be demonstrated that discriminatory hiring practices have left blacks disadvantaged. The opponents of affirmative action still outnumber its supporters, but the distribution of opinion shifts markedly, leaving a margin of more like three to two instead of the usual four to one. One no longer gets the impression that white opposition to affirmative action is so deep and unyielding that the issue need no longer be debated and, if peaceful race relations are to ensue, the programs had best be abandoned. One sees an issue that is controversial among whites, not settled, where opinion is polarized, not lopsided – where there is still plenty of room in which to carry out debate.

Once one thinks of affirmative action programs as being introduced in circumstances where established practices of discrimination have left blacks disadvantaged, it no longer makes sense to say that they allow "government apportionment of coveted positions to supersede the competition of the marketplace" (Sowell 1989, 21) or to describe the issue of affirmative action as one that forces a brute confrontation between equality of opportunity and equality of results:

> Affirmative action policies . . . have introduced a new approach to promoting equality in American life. The old approach, initially voiced in the Declaration of Independence, emphasized equality for *individuals*, defined as equality of opportunity. The new one focuses on equality for *groups*, defined as equality of result. It is the collision of these two views on equality that underlies the growing public controversy over affirmative action and quotas. (Lipset, 1991, 1)

In circumstances where racial discrimination had been operating, the "competition of the marketplace" itself had been distorted and equality of opportunity itself had been undermined, as Supreme Court decisions regularly point out and as Justice Brennan's opinion illustrates:

> Affirmative race-conscious relief may be the only means available to assure equalities of employment opportunities and to eliminate those discriminatory practices and devices which have fostered racially stratified job environments to the disadvantage of minority citizens. (*Local 25, Sheet Metal Workers' Intern. Ass'n v. E.E.O.C.*, 450)[16]

If one follows the Court in thinking of the practice of affirmative action as a remedial and compensatory response to discriminatory practices that have violated the norm of equal treatment, undermined the principle of equality of opportunity, and left blacks disadvantaged as a result, then no matter how complex the moral issues that remain, one can no longer simply describe it as replacing the practice of basing hiring decisions solely on merit with one in which blacks are given certain advantages in the name of equality of results.

Whether or not affirmative action programs are located in circumstances where discriminatory hiring practices had been operating is something that matters to the judgment one might make – and as I have argued, some in the public do make – about what justice requires. If people did not care about seeing justice done, it would not matter why they thought a given racial imbalance in the workforce had arisen. It does matter, however, and it matters because it enters into how people think about whether something wrong has in fact occurred and, further, how they think about what kind of response, if any, the victims are owed. The broader conclusion must be that the context in which affirmative action programs are implemented matters to opinions on affirmative

16 Quoted in Rosenfeld, 1991, 190.

action because it matters to the conclusions people reach as to whether justice demands a response.

LIBERAL PRINCIPLES AND PUBLIC OPINION ON POLICIES OF SOCIAL CONTROL

Ascertaining the point at which liberties cease to be protected because they become troublesome beyond a community's capacity to tolerate is among the most vexing problems faced by any modern democratic government. (McClosky and Brill, 1983, 20–21)

Why do some citizens support, and others oppose, public policies that restrict or prohibit activities that individuals might otherwise choose to engage in – abortion, for example, or the use of sexually explicit or pornographic materials? The model that I use to explain opinions on these issues gets its structure from the way in which a (classic) liberal would consider them. The liberal would be deeply concerned about the fact that governmental intervention inhibits people's ability to make their own decisions about the matter, and believes that government action should be undertaken only in limited circumstances – especially when it can be shown that the conduct is, in one way or another, seriously harmful. Analyzing the basis of opinions in this fashion lets us see the extent to which the moral contentions of liberalism, and those of its illiberal challengers, are represented in the way that the ordinary public comes to think about, and to disagree about, contemporary policies of social control.

The model I employ has a very simple logic, presented here in the form of three propositions:

1. The prospect of using government to inhibit particular modes of conduct initially arises in response to a judgment that the conduct is for some reason immoral or morally wrong. In what follows, I refer to this as the "moral judgment of the conduct."
2. Yet, using government to restrict or eradicate the objectionable conduct means limiting people's ability to make their own decisions about such matters. Thus, when considering imposing constraints on individual choices, people will not just consider whether those choices are being exercised in (what is to them) a morally objectionable way, but also where control over those decisions belongs. In other words, they will weigh the importance of preserving individual autonomy against the importance of limiting or eradicating the objectionable conduct. Liberalism gives great weight to a principle of individual autonomy – more, say, than does classic conservatism.

3. Whether action judged wrong may justifiably be subject to governmental intervention further depends on the perceived nature of
the wrong. Liberals will typically rely on some conception of harm
when scrutinizing "the nature of the wrong." Three different principles defended by liberals, each specifying circumstances under
which governmental intervention is justified and building on a
different notion of harm, are as follows:

*Utilitarian Harm Principle: Governments may intervene to protect
the welfare of the collectivity.* This conception is concerned with
the harmful consequences of an individual's actions for the collectivity. It builds roughly on the notion that unfettered individual actions (of a given sort) have consequences that threaten or
diminish the welfare of the society that such individual actors
form.

*Millian Harm Principle: Governments may intervene to prevent
one person from directly harming another.* This conception
focuses on dyadic relationships and the direct consequences that
one's actions have for others. The classic statement of this justification for governmental intervention is John Stuart Mill's:
"[T]he only purpose for which power can be rightfully exercised
over any member of a civilized community, against his will, is to
prevent harm to others" (Mill [1859] 1947, 9).[17]

*Paternalistic Harm Principle: Governments may intervene to
protect an individual from harming him- or herself.* This conception focuses on the consequences of a person's actions for
him- or herself. "The principle of legal paternalism justifies state
coercion to protect individuals from self-inflicted harm, or in its
extreme version, to guide them, whether they like it or not,
toward their own good" (Feinberg, 1971, 105).[18]

Disagreement may arise at each stage of the process this model identifies – about whether or not the conduct is morally objectionable, about

---

17 To call this the principle of Mill rather than citing Mill in reference to collective
harm is not to deny the importance of the former criterion to his thought. Social
utility is the final arbitrator for Mill, but his *On Liberty* relies upon "harm
to others" and individual rights (as indicative of where the greatest bad/good
will be found). His essay, however, also cites "damage, or a definite risk of
damage . . . to the public" as justifying constraints on liberty, as well as constraints
needed for the "protection [of] society" ([1859] 1947, 82, 95).

18 The Paternalist and Millian principles each concern what an individual may not
do (harm themselves or others) and thus fall under the nonconsequentialist rubric
discussed earlier. The Utilitarian principle is consequentialist, concerned with
advancing the welfare of the collectivity as a whole.

Political Value Judgments

the value of individual autonomy and the weight it should be given when in conflict with conduct objections, and about the harm (to oneself, others, and society at large) that the conduct causes.

Data to operationalize this model were gathered from a questionnaire distributed in 1986 to undergraduates at the University of Michigan.[19] Four sets of questions asked are pertinent here:

1. Social control policy questions with regard to four modes of conduct – abortion, homosexuality, reading pornographic books or watching pornographic movies, and euthanasia. In each case, respondents were asked to select one of four policy options: Abortion (alternatively: homosexuality, pornography, euthanasia) (a) should be prohibited by law, (b) should be regulated by law, (c) should be protected by law, or (d) government should stay out of this area altogether. (Since the last option introduces a second dimension, those selecting it were excluded from the analyses reported subsequently.)
2. Moral judgments of homosexuality, abortion, reading pornographic books or watching pornographic materials, and euthanasia. The questions asked of respondents involved a forced choice: "[Abortion] is immoral vs. There is nothing necessarily immoral about [abortion]."[20]
3. Four agree/disagree questions forming a scale designed to tap variation in people's general commitment to a principle of individual autonomy.
4. Perceptions of the degree of harm that the conduct (in turn: homosexuality, abortion, reading pornographic books or watching pornographic materials, and euthanasia) caused to the actor, to others, and to society in general. With respect to each of these referents, the respondents were given the following options: "no harmful effects," "not very harmful effects," "very harmful effects," or "extremely harmful effects."

The operationalized version of the model is as follows:

19 All cautions about using a student sample are in order here. See the Appendix for a full description of the measures.
20 The study employed a split-ballot test of alternative wordings. One random half of the sample was asked the wording given here, whereas the second was asked whether the conduct was "wrong" instead of "immoral": "[abortion] is wrong; there is nothing necessarily wrong with [abortion]." Differences between the versions were trivial, and the samples were pooled for the analyses reported here.

451

Social Control Policy Opinion
  (o = protect choice of conduct to 1 = prohibit conduct)
  = constant

+ b_1 (immoral)	[o = not immoral, 1 = immoral]
+ b_2 (autonomy)	[o = high to 1 = low commitment]
+ b_3 (immoral*autonomy)	[simple product term]
+ b_4 (harm to self)	[o = not harmful to 1 = extremely harmful]
+ b_5 (harm to others)	[o = not harmful to 1 = extremely harmful]
+ b_6 (harm to society)	[o = not harmful to 1 = extremely harmful]

where (model's normative logic follows in italics):

> b_1 represents the effect of one's moral judgment of the conduct among the strongest advocates of individual autonomy. A significant coefficient suggests that moral condemnation translates into support for policy intervention even among those who strongly affirm the importance of individual autonomy generally. [*A condemnatory judgment of some particular mode of conduct provides a prima facie basis for considering the use of state power to restrict the conduct.*]
>
> b_2 represents the effect of one's degree of commitment to a principle of individual autonomy among those who reject the condemnatory moral stance. A significant coefficient suggests that, among those viewing the practice as morally benign, a stronger principled commitment to autonomy generates greater support for a policy to protect that autonomy. [*Model fitting, no expectation.*]
>
> b_3 represents the differential effect of one's negative moral judgment as conditioned by the value given to individual autonomy. A significant coefficient suggests that the extent to which one's moral view is translated into a political response depends upon the strength of one's commitment to autonomy. The larger the coefficient, the greater the degree to which considerations of autonomy serve as a buffer between a condemnatory moral judgment and an interventionist political response. [*The condemnatory judgment must be weighed against the importance of preserving individual autonomy when one is considering a political proposal to restrict the conduct.*]
>
> b_4, b_5, and b_6 capture the effects of the assessments of harm to the self, to others, and to society, respectively. [*Ceteris paribus, the more "harmful" the conduct, the stronger the case for governmental intervention. Three distinctive categories of "harm" might be implicated, each reflecting a unique principle of governmental intervention.*]

This model of opinions has several important features. It is, first of all, a general model that may be applied to any question regarding the imposition of governmental measures aimed at controlling individual conduct.

Despite this generality, however, the model specifies judgments that are unique to each mode of conduct under consideration. In particular, it identifies moral objections to the conduct and beliefs about the extent to which the conduct is harmful – to the self, to others, or to society overall – as important to opinions regarding what government should do. At the same time, it represents one's strength of commitment to a principle of individual autonomy as a general consideration pertinent to any political judgment on questions of social control policy. Even so, this generalized commitment does not operate in a simple, additive fashion. In other words, people who vary in their strength of commitment to this individualist principle are not expected to vary simply in the extent to which they advocate an interventionist political response.[21] Instead, this model views people as weighing considerations of autonomy against any conduct objections when considering which political response is justified.

The results from estimating this policy opinion model are given in Table 15.1. I will begin by discussing the rather complex set of findings representing the conflict between conduct objections and the autonomy principle, and then turn to a brief discussion of the more straightforward findings regarding assessments of harm.

The first thing to note is that, with respect to each issue, questions of autonomy are of no consequence to the policy stances taken by those who view the conduct as morally benign (b_2 is small and insignificant in each case). In other words, absent a condemnatory moral judgment, issues of autonomy are not engaged when one considers the legislative response. At the same time, however, and across all four cases, the weighing of conduct objections and autonomy considerations is reflected in the robust effects of the immoral * autonomy interaction (b_3 is substantial in magnitude and significant in each case). The extent to which a condemnatory moral view is translated into a restrictive political response is strongly affected by the degree to which one values individual autonomy.

These results illustrate empirically what philosophers contend abstractly: that principles are evoked and engaged in a contingent, context-specific fashion. Without a prima facie reason for governmental intervention – in other words, among those who judge these practices as morally unobjectionable – questions about autonomy are not evoked and applied in judgment. Once moral condemnation provides a basis for considering governmental intervention, however, concerns about the preservation of personal autonomy are engaged, weighing in against an interventionist response. The weight people give to considerations of autonomy, moreover, shows a sensitivity to the particular practice being

21 The inclusion of the main effect term for autonomy, however, enables such an effect to emerge, if present.

Table 15.1. *Modeling Social Control Policy Opinions*

	Homosexuality	Abortion	Pornography	Euthanasia
(N)	(102)	(166)	(171)	(157)
Constant	−.01	.02	.22	.27
Immoral	.01	.18	.08	.16
	(.13)	(2.95)	(1.21)	(2.55)
Immoral ×	.68	.73	.44	.58
autonomy	(4.92)	(5.66)	(3.52)	(4.53)
Autonomy	−.10	−.002	−.03	−.01
	(−.64)	(−.02)	(−.27)	(−.01)
Harm to self	.16	−.03	.03	.17
	(1.62)	(−.45)	(.24)	(2.19)
Harm to others	−.01	.09	.05	.04
	(−.12)	(1.19)	(.48)	(.55)
Harm to society	.47	.40	.28	.24
	(4.48)	(4.72)	(2.96)	(3.04)
R^2	.74	.65	.40	.51
SE	.22	.22	.22	.22

Note: Entries are unstandardized regression coefficients, with *t*-ratios in parentheses below. Dependent and independent variables were scaled on the 0 to 1 interval. The dependent variables were coded such that 1 = the conservative response. The harm (self, others, and society) questions were scaled such that 0 = no harmful effects and 1 = extremely harmful effects. The autonomy index was coded such that 1 = least committed to a principle of individual autonomy. See the Appendix for question wording.

judged. The predicted policy scores, graphed in Figure 15.2, help illustrate these comparative results.

Comparing the magnitude of the interaction term across issues gives an indication of the relative weight given to considerations of autonomy in each case among those who judge the practice morally wrong.[22] In this respect, the results suggest a contrast between euthanasia and pornography, on the one hand, and between homosexuality and abortion, on the other. Among those condemning euthanasia and pornography, people rejecting the ideal of autonomy advocated more interventionist stances than those affirming that ideal; the differences in policy stances between those groups span roughly half of the policy scale. But these substantial autonomy effects are still overshadowed by those found with homosexuality and abortion, which generate differences of .68 and .73 (on the 0 to 1 scale), respectively.[23] This contrast between

22 This is illustrated in Figure 15.2a–d by the relative steepness of the slopes (for the morally condemning group) across the four issue areas.
23 Of course, as citizens in a liberal society, these respondents tend to be strong advocates of individual autonomy. Yet variation does exist, and as we see here, it is of great consequence to the positions taken on these issues.

the pairs of issues is complemented by the recognition that even those respondents with the most liberal profile showed an inclination toward government control of euthanasia and pornography but not of homosexuality and abortion; the estimated policy scores among those seeing no harmful effects, not judging the practice immoral, and showing the greatest affirmation of personal autonomy were .27 and .22 versus .02 and −.01 on these issues, respectively. Thus, more for homosexuality and abortion than for euthanasia and pornography, but in each case nonetheless, a concern with preserving individual autonomy powerfully militates against a restrictive political realization of a condemnatory moral view.

A different, but complementary, perspective on the conflict between a condemnatory moral judgment and the autonomy principle is afforded by focusing on the estimated main effects of one's moral judgment.[24] Whereas the magnitude of the interaction term that I have been discussing indicates the extent to which one's general commitment to preserving individual autonomy weighs against a condemnatory moral judgment, the magnitude of the main effect indicates the extent to which a condemnatory moral judgment overrides even a very strong commitment to the preservation of personal autonomy. Put another way, it represents the extent to which moral condemnation finds some political expression even among those with the strongest general commitments to autonomy.

In these results, there are no main effects of one's moral judgment for the issues of homosexuality and pornography (b_1 is small and insignificant). On these issues, the moral judgments made by those expressing a strong commitment to the principle of individual autonomy are fully disengaged from their policy opinions. In other words, their opposition to governmental restriction of homosexuality or pornography remains firm regardless of whether or not they judge the conduct immoral. Yet for abortion and euthanasia, which involve matters of life and death, a condemnatory moral conviction is influential in determining the policy stance taken by those who generally revere autonomy (b_1 is sizable and significant). On those issues we see a propensity for the moral judgment to trump considerations of personal autonomy, taking out of individuals' hands any unconditional right to make these choices.

In sum, across all four issues we see that the value one places on individual autonomy strongly conditions the extent to which a condemnatory moral judgment translates into an interventionist political response. The value given to autonomy especially divides those who morally

---

24 This is illustrated in Figure 15.2a–d by examining the gap between each pair of lines at the intercept and comparing that gap across issues.

A: Homosexuality

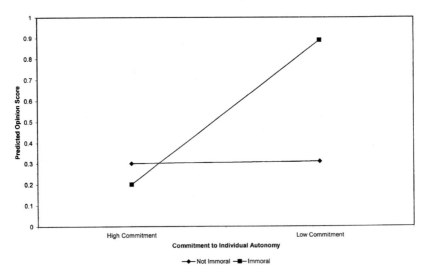

B: Abortion

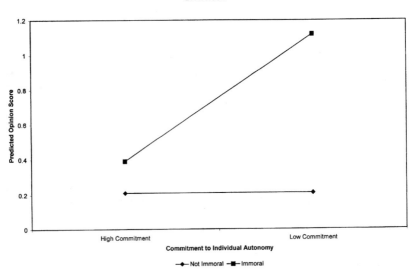

Figure 15.2. Predicted opinions on four social control policies. The policy opinion variables were scaled from 0 to 1; the most restrictive response was scored as 1. In generating these predicted values, I set each harm assessment at .5. This arbitrary selection accounts for the predicted values that extend beyond 1.

C: Pornography

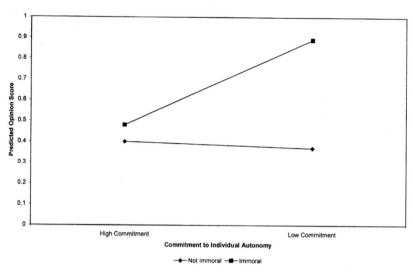

D: Euthanasia

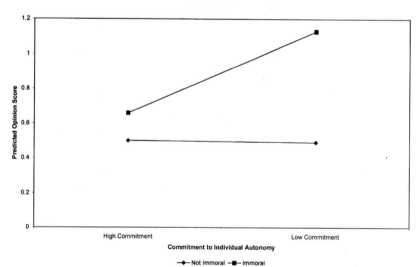

Figure 15.2 *(continued)*

condemn homosexuality and abortion, powerfully affecting whether or to what extent they will advocate state action that reflects their moral objection to the conduct. The parallel effects for pornography and euthanasia, although robust, are weaker by contrast; there is a tendency for everyone – even strong advocates of autonomy – to favor more governmental regulation of these practices. Further, even though considerations of autonomy may lead people to temper their political views, moral objections still carry some political weight even among those who generally valorize individual autonomy – though only when it comes to abortion and euthanasia. These findings contrast with those for homosexuality and pornography where concerns about the preservation of individual autonomy override an immoral judgment, fully muting its potential political effects. These comparative results clearly reveal the political implications of (nonconsequentialist) prohibitions against the taking of life.

Turning more briefly to the assessments of harm, we see in each estimation substantial and statistically significant effects of the assessment of harm to society (b_6 is sizable and significant in each case). The support for governmental intervention clearly increases as the perceived social damage from its inactivity increases. Considerations of collective welfare are felt most sharply for homosexuality, followed closely by abortion, again in contrast to euthanasia and pornography, where, as noted earlier, stronger general regulative tendencies are found. We also see an impact of judged harm to self in the positions taken regarding homosexuality and euthanasia (b_4), though no effects of perceived harm to others (b_5). But it is the aggregate effects, the troubles created for society at large, that are potent in these policy responses. Indeed, for each of these four practices, a concern for the welfare of the collectivity is prominent. In what was to me a surprising show of force, assessments of collective harm are strongly bound up with the political conclusions reached on these issues.

It appears, then, that these ordinary citizens are themselves grappling with what McClosky and Brill described as one of the "most vexing problems faced by any modern democratic government" (1983, 20–21) – the circumstances under which the government can justifiably restrict individual liberties. This model, though drawn from the arguments of political theorists, has yielded results that have accounted for major differences of opinion on these questions of social control while revealing the main points of contention that underlie them and that distinguish the four issues from one another.

The premise of this analysis has been that the limits to liberty are seriously contested in our society, resulting in explicable disagreements about which course of public policy is right. Even issues purportedly resolved by constitutional dictates – like abortion – may be contested by members of the American public who reject the Court's interpretation of what is justified. Once we recognize these contests over where the limits of liberty should be drawn, the question of how people understand and justify their opinions – whether "tolerant" or "intolerant" – arises. An investigation of this question does not supplant those that seek a deeper explanation in facets of individual personality, for example, or provide descriptions that probe the socioeconomic correlates of these views – raising questions of how the distribution of tolerant views is responsive to the life experiences that those variables summarize. It does, however, give us insight into the beliefs and principles that lend these opinions coherence and that set the terms for political debate. In this sense, this analysis has indicated that the moral contentions of liberalism, and those of its critics, form an integral part of the understanding of these issues among members of the American public and must be considered in any more complete explanation of the political controversies that have emerged.

DISCUSSION

I have suggested that differences of opinion in politics should not be conceptualized as differences in preferences (my favorite color is blue, yours is red), but instead as disagreements about what is the best or right course of policy to pursue. If so, we need to understand how and why people come to agree or disagree about which public policies are good or about which, in our present circumstances, is the right way to go. This requires theorizing about the basis of judgments about what is good or what is right and investigating the possible justificatory basis of opinions-as-value-judgments. It entails conceiving of people as judging particular practices or policies by reference to an array of different, and often incompatible, criteria of value – neither excluding nor limited to the value for oneself. These criteria of judgments are general, but the process of reaching a value judgment is thoroughly contextualized, contingent on perceptions of exactly what the policy does or seeks – what principles it instantiates, what values it advances, what problems it exacerbates, how it affects particular people or groups, society at large, or the particular person who is oneself. Value judgments, so understood, are not about symbols or intangibles or beyond the reach of scientific inquiry. They are, typically, intelligible claims about things in the world.

This approach to conceptualizing and organizing inquiry into public opinion provides a framework for integrating work on values with work on principles of justice or fairness, each of which has received substantial attention by social and political psychologists and public opinion analysts (e.g., Feldman, 1988; Folger, 1984; Gibson, 1993; Heath, Evans, and Martin, 1994; Hochschild, 1984; Inglehart, 1990; Jennings, 1991; Kinder, 1983; Lane, 1988; Lerner and Lerner, 1981; Lind and Tyler, 1988; Peffley and Hurwitz, 1987; Pollock, Lilie, and Vittes, 1993; Rasinski, 1987; Rescher, 1973; Rokeach, 1973, 1979; Searing, 1978; Sniderman and Hagen, 1985; Tetlock, 1986; Thibaut and Walker, 1975; Tyler, 1990; Verba et al., 1987; Zaller, 1992). At the same time that it seeks to draw this work together, it also draws other judgmental criteria into the same framework. Perhaps most glaringly absent from most previous public opinion work on values is the value of social welfare or social utility, the penultimate concern of utilitarians, social choice theorists, and welfare economists.[25] Moreover, principled claims about rights, duties, and obligations, with the exception of concerns about justice, have not received the attention given to values in public opinion research (but, for example, see Conover, Leonard, and Searing, 1993). And compensatory justice, which falls outside the dominant procedural versus distributive typology, has been neglected in work on justice. As well, this framework seeks to situate the concept of interests – in both its objective (e.g., material gain) and subjective (e.g., personal utility or satisfaction) forms – alongside the concepts of values and principles. This is something about which I have said little in this chapter. As I have argued at length elsewhere, however, judgments of right cannot be reduced to or be simply juxtaposed with claims about interests, but neither are they unresponsive to interest-based concerns (Stoker, 1992).

This approach also holds promise as a way of making sense of public opinion given what we have learned from decades of research. In the American context, it is well established that citizens are not ideological in the sense that their opinions are derived from a commitment to an abstract, organized ideology, but that there may be "sense" in those opinions nonetheless. Even opinions that are expressed in response to fictitious policies reveal a logic that belies simple description as randomly adopted "non-attitudes" (Bishop et al., 1989). From the perspective I have sketched out here, a citizen's views on any one issue may be coherent in the sense that they are felt to be justified. But because value judgments are sensitive to contextual contingencies and to cues or information about how the policy relates to one's values, principles, or beliefs,

---

25 Work on economic conditions and voting, however, although not framed as work pertaining to values, has focused on the contrast between personal and national economic circumstances (e.g., Kinder, Adams, and Gronke, 1989; Kinder and Kiewiet, 1981; Weatherford, 1983).

opinions qua value judgments may show considerable cross-situational or cross-temporal instability. Moreover, because the relevant justificatory considerations will vary across issues or issue areas, they will not exhibit the kind of constraint expected by the view of public opinion as ideologically driven (Converse, 1964).

At the same time, the thrust of my recommendation is that we incorporate what we might call political explanations of public opinion into our models. By this I mean that we should seek to discover what each side to a controversy finds compelling about its own positions and to model how disagreements about the merits of a policy might arise – by virtue of different values and principles, different means for reconciling conflict among them, and different vantage points on the world as it is or appears to be. Doing so would generate political explanations in that the explanations cite contentions about the collective enterprise we call government – what it, and thus we, should be doing or seeking, its relation to the people it serves and to the society in which it operates. Developing such explanations may require that we not merely situate our research in the context of some question addressed by liberal or democratic theorists, but that we rely on the work of political theorists to guide and organize our empirical inquiries as well.

This approach is oriented toward understanding how people make sense of, judge, and come to disagree about the activities or policies of government, and to reveal major points of contention in our political culture. But our empirical efforts must not stop with simply uncovering such self-understanding. We will want to know more. Questions like "Does education enhance political tolerance?" will remain important but, in the agenda I envision, they will be directly yoked to questions like these: "How does educational attainment alter how people adjudicate between competing values and principles?" "How does educational attainment change one's view of the world, and of the particular people and practices within it?" In short, "How does educational attainment alter the kinds of policies that people find justifiable?"

We must, then, ultimately place political value judgments in a larger explanatory framework. Such a larger framework would, first of all, contain a dynamic account of where political value judgments come from, something that I have not offered here. My argument has primarily been about what people might care about – whether or not some policy is good or right – and how we might conceptualize the ingredients of such judgments, not about where those views come from. Yet it draws, at least implicitly, on a philosophical model of opinion formation. That model, stylized, views value judgments as arising from a cognitive and deliberative process: citizens assess policies by reference to features they deem relevant to their conceptions of good or right. That model, idealized, conceives of value judgments as formed, and either maintained or changed, by virtue of reasoned arguments, bolstered by appropriate facts. Such descriptions, however, will surely fail to portray the actual process by which value judgments are formed and changed. Just as the cognitive and deliberative rational-choice model of preference formation has been found wanting, so too will this stylized and idealized philosophical model.

It is in this context that work in political psychology that is focused on process and not substance – especially work on learning and cognition and on mechanisms of social influence – can be joined with the approach and agenda I have outlined here. Empirical research will probably reveal, for example, that some value judgments learned early in childhood remain relatively immune to change as people enter new contexts and encounter new information that, from a philosophical perspective, ought to produce a new point of view. It will illuminate when and how opinions can be altered by the normative framing that an issue receives by elites or the mass media (e.g., Kinder and Sanders, 1990). And work on stereotyping or schema-driven information processing is clearly relevant to such questions as who are judged deserving or as having been harmed. More generally, the psychological work that has scrutinized the cognitive contentions of rational-choice models could also be brought to bear on the question of how political value judgments arise.

Developing a larger explanatory framework in which to place value judgments also requires that we elaborate and test competing explanations of opinion formation, again in reference to the stylized and idealized philosophical view. Viewed at an abstract level, I see two primary competitors. The first sees opinions as simple reflections of self-interested concerns, whether or not they are dressed up as contentions about what is good or right. People, in this view, are simply striving to enhance their own material interests or to advance their personal preferences. Thus, for example, research might reveal that people do adjust their value judgments as their life circumstances and information base change, but that changes in value judgments are simply driven by changes in what best advances their self-interest, with value judgments serving as public rationalizations. The second competitor sees opinions as purely affective responses, emerging, for example, as a consequence of inner personality dynamics and not a rational reflection of things going on in the world.

If we were to demonstrate that people articulate political value judgments as a purely strategic attempt to maximize personal gain, or that they are simply a public manifestation of personal fears and prejudices, this would mean that the philosophical account of where those value judgments come from was utterly false. I think this unlikely.[26] But even if true, this would not mean that those political value judgments were, as a consequence, unimportant as an object of study. They may remain of crucial importance to understanding public opinion and political controversy in a democratic society that expects opinion to be publicly justified, that expects people to offer opinions that transcend their own interests, fears, and prejudices. Important empirical questions would remain, but they would become questions like these: "Under what circumstances do people seek to mask their true motives and feelings?" "How does what counts as a publicly acceptable justification change over time?" "And what happens to those whose fears and prejudices find no publicly acceptable rationale?"

Finally, developing a larger framework in which to place political value judgments requires moving beyond a focus on how those judgments emerge in specific issue domains, the focus that I have both advocated and illustrated here, to consider ways in which our findings might be captured by and redescribed through a more parsimonious theoretical framework. This might, for example, entail a multidimensional depiction of competing ideologies (e.g., Maddox and Lilie, 1984) or cultures (e.g., Wildavsky, 1987) or involve what Shils (1968) called "quasi-ideological" phenomena, including "outlooks," "creeds," and "programs" (p. 71). As I have indicated, however, I think such general formulations will be most compelling if they build inductively on and are tied explicitly to work that explores the diverse problems of valuing and judgment that confront people in modern democracies.

CONCLUSION

Politics is full of claims about what ought to be done, about what good public policy is, about what is fair or unfair, about one's rights or duties, and about what is right or wrong. Despite the prominence of such contentions in political settings, however, we know surprisingly little about what it means to make such judgments, about how they differ from each other and from claims about interests or preferences, or about their

---

26 At the same time, however, I think it likely that self-interest and emotion play a role not unlike that outlined earlier, albeit not all-powerful. Thus it is probably less helpful to think of crude competitions among alternative motives (is it really values or self-interest/emotion?) than of how they work together in the process of opinion formation and change. This has been a major focus in social-psychological work on self-interest and justice (e.g., Conlon, 1993; Tyler, 1990) and is central to arguments about modern or symbolic racism (e.g., Kinder, 1986; Sniderman and Tetlock, 1986).

significance in structuring public opinion and political controversy. This is what I am striving to understand better with the approach that I have sketched out here.

In part, my recommendations are directed toward developing a better understanding of how people make sense of political goals and policies and judge them from their position as individuals in a democratic society. But I am also trying to direct our attention toward understanding what is taking place in political forums, not just what is happening in people's psyches. Here the question is how we are to understand political debate and disagreement as they emerge in public settings and the phenomenon of public justification itself. The concepts and arguments I have sketched out reflect this dual interest in trying to understand how people make sense of and formulate opinions in politics, and justify their views to others, without losing sight of the question of what it is that people actually care about.

The challenge for research will be to develop an account of public opinion that can capture what is at stake in particular political controversies and thus can provide a deep understanding of the debates that surround them and the different points of view that emerge; that can do this without developing ad hoc explanations that fail to cumulate toward a broader and more general understanding of public opinion and political conflict; and that remains fundamentally concerned with dynamic questions of how opinions develop and change. The result would be a portrait of public opinion that embraces its diversity and complexity, that illuminates the many sites and sources of political contestation, that forges a closer connection between the normative and empirical wings of political science, and that, despite all this, emerges from research that exhibits a scientific commitment to the development of general theories and cumulative knowledge.

APPENDIX: QUESTION WORDING

Social Control Policy Questions

These questions were designed with parallel wording for each issue. In each case, respondents were asked to select one of four policy options: Abortion (alternatively: homosexuality, reading pornographic books or watching pornographic movies, euthanasia):

a. should be prohibited by law. (scored 1)
b. should be regulated by law. (scored .5)
c. should be protected by law. (scored 0)
d. government should stay out of this area altogether. (excluded from analysis)

Political Value Judgments

Moral Judgments of Conduct

The questionnaire employed a split-ballot test of alternative moral evaluation wordings. Each question offered two response options to the respondents:

A [Abortion] is immoral. (scored 1)
There is nothing necessarily immoral about [abortion]. (scored 0)
B [Abortion] is wrong (scored 1)
There is nothing necessarily wrong with [abortion]. (scored 0)

The analysis presented is based on the pooled data.

Commitment to Individual Autonomy

An additive index designed to tap variation in people's general commitment to a principle of individual autonomy was built from the four following Likert questions:

1. We must respect people's own view of what is right and wrong, no matter what we think.
2. People have to decide for themselves what is right and wrong.
3. If we've decided something is morally wrong, it is wrong for everyone.
4. On most questions of right and wrong, it doesn't make sense to think of each person determining the answer for him- or herself.

After reflecting on the third and fourth items, responses to these questions were averaged to create a scale ranging from 0 (most committed) to 1 (least committed).

Harm Assessments

Respondents were asked to judge each practice as having "no harmful effects," "not very harmful effects," "very harmful effects," or "extremely harmful effects" for the following:

Self: "Individual(s) doing the act."
Others: "Other persons affected."
Society: "Society in general."

Each variable was scaled to range from 0 (no harmful effects) to 1 (extremely harmful effects).

465

Laura Stoker

References

Bishop, George F., Robert W. Oldendick, Alfred J. Tuchfarber, and Stephen E. Bennett. 1989. "Pseudo-Opinions on Public Affairs." In *Survey Research Methods*, ed. by Eleanor Singer and Stanley Presser. Chicago: University of Chicago Press.

Conlon, Donald E. 1993. "Some Tests of the Self-Interest and Group-Value Models of Procedural Justice: Evidence from an Organizational Appeal Procedure." *Academy of Management Journal*, 36: 1109–1124.

Conover, Pamela Johnston, Stephen T. Leonard, and Donald D. Searing. 1993. "Duty Is a Four-Letter Word: Democratic Citizenship in the Liberal Polity." In *Reconsidering the Democratic Public*, ed. by George E. Marcus and Russell L. Hanson. Philadelphia: Pennsylvania State Press.

Converse, Philip E. 1964. "The Nature of Belief Systems in Mass Publics." In *Ideology and Discontent*, ed. by David Apter. Glencoe, IL: Macmillan.

Dansicker, Andrew M. 1991. "A Sheep in Wolf's Clothing: Affirmative Action, Disparate Impact, Quotas, and the Civil Rights Act." *Columbia Journal of Law and Social Problems*, 25: 1–50.

Edwards, Rem B. 1979. *Pleasures and Pains: A Theory of Qualitative Hedonism.* Ithica, NY: Cornell University Press.

Feinberg, Joel. 1971. "Legal Paternalism." *Canadian Journal of Philosophy* 1: 105–124.

Feldman, Stanley. 1988. "Structure and Consistency in Public Opinion: The Role of Core Beliefs and Values." *American Journal of Political Science*, 32: 416–440.

Folger, R. 1984. (Ed.) *The Sense of Injustice.* New York: Plenum Press.

Gert, Bernard. 1988. *Morality: A New Justification of the Moral Rules.* Oxford: Oxford University Press.

Gibson, James L. 1993. "Political Freedom: A Sociopsychological Analysis." In *Reconsidering the Democratic Public*, ed. by George E. Marcus and Russell L. Hanson. Philadelphia: Pennsylvania State Press.

Groarke, Leo. 1990. "Affirmative Action as a Form of Restitution." *Journal of Business Ethics*, 9: 207–213.

Heath, Anthony, Geoffrey Evans, and Jean Martin. 1994. "The Measurement of Core Beliefs and Values: The Development of Balanced Socialist/Laissez Faire and Libertarian/Authoritarian Scales." *British Journal of Political Science*, 24: 115–132.

Hochschild, Jennifer. 1981. *What's Fair?* Cambridge, MA: Harvard University Press.

Hochschild, Jennifer L. 1984. *The New American Dilemma: Liberal Democracy & School Desegregation.* New Haven, CT: Yale University Press.

Inglehart, Ronald. 1990. *Culture Shift in Advanced Industrial Society.* Princeton, NJ: Princeton University Press.

Jennings, M. Kent. 1991. "Thinking about Social Injustice." *Political Psychology*, 12: 187–204.

Kinder, Donald R. 1983. "Diversity and Complexity in American Public Opinion." In *Political Science: The State of the Discipline*, ed. by Ada Finifter. Washington, DC: American Political Science Association.

1986. "The Continuing American Dilemma: White Resistance to Racial Change 40 Years After Myrdal." *Journal of Social Issues*, 42: 151–171.

Kinder, Donald R., Gordon S. Adams, and Paul W. Gronke. 1989. "Economics and Politics in the 1984 American Presidential Election." *American Journal of Political Science*, 33: 491–515.

Kinder, Donald R. and D. Roderick Kiewiet. 1981. "Sociotropic Politics: The American Case." *British Journal of Political Science*, 2: 129–161.

Kinder, Donald R. and Lynn M. Sanders. 1990. "Mimicking Political Debate with Survey Questions: The Case of White Opinion on Affirmative Action for Blacks." *Social Cognition*, 8: 73–103.

Kluckhohn, Clyde. 1951. "Values and Value Orientations in the Theory of Action: An Exploration in Definition and Classification." In *Toward a General Theory of Action*, ed. by Talcott Parsons and E. A. Shils. Cambridge, MA: Harvard University Press.

Lane, Robert E. 1988. "Procedural Goods in a Democracy: How One Is Treated versus What One Gets." *Social Justice Research*, 2: 177–192.

Lerner M. and S. Lerner. 1981. (Eds.). *The Justice Motive in Social Behavior.* New York: Plenum Press.

Lind, E. A. and T. R. Tyler. 1988. *The Social Psychology of Procedural Justice.* New York: Plenum Press.

Lipset, Seymour Martin. 1991. "Two Americas, Two Value Systems: Blacks and Whites." Hoover Institution Working Paper, P-91-1.

Maddox, William S. and Stuart Lilie. 1984. *Beyond Liberal and Conservative: Reassessing the Political Spectrum.* Washington, DC: Cato Institute.

Maikovich, Andrew J. and Michele D. Brown. 1989. *Employment Discrimination: A Claims Manual for Employees and Managers.* Jefferson, NC: McFarland & Co.

McClosky, Herbert and Alida Brill. 1983. *Dimensions of Tolerance: What Americans Believe about Civil Liberties.* New York: Russell Sage.

Meddin, Jay. 1975. "Attitudes, Values, and Related Concepts: A System of Classification." *Social Science Quarterly*, 55: 889–900.

Mill, John Stuart. 1947 [1859]. *On Liberty.* Arlington Heights, IL: Harlan Davidson.

Modood, Tariq. 1984. "J. L. Mackie's Moral Scepticism." *Journal of Value Inquiry*, 18: 237–246.

Nagel, Thomas. 1991. *Equality and Partiality.* New York: Oxford University Press.

Paul, Ellen Frankel. 1991. "Set-Asides, Reparations, and Compensatory Justice." In *Compensatory Justice: NOMOS XXXIII*, ed. John W. Chapman. New York: New York University Press.

Peffley, Mark A. and Jon Hurwitz. 1987. "A Hierarchical Model of Attitude Constraint." *American Journal of Political Science*, 29: 871–890.

Pollock, P. H., S. A. Lilie, and M. E. Vittes. 1993. "Hard Issues, Core Values and Vertical Constraint: The Case of Nuclear Power." *British Journal of Political Science*, 23: 29–50.

Rasinski, Kenneth A. 1987. "What's Fair Is Fair – Or Is it? Value Differences Underlying Public Views about Social Justice." *Journal of Personality and Social Psychology*, 53: 201–211.

Rescher, Nicholas. 1973. "The Study of Value Change." In *Value Theory in Philosophy and Social Science*, ed. by Ervin Laszlo and James B. Wilbur. New York: Gordon and Breach Science Publishers.

Rokeach, Milton. 1973. *The Nature of Human Values.* New York: Free Press.
  1979. (Ed.) *Understanding Human Values.* New York: Free Press.

Rosenfeld, Michel. 1991. *Affirmative Action and Justice*. New Haven, CT: Yale University Press.

Searing, Donald D. 1978. "Measuring Politicians' Values: Administering and Assessment of a Ranking Technique in the British House of Commons." *American Political Science Review*. 72: 65–79.

Sher, George. 1983. "Antecedentialism." *Ethics* 94: 6–17.

Shils, Edward. 1968. Ideology: The Concept and Function of Ideology. In *International Encyclopedia of the Social Sciences*, ed. by David Sills. Volume 7. New York: Macmillan.

Simon, Robert. 1977. "Preferential Hiring: A Reply to Judith Jarvis Thomson." In *Equality and Preferential Treatment*, ed. by Marshall Cohen, Thomas Nagel, and Thomas Scanlon. Princeton, NJ: Princeton University Press.

Sniderman, Paul M. and Michael Gray Hagen. 1985. *Race and Inequality: A Study in American Values*. Chatham, NJ: Chatham House.

Sniderman, Paul M. and Philip E. Tetlock. 1986. "Symbolic Racism: Problems of Motive Attribution in Political Analysis" and "Reflections on American Racism." *Journal of Social Issues*, 42: 129–150, 173–187.

Sowell, Thomas. 1989. "'Affirmative Action': A Worldwide Disaster." *Commentary*, 88: 21–41.

Spates, James L. 1983. "The Sociology of Values." *American Review of Sociology*, 9: 27–49.

Stoker, Laura. 1992. "Interests and Ethics in Politics." *American Political Science Review*, 86: 369–380.

Tetlock, Philip E. 1986. "A Value Pluralism Model of Ideological Reasoning." *Journal of Personality and Social Psychology*, 50: 819–827.

Thibaut, J. and L. Walker. 1975. *Procedural Justice: A Psychological Analysis*. Hillsdale, NJ: Erlbaum.

Tyler, Tom R. 1990. *Why People Obey the Law*. Chicago: University of Chicago Press.

Verba, Sidney, Steven Kelman, Gary R. Orren, Ichiro Miyake, Joji Watanuki, Ikuo Kabashima, and G. Donald Ferree, Jr. 1987. *Elites and the Idea of Equality*. Cambridge, MA: Harvard University Press.

Weatherford, M. Stephen. 1983. "Economic Voting and the 'Symbolic Politics' Argument: A Reinterpretation and Synthesis." *American Political Science Review*, 77(1): 158–174.

Wildavsky, Aaron. 1987. "Choosing Preferences by Constructing Institutions: A Cultural Theory of Preference Formation." *American Political Science Review*, 81: 45–66.

Williams, Robin M. 1979. "Change and Stability in Values and Value Systems: A Sociological Perspective." In *Understanding Human Values*, ed. by Milton Rokeach. New York: Free Press.

Zaller, John R. 1992. *The Nature and Origins of Mass Opinion*. New York: Cambridge University Press.

16

Commentary: The Study of Values

KENNETH A. RASINSKI

To the political scientist, the study of values represents an important challenge. On the one hand, the concept of citizen values has been used as a key component in theories of political behavior. On the other hand, it is not always clear exactly what is meant by values, how they differ from other kinds of political judgments, and exactly how to measure them. I will attempt to address these problems by presenting a working model of the study of values and by arguing that consideration of the components of this model can enhance the way values are used to explain political behavior. While I will draw from a number of sources, including my own research, a major source for many of the ideas comes from the chapters in this volume.

A value is a complex construct. From one perspective, values are considered to be attributes of a collective, that is, representing some shared norm, understanding, or view of the world (Hofstede, 1983; Triandis, Bontempo, Betancourt, and Bond, 1986), perhaps based on common experience (Inglehart, 1977). From another perspective, values have been located within individuals, and are associated with individual experiences and perceptions (Rasinski, 1987; Rokeach, 1973). I argue that both of these views must be considered in order to fully understand the role of values in political behavior. Even so, much research focuses on one or the other view.

For the sake of discussion, I offer the following premise: to undertake the study of how values affect political behavior, one must consider the following three elements: (1) a group's normative beliefs and expectations, (2) the social context within which values are formed and held, and (3) individual psychological dynamics.

The "normative dimension" refers to those shared beliefs and expectations within a culture or society. For example, societies are characterized as valuing industriousness, individualism, humanitarianism, communitarianism, and so forth. These shared beliefs and expectations provide important labels that can be used to characterize, classify, and differentiate societies (Triandis et al., 1986).

However descriptive the labels may be, though, they provide us with only superficial information about the groups they describe. A deeper understanding can be obtained by considering the social or historical reality giving rise to the values. As Stoker (this volume) puts it, the study of values should begin by recognizing "the diversity of problems that face people and governments in large-scale societies and the complexity of the problem of determining what it is that, in any given context, we ought to be doing."

To illustrate, consider a situation in which a brand new society is formed. Each member of this society is possessed with a single skill that she or he performs expertly. Further, members find that they need each other's expertise equally to survive as a group and thus ensure their individual survival. In this case, an appreciation of the expert practice of each different skill may become a social rule, so as to avoid the problems that would arise if one member of the society felt unappreciated and decided not to perform his or her skill. This social rule may become normative (that is, become a lasting expectation) over time. The norm may then grow to take the shape of a general principle – for example, the respect for individual differences and skilled practice.

At this point we have values. The raising of these practices to abstract level by giving them generality both underscores their importance and facilitates passing them on to others. For example, the lessons of many children's fables are presented in such general terms (as morals), specifically designed to illustrate and teach values to youth, thus ensuring the values' permanence.

The values that a society holds can be discovered through historical research by examining the social circumstances of a society and showing how a certain position emerged over time. Alternatively, values can be discovered through public opinion polls or assessment of contemporary political and social behavior. Often one society's values can be understood better by comparison and contrast to those held by other societies. In addition, as I shall argue later, an important method for understanding the role of values in political behavior involves studying their differential determinants and effects within and across societies (Rasinski, 1987; Rasinski and Scott, 1990; Rasinski, Smith, and Zuckerbraun, 1994).

I have argued that values emerge from social necessities. However, Stoker's statement also suggests that they develop within the context of changing social situations and new social challenges. When a novel social situation presents itself to the members of our new society, it seems reasonable to think that the members will try to apply rules that already exist, to try to bring some order to the new situation. Imagine that our group comes across a traveling scholar who is expert in the teaching of political science. They have never encountered such an individual before and are not sure what to do with the itinerant. As it turns out, for this group, the learning of political science is not considered to have survival value, and so it might be considered nonessential. Will the political scientist be run out of town, thrown into prison, killed, or (worse) simply ignored because she lacks what the society considers to be an essential skill? Not necessarily, because the society has learned to value expertise for its own sake, something that our itinerant political scientist can demonstrate through teaching of the discipline. Had the group not abstracted this general principle, the political scientist might have met an unhappy end.

Much contemporary political science research examines values within an economic context, but this need not be the only context. In a classic article, Deutsch (1975) argued that noneconomic social contexts – for example, those that are interpersonal or humanistic – can affect value-related social judgments such as whether equity, equality, or need-based distributions are considered fair. While group survival may be at the basis of all of these values, particular goals and circumstances may determine how this issue is played out.

It should be noted that values are not necessarily internalized uniformly across individuals (Rasinski, 1987). Differences in background, intelligence, education, and experience may lead to different understandings or interpretations of societal value. Like a language, these values may come to have many dialects, depending on the conditions surrounding their internalization. For example, as our small new society grows and subgroups take on functions formerly held by individuals (e.g., a group of political scientists emerges), an individual member of a particular subgroup may learn to value diversity and expertise only within the particular context of the subgroup. On the one hand, this may lead to the growth and development of this subspecialty, which may have positive effects on the survival of the subgroup. On the other hand, such emphasis on specialization may result in rifts between specialty groups, resulting in conflict within the society. Of course, conflict between subgroups may result in a new set of rules, norms, and values that contribute to the survival and progress of the now larger and more complex society.

VALUE AND VALUES

The terms "value" and "values" have been used in different ways by social scientists. Economists define "value" very narrowly in terms of the price a person would pay for a good. In contrast, other disciplines view "values" as representing beliefs about behavior shared by a group or a culture. Psychologists consider the internalization of these beliefs and have studied the dimensionality, cognitive structure, and function of values in determining individual behavior.

For example, Milton Rokeach, a psychologist who pioneered the study of values (Rokeach, 1973; Rokeach and Ball-Rokeach, 1989), stressed structure, function, and comparative valuation in his measurement of values. He argued that a core set of values exists, and he explored its structure. He also proposed that values must be measured comparatively. Rokeach also expanded the concept of values by positing different functions for them. He hypothesized that people may value some things because they are a means to an end and other things as ends in themselves. He termed these two types of valuation "instrumental" and "terminal," respectively.

Individual valuation can be studied from a purely economic perspective, while political values can be approached from a purely normative perspective. However, researchers of political behavior have realized that these two approaches are not sufficient because individual citizens' preferences (i.e., what they value) and their interpretation of norms (i.e., their values) both have a strong subjective component. This subjectivity and internalization imply that to understand the effect of political values on political behavior, one must also take into account principles of psychology.

CONTEMPORARY APPROACHES TO STUDYING VALUES

In her chapter in this volume, Stoker takes both an analytic and an empirical approach to studying values. She views values as the public expression of social norms (or "oughts"). She claims that public value expression, in the form of public opinion, is at the heart of collective, democratic decision making. Her goal is to discover how the public oughts are arrived at and how the public interprets them as being in their interest.

In Stoker's system, oughts (i.e., values) must be justified as in the public interest. She proposes four bases for justification. The first two concern the distinction between consequentialists and nonconsequentialists. Essentially, consequentialists consider outcomes of collective considerations as the basis for values, while nonconsequentialists consider societal rules independent of their outcomes. This distinction is reminiscent of the distributive/procedural distinction found in the social justice literature (Thibaut and Walker, 1975; Tyler and Caine, 1981; Tyler, Rasinski, and Griffin, 1986; Rasinski, 1987), which has also linked public opinion to values (Rasinski, 1987). Stoker's nonconsequentialist category is distinctive in that it covers a broader range of considerations than is usually included under the rubric of procedure.

The third and fourth ways of justifying values concern the impartial–partial distinction. Impartial judgments are said to concern either all people or each person, while partial judgments refer to a particular individual or to that person's group. This latter category is reminiscent of the individual–group level self-interest distinction proposed by Conover over fifteen years ago (1985). However, in Stoker's system, both partiality and impartiality must be principled. Thus, pure self-interest is not considered under this scheme.

Stoker's empirical results support her theory. The first study, a split-ballot experiment showing that public opinion on affirmative action depends on the value content of the prior questions, is reminiscent of context effects studies done by survey researchers. Others have interpreted findings similar to Stoker's as evidence invoking a cognitive structure (Tourangeau, Rasinski, Bradburn, and D'Andrade, 1989) rather than a social norm. This distinction is easily resolved by considering that social norms must be internalized to influence public opinion; in the process of internalization, norm-based cognitive structures are formed. The second study provides an interesting survey-based method for assessing whether certain values are operating by examining their effect on political judgments.

Stoker's chapter is valuable in presenting a general and coherent theoretical rationale for viewing public opinion as the expression of some value system or other. What is interesting about the system is that it implies a psychological process underlying value-based public opinion. The implication is that values are internalized societal oughts that can be detected from public opinion surveys. If this approach has a drawback, in my opinion it is the absence of an attempt to deal with why certain values (e.g., individualism, humanitarianism, communitarianism, as mentioned in the other chapters) are important within a culture.

It seems prophetic that Feldman and Steenbergen (in this volume) reminded us of the important differences underlying two major normative bases of social welfare – residual versus institutional welfare – shortly before the 1994 midterm elections. In part, the results of these elections seemed to be a public referendum on the two views, at least concerning health care. The health care debate that preceded those elections suggests that, while the majority of citizens are clearly concerned about whether adequate health care will be available for them, they seem willing, as a whole, to trust the market to provide their health care and unwilling to trust a health care system under government control.

473

The residual–institutional welfare distinction may also be helpful in explaining the results of a recent survey methodological study. Smith (1987) analyzed data from a split-ballot experiment included on the General Social Survey and found that the public is more willing to support programs "for the poor" than "welfare" programs. It is possible that welfare programs invoke the general anti-institutionalized welfare sentiment in this country, while programs for the poor may bring to mind charity-based, residual programs for the so-called deserving poor – those who have tried to do for themselves but have met with misfortune.

Feldman and Steenbergen go beyond normative considerations to take into account the psychological dimension of values. They examine two values, egalitarianism and humanitarianism, as they affect support for social welfare programs. Not only do the authors find value-based differences in support, they also identify psychological mechanisms underlying the differences. Their relatively small sample and high non-response rate are drawbacks, but the data seem adequate to support their points.

Finally, Markus argues that political science has suffered from over-reliance on two models of the political actor. The first model, based on economic theory, views the citizen as purely rational. Markus argues that this is a simplistic view of the citizen, and as part of his critique of this model, he cites examples such as support for health care reform, which was apparently overwhelming, according to public opinion polls, in 1993. It is interesting to view this also within the context of the 1994 Republican victory in congressional and state elections. As I mentioned earlier, while it is not clear that this was entirely a referendum on health care reform, it is possible that self-interest-based concerns about health care reform played a part in the election outcomes. A fairly strong self-interest explanation could be (and has been) given for his other examples against the economic view – support for civil rights, antiwar sentiment, environmentalism, and the women's movement.

The second model, based on the thoughts of past political theorists, and promoted by social psychologists and political attitude theorists in the 1950s and 1960s, posits a liberal or conservative ideology as a predominant motivating force. Rather than relying on the liberal–conservative dichotomy, Markus suggests that we study core values because they are likely to present a firmer, more realistic foundation for understanding political behavior. Markus relies upon political philosophy to champion the importance of what he calls the "core value of individualism" to understanding the American polity.

Similar to the approach taken by Feldman and Steenbergen, Markus's approach differentiates dimensions of individualism and proceeds to measure them. His findings are important in two respects. First, he demonstrates that there are distinctive subtypes of individualism. Second, he finds that individualism is not as widely endorsed by the public as traditional normative theory would predict. In fact, he finds substantial differences in support for the individualism ethic, depending on demographic factors.

It is interesting to observe that while criticizing the economic and ideological approaches, Markus defines as important and selects to study a value that is clearly aligned with conservative ideology and free market economics. Perhaps this suggests that economic and ideological models have some utility after all. While the two models he mentions may suffer from oversimplification, they may be useful in providing guidance in identifying concepts that could benefit from greater differentiation and explication.

VALUES AS A LENS THROUGH WHICH CITIZENS VIEW SOCIETY

Much of the preceding discussion can be summarized with a metaphor. Political values are like a lens through which the citizens view their political world. Judgments about specific political events, then, are consistent with the citizen's value-based perspective. One might argue from this metaphor that the psychological study of political values involves ascertaining properties of the lens and understanding how they affect individual citizens' views of contemporary political events and consequent political behaviors.

As one example of expanding the metaphor, my colleagues and I have conducted three studies examining the way in which values affect judgments of fairness in a number of social contexts, trying to determine, so to speak, the characteristics of the lenses of individual citizens by ascertaining their values and examining the impact of these values on their political judgments. In one study, I examined how individual values determine what individuals judge to be fair (Rasinski, 1987). A number of value-based survey items were rated as to their consistency with values of equity, equality, need, and individualism, four values thought to underlie judgments of fairness (Deutsch, 1975). Further examination of the structure, and of the convergent and discriminant validity of the items, indicated that two dimensions could summarize the four values. The first dimension seemed to measure a concern with "proportionality," or the belief that citizens should "reap what they sow," so to speak. The interesting thing about this dimension is that it included beliefs about economic individualism and equity. The second dimension, "egalitarianism," reflected the notions of human need, government responsibility for the well-being of citizens, and compassion for others.

College students' ratings of the values were correlated with their endorsement of Rokeach's instrumental values and with global liberalism–conservatism. Proportionality was associated with endorsing independence, imagination, ambition, and obedience as instrumental values and with self-identifying as conservative. Egalitarianism was associated with the instrumental values of being broad-minded, forgiving, helpful, and loving and with self-identifying as liberal. Men were more likely to endorse the proportionality values, but endorsement of egalitarianism was equally likely among men and women.

The point of the value measurement exercise was to develop a method for understanding the basis of fairness judgments. Respondents in a telephone survey of randomly selected Chicagoans were administered the value items, along with a number of items evaluating the current U.S. president. As part of the survey, respondents were also asked to make a number of judgments about the fairness of government economic policies and policy-making procedures. Results indicated that respondents who were egalitarian in their orientation applied judgments of fairness to government policies that directly affected the distribution of resources. Those who endorsed proportionality applied fairness judgments to government policies that dealt with the opportunity to access resources rather than to their actual distribution. Education played a role. The application of fairness judgments to opportunity versus distribution, based on value orientation, was more consistent for those with higher levels of education.

This study has similarities to the chapters of both Feldman and Steenbergen and Markus. Both begin by explaining policy preference from value-based positions. Markus's finding of different types of individualism supports the view expressed at the beginning of this chapter that subtypes, or different "dialects," of a value may emerge over time. However, neither study addresses how mediating judgments, such as conceptions of social justice, may bridge the value–policy preference gap. Deciding which values are important determinants of policy preference may depend on whether a mediating factor is included in the explanatory model. The choice of proportionality and egalitarianism values in my research was based on my belief that fairness judgments are important mediators of attitudes toward social distributive policies. Feldman and Steenbergen's choice of egalitarianism and humanism as determining values was based on an analysis of the function of social welfare in society. Each of these positions is legitimate. The different perspectives, and the results supporting each perspective, underscore the complexity of studying political values and policy preferences.

Commentary: The Study of Values

In two other studies (Rasinski and Scott, 1990; Rasinski, Smith, and Zuckerbraun, 1994), the effects of political values on policy judgments were examined across cultures. Rasinski and Scott (1990) used data from the 1984 General Social Survey and the 1984 West German ALLBUS; both surveys included identical questions on values and economic justice. Factor analysis of value items yielded a similar dimensionality for both countries for value items representing the proportionality and egalitarianism construct used in the Chicago study (Rasinski, 1987). However, the relationship between values and judgments about economic fairness differed by country. For Americans, beliefs about the fairness of the distribution of business profits were associated with conservative economic individualism values and with income level. Both of these factors were more strongly related to fairness judgments with increasing education. For West Germans, beliefs about the fairness of business profits were related both to economic individualism values and to socialist values, but the relationship was not moderated by education level. Nor was income a factor.

In a cross-cultural study, Rasinski, Smith, and Zuckerbraun (1994) used data from the International Social Survey Program to examine the linkage between values and support for government spending on the environment in nine countries. When only values and policy support were considered, a puzzling pattern of results emerged. Prosocialist values were associated with higher levels of support for environmental spending, while probusiness and government social responsibility values were both associated with less support. However, viewing these results within a social justice perspective provided some clarification. Those with prosocialist values endorsed support for government spending on many issues, including the environment. However, both the prosocialists and those endorsing government social responsibility were less likely to support spending on the environment at the expense of spending for other social programs, while those with probusiness attitudes were unlikely to endorse spending for any social programs, including the environment.

These results show the importance of taking a dynamic psychological approach to the study of values. If the first study had only examined the structure of values in the two countries, the conclusion would have been that the two countries were similar. However, though American and West German values were similar in structure, they presented different views of the social world, depending on socialization, culture, and the different political realities existing in the two countries. The results also show the importance of studying the value–policy preference relationship in a complex social policy domain. If the second study had not considered support for environmental policy within the context of many other policies, different conclusions about the value–policy preference relationship would have been drawn.

To my knowledge, citizen preferences of trade-offs among social programs, and the relationship of the trade-offs to value orientations, have not been studied widely. One wonders how the consideration of trade-offs, reflecting citizen judgments in a complex but realistic social context, might have affected the theory and research presented in the three chapters. Perhaps, although apparently introducing complexity into an already complex endeavor, some new clarity about the relationship between values, on the one hand, and citizen political judgments and behaviors, on the other, may have emerged, as was the case in the nine-nation International Social Survey Program study.

CONCLUSION

My approach to understanding the study of political values is to examine them against societal norms, social and political events, and the psychology of individual citizens. These are elements that I believe should be present in any practical study of political values. Most contemporary studies of values contain elements of each of these components but differ in how much each component is emphasized.

Often values are studied by examining public opinion. This is natural because measured public opinion is a prevalent source of expressed public desires. It is well to recognize that public opinion is not the only source of political expression and that public opinion is subject to many factors other than the expression of values. At times, other forms of public political expression (such as vote choice, policy preference, or social behavior) may contradict public opinion. That is, people do not always mean what they say and do not always behave consistently with their expressed opinions. My purpose in bringing attention to this point is to remind us that we must continually be aware of the variety of ways in which political values are expressed, as well as the limitations in our ability to measure these expressions. Our studies, while trying to capture value specificity, social context, and psychological underpinnings, should also pay close attention to the measurement process to the extent possible.

References

Conover, P. J. (1985). The Impact of Group Economic Interests on Political Evaluations. *American Politics Quarterly*, *13*(2), 139–166.

Commentary: The Study of Values

Deutsch, M. (1975). Equity, Equality, and Need: What Determines Which Value Will Be Used as the Basis for Distributive Justice. *Journal of Social Issues*, *31*, 137–150.

Hofstede. G. (1983). *Culture's Consequences*. Beverly Hills, CA: Sage.

Inglehart, R. (1977). *The Silent Revolution: Changing Values and Political Styles Among Western Publics*. Princeton, NJ: Princeton University Press.

Rasinski, K. A. (1987). What's Fair Is Fair – Or Is It? Value Differences Underlying Public Views About Social Justice. *Journal of Personality and Social Psychology*, *53*, 201–211.

Rasinski, K. A. and Scott, L. A. (1990). Culture, Values, and Beliefs about Economic Justice. *Social Justice Research*, 4, 307–323.

Rasinski, K. A., Smith, T. W., and Zuckerbraun, S. (1994). Fairness Motivations and Tradeoffs Underlying Public Support for Government Environmental Spending in Nine Nations. *Journal of Social Issues*, *50*, 179–197.

Rokeach, M. (1973). *The Nature of Human Values*. New York: Free Press.

Rokeach, M. and Ball-Rokeach, S. J. (1989). Stability and Change in American Value Priorities, 1968–1981. *American Psychologist*, 44, 775–784.

Smith, T. W. (1987). That Which We Call Welfare by Any Other Name Would Smell Sweeter: An Analysis of the Impact of Question Wording on Response Patterns. *Public Opinion Quarterly*, *51*, 75–83.

Thibaut, J. and Walker, L. (1975). *Procedural Justice: A Psychological Analysis*. Hillsdale, NJ: Erlbaum.

Tourangeau, R., Rasinski, K. A., Bradburn, N. M., and D'Andrade, R. (1989). Carryover Effects in Attitude Surveys. *Public Opinion Quarterly*, *53*, 388–394.

Triandis, Harry C., Bontempo, R., Betancourt, H., and Bond, M. (1986). The Measurement of the Etic Aspects of Individualism and Collectivism Across Cultures. *Australian Journal of Psychology*, *38*, 257–267.

Tyler, T. R. and Caine, A. (1981). The Influence of Outcomes and Procedures on Satisfaction with Formal Leaders. *Journal of Personality and Social Psychology*, *41*, 642–655.

Tyler, T. R., Rasinski, K. A., and Griffin, E. (1986). Alternative Images of the Citizen: Implications for Public Policy. *American Psychologist*, *41*, 970–978.

17

Commentary: The Value of Politics

MELISSA A. ORLIE

A significant group of empirical researchers are beginning to engage questions that, at least according to recent convention, have been considered the province of political philosophers. Some political scientists are taking so-called normative issues more seriously and centrally. They are looking for ways to join questions of value to their more usual topics of interest and power. Arguably, a complementary shift is at work in political philosophy, where many increasingly regard issues of power, hegemony, interest, and the like to be inseparable from more traditional concerns with principles and ideals. Both of these shifts suggest the need to rethink some of our most basic ideas. For instance, predominant understandings that oppose value and interest, principle and power, may require rethinking. What is more, reconceiving the relationship between these issues may yield a reappraisal of politics.

THE POLITICS OF PUBLIC OPINION RESEARCH

The array of issues encompassed by the catchall term "opinion formation" pose and pursue a variety of crucial questions: What mix of emotion, interest, and value prevails in citizens' opinions? What are interests, feelings, and values? In what measure are political opinions affective or cognitive? More generally, what is a political opinion, where do political opinions come from, and what do they express? Recent efforts to recover the evaluative basis of public opinion pursue these as political theoretical questions. But even these new approaches to survey research continue to be animated by a "logic of discovery" that casts questions of opinion formation as factual and empirically answerable. But questions of political opinion formation are only *partly* factual matters. Empirical research can represent current public opinion as well as offer accounts of how such opinion is formed, but it cannot tell us what political opinion necessarily is or should be. It is not especially controversial to say that empirical research cannot tell us what political opinion should be. Indeed, the discipline of political science remains structured by a distinction between what politics is and what politics ought to be. Thus, we have a division of labor between empirical researchers and political philosophers.[1]

It may be more controversial, however, to claim that empirical research cannot tell us what political opinions necessarily are. How political opinions are formed and what they express are not, strictly speaking, empirically answerable questions because what mix of emotion, interest, and value prevails in political opinions, how political opinions are formed, and what political opinions manifest are themselves politically conditioned. Not only particular citizen opinions, but also scholarly representations of them, are political, which is to say, contestable and alterable.

The questions we pose and the methods we deploy in studying political opinion affect to a significant degree what political opinion is or is allowed to be. These expectations and their effects accumulate over time and profoundly influence political discourse and culture. To the degree that survey researchers cast questions of opinion formation as susceptible to a logic of discovery, they might reject my claim. I shall try to show why they should not.

What is at stake here? If I am right that the questions public opinion researchers engage are finally political questions – not only answerable by empirical verification but also necessarily involving political contestation – then every account of public opinion projects a vision of politics for which in principle it should be accountable. In this sense, methodological reflexivity entails political theorizing. If I am right, then the division of labor between political philosophers and empirical researchers must be transfigured. If I am right, then we need more concerted reflection upon the theory of politics manifest both in citizens' opinions and in our representations of them. If I am right, our research not only measures the political values animating citizen opinion, but also in part constitutes the value we and they find in politics.

Political forms and culture condition how emotion, interest, and value inform political opinion. Moreover, particular political opinions are efforts to shape that mix. When citizens register their opinions, they endeavor to make, reinforce, or initiate something new within our

---

1 All of the chapters considered here take political theory or philosophy to be a primarily prescriptive enterprise. But political theory is also an interpretive and explanatory practice. Likewise, empirical research is (if sometimes only implicitly) prescriptive and interpretive, as well as explanatory. Throughout, my discussion evinces examples of both claims.

collective condition. Thus, political opinions are not only givens to be measured or explained, but also forms of action that challenge and seek to change or maintain political discourse and social life.[2] Because our research facilitates citizen opinion, every representation and explanation of political opinion (including my own) is itself political. Calling these matters political, however, is not to say that they are therefore merely arbitrary, assertive, or unprincipled, though they can be. Unfortunately, the political theories that inform much survey research often countenance, however unwittingly, a politics of thoughtless assertion.[3]

VALUES, POLITICAL JUDGMENTS, AND DEMOCRATIC LEGITIMACY

I begin with a conception of public opinion closest to that which informs my perspective. Laura Stoker's chapter in this volume studies political opinions as judgments about what is "valuable" or of "value" to "anyone" or to "us." Stoker believes that public opinion research has only a murky understanding of the normative issues that animate political debate, "of the bases of agreement and disagreement about the policies that governments *ought* to be implementing or the actions they *should* be undertaking." She seeks and offers "an approach to the study of public opinion that tries to systematically illuminate this normative terrain."

In my view, Stoker's hypothesis that political opinions express the values people hold has simultaneously descriptive and normative implications. It is descriptive because Stoker's data and her interpretations of it demonstrate the values and principles at issue in different political opinions. But her account is also normative because it delimits what counts as a political opinion. (As I have said, such delimitation is unavoidable.) According to the theory of democratic legitimacy that implicitly informs Stoker's hypothesis, personal preferences or bald assertions of interest are not properly political opinions. This is not to say that Stoker does not measure such assertive expression. But by attending to the context of political expression, she notes that citizens and actors are often called on to give reasons for their views.[4] When this

---

2 Every theory of politics also makes certain ontological presumptions; I offer a more extended account of the social ontology informing my own account in Orlie, 1997.
3 Throughout I deploy ideas more fully developed in Orlie, 1994.
4 Stoker's attention to historical and institutional context is a crucial development. Many of my criticisms of the other chapters in this volume in subsequent sections of this chapter are related to issues of contextualization and historicization.

happens, personal preferences become political opinions, matters not only of interest but also of value.[5]

Stoker emphasizes the cognitive and deliberative rather than the affective aspects of opinion formation. From this perspective, when citizens register their political opinions, they express more than their personal feelings or self-interest. They offer their views of what they think is "right" or "wrong," "good" or "bad" for us to do. Such political value judgments may be supported by objective or intersubjective reasons. To say that political value judgments are supported by reasons is to say that they are publicly justified or justifiable. "Objective" reasons make claims about what anyone should do, while "intersubjective" reasons make claims about what "we" (as a particular community) should do. These reasons, Stoker suggests, are informed by self-interest while also transcending it. In other words, the values political opinions express are informed by our feelings and interests but also exceed them as judgments about who we are (as citizens or human beings) and about what it is right or good for us to do as such.

Stoker is right, I think, that in a democratic polity all political opinions – even those that in our judgment are less than reasonable – make claims about what is good or right, which is to say that they are regarded by their advocates as reasonable. Individuals and groups sometimes simply do assert their interests or preferences over and against those of other citizens. But when they do, others may demand a more principled basis for their views and, when those reasons are not forthcoming, their views are often considered less legitimate.[6] To put the point another way, when assertive preferences or thoughtless interests are allowed to prevail without account, we may surmise that the quality of collective life and political discourse suffer. In contrast to Stoker, this seems to be the politics discovered and documented by much public opinion research.

---

5 Habermas, 1996, offers an account of democratic legitimacy akin to Stoker's analysis. In what I read as an improvement upon previous formulations, Habermas more squarely confronts the tension between facticity and normativity, just as Stoker queries the opposition between interests and values (Stoker, 1992). Still, though Habermas now places greater emphasis upon how the "always already familiar" resists critical evaluation, I think he underestimates the "normalizing" affects of the "leveling out of the tension between facticity and validity" even in communicative action (see Habermas's first chapter for an introduction to this theme). Likewise, what Stoker calls "political value judgments" always presume more than they can justify. For a problematization of the invisible boundaries of political judgments, see Orlie, 1997.

6 For a useful, if partial, overview of different conceptions of the relationship between reason-giving, democracy, and legitimacy see Benhabib, 1994.

Viewing citizens' opinions as political value judgments projects a vision of political discourse animated by politically justified or justifiable claims. If we allow perspectives like Stoker's to structure our views of political opinion, it would influence what we count (literally, how we survey) public opinion, how we understand and interpret it. Over time, this practice could transform the character and quality of public opinion and political discourse more generally. Though Stoker herself does not say so, the plausibility and appeal of her account depend upon the acquisition of our values being (at least in part) political and susceptible to change. In other words, public opinion research not only envisions a politics, it also projects a vision of the self. Contrasting Stoker's deliberative theory of politics to a more affective account will enable me to clarify the relationship between conceptions of politics and of selves. Moreover, we may then better understand the prevalence of thoughtless assertion over deliberate political opinion in the contemporary political life of the United States.

THE POLITICS OF FEELINGS

Like Stoker, Stanley Feldman and Marco Steenbergen are interested in recovering the evaluative basis of public opinion, though they emphasize its affective aspects. In their chapter, they seek to understand not only whether citizens support social welfare policies, but why they do or do not support them. Like Stoker, they do not regard self-interest *simpliciter* as an adequate account of citizens' views. But Feldman and Steenbergen emphasize "feelings" rather than "values" to explicate political opinions. Nonetheless, they are interested in the different "philosophies that people may hold as far as social policies are concerned."

Humanitarianism

Understanding Americans' views regarding social welfare policy, Feldman and Steenbergen argue, requires attending to both the specific characteristics of these programs (whether they are typical of a residual or an institutional welfare state) and the basis or "justifications" for that support. In their view, previous research has neglected the "underlying goals of specific welfare programs" and emphasized "values" and "norms" as predictors of behavior and opinion. But Feldman and Steenbergen find the "presocial orientation" of "humanitarianism" a better predictor of Americans' support for social welfare programs, especially if we are to explain Americans' apparent preference for a residual rather than an institutional welfare state.

Commentary: The Value of Politics

Once again, I am interested in the *implicit* politics envisioned by Feldman and Steenbergen's conception of public opinion. Understanding that vision of politics requires interpreting what they find in their data. In matters of social welfare policy, Feldman and Steenbergen find feelings like empathy and sympathy for others – what they call the "presocial orientation" of humanitarianism – to have greater explanatory power than "principles" like "egalitarianism" or "ideologies" like "liberal" and "conservative." While values (at least on their understanding) imply societal rules about how social and political arrangements should be constructed, a presocial orientation like humanitarianism involves our feelings for others. Such presocial orientations do not involve "impersonal rules" but engage our personal reactions to the conditions of others.[7] By definition, such feelings are affective responses rather than cognitive claims. Such affective reactions, they believe, are the key to understanding Americans' attitudes toward social welfare programs.

Feldman and Steenbergen find that Americans are at best polarized with regard to the principle of egalitarianism. Because egalitarianism generally correlates with support for an institutional welfare state, this polarization may explain why such programs receive divided or minimal support among Americans. But they also find that Americans are fairly united in their "humanitarian" feelings, or at least in their opinion about such feelings: The vast majority of those surveyed seem "quite willing to go out of their way to help others and they deem the well-being of others of the utmost importance." Such charitable feelings toward others, Feldman and Steenbergen claim, translate into support for a residual welfare state. By contrast, according to their account, egalitarians' cognitive appraisal of the sources of poverty tends to hold society responsible for individual well-being because they interpret individuals' fate in light of prevalent social arrangements. Thus, egalitarians tend to support an institutional welfare state to ameliorate these negative, socially generated effects. Humanitarians, however, do not depend upon, or may even shy away from, a cognitive appraisal of social conditions. From their perspective, neither the individual nor society is responsible for poverty; humanitarians simply feel sympathy for the unfortunate. Where egalitarians desire preventive measures to protect against misfortune and support the redistribution of resources to achieve this goal, humanitarians simply feel for the needy and support residual welfare programs (analogous to charity) to help them.

But are presocial orientations like humanitarianism justly called political opinions? What sort of politics follows from the characterization of

7 "The distinction between presocial orientation and impersonal rules might be false; see Benhabib, 1992, 147–148.

485

such feelings as a "philosophy" or "justification" of a political judgment? I offer both a short and a more extended answer to these questions.

First, consider Feldman and Steenbergen's characterization of the individual impelled by humanitarian feelings. What sort of citizen is he?[8] For instance, what (if any) sense does he have of common concerns or of modes of action for realizing them? The answer may be "little" on both counts. Arguably, the humanitarian citizen's cognitive stance (or lack thereof) toward social conditions is a sign of intellectual disempowerment and political disenfranchisement. Leaving aside the question of what actions are politically good or possible in relation to poverty or social dislocation and the like, the humanitarian's passivity in the face of them – misfortune is something that just happens, about which little preventive action can be taken, and for which no one is responsible – suggests that this affective reaction masks cognitive disorientation and a sense of individual and collective inefficacy.[9] At least on some understandings, a political attitude is distinct from a feeling or mood precisely in its deliberate and powerful potentialities and manifestations, in its action rather than reaction.[10] By contrast, humanitarian feeling may stem from a sense of one's own vulnerability or powerlessness and, as Rousseau might say, pity for the similar plight of others.

But feelings of political impotence and fear of social dependence may also yield less estimable reactions. We can observe humanitarian feelings engendering less humane responses in the politics of resentment so palpable in contemporary American political life.

The Limits of Humanitarianism

The long answer to my questions about the politics of feelings begins with an apparent contradiction. On the one hand, Feldman and Steenbergen document substantial humanitarian support for social welfare programs (albeit residual and not institutional ones). On the other hand,

8 I use the masculine pronoun here intentionally for reasons that I clarify in footnote 15.
9 I am not at all sure that the welfare state is an unadulterated good. For some political theoretical reasons why one might be ambivalent about the welfare state, especially in regard to its effects on citizen sensibility and practice, see Wolin, 1989, 79, 151–179 and Brown, 1995, 166–196. In the next section, I address further the issue of citizens' attitudes toward and dependence upon government.
10 Hannah Arendt often distinguished between political action and the passivity of perceiving things as simply happening. I further elaborate this distinction in the next section when I use Arendt's writings to discuss the differences between feelings, interests, and opinions and a politics of *ressentiment* in which imaginary revenge displaces actual deeds.

the welfare state as we have known it appears to be in crisis. What is the relationship between Americans' pervasive humanitarianism and the current dismantling of the welfare state? Pursuing this question yields insight into the dynamics of resentment in contemporary American political life, as well as clarifying the implications of primarily affective interpretations of citizens' sensibilities in contrast to more deliberative accounts.

I do not doubt Feldman and Steenbergen's finding that most Americans express high degrees of humanitarianism. At the same time, it seems difficult to deny that many Americans are at least somewhat reticent, if not increasingly hostile, toward helping others, or at least toward helping certain others. The widespread support for welfare reform and, more important, the ubiquitous moralizing mantra "work, not welfare" suggest that more than social concern and fiscal responsibility infuse many opinions of this matter.[11] How are we to understand the apparent contradiction between the prevalent humanitarian sentiment that we should and will readily help others, on the one hand, and actual resentment and rejection of programs such as Aid to Families with Dependent Children (AFDC), on the other hand? One element of an answer lies in the relationship between conceptions of self and politics. More specifically, I argue subsequently, political opinions advance, by unwittingly presuming, the perceptions and experiences of particular selves in contrast to others.[12]

A humanitarian outlook, Feldman and Steenbergen claim, involves "a positive evaluation of human beings," "concern about," and "feelings of personal responsibility for" their welfare. They invoke Jencks's account of empathetic unselfishness to describe the humanitarian: "We incorporate their [other people's] interests into our subjective welfare function, so that their interests become our own." We might say that humanitarian sentiment grows out of the self's sense of interdependence and of its shared existence with others. But to whom do selves feel bound and why?

The interdependent self-interest described by Feldman and Steenbergen suggests a self who combines his or her interests with those of others to whom he or she feels bound. But we do not perceive all relationships as of the same centrality or importance in our self-conception.

11 I remind the reader that I am far from unambivalent about such programs (see footnote 8). What I am questioning here are the images and sentiments suffusing public discourse about such programs and what they might tell us about American political culture and citizenship more generally.
12 The following analysis was suggested to me in the course of reading Conover and Searing, 1993.

Some relationships appear essential to our selves, while others appear more contingent and thus less important. In contexts where others appear essential to our self-conception, humanitarian regard for the well-being of others and willingness to go out of our way to help them become explicable. Yet our experience of interdependence, especially when it appears to transcend politics, also suggests the boundaries of humanitarian feeling. When faced with others whom we take to be inessential to ourselves, we may come to resent and reject offering aid to those others even as we generally express humanitarian sentiment.

Contemporary political theorists contest what is essential and contingent to selves. For example, liberal political theorists have tended to assume that individuals can distance themselves from their social relationships and roles. As a consequence, most liberal political theorists presume that we can critically evaluate and, if need be, abandon those relationships and roles. By contrast, communitarians have tended to conceive social relationships as essentially constitutive of selves and, thus, set significant limits on our capacity for reflection and choice in these matters.[13] Empirical researchers might favor a turn to recent psychological research to adjudicate this theoretical dispute between liberals and communitarians. As I have said, however, conceptions of politics and selves are only partly factual matters. More specifically, the capacity of selves to change or remain the same is politically conditioned. Conceptions of the independence and interdependence of selves, of how essential or contingent their social roles and relations are, emerge in a political culture that is itself politically contingent.

How much room for reflection and choice do our social relationships, especially those that appear essential to who we are, allow us? If liberals have tended to underestimate the political conditions of transforming our selves and relationships, communitarians have tended to represent these relations as prior to or beyond politics. While acknowledging the contextual variability of selves and the communities in which they find themselves, communitarians have tended to underscore the limits of our capacity to critically reflect upon and evaluate, let alone change, our selves and relationships. But the agility of selves in making and altering connections with others is not only contextually variable but also a matter of politics.

Some relationships – and the interests, feelings, and values that accompany them – may appear so constitutive of what we are that they appear to preclude meaningful reflection and change. We appear unable to evaluate them critically or imagine what or who they exclude. This other

13 For an introduction to these positions geared to empirical researchers, see Neal and Paris, 1990.

or excluded side of essentially shared relationships may help us understand the dynamics of public feeling about social welfare programs. So
long as social welfare programs serve those we perceive as essential to
our selves, we can expect humanitarian feelings to flow unabated. So
long as we recognize them as part of who we are, we will regard their
well-being as related to our own, perhaps even of the utmost importance,
so that we willingly go out of our way to help them. To the extent that
we do not feel essentially bound to others, however, we may not feel
their claim upon us. Indeed, if we do not imagine others as essential to
our selves, we may find it difficult, even impossible, to imagine who they
are or to evaluate critically our relationship to them.

But whom do social welfare programs serve, and to whom and what
are they contingently and essentially bound? The situation is complex,
and no linear narrative or causal explanation, I think, can do it justice.
But a few crucial factors can be noted. First, we must note the demise
of the family-wage ideal that was "inscribed in the structure of most
industrial-era welfare states," whether in social insurance programs or
those like AFDC that serve the "residuum."[14] Second, we may note "a
dramatic increase in impoverished, woman-supported households
over the last two decades."[15] Third, both facts are intimately bound up
with what William E. Connolly calls the "globalization of contingency"
(Connolly, 1991, 22–26 passim): "[L]ate modernity is a time when the
worldwide web of systemic interdependencies has become more tightly
drawn, while no political entity or alliance can attain the level of efficiency needed to master this system and its effects" (Connolly, 1991, 23).
Individual lives grow more insecure as the forces that shape them increasingly exceed our control and that of the larger associations upon which
we depend. Connolly has explored links between world systematicity,
state inefficacy, and the increasingly strident politics of resentment and
recrimination infusing U.S. public life, of which campaigns for "work,
not welfare" are prime examples. The "late-modern state is becoming a
medium through which world-systemic pressures are transmitted to its

14 On this theme and possible alternatives, see Fraser, 1994, 591–618.
15 Wendy Brown summarizes the statistics: "[T]oday, approximately one-fifth of all
    women are poor and two out of three poor adults are women; women literally
    replaced men on state poverty roles over the past twenty years. The poverty rate
    for children under six is approximately 25 percent – and is closer to 50 percent
    for African American and Hispanic children. Nearly one-fifth of U.S. families are
    officially 'headed by women,' but this fifth accounts for half of all poor families
    and harbors almost one-third of all children between three and thirteen. Approxi-
    mately half of poor 'female-headed' households are on welfare; over ten percent
    of all U.S. families thus fit the profile of being headed by women, impoverished,
    and directly dependent upon the state for survival" (Brown, 1995, 171).

most vulnerable constituencies as imperatives of domestic discipline";
"[a]s obstacles to its efficacy multiply, the state increasingly sustains collective identity through theatrical displays of punishment and revenge
against those elements that threaten to signify its inefficacy."[16] For
instance, global economic conditions (not to mention social movements
for freedom) have rendered the sole male breadwinner household an
object of nostalgia for all but the most privileged families. To a great
extent, these global conditions seem impervious to national political
control.[17] Under these circumstances, in Connolly's formulation, the state
increasingly functions as a "ministry for collective salvation through a
politics of generalized resentment."[18] Indeed, we might understand the
loose coalition between the conservatives who have overtaken the Southern Baptist Convention (Bloom, 1992, 191–233) and disaffected blue-
collar workers against "blacks" (read "lazy welfare cheats"), "women"
(read "destroyers of the male-headed heterosexual nuclear family"), and
"liberals" (read "elites who push un-American values") that undermined
the New Deal coalition of the Democratic Party as among the most
graphic displays of this functional state dynamic.[19] But are "blacks and
women" (because the liberal state purportedly spent so lavishly upon
them) to be blamed for the greater insecurity and declining real wages
that characterize the majority of U.S. workers' lives? Or might global

16 Connolly, 1991, 24, 206. So, for example, the mantra "work, not welfare" is
often deployed to suggest that if people are without a job, it must be due to a
failing of character (their laziness) rather than the absence of jobs that pay wages
that could support a family (child care, health insurance, and the like).

17 Consider, for instance, popular rhetoric of economic development that evokes
preparing ourselves for a future made elsewhere (in a global economy) rather than
making that future ourselves (which is no longer, if it ever was, within our power).

18 Connolly elaborates: "The state becomes, first, the screen upon which much of
the resentment against the adverse effects of the civilization of productivity and
private affluence is projected; second, the vehicle through which rhetorical reas-
surances about the glory and durability of that civilization are transmitted back
to the populace; and third, the instrument of campaigns against those elements
most disturbing to the collective identity. In the first instance, the welfare apparatus of the state is singled out for criticism and reformation. In the second, the
presidency is organized into a medium of rhetorical diversion and reassurance. In
the third, the state disciplinary-police-punitive apparatus is marshaled to constitute and stigmatize constituencies whose terms of existence might otherwise
provide signs of defeat, injury, and sacrifice engendered by the civilization of productivity itself" (Connolly, 1991, 206).

19 For a reading along these lines, see Connolly, 1995, 109–128. Connolly does not
neglect liberalism's "fundamentalisms" and inefficacies that have contributed to
this situation; indeed, that element may be the most provocative aspect of his
argument.

Commentary: The Value of Politics

economic commitments and conditions define these circumstances? If their opinion were asked, many Americans might acknowledge the determinative effects of the latter. Yet representations of public feeling often suggest that the former weighs heavily upon our minds. To put the matter too simply, global economic systematicity and state inefficacy appear to be decisive factors in the decline of the family-wage ideal and the feminization of poverty, but public feeling vents frustration at the increased contingency of our lives via resentful representations and recriminations against the more vulnerable and dependent among us.[20] Friedrich Nietzsche named this dynamic cycle – of insecurity, resentment of suffering, and punishment – *ressentiment*, and, as we shall see in the next section, it has become a virtually constitutive feature of American political culture (Nietzsche, 1969, 37).

The extent of Americans' resistance, even hostility, to social welfare programs amidst their professed humanitarianism can be attributed to their feeling that those served by such programs are alien to their essential selves.[21] Those "others" are simply felt not to be part of "us" – and this may be especially the case when gender, race/ethnicity, or other aspects of social identity underscore, or appear to justify, their essential difference.[22] Thus, for a self who feels that some social relationships are essentially shared and others are not, humanitarian feelings are perfectly compatible with reticence to help others who request our aid or with resentment of those who require it. In other words, those who express unqualified humanitarianism may constrict or contradict those expressions in practice, perhaps without even recognizing it. But this is neither necessarily nor essentially so. Rather, these facts are constituted by and through a political condition. A political condition that fosters

---

20 Connolly describes those who best fill this need: "The primary targets of state negation are most functional if (a) they can be constituted as evils responsible for threats to the common identity, (b) their visibility might otherwise signify defects and failings in the established identity, (c) they are strategically weak enough to be subjected to punitive measures, and (d) they are resilient enough to renew their status as sources of evil in the face of such measures" (Connolly, 1991, 207). Connolly wants to problematize our notion of "evil," and the preceding passage must be read in this light. In his view, we judge those who are different as evil when we need to guard against the contingencies of our own identity; the more virulent our attacks upon others, the more insecure the identity we dogmatically assert.

21 Thus, the greater popularity of so-called social insurance welfare programs that serve "us" and others "like us."

22 This suggests the import of gender-coded and racially coded messages (even extremely subtle ones), for they establish or reinscribe bounds to humanitarian feeling; they govern whose interest we do and do not regard as tied to our own.

491

Melissa A. Orlie

displacements such as those evinced in relation to social welfare programs not only may harm others but also may prove self-defeating, so to speak. In a political culture of resentment, citizen action becomes reaction.

Recognition of the relational, interdependent character of selves can, however, yield conclusions nearly opposite to those I have thus far explored. From another perspective, the relational character of the self – its dependence upon others for its identity – continually subverts the stability of the self, so that it becomes essentially fluid (which is to say, not essential at all). Indeed, this vision of the self might form the basis for an alternative to a politics of thoughtless assertion and *ressentiment*. On this account, the self's dependence upon others continually upsets its assurance about the boundaries between self and other. Interdependence may thereby become a source of perpetual political questioning of the self's effects upon others, of the feelings it has for others, and of what it owes them.[23]

Conventionally, political theory is represented as prescriptive and psychology descriptive. Political theorists speculate about what selves and citizens should be, while psychologists tell us what selves can be by telling us what they are. Indeed, on this understanding, this is the contribution empirical research can make to debates about citizenship: It can tell us whether or not political theorists are realistic in the demands they make of selves and citizens. Empirical researchers do so by evaluating political theorists' prescriptive claims in light of the reality that emerges by joining current psychological research to social scientific explanations of particular contexts. But, as I maintained at the outset, what selves are, and the character of the opinions they hold, are not factual matters alone. The problem with applying a logic of discovery to selves – whether independent or interdependent, contingently or essentially bound – is that it obscures the degree to which selves and their boundaries are perpetually politically constituted. Indeed, this is the significance of citizens' words, deeds, and associations. Citizen opinion, whether measured in surveys or enacted in everyday life, seeks to make and remake its own and others' selves and the world in which they are joined. In short, political opinions seek to render some things essential, others contingent. We assert our independence and guard our dependencies; we challenge others' independence and dependence when it threatens our own. As a consequence, what appears contingent and what appears essential are con-

23 Experiencing the fluidity and instability of the self may breed discomfort and resentment, but noting this is different from saying that recognition or responsiveness to others is impossible because of who we "essentially" are (see Connolly, 1991, 16–35, passim).

tinually contested and potentially altered, whether we recognize it or not. But a logic of discovery casts selves as impervious to political transfiguration, and does so at the point where political claims are most likely to arise. A self's feelings are most likely to authorize its ignorance of, or resistance to, others at precisely the point where that self is actually related to others. We may not feel that such relations are essential to our selves, but resentment and resistance are bred by proximity, not by the absence of relation. In short, we may be inclined to deny the reach of politics exactly when we are most fully implicated in politics. A logic of discovery gives us no way of seeing or challenging this tendency in our selves or others.

Politics entails imagining one's relationship to fellow citizens, recognizing and responding to different (sometimes profoundly so) others within a collectivity. Politics involves responding to the diverse competing claims of those to whom we are contingently yet actually bound, not only imagining those whom we see as essentially the same.[24] The selves to whom we feel bound and those to whom we feel only contingently related are politically conditioned and, thus, open to challenge. But when we cast these relations as essential (or not), they are rendered pre- and nonpolitical. As a consequence, opinions qua feelings proceed without public account because they are cast beyond politics.[25]

In my view, this is a principal and typical shortcoming of predominantly affective accounts of citizen sensibility and reveals the *politics of feelings*. Feldman and Steenbergen equate a feeling like humanitarianism with a philosophy or justification. To be sure, affective predispositions are crucial factors in political discourse and may greatly influence our ability and willingness to offer an account of our political opinions or to explicate the principles that have led us to hold the views that we do. But such feelings are not specifically political opinions, not when they are shorn of political deliberation, at least according to the vision of politics I advance here. Without a principled, deliberate political contest among competing claims, feelings are simple assertions of self, albeit of a more sophisticated kind than appeals to self-interest *simpliciter*.

Politics is the means by which we determine who we are and what we owe one another. Both individual and collective identities are not given once and for all but are continually renegotiated and reconstituted.

---

24 I am simply reiterating Aristotle's claim that politics involves deliberation and decision making between the likes of physicians and farmers, not among physicians or farmers alone.

25 For a complementary and more extended critique of the "communitarian" position, see Bonnie Honig's critique of Michael Sandel's writings (Honig, 1993, 162–199).

Citizens' opinions are political actions that endeavor to make, reinforce, or initiate something new within our collective condition. But when we regard selves as prepolitically bound (or indifferent) to others in essential ways, we represent them and their opinions as outside politics. Personal feelings express how selves feel about others and their relationship to them. Political opinions require reflection upon how those feelings are publicly justified or justifiable. When feelings are shorn of deliberation, they place our beliefs, interests, and habits toward our selves and others beyond political contestation, even as those beliefs, interests, and habits are politically constituted and politically significant.

Surveys of political views that represent feelings as deliberate opinions may authorize – as they accept and evoke – a politics that is finally assertive, unprincipled, and arbitrary. No doubt, such surveys did not create such a politics, but they do perpetuate, when they do not question, it.

A CONUNDRUM OF AMERICAN PUBLIC OPINION

There is a more obvious explanation for Americans' apparent ambivalence toward social welfare programs, namely, that they are likely to be independent, not interdependent, selves. Americans might express humanitarian feelings, but their feelings flow in a more constricted circle, toward their children and personal friends, as Alexis de Tocqueville might say. If this is the case, then Americans would be wary of social welfare programs because they have a profound sense of their separateness from others. On this view, Americans value their independence and expect the same from others. The literature documenting the predominance of individualism in American political culture is voluminous. But Gregory Markus's chapter in this volume casts doubt upon this truism, or at least reveals a more complex reality beneath individualism and Americans' declarations of independence.

Markus's effort to assess the evaluative aspects of public opinion centers on the possible linkages between "abstract values" and policy attitudes. He looks for evidence of "core American values" and seeks to identify how they are used. For some time, commentators have maintained the "centrality of individualistic values to the American ethos." Ideals such as autonomy, self-reliance, and limited government have seemed definitive of American political culture. But researchers are only beginning to collect data on ordinary citizens' views of individualism. Surprisingly, Markus finds that "[o]rdinary Americans are far from consistently supportive of basic tenets of individualism." Markus summarizes his findings:

Commentary: The Value of Politics

[T]he evidence suggests an ethos that is a complex mix of relatively strong support for the idea of individual autonomy tempered with an understanding and affirmation of the idea that individual citizens are embedded in a social context. A majority of Americans endorse the idea that people should "take care of themselves," but at the same time they believe that circumstances beyond one's control can frustrate that effort, particularly in the economic realm. And as societal problems increase in size and complexity, government should step in rather than leave it to individuals or market forces to right matters.

Markus asks whether there might not be some dissonance between professing to value independence and simultaneously supporting an activist role for government. He wonders what kind of story might make sense of this complex mix. Alexis de Tocqueville's *Democracy in America* provides such a story. Tocqueville not only enables us to explicate this apparent contradiction, but also suggests that a political danger lurks at its heart. Tocqueville enables us to take a longer and broader view of the politics of Americans' feelings about themselves and others.

Tocqueville witnessed the birth of our democratic age, and among his most startling insights was the possibility of a democratic form of despotism. He foresaw, however paradoxical it may seem, a culture of professed individualists coming to love or rely upon a strong, activist central power because of their preoccupation with equality and independence.[26] "Individualism, Tocqueville wrote, "is a calm and considered feeling which disposes each citizen to isolate himself from the mass of his fellows and withdraw into the circle of family and friends; with this little society formed to his taste, he gladly leaves the greater society to look after itself" (Tocqueville, 1969, 506, 508). Tocqueville worried that citizens' *imaginary* self-sufficiency coupled with their real isolation would make them reticent to respond to or lean upon those proximate to them (neighbors and fellow citizens) for fear of becoming dependent upon them. They would resist the authoritative claims of identifiable others because of their fear of appearing less than equal and resent those who seem to embody the weakness they fear in themselves.

This cultural ethos corresponds with distinctive institutional tendencies and developmental trajectories: "It is always an effort for such men to tear themselves away from their private affairs and pay attention to those of the community; the natural inclination is to leave the only visible and permanent representative of collective interests, that is to say, the state, to look after them" (Tocqueville, 1969, 671). There are two things at work here.

---

26 He feared most for France, but American political development and Markus's data suggest that we may rightly fear as well.

Since in times of equality no man is obliged to put his powers at the disposal of another, and no one has any claim of right to substantial support from his fellow man, each is both independent and weak. These two conditions . . . give the citizen of democracy two extremely contradictory instincts. He is full of confidence and pride in his independence among his equals, but from time to time his weakness makes him feel the need for some outside help which he cannot expect from any of his fellows, for they are both impotent and cold. In this extremity he naturally turns his eyes toward that huge entity which alone stands out above the universal level of abasement. His needs, and even more his longings, continually put him in mind of that entity, and he ends by regarding it as the sole and necessary support of his individual weakness. (Tocqueville, 1969, 672)

Thus, we are not far from the paradox Markus finds: Americans profess belief in individual independence while supporting an increasingly activist government coupled, we might add, with feelings of resentment toward others who embody the dependence they fear in themselves. Because governmental powers appear far off, and thus not immediately recognizable, they seem neither an affront to democratic citizens' dignity nor a threat to their freedom. Instinctual preoccupation with self combined with reticence to depend upon others, Tocqueville surmised, might engender citizens' increased willingness (out of felt necessity) to turn to distant powers to meet their needs. Though jealous of their independence, they would see no danger in doing so: "The sovereign, being of necessity and incontestably above all the citizens, does not excite their envy, and each thinks that he is depriving his equals of all those prerogatives which he concedes to the state" (Tocqueville, 1969, 673).

But here Tocqueville identified a colossal miscalculation and misrecognition on the part of the citizen of democracy. In essence, we freely choose bonds of servitude. The strategy we adopt to assuage our feelings of weakness and isolation ultimately only heightens such feelings. "It is easy to see," Tocqueville writes (as if he senses the globalization of contingency looming upon the horizon), "the time coming in which men will be less and less able to produce, by each alone, the commonest bare necessities of life. The tasks of government must therefore perpetually increase, and its efforts to cope with them must spread its net ever wider. The more government takes the place of associations, the more will individuals lose the idea of forming associations and need the government to come to their help" (Tocqueville, 1969, 515). The more unwilling or unable we are to act together politically, which is to say deliberately and collaboratively, the more we come to need and engender a strong government, if all the while professing our independence and, at times, denigrating or resenting those in need. What we fail to recognize, as we cast aspersions on others, is our own dependence

Commentary: The Value of Politics

and waning freedom. The result may be something resembling the democratic form of despotism Tocqueville so feared (Tocqueville, 1969, 691–693).

We could understand Tocqueville to mean that the stronger government grows, the less we are related to one another. But what Tocqueville means by association, and our own experience of increased interdependence within a globalizing world, suggests that the crucial issue is whether our associations are free and deliberate, not whether we are related at all. We are related; we press upon and are pressed upon by others. When we press upon others thoughtlessly and assertively, or are so pressed upon, we may evoke resentment or feel resentful. Feeling isolated and weak, we turn to governing powers to aid our efforts to live or to surpass our fellows. But our dependence upon governance renders us weaker and more isolated, not less so.

Their imagination conceives a government which is unitary, protective, and all-powerful, but elected by the people. Centralization is combined with sovereignty of the people. That gives them a chance to relax. They console themselves for being under schoolmasters by thinking that they have chosen them themselves. Each individual lets them put the collar on, for he sees that it is not a person, or a class of persons, but society itself which holds the chain. Under this system the citizens quit their state of dependence just long enough to choose their masters and then fall back into. (Tocqueville, 1969, 693)

Of course, Tocqueville says, "[d]emocratic peoples often hate those in whose hands the central power is vested, but they always love that power itself" (Tocqueville 1969, 673). The latter statement seems to me a highly apt characterization of contemporary popular sentiments about government.

Political freedom alone, Tocqueville claimed, can chasten the individual and collective manifestations of democracy's despotic tendencies. Surveying America in the early nineteenth century, Tocqueville found an abundance of local liberties and the civil associations that fostered and secured them. Why did active citizen presence in the business of municipalities and countless civil associations bode well for American democracy?

[A]mong democratic peoples all the citizens are independent and weak. They can do hardly anything for themselves, and none of them is in a position to force his fellows to help him. They would all therefore find themselves helpless if they did not learn to help each other voluntarily. If the inhabitants of democratic countries had neither the right nor the taste for uniting for political objects, their independence would run great risks. (Tocqueville, 1969, 514)

The democratic individual is weak, and her only access to power is through deliberate association and collaborative action with others. Both

497

an active imagination of others and actual association with them counteract the fact of isolation and the myth of self-sufficiency by bringing our interests in touch with larger principles: "Citizens who are bound to take part in public affairs must turn from private interests and occasionally take a look at something other than themselves. As soon as common affairs are treated in common, *each man notices that he is not as independent of his fellows as he used to suppose* and that to get their help he must often offer his aid to them" (Tocqueville, 1969, 510, my emphasis). Political association cultivates an imagination of social relations that problematizes what we assume to be essential and contingent to our selves, and in ways that create opportunities for further deliberation and action. Tocqueville noted Americans' peculiar genius for deliberately associating and proclaimed: "The Americans have used liberty to combat individualism born of equality, and they have won" (Tocqueville, 1969, 511).

More recent commentators, however, have not been so sanguine.[27] Viewing American politics from the perspective of the twentieth century, Hannah Arendt regarded the passage from the colonies' Declaration of Independence to the United States Constitution to be the first episode in a story of the transformation of public freedom into civil liberties, public happiness into individual welfare of the greatest number, and public spirit into public opinion as the greatest force ruling an egalitarian, democratic society (Arendt, 1977, 221). In other words, she tells a story of the withering of Americans' genius for deliberate and deliberative association so praised and counted upon by Tocqueville.

In Arendt's view, the American founding fathers failed to encourage public spiritedness because it did not provide lasting institutions where ordinary citizens might experience the essence of political freedom – expression, discussion, decision (Arendt, 1977, 232, 235, 238). When public opinion and rule in the people's name prevail without the salutary effect of intermediate forms of citizen deliberation, both Tocqueville and Arendt find a recipe for majoritarian thoughtlessness and the crude assertion of interest. Why is this the politics fostered by unmediated mass opinion? Because opinion constituted without actual, or at least imaginative, association with others is more apt to express the narrowest personal feelings rather than a considered political view. Specifically political opinion becomes deliberate through contrast and contest among the

27 Tocqueville also had his doubts, not just about France, but also about America. For instance: "The Americans believe that in each state supreme power should emanate directly from the people, but once this power has been constituted, they can hardly conceive any limits to it. They freely recognize that it has the right to do anything" (Tocqueville 1969, 669).

diverse perspectives of those to whom we are actually bound, whether or not we feel they are essential to our selves.[28] According to Arendt, there is no formation of opinion without the benefit of a multitude of opinions held by others; only then is there true freedom of opinion (Arendt, 1977, 225). Why is this so? As Tocqueville puts it, "[f]eelings and ideas are renewed, the heart enlarged, and the understanding developed only by the reciprocal action of men upon one another" (Tocqueville, 1969, 515). Opinions, Arendt says, are "formed and tested in a process of exchange of opinion against opinion" (Arendt, 1977, 227); without such deliberative reflection, there are only moods (Arendt, 1977, 253). As a consequence, the associations forged among citizens, and between citizens and the state, are thoughtless rather than deliberative, arbitrary rather than deliberate, assertive rather than principled. As a result, the corruption of the government and the people mirror one another (Arendt, 1977, 252).

In the United States and other modern democratic nations, the people are proclaimed sovereign, their name constantly invoked to ratify government action while public opinion seems to hold some sway over state direction. But such public opinion is bereft of the salutary effects of the "reciprocal action of men upon men" because the people's powers always appear to be symbolic rather than actual. Indeed, no one seems more convinced of that fact than the people themselves. In many respects we are right to feel this way, for we receive power not as public citizens but mainly in our private capacities. When the American dream was vibrant, citizens' political impotence appeared as the freedom from public concerns that enabled (at least some of) us to enjoy private benefits and pleasures. But as global contingencies increase our insecurity and potential suffering, denied the true reaction of deeds we are tempted to compensate ourselves with an imaginary revenge (Nietzsche, 1969, 36). Nietzsche describes the political psychology of *ressentiment*:

For every sufferer instinctively seeks a cause for his suffering; more exactly, an agent; still more specifically, a *guilty* agent who is susceptible to suffering – in short, some living thing upon which he can, on some pretext or other, vent his affects, actually or in effigy. . . . This alone, I surmise, constitutes the actual physiological cause of *ressentiment*, vengefulness and the like: a desire to *deaden pain by means of affects*. (Nietzsche, 1969, 127)

Wendy Brown offers an extremely apt summary of this psychological process: "*Ressentiment* in this context is a triple achievement: it produces an affect (rage, righteousness) that overwhelms the hurt [in this case,

---

28 See Orlie 1994 for a more extended account of the role of others' perspectives in the formation of opinion.

feelings of insecurity, weakness, and isolation]; it produces a culprit responsible for the hurt; and it produces a site of revenge to displace the hurt (a place to inflict hurt as the sufferer has been hurt)" (Brown, 1995, 68). Might not something like this be at work in public feelings about social welfare programs? We feel at once righteous by virtue of our humanitarian feelings and rage at others whom we imagine to be unworthy of our sentiment; our feelings of recrimination toward the unworthy displace the pain and anger generated by the contingencies we suffer and reconstitute our imaginary independence in contradistinction to the (more) needy ones.

But Tocqueville and Arendt help us see how this process may not only harm others but also undermine our own freedom, which is to say that such thoughtlessness may prove self-defeating. As we, out of feelings of weakness and isolation, embolden governing institutions to master conditions that exceed our (and its) control, we increasingly satisfy ourselves with reactive feelings and imaginary revenge that displace our actual opinions and deeds. Such a politics of *ressentiment* only defeats the self as it empowers the state. By symbolically and actually displacing our power elsewhere, we only increase the feeling and actuality of our isolation and weakness and, in turn, the affects of *ressentiment* only increase, as do the powers through which we hope to vent them. But *ressentiment* is self-defeating in another sense as we become unable to discern the actual effects of our words and deeds.

Ressentiment displaces actual deeds, which does not mean that our opinions and actions do not matter. It does mean that we tend to regard relations between our selves and others as essential rather than seeing how they are perpetually politically constituted. As a result, our relations and associations tend to be thoughtless, not deliberate and deliberative. In sum, we displace our power, with the result that we increasingly feel, and actually are, isolated and weak even as the globalization of contingency renders us increasingly (inter)dependent.

This brief sketch adds elements of national and historical context to my critique of the politics of feelings. In my view, Tocqueville and Arendt offer powerful illustrations of how political forms and culture condition public opinion, especially what mix of emotion, interest, and value or principle prevails in them. The existence or absence of deliberate and deliberative association is crucial to the shape of individual and collective life; it conditions whether feelings and interests are chastened, encouraged, affirmed, and emboldened by principles and the perspectives of others or whether they thoughtlessly prevail against them. And how we survey public opinion – the questions we ask and the character of the answers we evoke – affects whether predominant political forms and culture are reinforced or challenged.

Commentary: The Value of Politics

Critical reflection and change require personally meaningful exercises in imagination at least and, sometimes, in action. Whether or not we feel essentially or contingently bound, and to whom, is profoundly affected by political forms and culture. If I have no means of associating (whether physically or imaginatively) with my fellow citizens, it is unlikely that I will be able to recognize the actual relations among us. But neither my feelings about others nor those about myself are the product of ineradicable boundaries, but rather are the effect of a political constitution.

The individualism Markus explores is, I suggest, an ideology. By "ideology" I do not mean a decided position on a political spectrum (liberal–conservative, right–left) or a coherent political program. Rather, ideology is our imaginary relationship to actual social relations (Althusser, 1971, 162). Real isolation and fictional self-sufficiency obscure the political constitution of selves and their relations, as well as frustrating their deliberate evaluation and transformation. "Individualism" is a name for this set of beliefs and practices that enable us to conceive feelings and interests as individual expressions. But individual expressions of opinion are more aptly understood as signs of competing collective ways of life – structures of feeling, amalgamations of interest, habitual practices, and evaluative perspectives. Politics can be represented, at its worst, as a thoughtless, assertive battle among divided individuals and competing ways of life. At its best, politics is a collaborative and deliberative contestation, accommodation, and transfiguration of selves and the ways of life they bear. Which prevails is itself politically decided. Representations and explanations of public opinion contribute to this decision.[29]

DEMOCRATIC DELIBERATION

I began my discussion with the claim that how we study public opinion to a very significant degree affects what political opinion is or is allowed to be. I have endeavored to elicit the theory of politics implicit in citizens' opinions, and in representations of them, and to suggest why they are worthy of more concerted reflection. I have criticized primarily affective representations of citizen sensibility for their implicit theory of politics because I think they, however unwittingly, authorize and enable assertive preferences and unreflective feelings to prevail without account, or as if they were deliberate opinions, which I have argued they are not. As a consequence, the quality of collective life and public discourse continues to suffer.

29 For example, consider Stoker's discussion of how public opinion regarding affirmative action is surveyed affects the opinions expressed.

Against this prevalent conception, I have deployed something more akin to Stoker's account of public opinion as informed by political value judgments. Stoker not only enables us to recover and consider the principled basis for political agreement and disagreement, but her implicit theory of politics entreats us to be accountable to others for who we are, for what we believe and do. But the plausibility and appeal of Stoker's implicit theory of politics depends upon our values being (at least in part) politically acquired and alterable. If they are not, then public debate is fruitless, perhaps even intolerably dangerous. If our values and judgments are not politically informed and transfigurable, then public debate will only highlight our differences and fuel conflict, not provide a means for recognizing and either resolving or learning to live together amid our differences. If there are severe constitutive and thus, for all intents and purposes, unalterable restrictions on who we are, on what we can imagine and change, then politics may be of little value. Obviously, this is not my view.

Political opinions are forms of action that advance competing ways of life. Specific opinions not only emanate from and manifest particular locations in the world (the emotions, interests, and values that characterize ways of life and senses of self). Political opinions also seek to shape the world, to establish or sustain particular selves and their ways of life amid competing alternatives.[30] In this respect, liberals and communitarians could both be right in the claims they make about selves and their relationship to others. Such diverse and even conflicting accounts may prove equally compelling, however, not because they have captured what selves necessarily are, but when they seek to account deliberately for their views of what selves should be, what we owe to ourselves and others. Such perspectives and claims are fundamentally political. They call for us, and others, to change or to remain the same. As Aristotle maintained, politics inevitably changes who you are. Whether such change occurs primarily by choice or imposition is itself politically decided. Whether the claims of those who are proximate and to whom we are contingently related are accepted and affirmed, or resented, in large measure depends upon the quality of political life and decision making. In my view, some form of a deliberative theory of politics is more likely to cultivate acceptance and affirmation of our actual relations with others, while affective conceptions of public opinion are more likely to foster resentment of them.

Political opinions and judgments – even when they are motivated by "values" or other-regarding "feelings" rather than by the goal of "maximizing self-interest" – have power effects as they endeavor to shape the

30 For a fuller elaboration of this account, see Orlie 1994.

Commentary: The Value of Politics

world in some ways rather than others. When a political opinion prevails, some understandings and courses of action, themselves often viable and justifiable, are precluded. But this proximity of opinion and judgment to interest and power – the fundamentally political character of opinion and judgment – need not mean that they are therefore wholly arbitrary, assertive, unprincipled, or illegitimate, though they can be. The sufficiency of the deliberation that actualizes political opinions and judgments may delimit their arbitrariness and chasten their assertiveness. Evaluating the complexity of decisions (e.g., do they do justice to the diversity of different, competing, often equally valid claims?) and the inclusiveness of the political forms in which they are made are ways of "measuring" the values and value of political opinions. Public opinion research not only represents citizens' opinions, it also projects a vision of politics. In this sense, our research, like the citizens' opinions we survey, is political action. The theory of politics our research affirms decisively conditions the value(s) we and others find in politics.

Reference

Althusser, Louis (1971). *Lenin and Philosophy and Other Essays.* Trans. Ben Brewster. New York: Monthly Review Press.

Arendt, Hannah (1977). *On Revolution.* New York: Penguin.

Benhabib, Seyla (1992). *Situating the Self.* New York: Routledge.

(1994). "Deliberative Democracy and Models of Democratic Legitimacy." *Constellations* 1(1):26–52.

Bloom, Harold (1992). *The American Religion: The Emergence of a Post-Christian Nation.* New York: Simon and Schuster.

Brown, Wendy (1995). *States of Injury.* Princeton: Princeton University Press.

Connolly, William E. (1991). *Identity/Difference: Democratic Negotiations of Political Paradox.* Ithaca: Cornell University Press.

(1995). *The Ethos of Pluralization.* Minneapolis: University of Minnesota Press.

Fraser, Nancy (1994). "After the Family Wage: Gender Equity and the Welfare State." *Political Theory* 22(4):591–618.

Habermas, Jürgen (1996). *Between Facts and Norms: Contributions to a Discourse Theory of Law and Democracy.* Cambridge, Mass.: MIT Press.

Honig, Bonnie (1993). *Political Theory and the Displacement of Politics.* Ithaca: Cornell University Press.

Neal, Patrick, and David Paris (1990). "Liberalism and Communitarian Critique: A Guide for the Perplexed." *Canadian Journal of Political Science* 23:421–439.

Nietzsche, Friedrich (1969). *On the Genealogy of Morals.* Trans. Kaufmann and Hollingdale. New York: Vintage Books.

Orlie, Melissa A. (1994). "Thoughtless Assertion and Political Deliberation." *American Political Science Review* 88(3):684–695.

(1997). *Living Ethically, Acting Politically*. Ithaca: Cornell University Press.

Stoker, Laura (1992). "Interests and Ethics in Politics." *American Political Science Review* 86(2):369–380.

Tocqueville, Alexis de (1969). *Democracy in America*. Trans. Lawrence. New York: Harper and Row.

Wolin, Sheldon S. (1989). *The Presence of the Past: Essays on the State and the Constitution*. Baltimore: Johns Hopkins University Press.

Index

Index

American Revolution, 14
anchoring and adjustment process,
  and evaluation of political
  candidates, 205
Anderson, J. A., 203
Anderson, N. H., 205, 218
anxiety, and electoral decision
  making, 9–10, 12–13, 55–61,
  116–17, 119
appropriate categories, and category-
  based processing, 31
Arendt, H., 486n10, 498–500
Aristotle, 493n24, 502
Arnold, R. D., 164
Asch, S. E., 24
associative model, and evaluation of
  political candidates, 202–6
"associative network," and memory,
  25
attention, and social psychology,
  50–1
attitudes: accessibility and strength
  of, 28–9
  automatic activation of, 24–9
  and collective emotion, 120
  concepts of, 243–51
  construction of political, 200–1
  and evaluation of political
  candidates, 24–9, 230–2, 234–5
  grounding of political, 347–51
  and limbic system, 73
  and motivation, 133
  perceptions and policy, 324–7
  psychological structure of,
  290–4
  and public opinion, 243, 259,
  280–4
  and quality of political judgments,
  12, 251–3
  and recomputation, 233f
  and representative democracies,
  342–7
  self-interest and political, 32
  and symbolic predispositions,
  16–18
  television and responses to political
  leaders, 75, 81–3

attribution processes, in social and
  political judgment, 161–3,
  169–86
Austen-Smith, D., 170
Austin, J. L., 168
automatic activation, of attitudes,
  24–9
automatic processing, 8, 25–7
autonomy: and individualism, 361,
  407, 410t, 414–16, 428
  and public opinion on social
  control, 453–5, 458
  and question-wording in survey
  research, 465
awareness-predisposition model, and
  public opinion, 259–65

Baird, Zoe, 247, 305
Bargh, J. A., 25, 28–9
Baumeister, R. F., 208, 218
Becker, G., 317n3
Behavioral Approach System (BAS),
  9, 44–6, 54–5, 116
behavioral decision theory, 138–40,
  156–7
Behavioral Inhibition System (BIS), 9,
  44, 46–8, 54–5, 71, 116
beliefs: and evaluation of political
  candidates, 206
  and survey measures of emotion,
  11
  and threat perceptions, 52
  See also values
Bellah, R. N., 404–5, 428
Benhabib, S., 483n6
Bennett, W. L., 168
Berelson, B., 207
Bettman, J. R., 138
biased spreading activation, and
  memory, 218
black box model, of electoral choice,
  198
blame, and attributions of
  responsibility, 174–7, 184–6
Bloom, H., 490
Bodenhausen, G. V., 234
Bontempo, R., 403

506

Index

Index

Index

Public Affairs Research Institute,
335
public opinion: attitudes in research
on, 243, 280–4
on compensatory justice and
affirmative action, 440–9, 473
expression of, 289–90
and helping hand experiment,
276–9
and latitude theory, 295–310
liberalism and social control,
449–59
and political value judgments in
political psychology literature,
459–64
and probable cause experiment,
268–76
and response models, 259–65
and self-interest, 402
and values, 313–15, 365–7, 478,
480–2, 494–503
and view of citizen, 255–6
Pyszczynski, T., 209, 215

Quayle, Dan, 69–70, 93
question-wording effects: and
political attitudes, 347
and political value judgments,
464–5
and research on public opinion,
262, 265–66, 269–71, 281,
283
See also wording variations

Rabinowitz, G., 57
race: and egalitarianism, 382, 383t
and individualism, 358
and influence of values on political
perceptions, 327–9
and poverty rates, 489n15
and stereotyping, 396–7
See also demographics; racism
Race and American Values Study,
284–6
racism: and influence of values on
public opinion, 317, 322–5
and symbolic meaning, 21–2

and symbolic predispositions, 18
See also race
Raden, D., 29n7
Rahn, W. M., 24, 55
"rank order invariance" hypothesis,
on public opinion, 264
Rasinki, K. A., 235, 362–3, 472,
475, 477
rational choice models, 52–3, 57,
60–2
Reagan, Ronald, 22, 69, 169, 178,
404, 423, 424t, 425–6
reason and reasoning: and
emotionality, 41–2, 61, 103
motivation of political, 206–8
nonattitudes and critique of citizen,
255–9, 265–8
Redlawsk, D. P., 128–9, 131, 133–4,
142–3, 148, 150, 227–30, 233
refusals, and accountability of public
officials, 167
Reich, R., 406
reinforcers, and emotion, 43–4
Reiss, H., 165
relational values, 356, 371–6
relevance, of attitudes in evaluation
process for political candidates,
234–5
Rempel, J. K., 235
Reno, Janet, 167
response models, of public opinion,
259–65
responsibility, and accountability of
public officials, 162, 174–7
revisionist theory: on symbolic
predispositions and attitude
change, 19
Richmond v. J. A. Croson Co.
(1988), 441
Riggle, E., 53n7
Riker, W. H., 170
Rimlinger, G. V., 368
"rock-throwing," and political
debates, 301–2
Rokeach, M., 372–3, 403, 436, 472,
476
Rolls, E. T., 71

Other books in the series (*continued from front of book*)

LaVergne, TN USA
08 December 2009
166271LV00003B/4/P